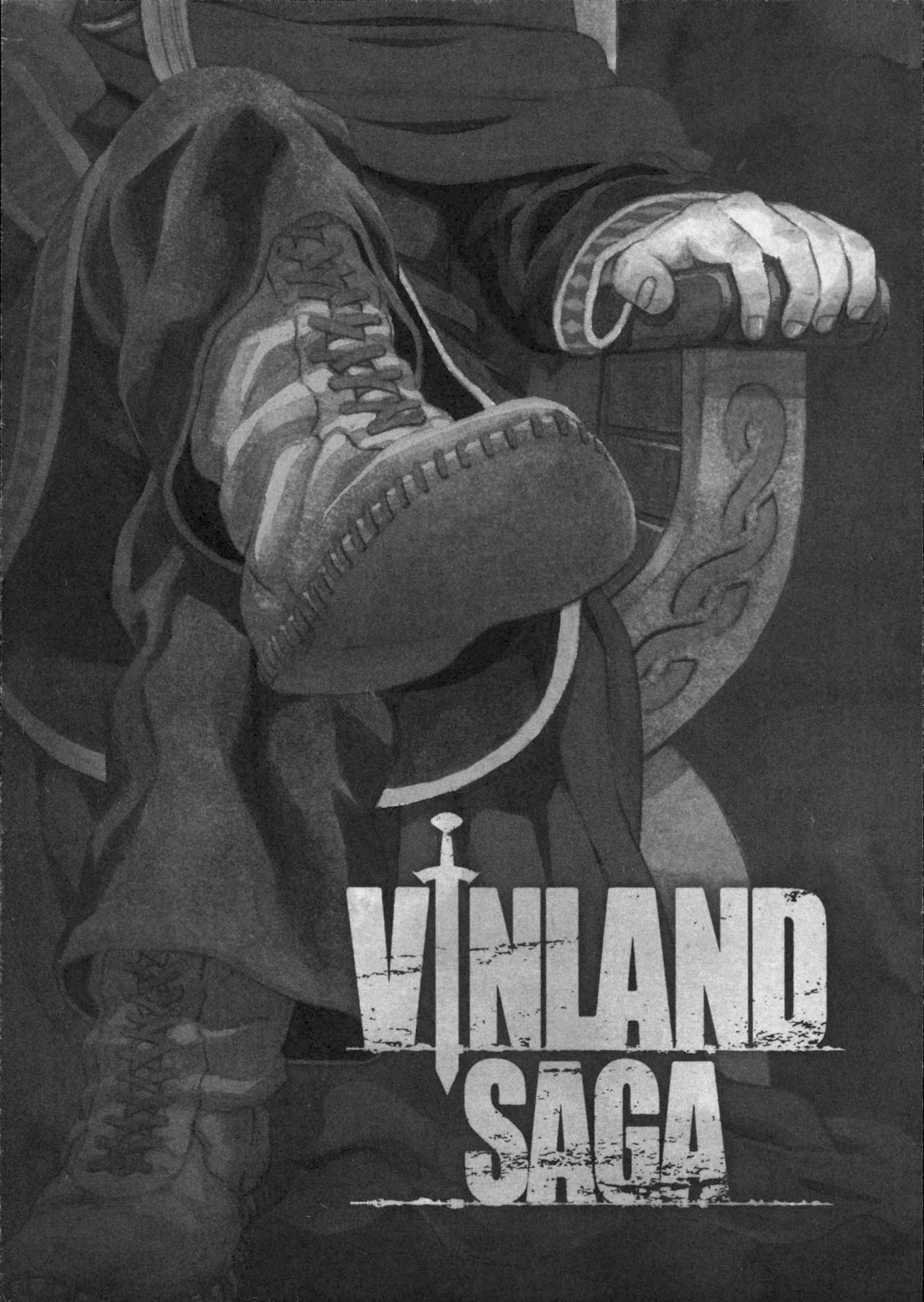
VINLAND
SAGA

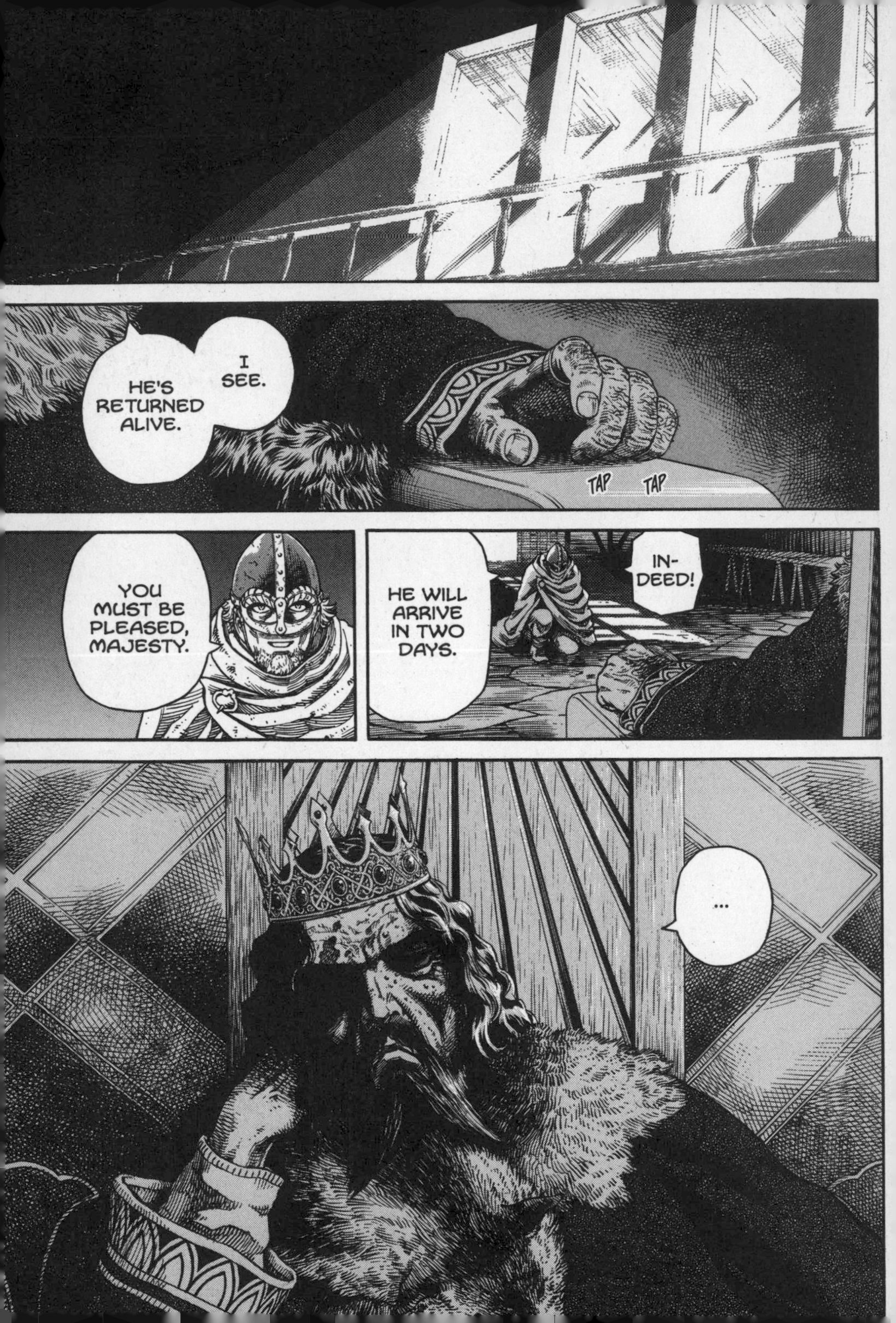
I SEE.
HE'S RETURNED ALIVE.
TAP TAP
IN-DEED!
HE WILL ARRIVE IN TWO DAYS.
YOU MUST BE PLEASED, MAJESTY.
...

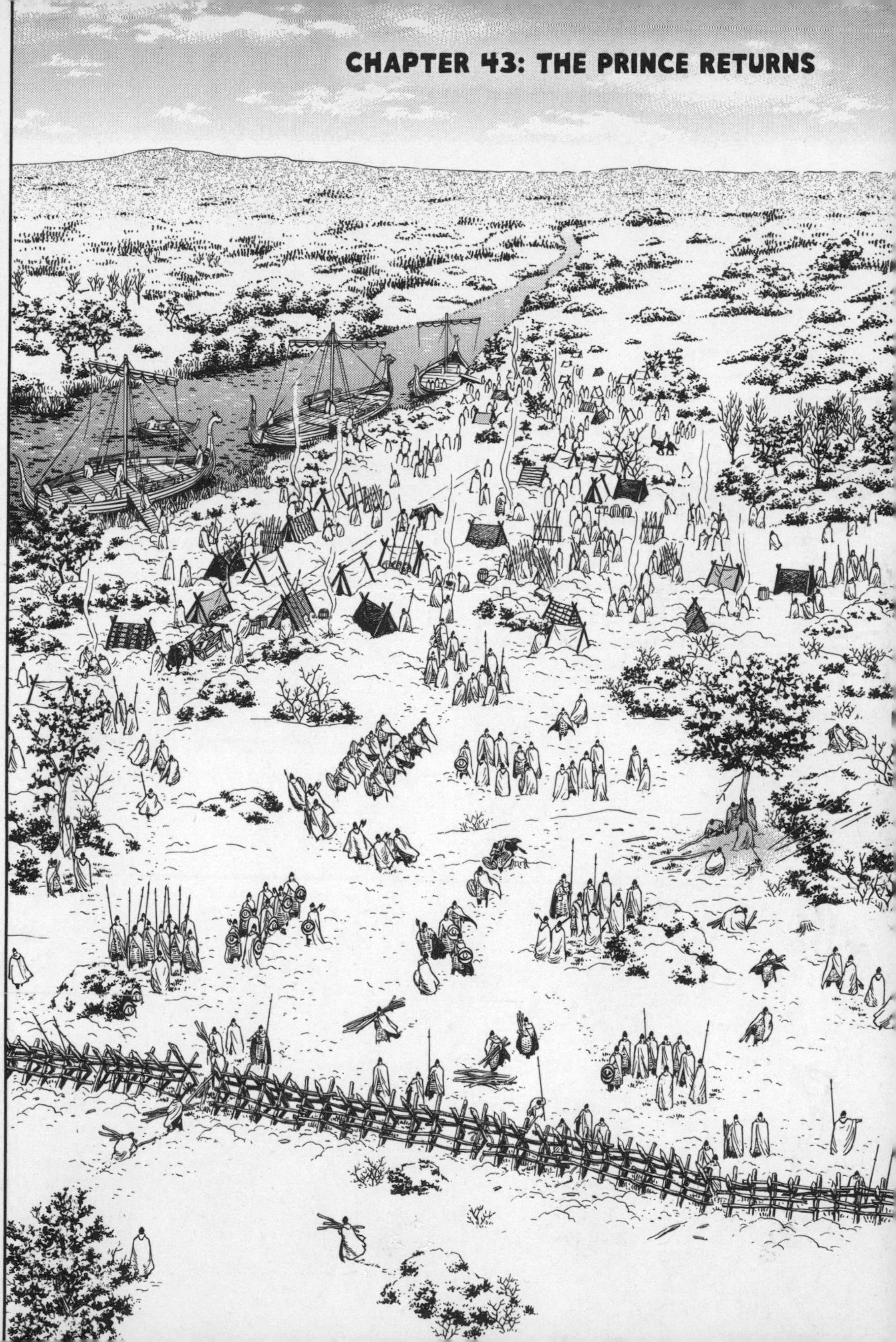
CHAPTER 43: THE PRINCE RETURNS

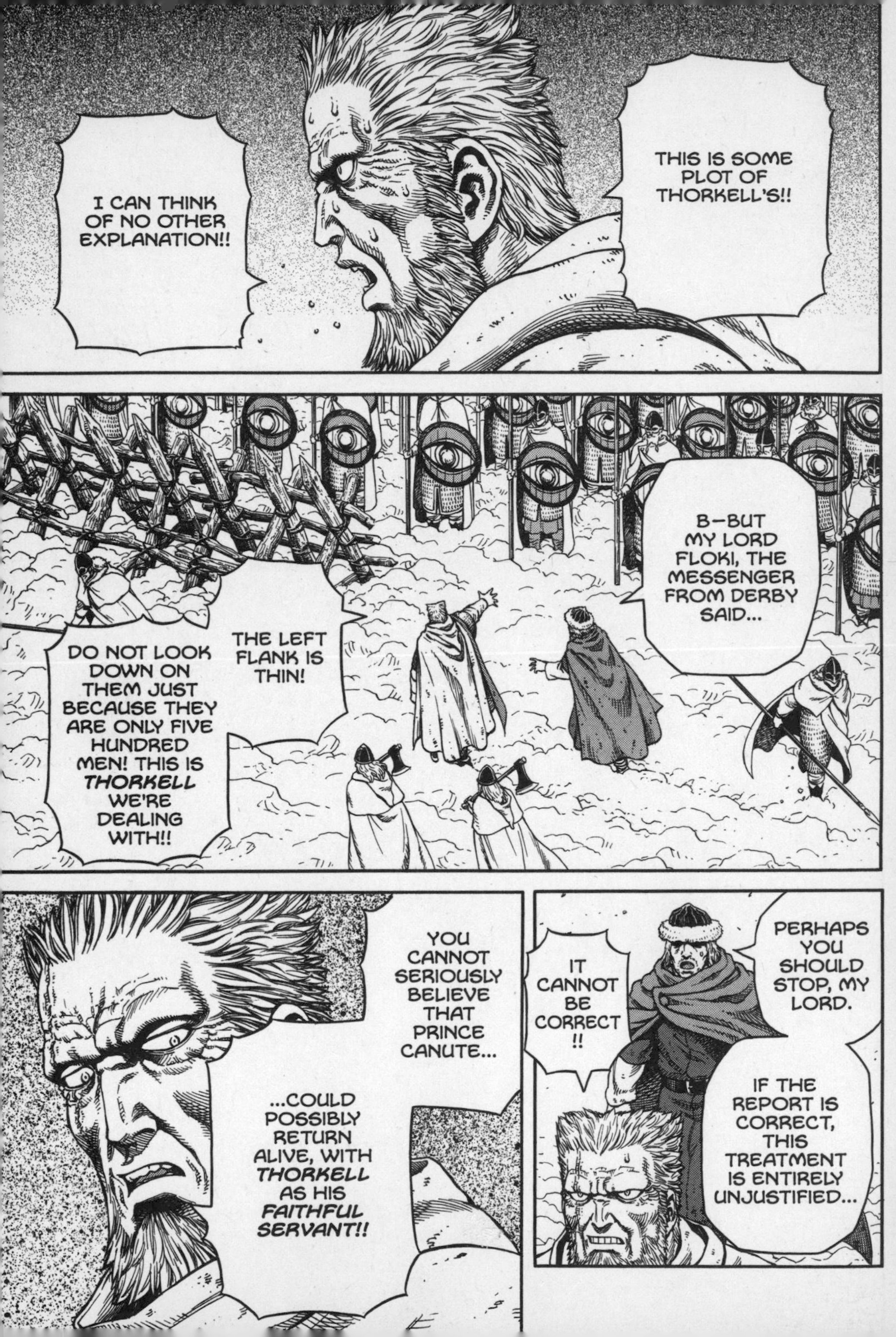
THIS IS SOME PLOT OF THORKELL'S!!
I CAN THINK OF NO OTHER EXPLANATION!!
B—BUT MY LORD FLOKI, THE MESSENGER FROM DERBY SAID...
THE LEFT FLANK IS THIN!
DO NOT LOOK DOWN ON THEM JUST BECAUSE THEY ARE ONLY FIVE HUNDRED MEN! THIS IS THORKELL WE'RE DEALING WITH!!
PERHAPS YOU SHOULD STOP, MY LORD.
IT CANNOT BE CORRECT!!
IF THE REPORT IS CORRECT, THIS TREATMENT IS ENTIRELY UNJUSTIFIED...
YOU CANNOT SERIOUSLY BELIEVE THAT PRINCE CANUTE...
...COULD POSSIBLY RETURN ALIVE, WITH THORKELL AS HIS FAITHFUL SERVANT!!

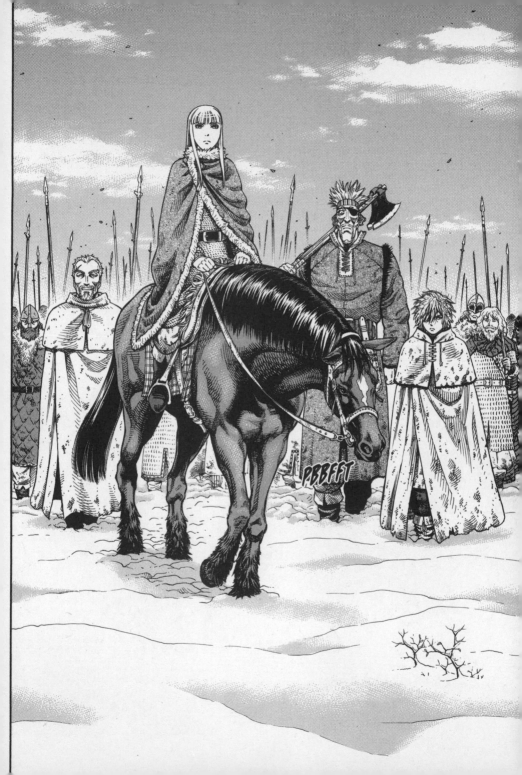

PBBFFT

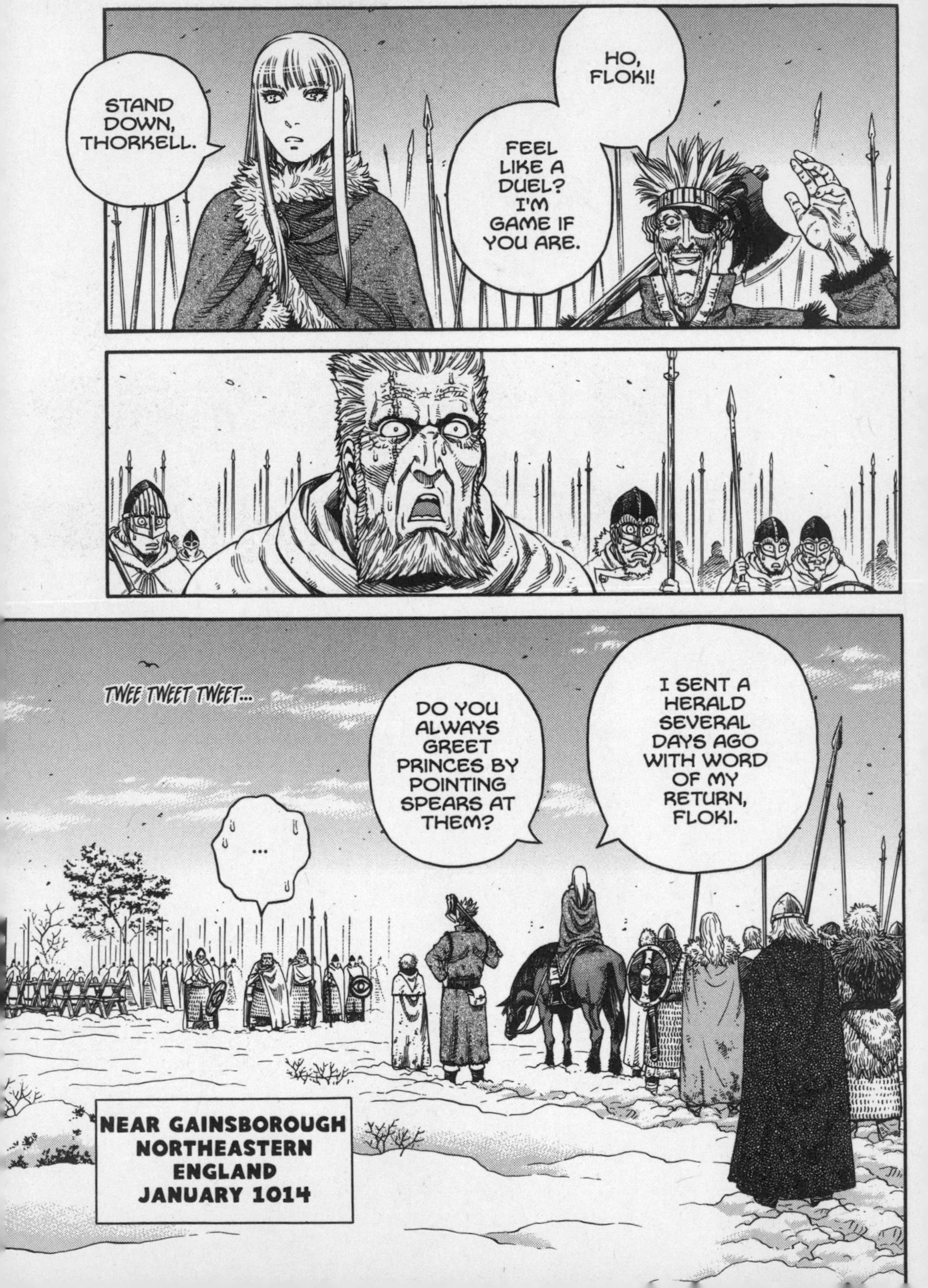
HO, FLOKI!
FEEL LIKE A DUEL? I'M GAME IF YOU ARE.
STAND DOWN, THORKELL.
I SENT A HERALD SEVERAL DAYS AGO WITH WORD OF MY RETURN, FLOKI.
DO YOU ALWAYS GREET PRINCES BY POINTING SPEARS AT THEM?
TWEE TWEET TWEET...
...
NEAR GAINSBOROUGH NORTHEASTERN ENGLAND JANUARY 1014

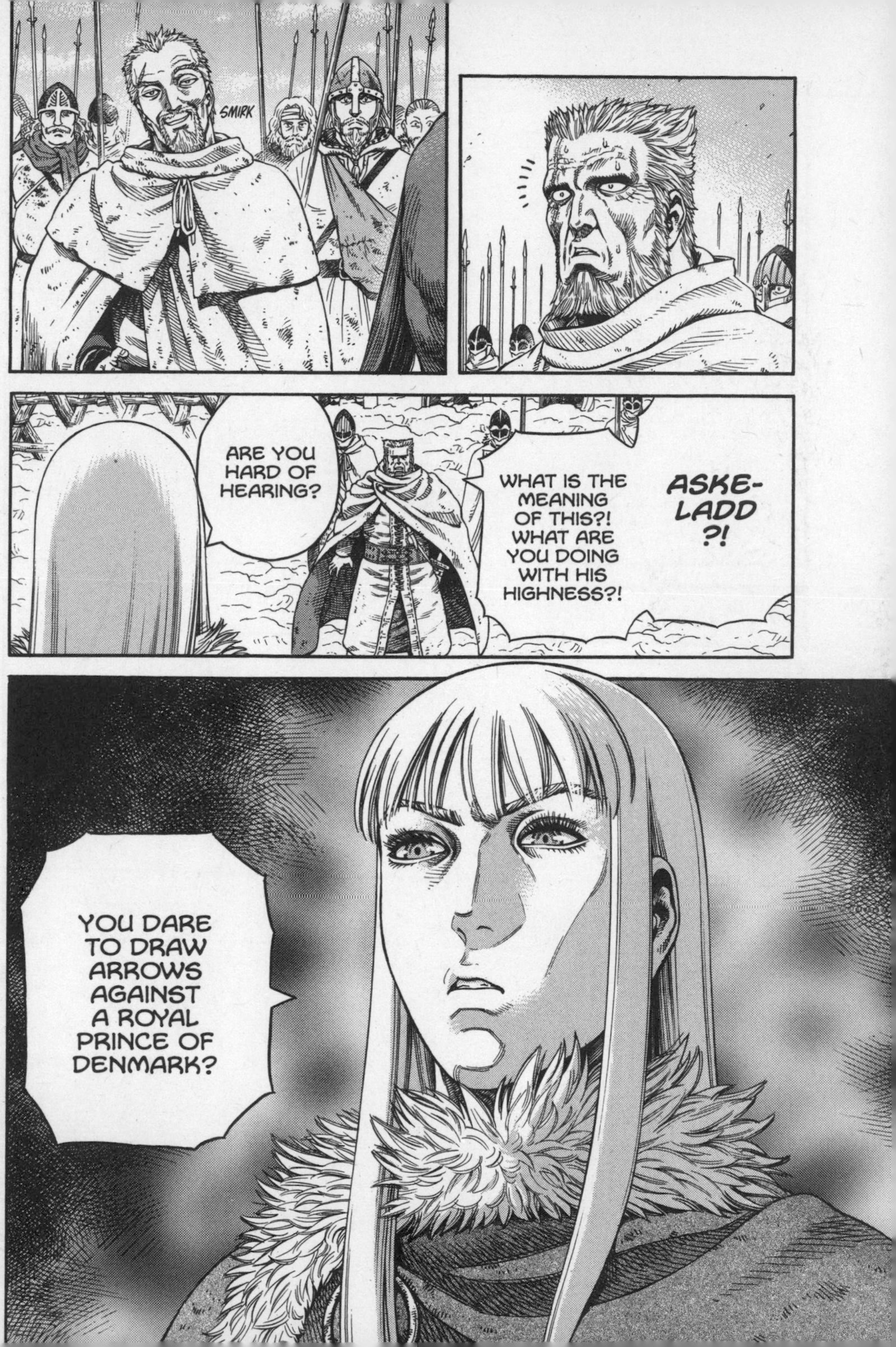
SMIRK
ASKE-LADD ?!
WHAT IS THE MEANING OF THIS?! WHAT ARE YOU DOING WITH HIS HIGHNESS?!
ARE YOU HARD OF HEARING?
YOU DARE TO DRAW ARROWS AGAINST A ROYAL PRINCE OF DENMARK?

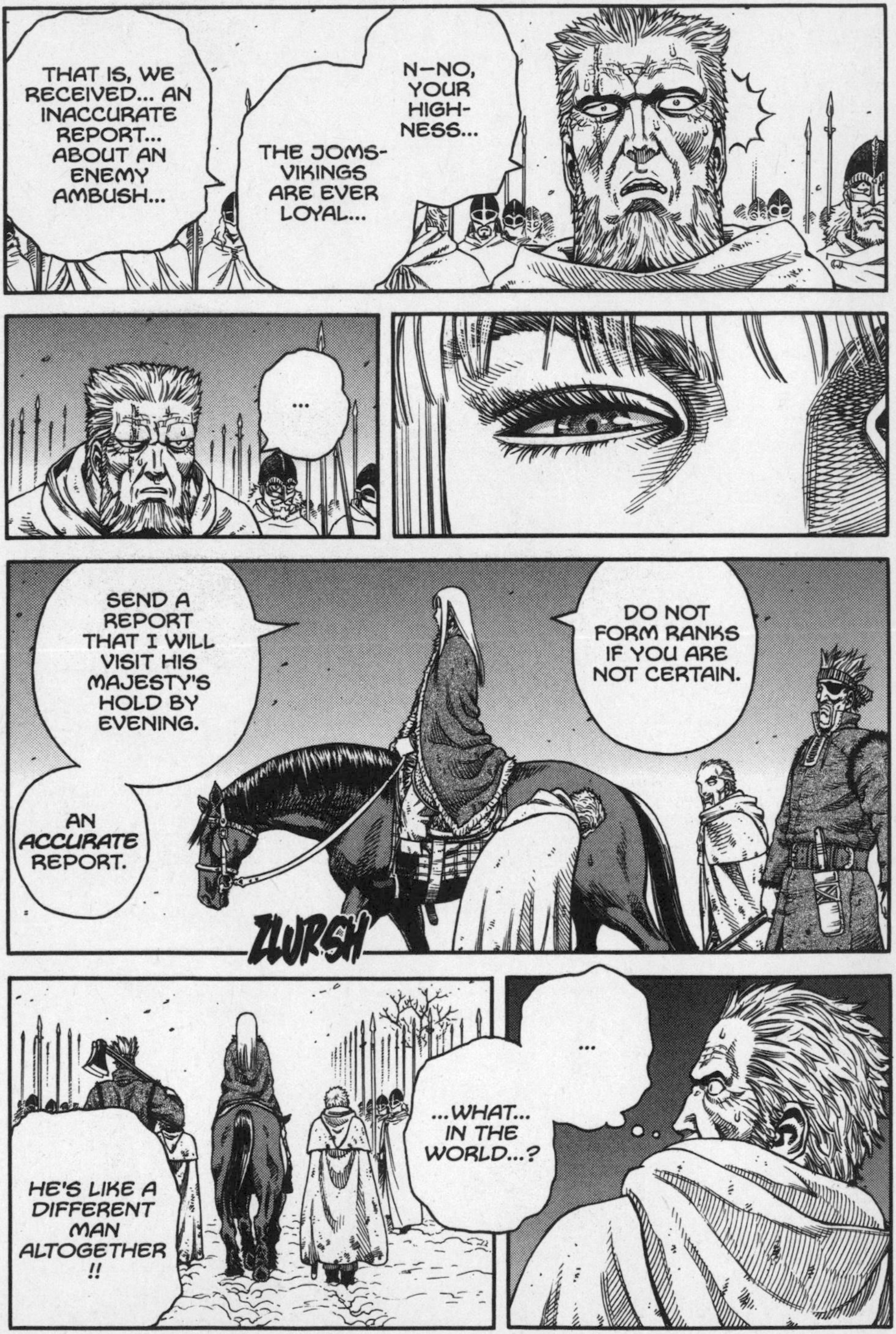
N—NO, YOUR HIGHNESS...
THE JOMS-VIKINGS ARE EVER LOYAL...
THAT IS, WE RECEIVED... AN INACCURATE REPORT... ABOUT AN ENEMY AMBUSH...
...
DO NOT FORM RANKS IF YOU ARE NOT CERTAIN.
SEND A REPORT THAT I WILL VISIT HIS MAJESTY'S HOLD BY EVENING.
AN ACCURATE REPORT.
ZLURSH
...
...WHAT... IN THE WORLD...?
HE'S LIKE A DIFFERENT MAN ALTOGETHER !!

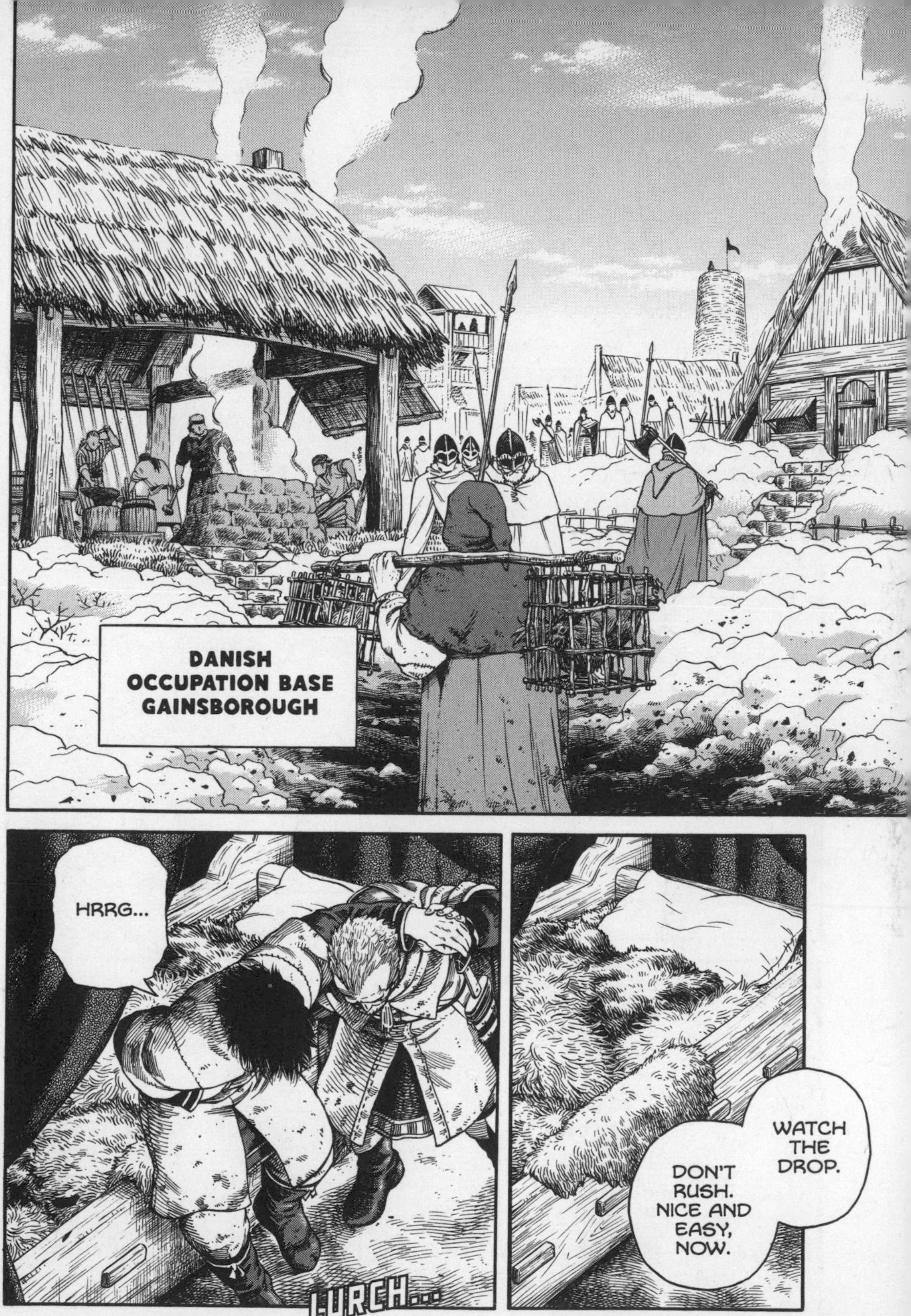
DANISH OCCUPATION BASE GAINSBOROUGH
WATCH THE DROP.
DON'T RUSH. NICE AND EASY, NOW.
HRRG...
LURCH...

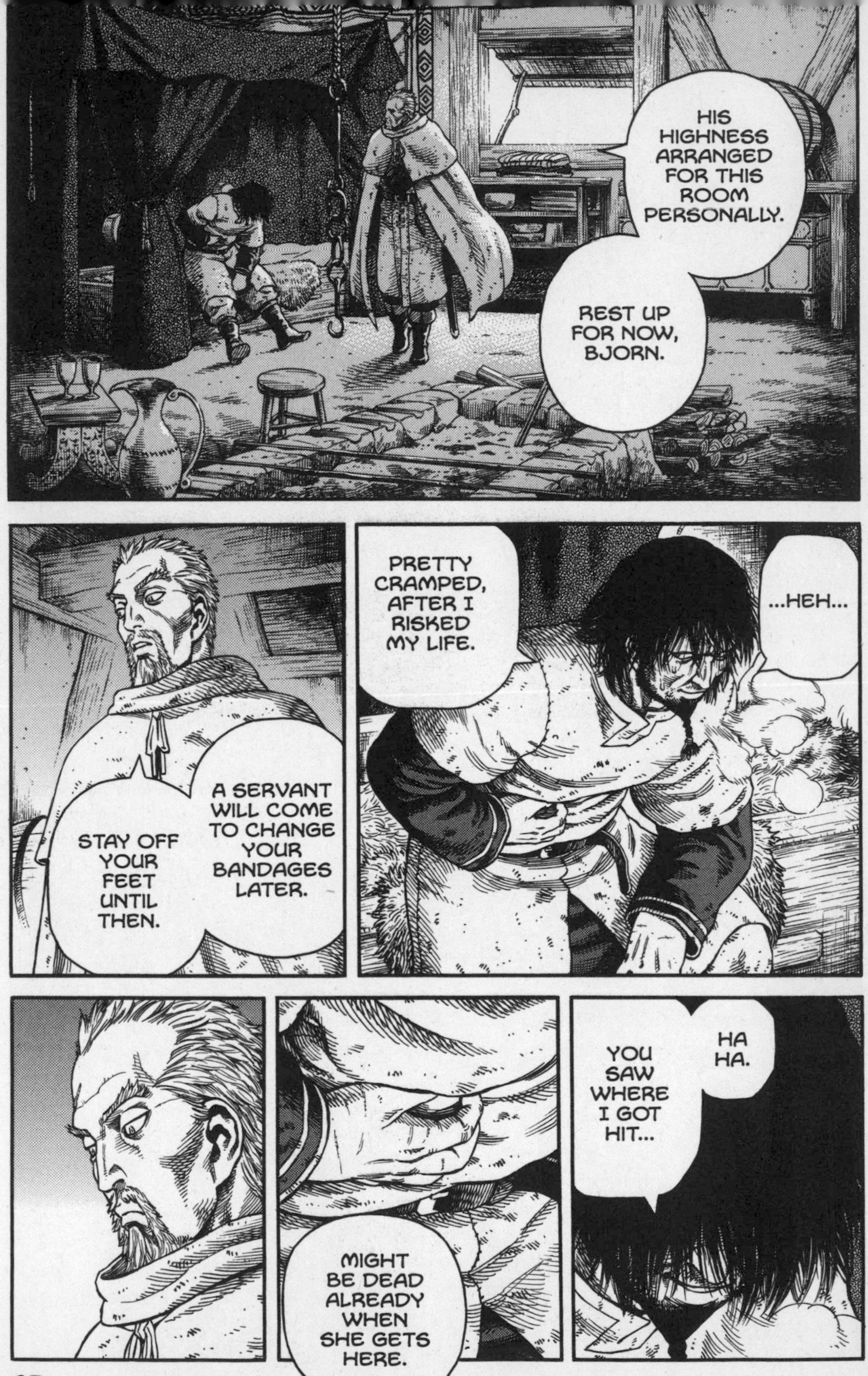
HIS HIGHNESS ARRANGED FOR THIS ROOM PERSONALLY.
REST UP FOR NOW, BJORN.
...HEH...
PRETTY CRAMPED, AFTER I RISKED MY LIFE.
A SERVANT WILL COME TO CHANGE YOUR BANDAGES LATER.
STAY OFF YOUR FEET UNTIL THEN.
HA HA.
YOU SAW WHERE I GOT HIT...
MIGHT BE DEAD ALREADY WHEN SHE GETS HERE.

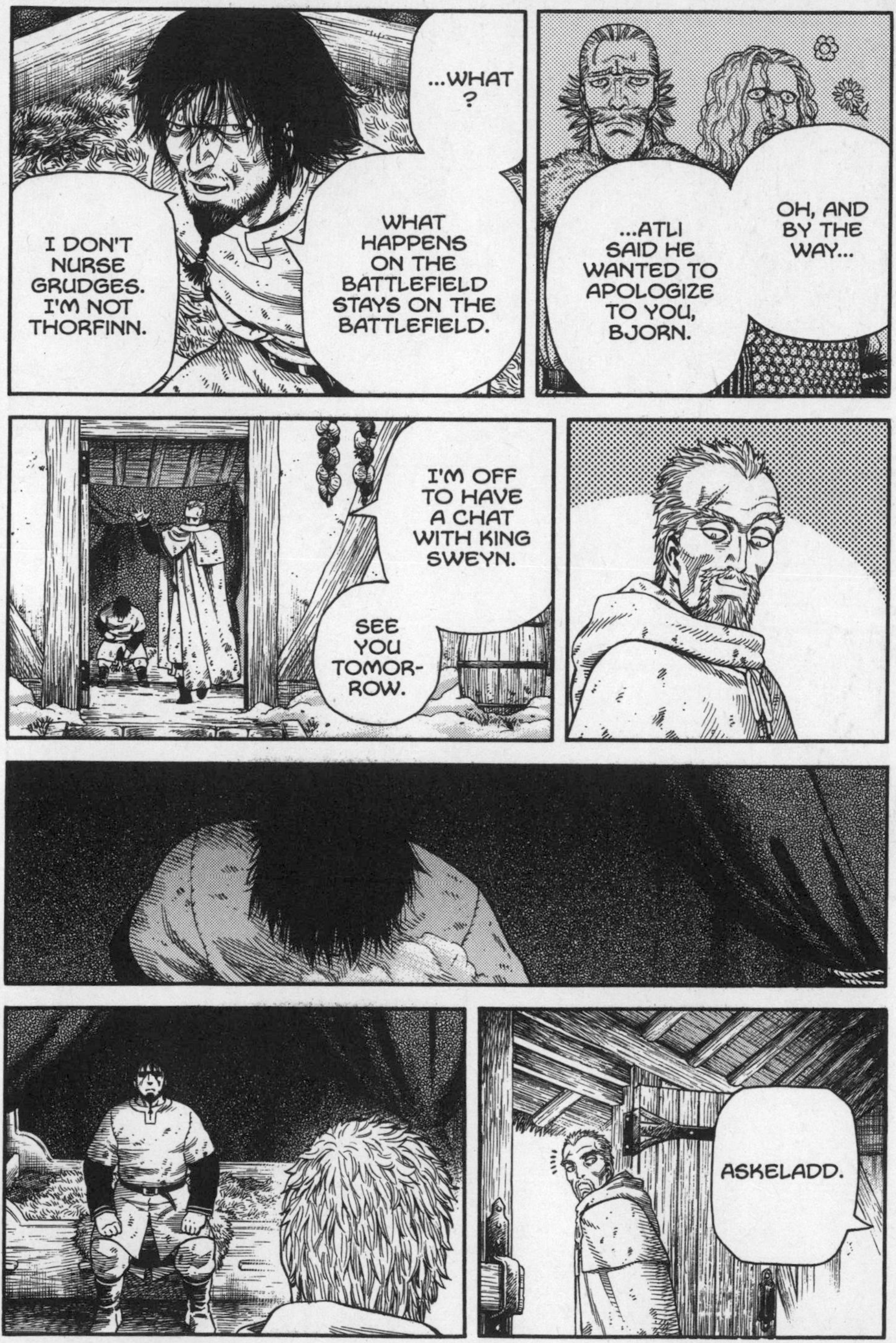
OH, AND BY THE WAY...
...ATLI SAID HE WANTED TO APOLOGIZE TO YOU, BJORN.
...WHAT ?
WHAT HAPPENS ON THE BATTLEFIELD STAYS ON THE BATTLEFIELD.
I DON'T NURSE GRUDGES. I'M NOT THORFINN.
I'M OFF TO HAVE A CHAT WITH KING SWEYN.
SEE YOU TOMOR-ROW.
ASKELADD.

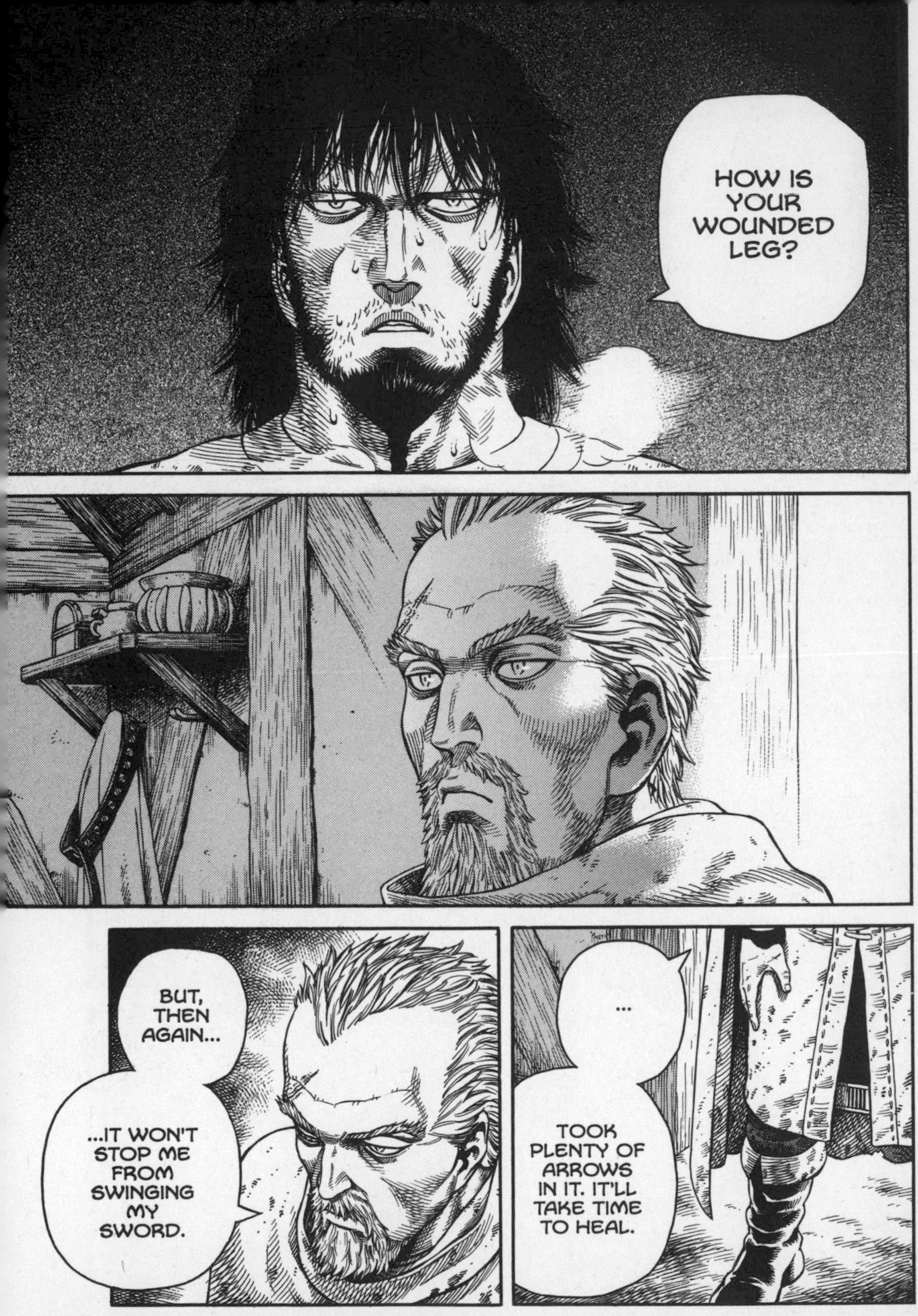
HOW IS YOUR WOUNDED LEG?
...
TOOK PLENTY OF ARROWS IN IT. IT'LL TAKE TIME TO HEAL.
BUT, THEN AGAIN...
...IT WON'T STOP ME FROM SWINGING MY SWORD.

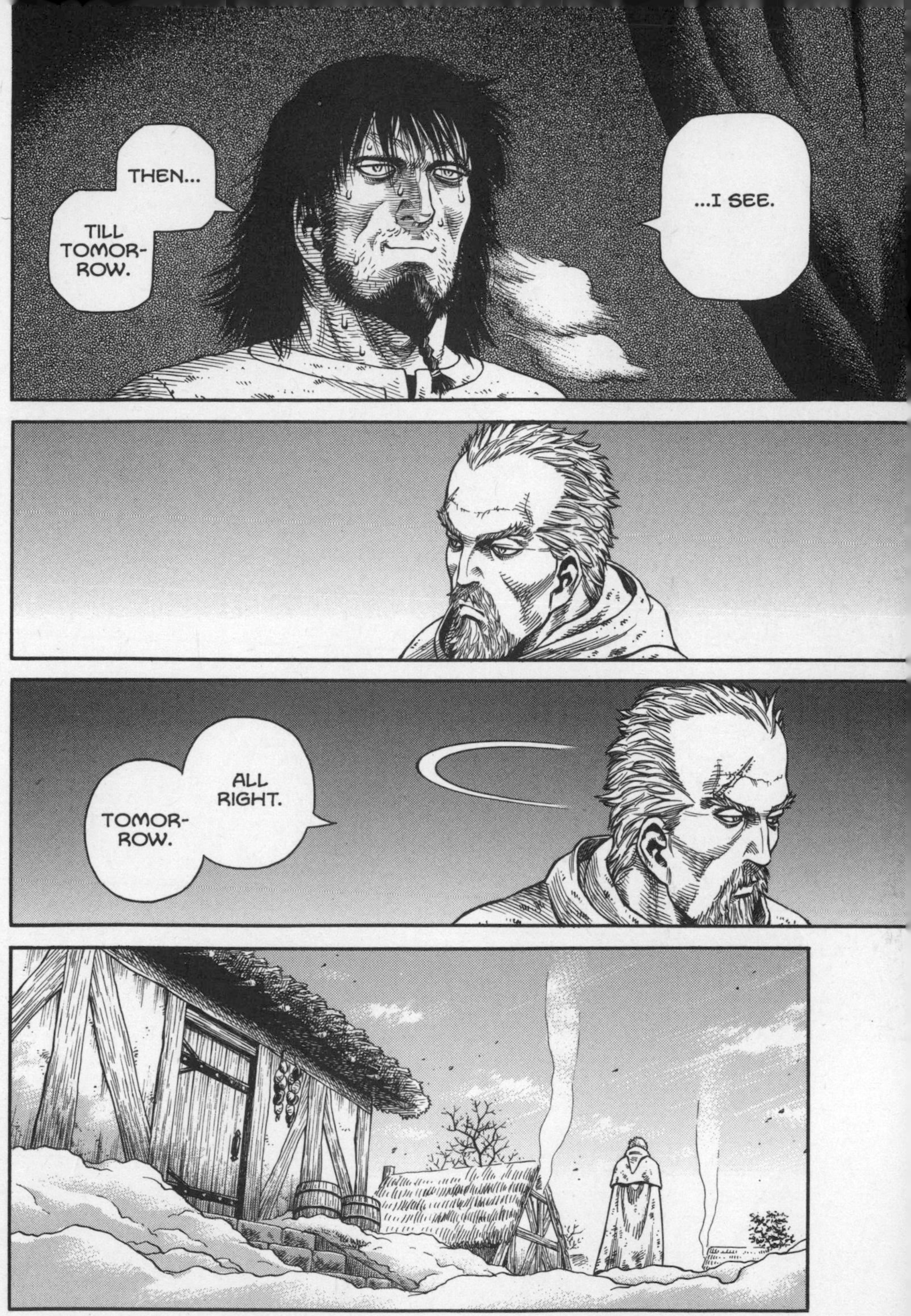
...I SEE.
THEN...
TILL TOMOR-ROW.
ALL RIGHT.
TOMOR-ROW.

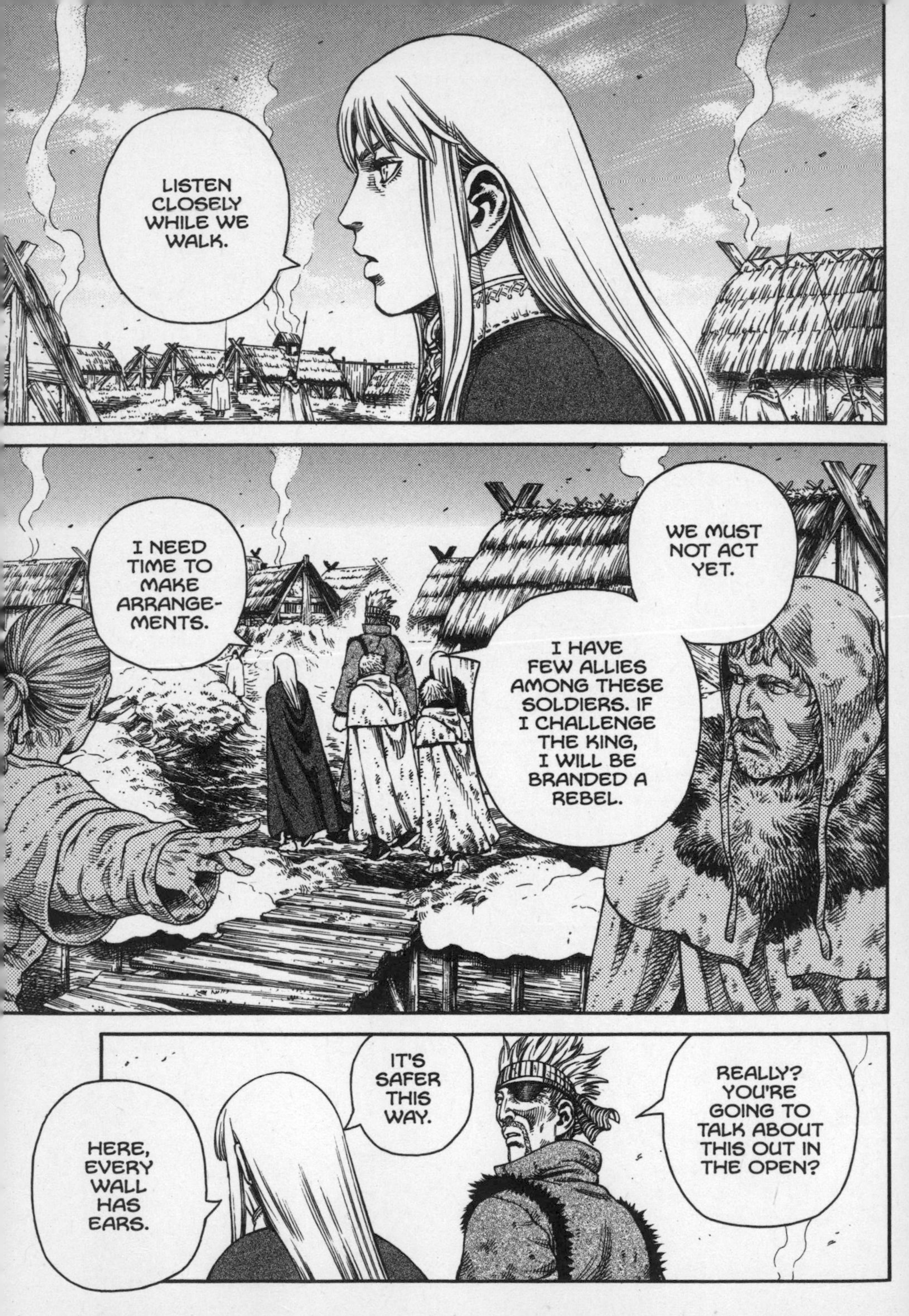
LISTEN CLOSELY WHILE WE WALK.
WE MUST NOT ACT YET.
I HAVE FEW ALLIES AMONG THESE SOLDIERS. IF I CHALLENGE THE KING, I WILL BE BRANDED A REBEL.
I NEED TIME TO MAKE ARRANGE-MENTS.
REALLY? YOU'RE GOING TO TALK ABOUT THIS OUT IN THE OPEN?
IT'S SAFER THIS WAY.
HERE, EVERY WALL HAS EARS.

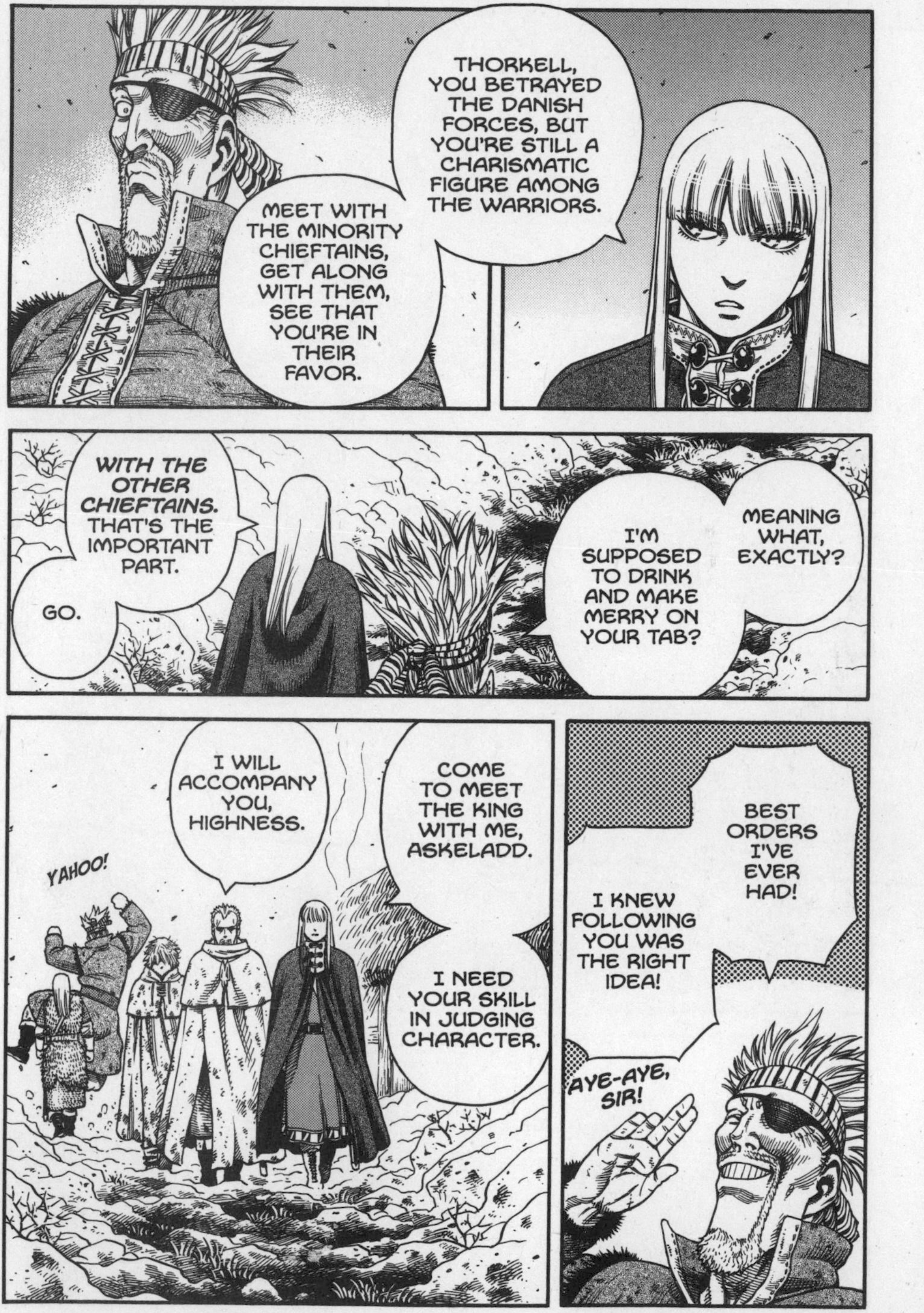
THORKELL, YOU BETRAYED THE DANISH FORCES, BUT YOU'RE STILL A CHARISMATIC FIGURE AMONG THE WARRIORS.
MEET WITH THE MINORITY CHIEFTAINS, GET ALONG WITH THEM, SEE THAT YOU'RE IN THEIR FAVOR.
MEANING WHAT, EXACTLY?
I'M SUPPOSED TO DRINK AND MAKE MERRY ON YOUR TAB?
WITH THE OTHER CHIEFTAINS. THAT'S THE IMPORTANT PART.
GO.
BEST ORDERS I'VE EVER HAD!
I KNEW FOLLOWING YOU WAS THE RIGHT IDEA!
AYE-AYE, SIR!
COME TO MEET THE KING WITH ME, ASKELADD.
I NEED YOUR SKILL IN JUDGING CHARACTER.
I WILL ACCOMPANY YOU, HIGHNESS.
YAHOO!

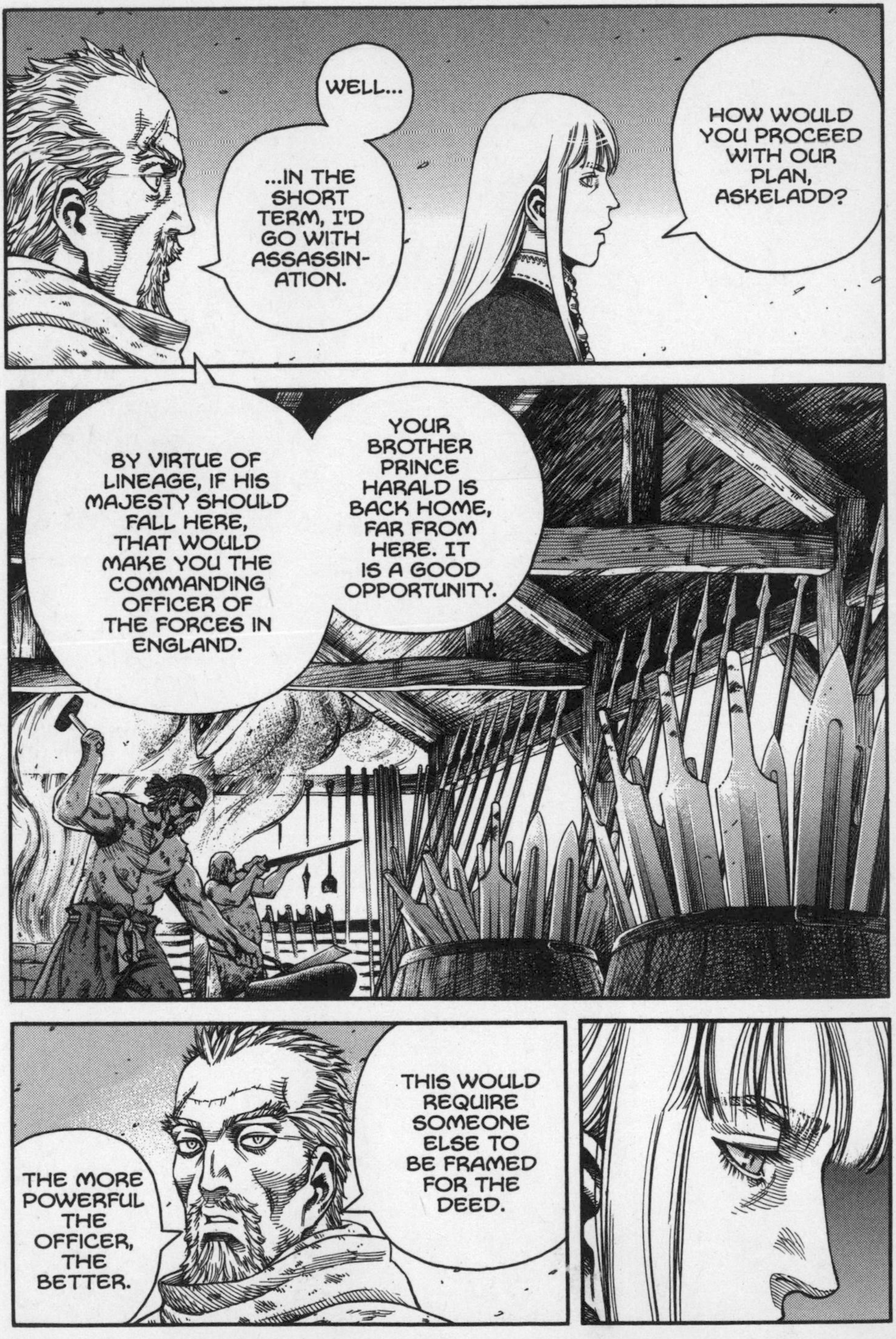
HOW WOULD YOU PROCEED WITH OUR PLAN, ASKELADD?
WELL...
...IN THE SHORT TERM, I'D GO WITH ASSASSIN-ATION.
YOUR BROTHER PRINCE HARALD IS BACK HOME, FAR FROM HERE. IT IS A GOOD OPPORTUNITY.
BY VIRTUE OF LINEAGE, IF HIS MAJESTY SHOULD FALL HERE, THAT WOULD MAKE YOU THE COMMANDING OFFICER OF THE FORCES IN ENGLAND.
THIS WOULD REQUIRE SOMEONE ELSE TO BE FRAMED FOR THE DEED.
THE MORE POWERFUL THE OFFICER, THE BETTER.

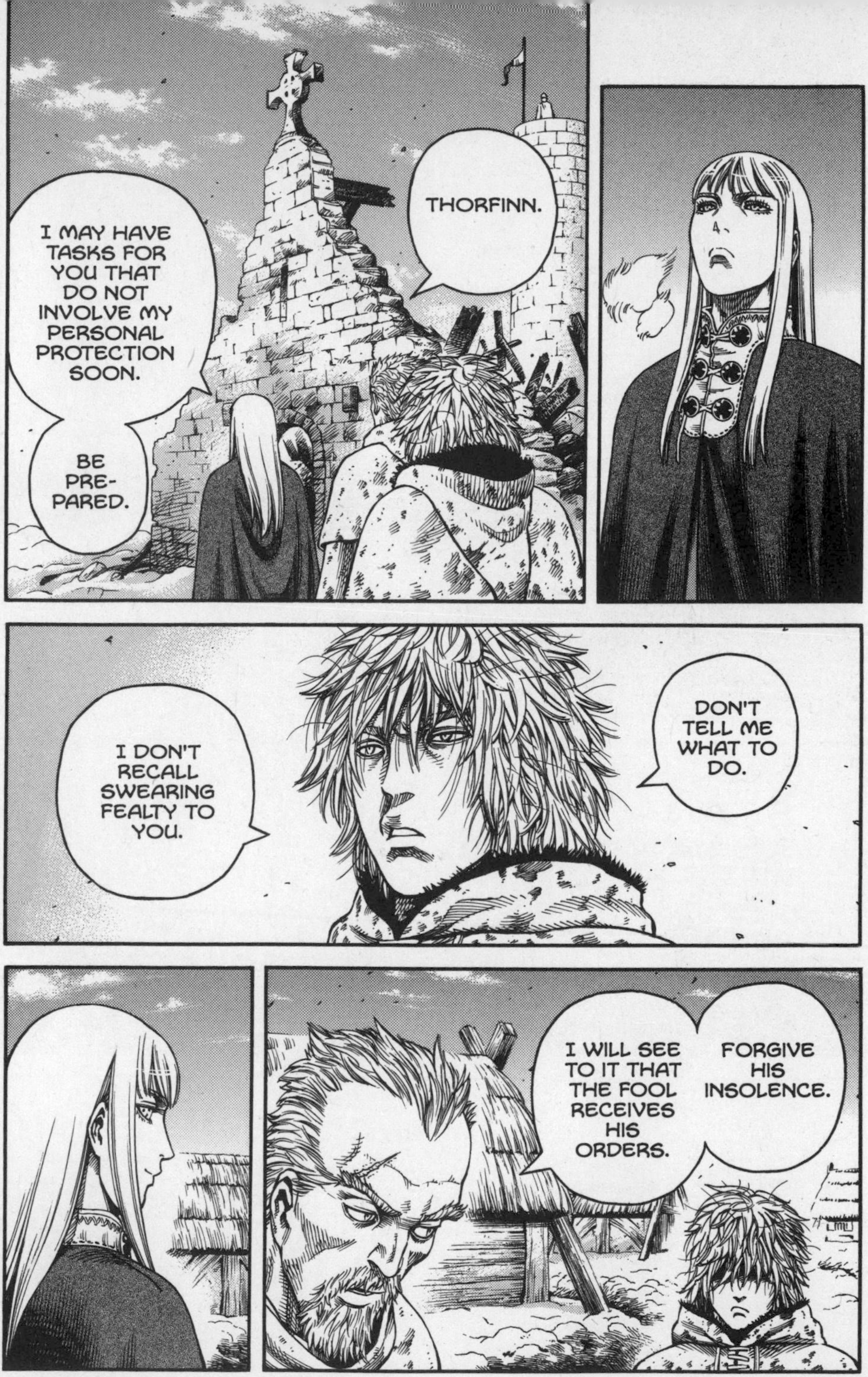
THORFINN.
I MAY HAVE TASKS FOR YOU THAT DO NOT INVOLVE MY PERSONAL PROTECTION SOON.
BE PRE-PARED.
DON'T TELL ME WHAT TO DO.
I DON'T RECALL SWEARING FEALTY TO YOU.
FORGIVE HIS INSOLENCE.
I WILL SEE TO IT THAT THE FOOL RECEIVES HIS ORDERS.

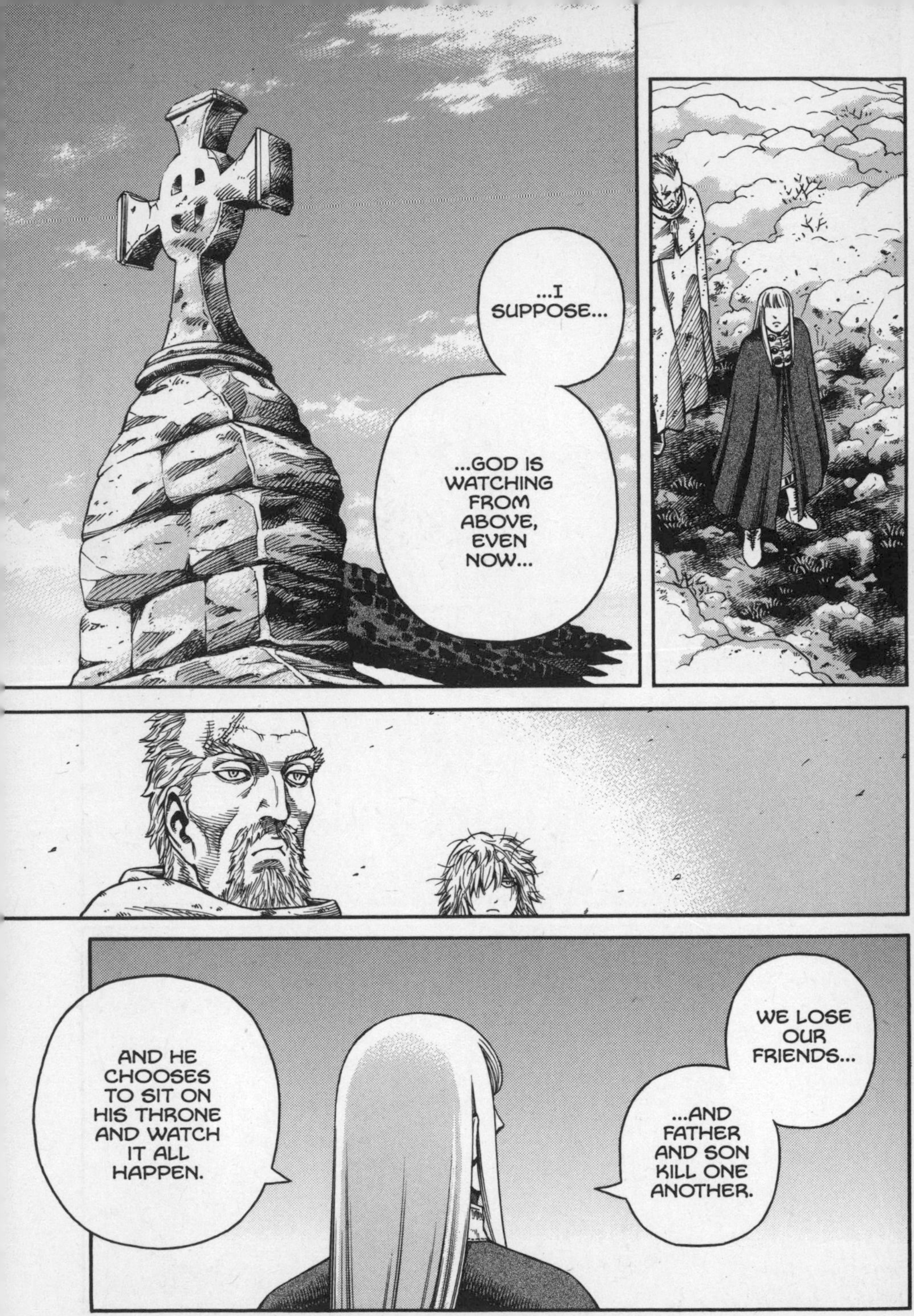
...I SUPPOSE...
...GOD IS WATCHING FROM ABOVE, EVEN NOW...
WE LOSE OUR FRIENDS...
...AND FATHER AND SON KILL ONE ANOTHER.
AND HE CHOOSES TO SIT ON HIS THRONE AND WATCH IT ALL HAPPEN.

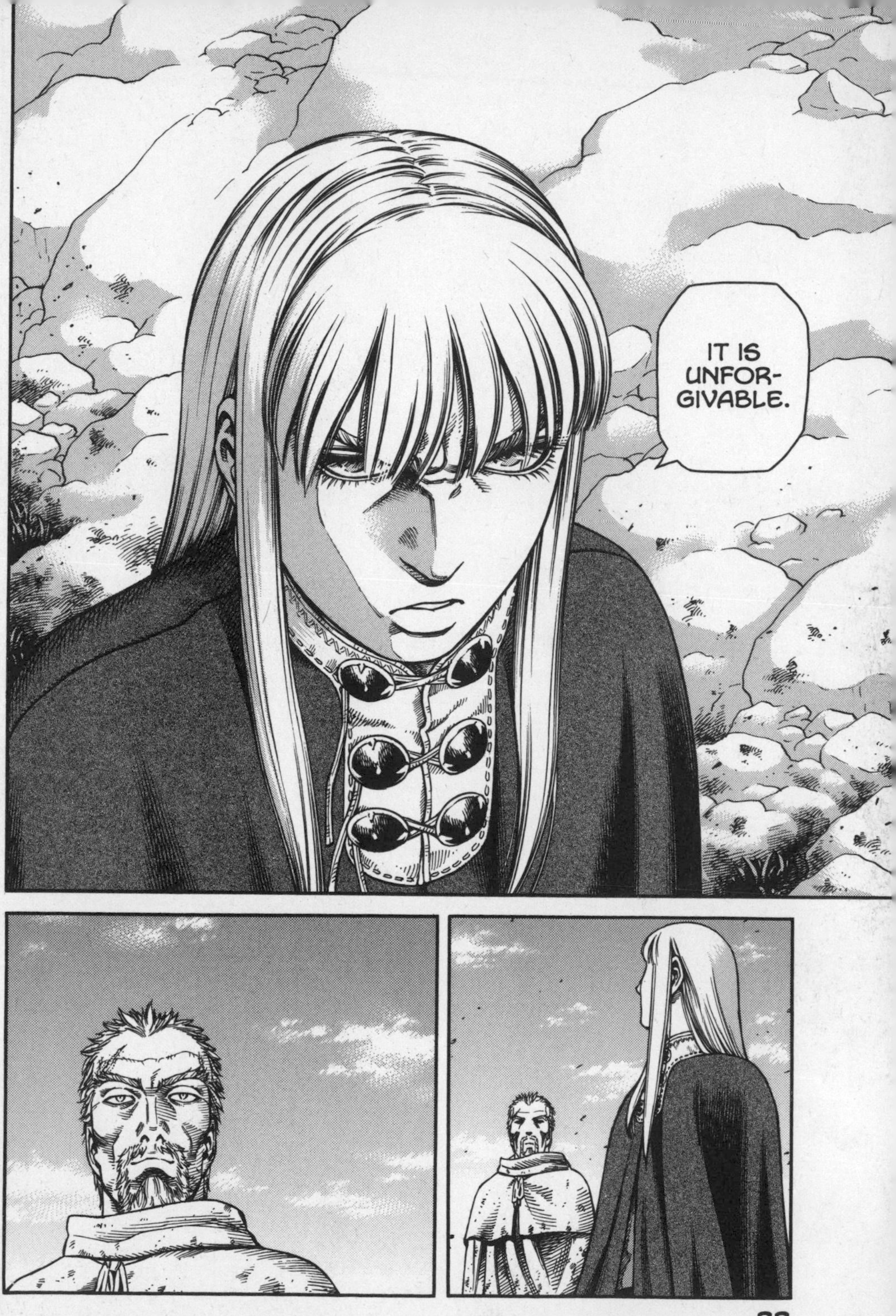
IT IS UNFORGIVABLE.

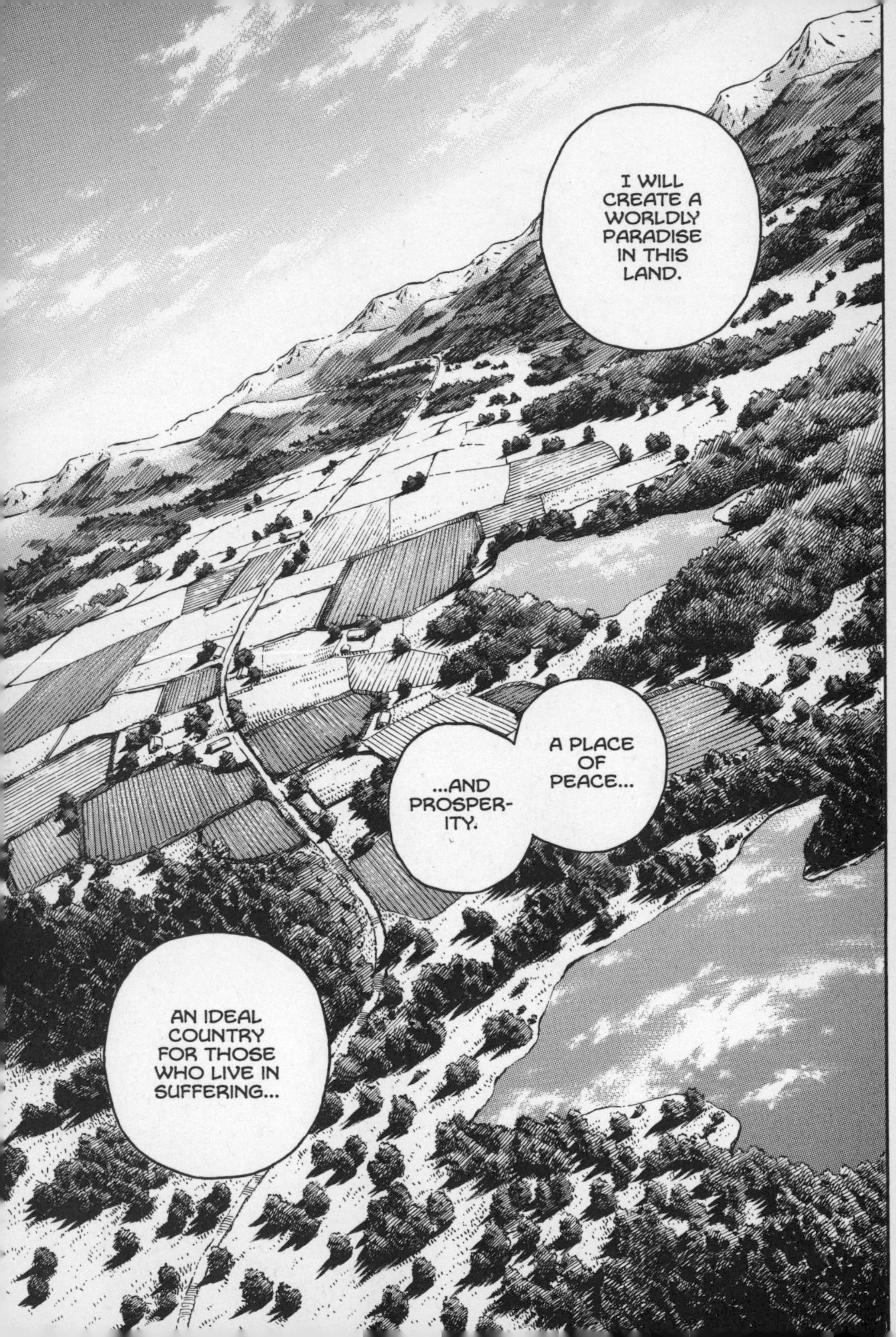
I WILL CREATE A WORLDLY PARADISE IN THIS LAND.
A PLACE OF PEACE...
...AND PROSPER-ITY.
AN IDEAL COUNTRY FOR THOSE WHO LIVE IN SUFFERING...

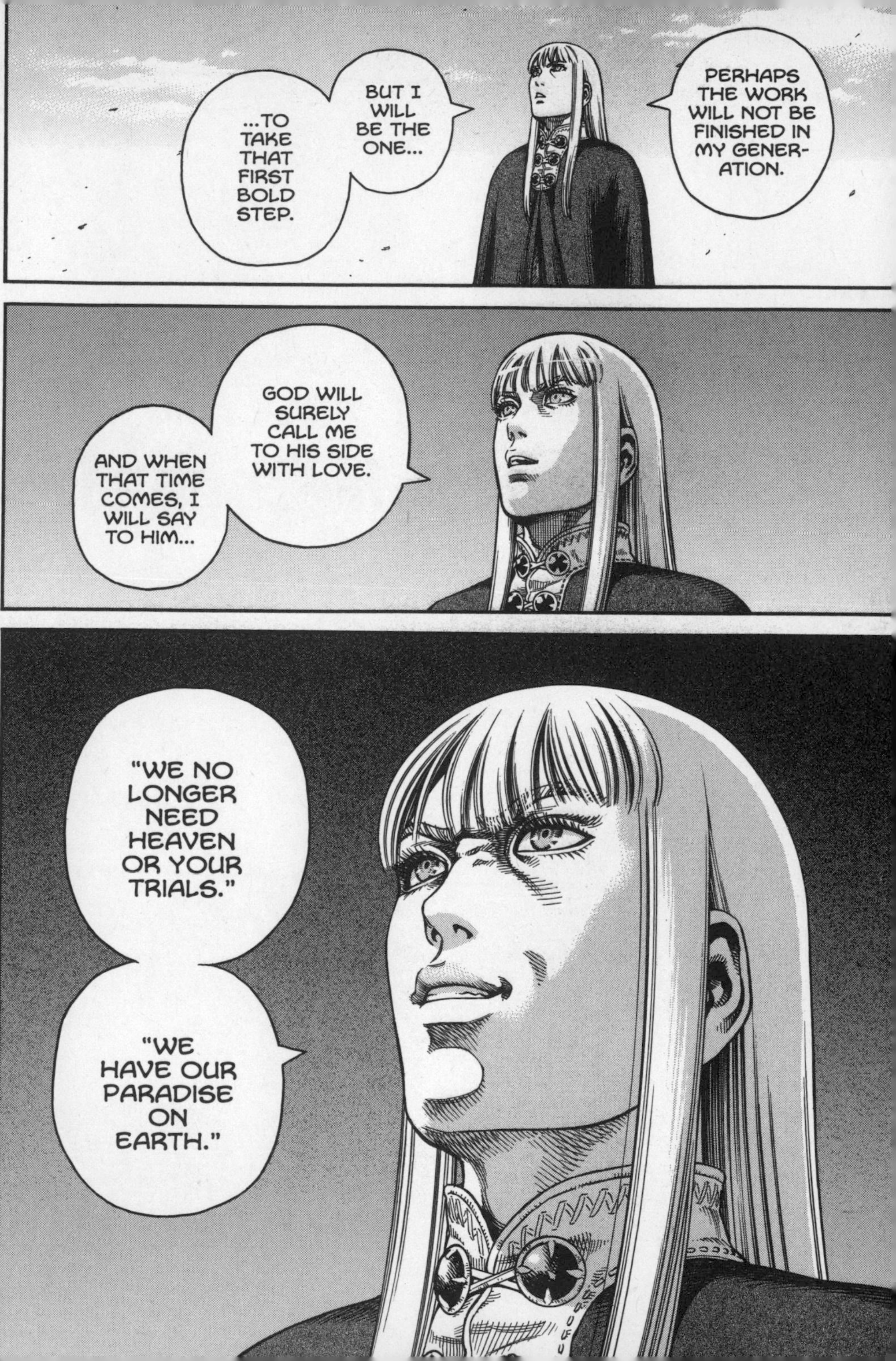
PERHAPS THE WORK WILL NOT BE FINISHED IN MY GENER-ATION.
BUT I WILL BE THE ONE...
...TO TAKE THAT FIRST BOLD STEP.
GOD WILL SURELY CALL ME TO HIS SIDE WITH LOVE.
AND WHEN THAT TIME COMES, I WILL SAY TO HIM...
"WE NO LONGER NEED HEAVEN OR YOUR TRIALS."
"WE HAVE OUR PARADISE ON EARTH."

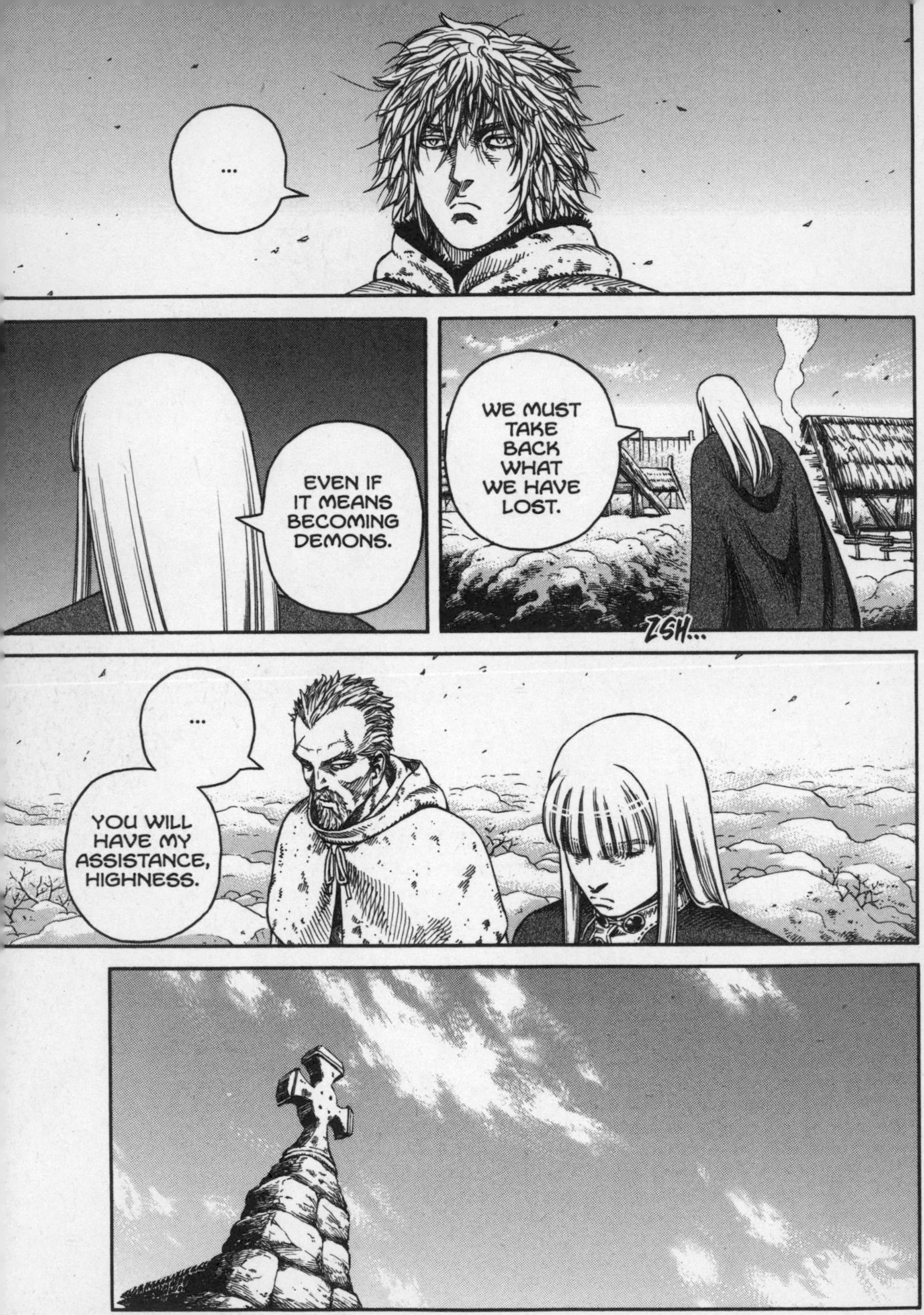
...
WE MUST TAKE BACK WHAT WE HAVE LOST.
ZSH...
EVEN IF IT MEANS BECOMING DEMONS.
...
YOU WILL HAVE MY ASSISTANCE, HIGHNESS.

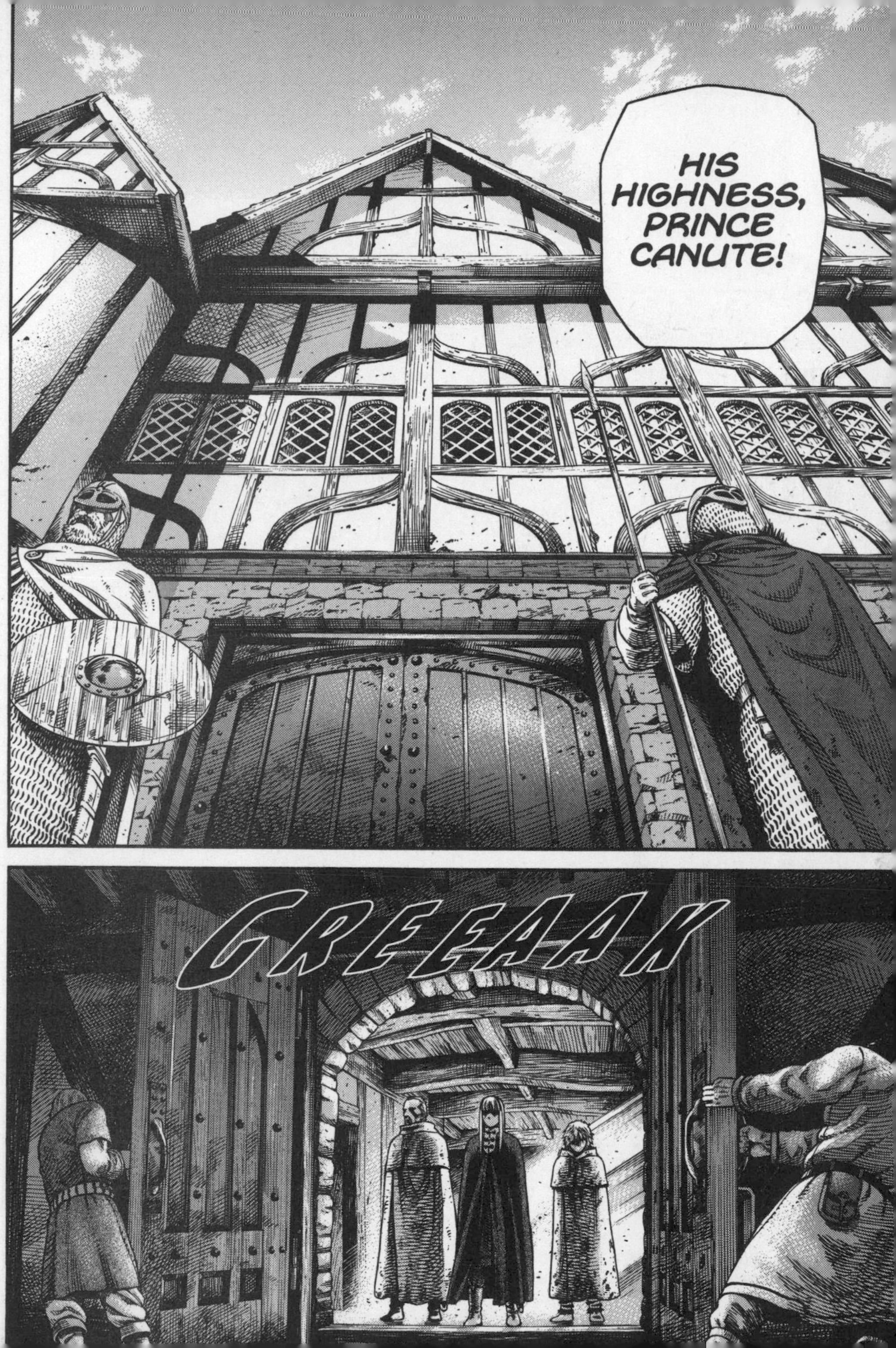
HIS HIGHNESS, PRINCE CANUTE!
CREEAAK

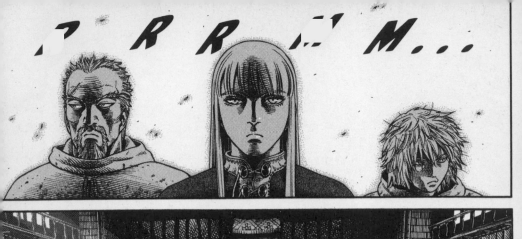

PRRRM...

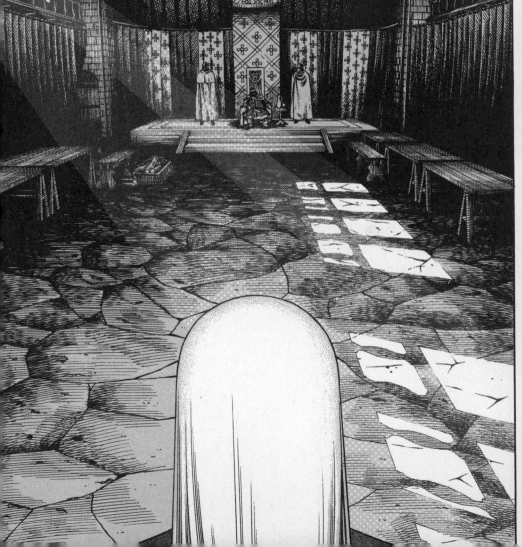

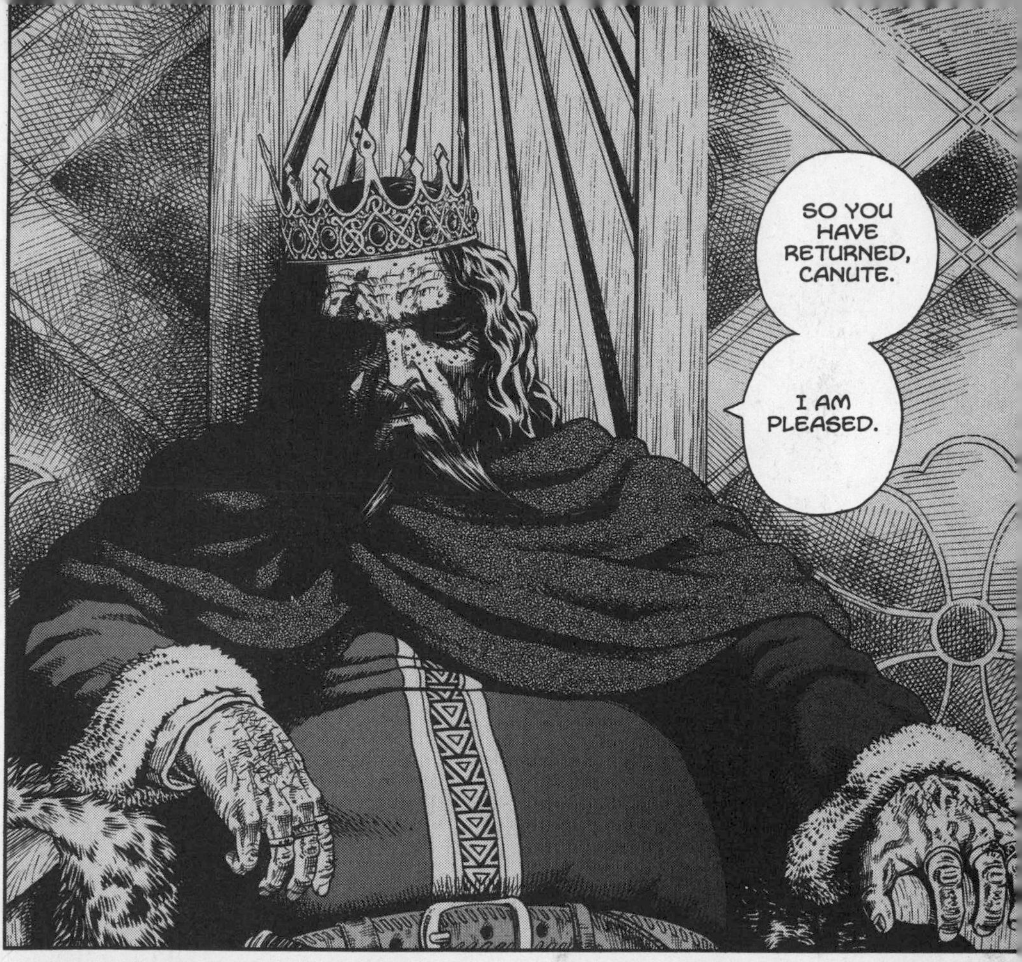
SO YOU HAVE RETURNED, CANUTE.
I AM PLEASED.
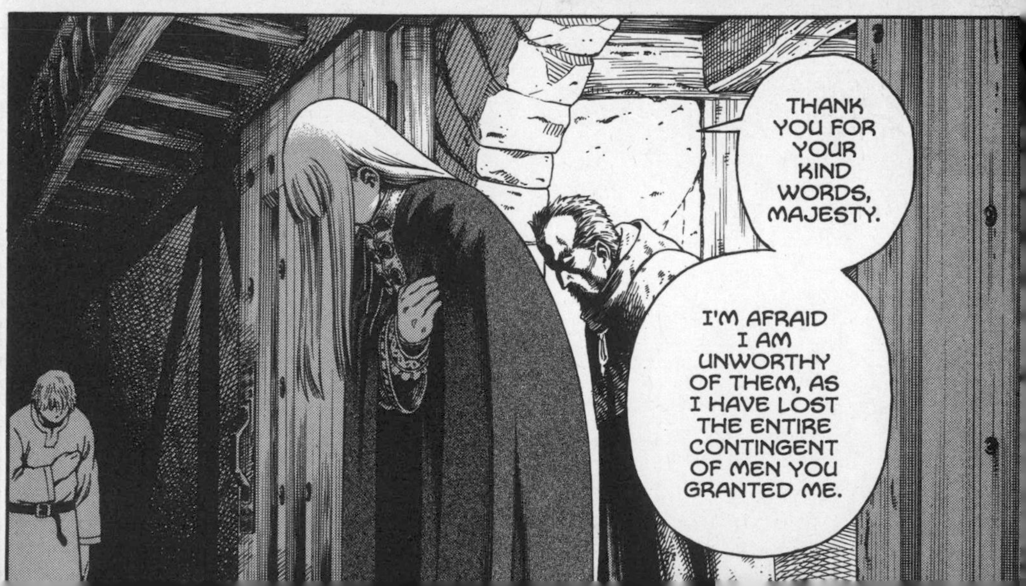
THANK YOU FOR YOUR KIND WORDS, MAJESTY.
I'M AFRAID I AM UNWORTHY OF THEM, AS I HAVE LOST THE ENTIRE CONTINGENT OF MEN YOU GRANTED ME.

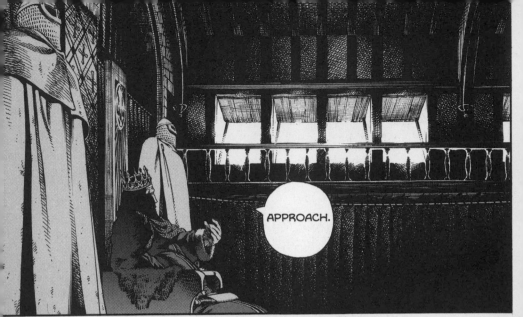

APPROACH.

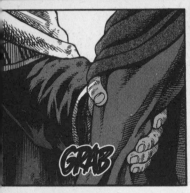

GRAB

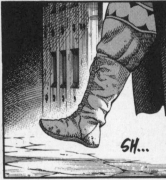

SH...

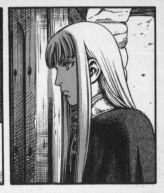

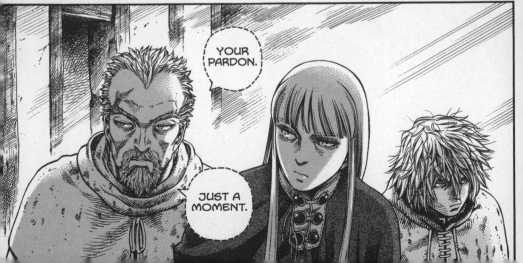

YOUR PARDON.

JUST A MOMENT.

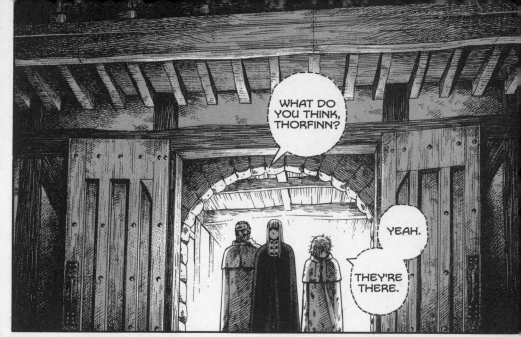

WHAT DO YOU THINK, THORFINN?

YEAH.

THEY'RE THERE.

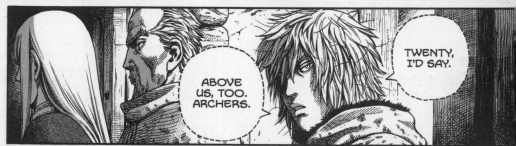

ABOVE US, TOO. ARCHERS.

TWENTY, I'D SAY.

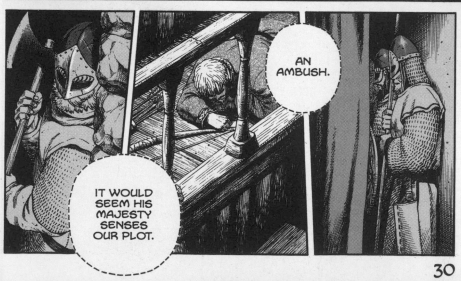

AN AMBUSH.

IT WOULD SEEM HIS MAJESTY SENSES OUR PLOT.

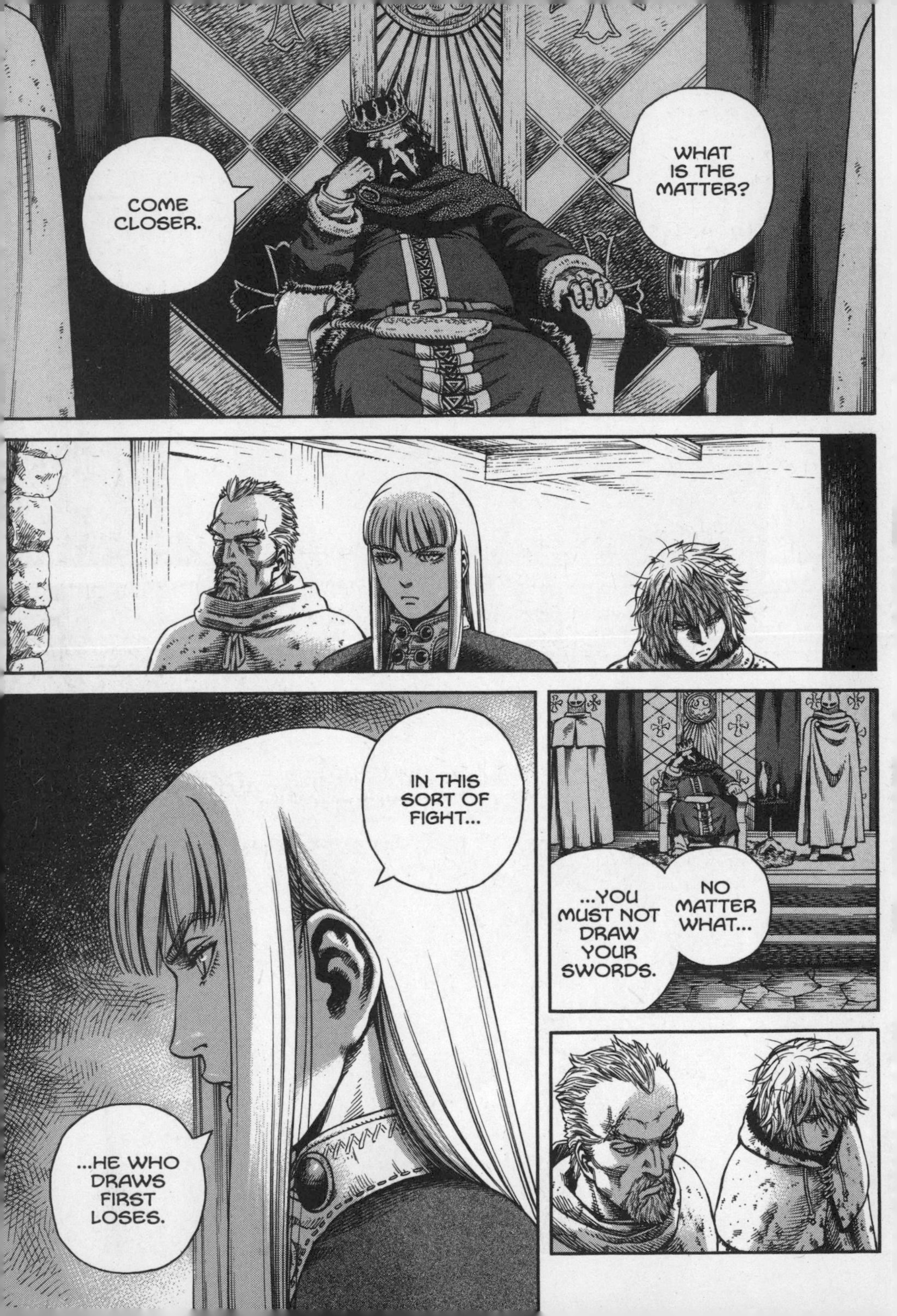
WHAT IS THE MATTER?
COME CLOSER.
NO MATTER WHAT...
...YOU MUST NOT DRAW YOUR SWORDS.
IN THIS SORT OF FIGHT...
...HE WHO DRAWS FIRST LOSES.

CHAPTER 44: THE CURSE OF THE CROWN

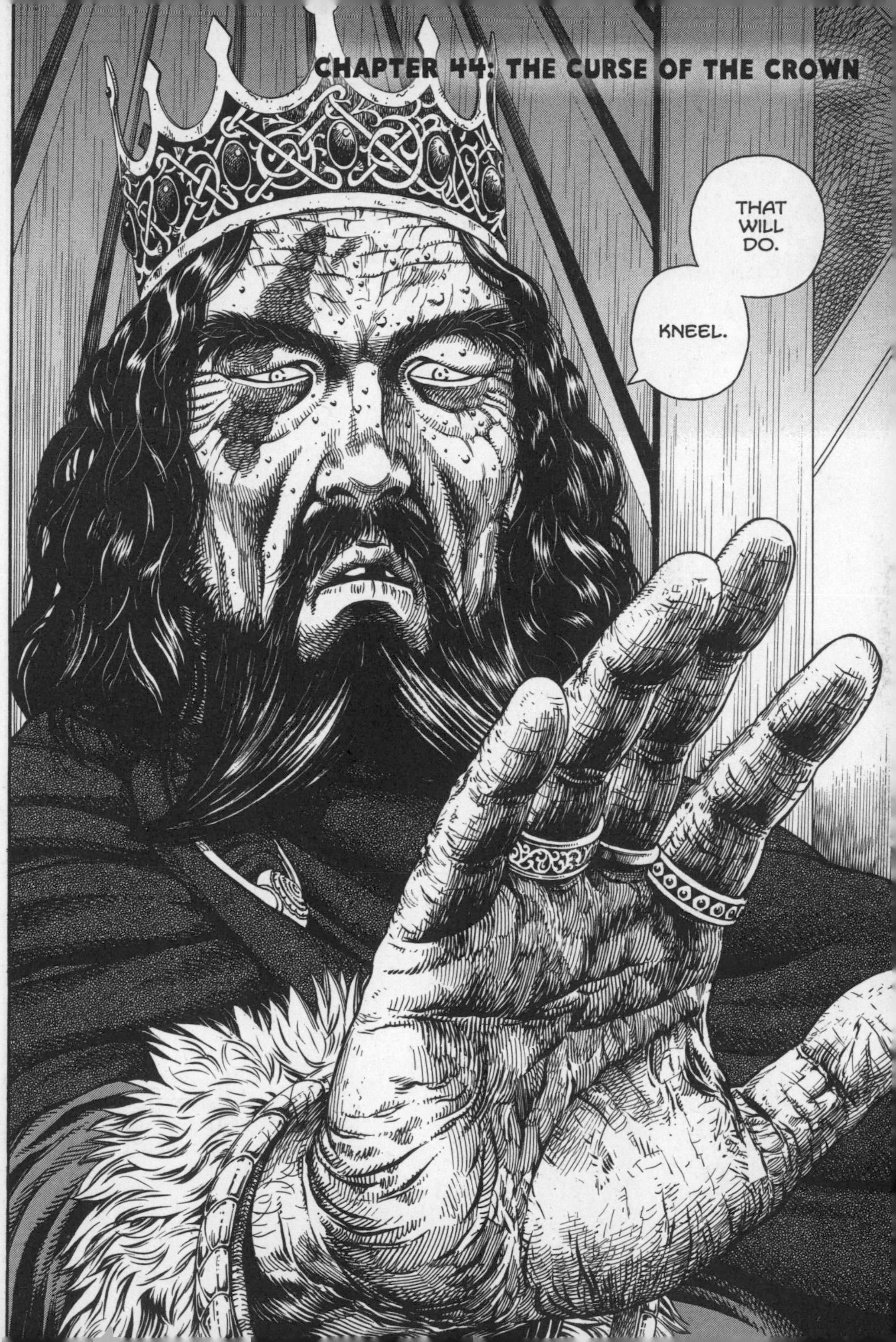
THAT WILL DO.
KNEEL.

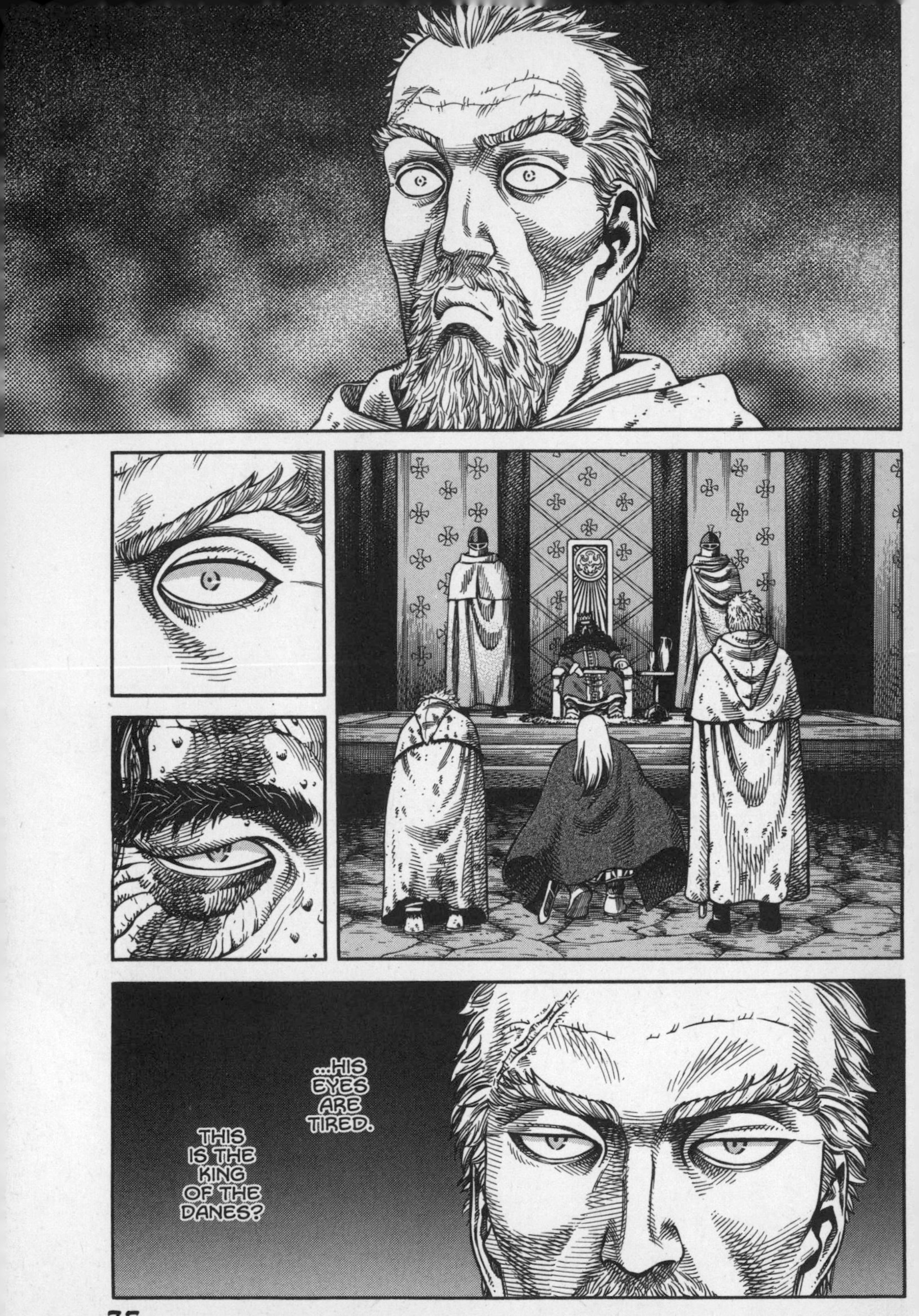
...HIS EYES ARE TIRED.
THIS IS THE KING OF THE DANES?

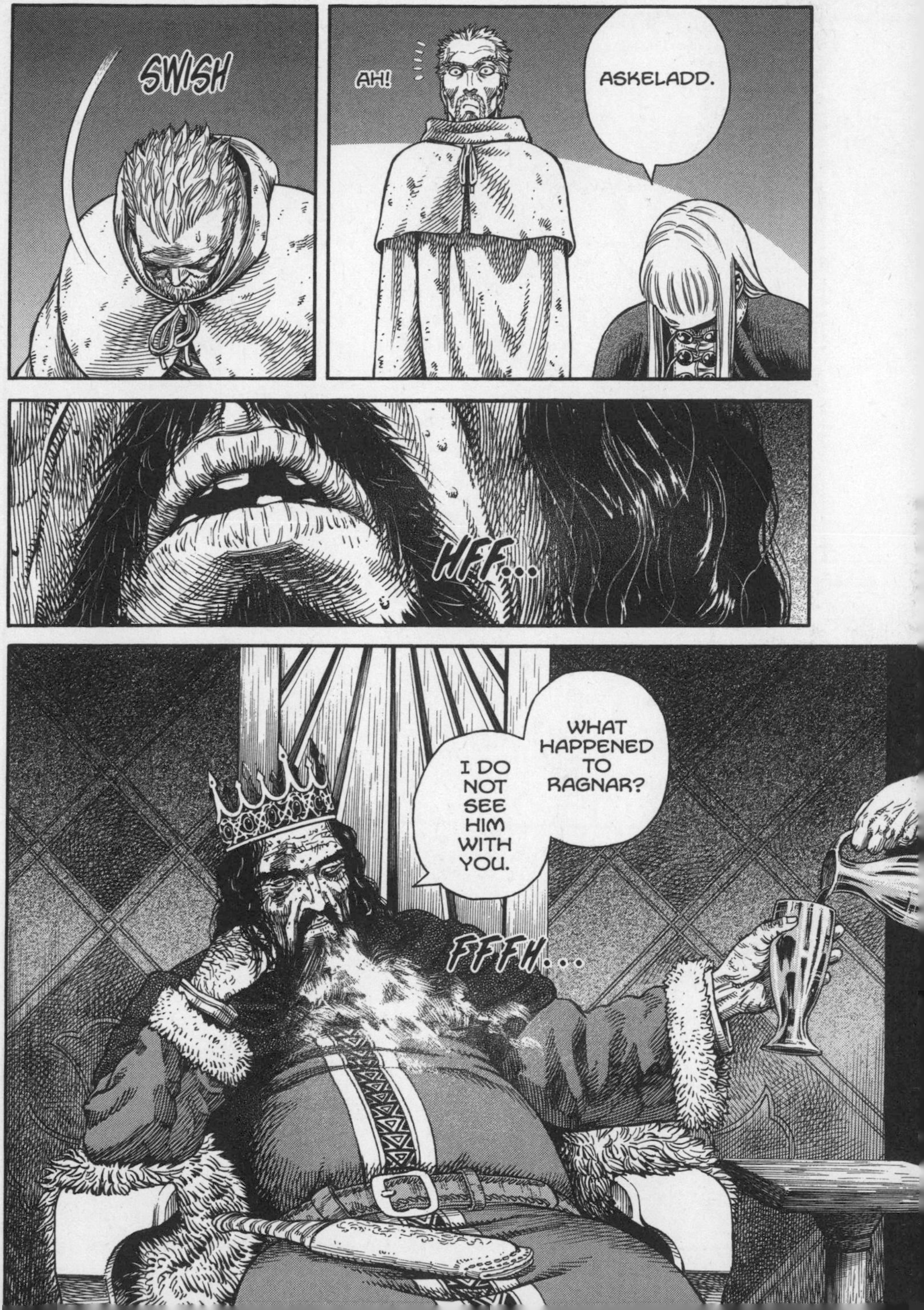
ASKELADD.
AH!
SWISH
HFF...
WHAT HAPPENED TO RAGNAR?
I DO NOT SEE HIM WITH YOU.
FFFH...

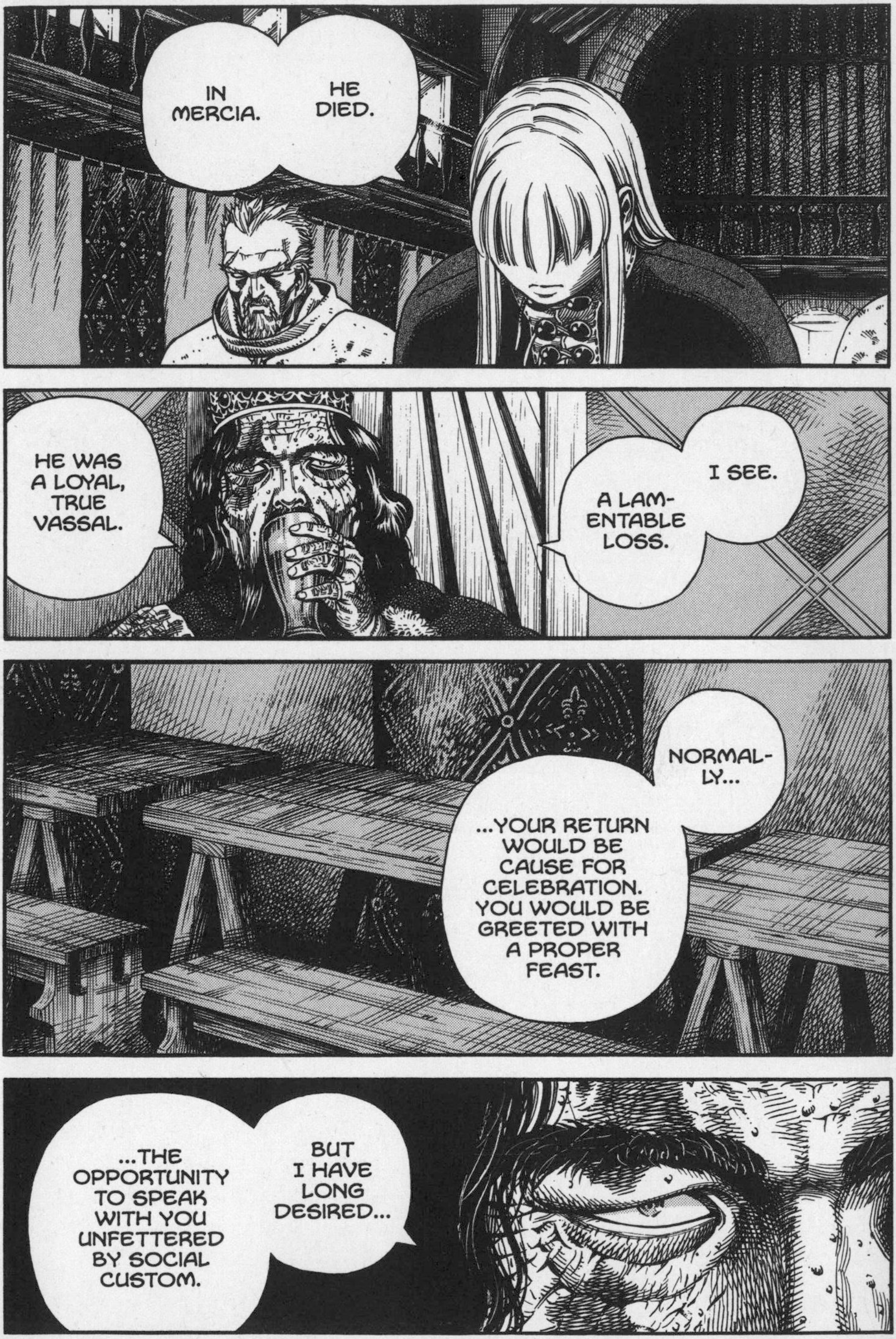
HE DIED.
IN MERCIA.
I SEE. A LAMENTABLE LOSS.
HE WAS A LOYAL, TRUE VASSAL.
NORMALLY...
...YOUR RETURN WOULD BE CAUSE FOR CELEBRATION. YOU WOULD BE GREETED WITH A PROPER FEAST.
BUT I HAVE LONG DESIRED...
...THE OPPORTUNITY TO SPEAK WITH YOU UNFETTERED BY SOCIAL CUSTOM.

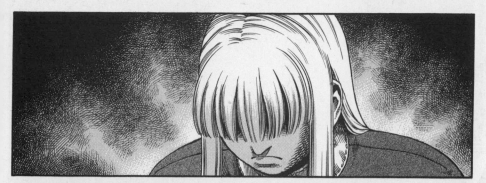

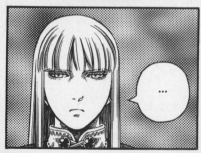

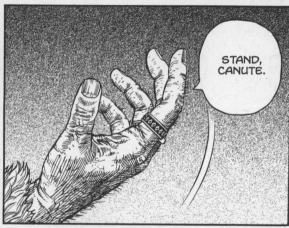

STAND, CANUTE.

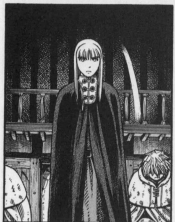

...

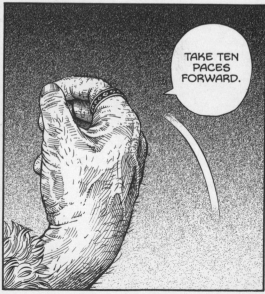

TAKE TEN PACES FORWARD.

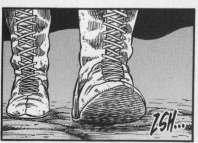

ZSH...

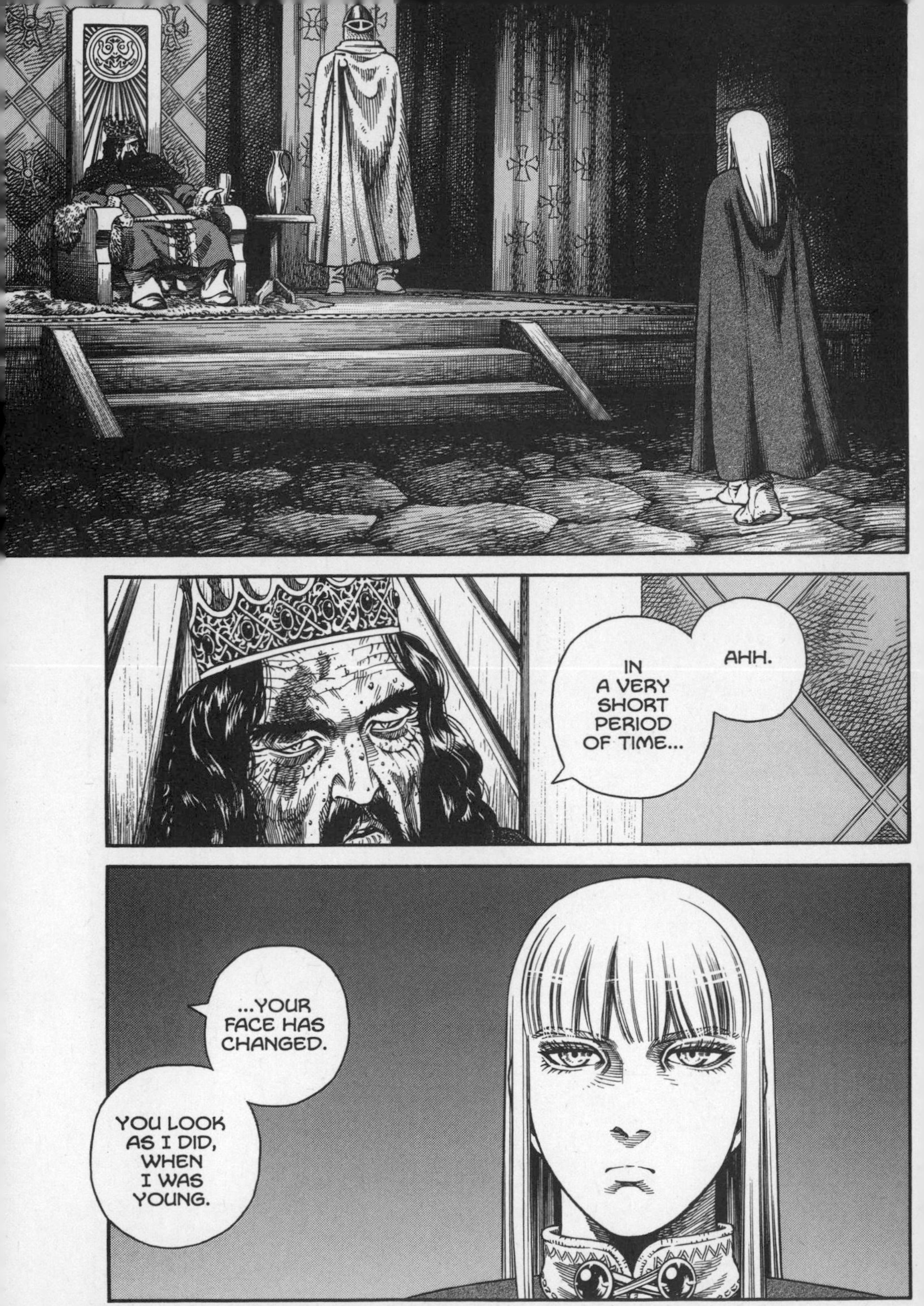
AHH.
IN A VERY SHORT PERIOD OF TIME...
...YOUR FACE HAS CHANGED.
YOU LOOK AS I DID, WHEN I WAS YOUNG.

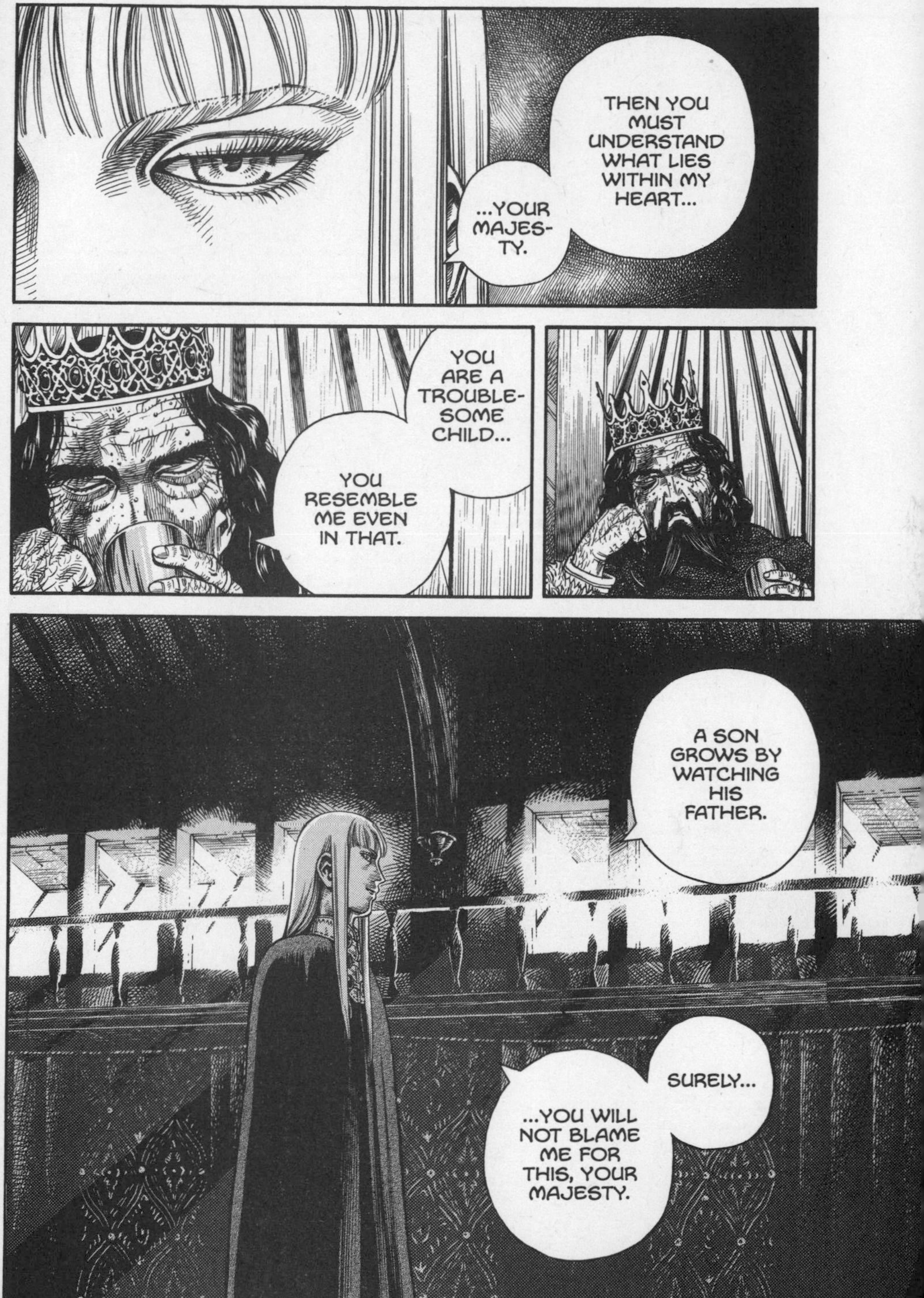
THEN YOU MUST UNDERSTAND WHAT LIES WITHIN MY HEART...
...YOUR MAJES-TY.
YOU ARE A TROUBLE-SOME CHILD...
YOU RESEMBLE ME EVEN IN THAT.
A SON GROWS BY WATCHING HIS FATHER.
SURELY...
...YOU WILL NOT BLAME ME FOR THIS, YOUR MAJESTY.

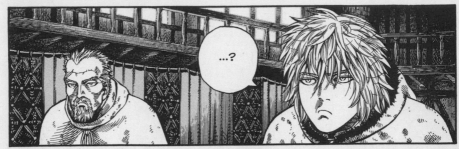

...?

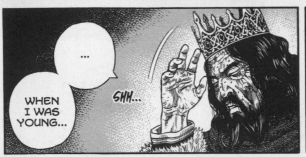

...

WHEN
I WAS
YOUNG...

SHH...

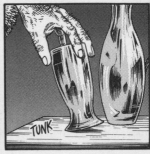

TUNK

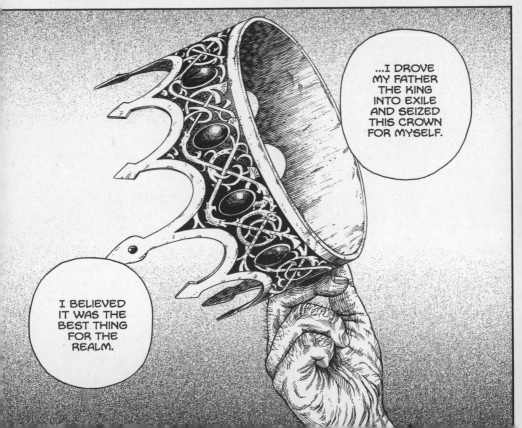

...I DROVE
MY FATHER
THE KING
INTO EXILE
AND SEIZED
THIS CROWN
FOR MYSELF.

I BELIEVED
IT WAS THE
BEST THING
FOR THE
REALM.

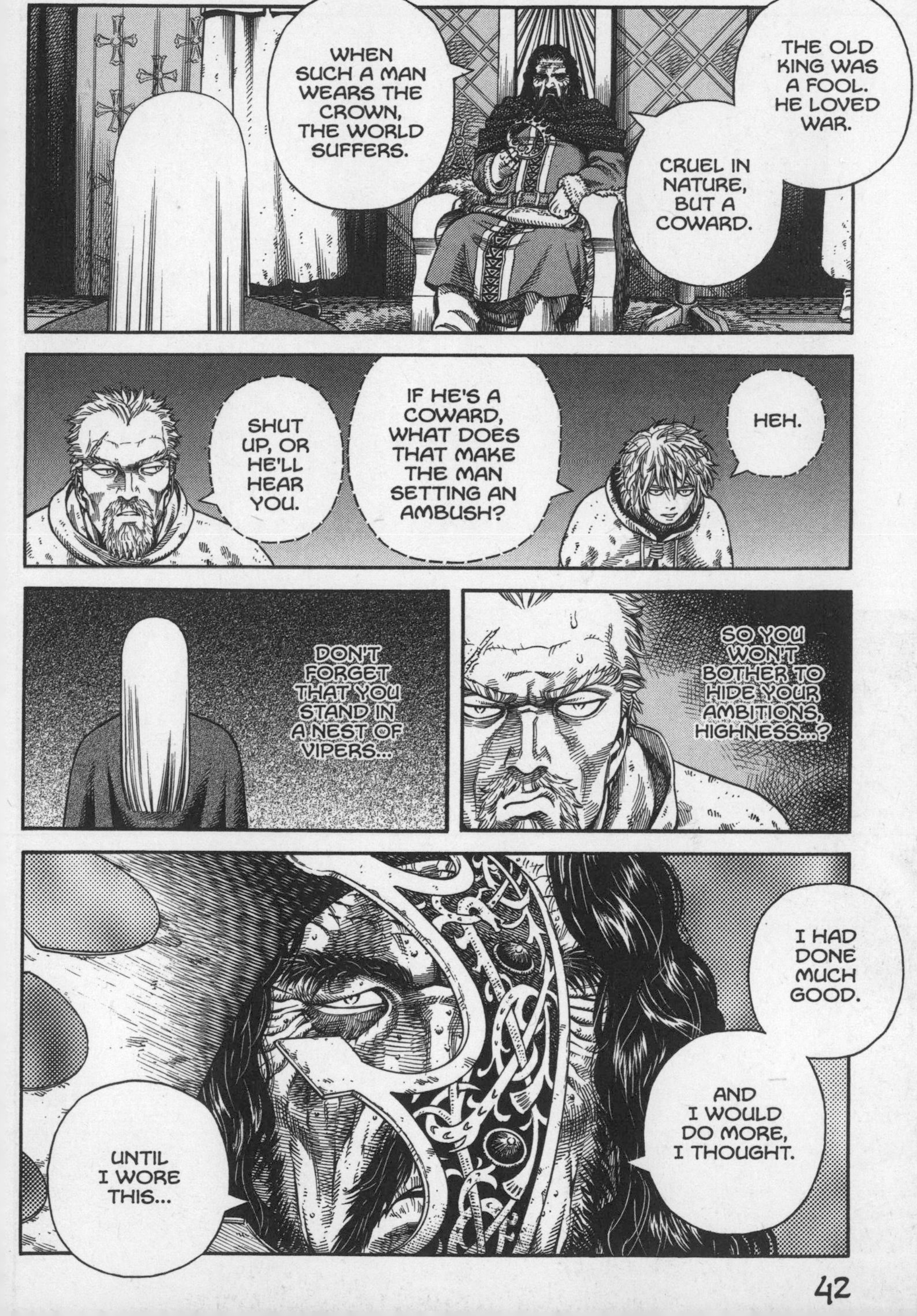
THE OLD KING WAS A FOOL. HE LOVED WAR.
CRUEL IN NATURE, BUT A COWARD.
WHEN SUCH A MAN WEARS THE CROWN, THE WORLD SUFFERS.
HEH.
IF HE'S A COWARD, WHAT DOES THAT MAKE THE MAN SETTING AN AMBUSH?
SHUT UP, OR HE'LL HEAR YOU.
SO YOU WON'T BOTHER TO HIDE YOUR AMBITIONS, HIGHNESS...?
DON'T FORGET THAT YOU STAND IN A NEST OF VIPERS...
I HAD DONE MUCH GOOD.
AND I WOULD DO MORE, I THOUGHT.
UNTIL I WORE THIS...

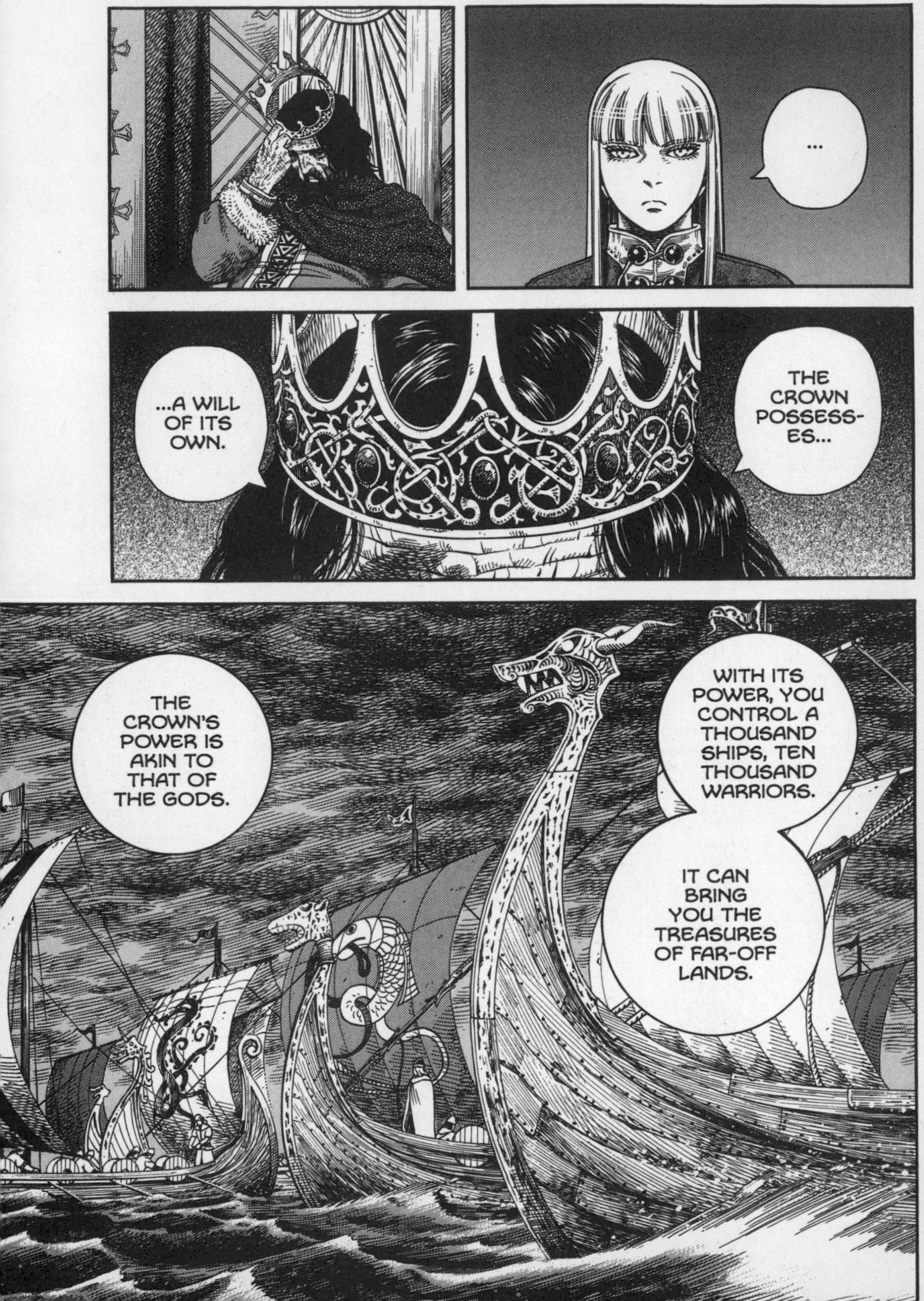
...
THE CROWN POSSESS-ES...
...A WILL OF ITS OWN.
WITH ITS POWER, YOU CONTROL A THOUSAND SHIPS, TEN THOUSAND WARRIORS.
IT CAN BRING YOU THE TREASURES OF FAR-OFF LANDS.
THE CROWN'S POWER IS AKIN TO THAT OF THE GODS.

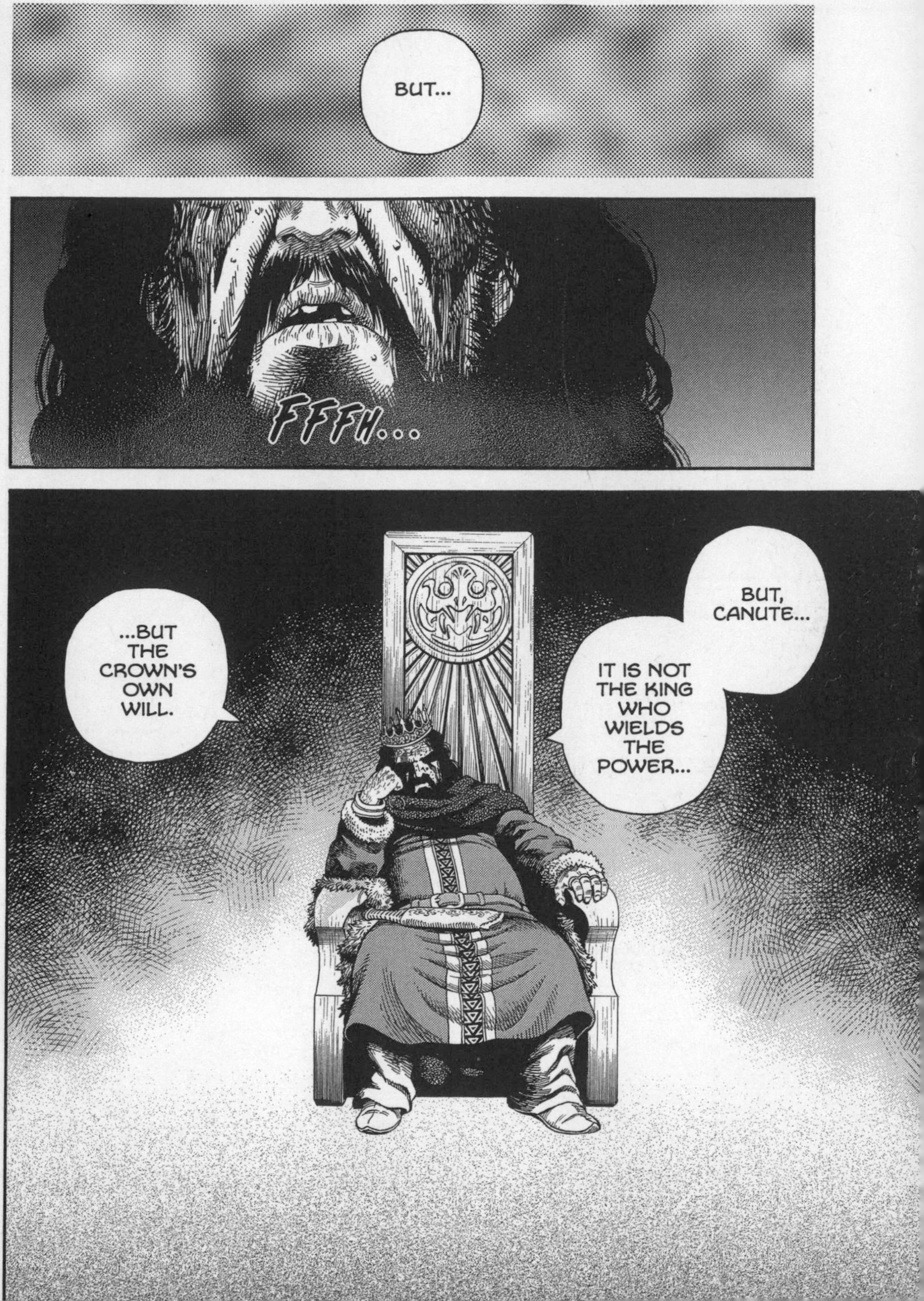
BUT...
FFFH...
BUT, CANUTE...
IT IS NOT THE KING WHO WIELDS THE POWER...
...BUT THE CROWN'S OWN WILL.

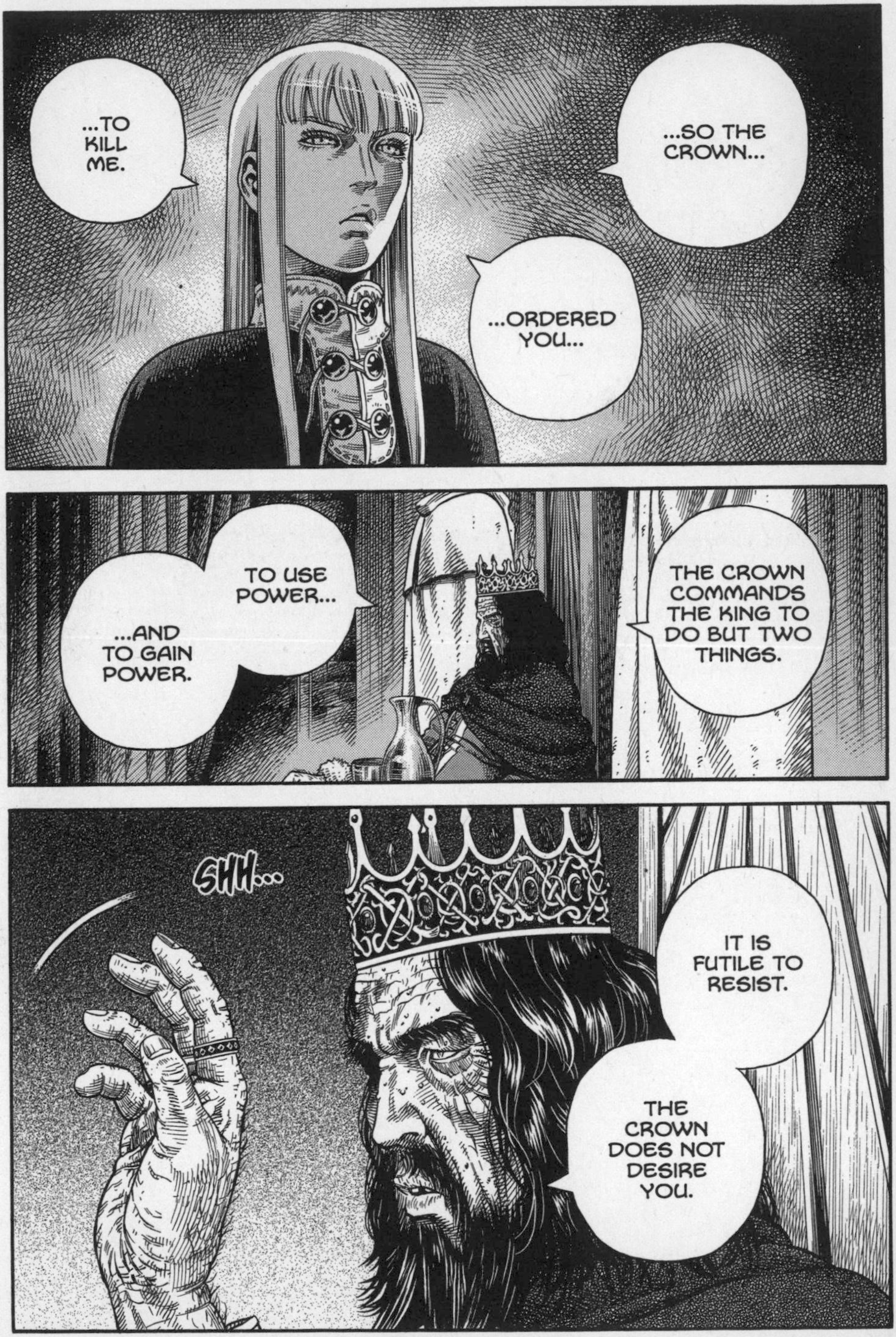
...SO THE CROWN...
...ORDERED YOU...
...TO KILL ME.
THE CROWN COMMANDS THE KING TO DO BUT TWO THINGS.
TO USE POWER...
...AND TO GAIN POWER.
IT IS FUTILE TO RESIST.
THE CROWN DOES NOT DESIRE YOU.
SHH...

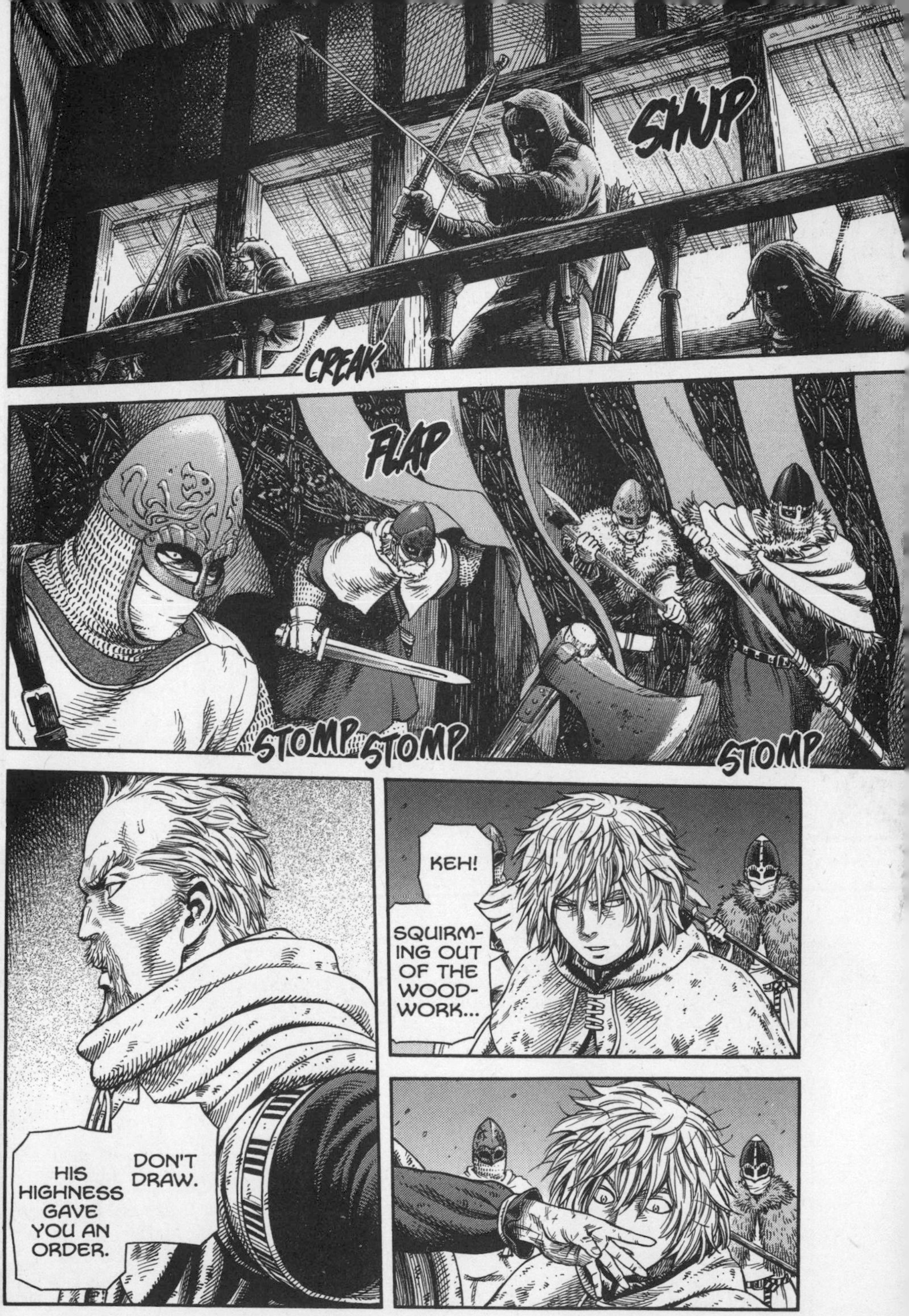
SHUP
CREAK
FLAP
STOMP
STOMP
STOMP
KEH!
SQUIRMING OUT OF THE WOODWORK...
DON'T DRAW.
HIS HIGHNESS GAVE YOU AN ORDER.

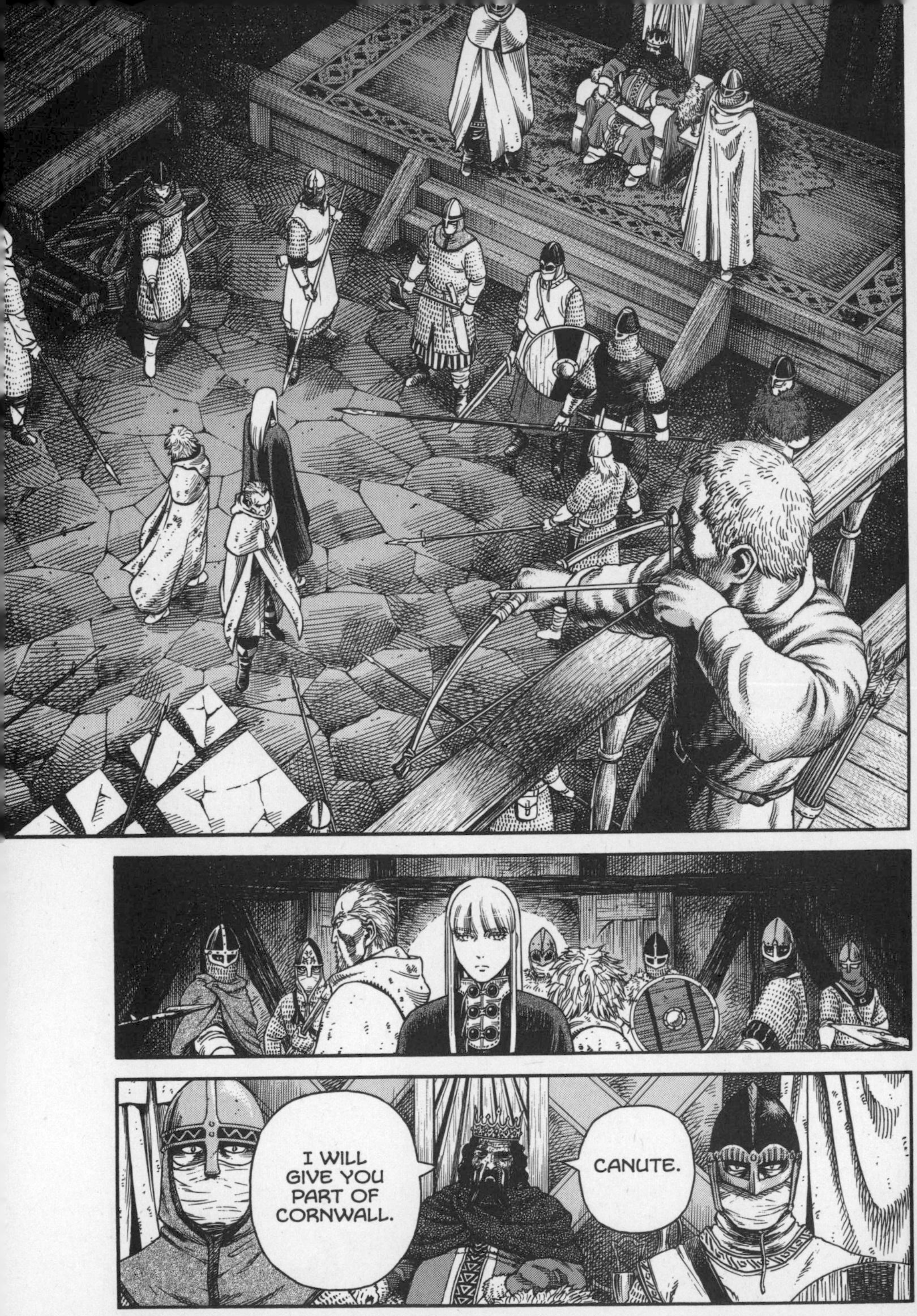
CANUTE.
I WILL GIVE YOU PART OF CORNWALL.

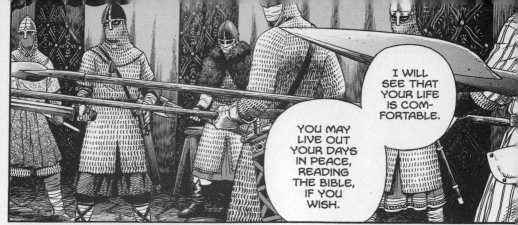

I WILL SEE THAT YOUR LIFE IS COMFORTABLE.

YOU MAY LIVE OUT YOUR DAYS IN PEACE, READING THE BIBLE, IF YOU WISH.

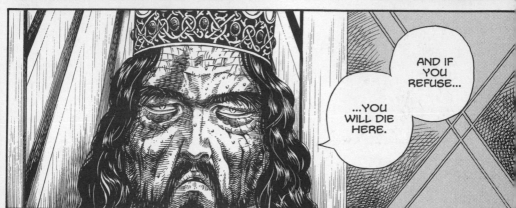

AND IF YOU REFUSE...

...YOU WILL DIE HERE.

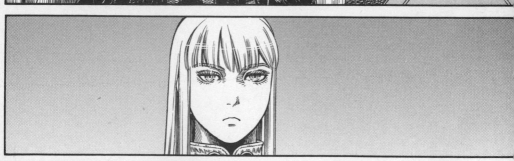

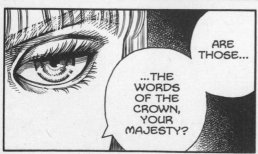

ARE THOSE...

...THE WORDS OF THE CROWN, YOUR MAJESTY?

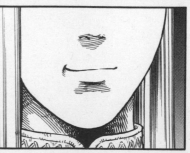

48

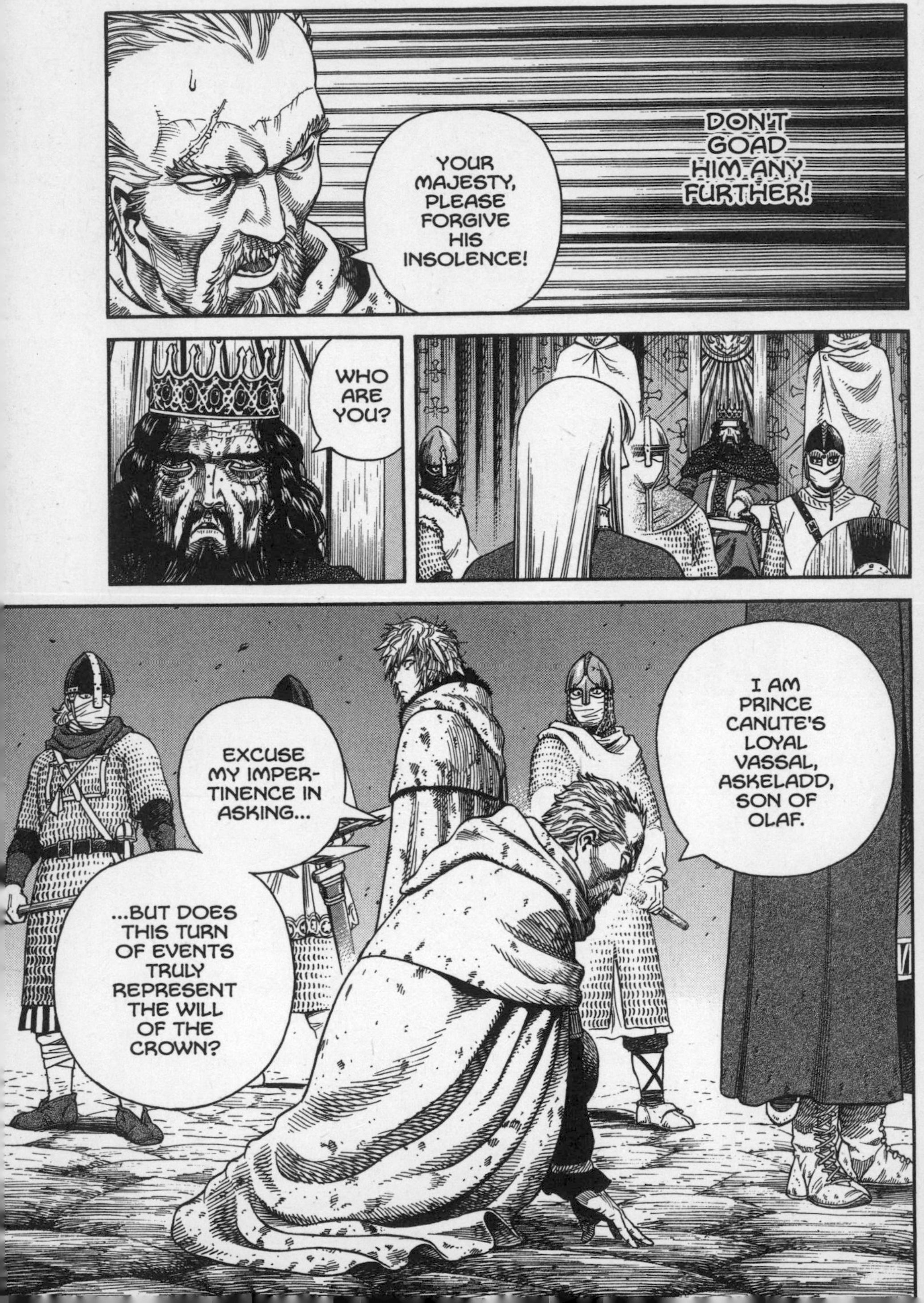
DON'T GOAD HIM ANY FURTHER!
YOUR MAJESTY, PLEASE FORGIVE HIS INSOLENCE!
WHO ARE YOU?
I AM PRINCE CANUTE'S LOYAL VASSAL, ASKELADD, SON OF OLAF.
EXCUSE MY IMPERTINENCE IN ASKING...
...BUT DOES THIS TURN OF EVENTS TRULY REPRESENT THE WILL OF THE CROWN?

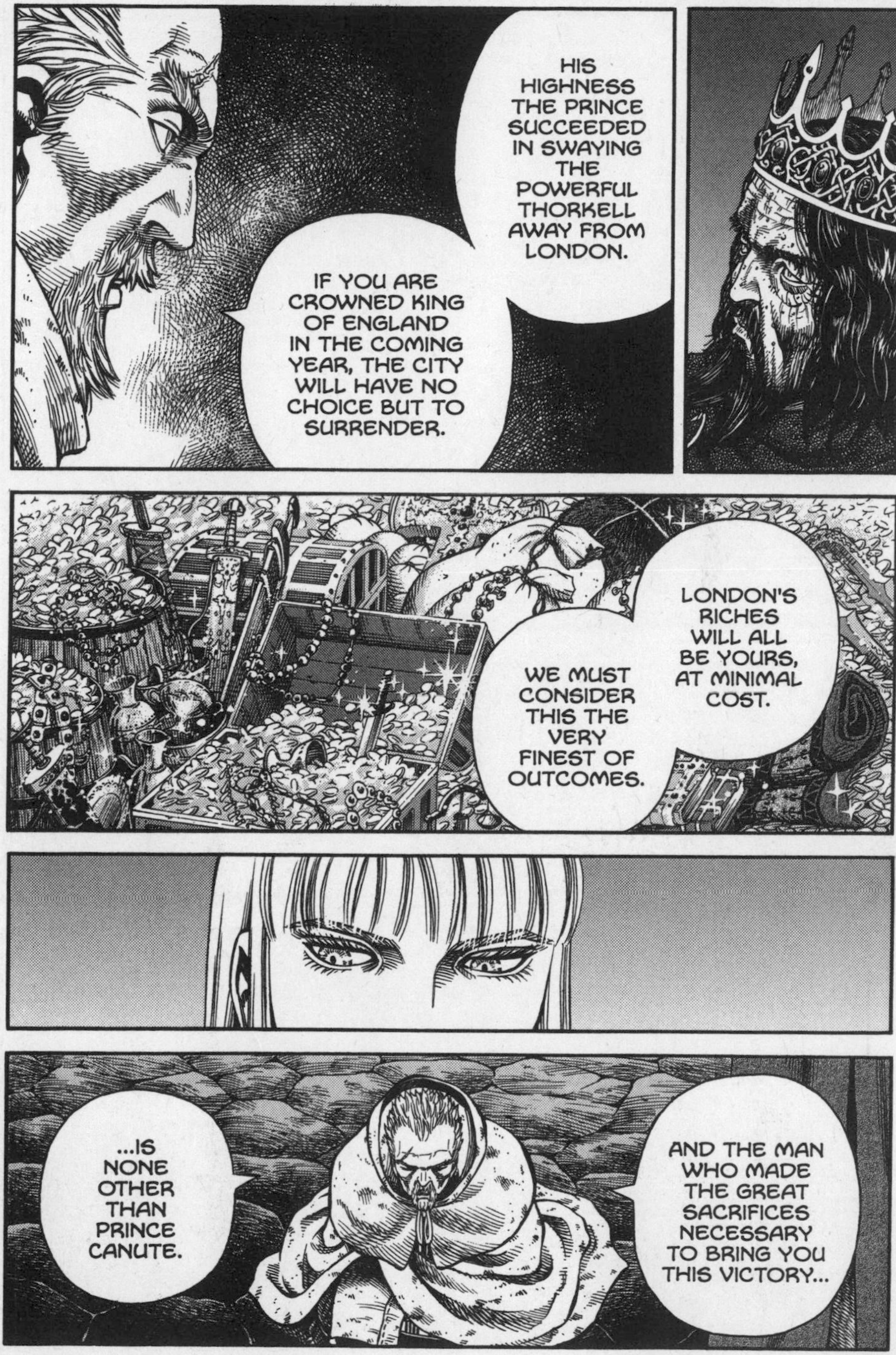
HIS HIGHNESS THE PRINCE SUCCEEDED IN SWAYING THE POWERFUL THORKELL AWAY FROM LONDON.
IF YOU ARE CROWNED KING OF ENGLAND IN THE COMING YEAR, THE CITY WILL HAVE NO CHOICE BUT TO SURRENDER.
LONDON'S RICHES WILL ALL BE YOURS, AT MINIMAL COST.
WE MUST CONSIDER THIS THE VERY FINEST OF OUTCOMES.
AND THE MAN WHO MADE THE GREAT SACRIFICES NECESSARY TO BRING YOU THIS VICTORY...
...IS NONE OTHER THAN PRINCE CANUTE.

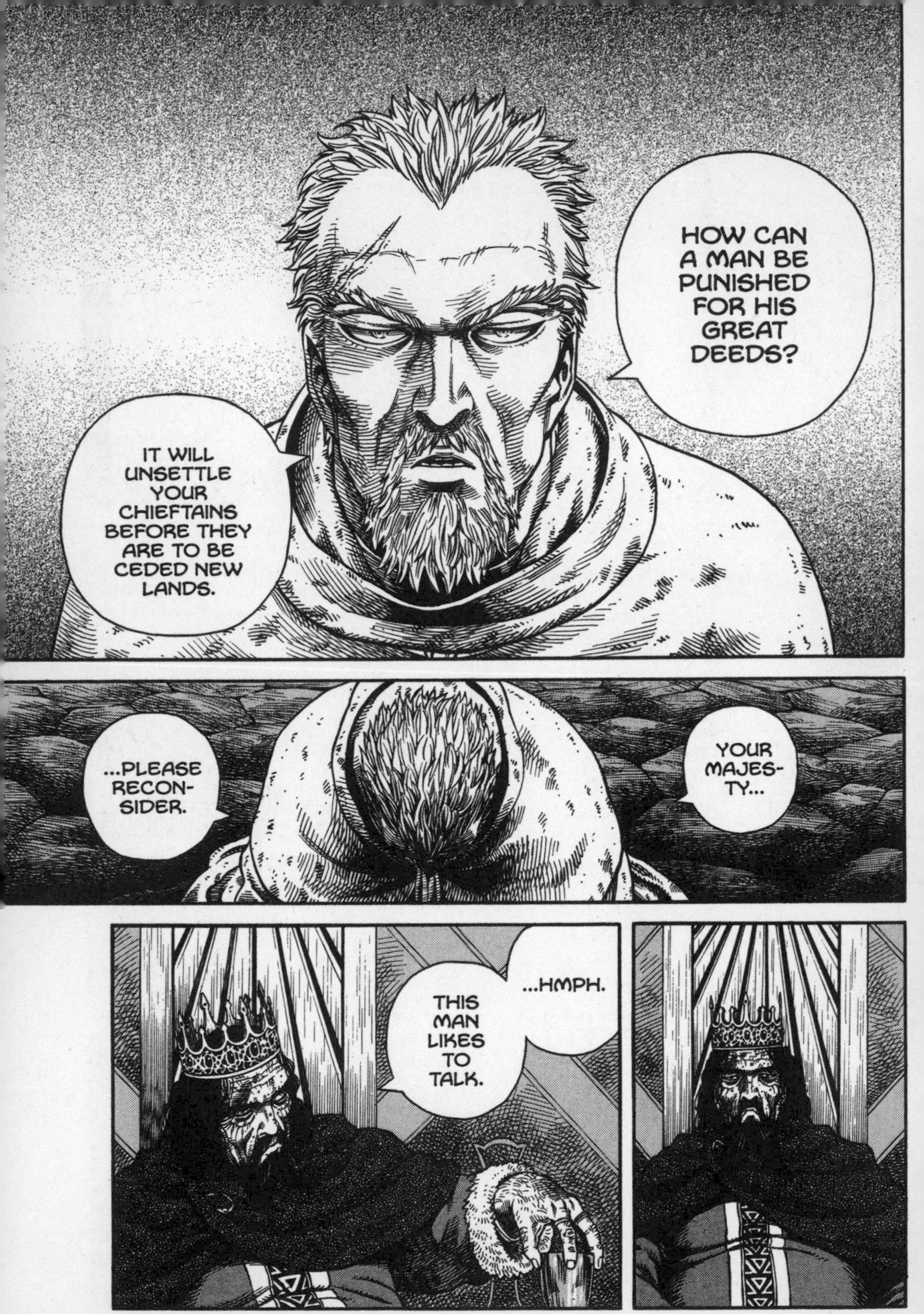
HOW CAN A MAN BE PUNISHED FOR HIS GREAT DEEDS?
IT WILL UNSETTLE YOUR CHIEFTAINS BEFORE THEY ARE TO BE CEDED NEW LANDS.
YOUR MAJESTY...
...PLEASE RECONSIDER.
...HMPH.
THIS MAN LIKES TO TALK.

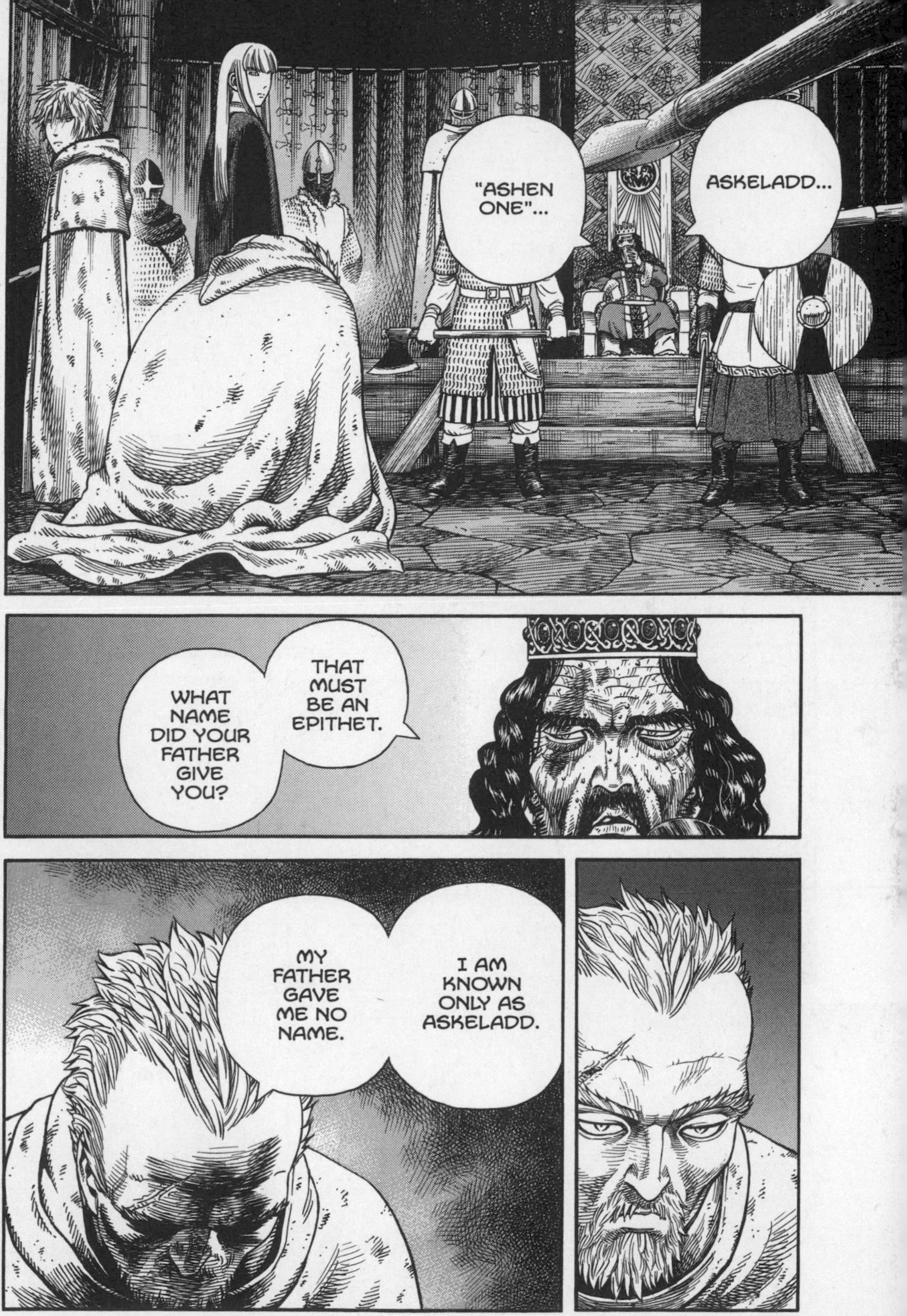
ASKELADD...
"ASHEN ONE"...
THAT MUST BE AN EPITHET.
WHAT NAME DID YOUR FATHER GIVE YOU?
I AM KNOWN ONLY AS ASKELADD.
MY FATHER GAVE ME NO NAME.

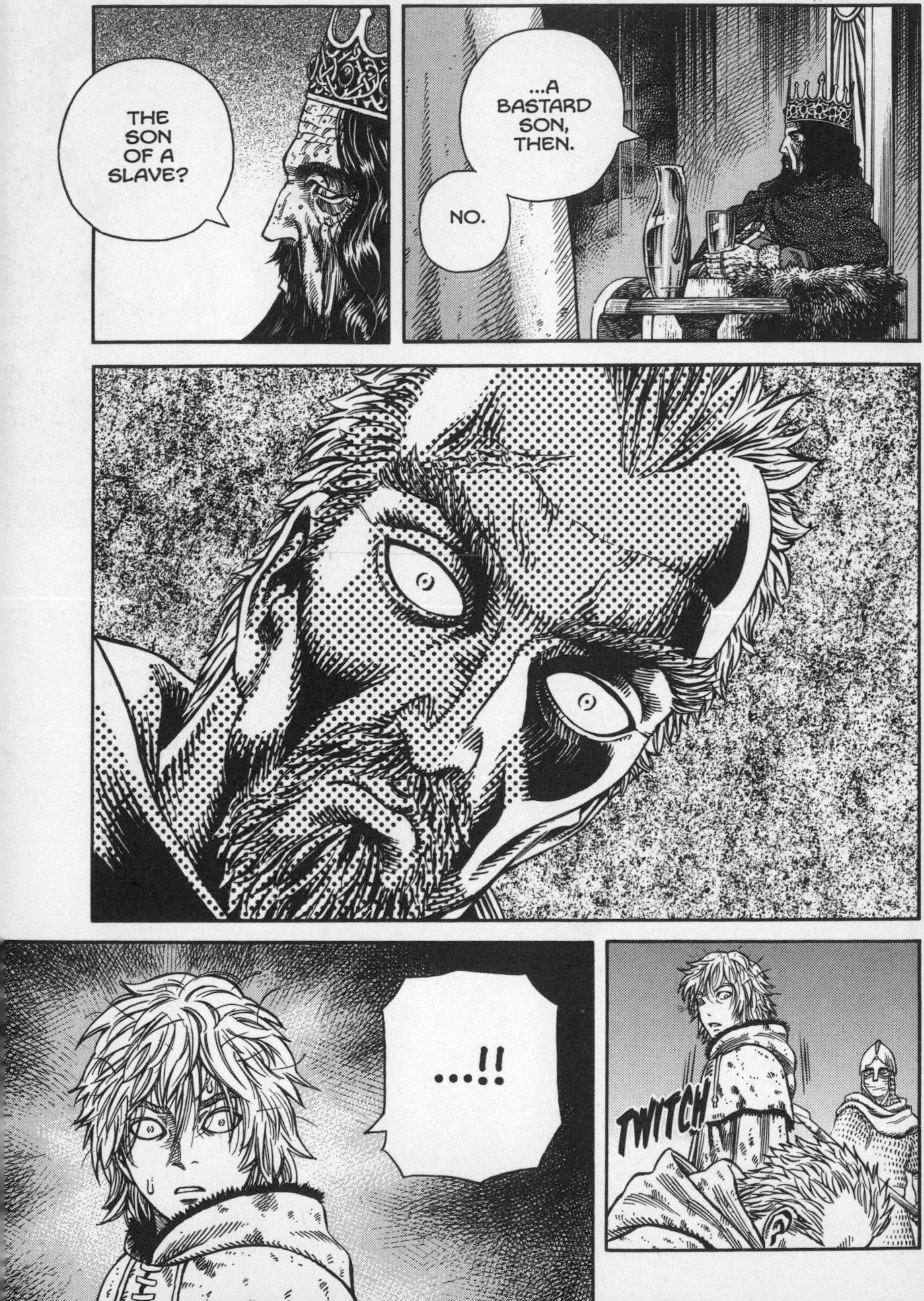
...A BASTARD SON, THEN.
NO.
THE SON OF A SLAVE?
TWITCH
...!!

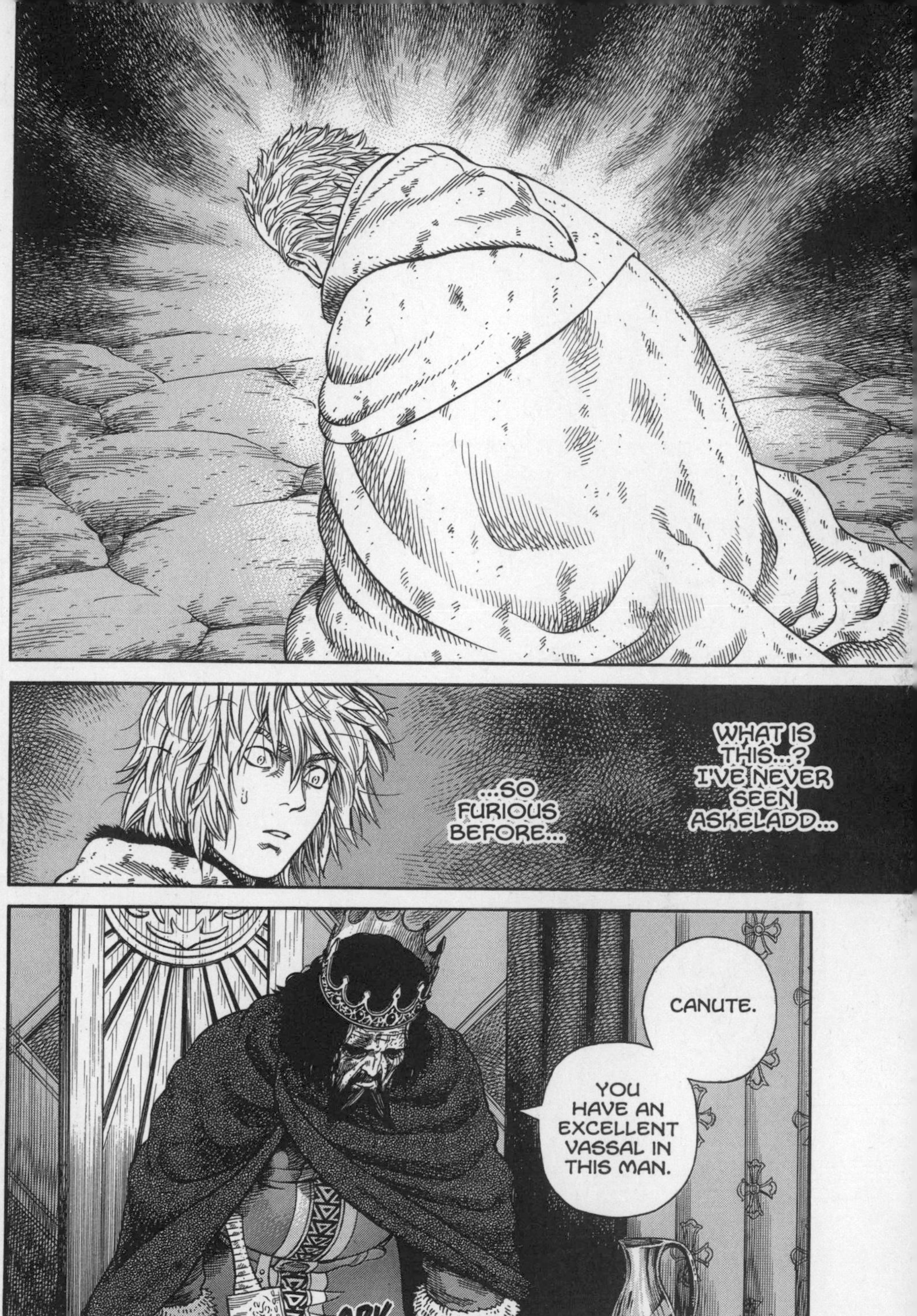

WHAT IS THIS...? I'VE NEVER SEEN ASKELADD...
...SO FURIOUS BEFORE...
CANUTE.
YOU HAVE AN EXCELLENT VASSAL IN THIS MAN.
CRK...

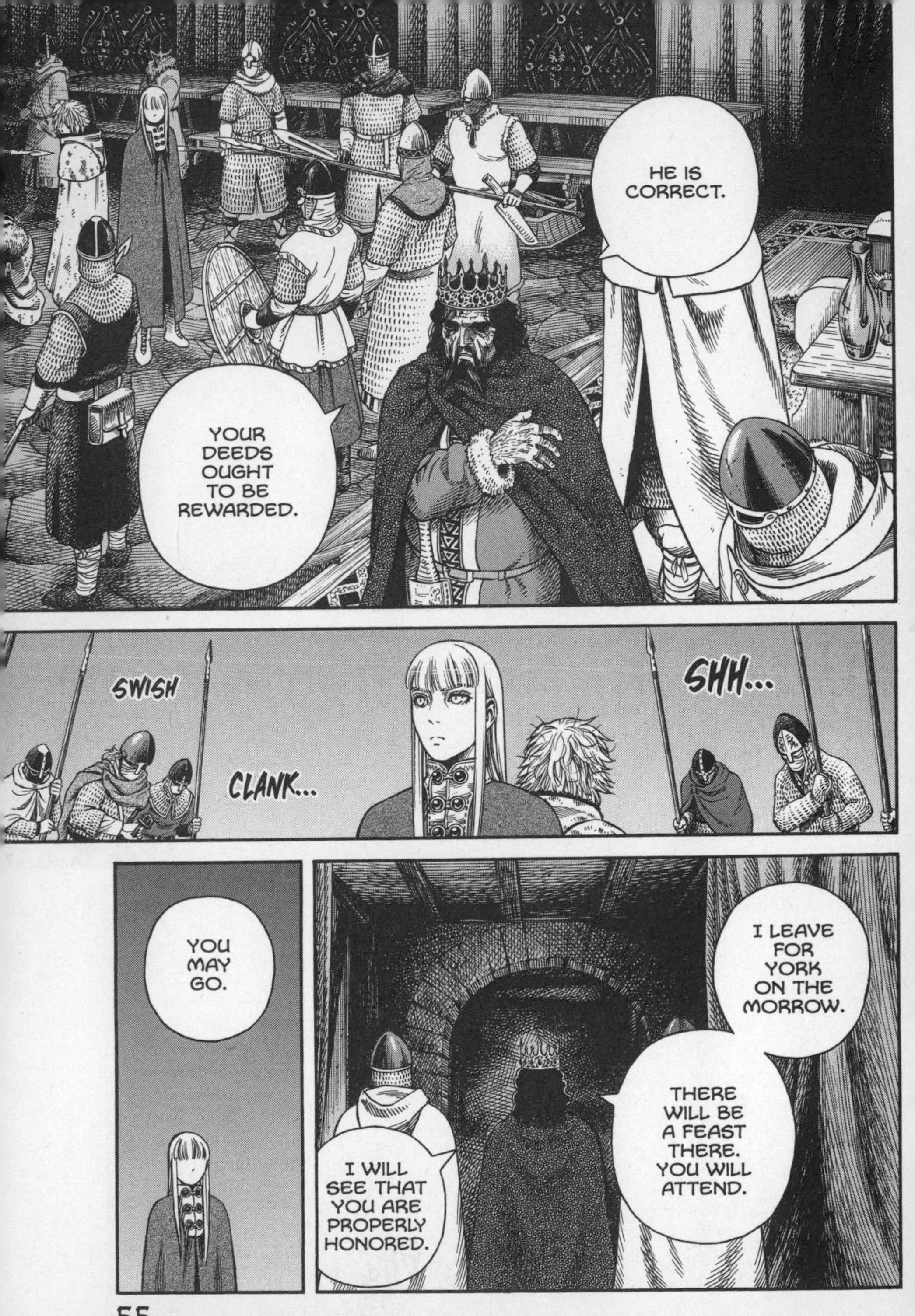
HE IS CORRECT.
YOUR DEEDS OUGHT TO BE REWARDED.
SHH...
CLANK...
SWISH
I LEAVE FOR YORK ON THE MORROW.
THERE WILL BE A FEAST THERE. YOU WILL ATTEND.
I WILL SEE THAT YOU ARE PROPERLY HONORED.
YOU MAY GO.

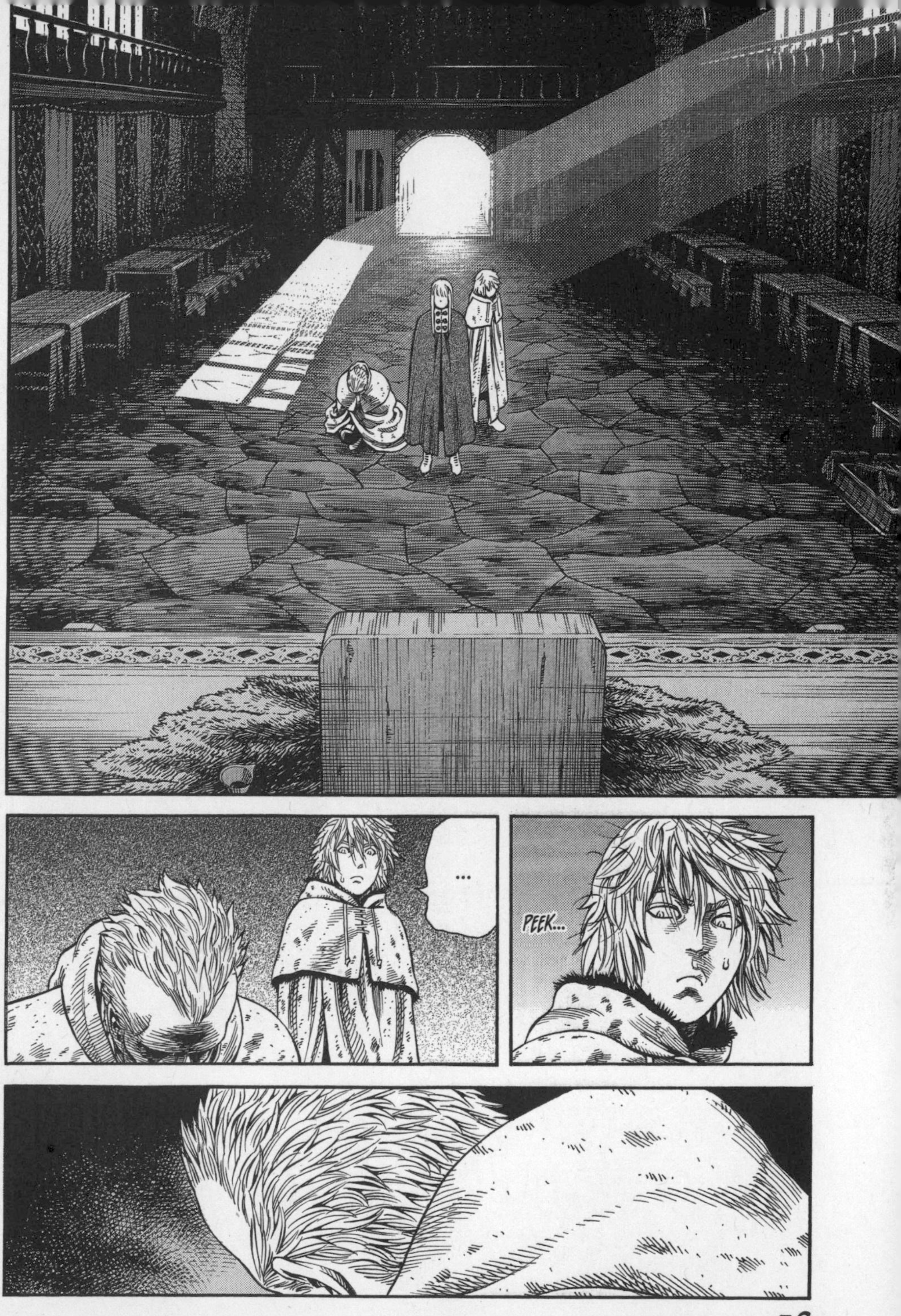
PEEK...
...

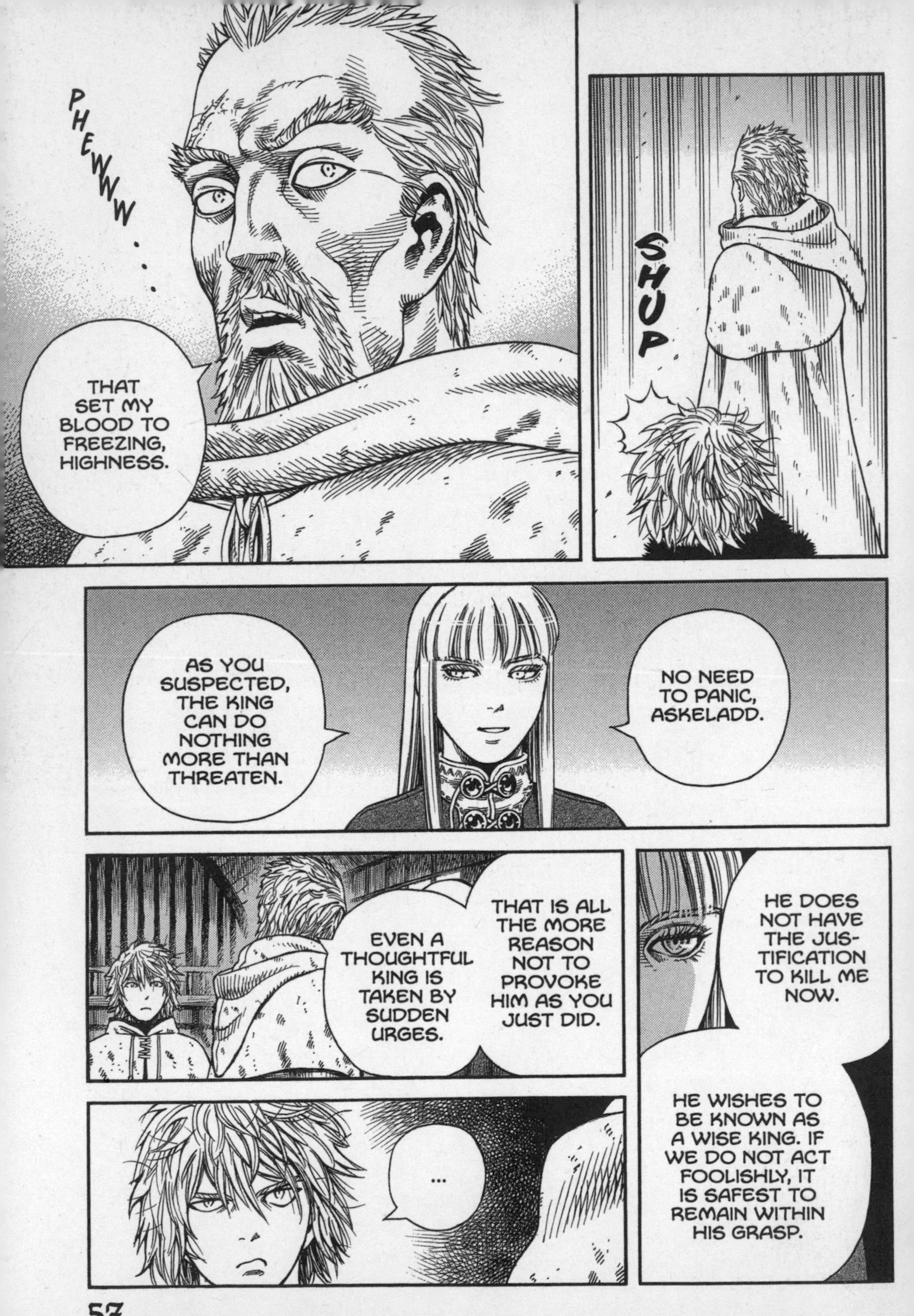
SHUP
PHEWWW...
THAT SET MY BLOOD TO FREEZING, HIGHNESS.
NO NEED TO PANIC, ASKELADD.
AS YOU SUSPECTED, THE KING CAN DO NOTHING MORE THAN THREATEN.
HE DOES NOT HAVE THE JUS-TIFICATION TO KILL ME NOW.
HE WISHES TO BE KNOWN AS A WISE KING. IF WE DO NOT ACT FOOLISHLY, IT IS SAFEST TO REMAIN WITHIN HIS GRASP.
THAT IS ALL THE MORE REASON NOT TO PROVOKE HIM AS YOU JUST DID.
EVEN A THOUGHTFUL KING IS TAKEN BY SUDDEN URGES.
...

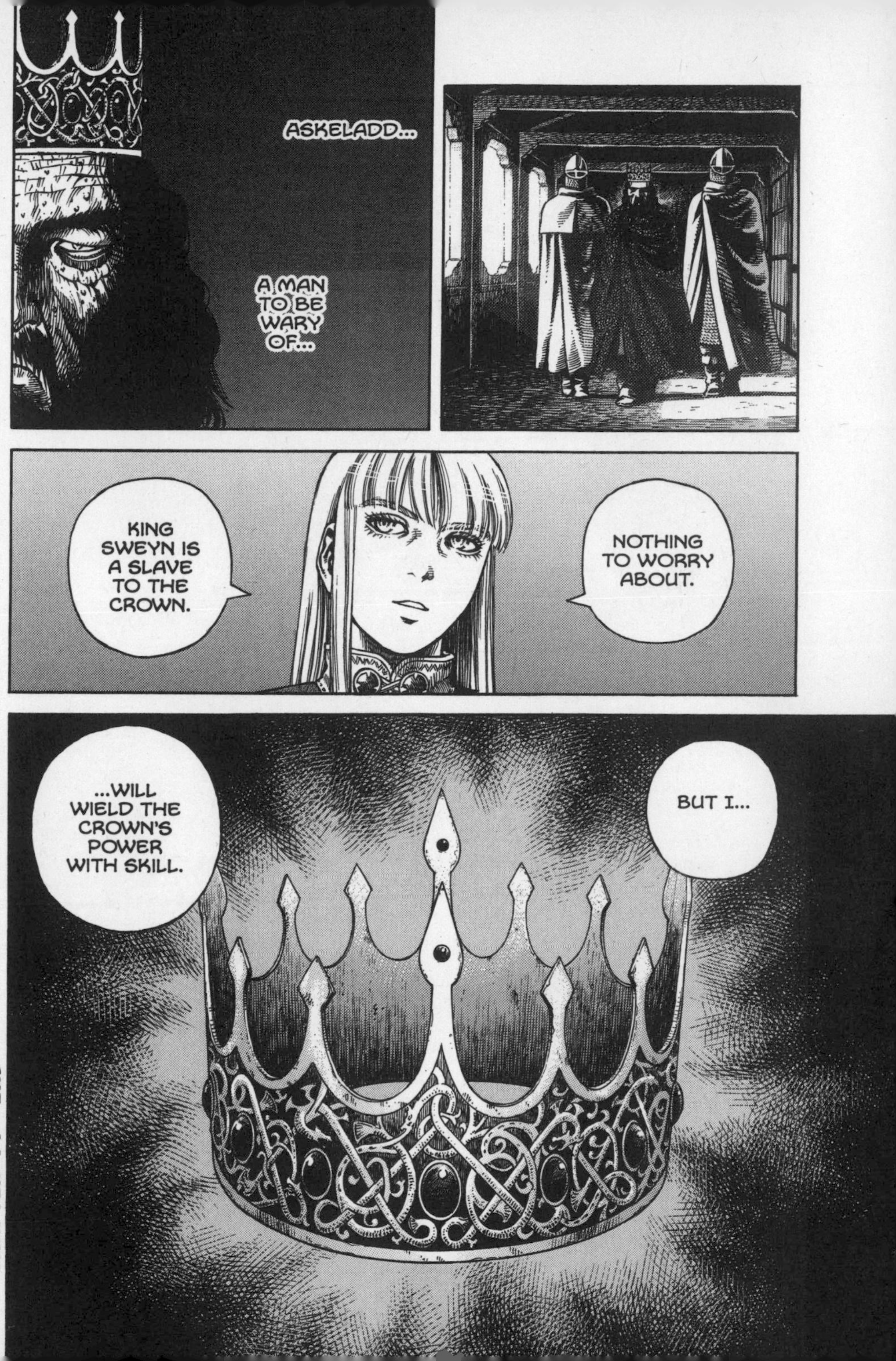
ASKELADD...
A MAN TO BE WARY OF...
NOTHING TO WORRY ABOUT.
KING SWEYN IS A SLAVE TO THE CROWN.
BUT I...
...WILL WIELD THE CROWN'S POWER WITH SKILL.

CHAPTER 44 • END

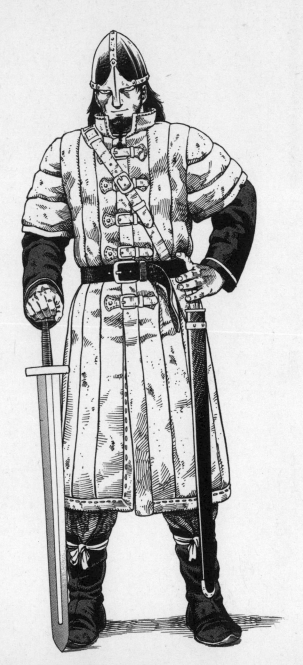

CHAPTER 45: HIS LAST FRIEND

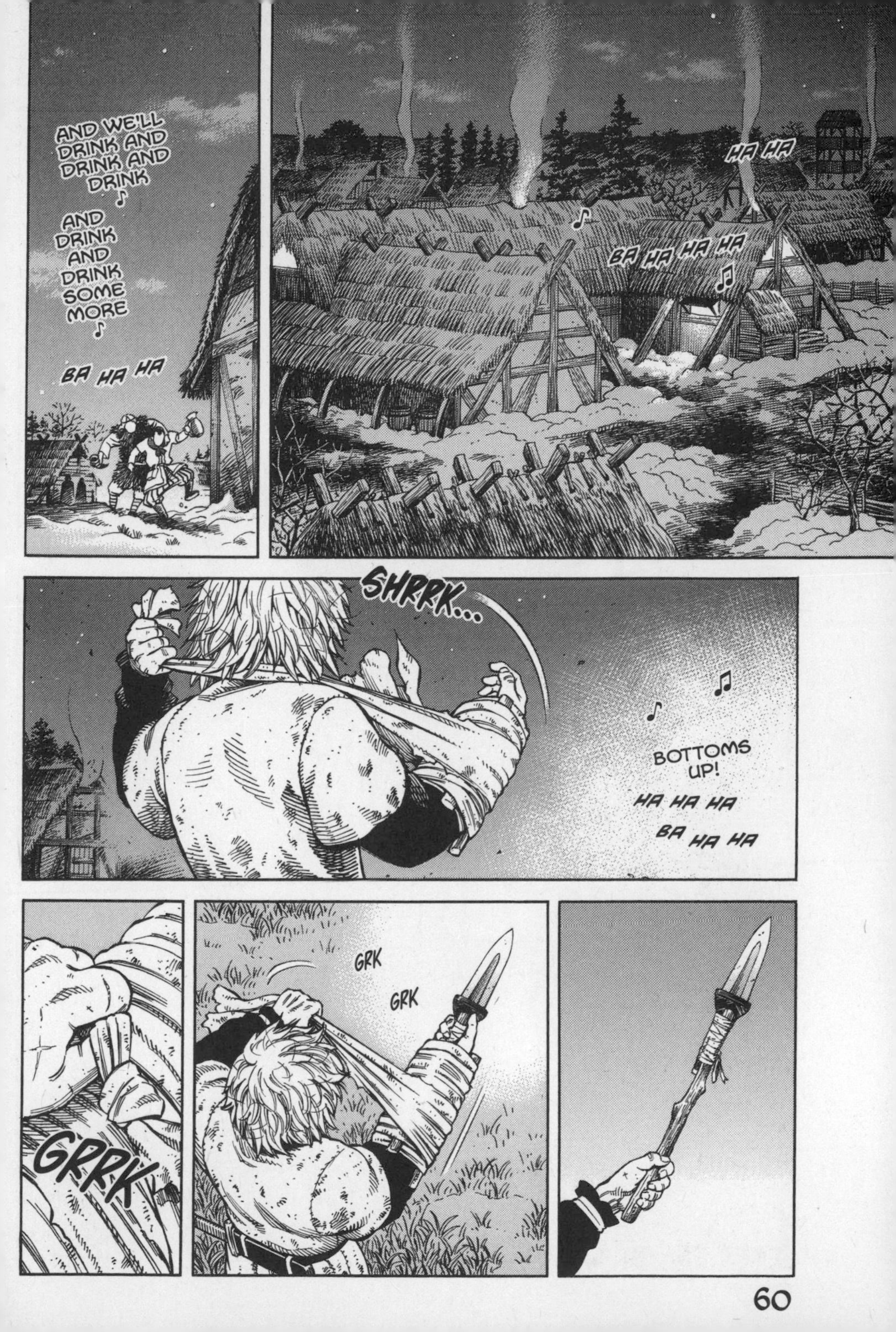
HA HA
BA HA HA HA
AND WE'LL DRINK AND DRINK AND DRINK
AND DRINK AND DRINK SOME MORE
BA HA HA
SHRRK...
BOTTOMS UP!
HA HA HA
BA HA HA
GRK
GRK
GRRK

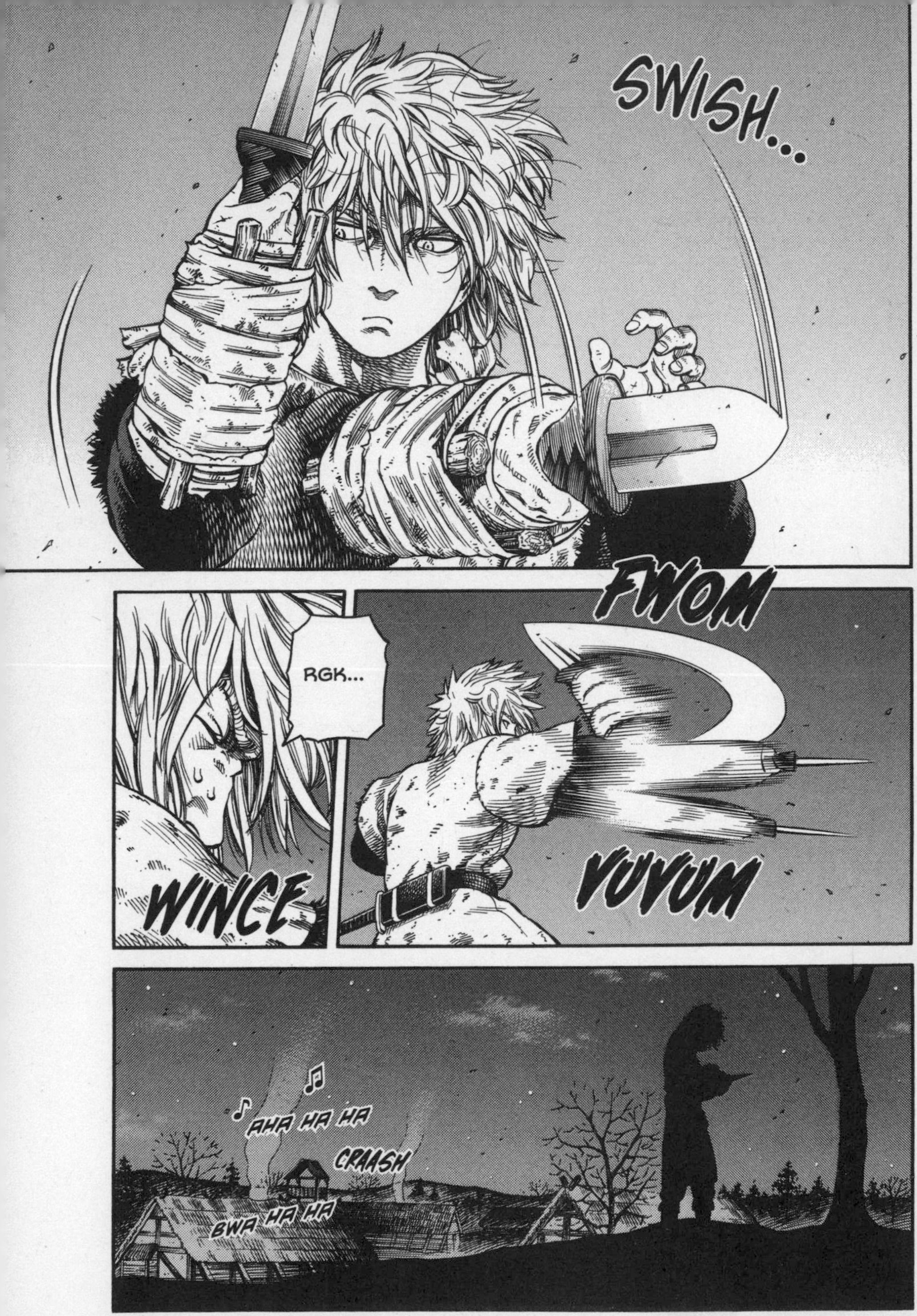
SWISH...
FWOM
VUVUM
RGK...
WINCE
AHA HA HA
CRAASH
BWA HA HA

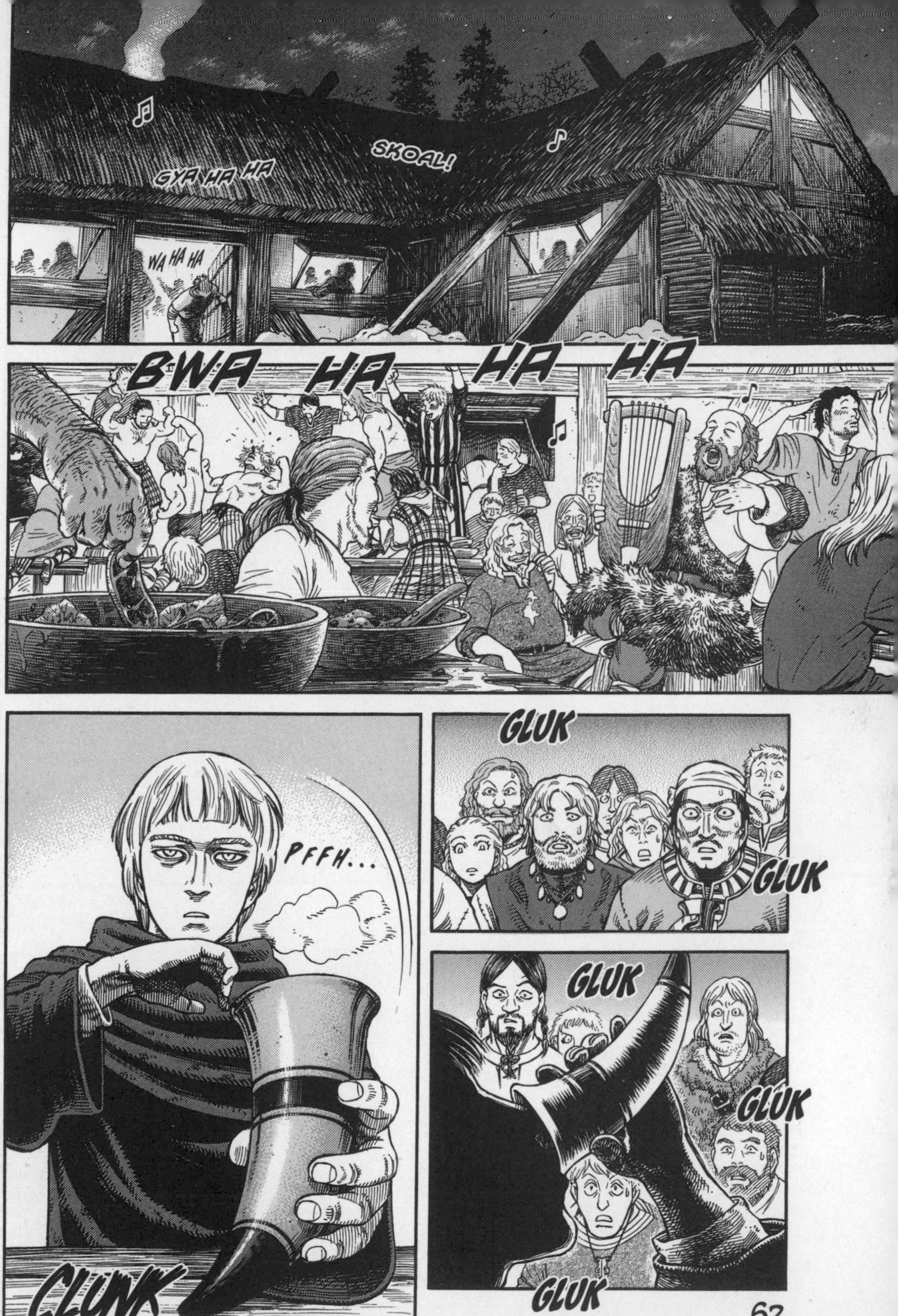
SKOAL!
GYA HA HA
WA HA HA
BWA HA HA HA
GLUK
GLUK
GLUK
GLUK
GLUK
PFFH...
CLUNK

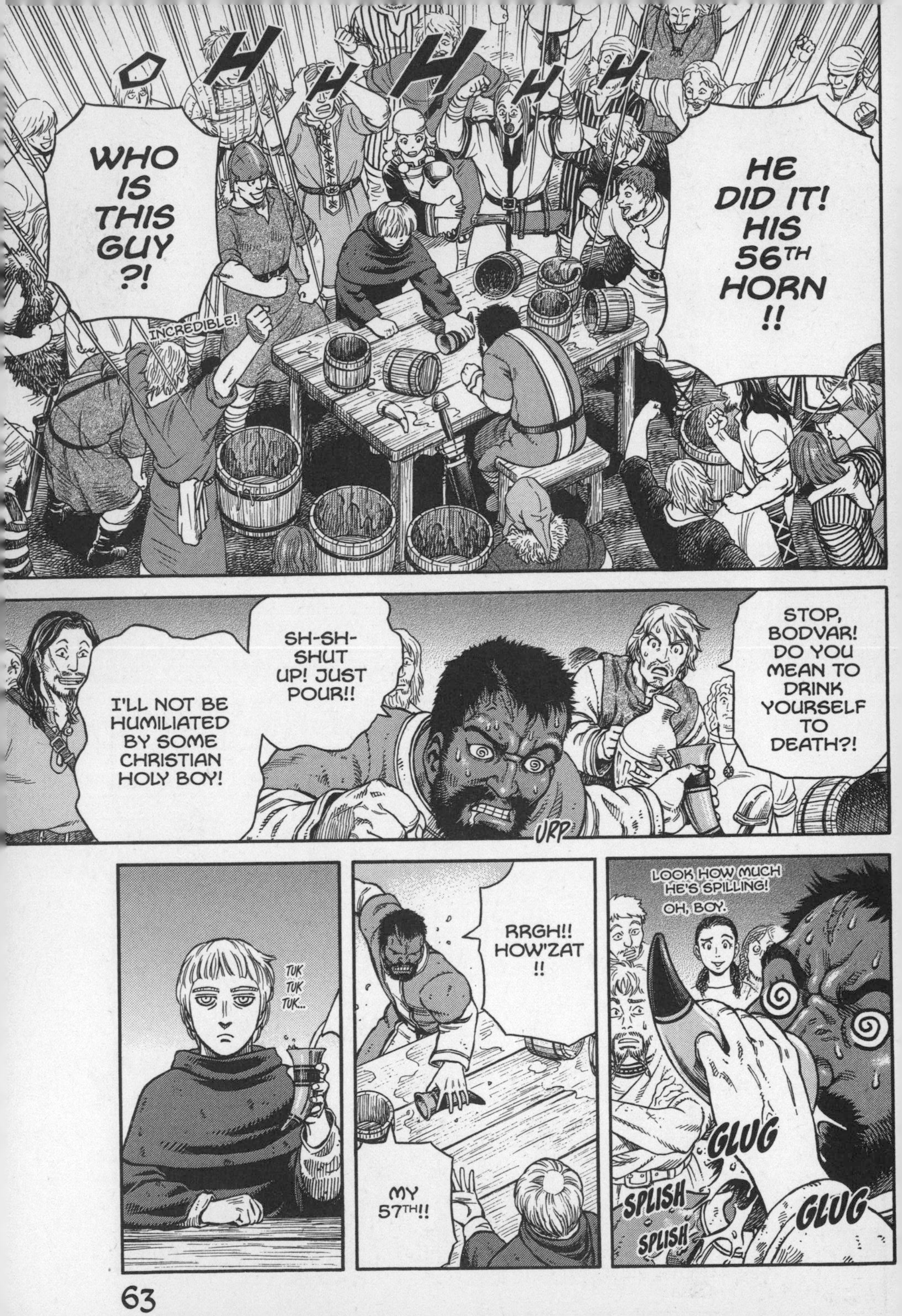
OHHHHHH
HE DID IT! HIS 56TH HORN!!
WHO IS THIS GUY?!
INCREDIBLE!
STOP, BODVAR! DO YOU MEAN TO DRINK YOURSELF TO DEATH?!
SH-SH-SHUT UP! JUST POUR!!
I'LL NOT BE HUMILIATED BY SOME CHRISTIAN HOLY BOY!
URP
LOOK HOW MUCH HE'S SPILLING!
OH, BOY.
GLUG
GLUG
SPLISH
SPLISH
RRGH!! HOW'ZAT!!
MY 57TH!!
TUK TUK TUK...

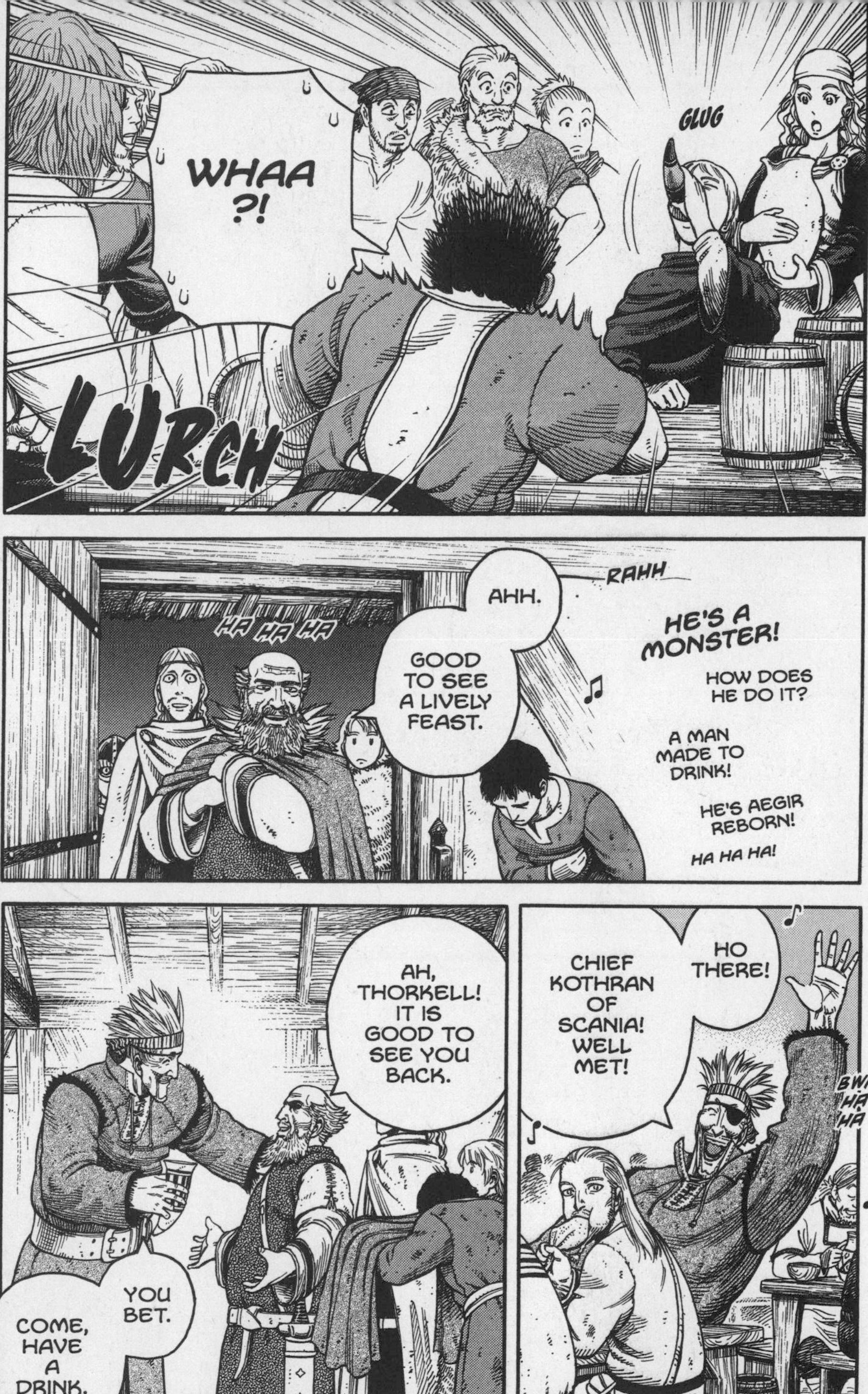
GLUG
WHAA?!
LURCH
RAHH
HE'S A MONSTER!
HOW DOES HE DO IT?
A MAN MADE TO DRINK!
HE'S AEGIR REBORN!
HA HA HA!
AHH.
GOOD TO SEE A LIVELY FEAST.
HA HA HA
BWA HA HA
HO THERE!
CHIEF KOTHRAN OF SCANIA! WELL MET!
AH, THORKELL! IT IS GOOD TO SEE YOU BACK.
YOU BET.
COME, HAVE A DRINK.

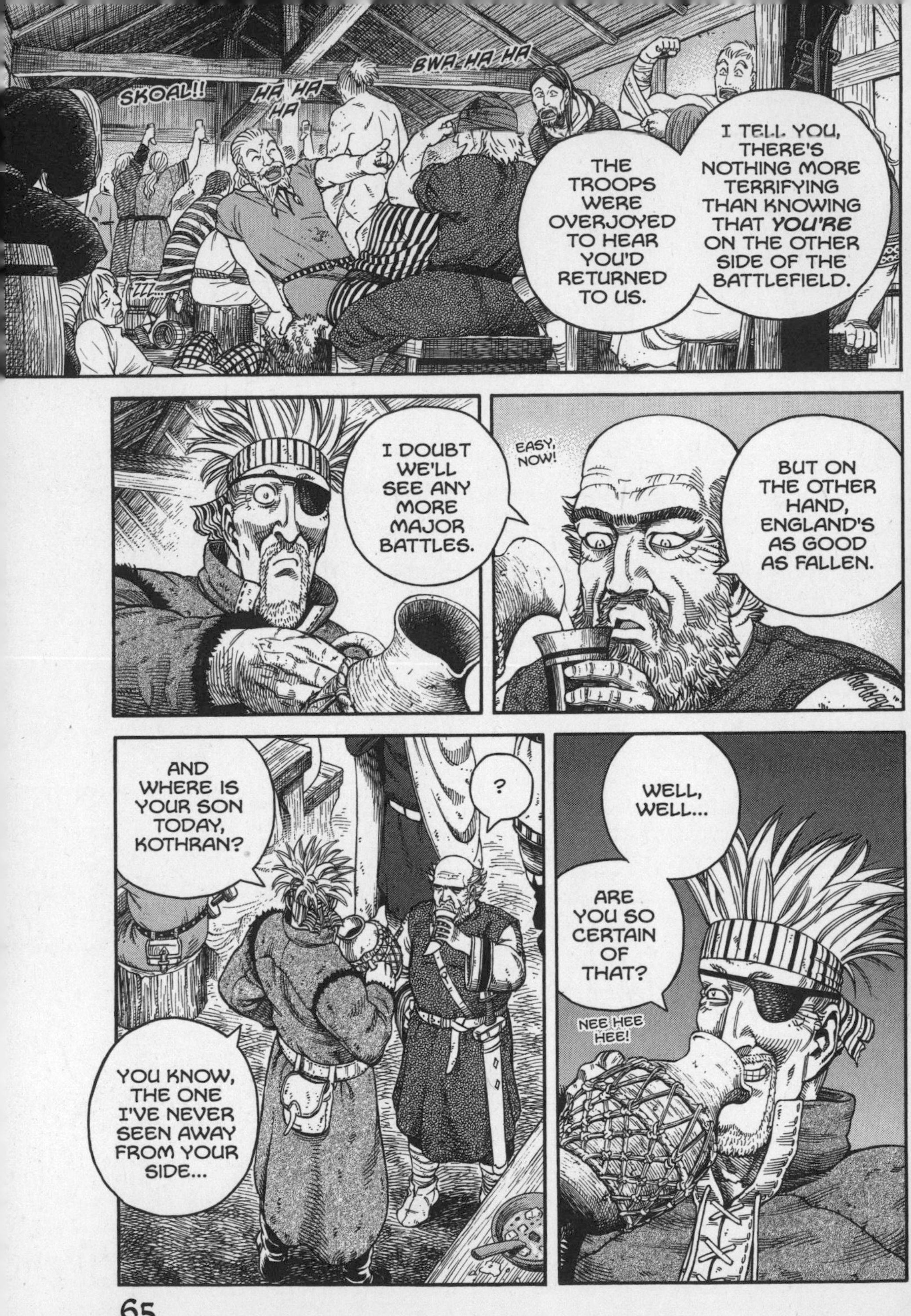
BWA-HA-HA
HA HA HA
SKOAL!!
I TELL YOU, THERE'S NOTHING MORE TERRIFYING THAN KNOWING THAT *YOU'RE* ON THE OTHER SIDE OF THE BATTLEFIELD.
THE TROOPS WERE OVERJOYED TO HEAR YOU'D RETURNED TO US.
BUT ON THE OTHER HAND, ENGLAND'S AS GOOD AS FALLEN.
EASY, NOW!
I DOUBT WE'LL SEE ANY MORE MAJOR BATTLES.
WELL, WELL...
ARE YOU SO CERTAIN OF THAT?
NEE HEE HEE!
AND WHERE IS YOUR SON TODAY, KOTHRAN?
?
YOU KNOW, THE ONE I'VE NEVER SEEN AWAY FROM YOUR SIDE...

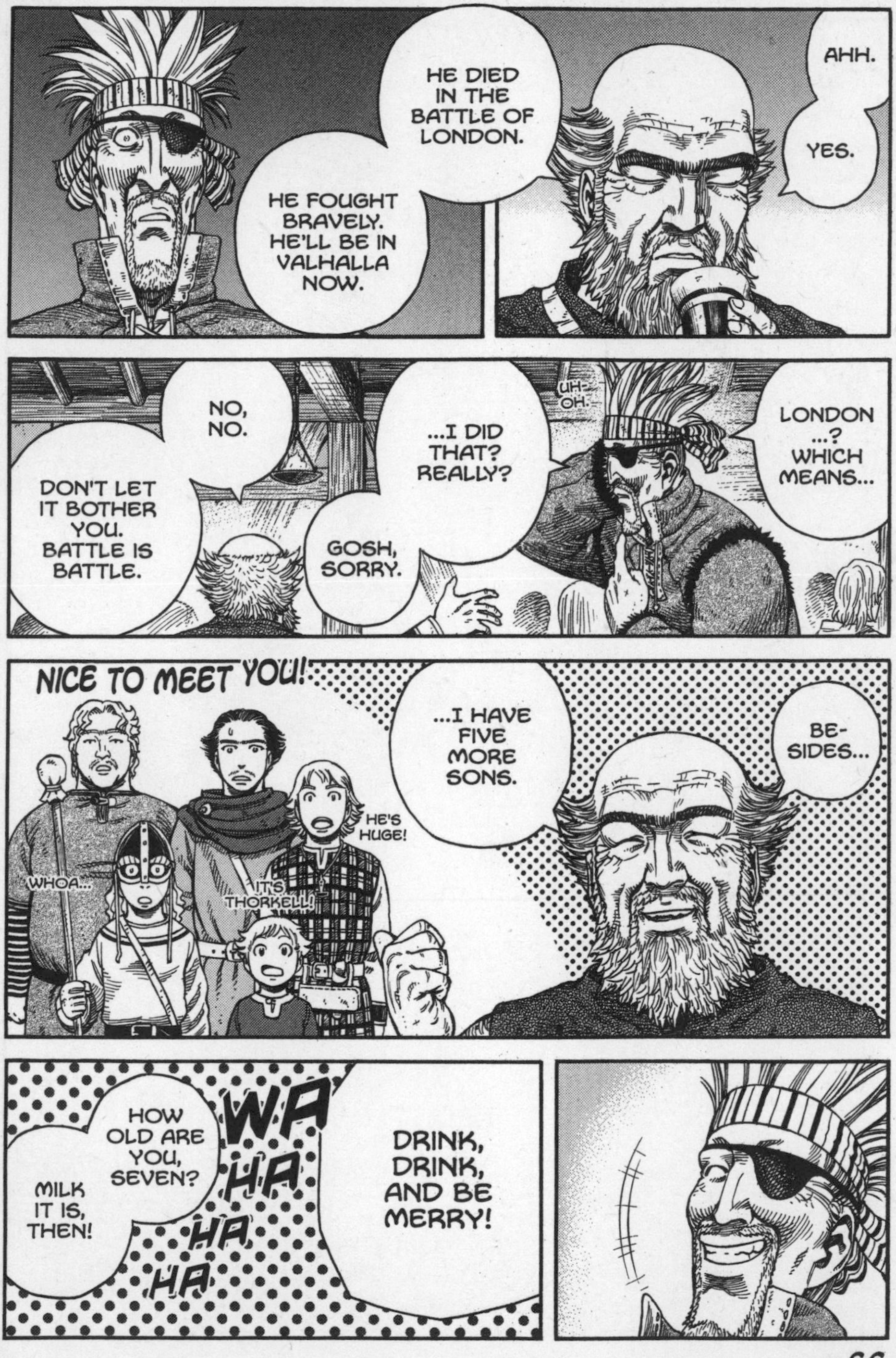
AHH.
YES.
HE DIED IN THE BATTLE OF LONDON.
HE FOUGHT BRAVELY. HE'LL BE IN VALHALLA NOW.
LONDON ...? WHICH MEANS...
UH-OH.
...I DID THAT? REALLY?
GOSH, SORRY.
NO, NO.
DON'T LET IT BOTHER YOU. BATTLE IS BATTLE.
BE-SIDES...
...I HAVE FIVE MORE SONS.
HE'S HUGE!
NICE TO MEET YOU!
IT'S THORKELL!
WHOA...
DRINK, DRINK, AND BE MERRY!
WA HA HA HA
HOW OLD ARE YOU, SEVEN?
MILK IT IS, THEN!

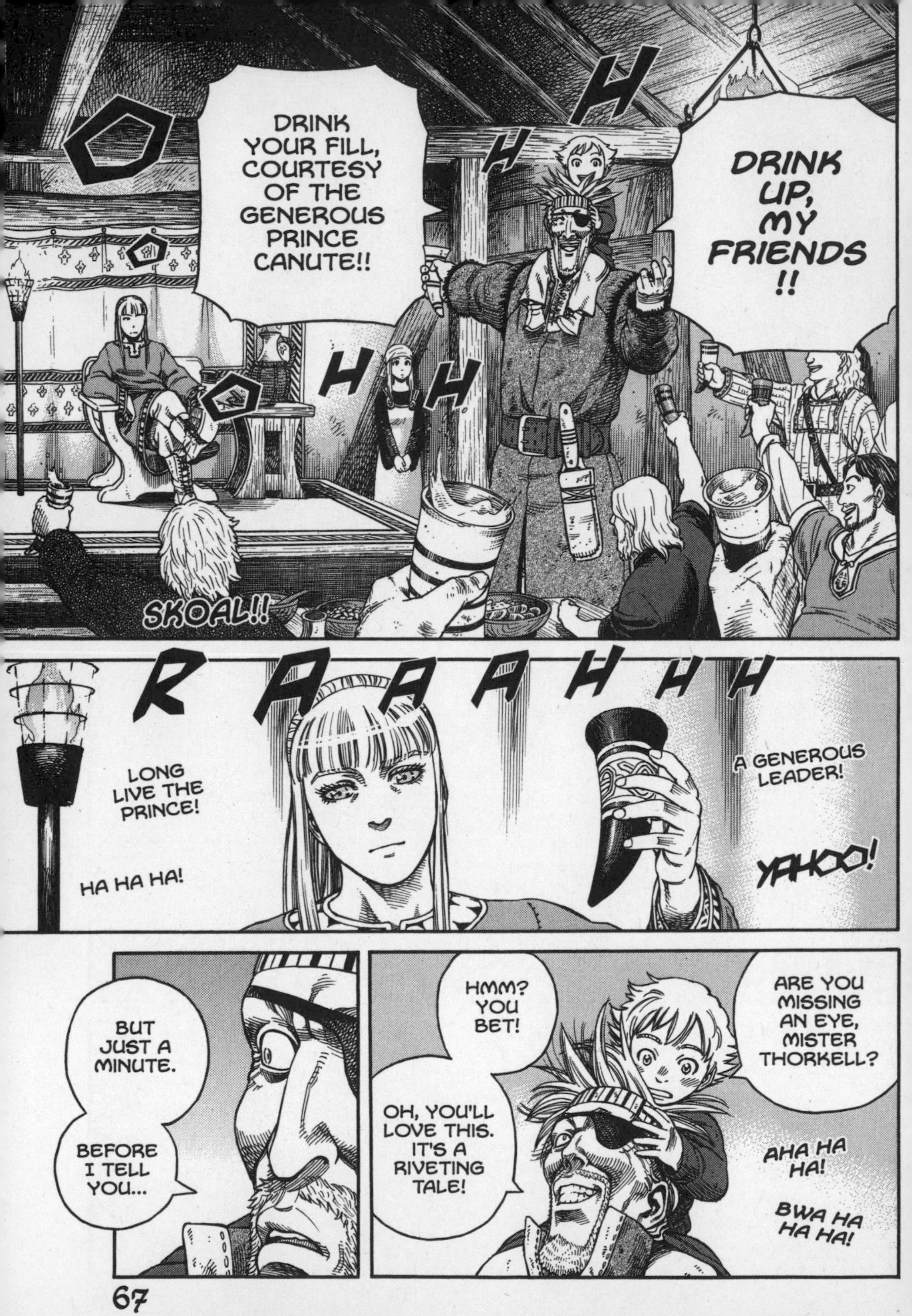
DRINK UP, MY FRIENDS!!
H H
DRINK YOUR FILL, COURTESY OF THE GENEROUS PRINCE CANUTE!!
O O O
H H
SKOAL!!
R A A A H H H H
A GENEROUS LEADER!
YAHOO!
LONG LIVE THE PRINCE!
HA HA HA!
ARE YOU MISSING AN EYE, MISTER THORKELL?
HMM? YOU BET!
AHA HA HA!
BWA HA HA HA!
OH, YOU'LL LOVE THIS. IT'S A RIVETING TALE!
BUT JUST A MINUTE.
BEFORE I TELL YOU...

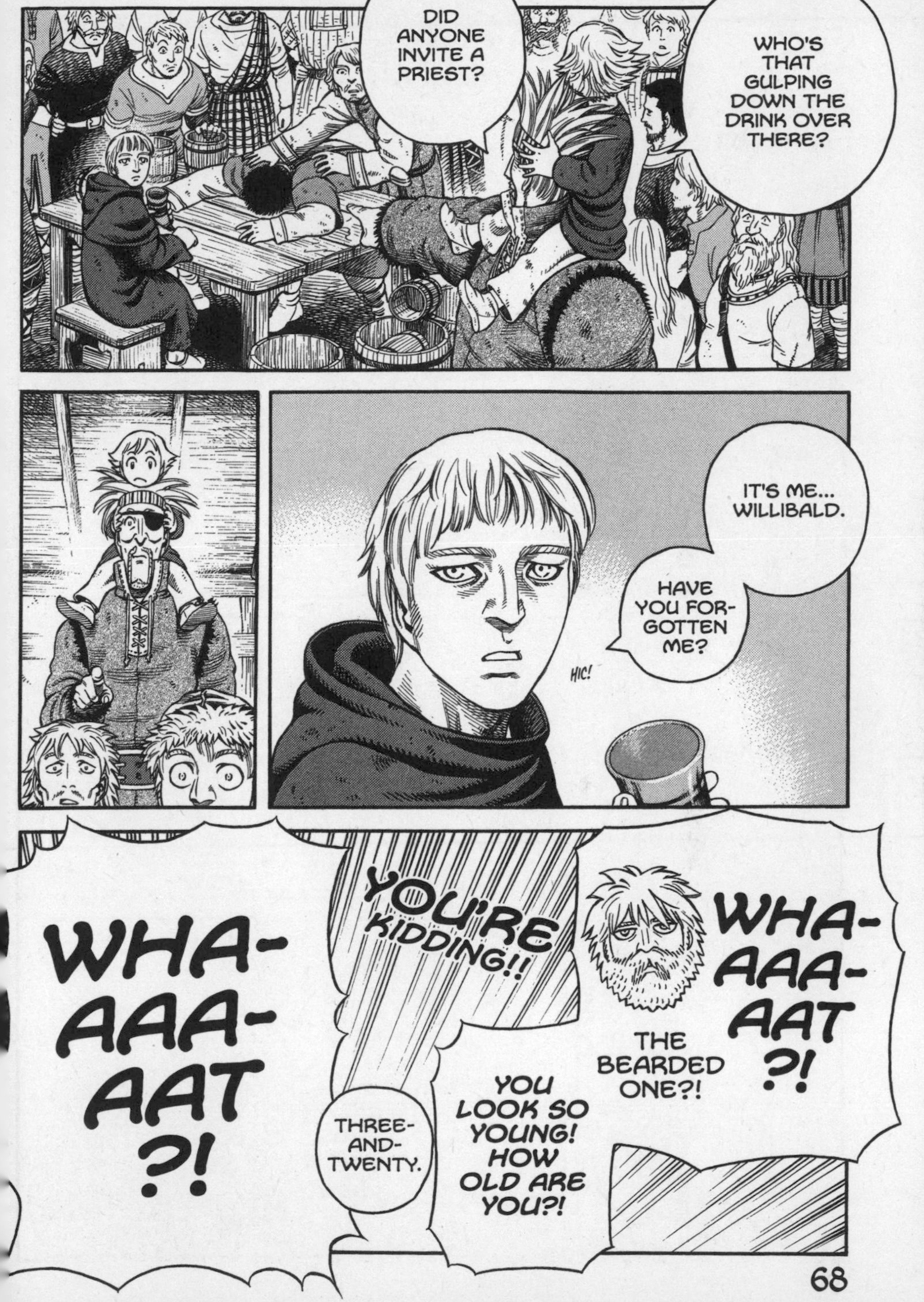
WHO'S THAT GULPING DOWN THE DRINK OVER THERE?
DID ANYONE INVITE A PRIEST?
IT'S ME... WILLIBALD.
HAVE YOU FOR-GOTTEN ME?
HIC!
WHA-AAA-AAT?!
THE BEARDED ONE?!
YOU'RE KIDDING!!
YOU LOOK SO YOUNG! HOW OLD ARE YOU?!
THREE-AND-TWENTY.
WHA-AAA-AAT?!

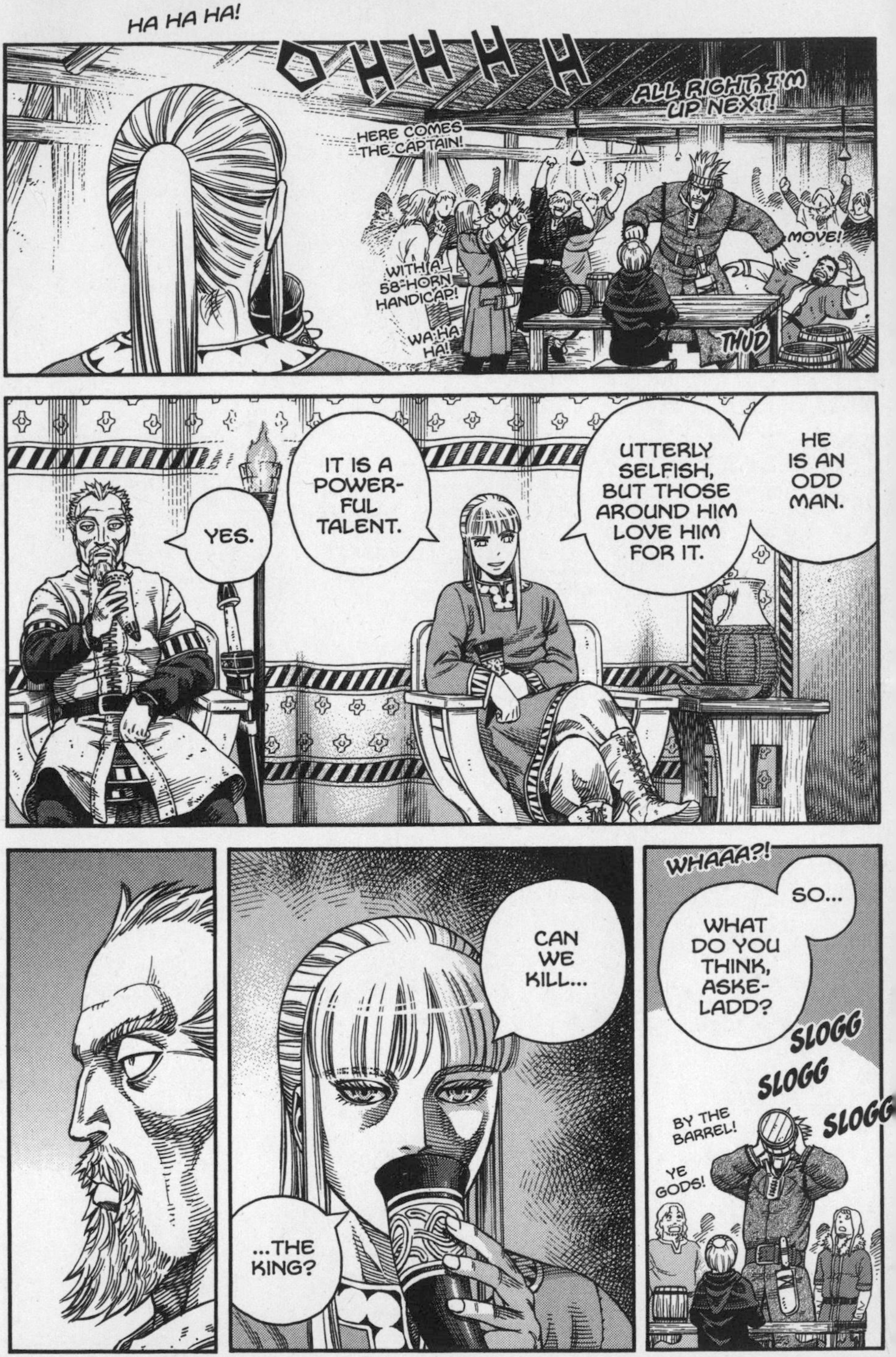
HA HA HA!
ALL RIGHT, I'M UP NEXT!
MOVE!
THUD
HERE COMES THE CAPTAIN!
OHHHHH
WITH A 58-HORN HANDICAP!
WA HA HA!
HE IS AN ODD MAN.
UTTERLY SELFISH, BUT THOSE AROUND HIM LOVE HIM FOR IT.
IT IS A POWERFUL TALENT.
YES.
WHAAA?!
SO...
WHAT DO YOU THINK, ASKELADD?
SLOGG
SLOGG
SLOGG
BY THE BARREL!
YE GODS!
CAN WE KILL...
...THE KING?

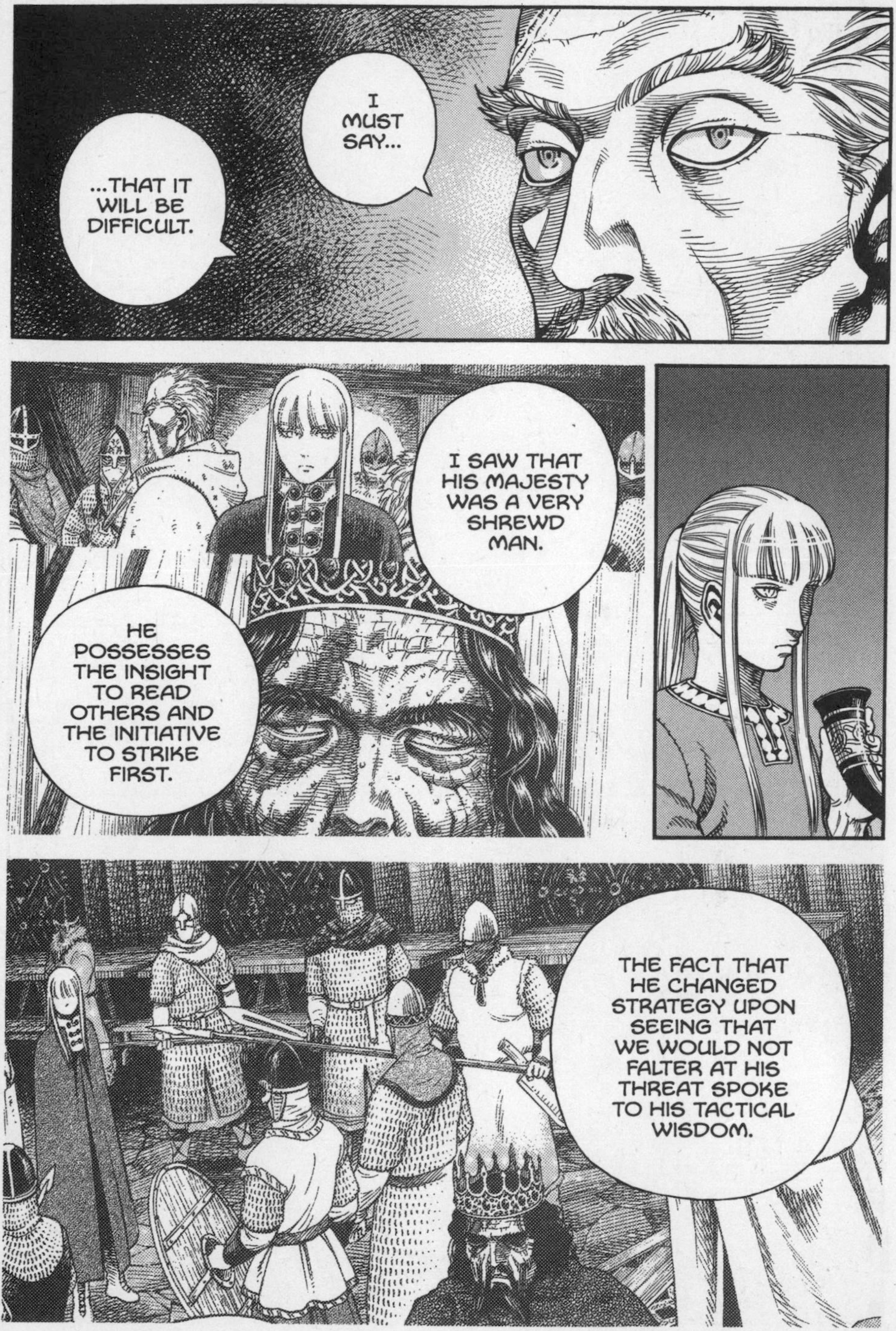
I MUST SAY...
...THAT IT WILL BE DIFFICULT.
I SAW THAT HIS MAJESTY WAS A VERY SHREWD MAN.
HE POSSESSES THE INSIGHT TO READ OTHERS AND THE INITIATIVE TO STRIKE FIRST.
THE FACT THAT HE CHANGED STRATEGY UPON SEEING THAT WE WOULD NOT FALTER AT HIS THREAT SPOKE TO HIS TACTICAL WISDOM.

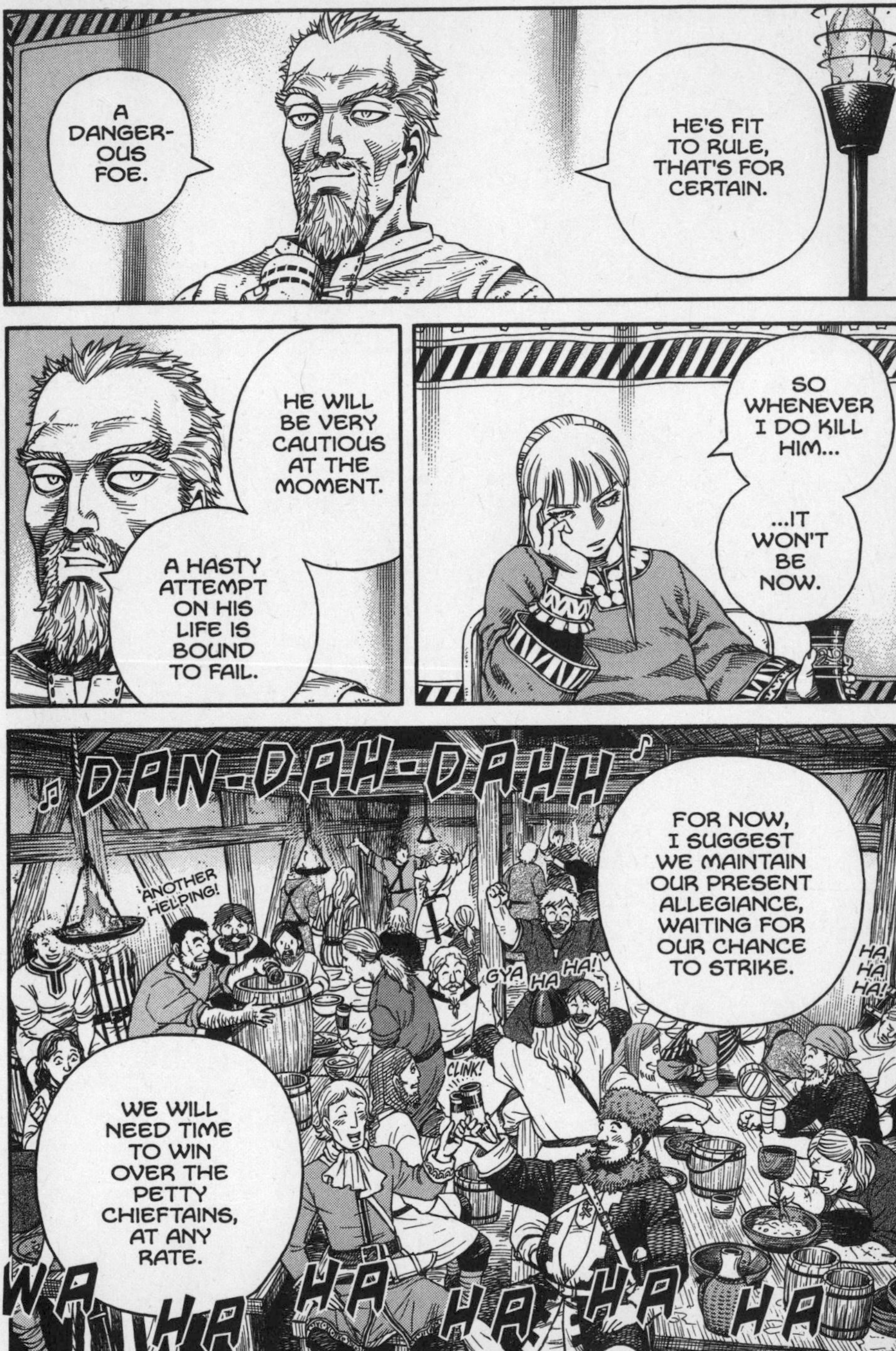
HE'S FIT TO RULE, THAT'S FOR CERTAIN.
A DANGER-OUS FOE.
SO WHENEVER I DO KILL HIM...
...IT WON'T BE NOW.
HE WILL BE VERY CAUTIOUS AT THE MOMENT.
A HASTY ATTEMPT ON HIS LIFE IS BOUND TO FAIL.
DAN-DAH-DAHH
FOR NOW, I SUGGEST WE MAINTAIN OUR PRESENT ALLEGIANCE, WAITING FOR OUR CHANCE TO STRIKE.
HA HA HA!
GYA HA HA!
ANOTHER HELPING!
CLINK!
WE WILL NEED TIME TO WIN OVER THE PETTY CHIEFTAINS, AT ANY RATE.
WA HA HA HA HA HA

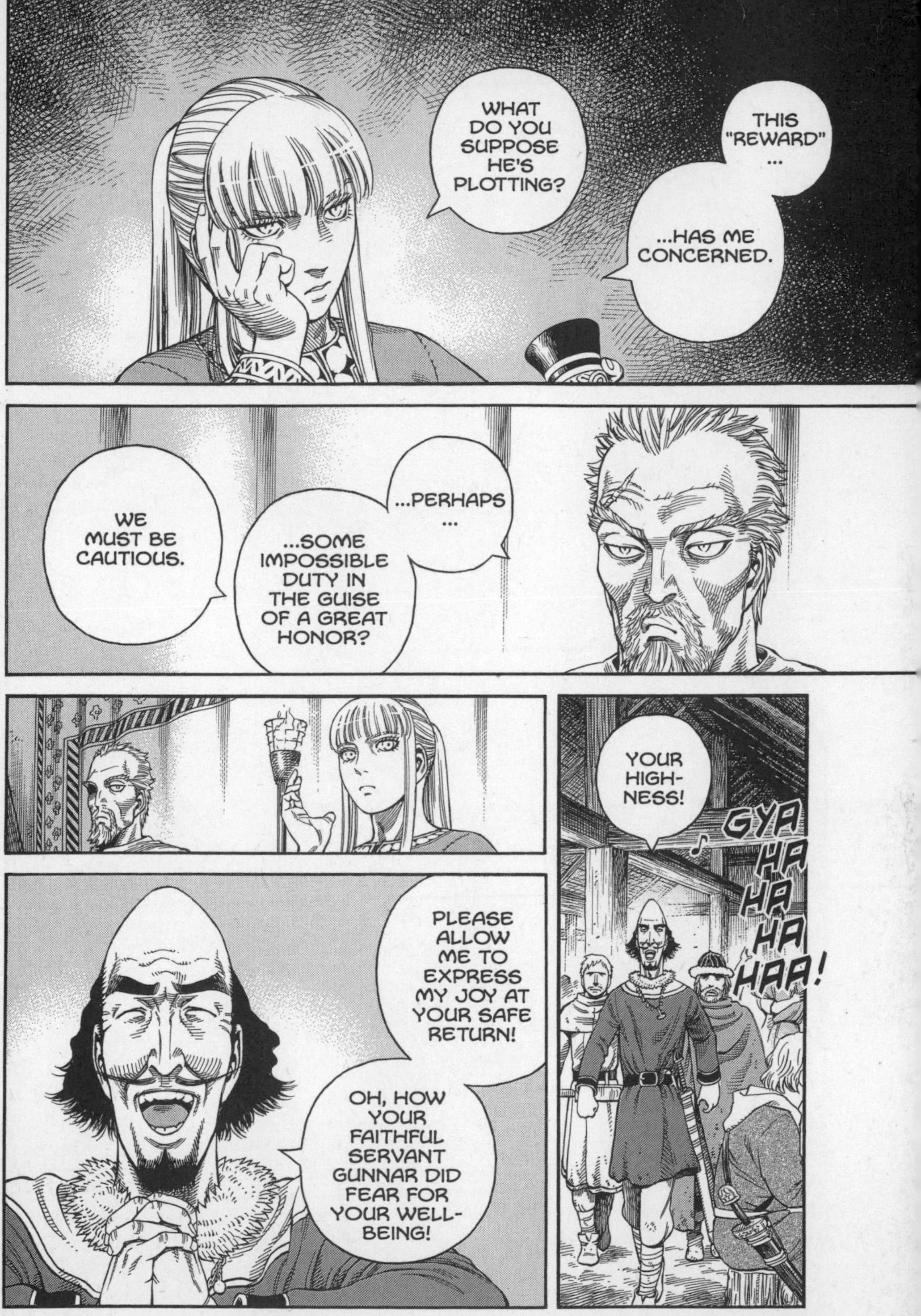
THIS "REWARD" ...
...HAS ME CONCERNED.
WHAT DO YOU SUPPOSE HE'S PLOTTING?
...PERHAPS ...
...SOME IMPOSSIBLE DUTY IN THE GUISE OF A GREAT HONOR?
WE MUST BE CAUTIOUS.
YOUR HIGH-NESS!
GYA HA HA HA HAA!
PLEASE ALLOW ME TO EXPRESS MY JOY AT YOUR SAFE RETURN!
OH, HOW YOUR FAITHFUL SERVANT GUNNAR DID FEAR FOR YOUR WELL-BEING!

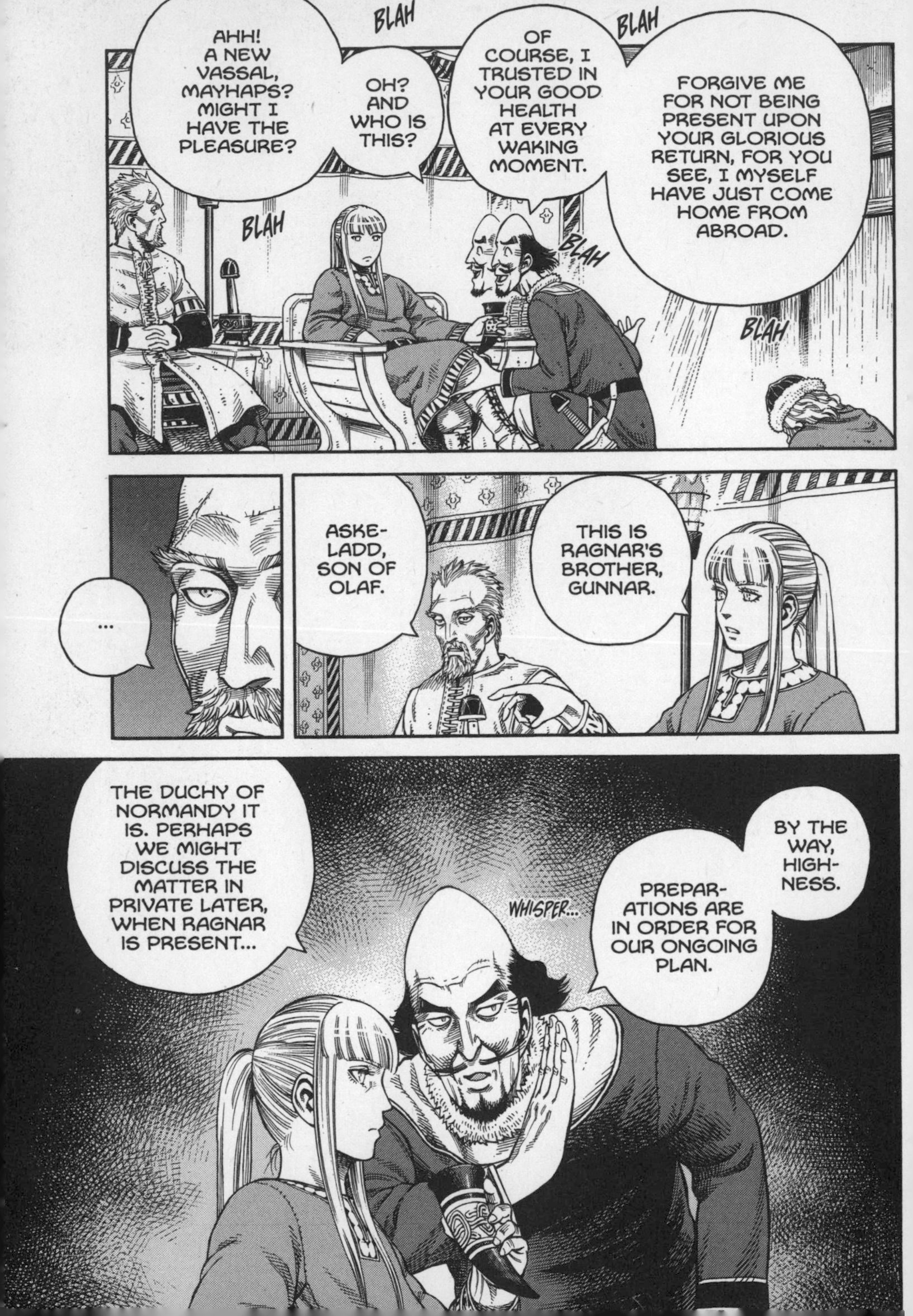
BLAH
FORGIVE ME FOR NOT BEING PRESENT UPON YOUR GLORIOUS RETURN, FOR YOU SEE, I MYSELF HAVE JUST COME HOME FROM ABROAD.
BLAH
BLAH
OF COURSE, I TRUSTED IN YOUR GOOD HEALTH AT EVERY WAKING MOMENT.
BLAH
OH? AND WHO IS THIS?
AHH! A NEW VASSAL, MAYHAPS? MIGHT I HAVE THE PLEASURE?
BLAH
THIS IS RAGNAR'S BROTHER, GUNNAR.
ASKE-LADD, SON OF OLAF.
...
BY THE WAY, HIGH-NESS.
PREPAR-ATIONS ARE IN ORDER FOR OUR ONGOING PLAN.
WHISPER...
THE DUCHY OF NORMANDY IT IS. PERHAPS WE MIGHT DISCUSS THE MATTER IN PRIVATE LATER, WHEN RAGNAR IS PRESENT...

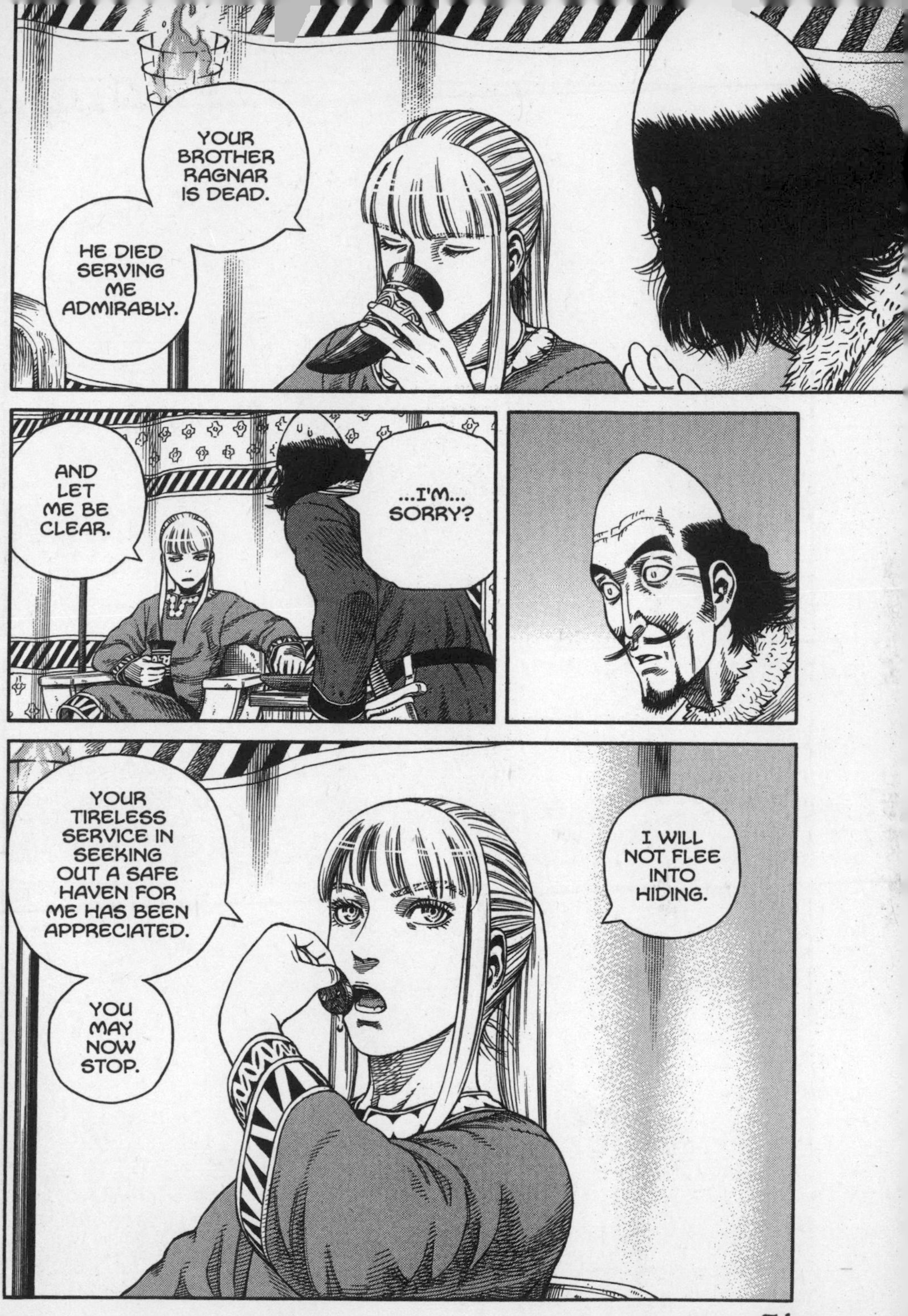
YOUR BROTHER RAGNAR IS DEAD.
HE DIED SERVING ME ADMIRABLY.
...I'M... SORRY?
AND LET ME BE CLEAR.
I WILL NOT FLEE INTO HIDING.
YOUR TIRELESS SERVICE IN SEEKING OUT A SAFE HAVEN FOR ME HAS BEEN APPRECIATED.
YOU MAY NOW STOP.

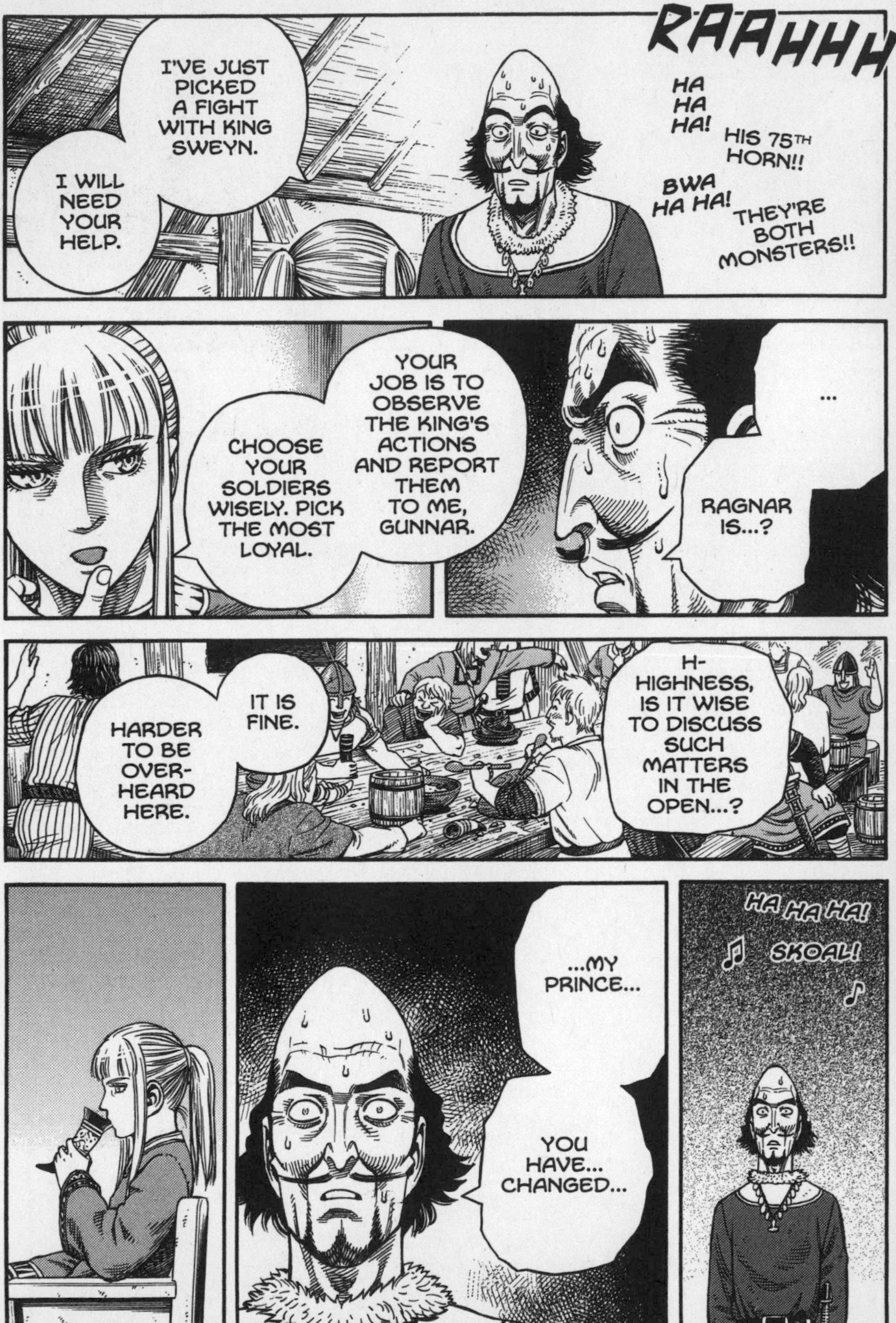
RAAHHH
HA HA HA!
HIS 75TH HORN!!
BWA HA HA!
THEY'RE BOTH MONSTERS!!
I'VE JUST PICKED A FIGHT WITH KING SWEYN.
I WILL NEED YOUR HELP.
...
RAGNAR IS...?
YOUR JOB IS TO OBSERVE THE KING'S ACTIONS AND REPORT THEM TO ME, GUNNAR.
CHOOSE YOUR SOLDIERS WISELY. PICK THE MOST LOYAL.
H-HIGHNESS, IS IT WISE TO DISCUSS SUCH MATTERS IN THE OPEN...?
IT IS FINE.
HARDER TO BE OVER-HEARD HERE.
HA HA HA!
SKOAL!
...MY PRINCE...
YOU HAVE... CHANGED...

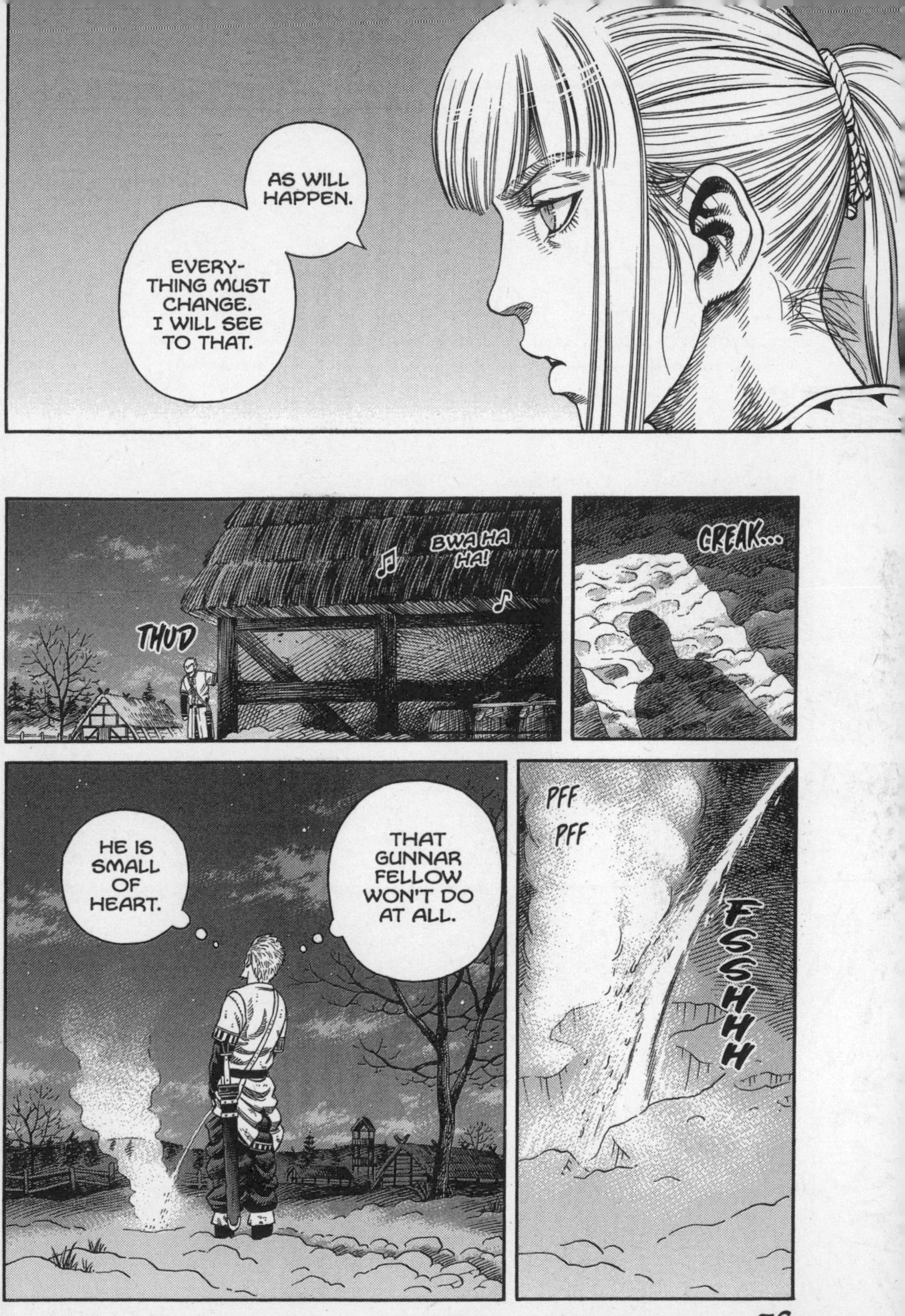
AS WILL HAPPEN.
EVERY-THING MUST CHANGE. I WILL SEE TO THAT.
CREAK...
BWA HA HA!
THUD
PFF
PFF
FSSHHH
THAT GUNNAR FELLOW WON'T DO AT ALL.
HE IS SMALL OF HEART.

MM?

HE WON'T BE NEARLY AS LOYAL TO THE PRINCE AS HE SAYS...

AND WHEN PUSH COMES TO SHOVE, THE SMALL-HEARTED PROTECT THEM-SELVES.

PSH PSH PSH

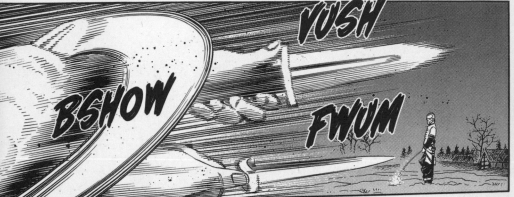

VUSH

BSHOW

FWUM

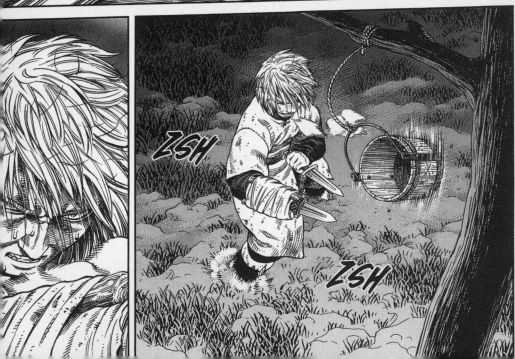

ZSH

ZSH

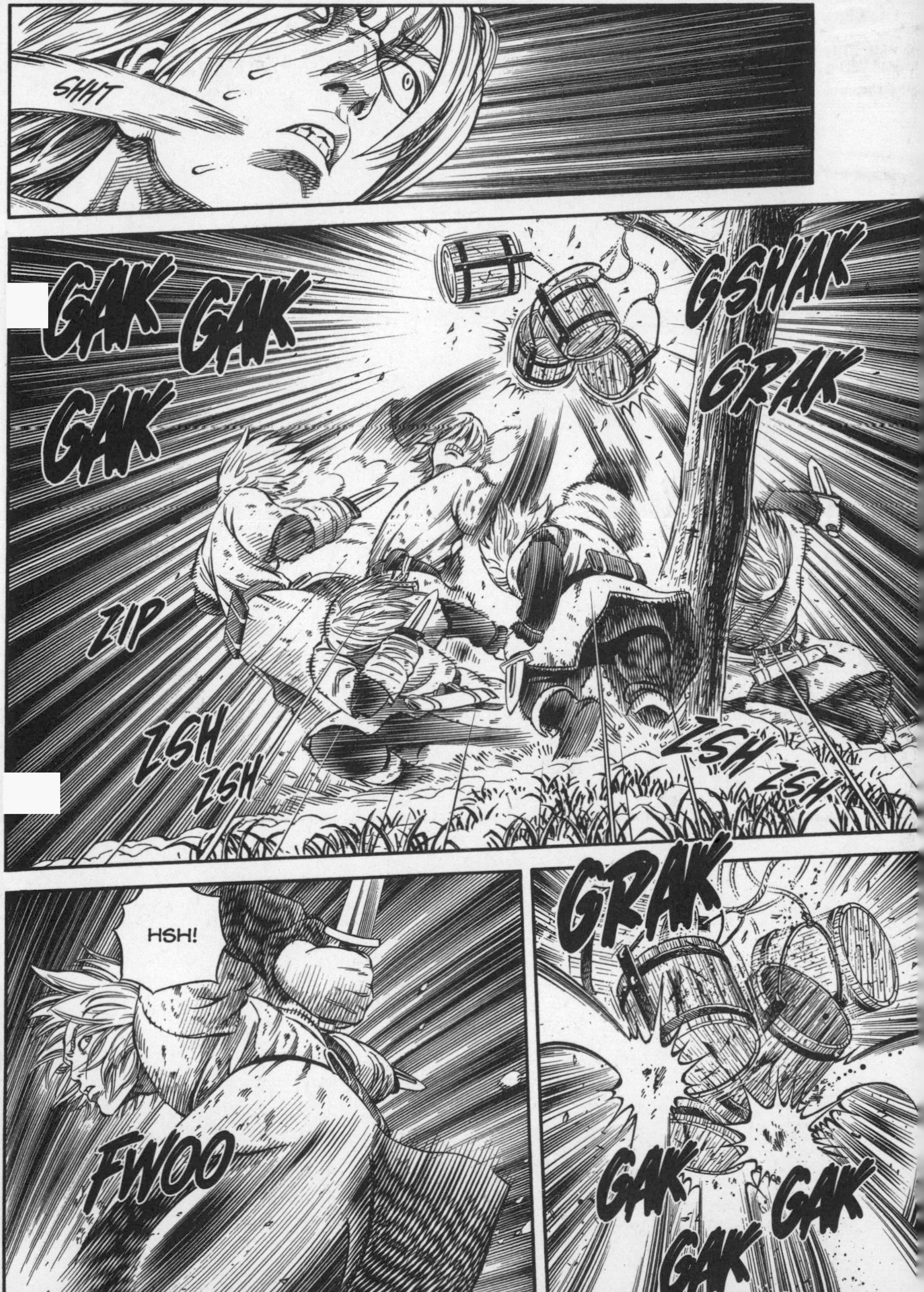

SHHT
GSHAK
GRAK
GAK GAK
GAK
ZIP
ZSH ZSH
ZSH ZSH
GRAK
GAK
GAK
GAK
HSH!
FWOO

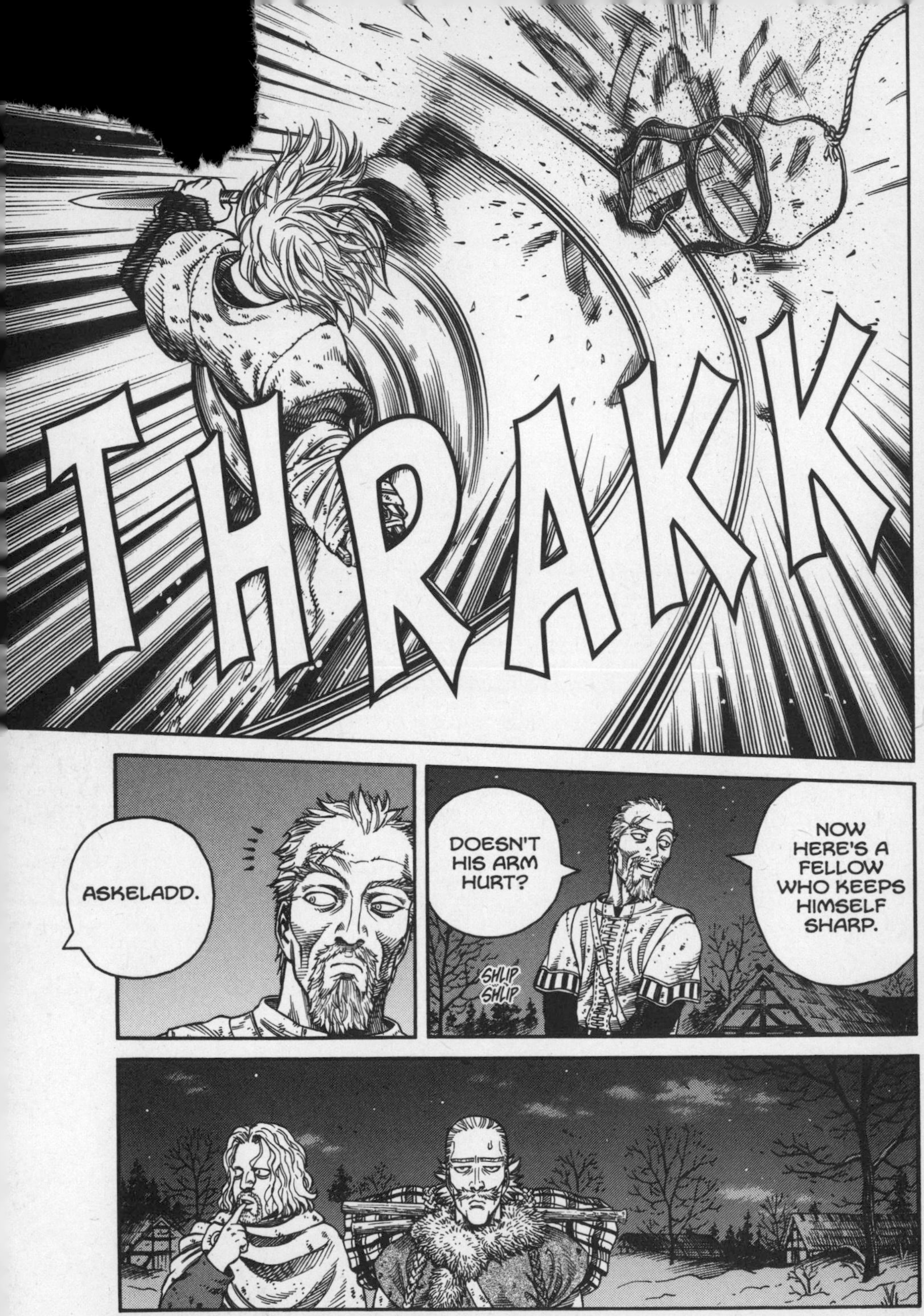
THRAKK
NOW HERE'S A FELLOW WHO KEEPS HIMSELF SHARP.
DOESN'T HIS ARM HURT?
SHLIP SHLIP
ASKELADD.

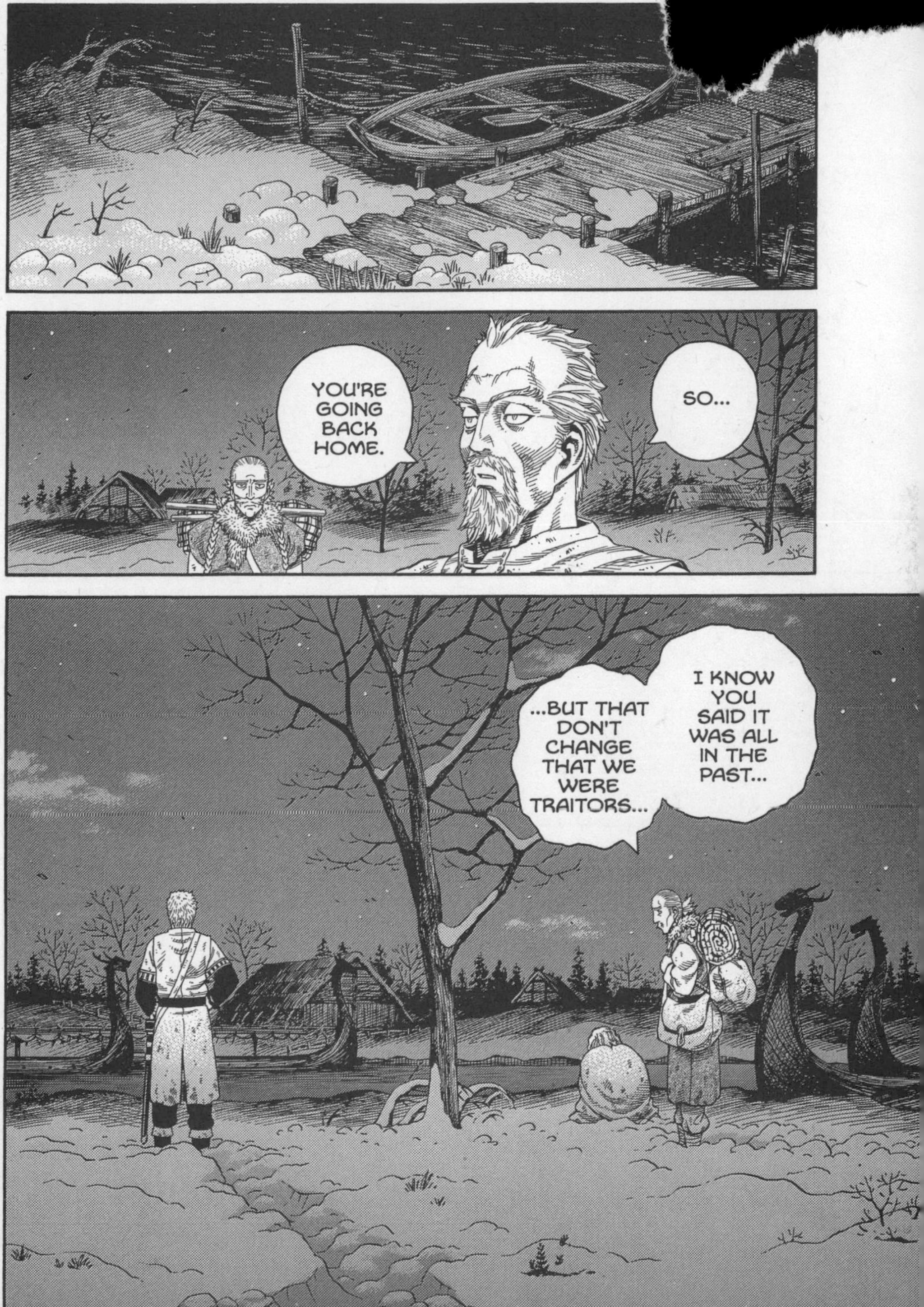
SO...
YOU'RE GOING BACK HOME.
I KNOW YOU SAID IT WAS ALL IN THE PAST...
...BUT THAT DON'T CHANGE THAT WE WERE TRAITORS...

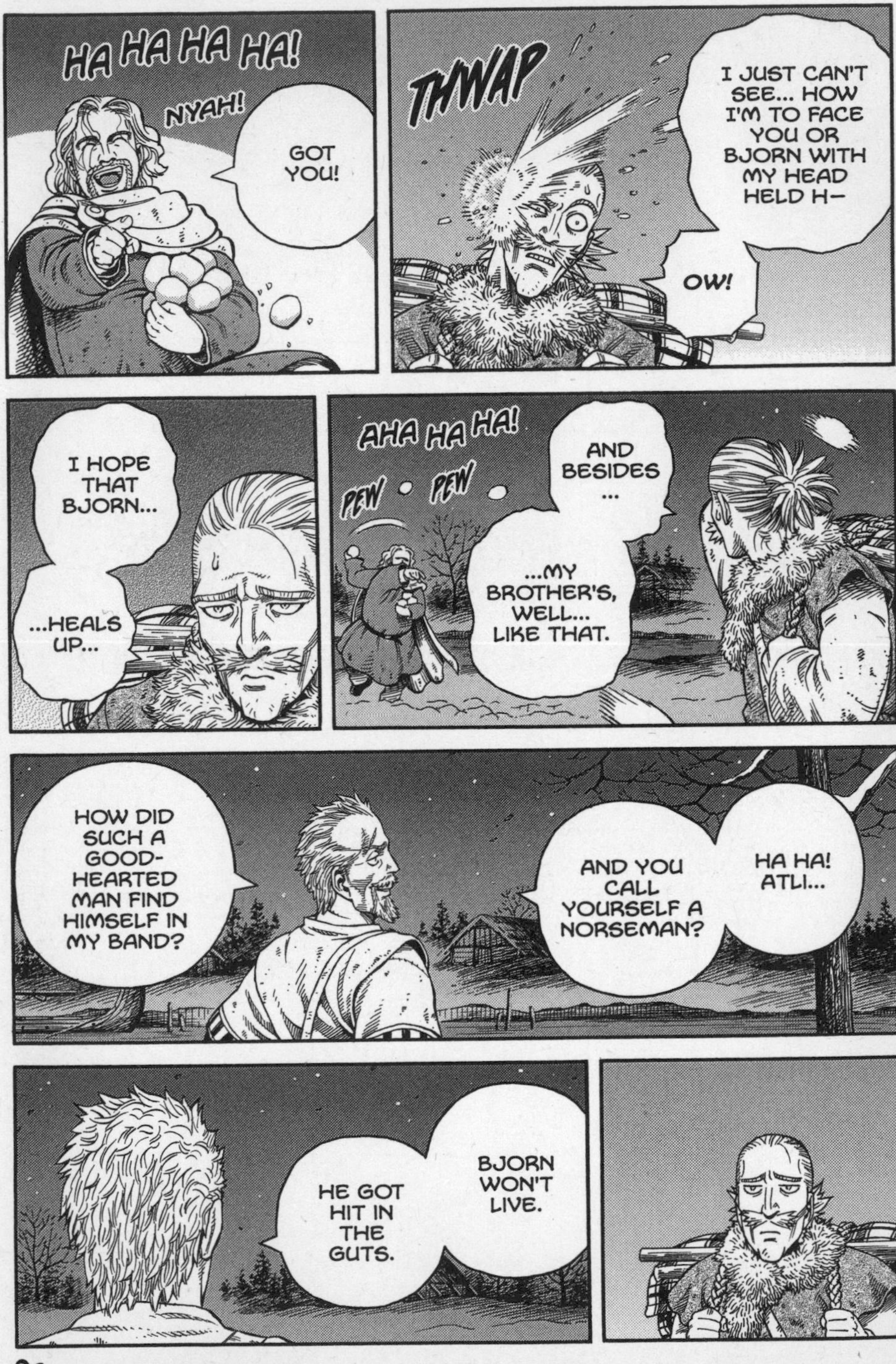
THWAP
I JUST CAN'T SEE... HOW I'M TO FACE YOU OR BJORN WITH MY HEAD HELD H–
OW!
HA HA HA HA!
NYAH!
GOT YOU!
AHA HA HA!
PEW
PEW
AND BESIDES ...
...MY BROTHER'S, WELL... LIKE THAT.
I HOPE THAT BJORN...
...HEALS UP...
HA HA! ATLI...
AND YOU CALL YOURSELF A NORSEMAN?
HOW DID SUCH A GOOD-HEARTED MAN FIND HIMSELF IN MY BAND?
BJORN WON'T LIVE.
HE GOT HIT IN THE GUTS.

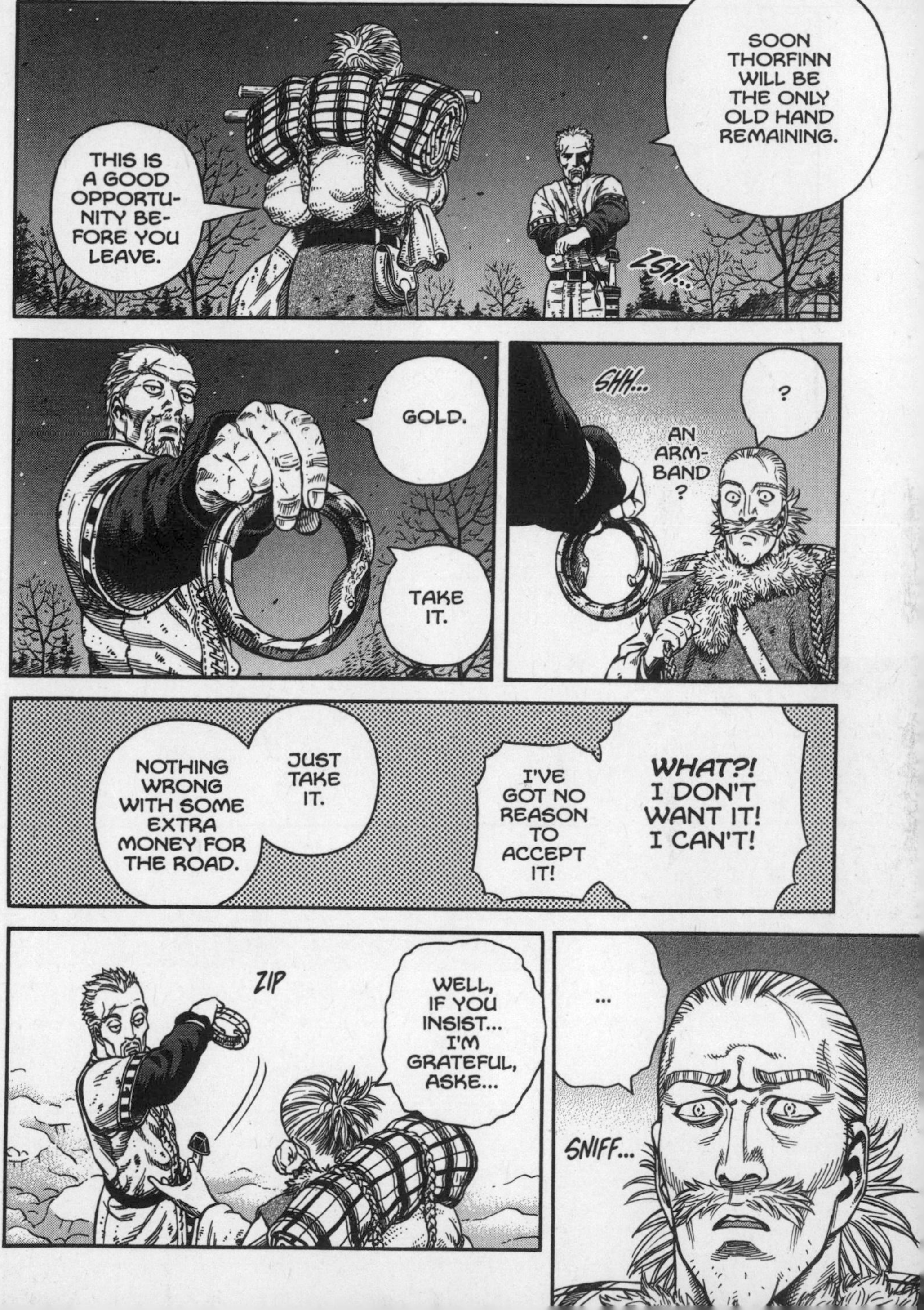
SOON THORFINN WILL BE THE ONLY OLD HAND REMAINING.
ZSH...
THIS IS A GOOD OPPORTUNITY BEFORE YOU LEAVE.
?
SHH...
AN ARMBAND?
GOLD.
TAKE IT.
WHAT?! I DON'T WANT IT! I CAN'T!
I'VE GOT NO REASON TO ACCEPT IT!
JUST TAKE IT.
NOTHING WRONG WITH SOME EXTRA MONEY FOR THE ROAD.
...
SNIFF...
WELL, IF YOU INSIST... I'M GRATEFUL, ASKE...
ZIP

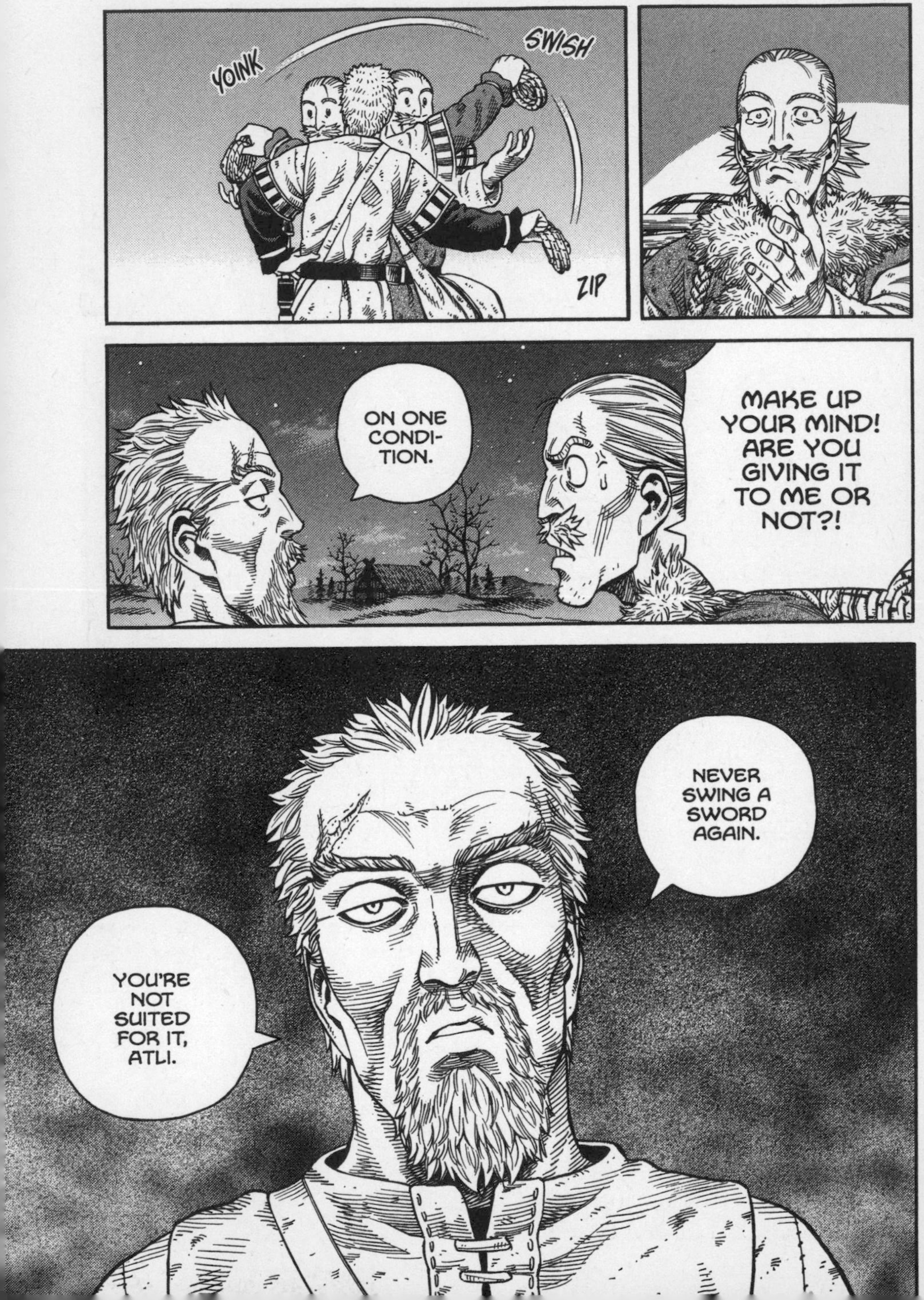
SWISH
YOINK
ZIP
MAKE UP YOUR MIND! ARE YOU GIVING IT TO ME OR NOT?!
ON ONE CONDITION.
NEVER SWING A SWORD AGAIN.
YOU'RE NOT SUITED FOR IT, ATLI.

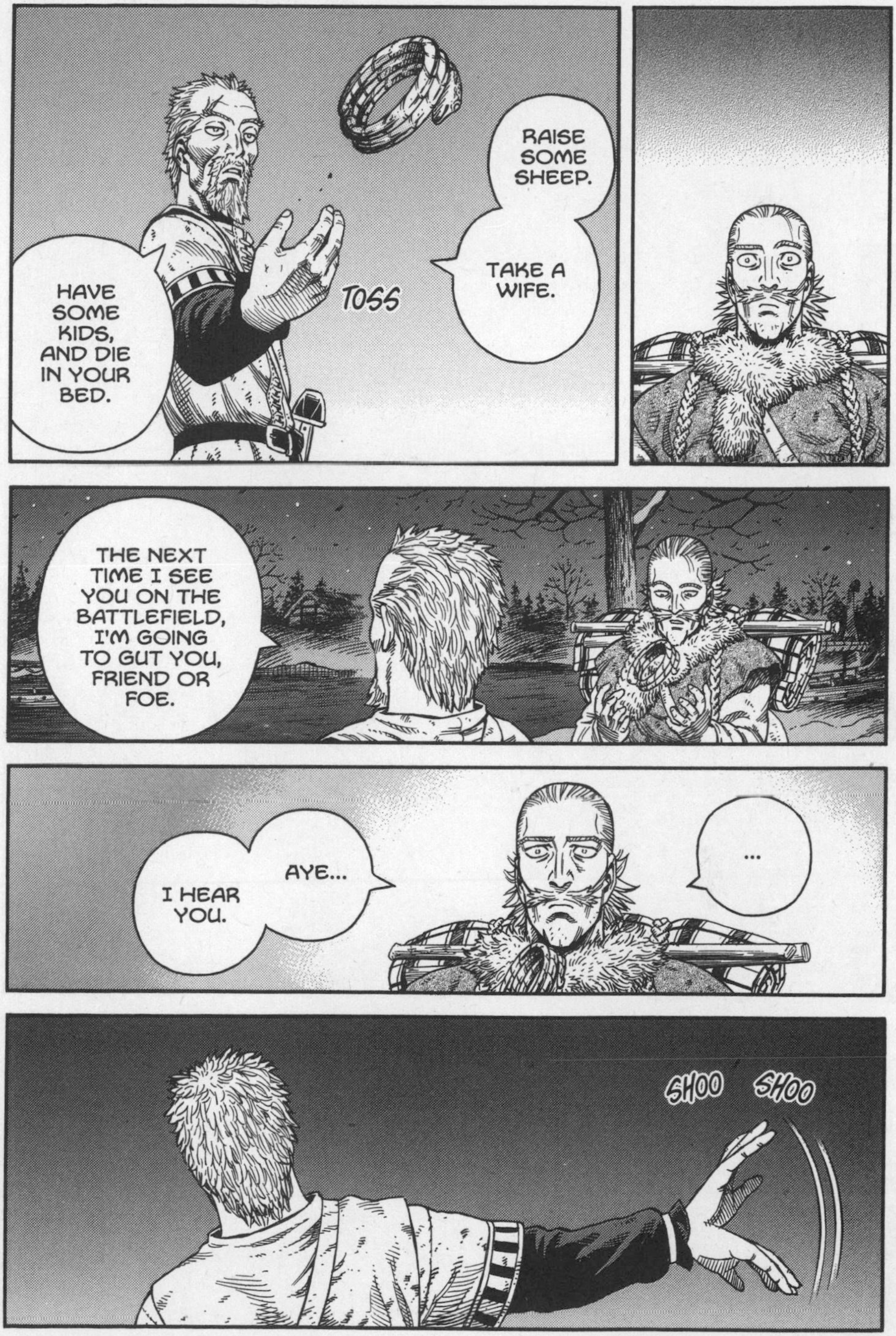
RAISE SOME SHEEP.
TAKE A WIFE.
TOSS
HAVE SOME KIDS, AND DIE IN YOUR BED.
THE NEXT TIME I SEE YOU ON THE BATTLEFIELD, I'M GOING TO GUT YOU, FRIEND OR FOE.
...
AYE...
I HEAR YOU.
SHOO SHOO

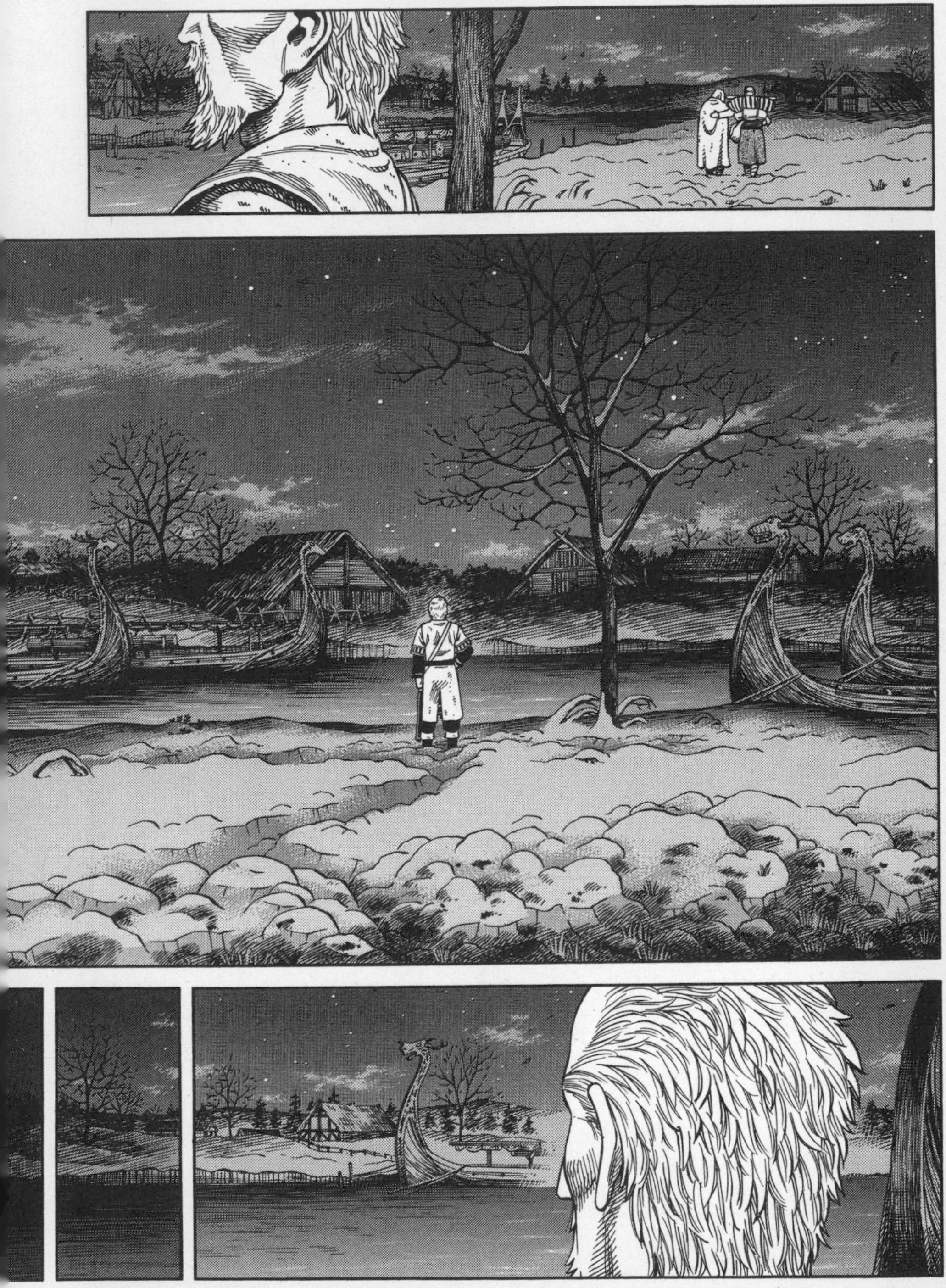

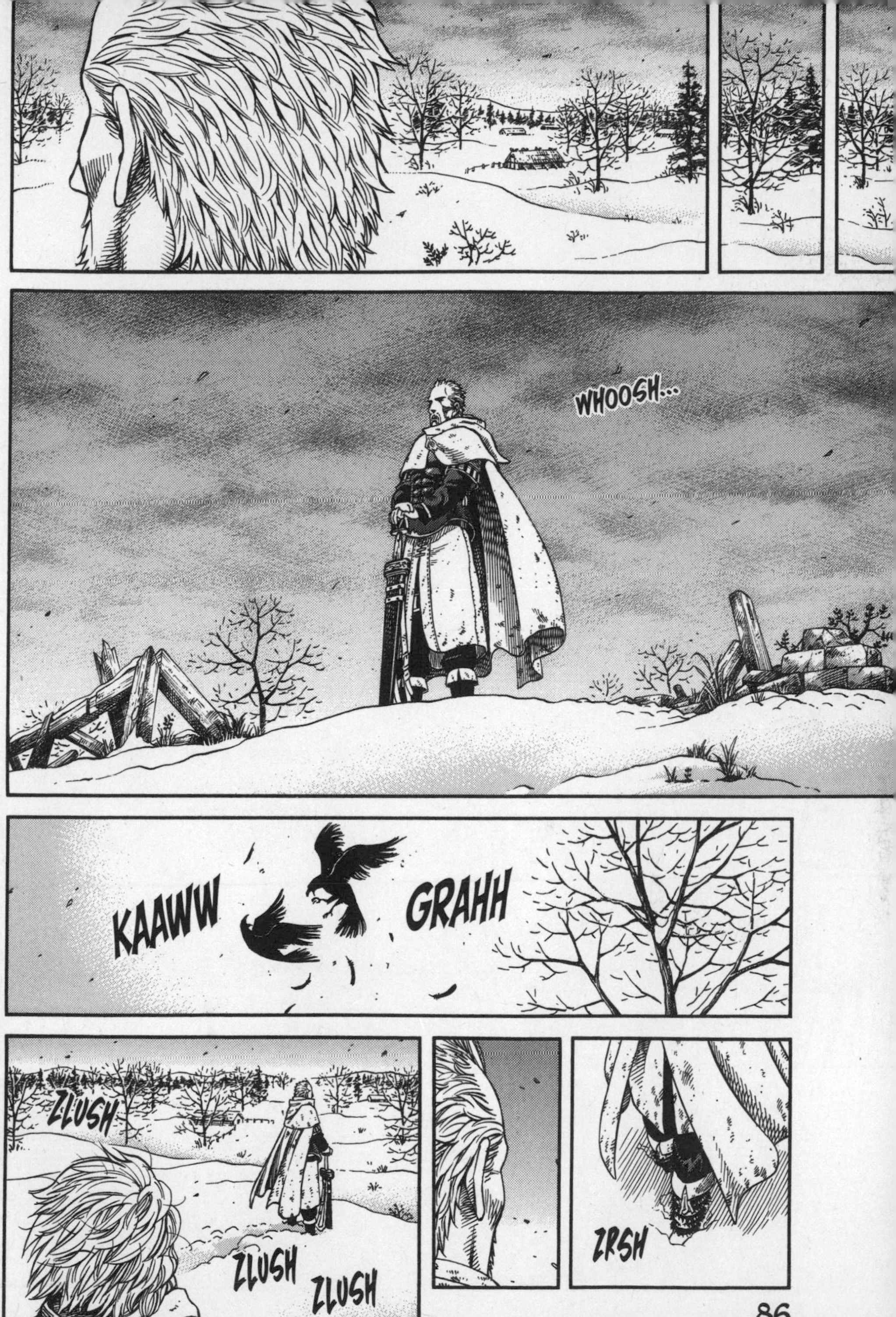
WHOOSH...
GRAHH
KAAWW
ZRSH
ZLUSH
ZLUSH
ZLUSH

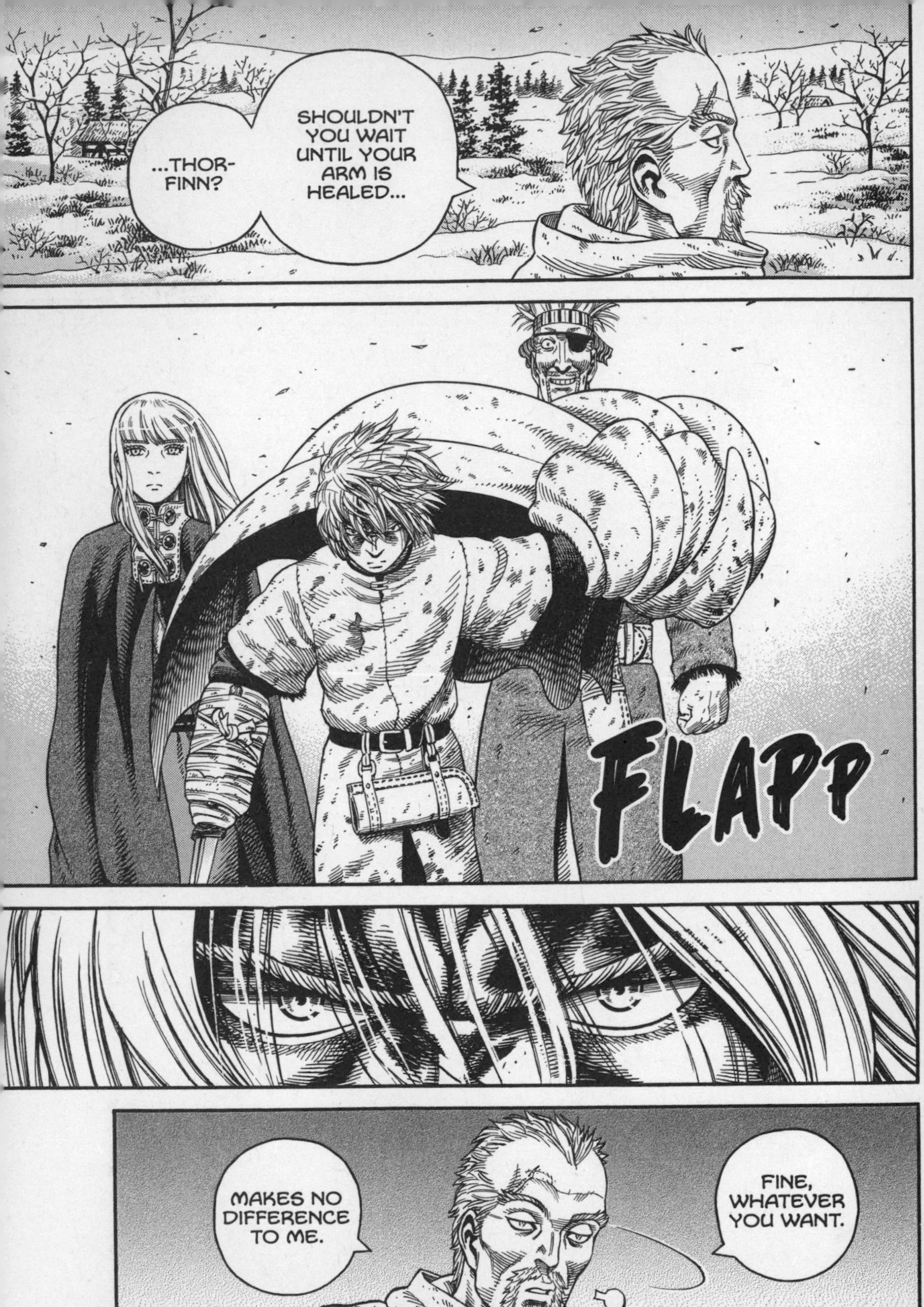
SHOULDN'T YOU WAIT UNTIL YOUR ARM IS HEALED...
...THOR-FINN?
FLAPP
FINE, WHATEVER YOU WANT.
MAKES NO DIFFERENCE TO ME.

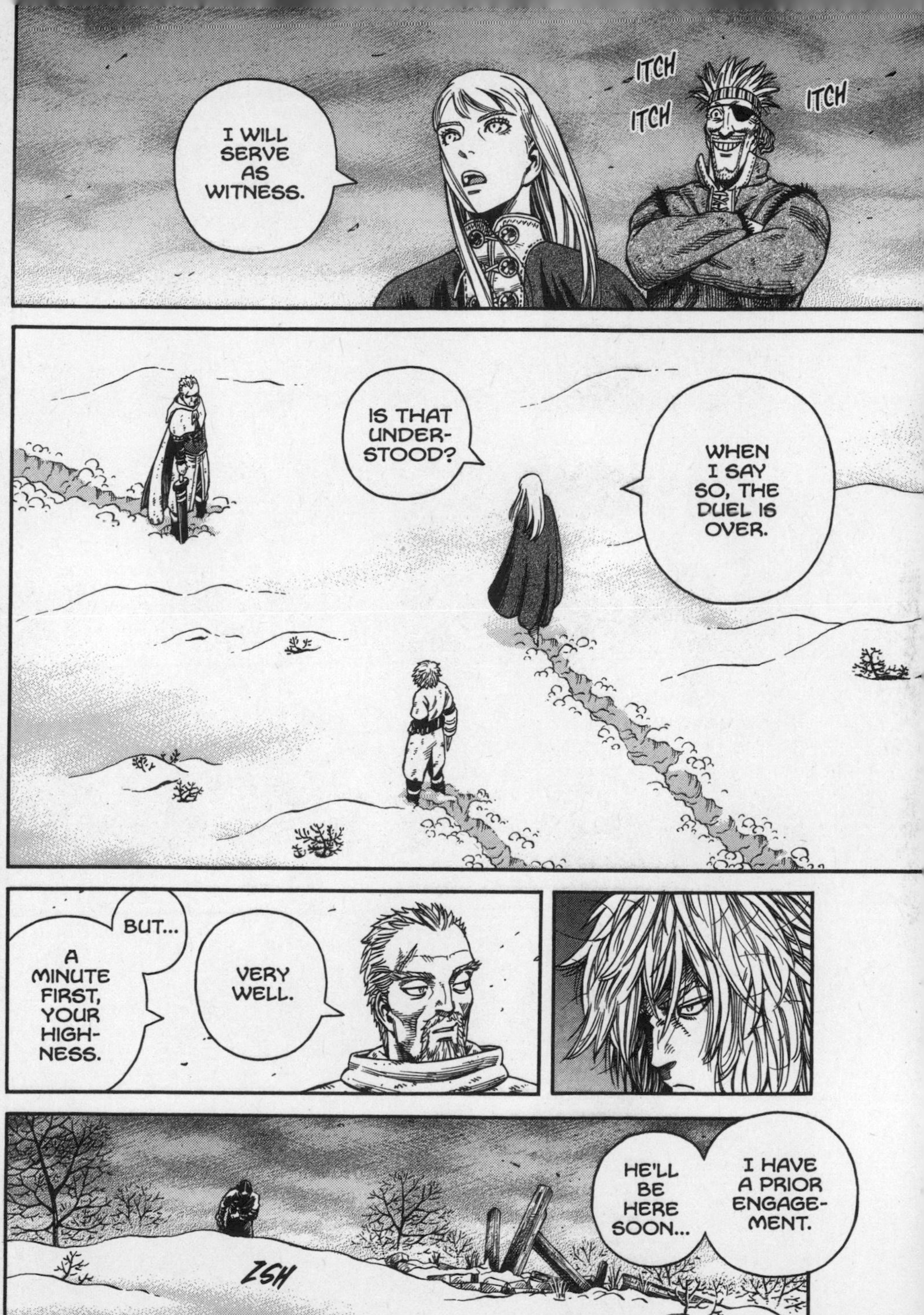
ITCH
ITCH
ITCH
I WILL SERVE AS WITNESS.
WHEN I SAY SO, THE DUEL IS OVER.
IS THAT UNDERSTOOD?
VERY WELL.
BUT...
A MINUTE FIRST, YOUR HIGHNESS.
I HAVE A PRIOR ENGAGEMENT.
HE'LL BE HERE SOON...
ZSH

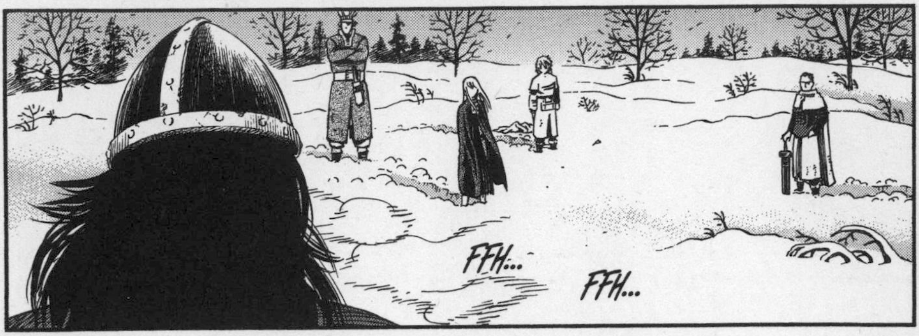
FFH...
FFH...

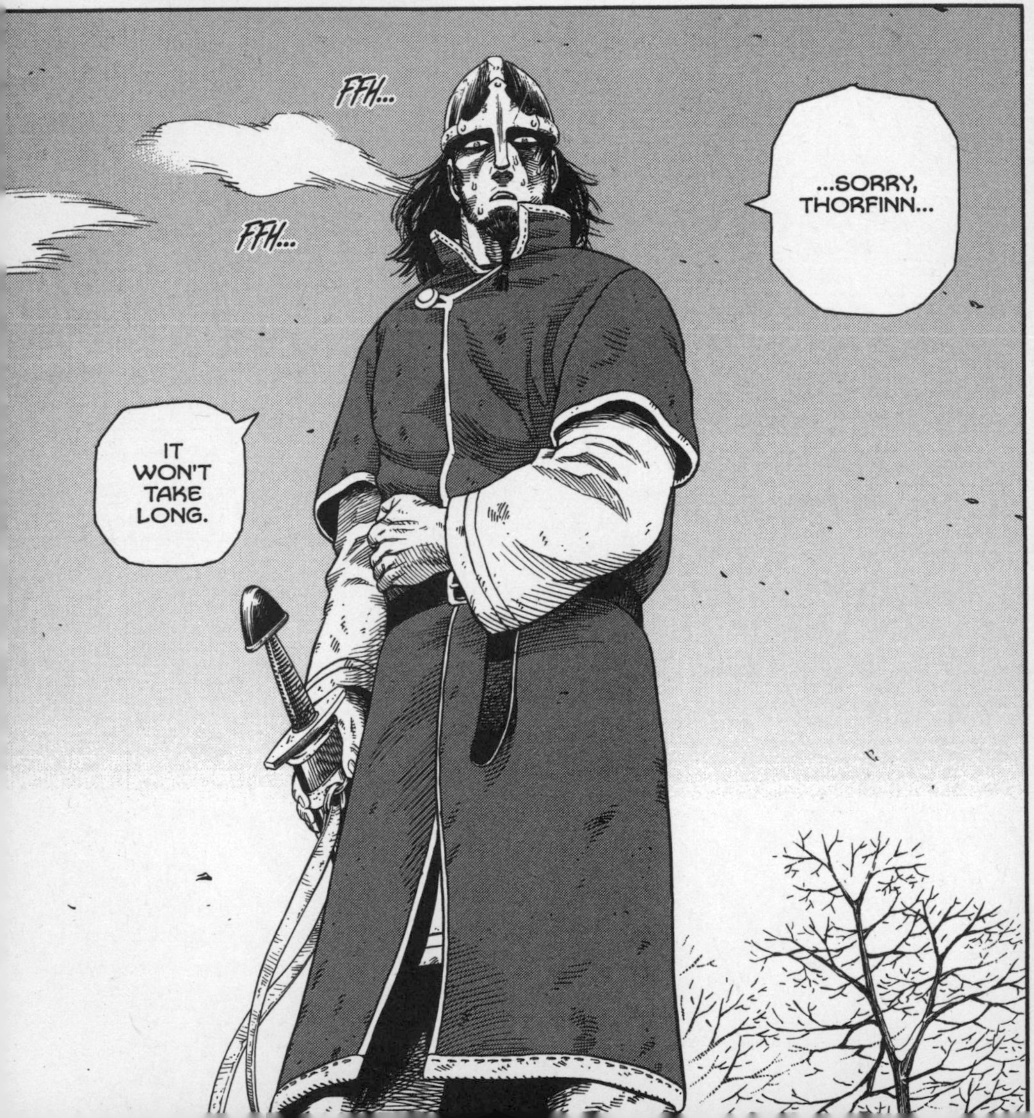
...SORRY, THORFINN...
FFH...
FFH...
IT WON'T TAKE LONG.

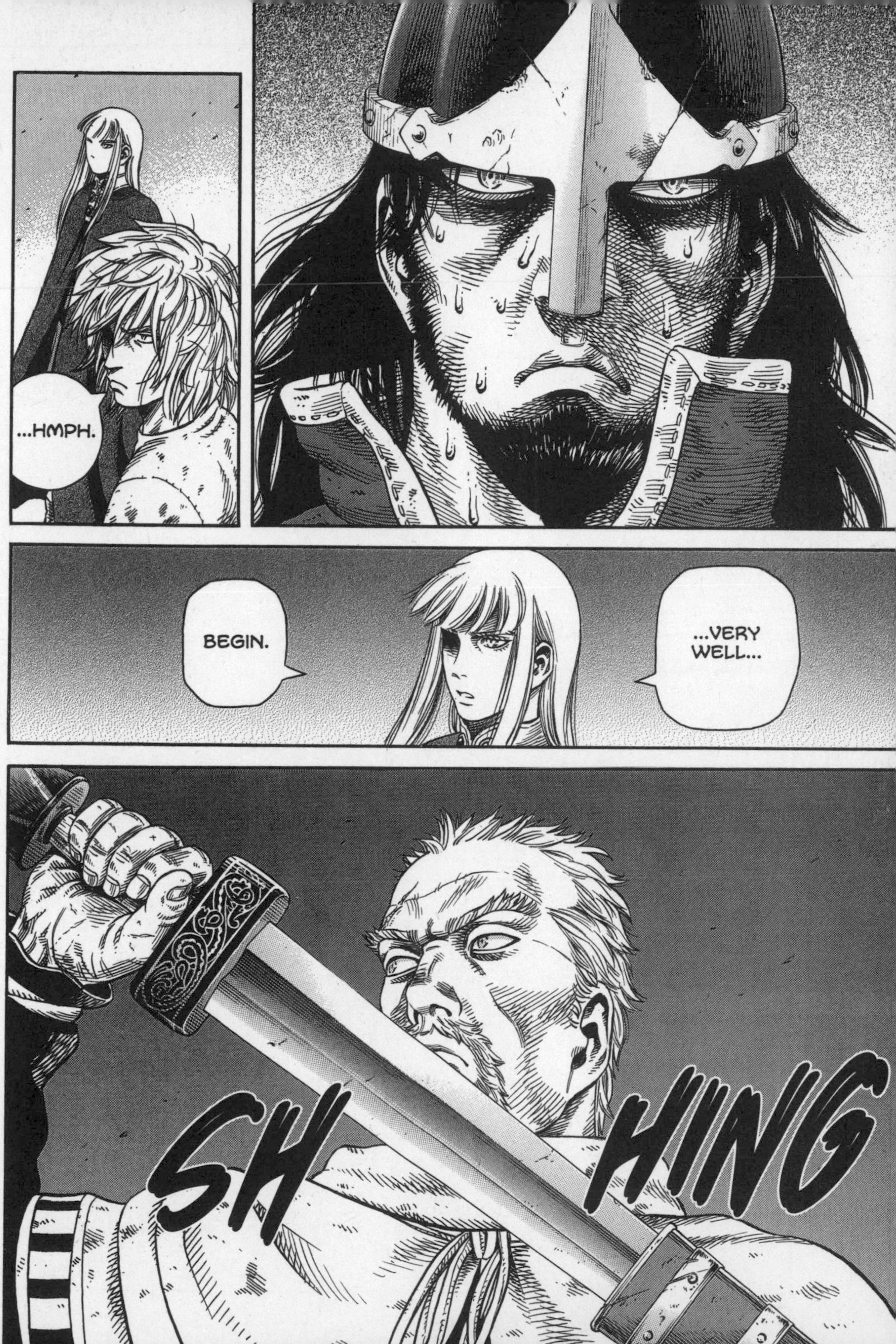
...HMPH.
...VERY WELL...
BEGIN.
SH HING

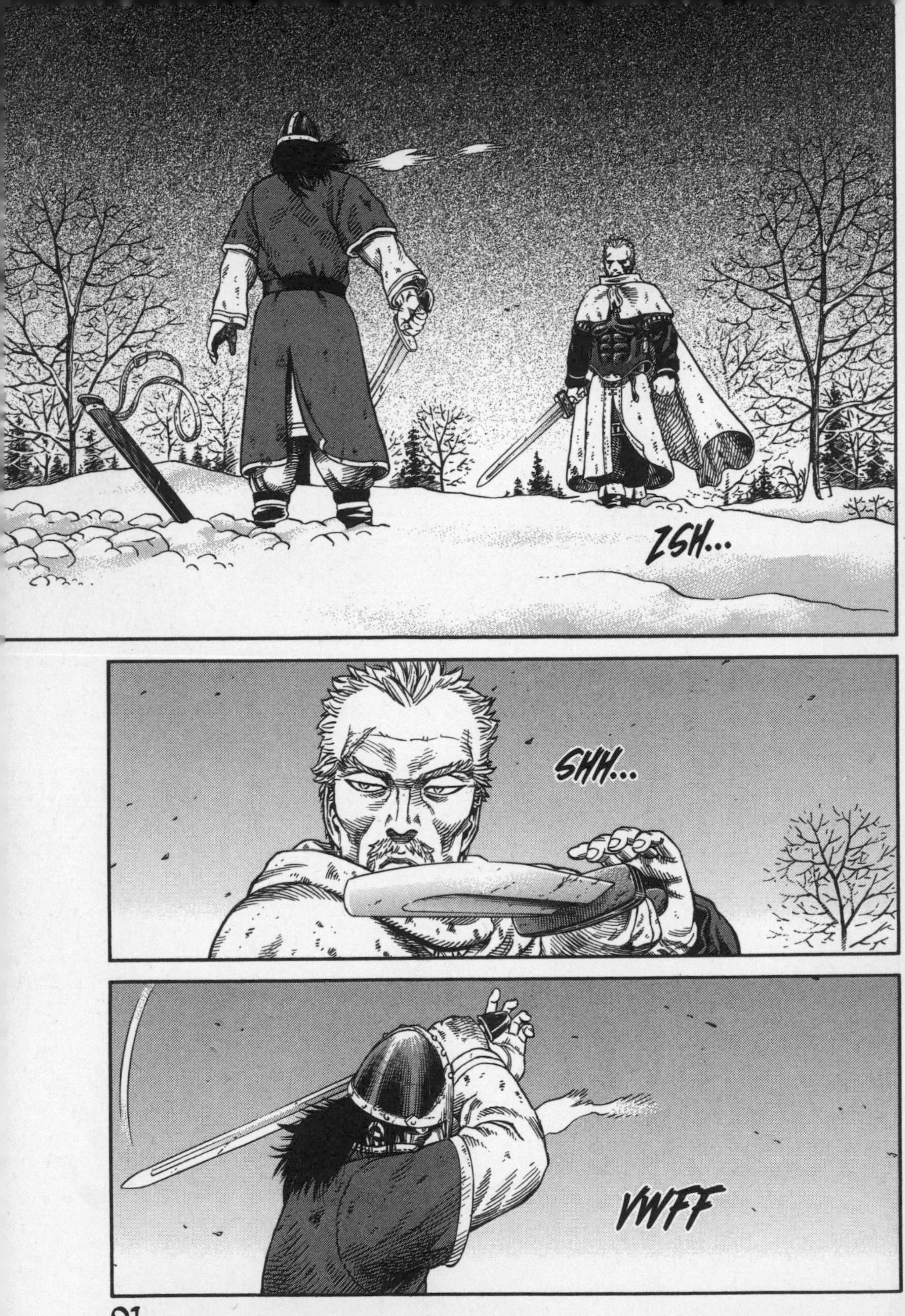
ZSH...
SHH...
VWFF

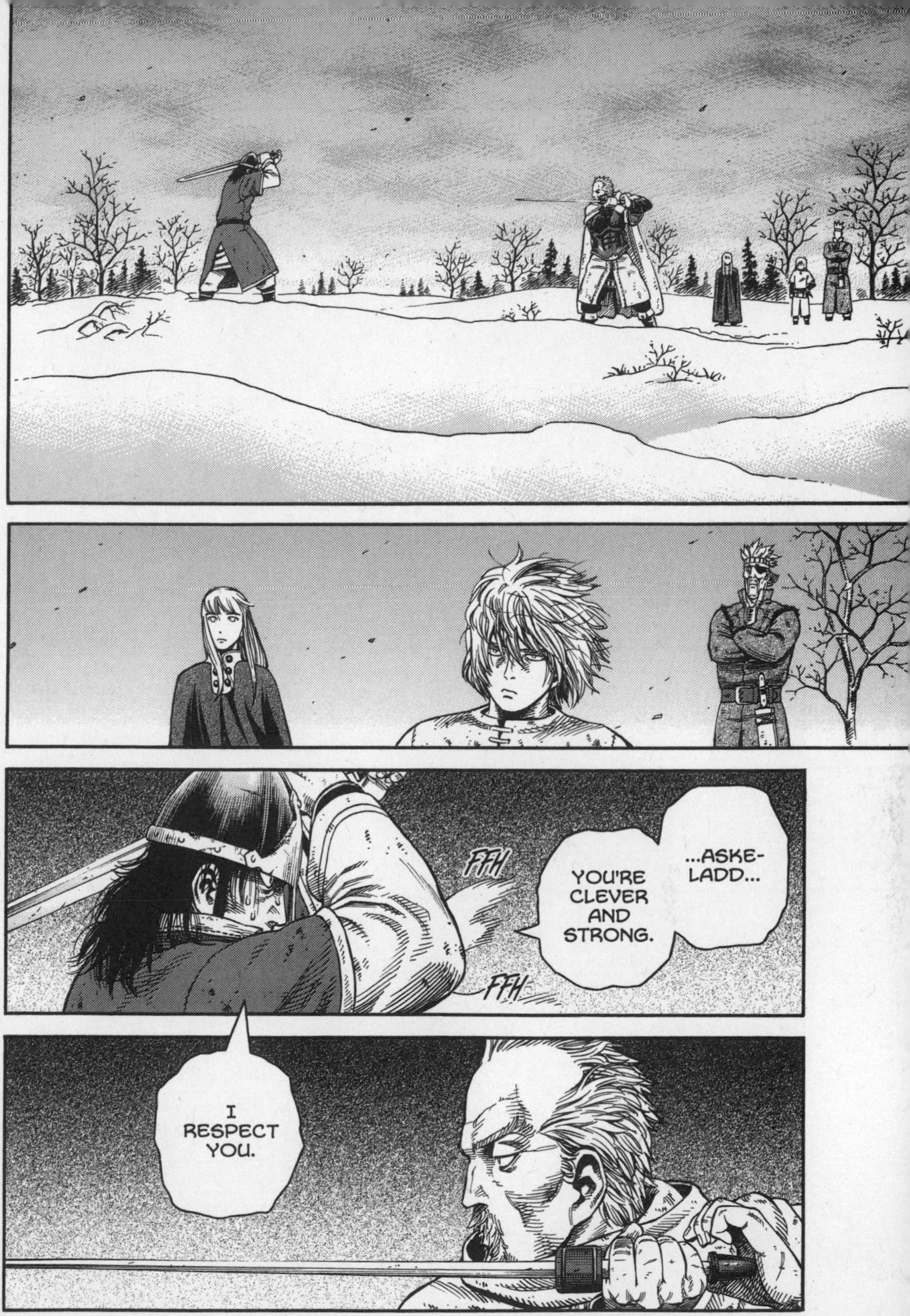
...ASKE-
LADD...
YOU'RE CLEVER AND STRONG.
FFH
FFH
I RESPECT YOU.

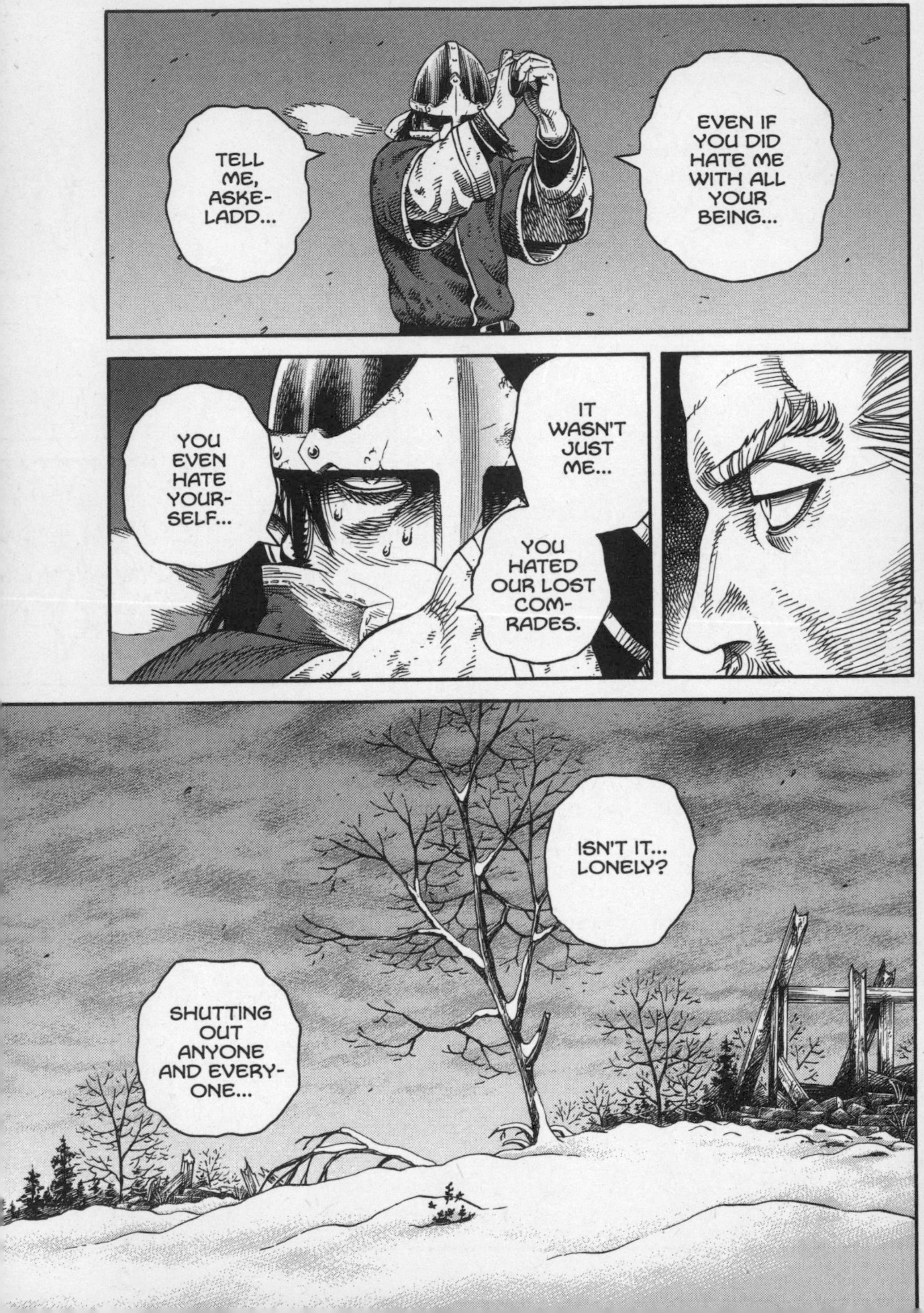
EVEN IF YOU DID HATE ME WITH ALL YOUR BEING...
TELL ME, ASKE-LADD...
IT WASN'T JUST ME...
YOU HATED OUR LOST COM-RADES.
YOU EVEN HATE YOUR-SELF...
ISN'T IT... LONELY?
SHUTTING OUT ANYONE AND EVERY-ONE...

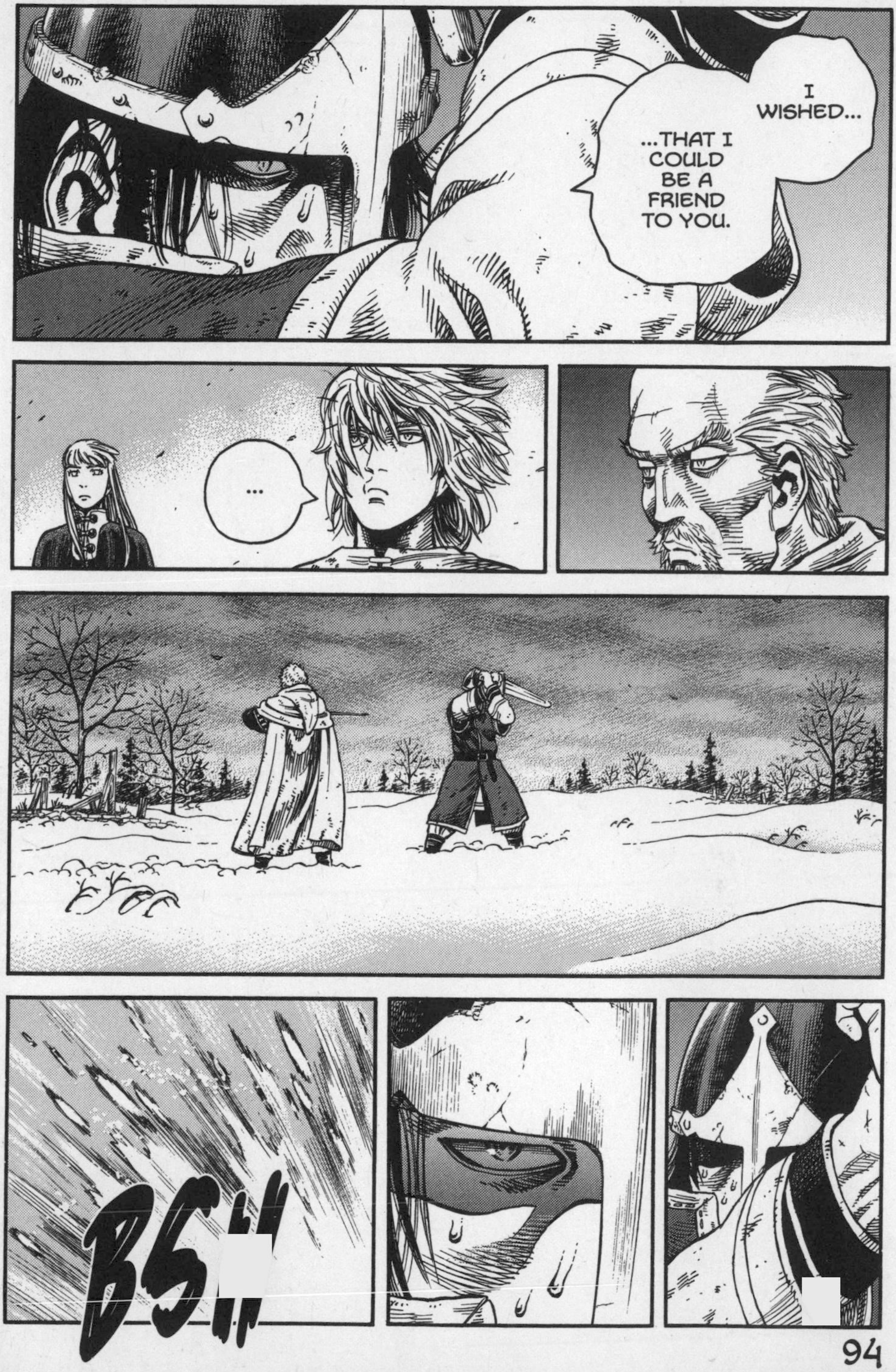
I WISHED...
...THAT I COULD BE A FRIEND TO YOU.
...
BS

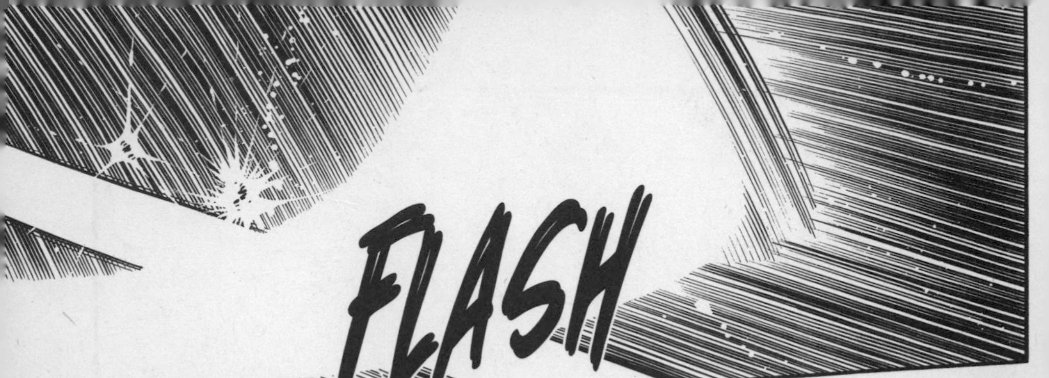
FLASH
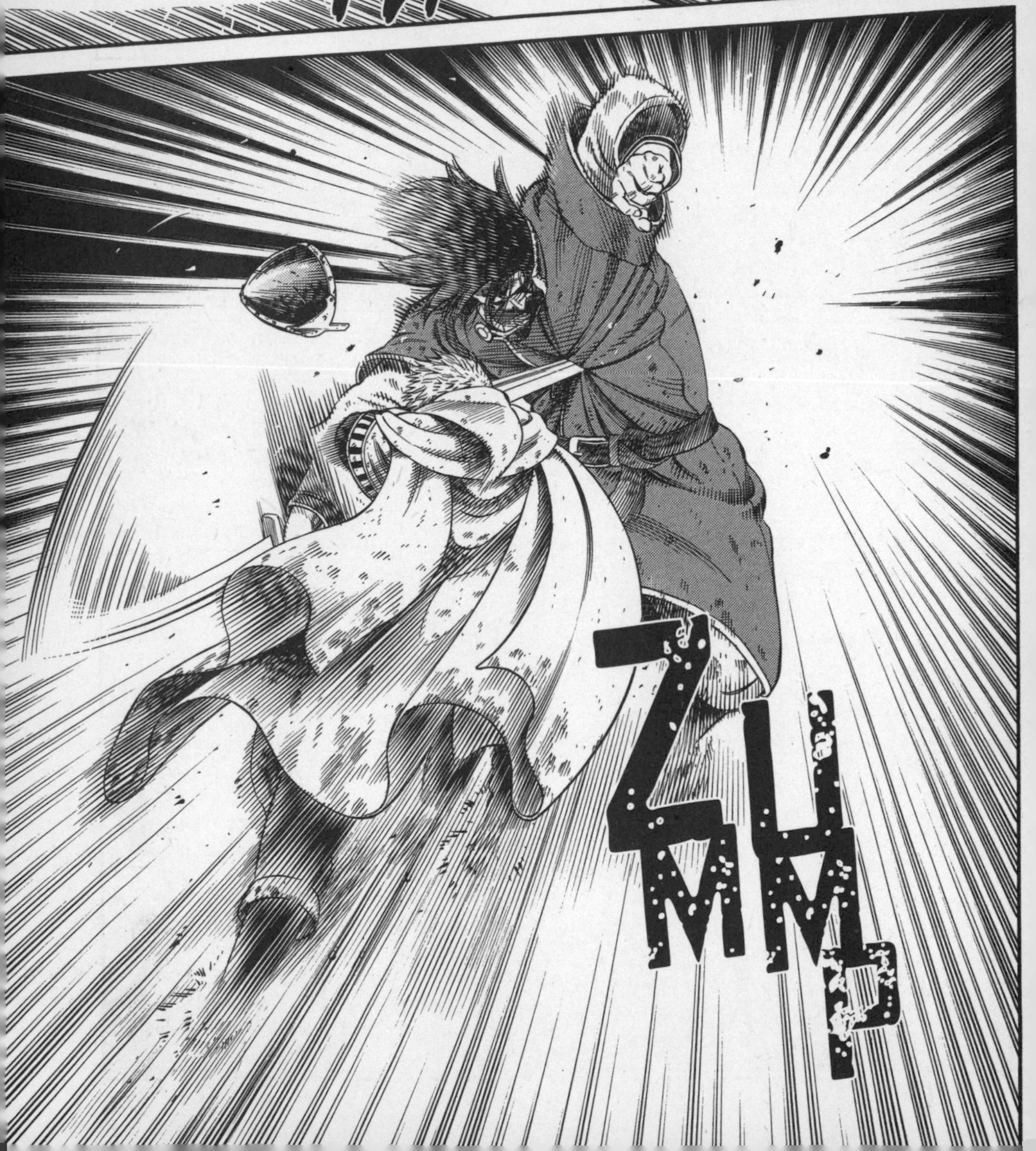
ZUMMP

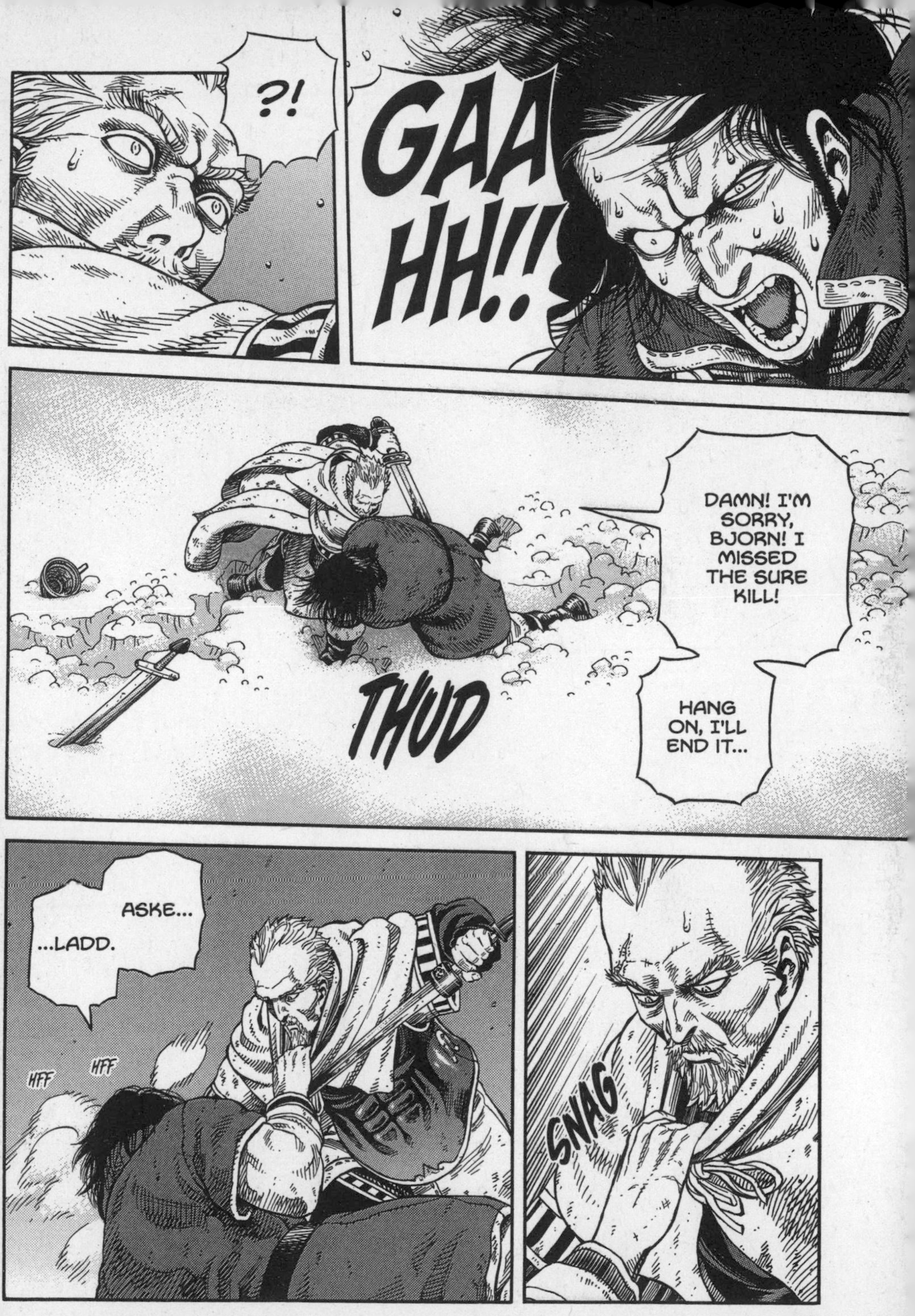
GAA HH!!
?!
DAMN! I'M SORRY, BJORN! I MISSED THE SURE KILL!
HANG ON, I'LL END IT...
THUD
SNAG
ASKE...
...LADD.
HFF
HFF

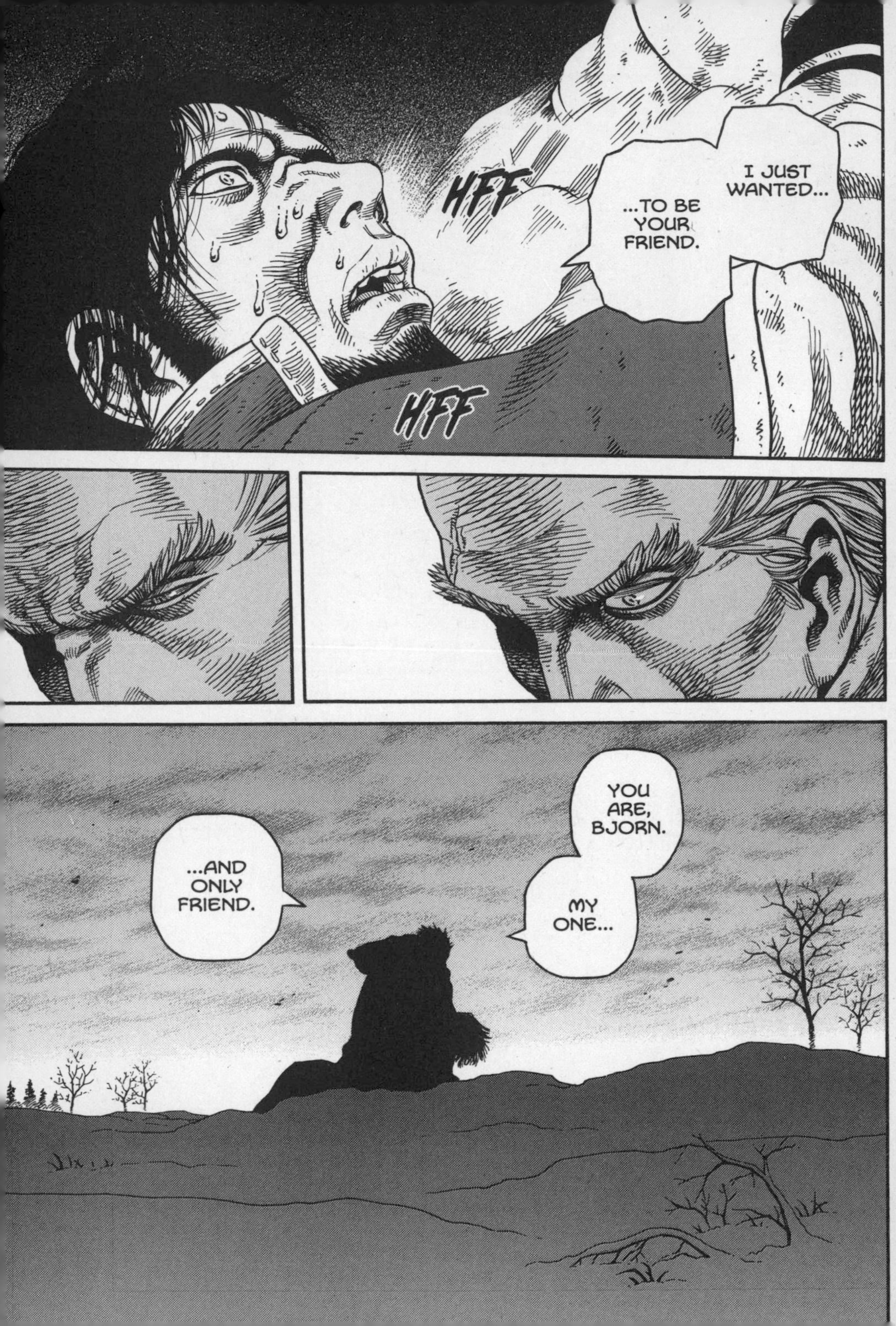
I JUST WANTED...
...TO BE YOUR FRIEND.
HFF
HFF
YOU ARE, BJORN.
MY ONE...
...AND ONLY FRIEND.

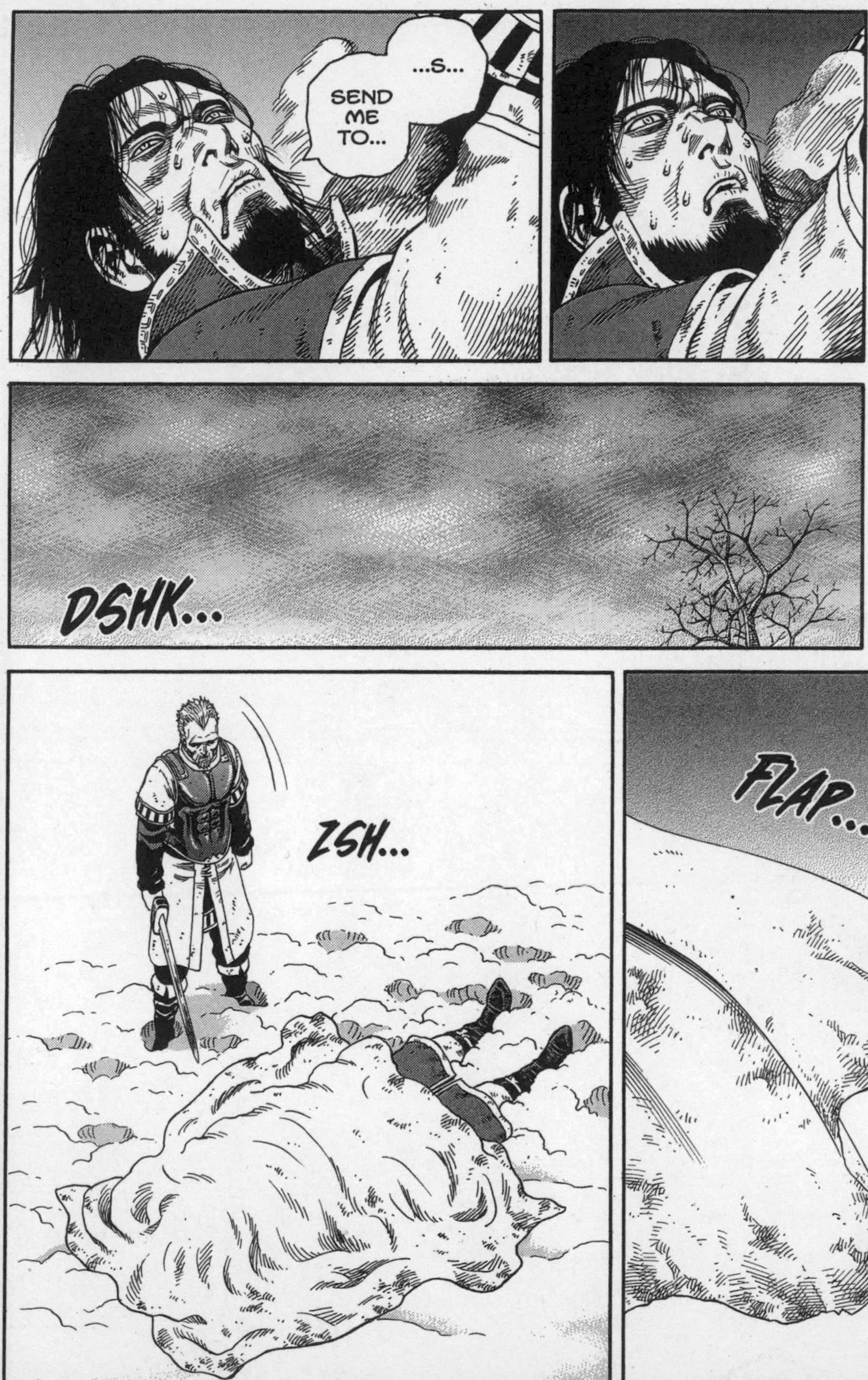
...S...
SEND ME TO...
DSHK...
FLAP...
ZSH...

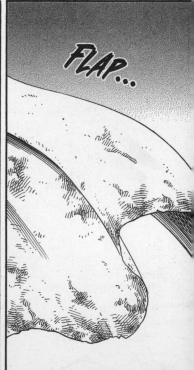

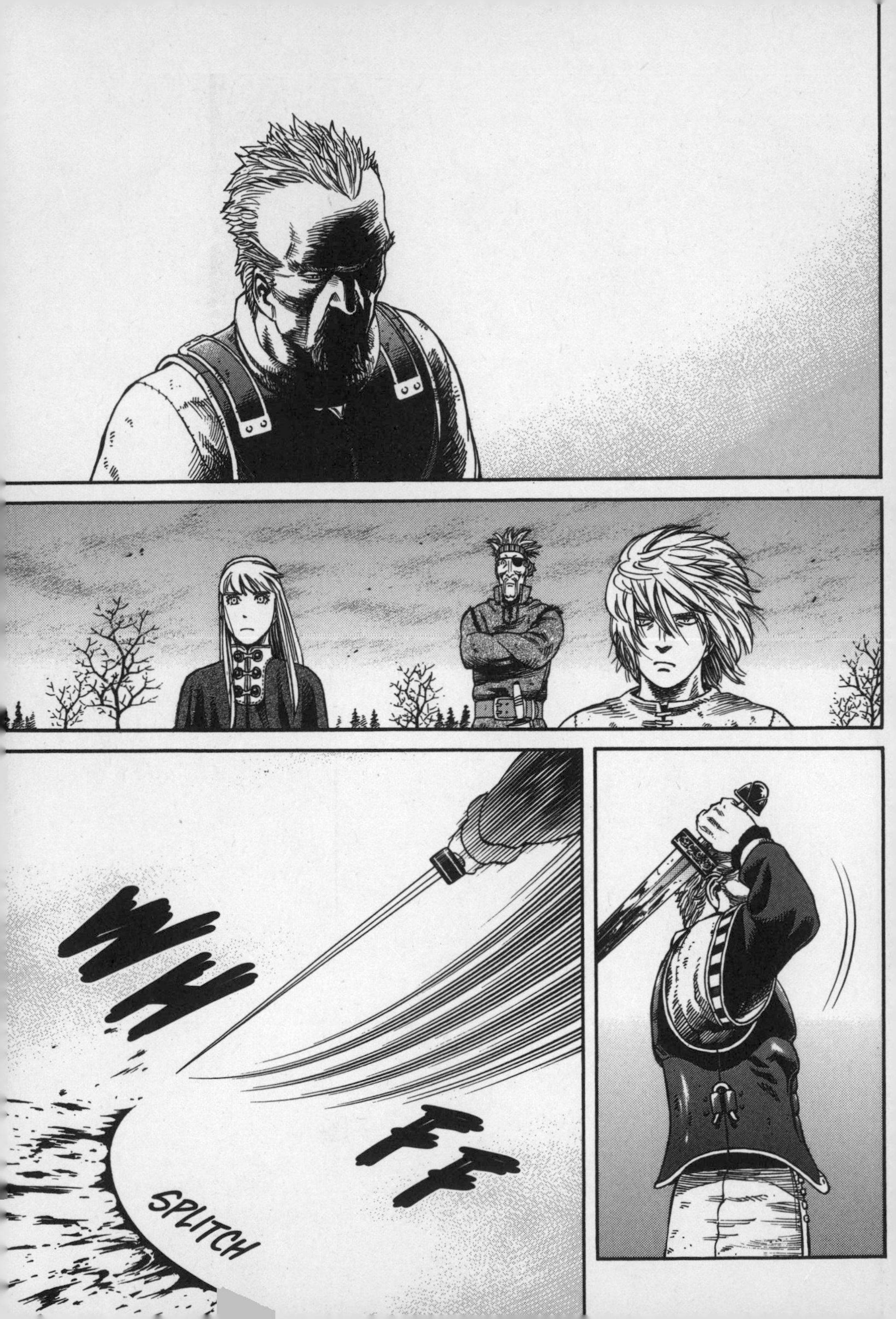
WHFF
SPLITCH

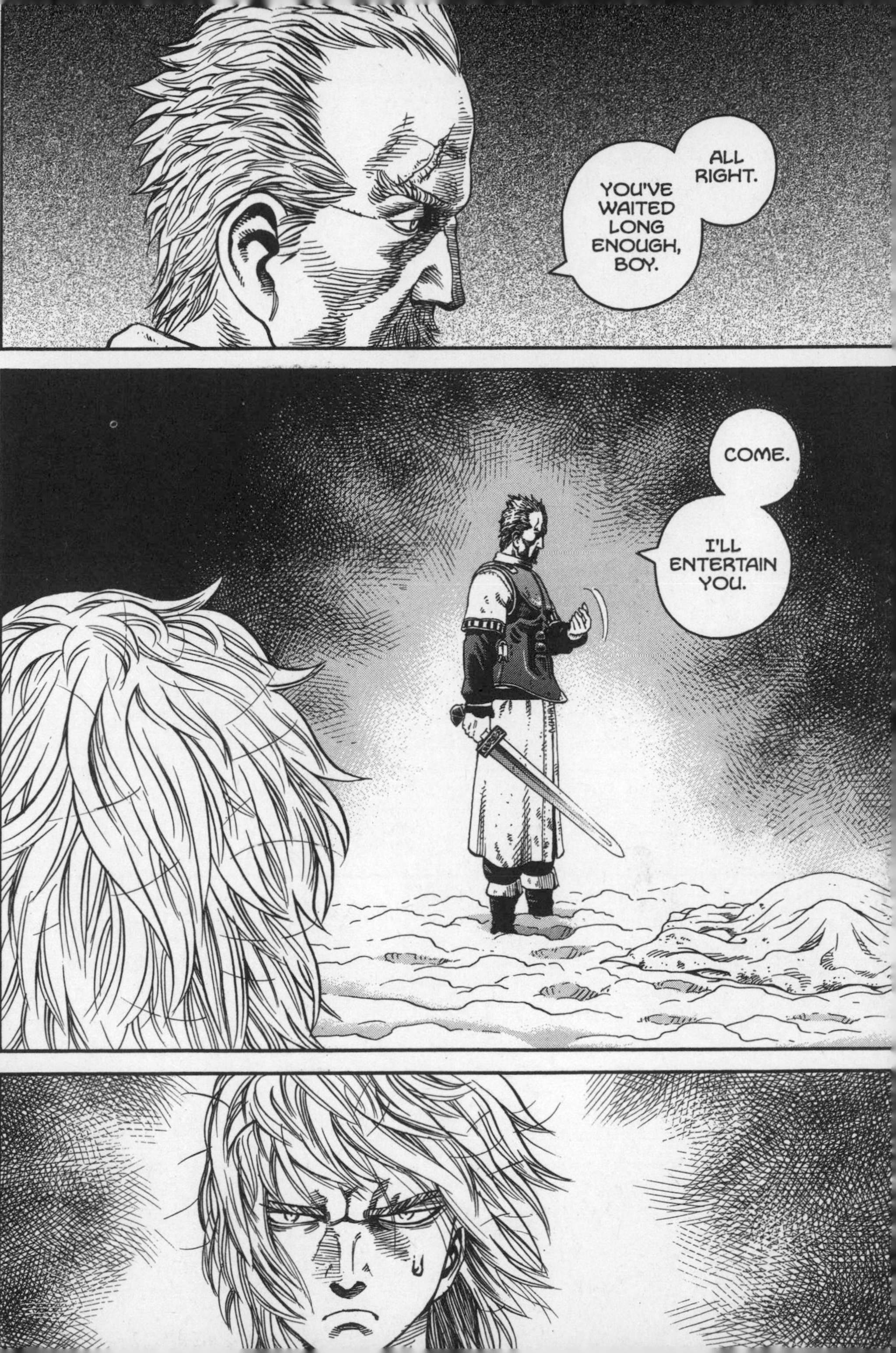
ALL RIGHT.
YOU'VE WAITED LONG ENOUGH, BOY.
COME.
I'LL ENTERTAIN YOU.

CHAPTER 3 - END

CHAPTER 46: TWO LONE WOLVES

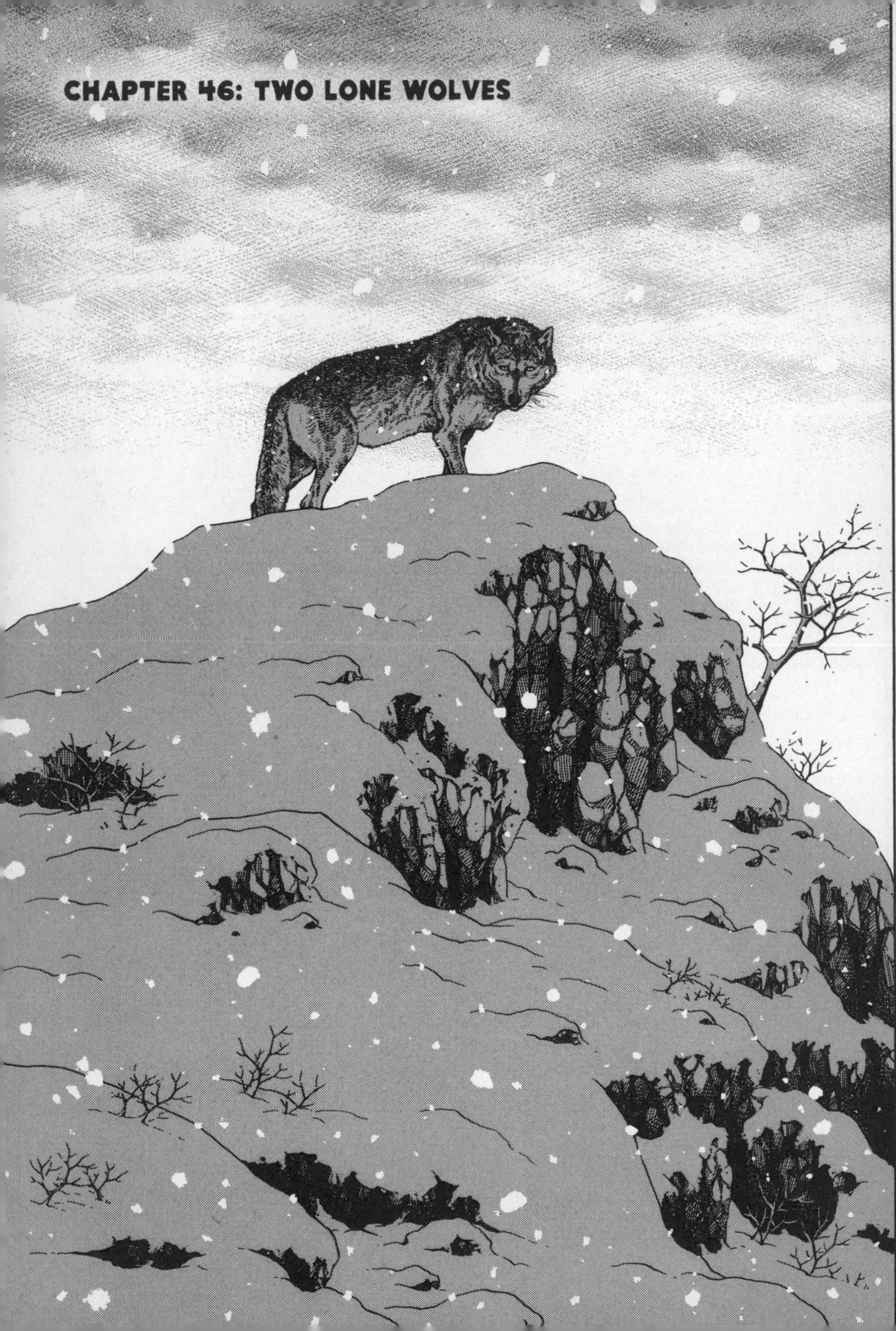

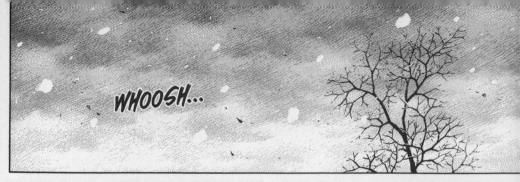

WHOOSH...

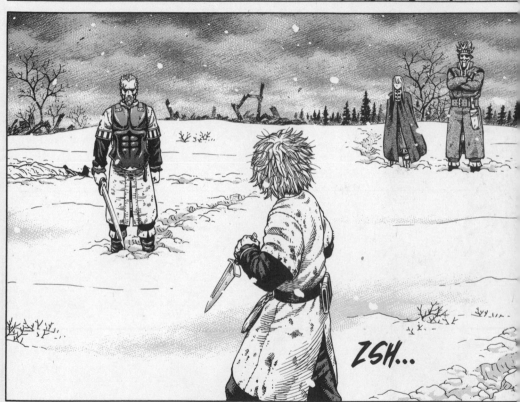

ZSH...

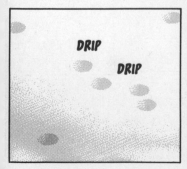

DRIP

DRIP

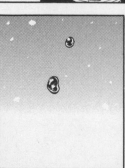

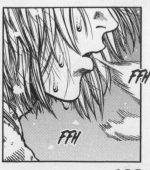

FFH

FFH

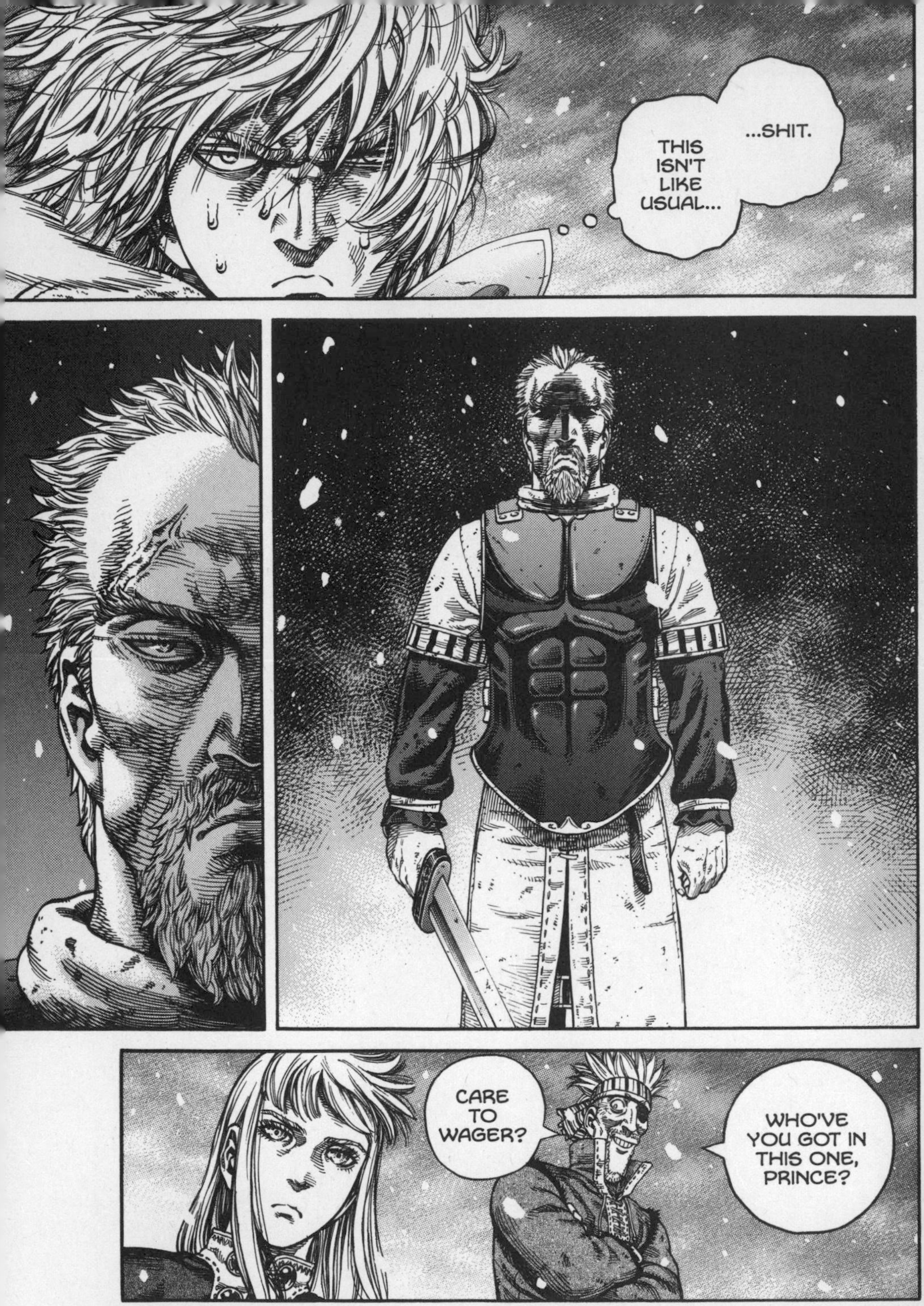
...SHIT.
THIS ISN'T LIKE USUAL...
WHO'VE YOU GOT IN THIS ONE, PRINCE?
CARE TO WAGER?

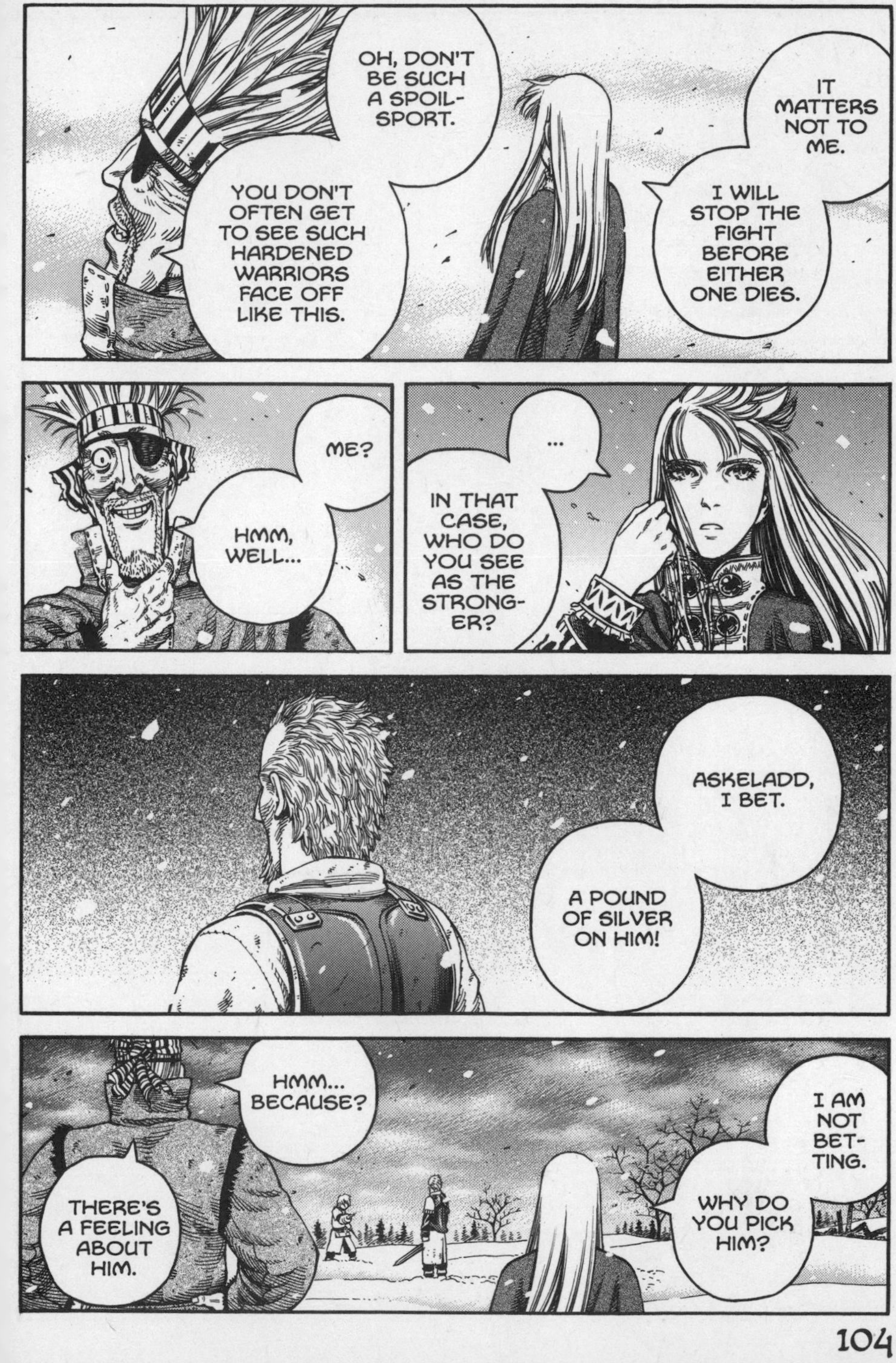
IT MATTERS NOT TO ME.
I WILL STOP THE FIGHT BEFORE EITHER ONE DIES.
OH, DON'T BE SUCH A SPOIL-SPORT.
YOU DON'T OFTEN GET TO SEE SUCH HARDENED WARRIORS FACE OFF LIKE THIS.
...
IN THAT CASE, WHO DO YOU SEE AS THE STRONGER?
ME?
HMM, WELL...
ASKELADD, I BET.
A POUND OF SILVER ON HIM!
I AM NOT BETTING.
WHY DO YOU PICK HIM?
HMM... BECAUSE?
THERE'S A FEELING ABOUT HIM.

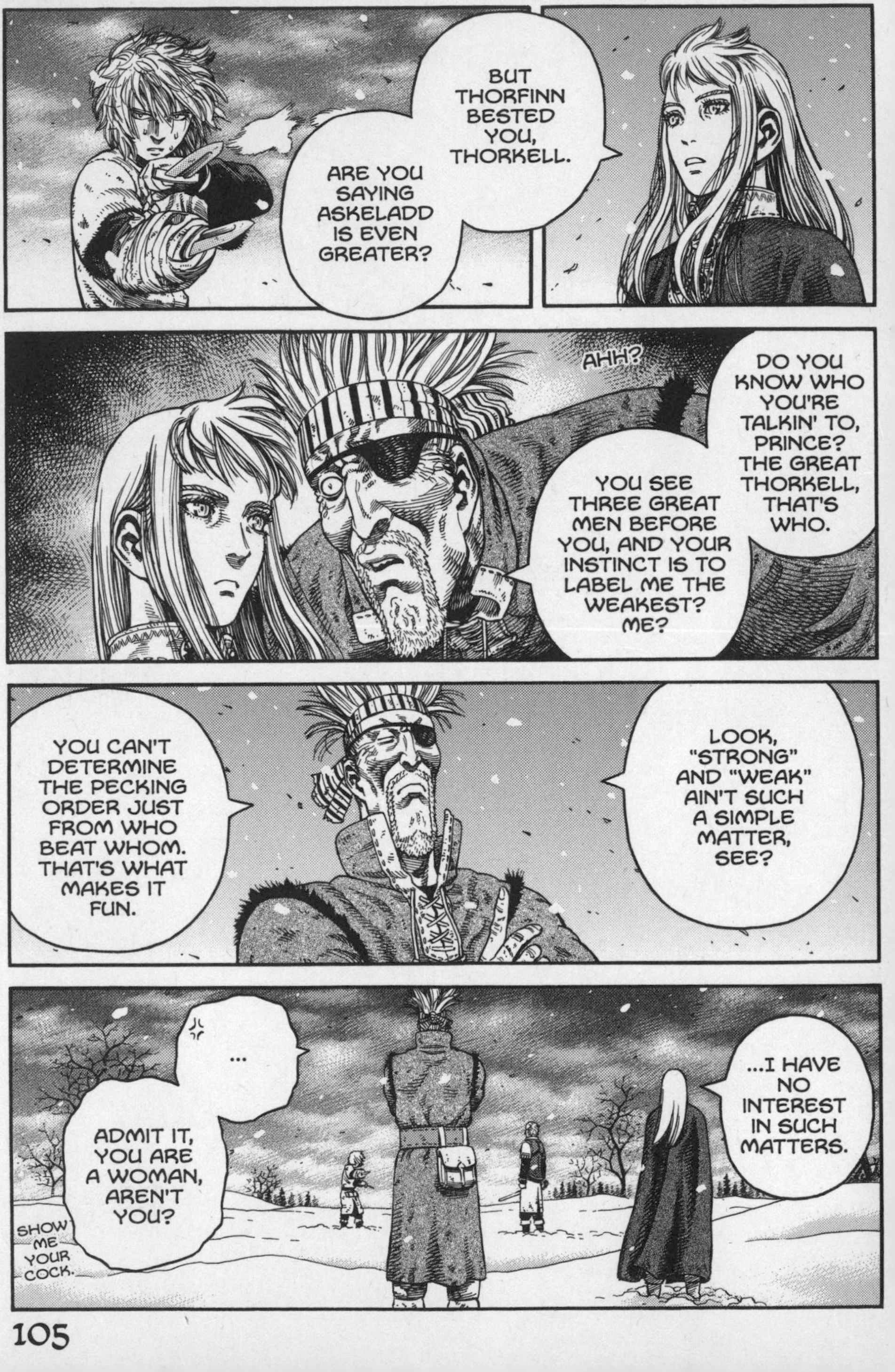
BUT THORFINN BESTED YOU, THORKELL.
ARE YOU SAYING ASKELADD IS EVEN GREATER?
AHH?
DO YOU KNOW WHO YOU'RE TALKIN' TO, PRINCE? THE GREAT THORKELL, THAT'S WHO.
YOU SEE THREE GREAT MEN BEFORE YOU, AND YOUR INSTINCT IS TO LABEL ME THE WEAKEST? ME?
LOOK, "STRONG" AND "WEAK" AIN'T SUCH A SIMPLE MATTER, SEE?
YOU CAN'T DETERMINE THE PECKING ORDER JUST FROM WHO BEAT WHOM. THAT'S WHAT MAKES IT FUN.
...I HAVE NO INTEREST IN SUCH MATTERS.
...
ADMIT IT, YOU ARE A WOMAN, AREN'T YOU?
SHOW ME YOUR COCK.

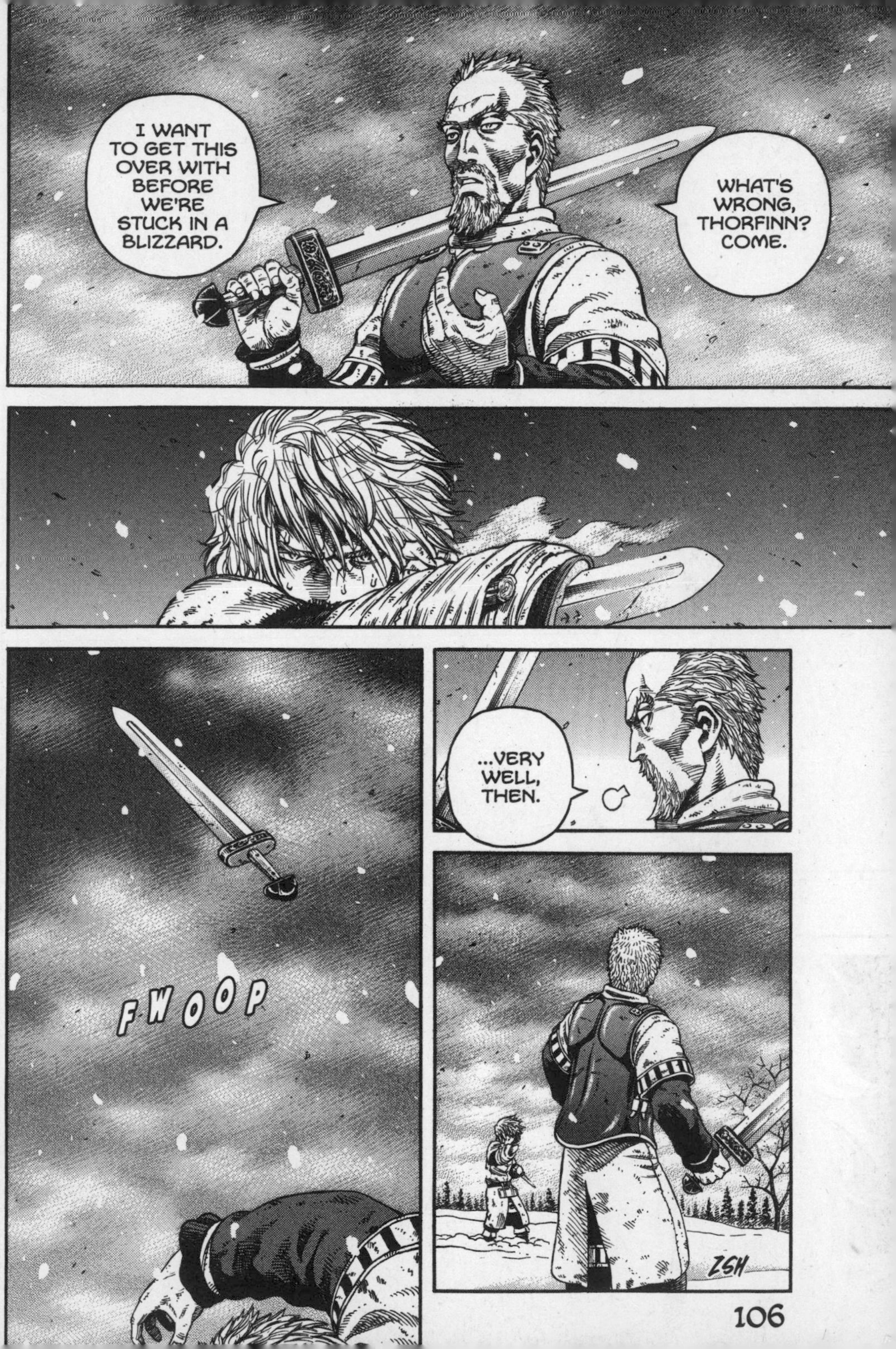
I WANT TO GET THIS OVER WITH BEFORE WE'RE STUCK IN A BLIZZARD.
WHAT'S WRONG, THORFINN? COME.
...VERY WELL, THEN.
ZSH
FWOOP

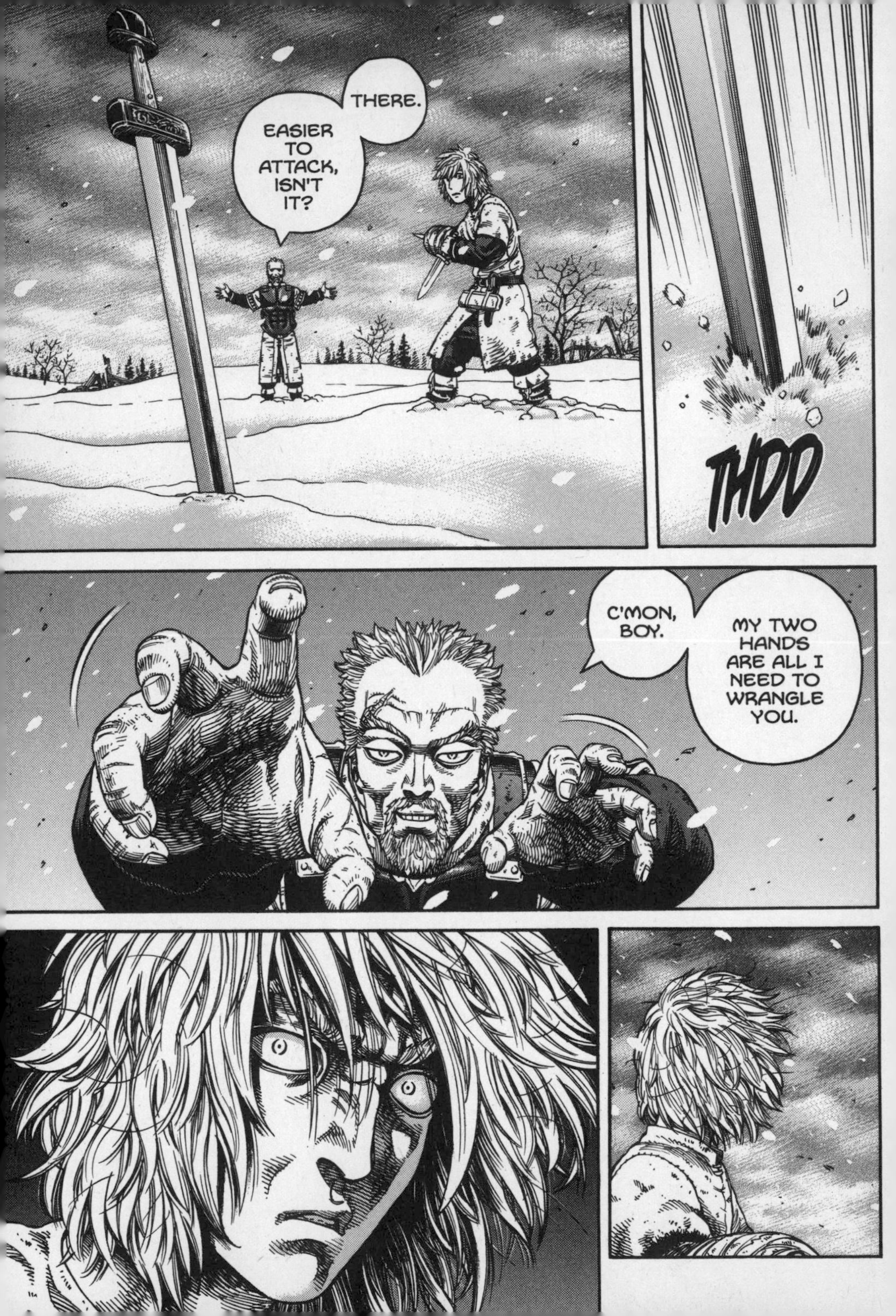
THDD
THERE.
EASIER TO ATTACK, ISN'T IT?
C'MON, BOY.
MY TWO HANDS ARE ALL I NEED TO WRANGLE YOU.

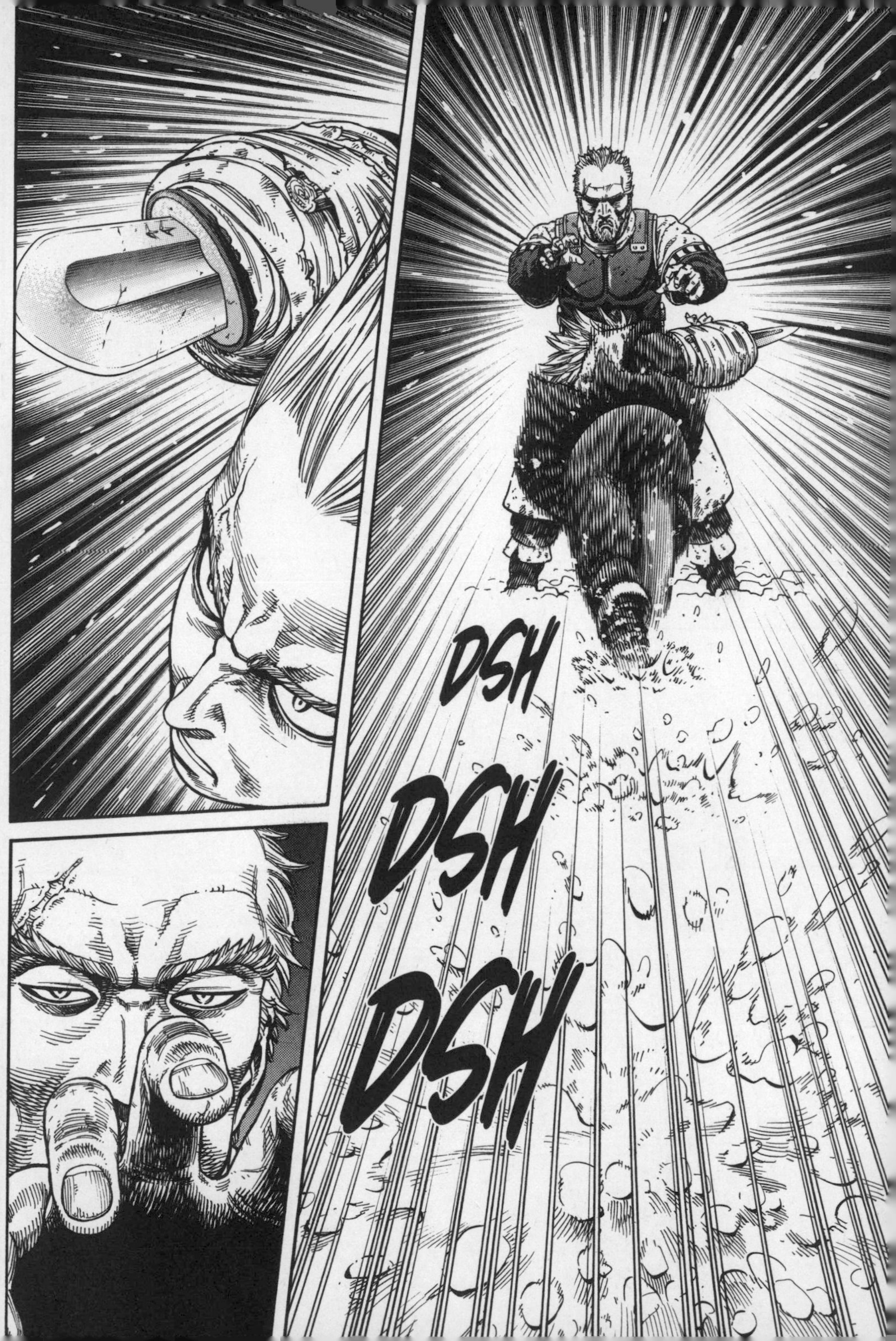
DSH
DSH
DSH

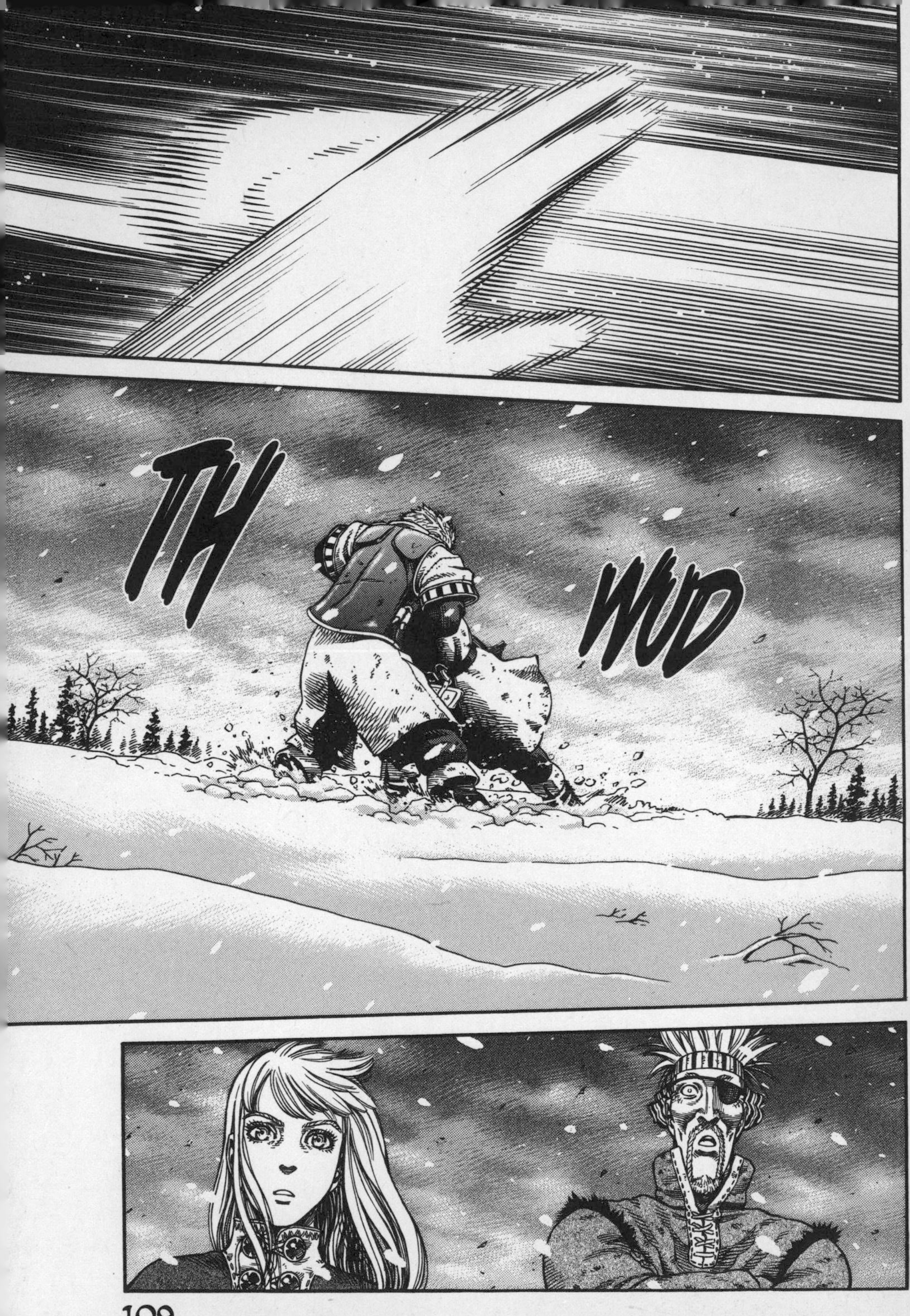
THWUD

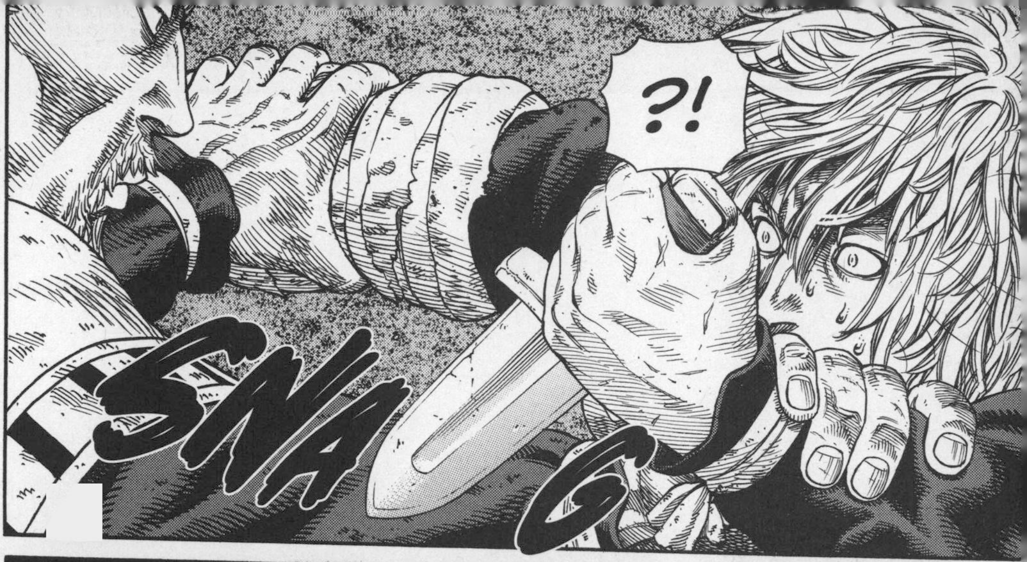
?!
SNAG
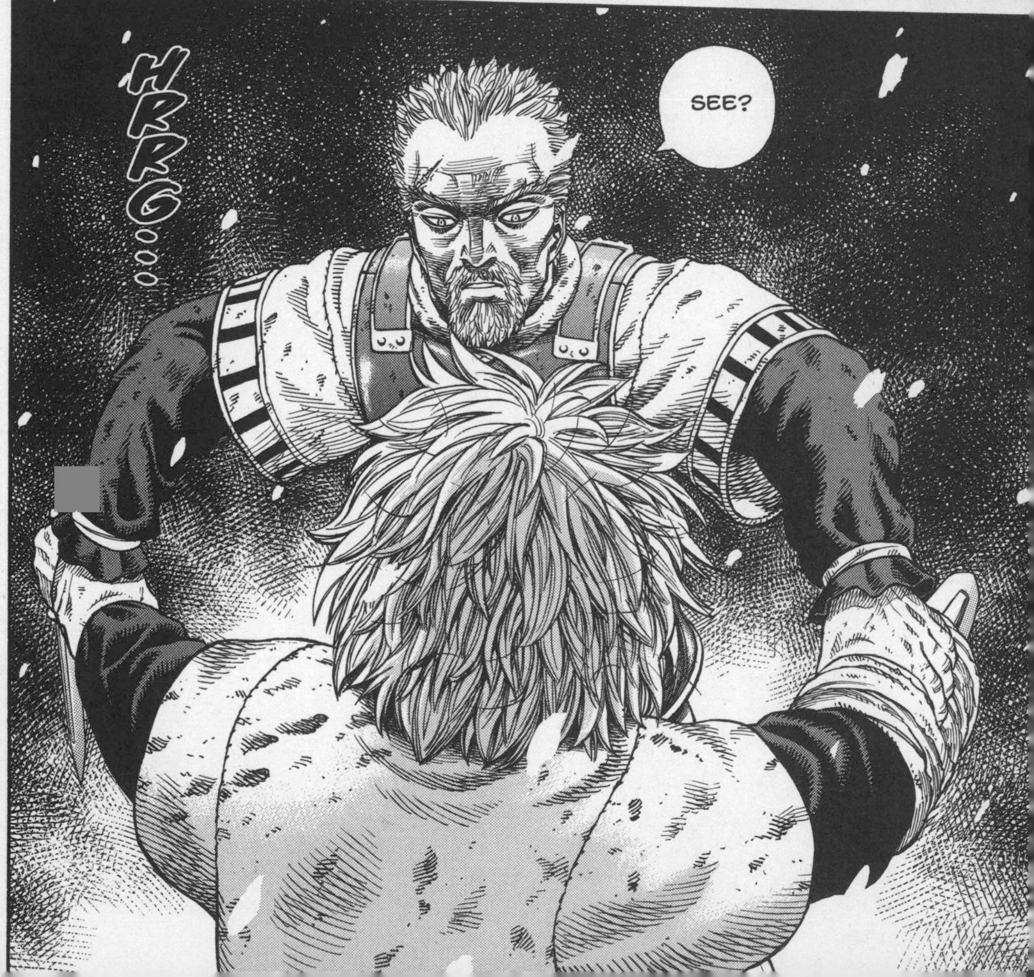
SEE?
HRRGooo

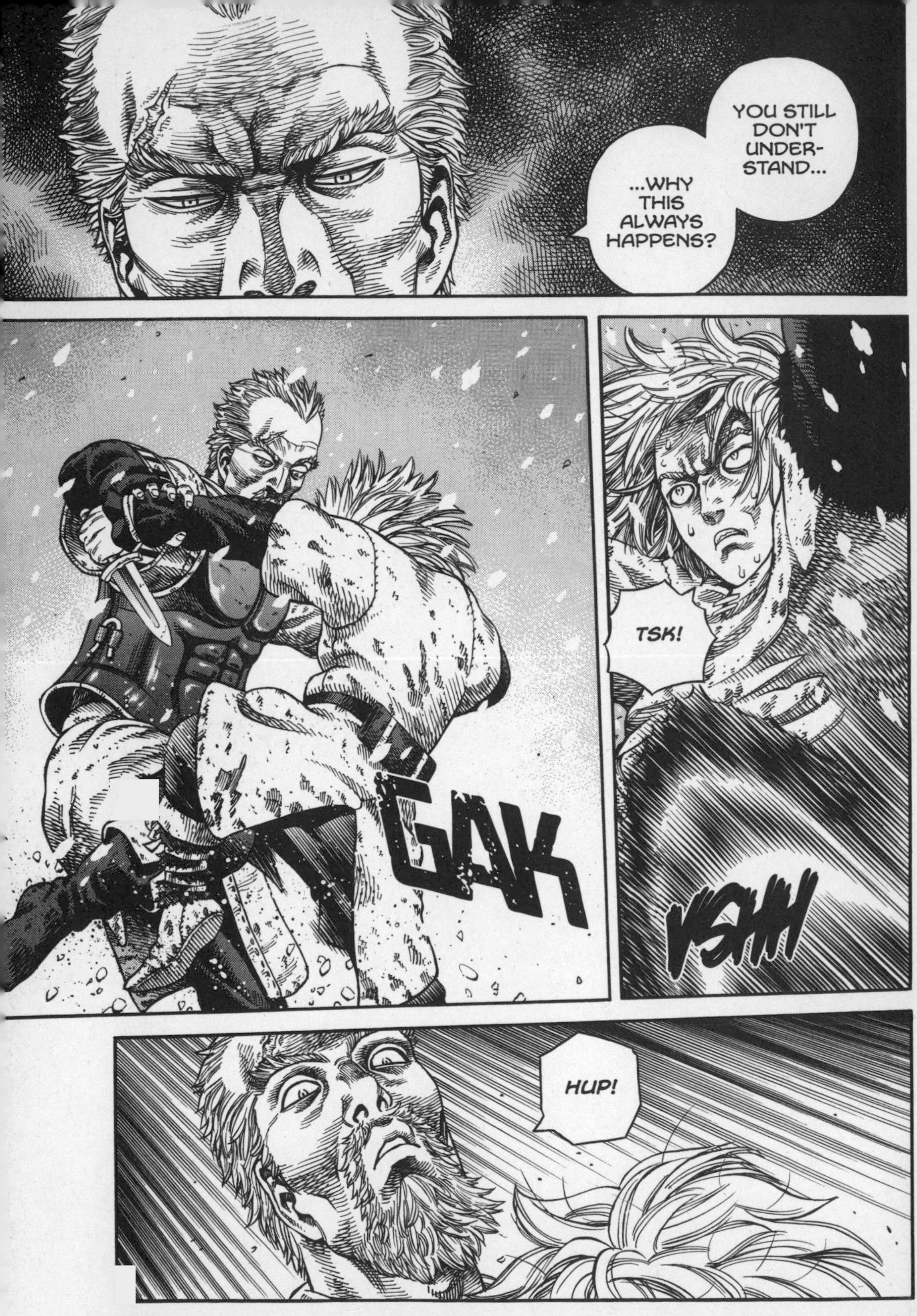
YOU STILL DON'T UNDER-STAND...
...WHY THIS ALWAYS HAPPENS?
TSK!
VSHH
GAK
HUP!

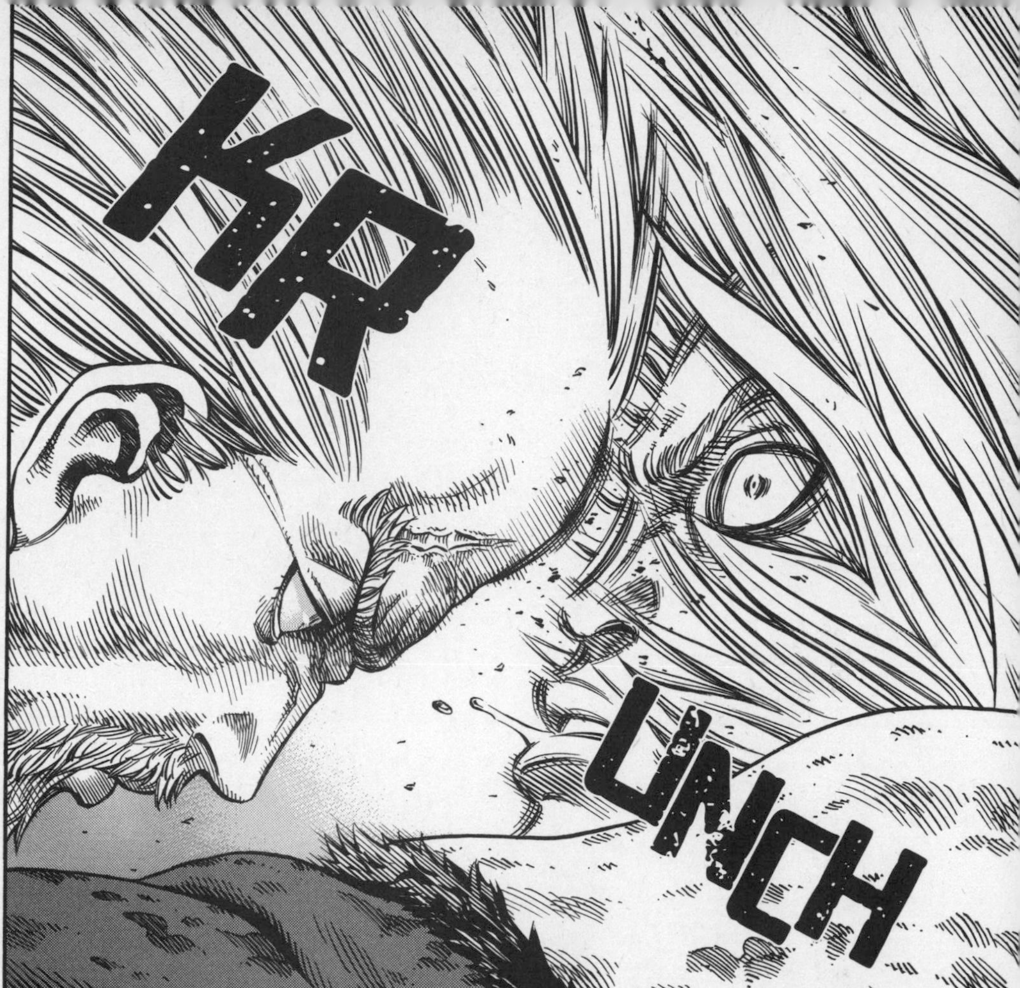
KR
UNCH
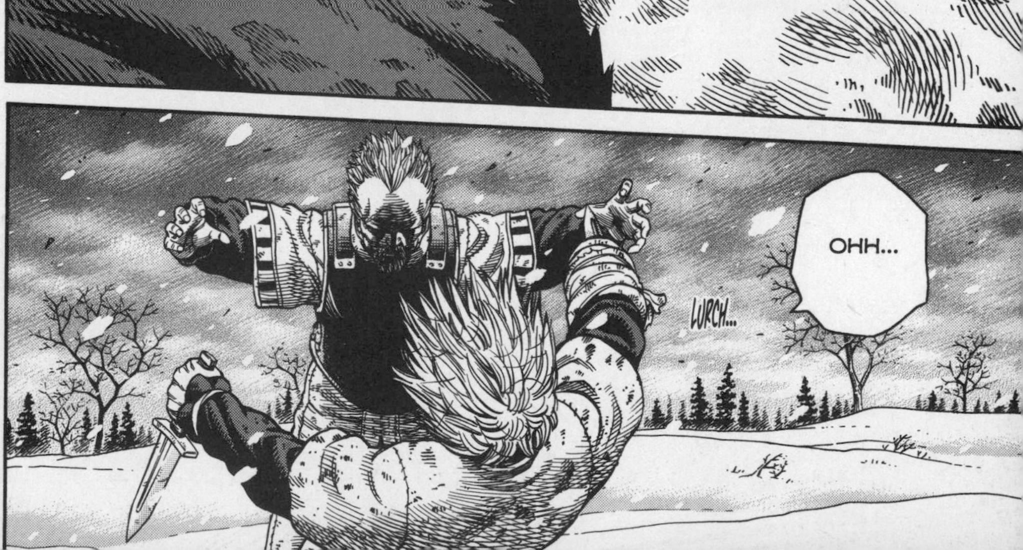
OHH...
LURCH...

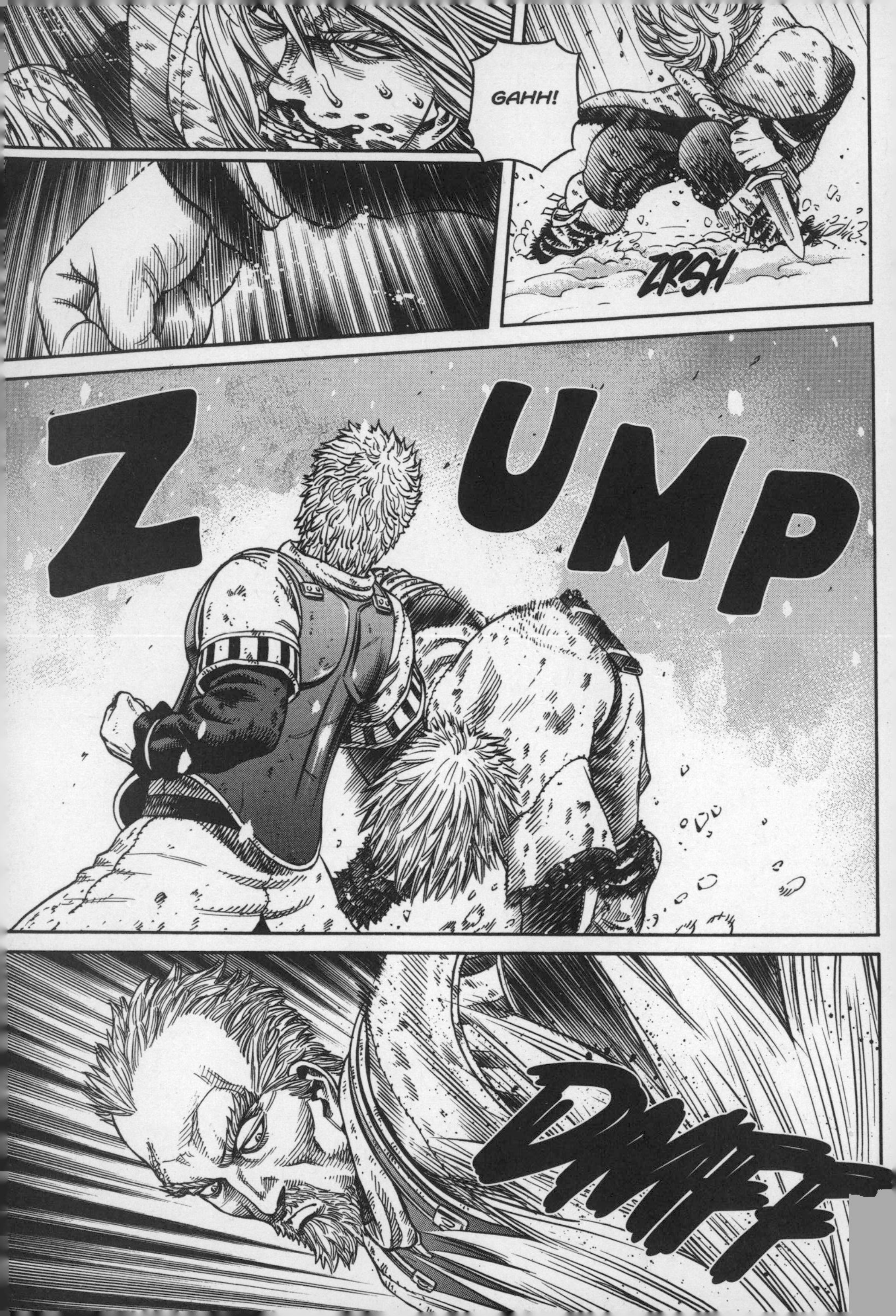
GAHH!
ZRSH
Z UMP
DMPF

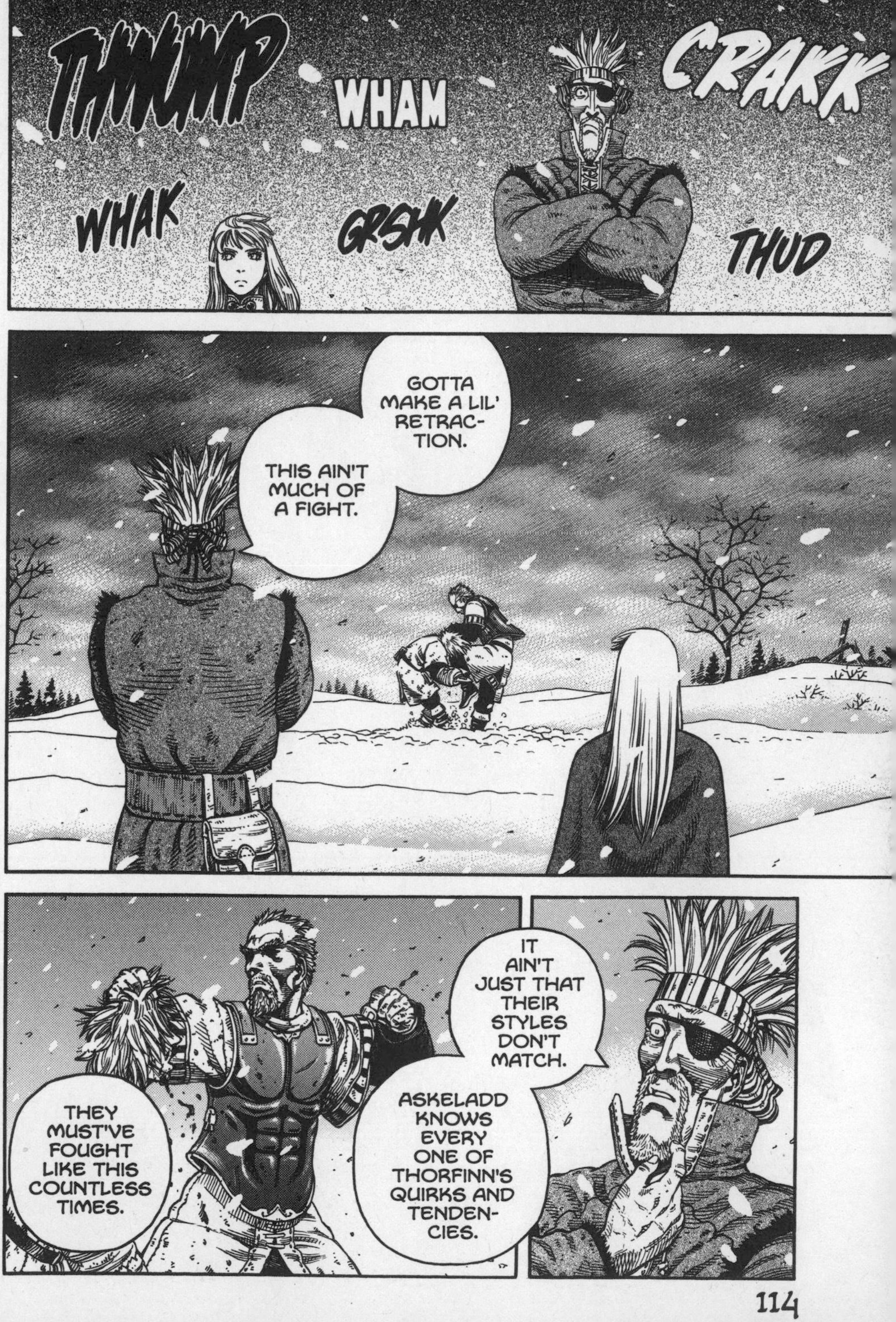
CRAKK
WHAM
THWUMP
THUD
GRSHK
WHAK
GOTTA MAKE A LIL' RETRAC- TION.
THIS AIN'T MUCH OF A FIGHT.
IT AIN'T JUST THAT THEIR STYLES DON'T MATCH.
ASKELADD KNOWS EVERY ONE OF THORFINN'S QUIRKS AND TENDEN- CIES.
THEY MUST'VE FOUGHT LIKE THIS COUNTLESS TIMES.

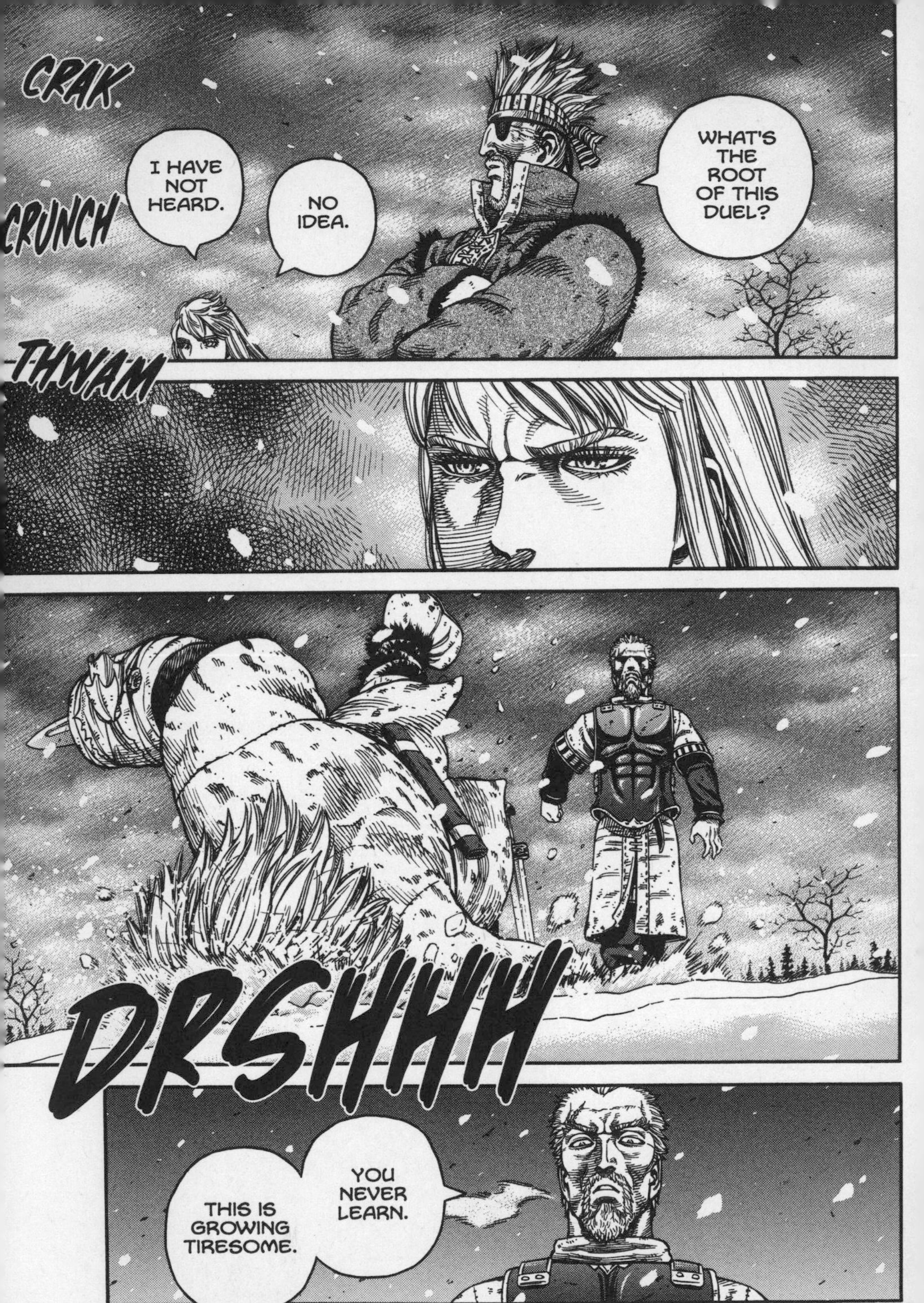
WHAT'S THE ROOT OF THIS DUEL?
CRAK
NO IDEA.
I HAVE NOT HEARD.
CRUNCH
THWAM
DRSHHH
YOU NEVER LEARN.
THIS IS GROWING TIRESOME.

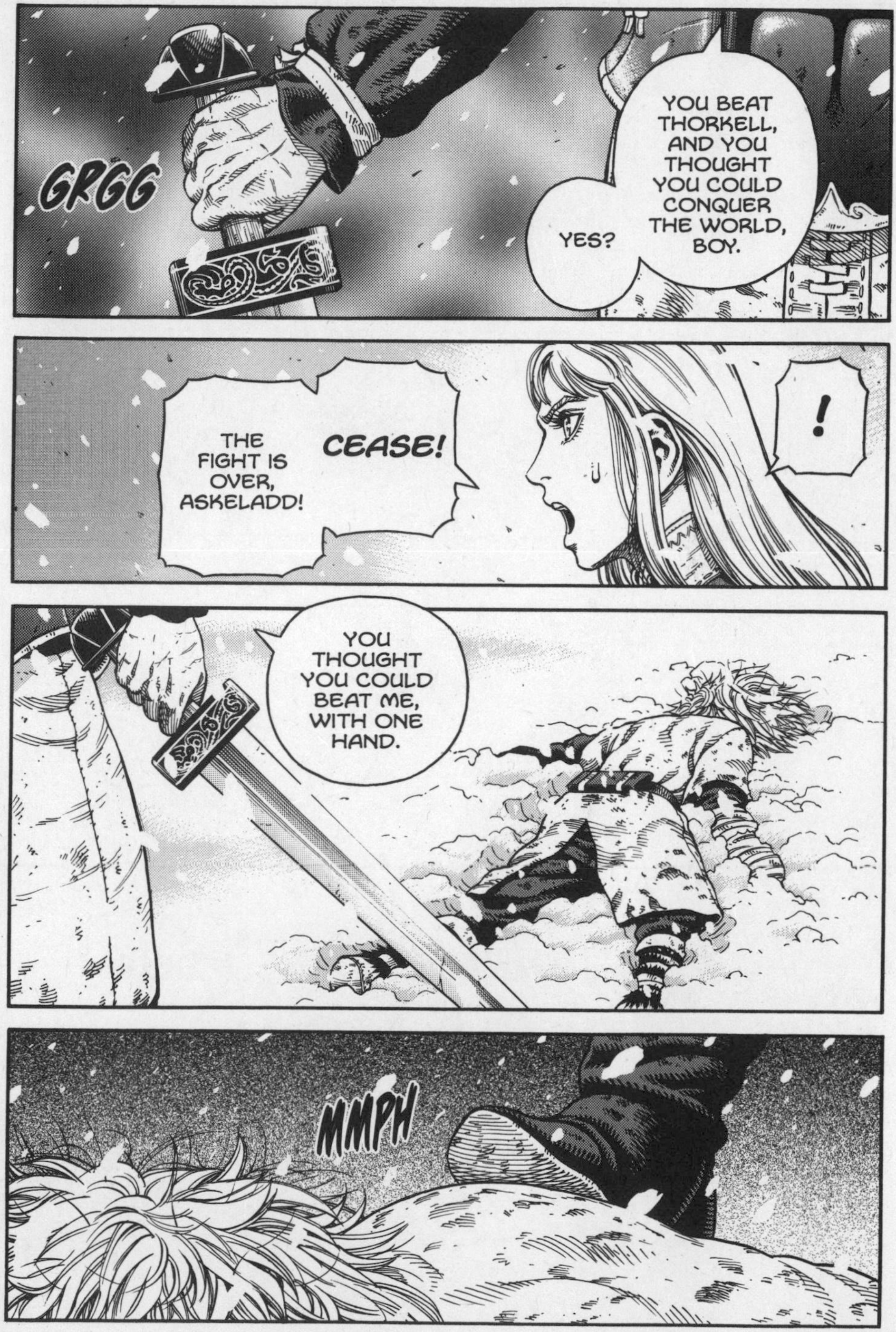
YOU BEAT THORKELL, AND YOU THOUGHT YOU COULD CONQUER THE WORLD, BOY.
YES?
GRGG
!
CEASE!
THE FIGHT IS OVER, ASKELADD!
YOU THOUGHT YOU COULD BEAT ME, WITH ONE HAND.
MMPH

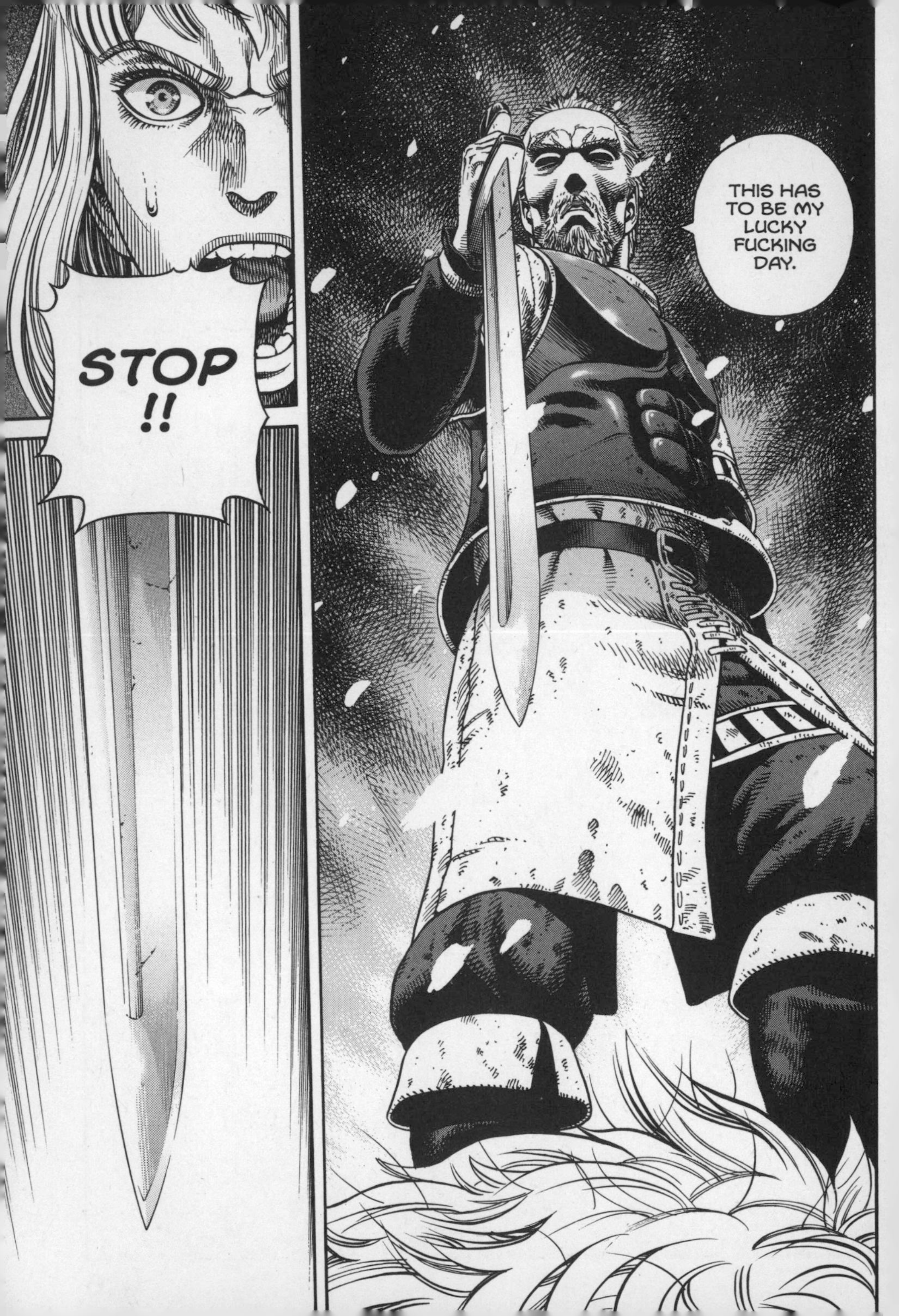
THIS HAS TO BE MY LUCKY FUCKING DAY.
STOP !!

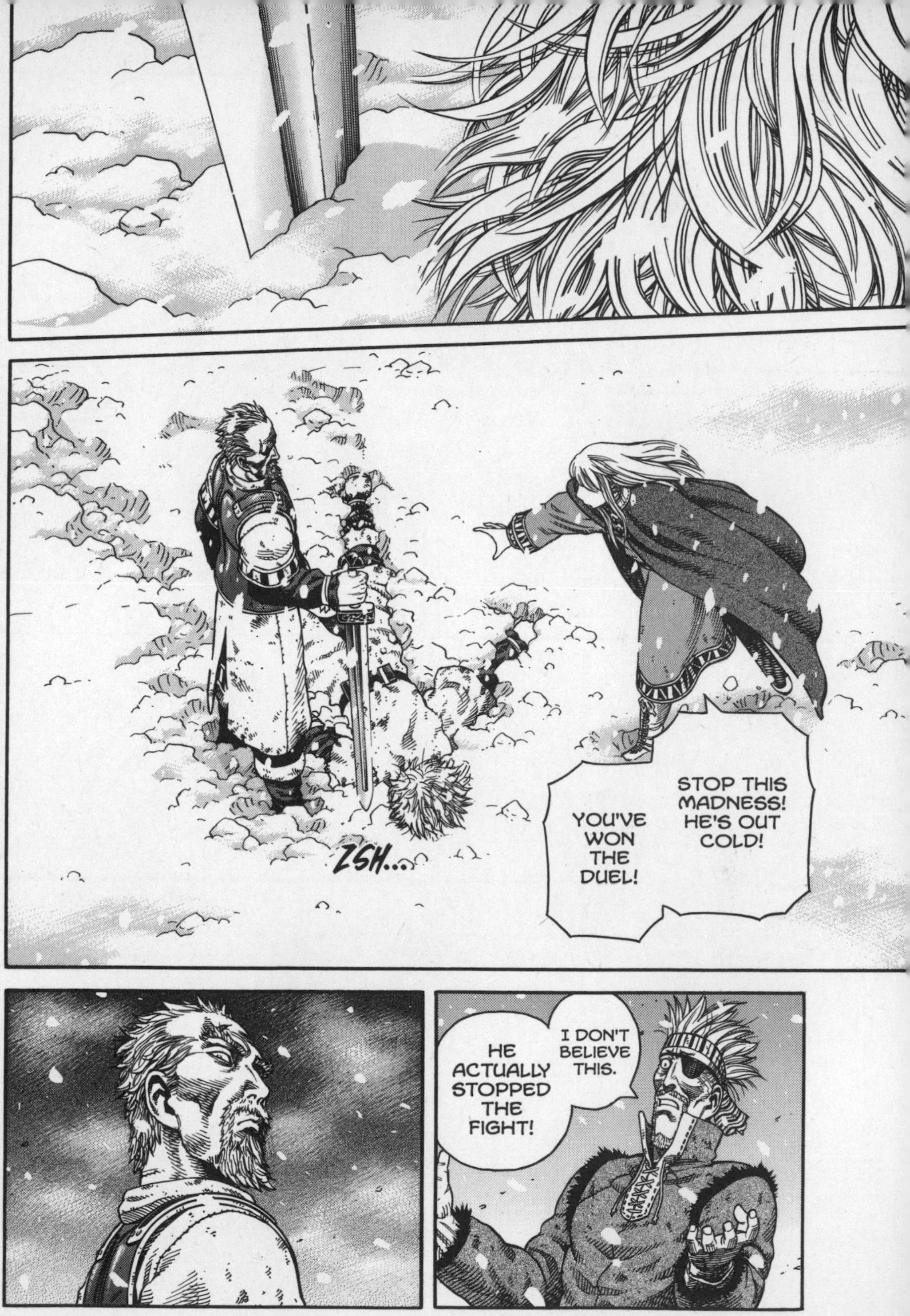
STOP THIS MADNESS! HE'S OUT COLD!
YOU'VE WON THE DUEL!
ZSH...
I DON'T BELIEVE THIS.
HE ACTUALLY STOPPED THE FIGHT!

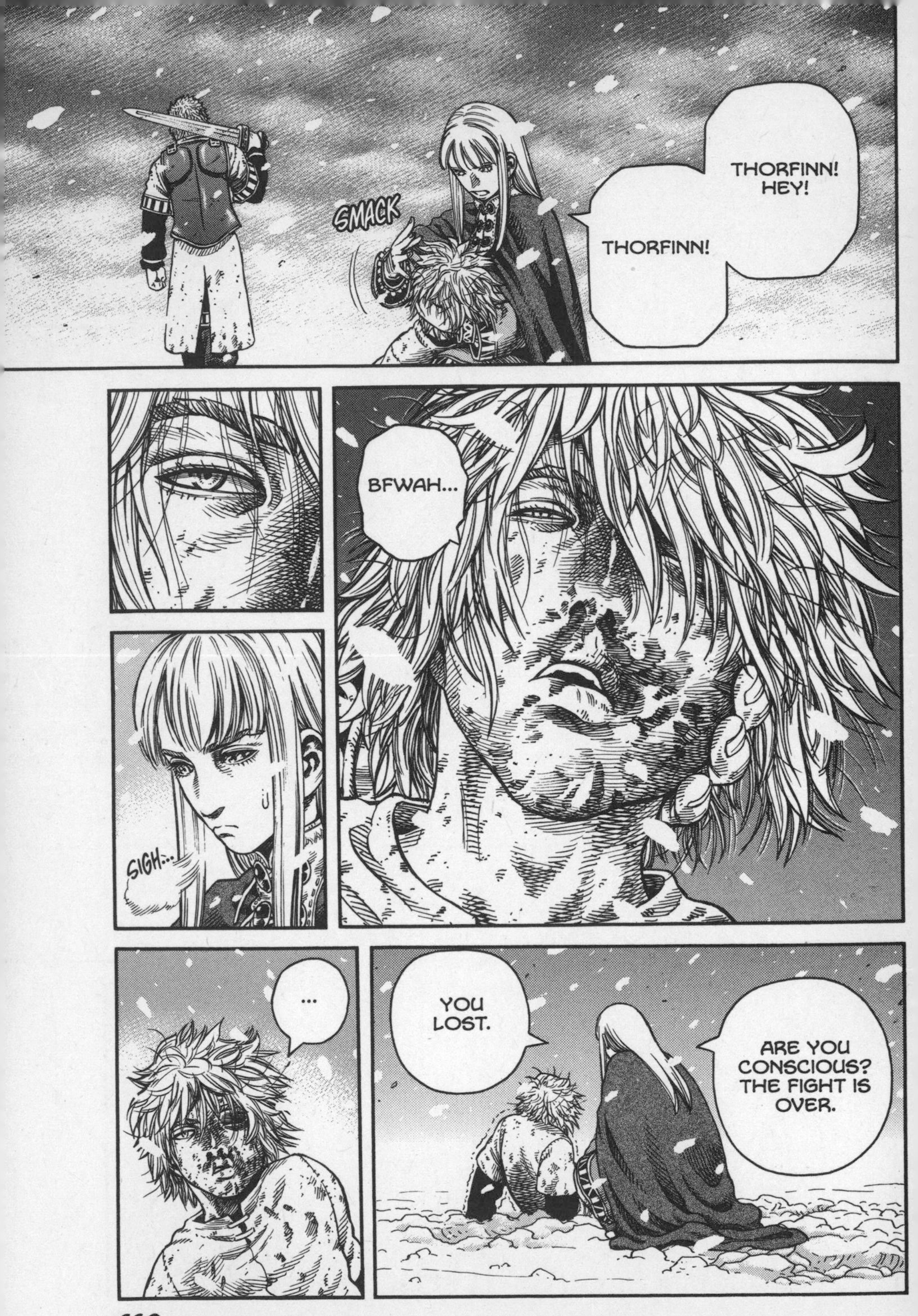
THORFINN! HEY!
THORFINN!
SMACK
BFWAH...
SIGH...
ARE YOU CONSCIOUS? THE FIGHT IS OVER.
YOU LOST.
...

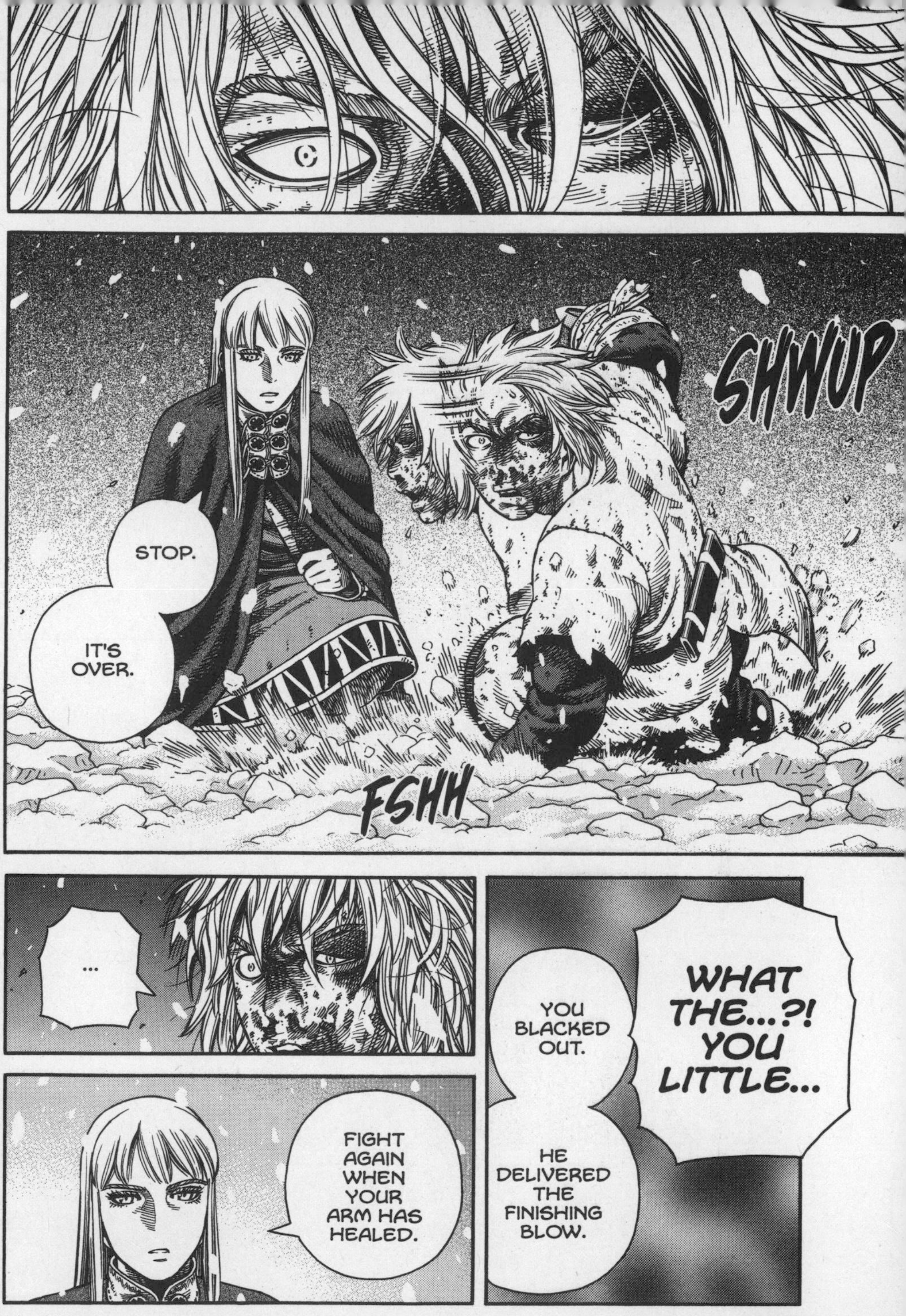
SHWUP
STOP.
IT'S OVER.
FSHH
WHAT THE...?! YOU LITTLE...
YOU BLACKED OUT.
HE DELIVERED THE FINISHING BLOW.
...
FIGHT AGAIN WHEN YOUR ARM HAS HEALED.

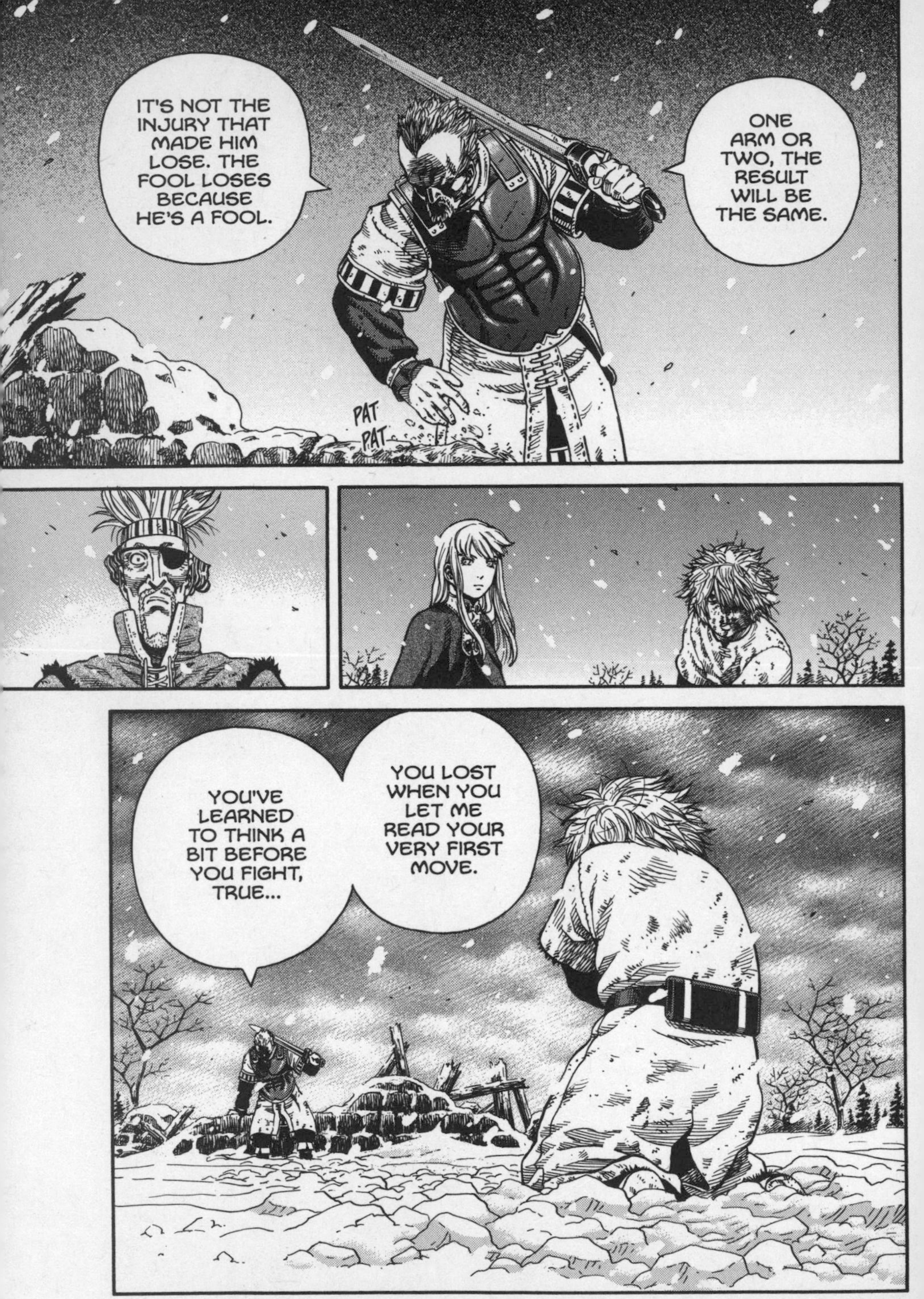
ONE ARM OR TWO, THE RESULT WILL BE THE SAME.
IT'S NOT THE INJURY THAT MADE HIM LOSE. THE FOOL LOSES BECAUSE HE'S A FOOL.
PAT PAT
YOU LOST WHEN YOU LET ME READ YOUR VERY FIRST MOVE.
YOU'VE LEARNED TO THINK A BIT BEFORE YOU FIGHT, TRUE...

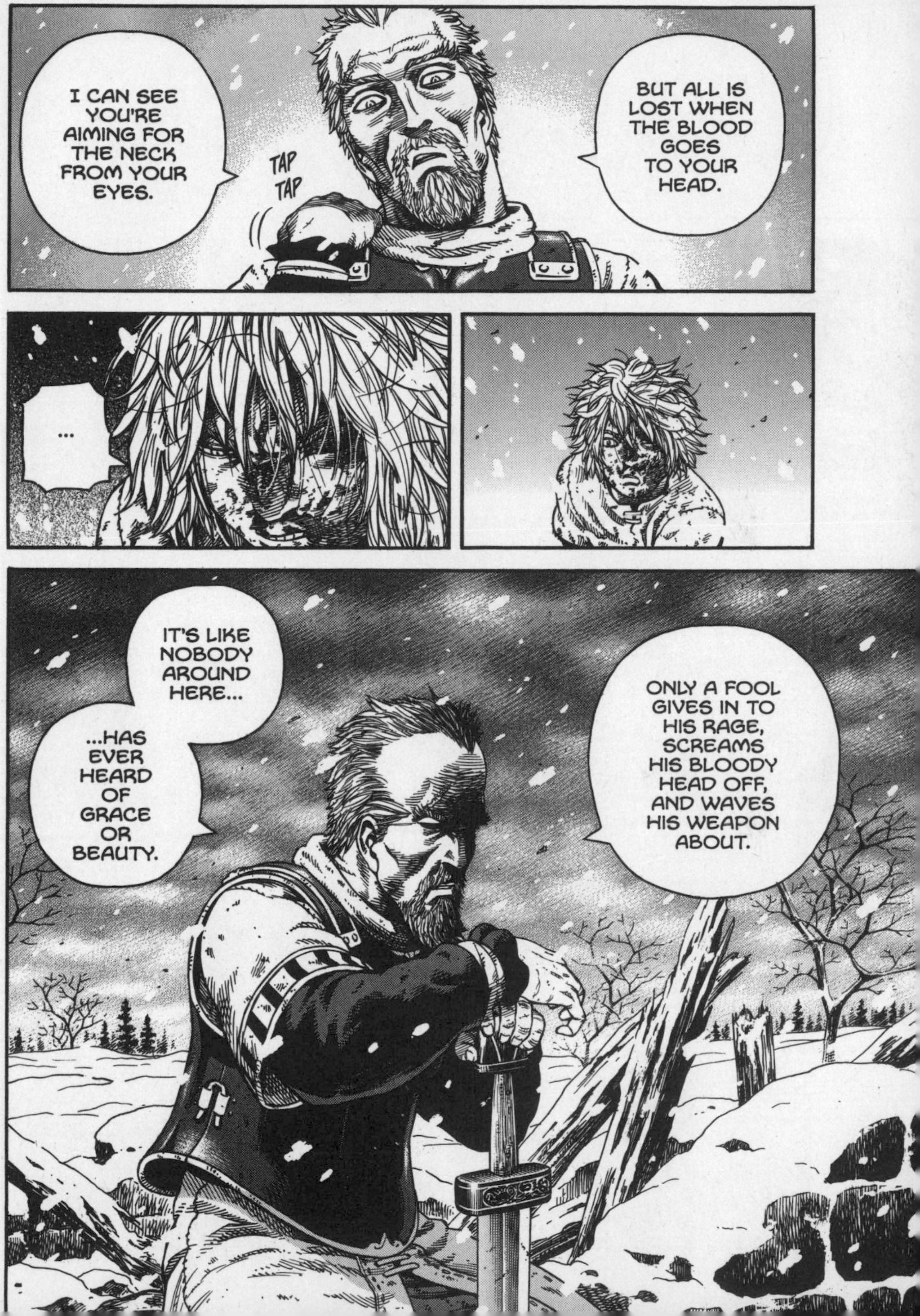
I CAN SEE YOU'RE AIMING FOR THE NECK FROM YOUR EYES.
TAP TAP
BUT ALL IS LOST WHEN THE BLOOD GOES TO YOUR HEAD.
...
ONLY A FOOL GIVES IN TO HIS RAGE, SCREAMS HIS BLOODY HEAD OFF, AND WAVES HIS WEAPON ABOUT.
IT'S LIKE NOBODY AROUND HERE...
...HAS EVER HEARD OF GRACE OR BEAUTY.

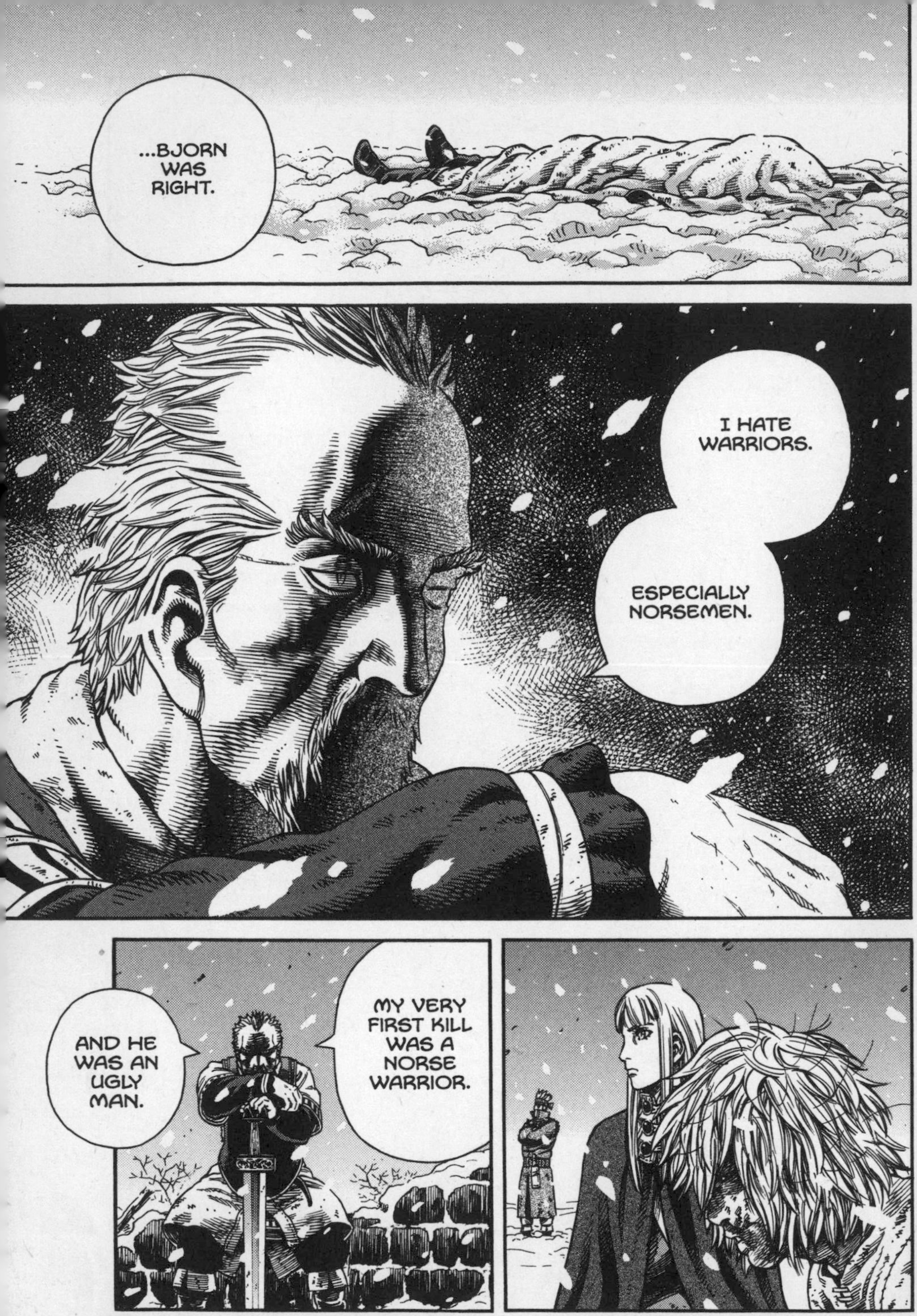
...BJORN WAS RIGHT.
I HATE WARRIORS.
ESPECIALLY NORSEMEN.
MY VERY FIRST KILL WAS A NORSE WARRIOR.
AND HE WAS AN UGLY MAN.

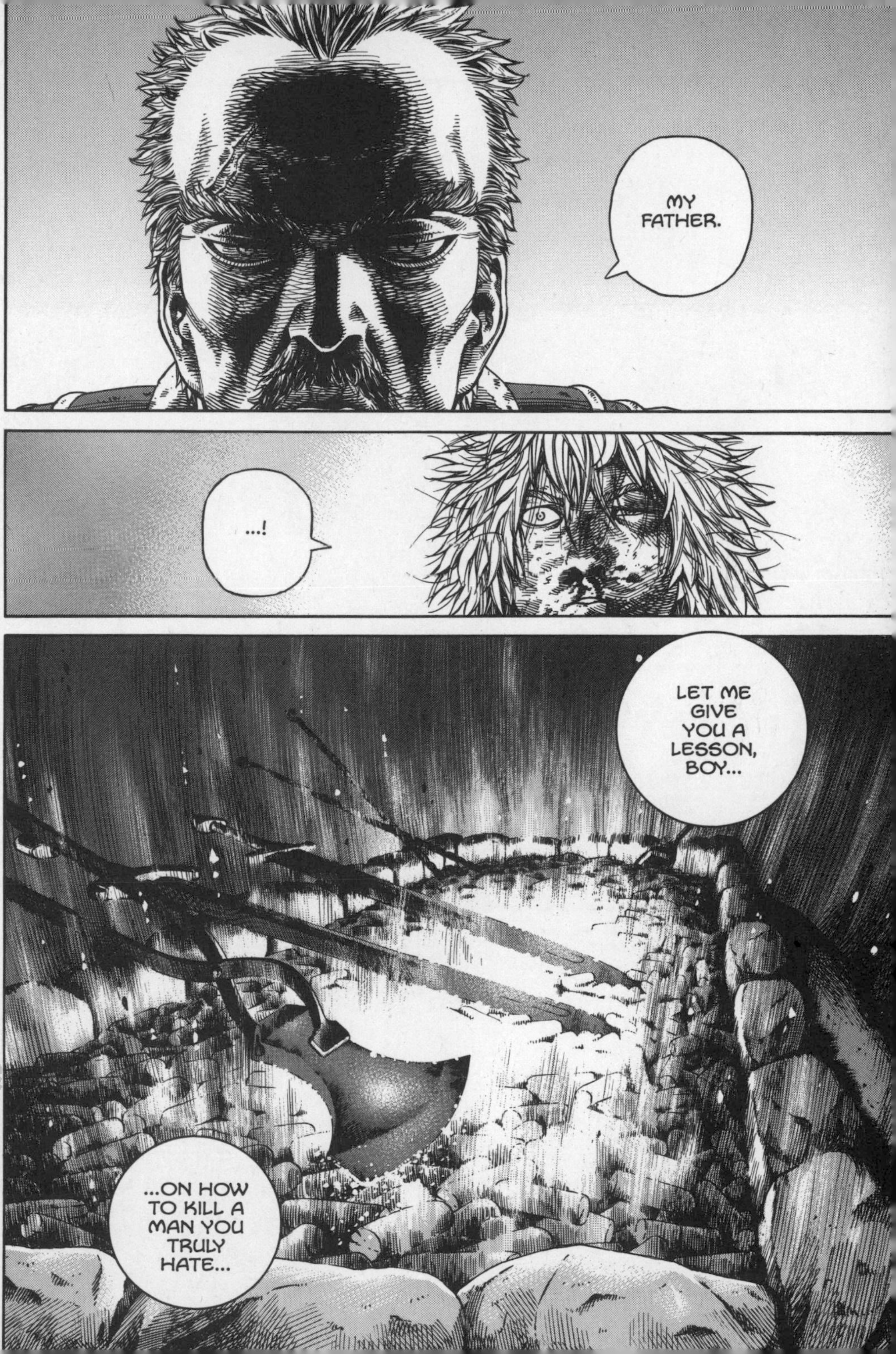
MY FATHER.
...!
LET ME GIVE YOU A LESSON, BOY...
...ON HOW TO KILL A MAN YOU TRULY HATE...

CHAPTER 47: THE HERO IS GONE

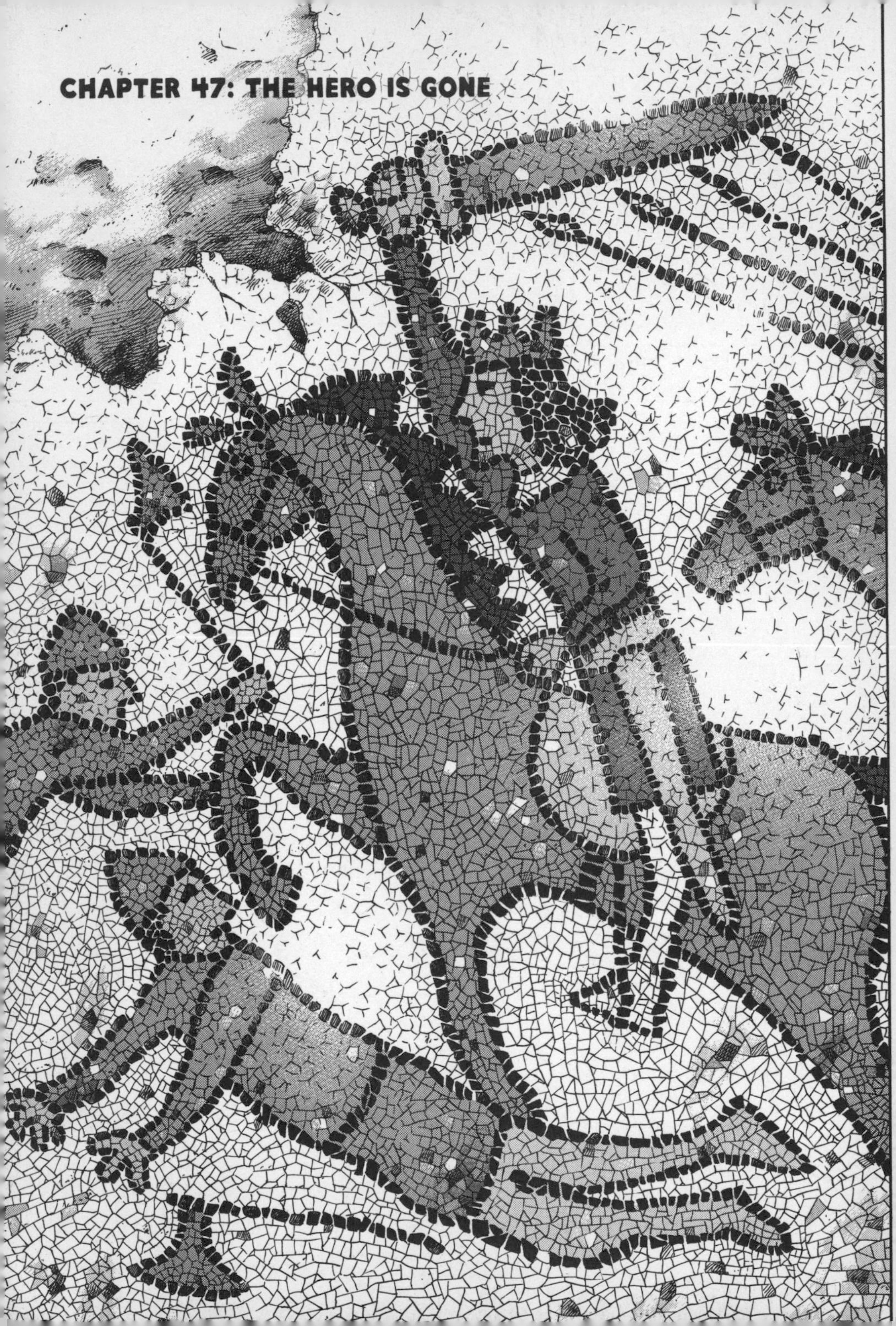

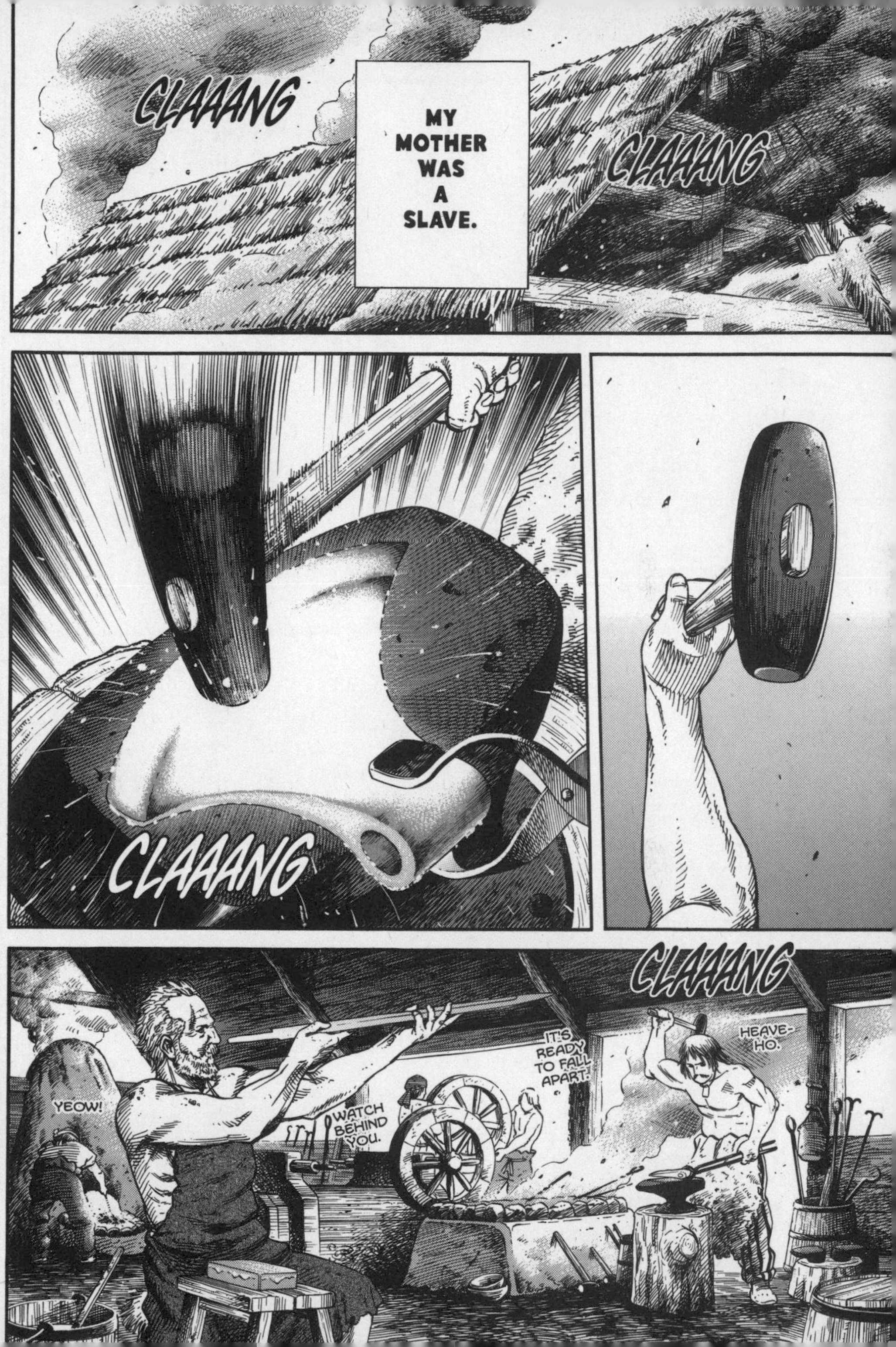
MY MOTHER WAS A SLAVE.
CLAAANG
CLAAANG
CLAAANG
CLAAANG
HEAVE-HO.
IT'S READY TO FALL APART.
WATCH BEHIND YOU.
YEOW!

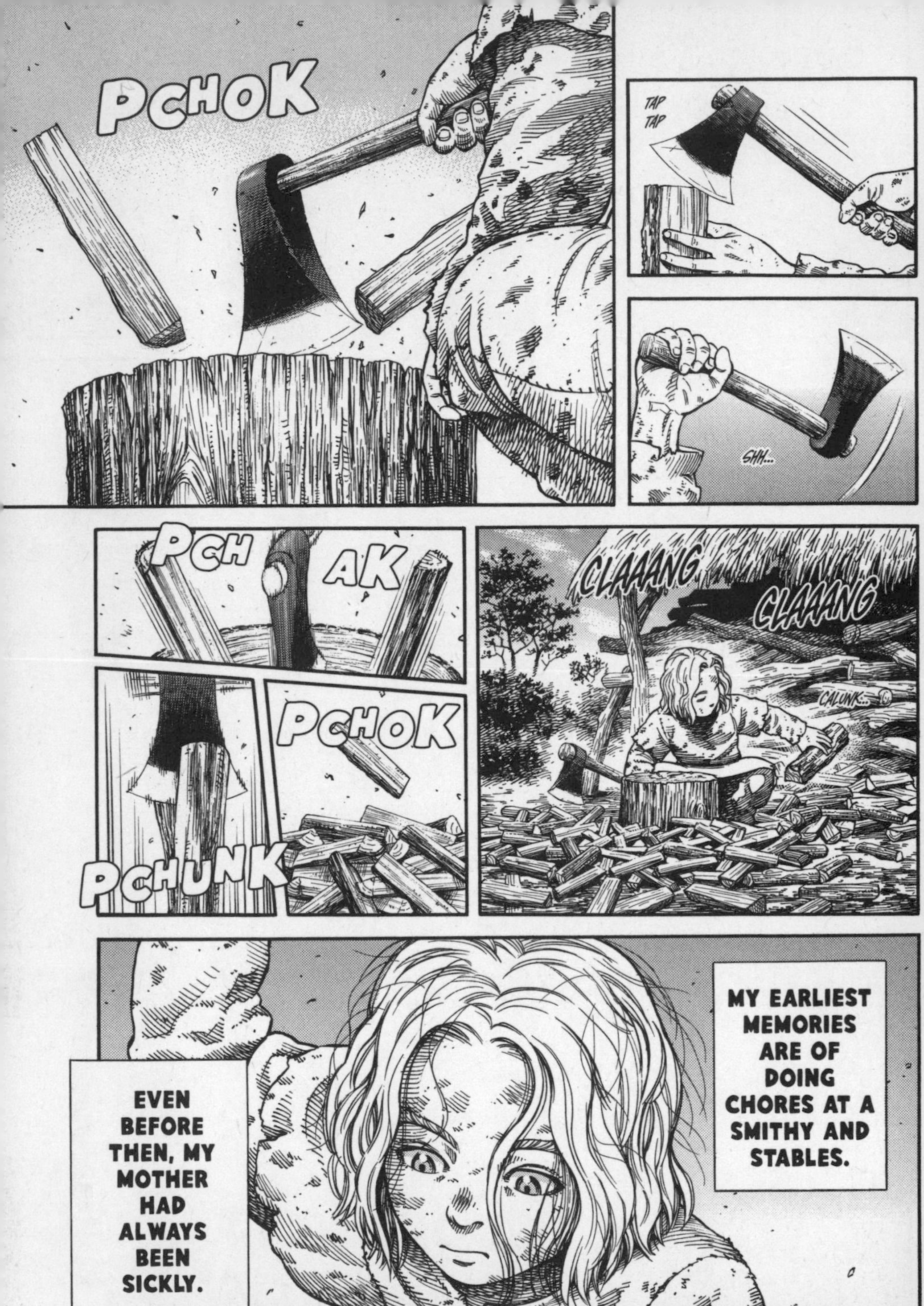
TAP TAP
SHH...
PCHOK
CLAAANG
CLAAANG
CALUNK...
PCH AK
PCHOK
PCHUNK
MY EARLIEST MEMORIES ARE OF DOING CHORES AT A SMITHY AND STABLES.
EVEN BEFORE THEN, MY MOTHER HAD ALWAYS BEEN SICKLY.

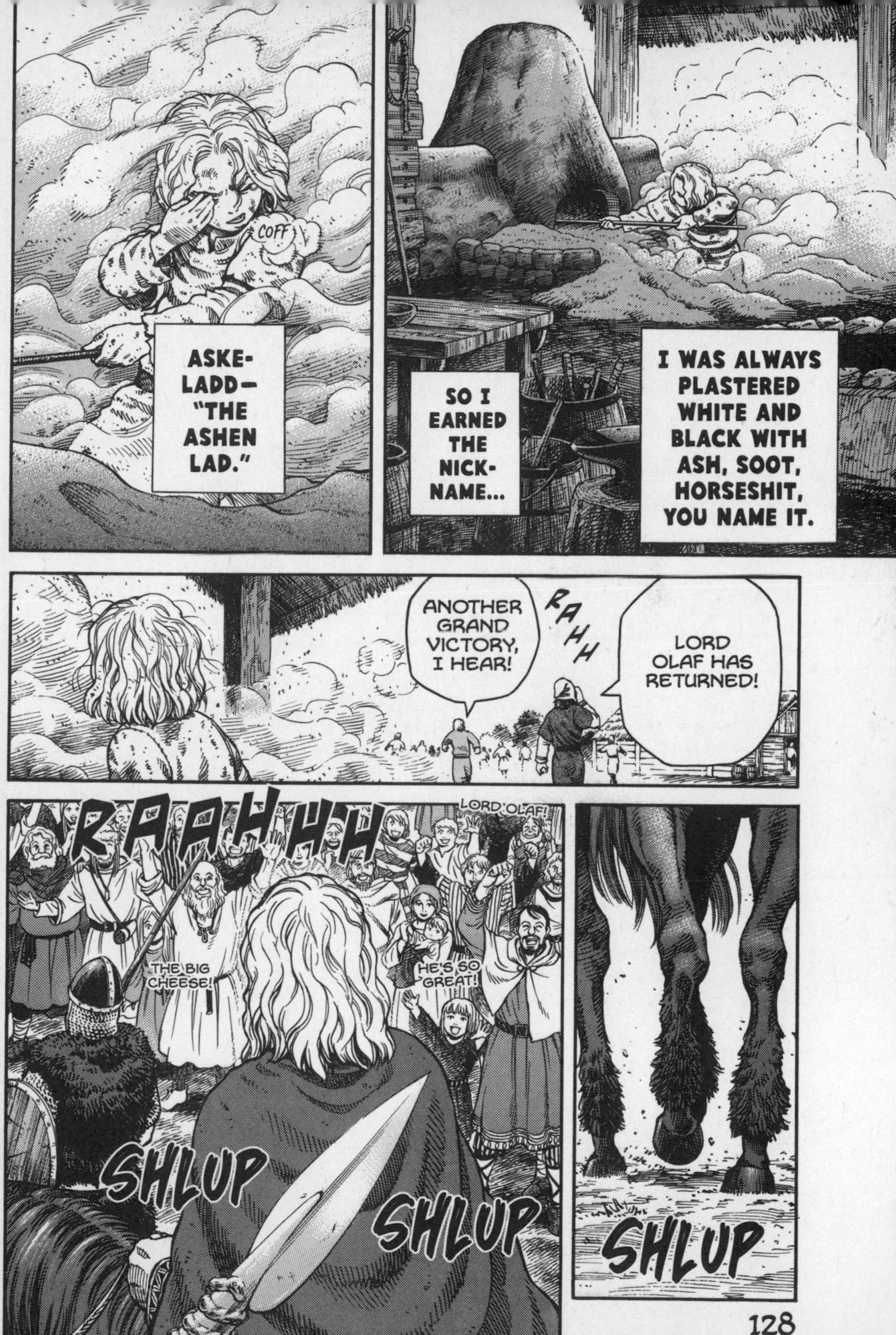
I WAS ALWAYS PLASTERED WHITE AND BLACK WITH ASH, SOOT, HORSESHIT, YOU NAME IT.
SO I EARNED THE NICK-NAME...
ASKE-LADD— "THE ASHEN LAD."
COFF
LORD OLAF HAS RETURNED!
RAHH
ANOTHER GRAND VICTORY, I HEAR!
SHLUP
LORD OLAF!
RAAHHH
HE'S SO GREAT!
THE BIG CHEESE!
SHLUP
SHLUP

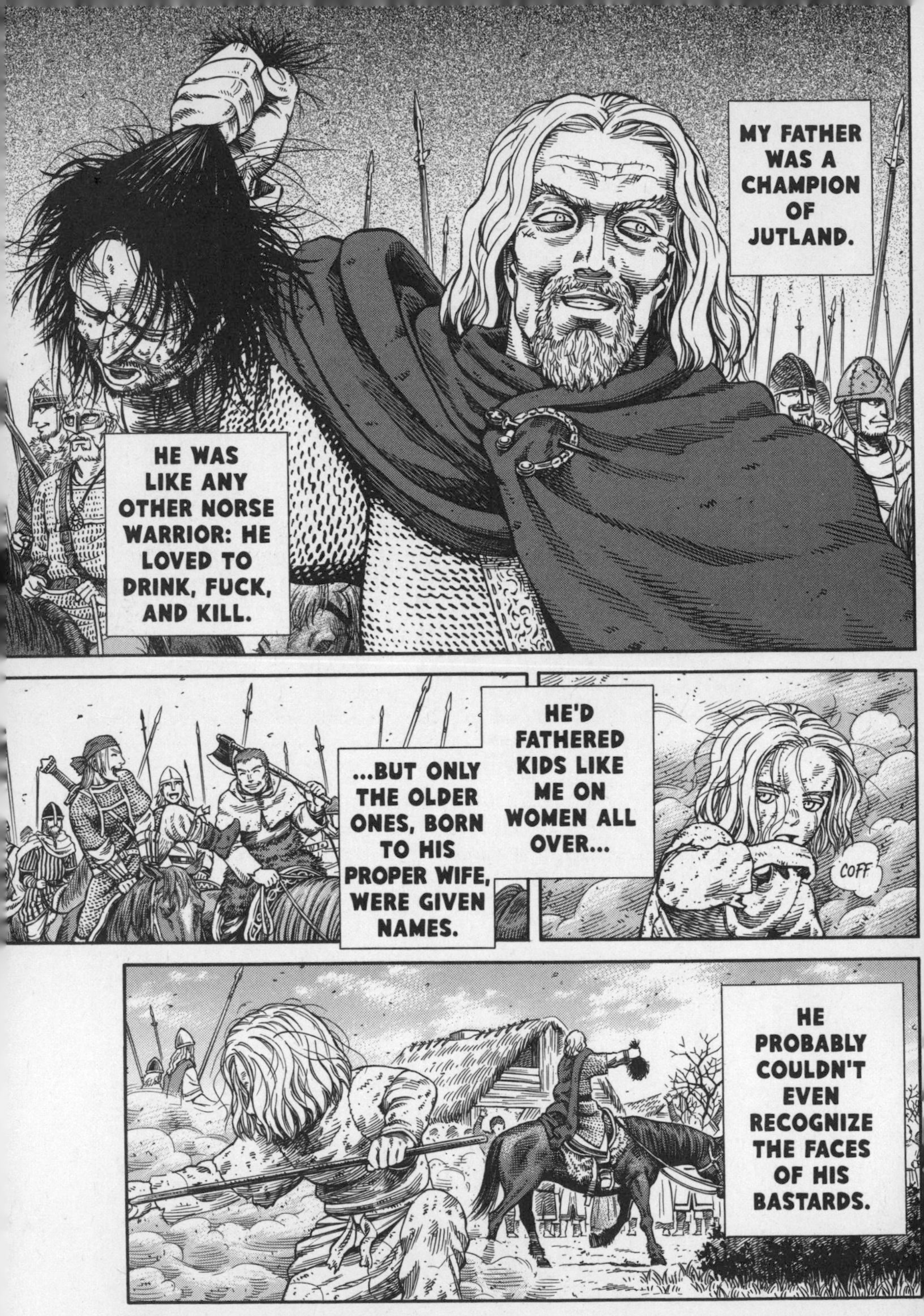
MY FATHER WAS A CHAMPION OF JUTLAND.
HE WAS LIKE ANY OTHER NORSE WARRIOR: HE LOVED TO DRINK, FUCK, AND KILL.
HE'D FATHERED KIDS LIKE ME ON WOMEN ALL OVER...
COFF
...BUT ONLY THE OLDER ONES, BORN TO HIS PROPER WIFE, WERE GIVEN NAMES.
HE PROBABLY COULDN'T EVEN RECOGNIZE THE FACES OF HIS BASTARDS.

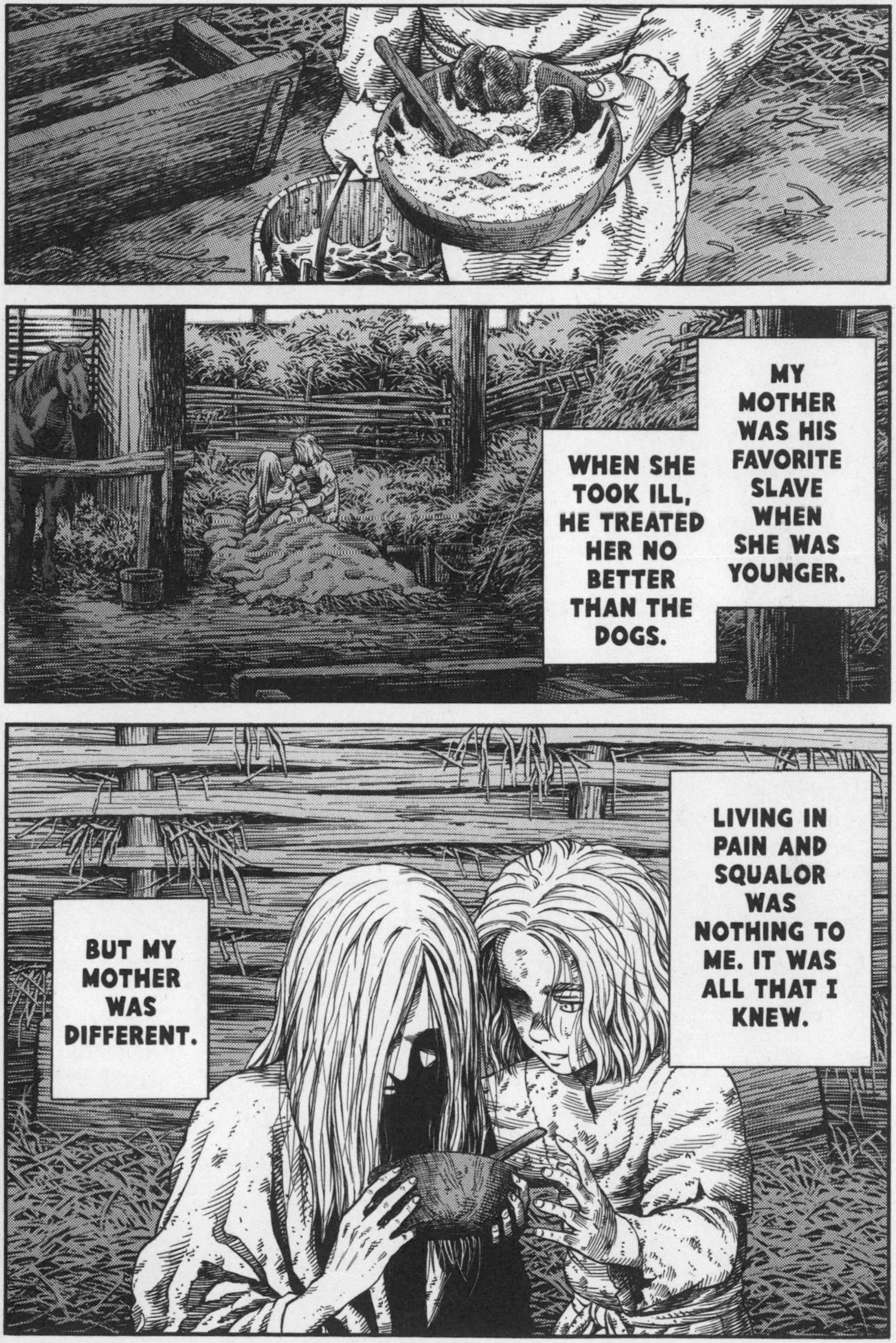
MY MOTHER WAS HIS FAVORITE SLAVE WHEN SHE WAS YOUNGER.
WHEN SHE TOOK ILL, HE TREATED HER NO BETTER THAN THE DOGS.
LIVING IN PAIN AND SQUALOR WAS NOTHING TO ME. IT WAS ALL THAT I KNEW.
BUT MY MOTHER WAS DIFFERENT.

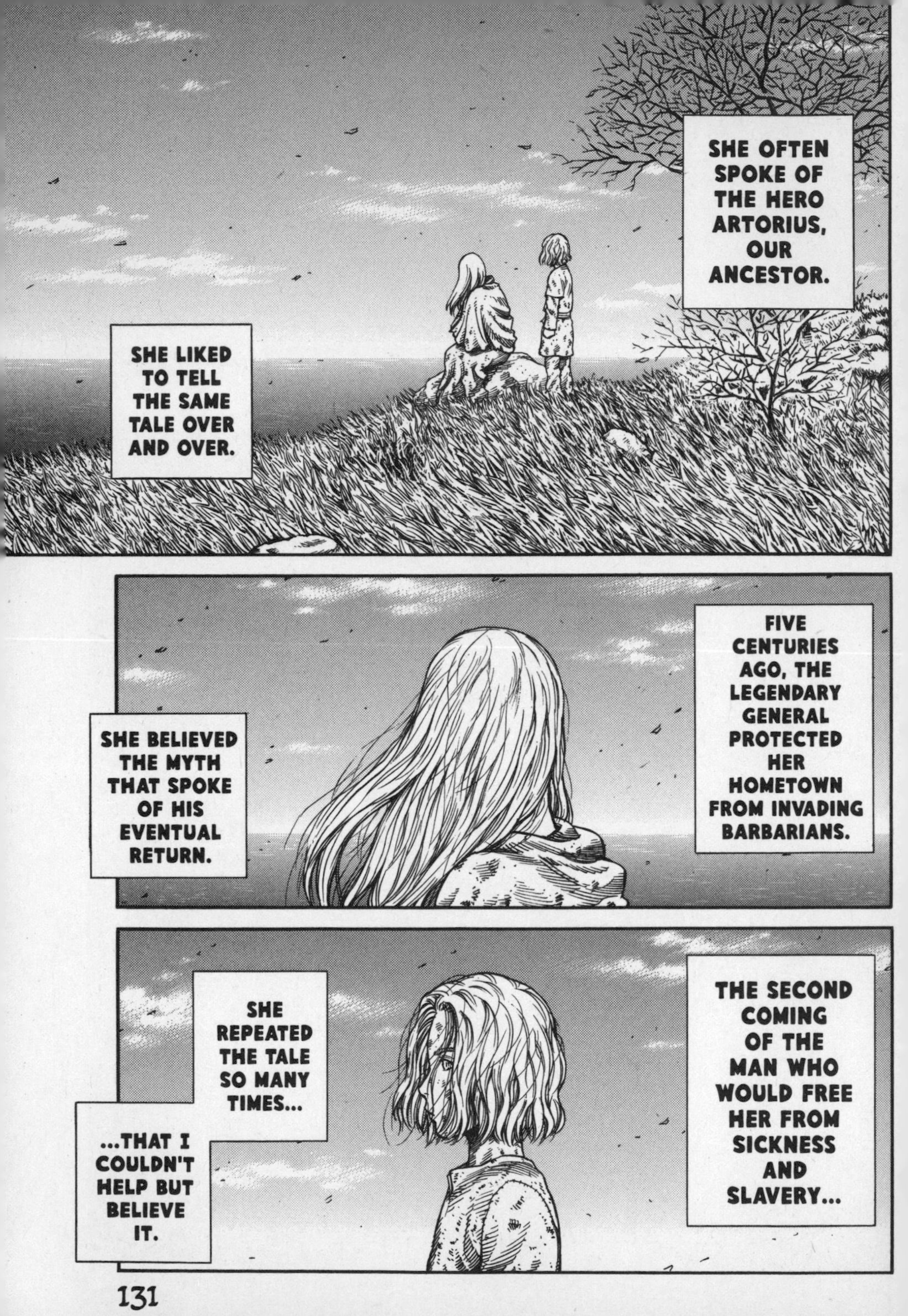
SHE OFTEN SPOKE OF THE HERO ARTORIUS, OUR ANCESTOR.
SHE LIKED TO TELL THE SAME TALE OVER AND OVER.
FIVE CENTURIES AGO, THE LEGENDARY GENERAL PROTECTED HER HOMETOWN FROM INVADING BARBARIANS.
SHE BELIEVED THE MYTH THAT SPOKE OF HIS EVENTUAL RETURN.
THE SECOND COMING OF THE MAN WHO WOULD FREE HER FROM SICKNESS AND SLAVERY...
SHE REPEATED THE TALE SO MANY TIMES...
...THAT I COULDN'T HELP BUT BELIEVE IT.

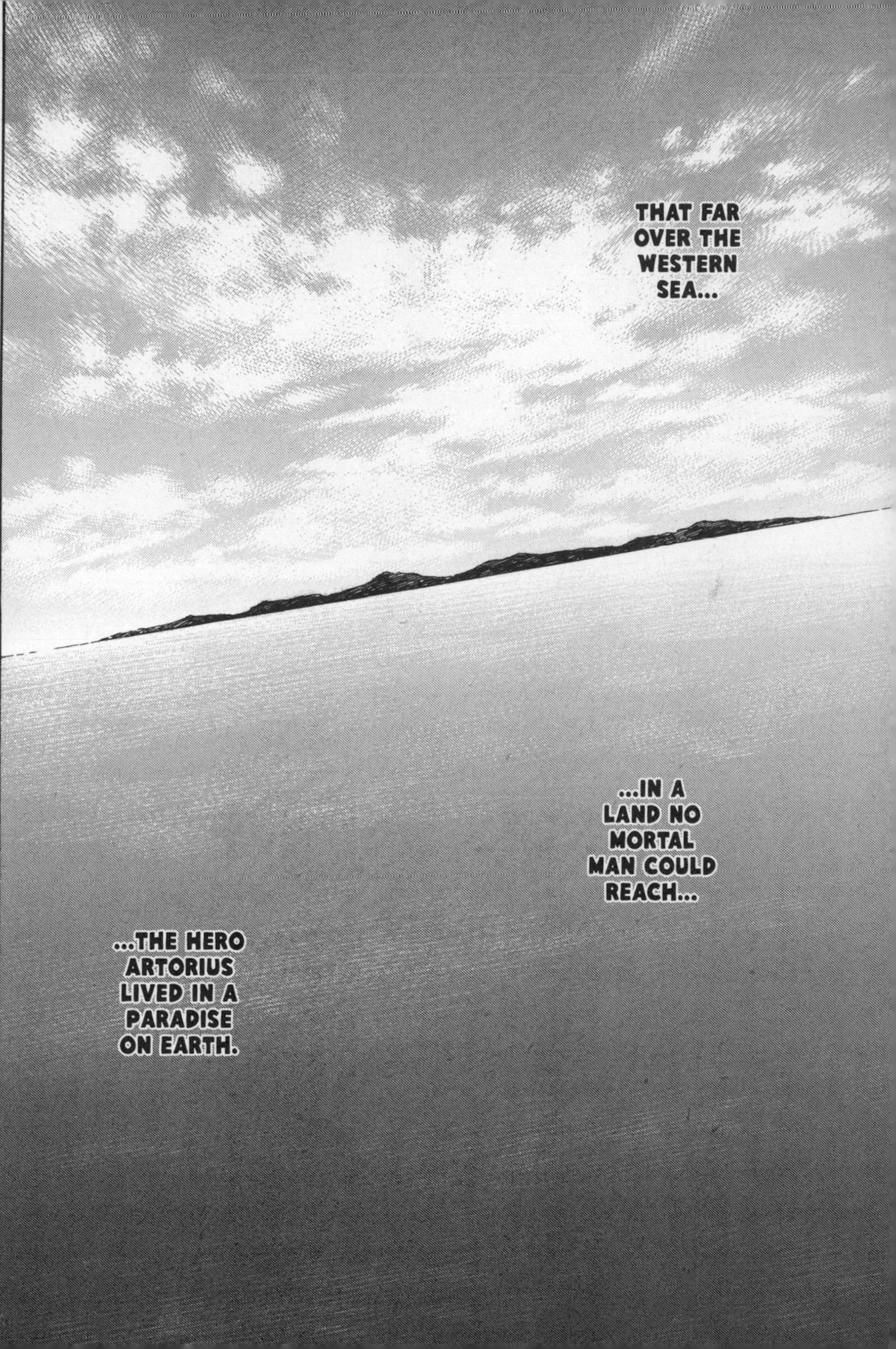
THAT FAR OVER THE WESTERN SEA...
...IN A LAND NO MORTAL MAN COULD REACH...
...THE HERO ARTORIUS LIVED IN A PARADISE ON EARTH.

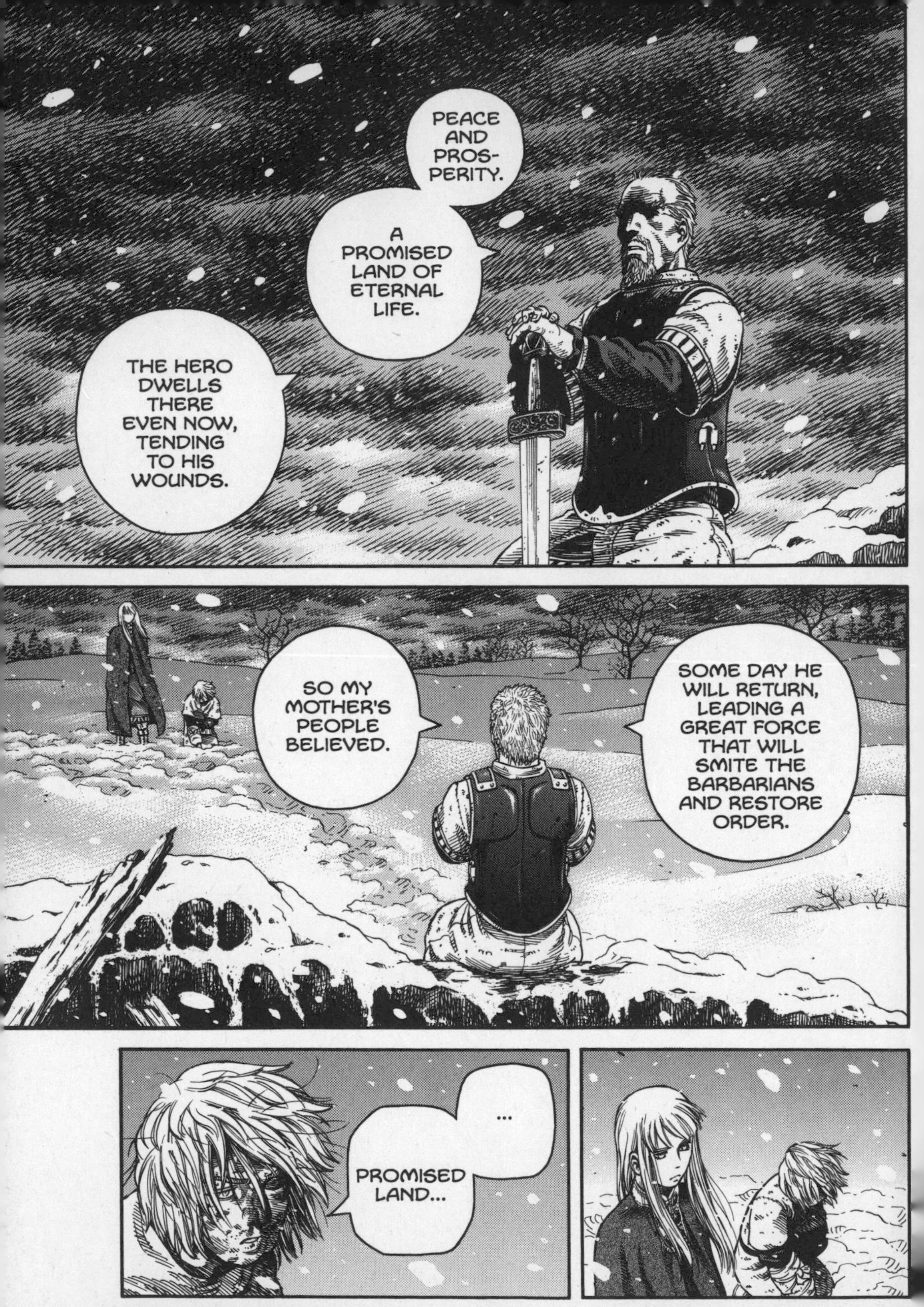
PEACE AND PROS-PERITY.
A PROMISED LAND OF ETERNAL LIFE.
THE HERO DWELLS THERE EVEN NOW, TENDING TO HIS WOUNDS.
SOME DAY HE WILL RETURN, LEADING A GREAT FORCE THAT WILL SMITE THE BARBARIANS AND RESTORE ORDER.
SO MY MOTHER'S PEOPLE BELIEVED.
...
PROMISED LAND...

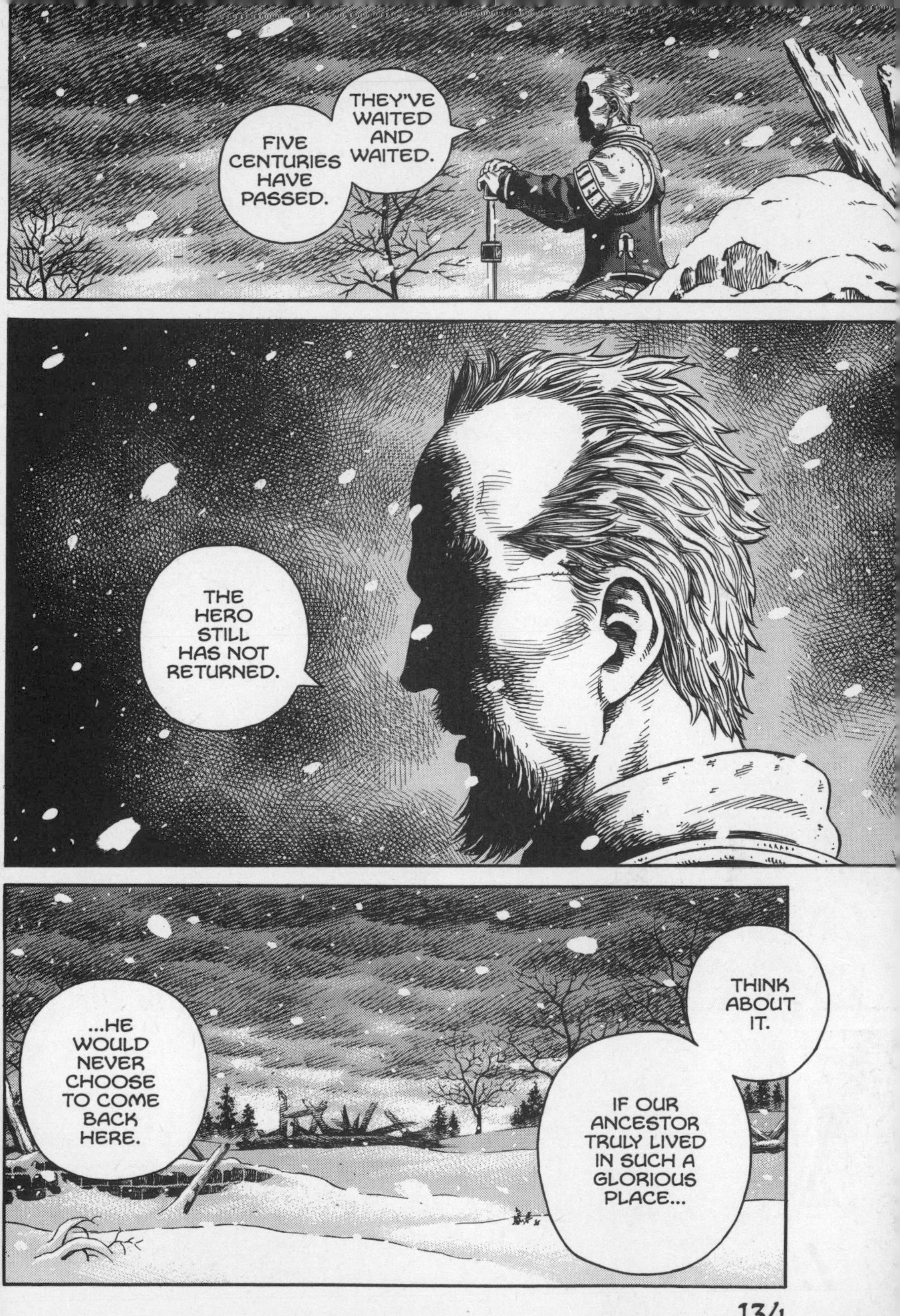
THEY'VE WAITED AND WAITED.
FIVE CENTURIES HAVE PASSED.
THE HERO STILL HAS NOT RETURNED.
THINK ABOUT IT.
IF OUR ANCESTOR TRULY LIVED IN SUCH A GLORIOUS PLACE...
...HE WOULD NEVER CHOOSE TO COME BACK HERE.

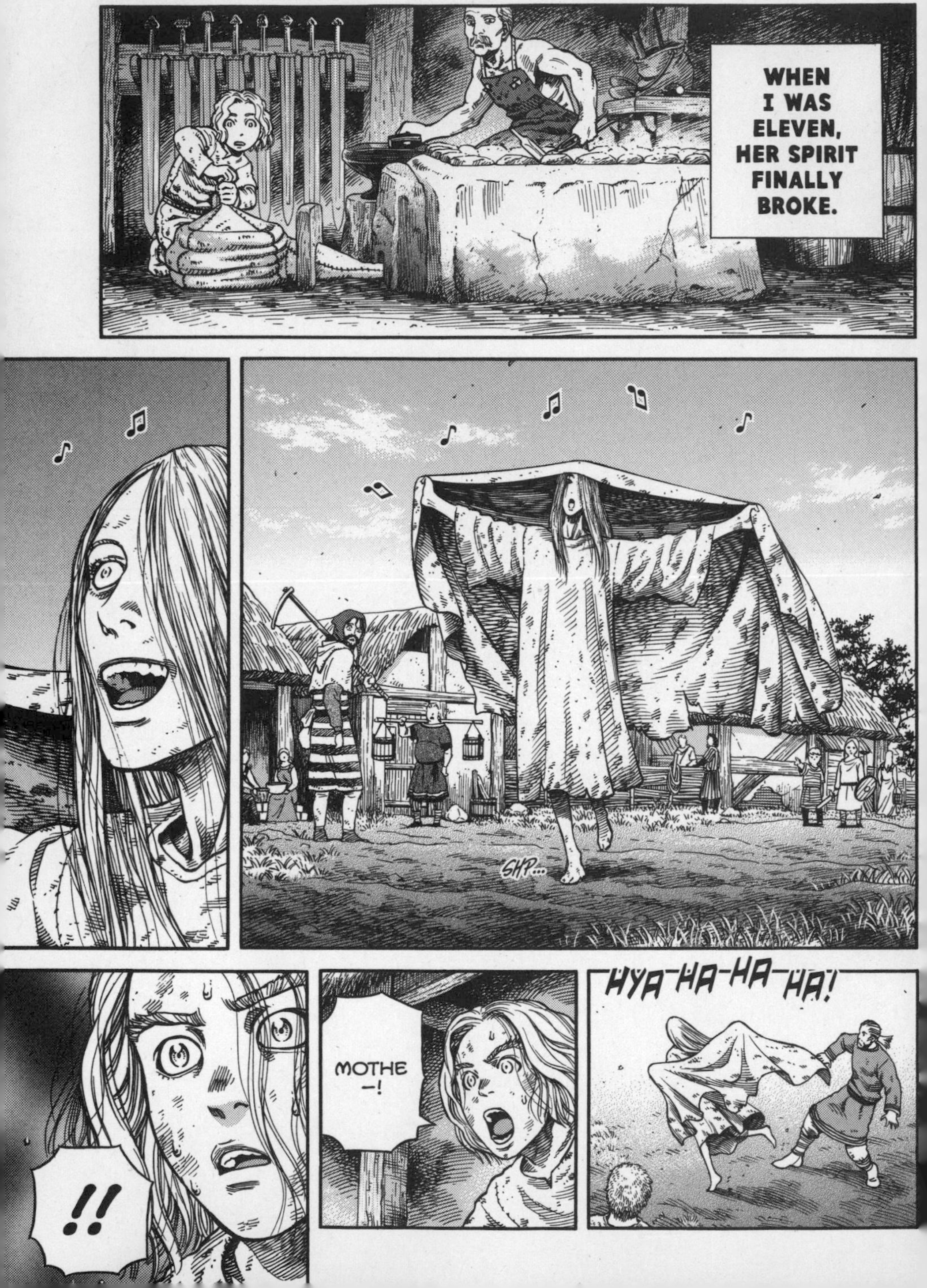
WHEN I WAS ELEVEN, HER SPIRIT FINALLY BROKE.
SHP...
HYA-HA-HA-HA!
MOTHE—!
!!

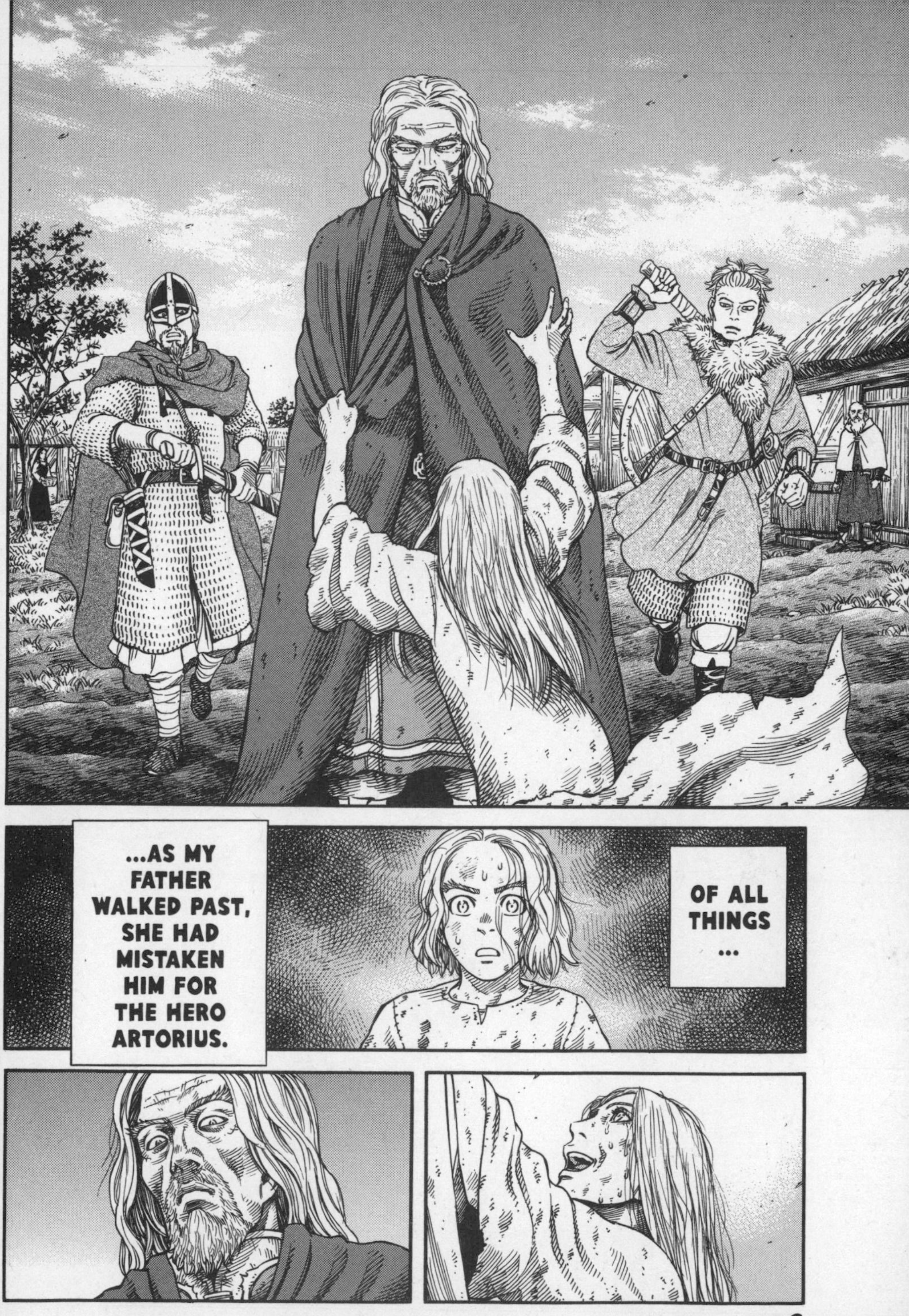
OF ALL THINGS ...
...AS MY FATHER WALKED PAST, SHE HAD MISTAKEN HIM FOR THE HERO ARTORIUS.

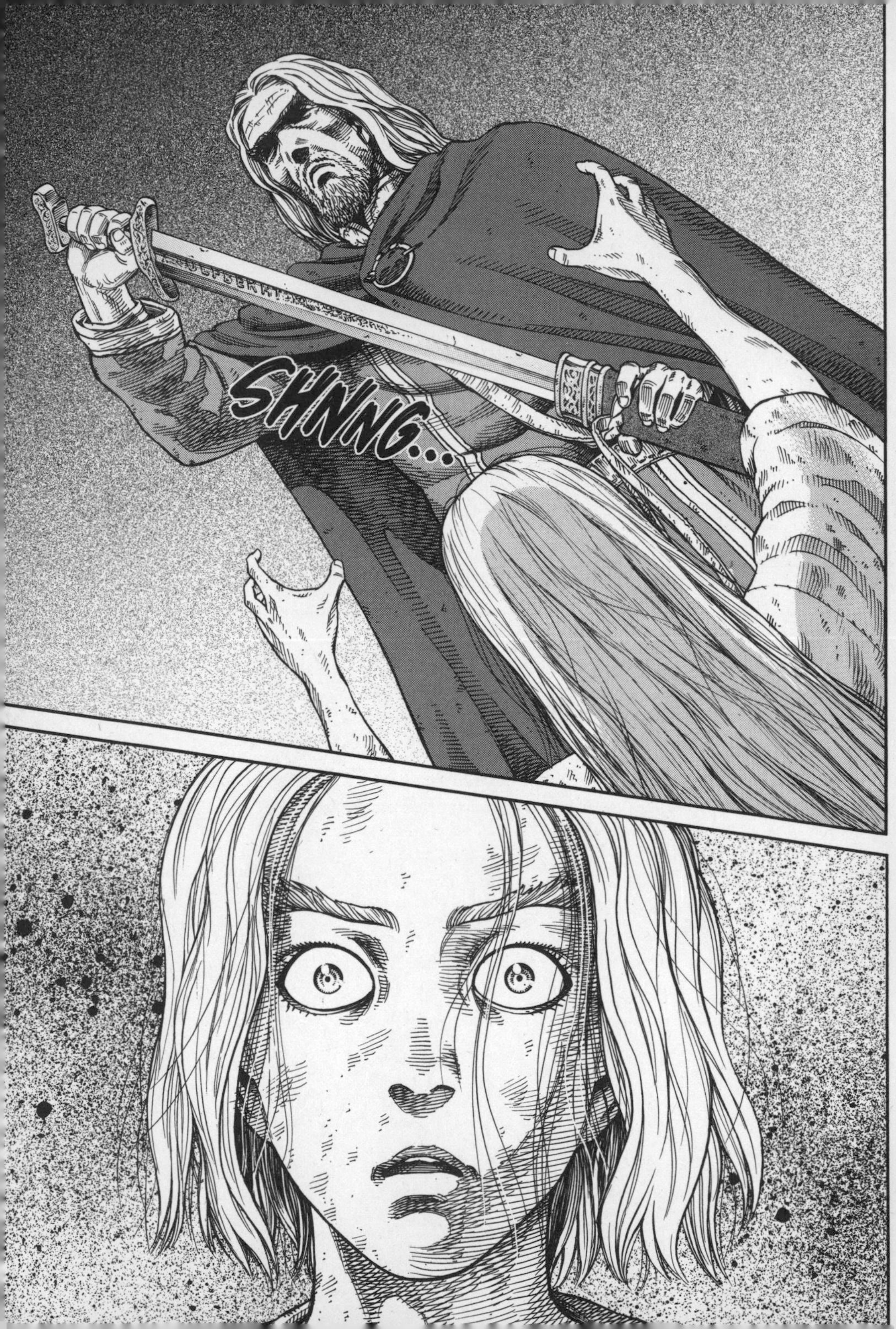
SHNNG...

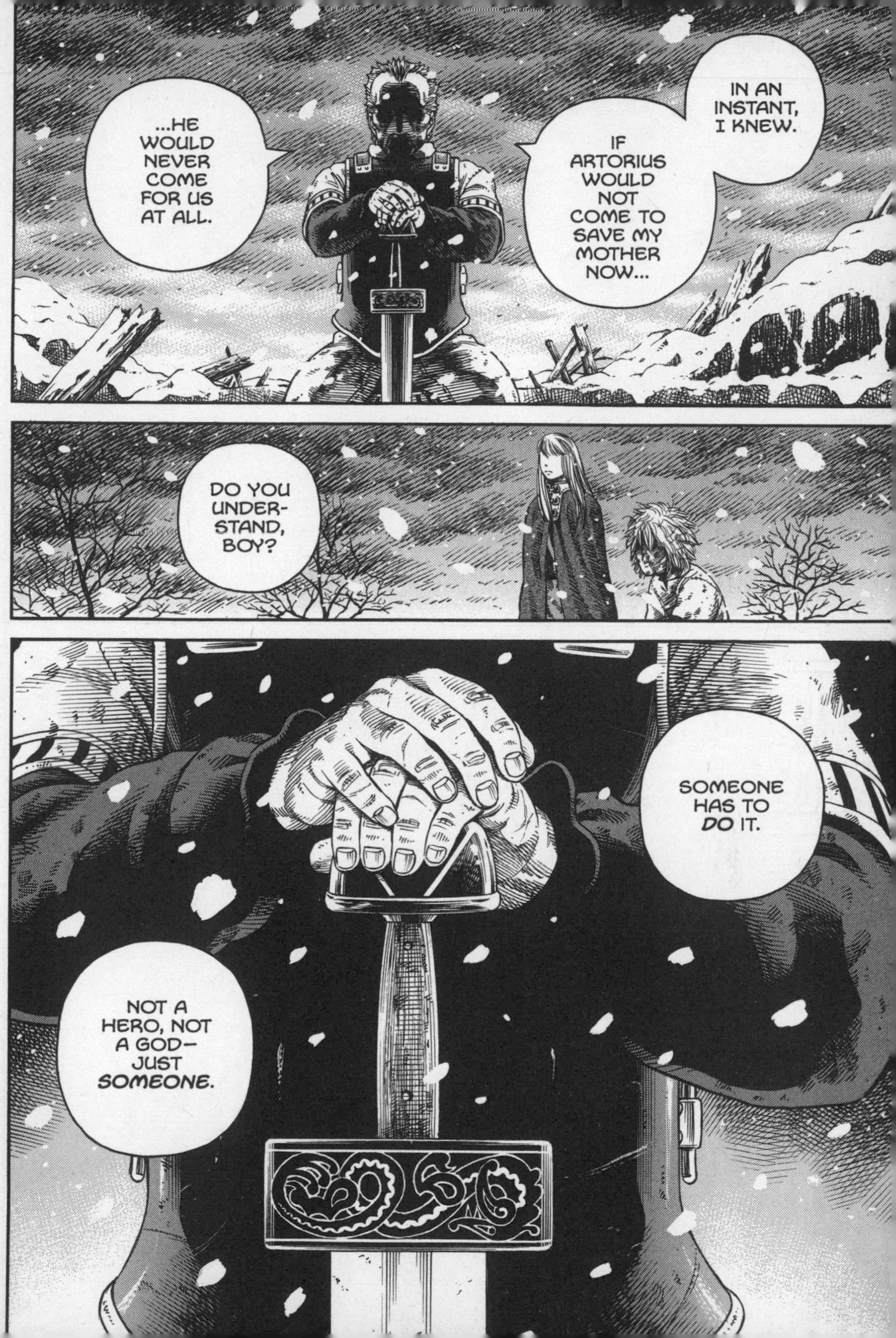
IN AN INSTANT, I KNEW.
IF ARTORIUS WOULD NOT COME TO SAVE MY MOTHER NOW...
...HE WOULD NEVER COME FOR US AT ALL.
DO YOU UNDER-STAND, BOY?
SOMEONE HAS TO *DO* IT.
NOT A HERO, NOT A GOD— JUST *SOMEONE*.

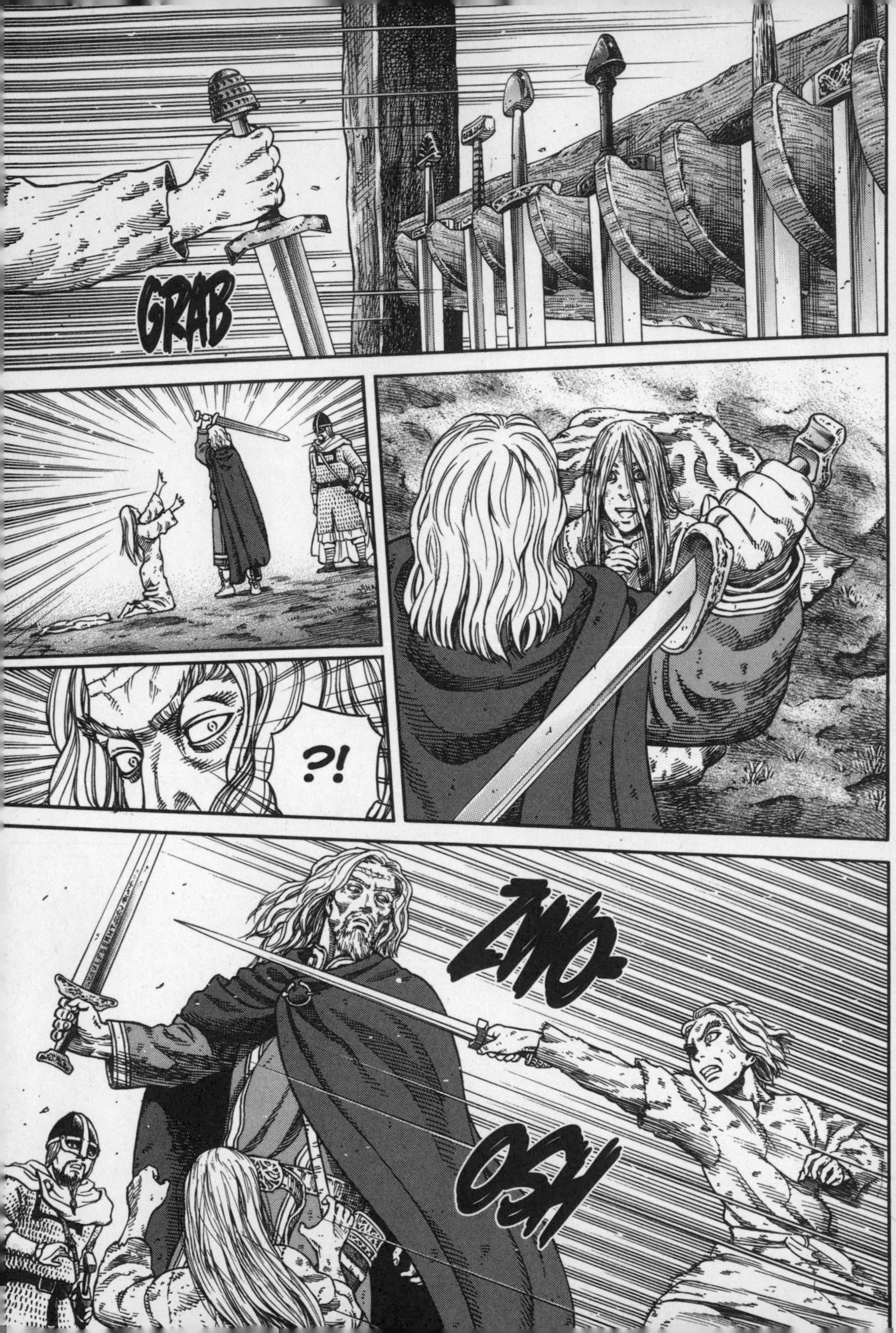
GRAB
?!
ZWO
OSH

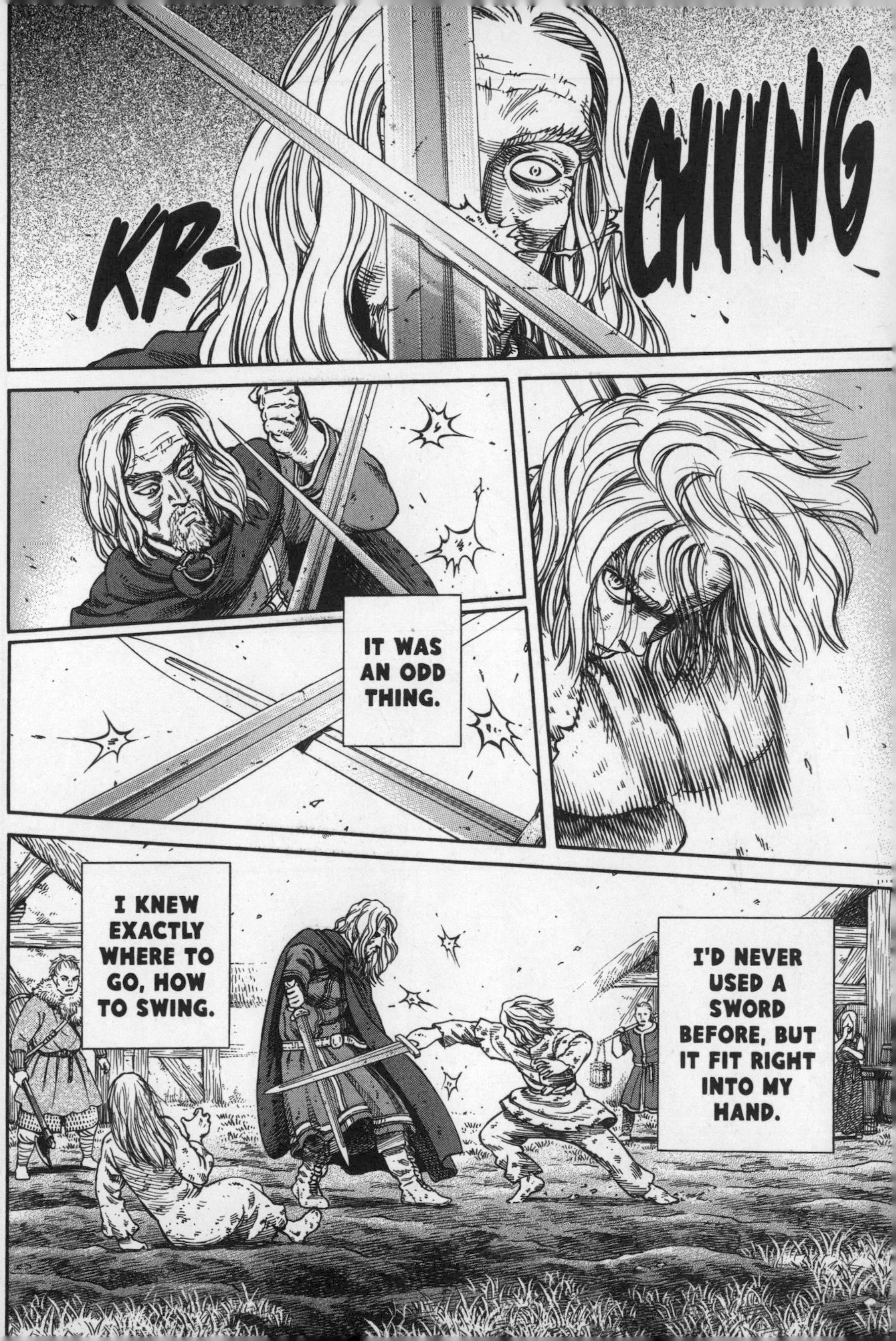
KR-
CHIING
IT WAS AN ODD THING.
I'D NEVER USED A SWORD BEFORE, BUT IT FIT RIGHT INTO MY HAND.
I KNEW EXACTLY WHERE TO GO, HOW TO SWING.

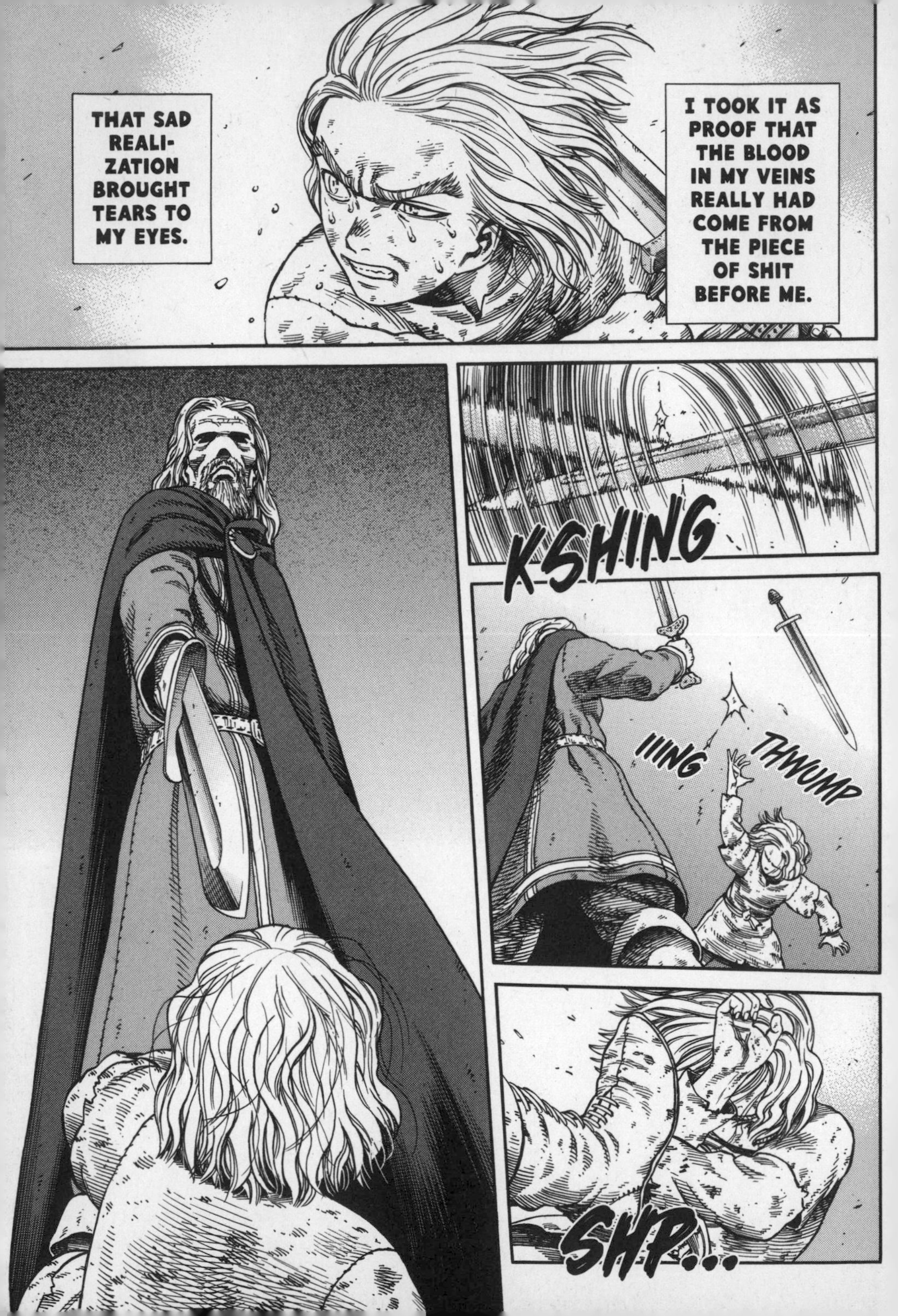
I TOOK IT AS PROOF THAT THE BLOOD IN MY VEINS REALLY HAD COME FROM THE PIECE OF SHIT BEFORE ME.
THAT SAD REALI-ZATION BROUGHT TEARS TO MY EYES.
KSHING
THWUMP
IIING
SHP...

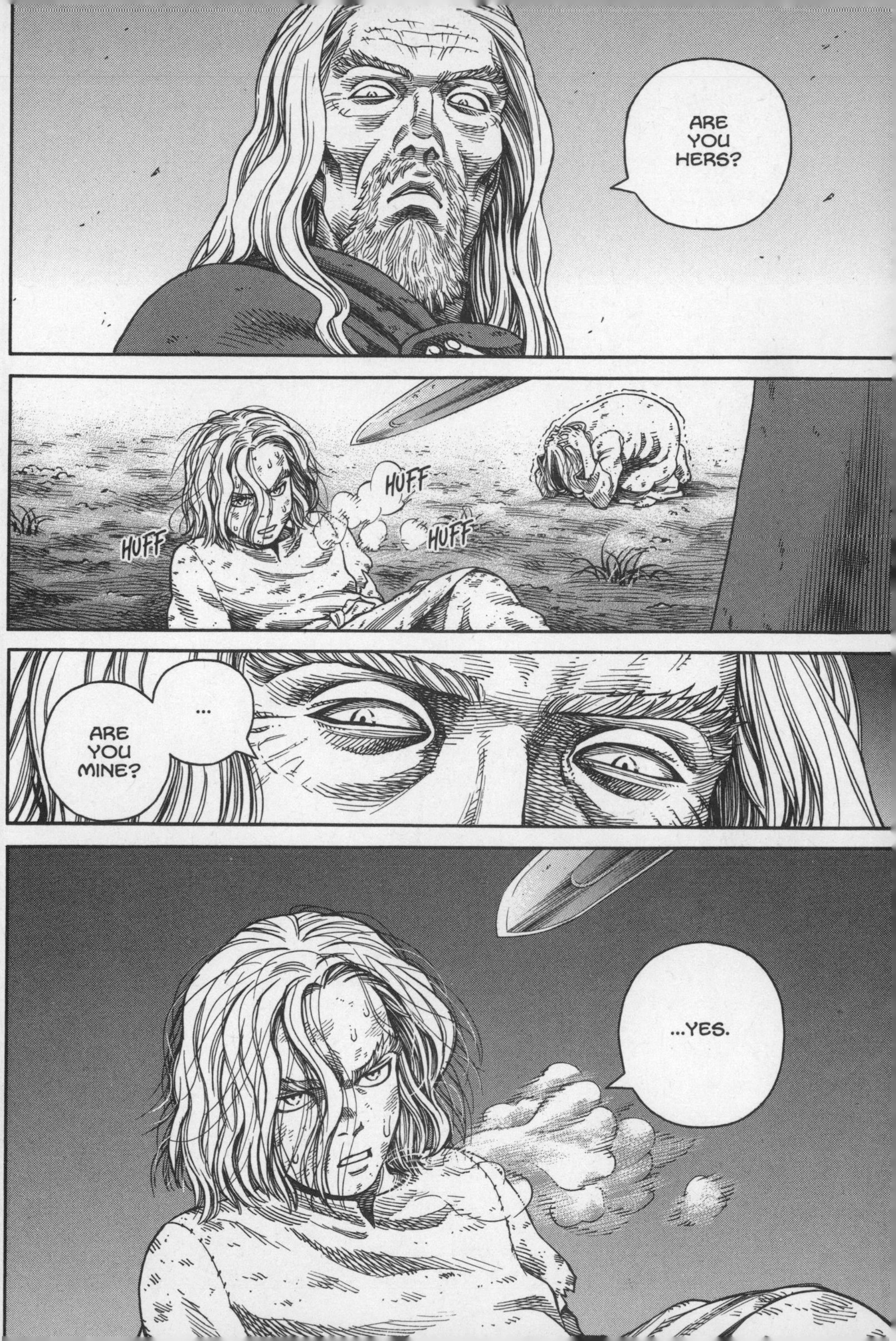
ARE YOU HERS?
HUFF
HUFF
HUFF
...
ARE YOU MINE?
...YES.

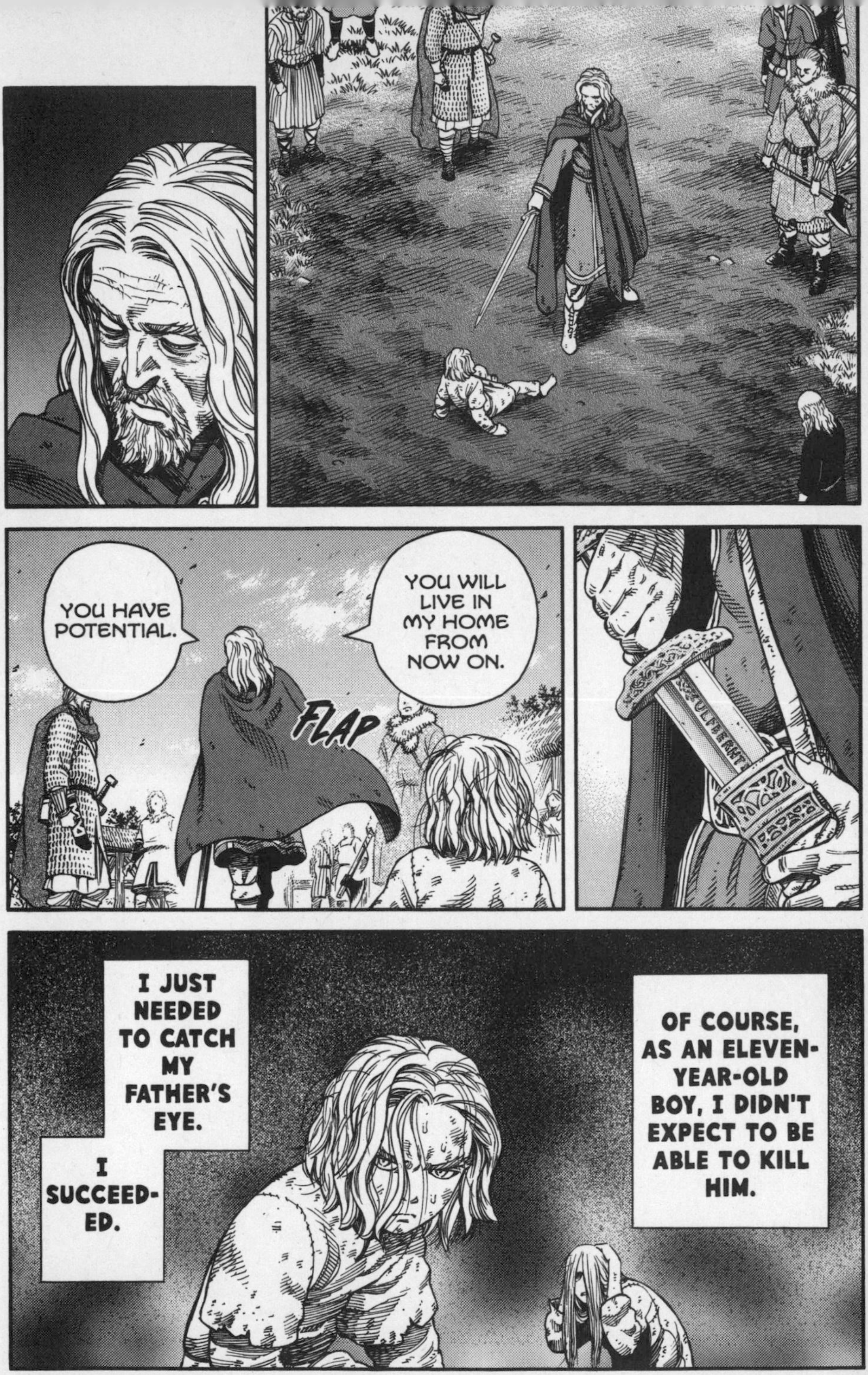
YOU WILL LIVE IN MY HOME FROM NOW ON.
YOU HAVE POTENTIAL.
FLAP
OF COURSE, AS AN ELEVEN-YEAR-OLD BOY, I DIDN'T EXPECT TO BE ABLE TO KILL HIM.
I JUST NEEDED TO CATCH MY FATHER'S EYE.
I SUCCEED-ED.

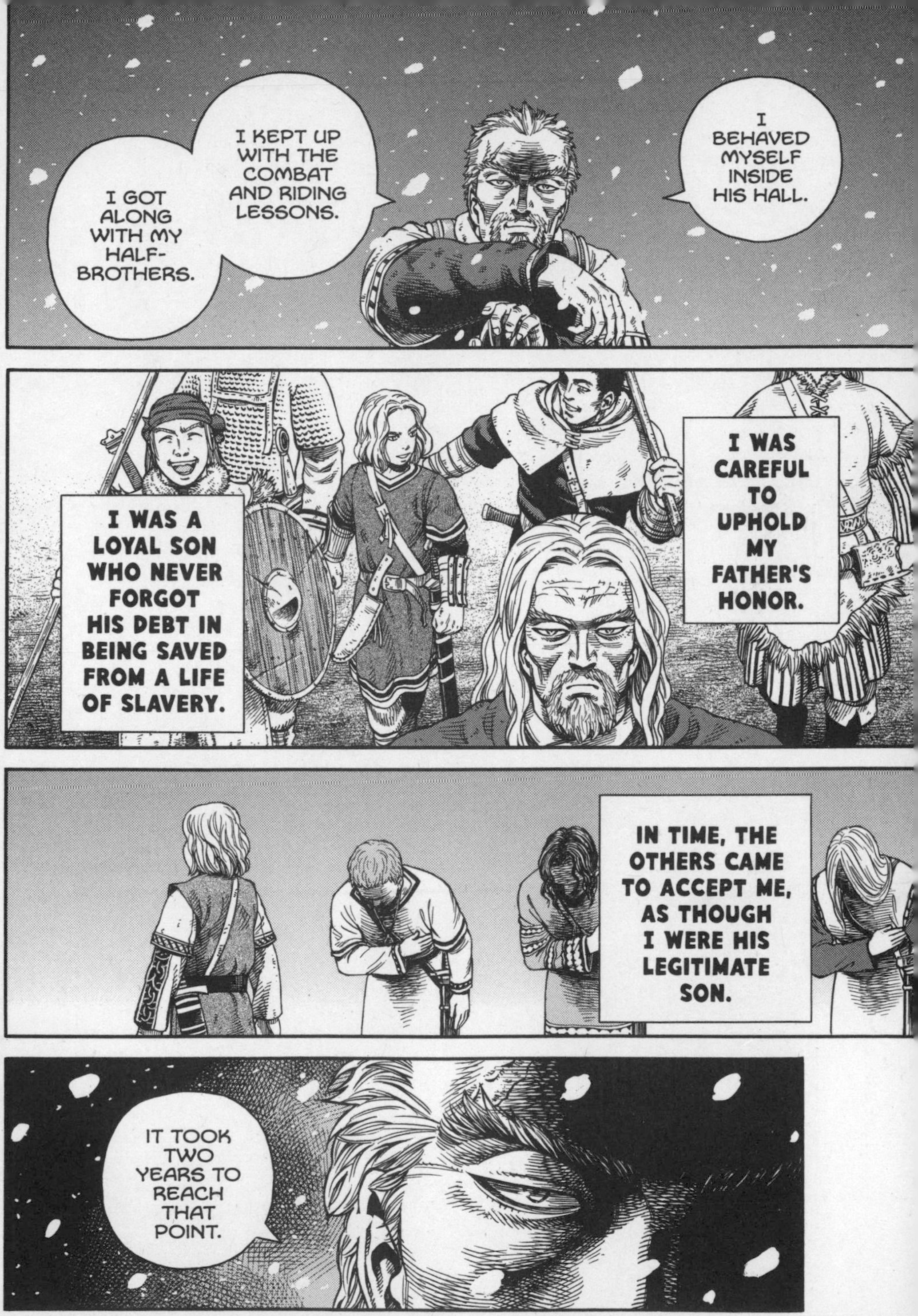
I BEHAVED MYSELF INSIDE HIS HALL.
I KEPT UP WITH THE COMBAT AND RIDING LESSONS.
I GOT ALONG WITH MY HALF-BROTHERS.
I WAS CAREFUL TO UPHOLD MY FATHER'S HONOR.
I WAS A LOYAL SON WHO NEVER FORGOT HIS DEBT IN BEING SAVED FROM A LIFE OF SLAVERY.
IN TIME, THE OTHERS CAME TO ACCEPT ME, AS THOUGH I WERE HIS LEGITIMATE SON.
IT TOOK TWO YEARS TO REACH THAT POINT.

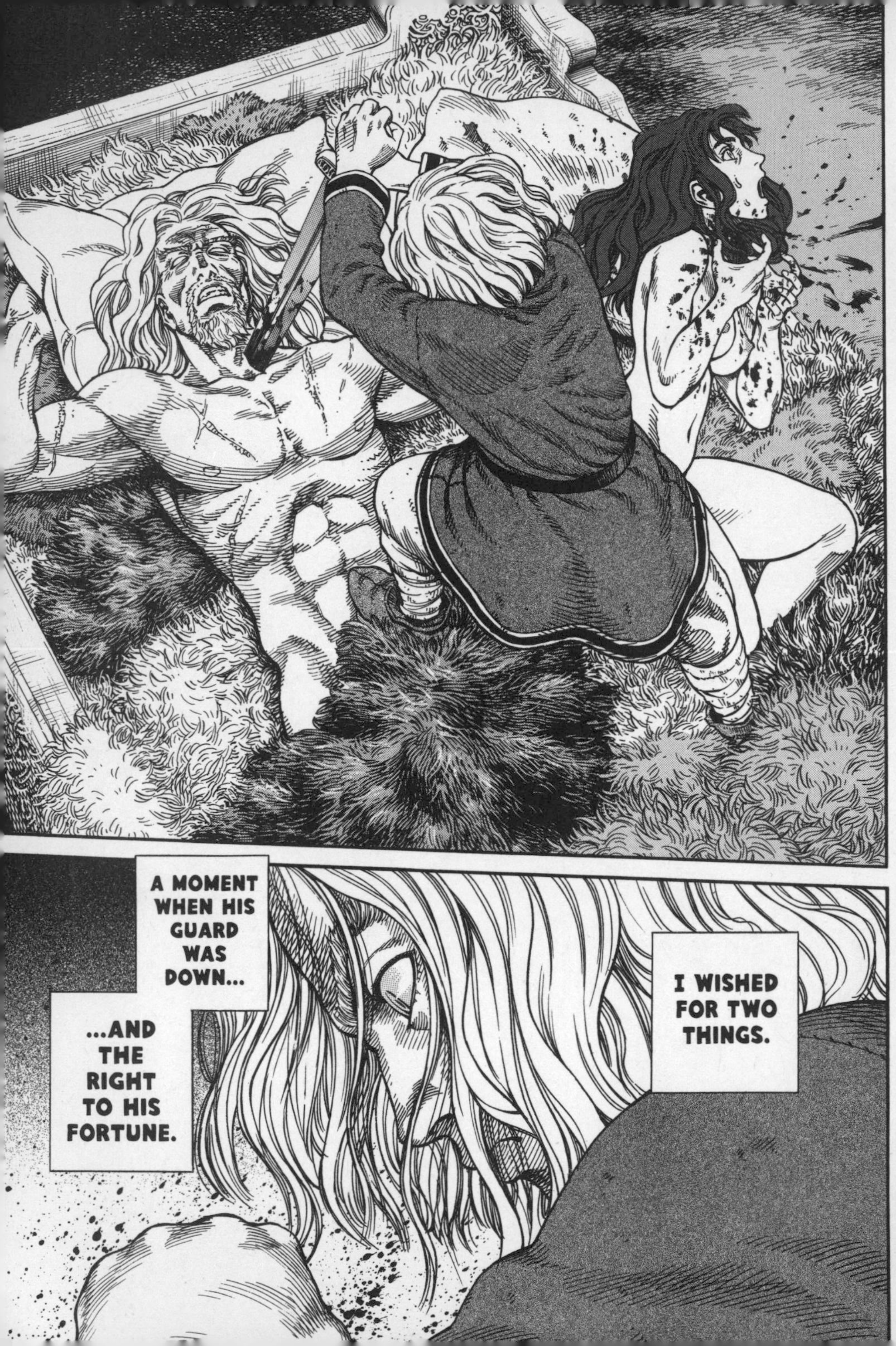
I WISHED FOR TWO THINGS.
A MOMENT WHEN HIS GUARD WAS DOWN...
...AND THE RIGHT TO HIS FORTUNE.

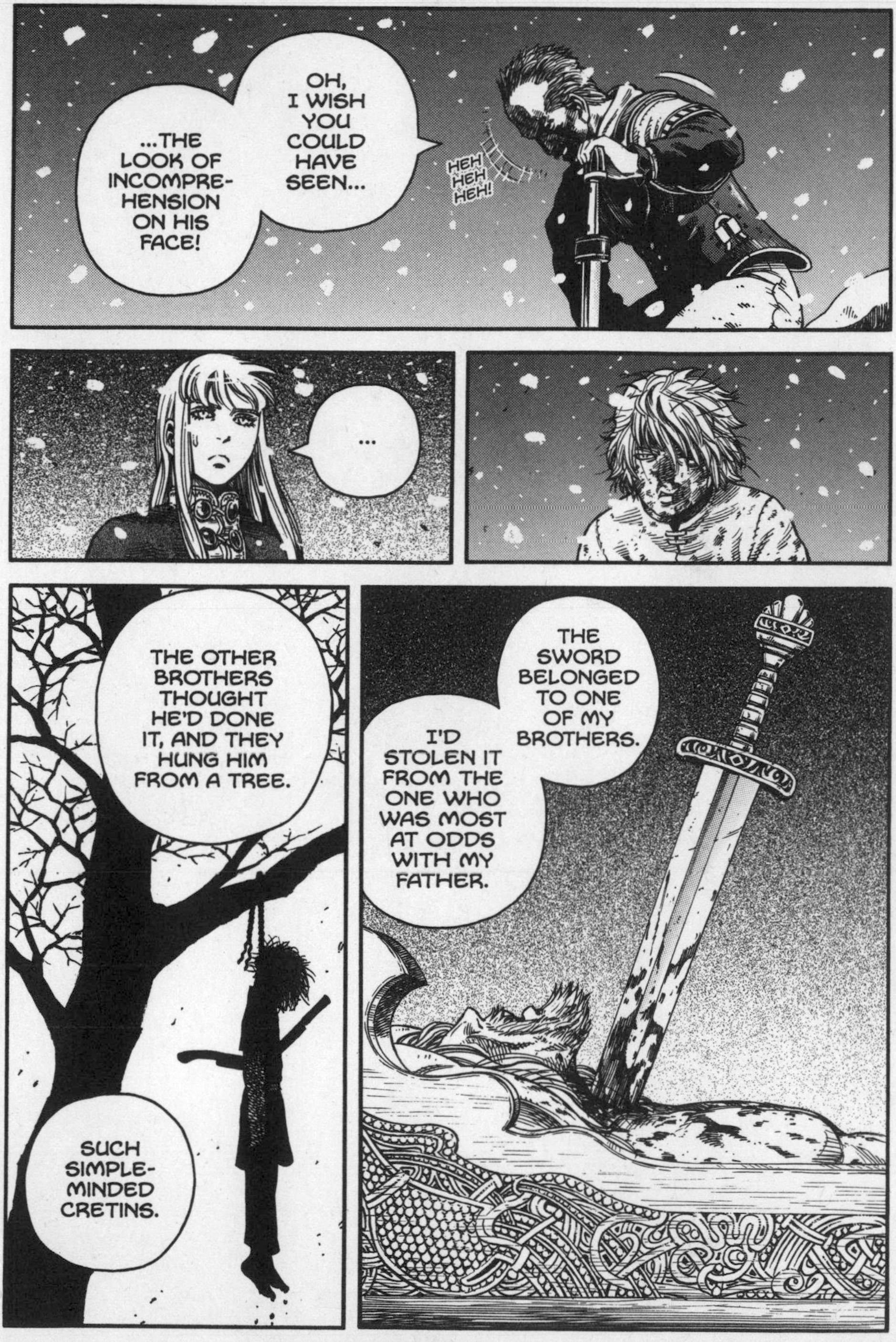

OH, I WISH YOU COULD HAVE SEEN...
HEH HEH HEH!
...THE LOOK OF INCOMPREHENSION ON HIS FACE!
...
THE SWORD BELONGED TO ONE OF MY BROTHERS.
I'D STOLEN IT FROM THE ONE WHO WAS MOST AT ODDS WITH MY FATHER.
THE OTHER BROTHERS THOUGHT HE'D DONE IT, AND THEY HUNG HIM FROM A TREE.
SUCH SIMPLE-MINDED CRETINS.

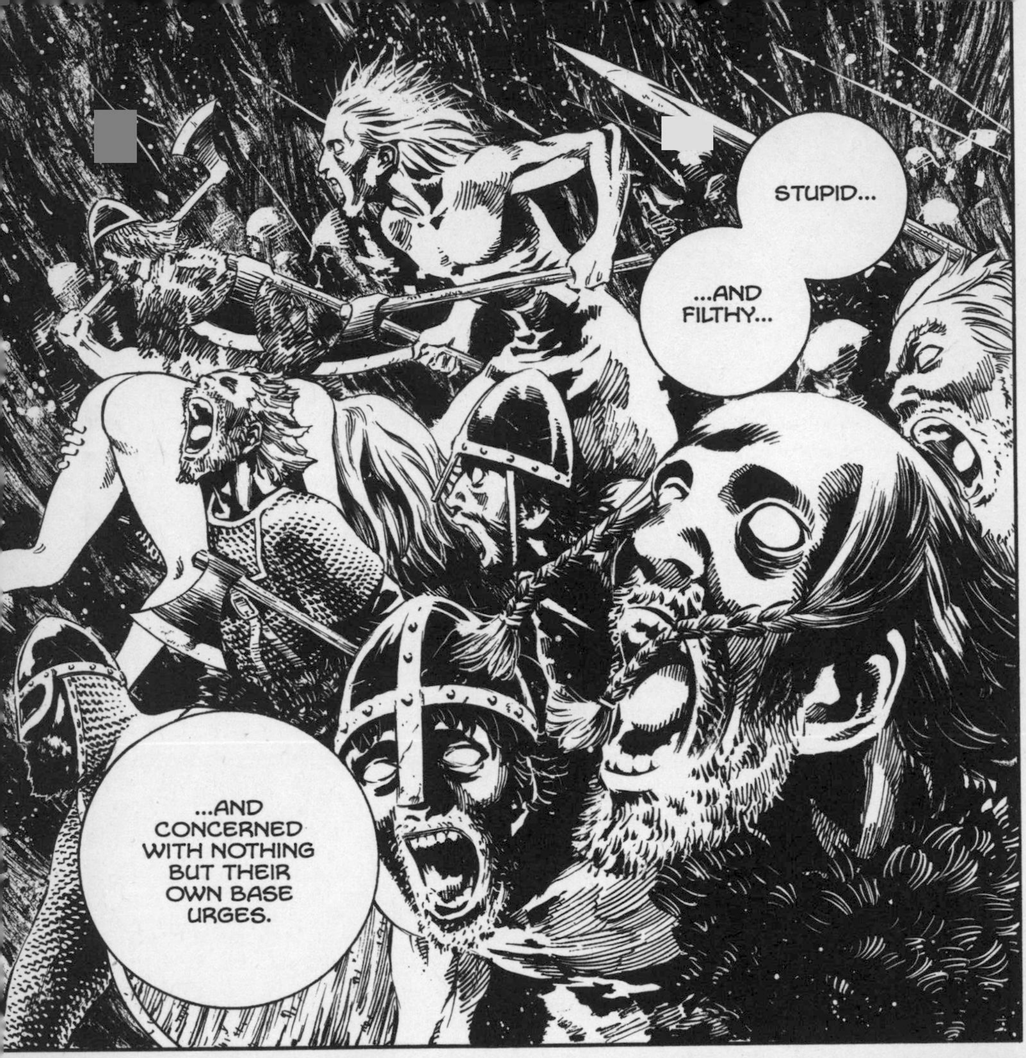
STUPID...
...AND FILTHY...
...AND CONCERNED WITH NOTHING BUT THEIR OWN BASE URGES.
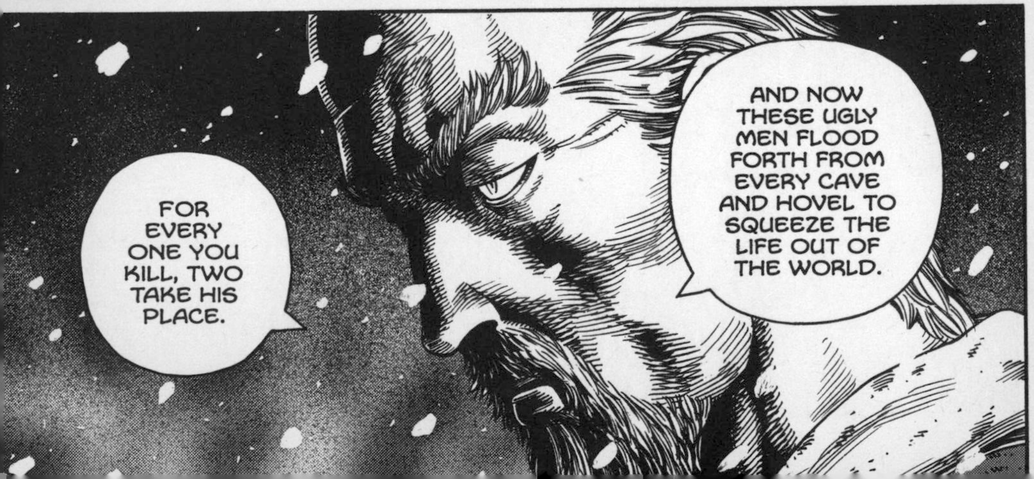
AND NOW THESE UGLY MEN FLOOD FORTH FROM EVERY CAVE AND HOVEL TO SQUEEZE THE LIFE OUT OF THE WORLD.
FOR EVERY ONE YOU KILL, TWO TAKE HIS PLACE.

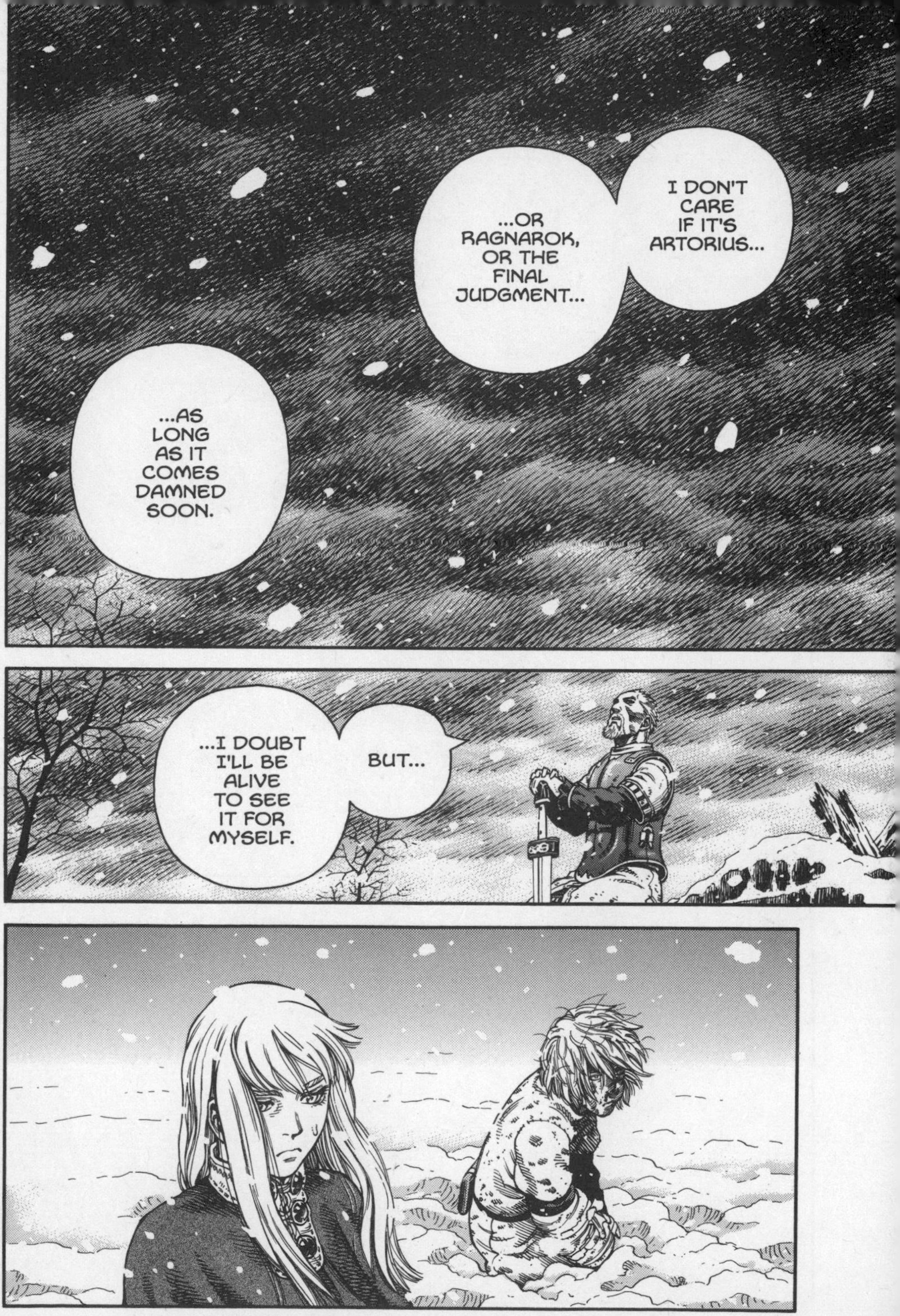
I DON'T CARE IF IT'S ARTORIUS...
...OR RAGNAROK, OR THE FINAL JUDGMENT...
...AS LONG AS IT COMES DAMNED SOON.
BUT...
...I DOUBT I'LL BE ALIVE TO SEE IT FOR MYSELF.

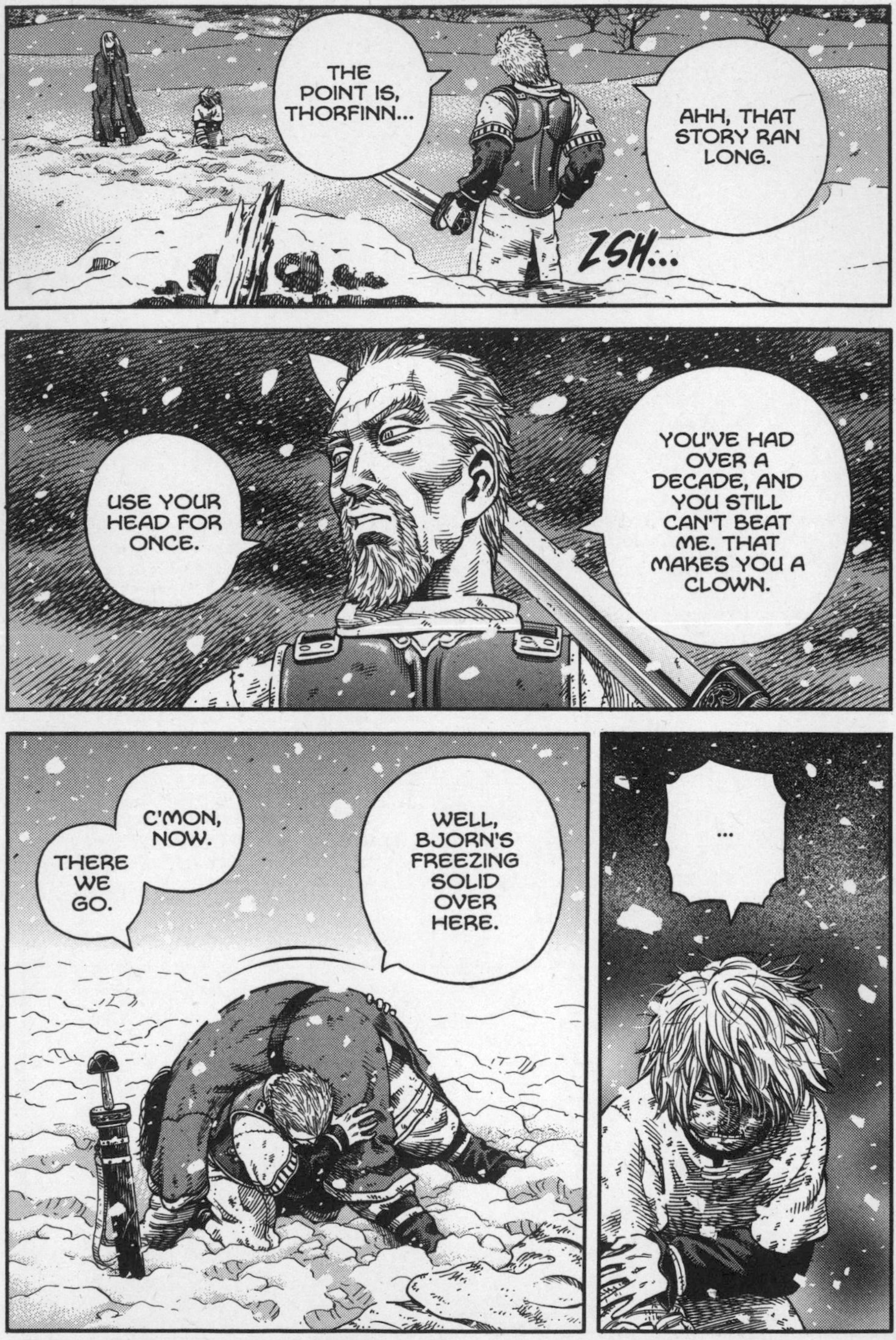
AHH, THAT STORY RAN LONG.
THE POINT IS, THORFINN...
ZSH...
YOU'VE HAD OVER A DECADE, AND YOU STILL CAN'T BEAT ME. THAT MAKES YOU A CLOWN.
USE YOUR HEAD FOR ONCE.
...
WELL, BJORN'S FREEZING SOLID OVER HERE.
C'MON, NOW.
THERE WE GO.

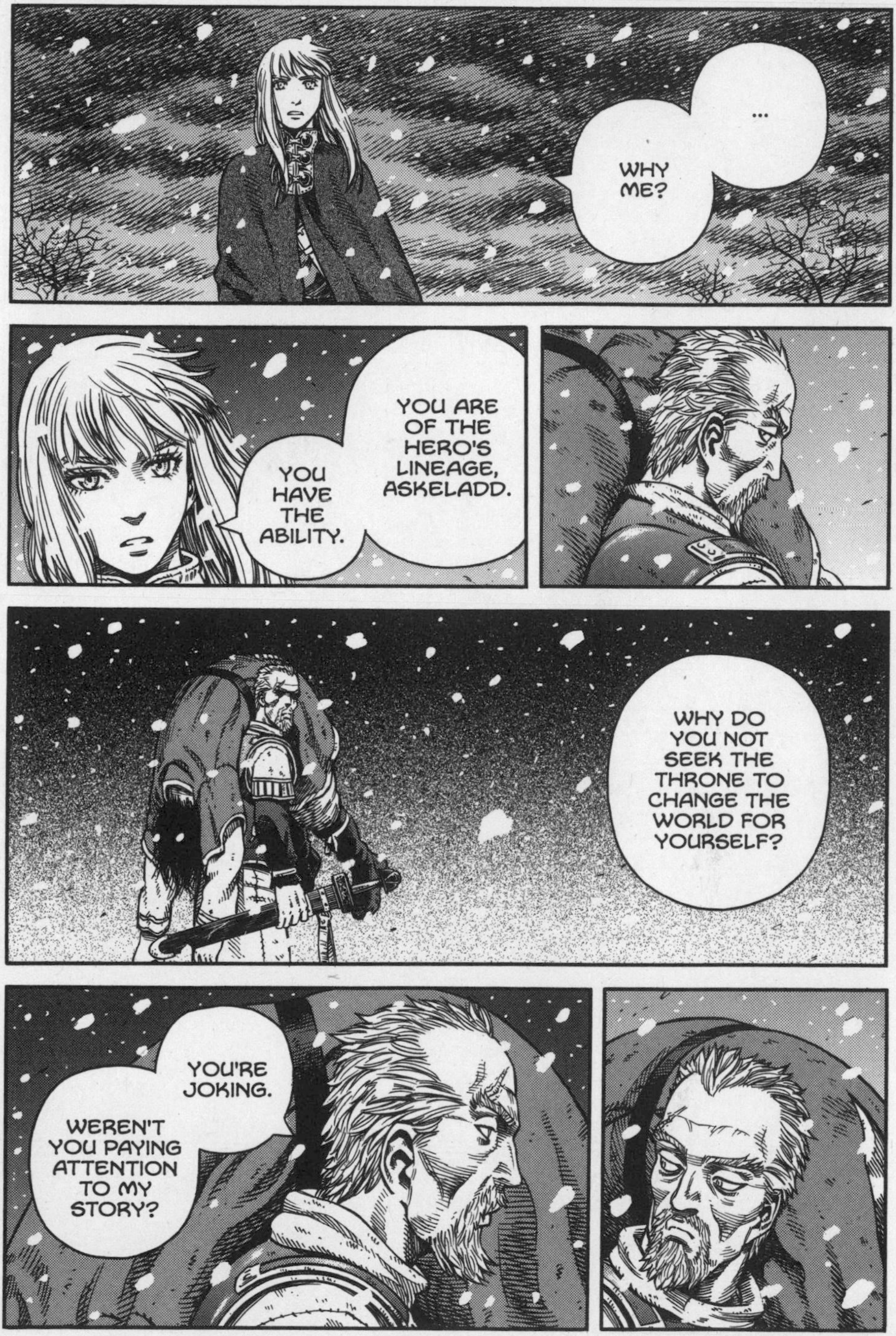
...
WHY ME?
YOU ARE OF THE HERO'S LINEAGE, ASKELADD.
YOU HAVE THE ABILITY.
WHY DO YOU NOT SEEK THE THRONE TO CHANGE THE WORLD FOR YOURSELF?
YOU'RE JOKING.
WEREN'T YOU PAYING ATTENTION TO MY STORY?

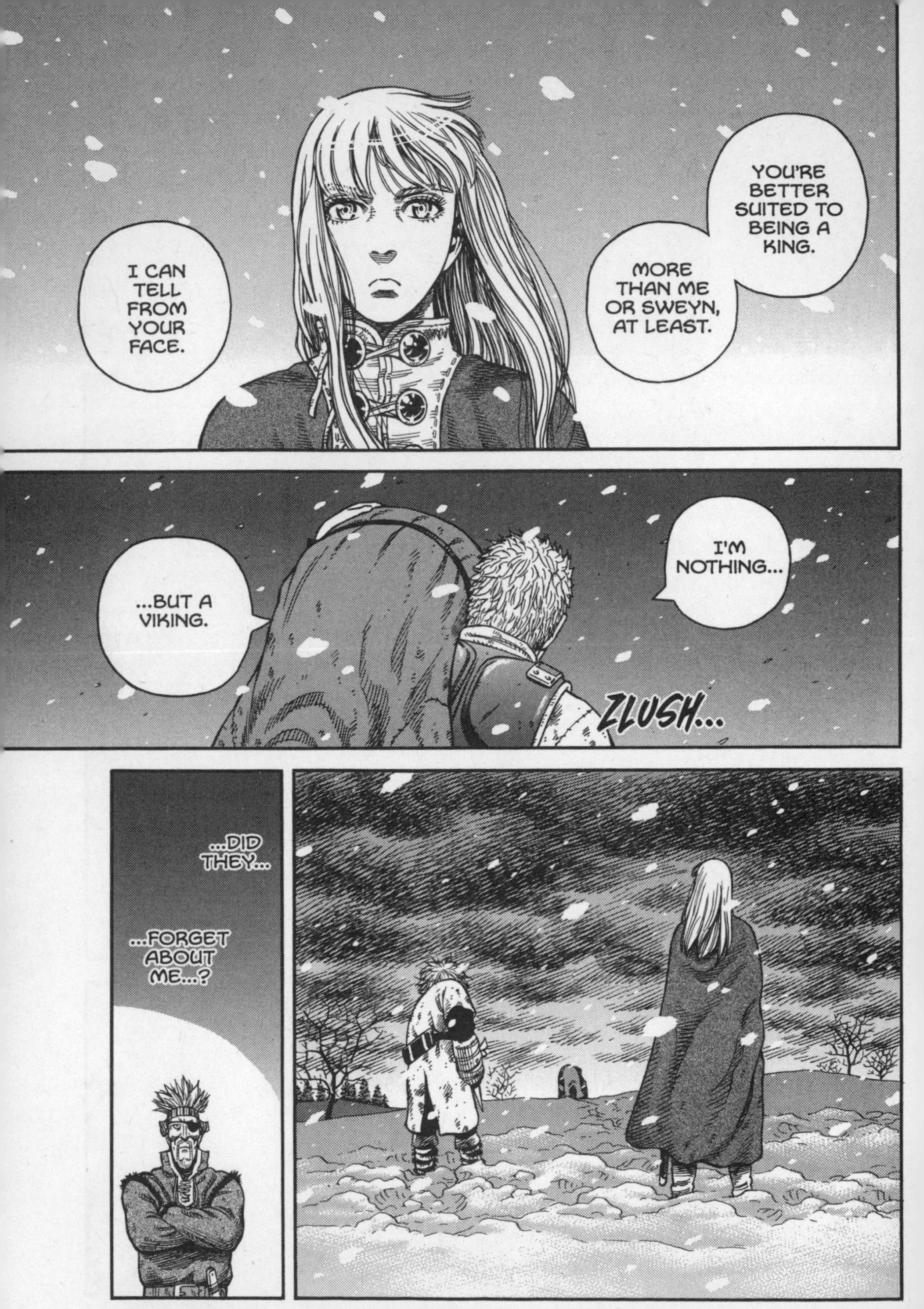
YOU'RE BETTER SUITED TO BEING A KING.
MORE THAN ME OR SWEYN, AT LEAST.
I CAN TELL FROM YOUR FACE.
I'M NOTHING...
...BUT A VIKING.
ZLUSH...
...DID THEY...
...FORGET ABOUT ME...?

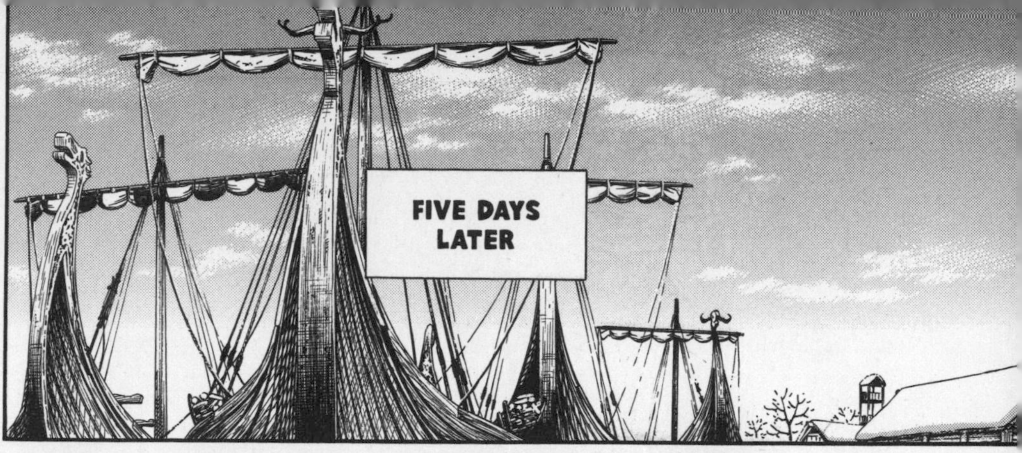
FIVE DAYS LATER

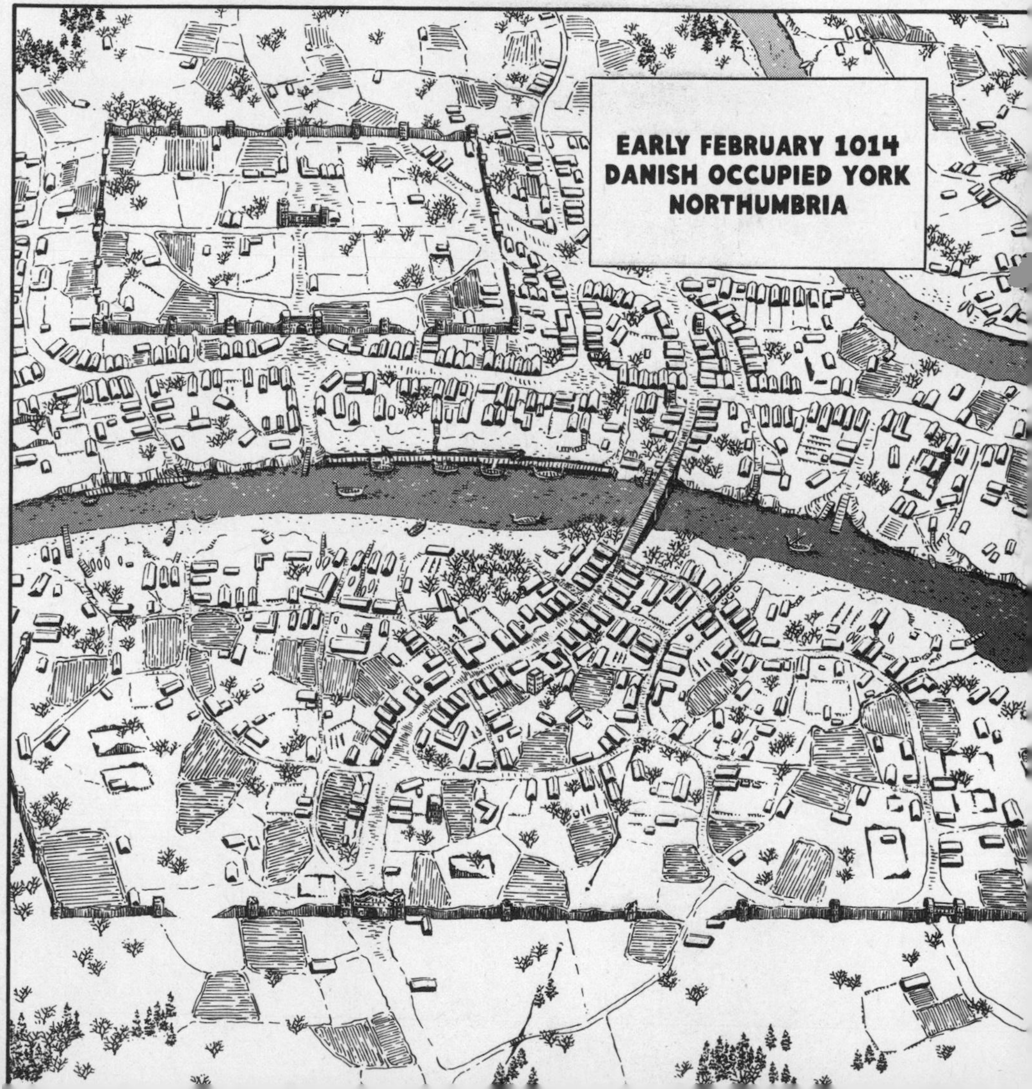
EARLY FEBRUARY 1014
DANISH OCCUPIED YORK
NORTHUMBRIA

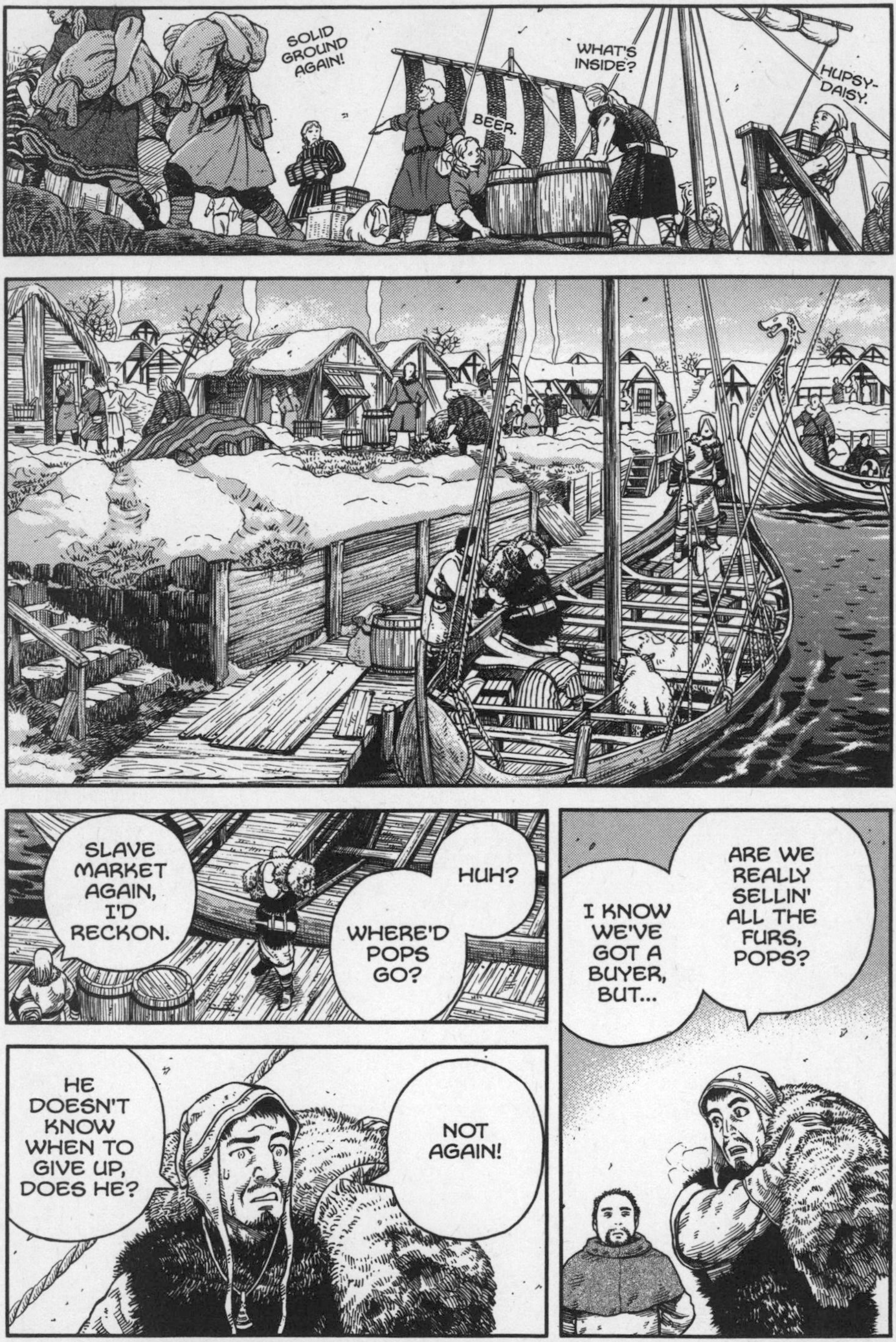
HUPSY-DAISY.
WHAT'S INSIDE?
BEER.
SOLID GROUND AGAIN!
ARE WE REALLY SELLIN' ALL THE FURS, POPS?
I KNOW WE'VE GOT A BUYER, BUT...
HUH?
WHERE'D POPS GO?
SLAVE MARKET AGAIN, I'D RECKON.
NOT AGAIN!
HE DOESN'T KNOW WHEN TO GIVE UP, DOES HE?

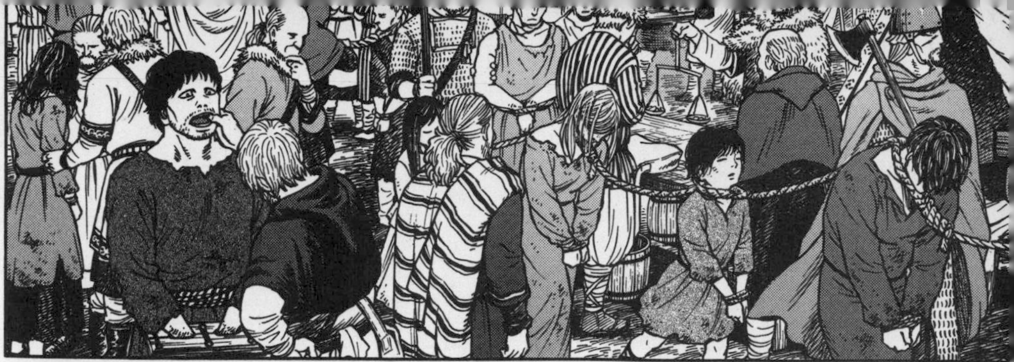

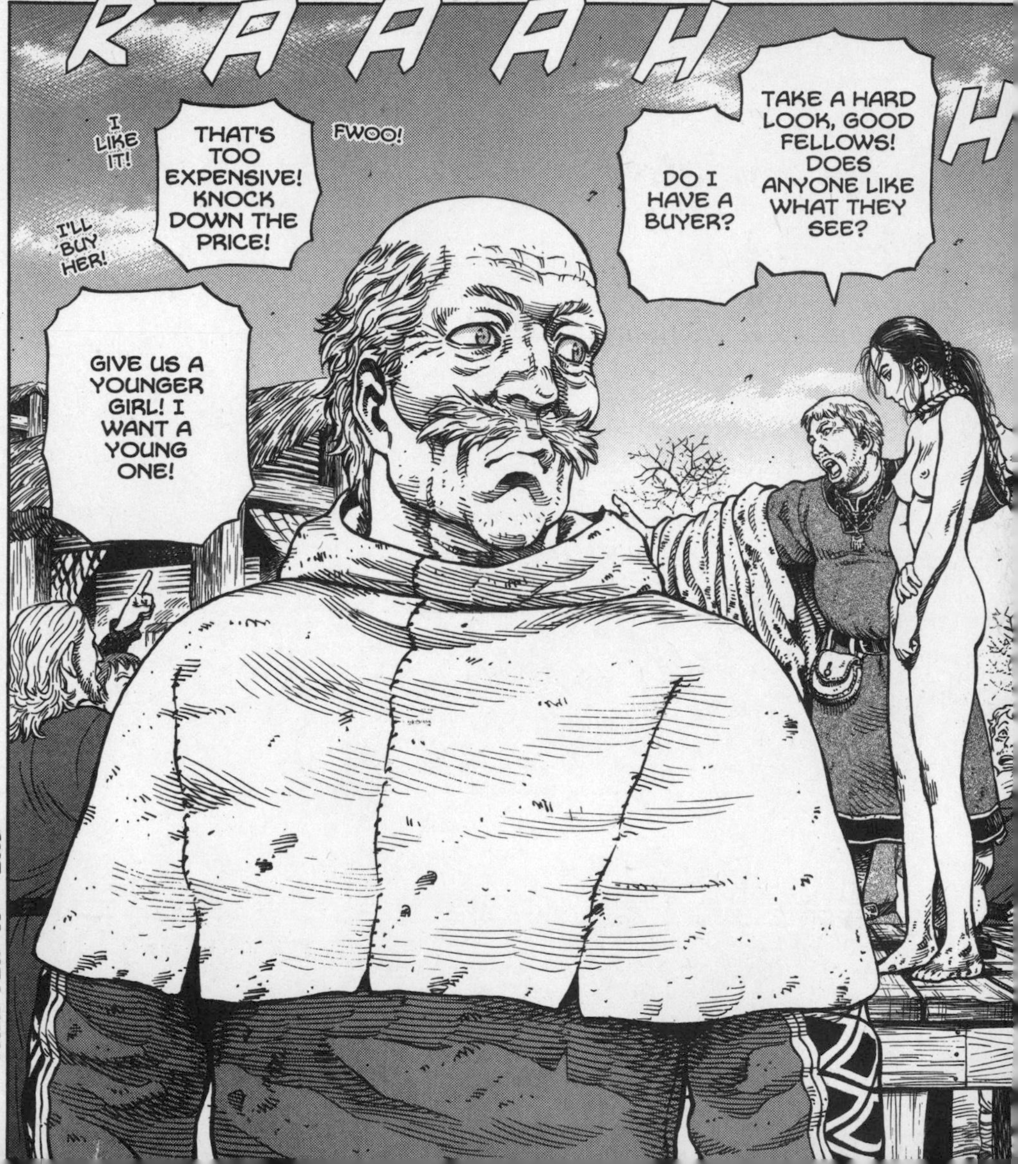
RAAAAHH
TAKE A HARD LOOK, GOOD FELLOWS! DOES ANYONE LIKE WHAT THEY SEE?
DO I HAVE A BUYER?
FWOO!
THAT'S TOO EXPENSIVE! KNOCK DOWN THE PRICE!
I LIKE IT!
I'LL BUY HER!
GIVE US A YOUNGER GIRL! I WANT A YOUNG ONE!

CHAPTER 47 - END

CHAPTER 48: REUNION

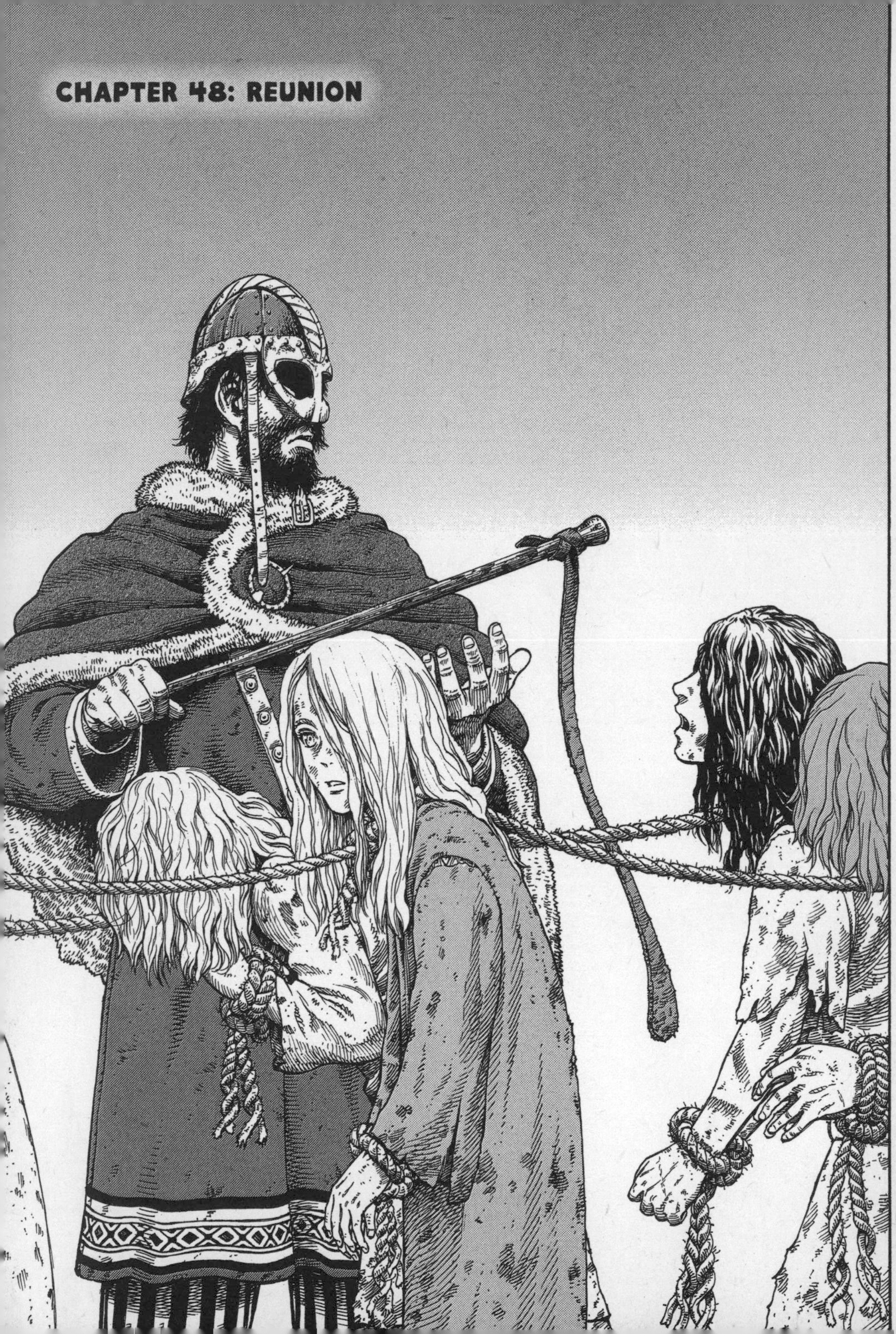

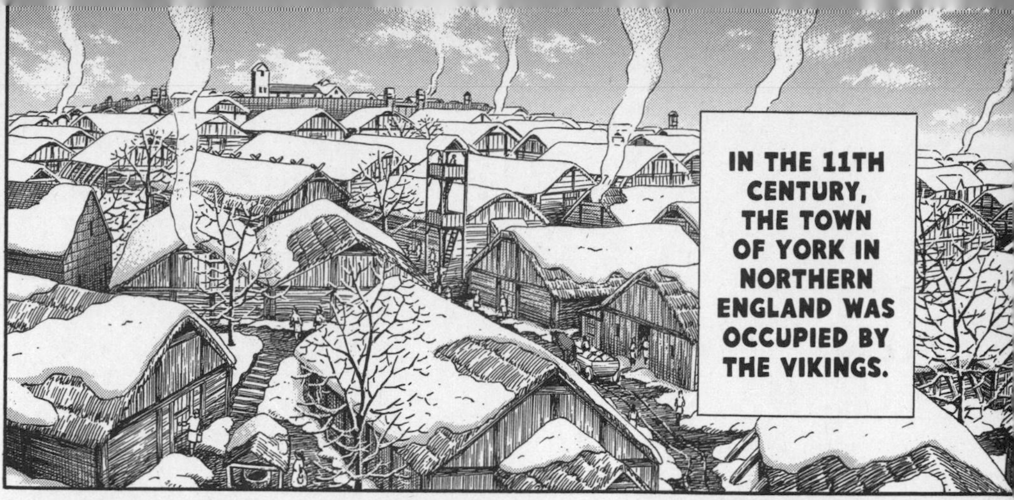
IN THE 11TH CENTURY, THE TOWN OF YORK IN NORTHERN ENGLAND WAS OCCUPIED BY THE VIKINGS.

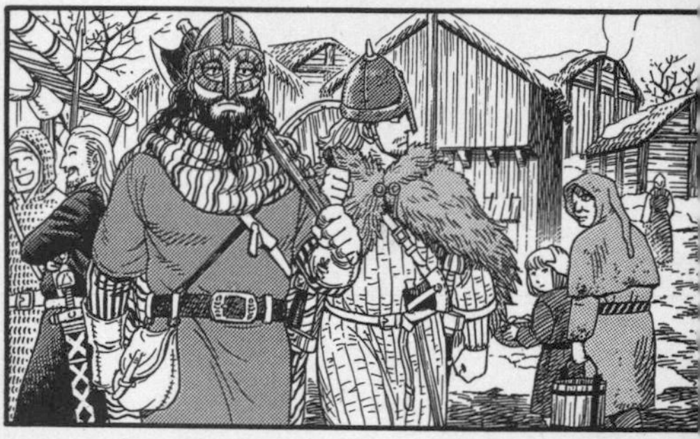

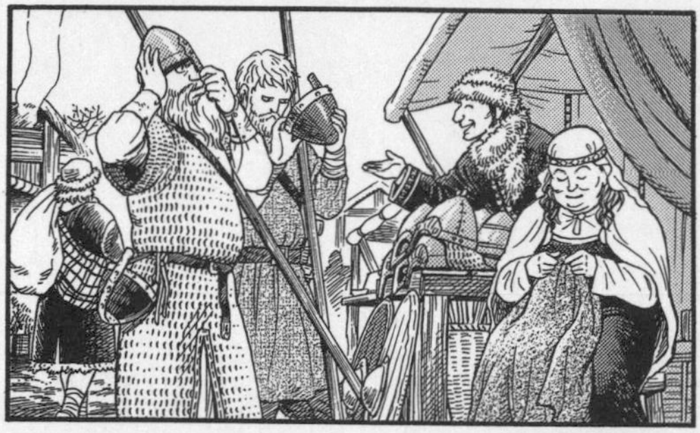

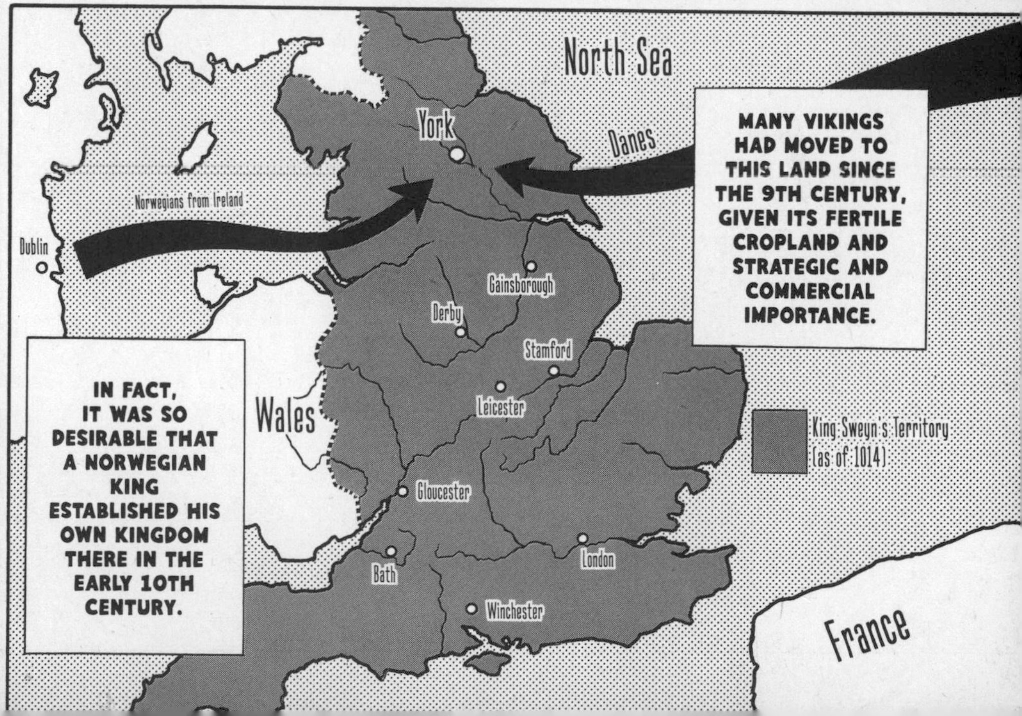
North Sea
MANY VIKINGS HAD MOVED TO THIS LAND SINCE THE 9TH CENTURY, GIVEN ITS FERTILE CROPLAND AND STRATEGIC AND COMMERCIAL IMPORTANCE.
Danes
York
Norwegians from Ireland
Dublin
Gainsborough
Derby
Stamford
Leicester
Wales
King Sweyn's Territory (as of 1014)
Gloucester
Bath
London
Winchester
France
IN FACT, IT WAS SO DESIRABLE THAT A NORWEGIAN KING ESTABLISHED HIS OWN KINGDOM THERE IN THE EARLY 10TH CENTURY.

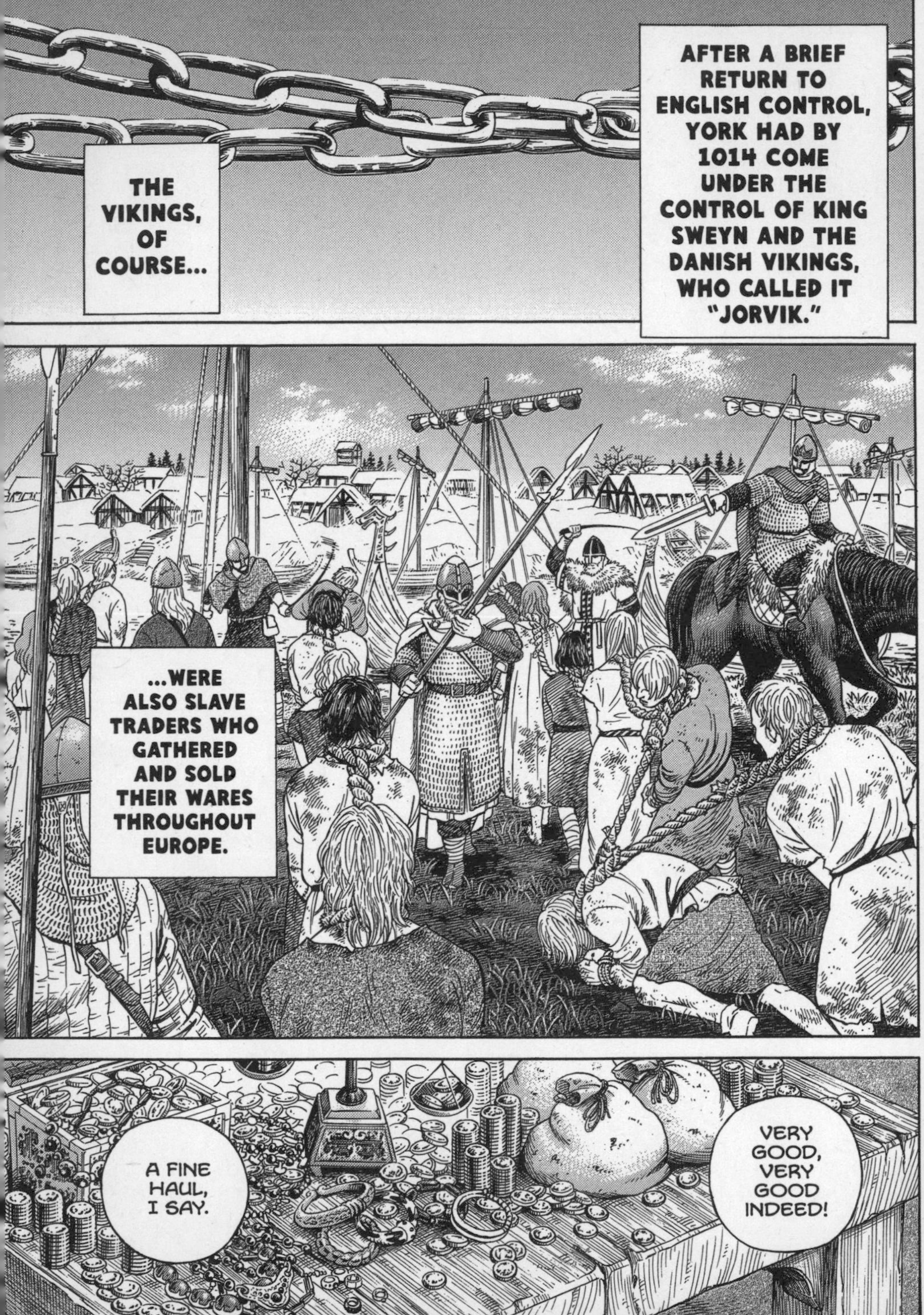
AFTER A BRIEF RETURN TO ENGLISH CONTROL, YORK HAD BY 1014 COME UNDER THE CONTROL OF KING SWEYN AND THE DANISH VIKINGS, WHO CALLED IT "JORVIK."
THE VIKINGS, OF COURSE...
...WERE ALSO SLAVE TRADERS WHO GATHERED AND SOLD THEIR WARES THROUGHOUT EUROPE.
VERY GOOD, VERY GOOD INDEED!
A FINE HAUL, I SAY.

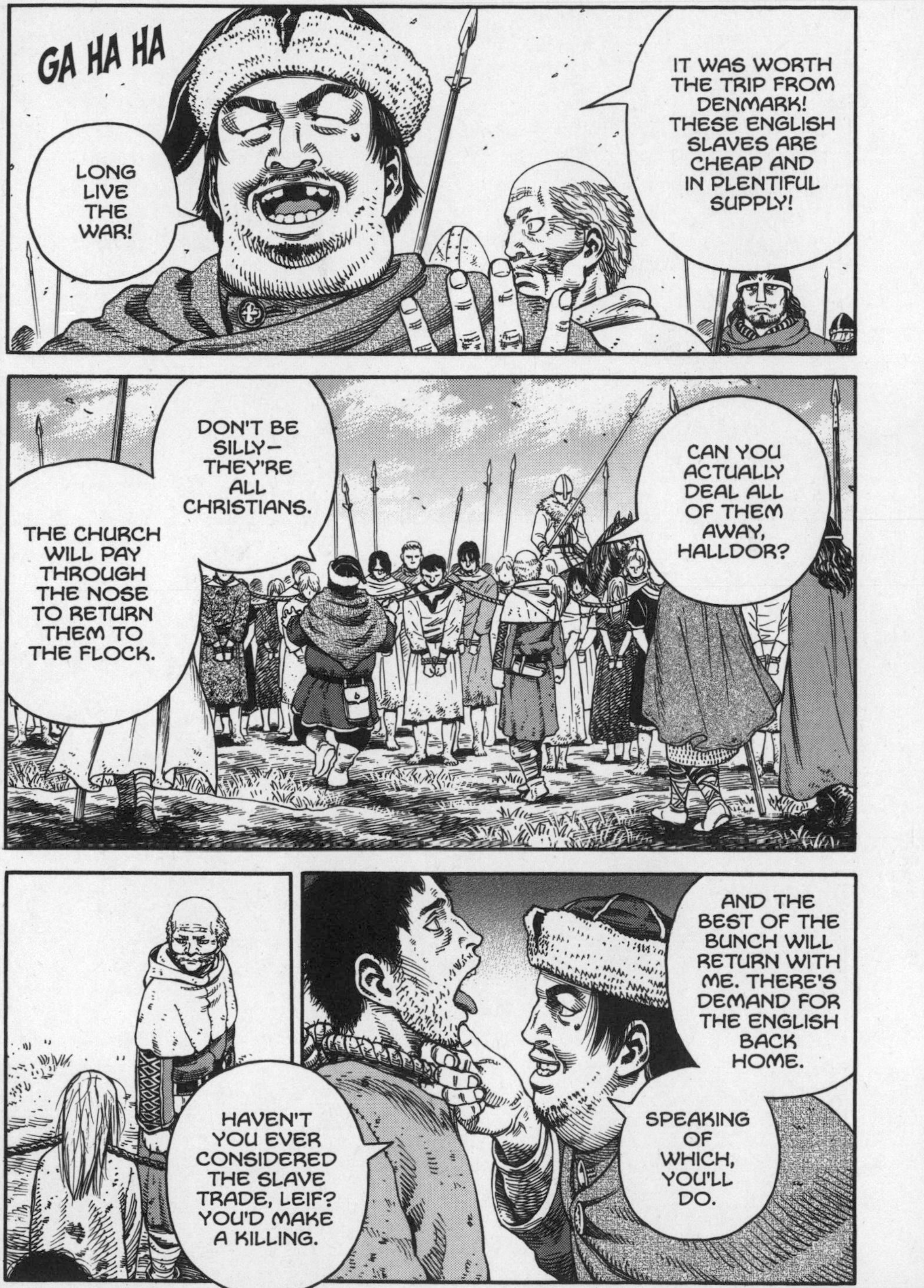
IT WAS WORTH THE TRIP FROM DENMARK! THESE ENGLISH SLAVES ARE CHEAP AND IN PLENTIFUL SUPPLY!
GA HA HA
LONG LIVE THE WAR!
CAN YOU ACTUALLY DEAL ALL OF THEM AWAY, HALLDOR?
DON'T BE SILLY—THEY'RE ALL CHRISTIANS.
THE CHURCH WILL PAY THROUGH THE NOSE TO RETURN THEM TO THE FLOCK.
AND THE BEST OF THE BUNCH WILL RETURN WITH ME. THERE'S DEMAND FOR THE ENGLISH BACK HOME.
SPEAKING OF WHICH, YOU'LL DO.
HAVEN'T YOU EVER CONSIDERED THE SLAVE TRADE, LEIF? YOU'D MAKE A KILLING.

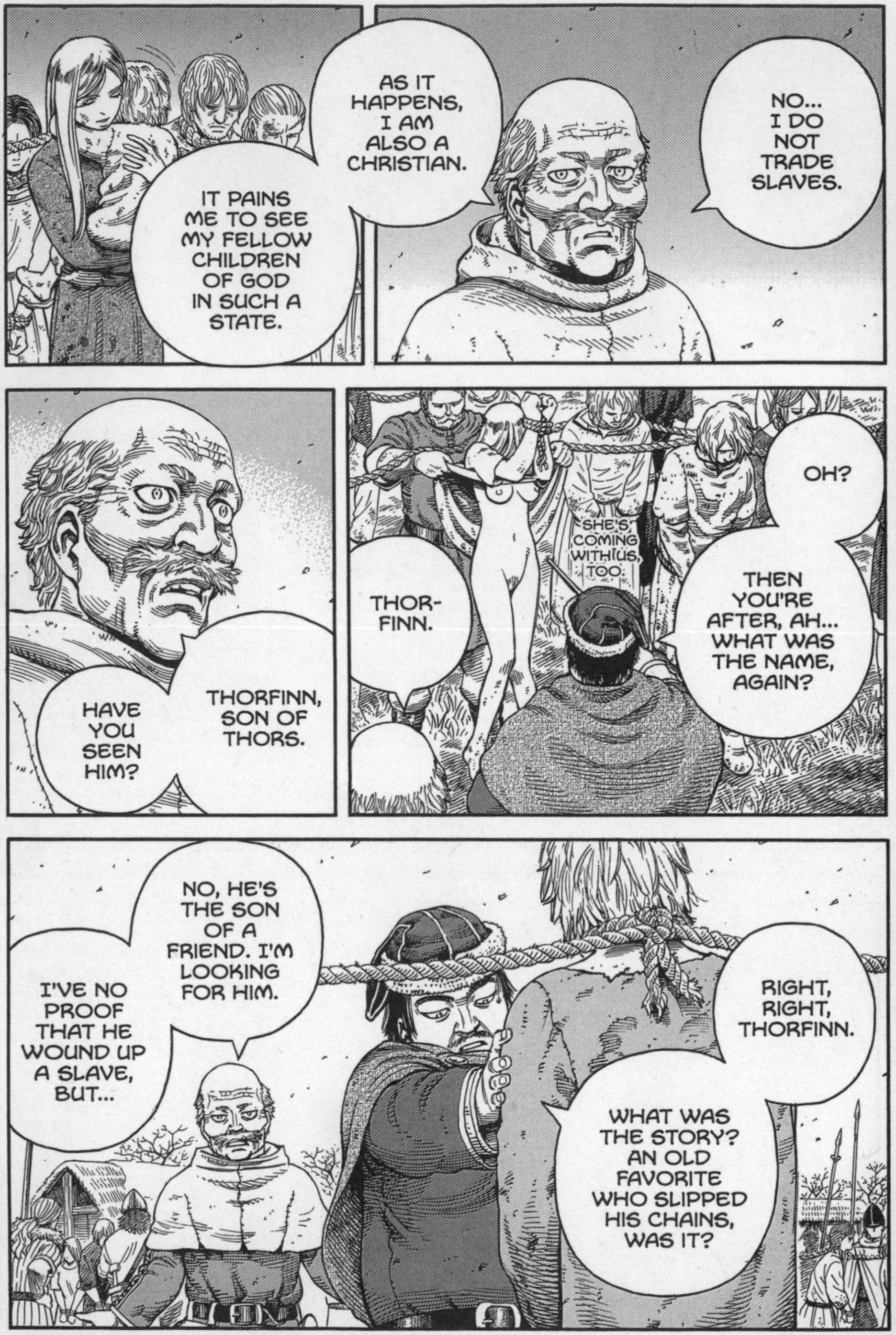
NO... I DO NOT TRADE SLAVES.
AS IT HAPPENS, I AM ALSO A CHRISTIAN.
IT PAINS ME TO SEE MY FELLOW CHILDREN OF GOD IN SUCH A STATE.
OH?
THEN YOU'RE AFTER, AH... WHAT WAS THE NAME, AGAIN?
SHE'S COMING WITH US, TOO.
THORFINN.
THORFINN, SON OF THORS.
HAVE YOU SEEN HIM?
RIGHT, RIGHT, THORFINN.
WHAT WAS THE STORY? AN OLD FAVORITE WHO SLIPPED HIS CHAINS, WAS IT?
NO, HE'S THE SON OF A FRIEND. I'M LOOKING FOR HIM.
I'VE NO PROOF THAT HE WOUND UP A SLAVE, BUT...

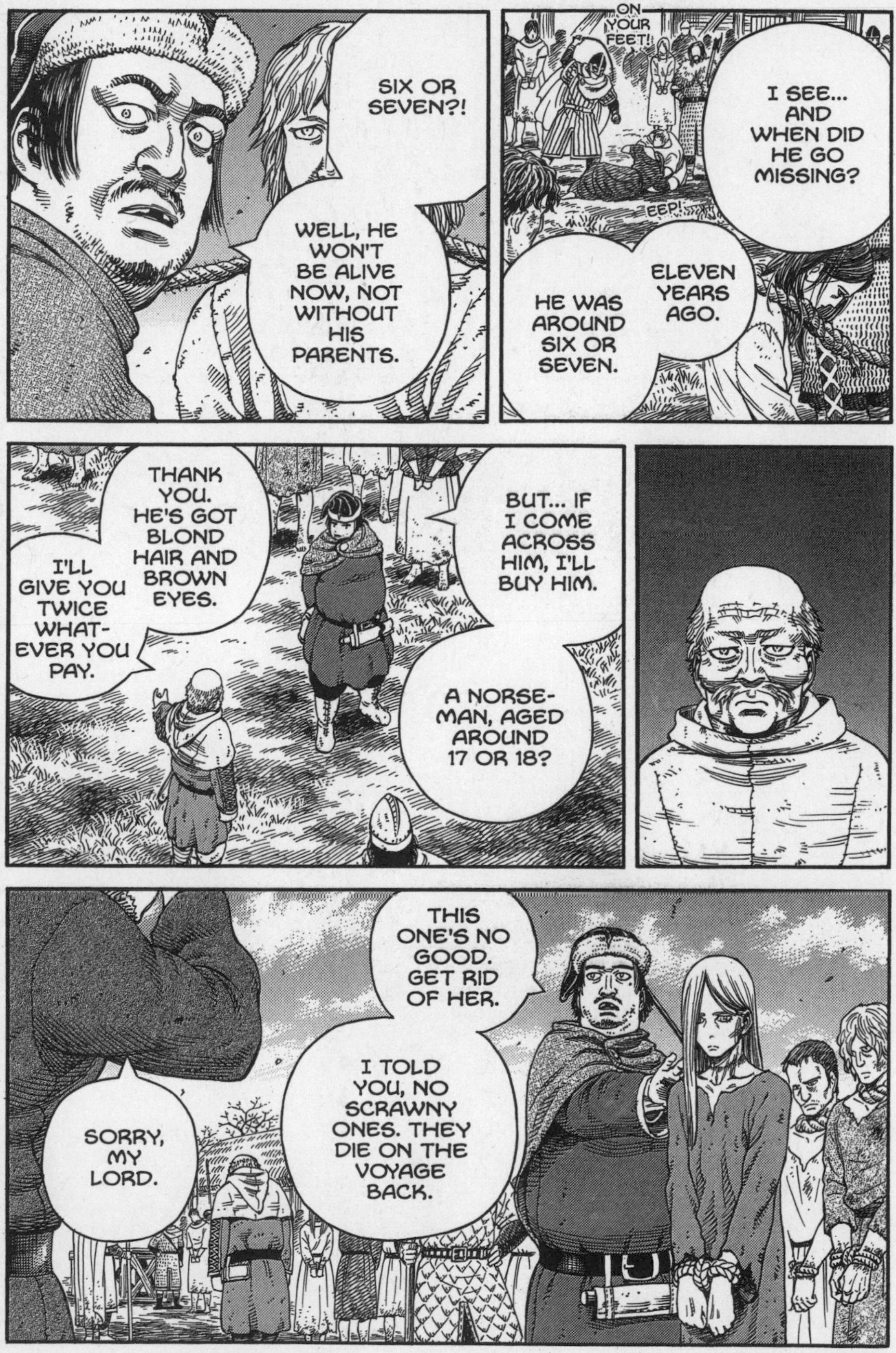
ON YOUR FEET!
I SEE... AND WHEN DID HE GO MISSING?
EEP!
ELEVEN YEARS AGO.
HE WAS AROUND SIX OR SEVEN.
SIX OR SEVEN?!
WELL, HE WON'T BE ALIVE NOW, NOT WITHOUT HIS PARENTS.
BUT... IF I COME ACROSS HIM, I'LL BUY HIM.
A NORSE-MAN, AGED AROUND 17 OR 18?
THANK YOU. HE'S GOT BLOND HAIR AND BROWN EYES.
I'LL GIVE YOU TWICE WHAT-EVER YOU PAY.
THIS ONE'S NO GOOD. GET RID OF HER.
I TOLD YOU, NO SCRAWNY ONES. THEY DIE ON THE VOYAGE BACK.
SORRY, MY LORD.

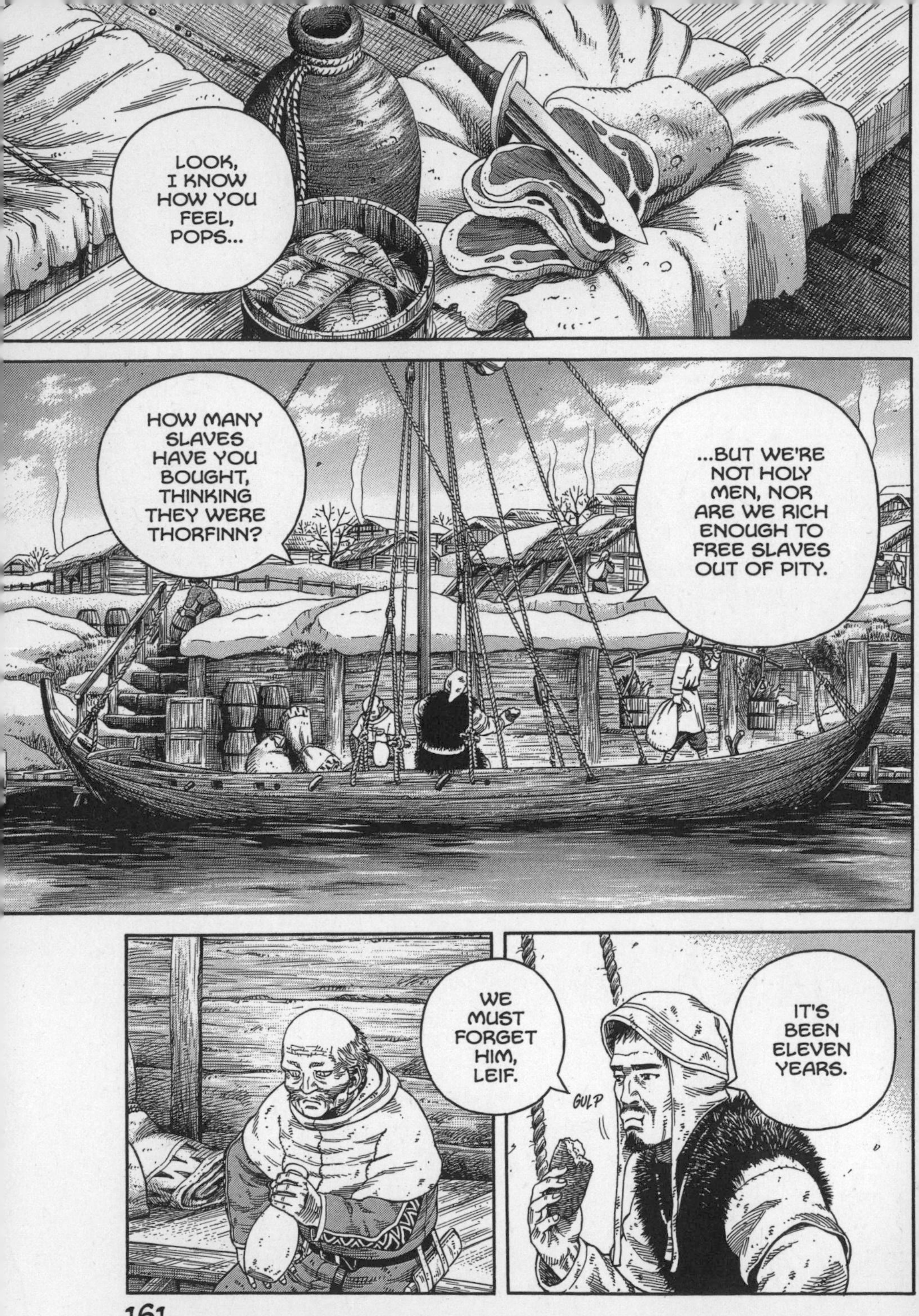
LOOK, I KNOW HOW YOU FEEL, POPS...
...BUT WE'RE NOT HOLY MEN, NOR ARE WE RICH ENOUGH TO FREE SLAVES OUT OF PITY.
HOW MANY SLAVES HAVE YOU BOUGHT, THINKING THEY WERE THORFINN?
IT'S BEEN ELEVEN YEARS.
WE MUST FORGET HIM, LEIF.
GULP

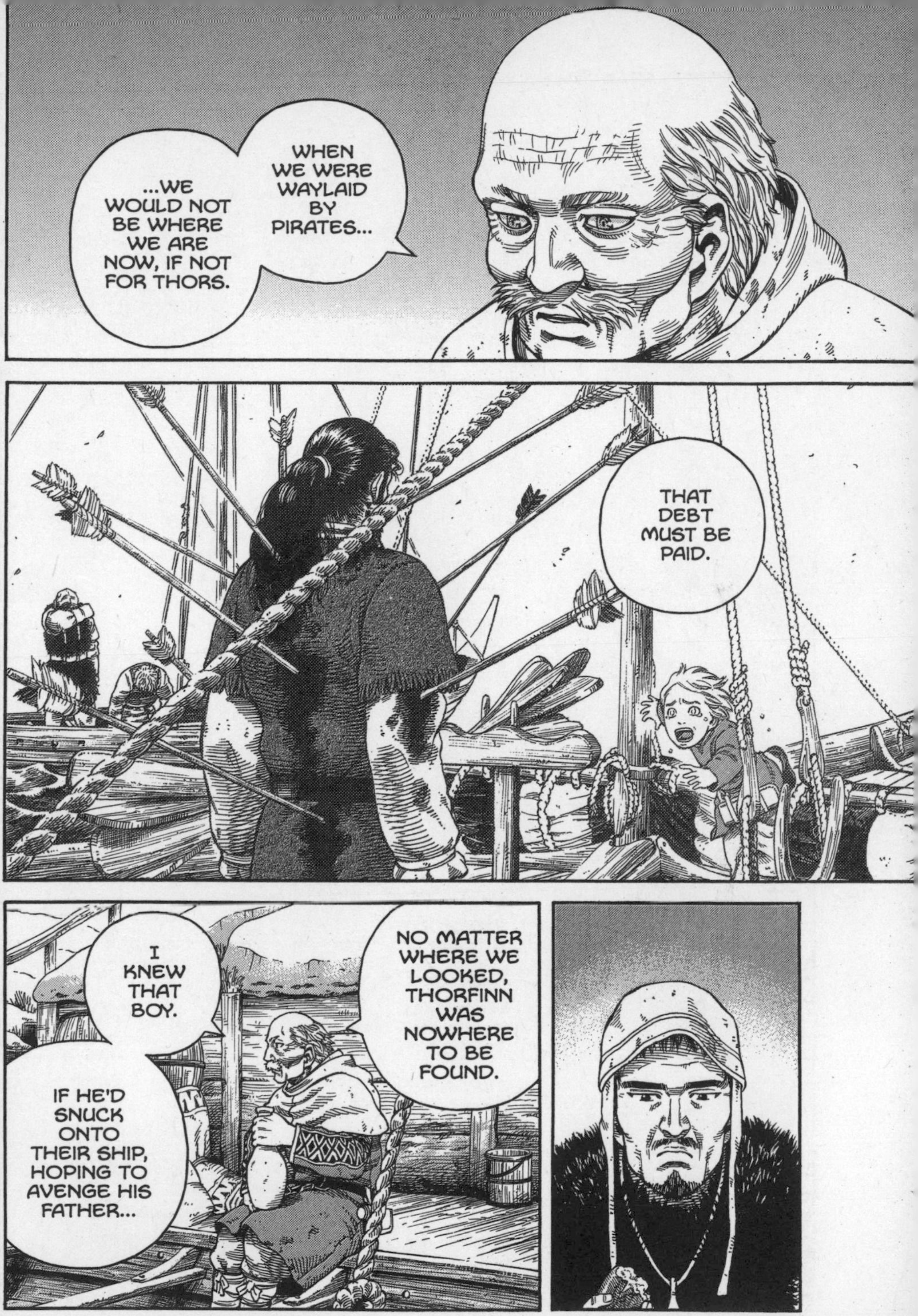
WHEN WE WERE WAYLAID BY PIRATES...
...WE WOULD NOT BE WHERE WE ARE NOW, IF NOT FOR THORS.
THAT DEBT MUST BE PAID.
NO MATTER WHERE WE LOOKED, THORFINN WAS NOWHERE TO BE FOUND.
I KNEW THAT BOY.
IF HE'D SNUCK ONTO THEIR SHIP, HOPING TO AVENGE HIS FATHER...

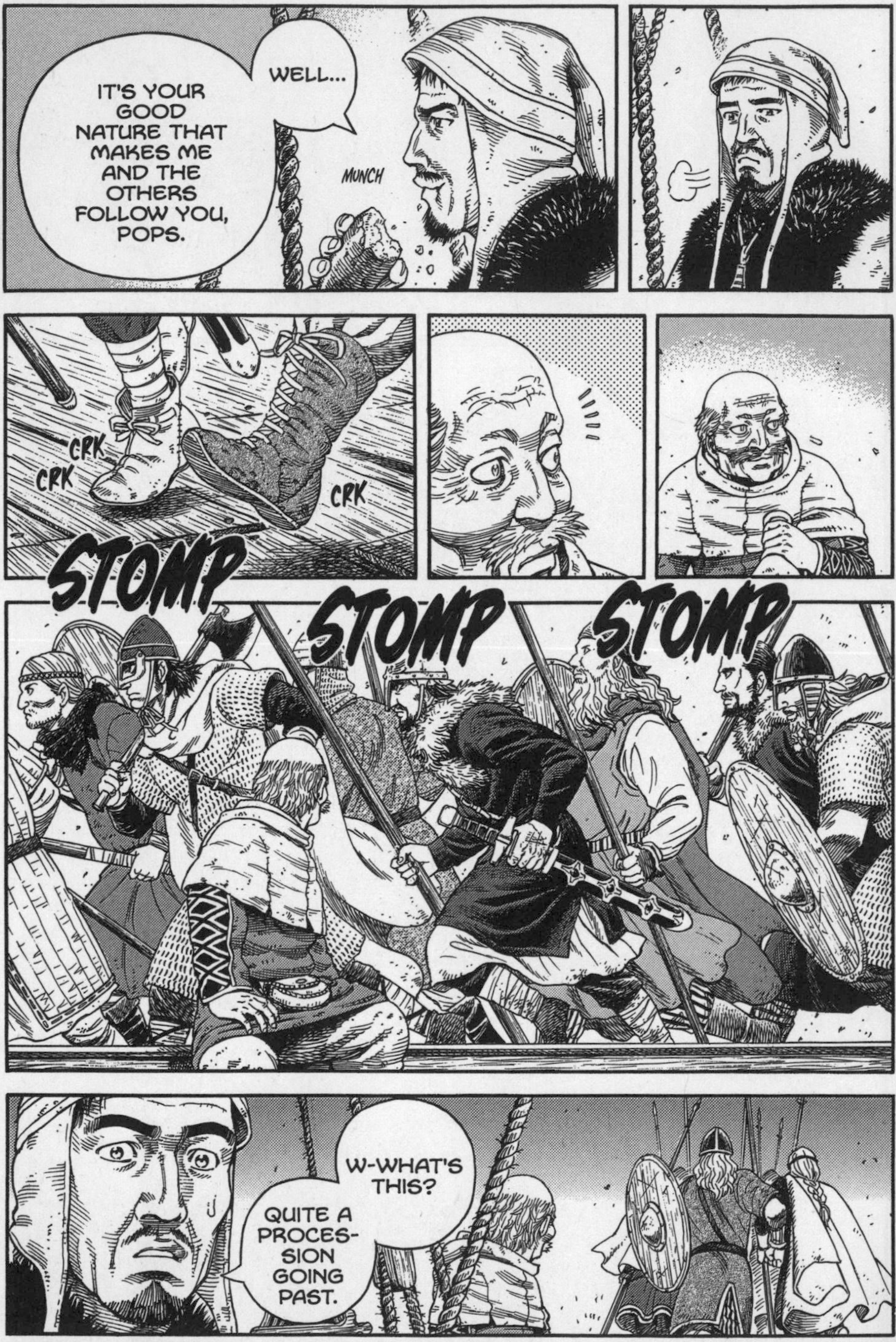
WELL...
IT'S YOUR GOOD NATURE THAT MAKES ME AND THE OTHERS FOLLOW YOU, POPS.
MUNCH
CRK
CRK
CRK
STOMP
STOMP
STOMP
W-WHAT'S THIS?
QUITE A PROCES-SION GOING PAST.

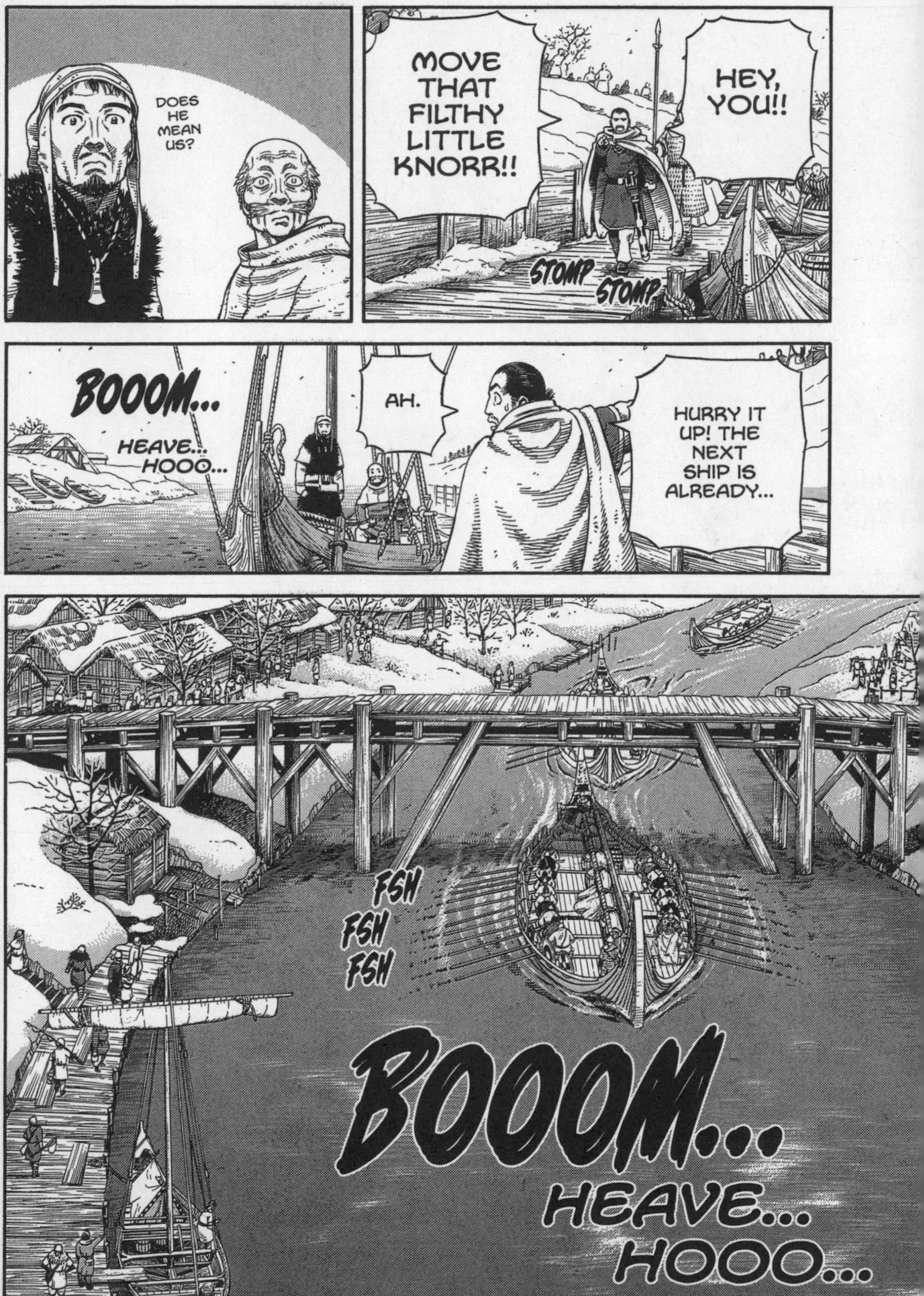
HEY, YOU!!
MOVE THAT FILTHY LITTLE KNORR!!
STOMP
STOMP
DOES HE MEAN US?
HURRY IT UP! THE NEXT SHIP IS ALREADY...
AH.
BOOOM...
HEAVE... HOOO...
FSH
FSH
FSH
BOOOM...
HEAVE... HOOO...

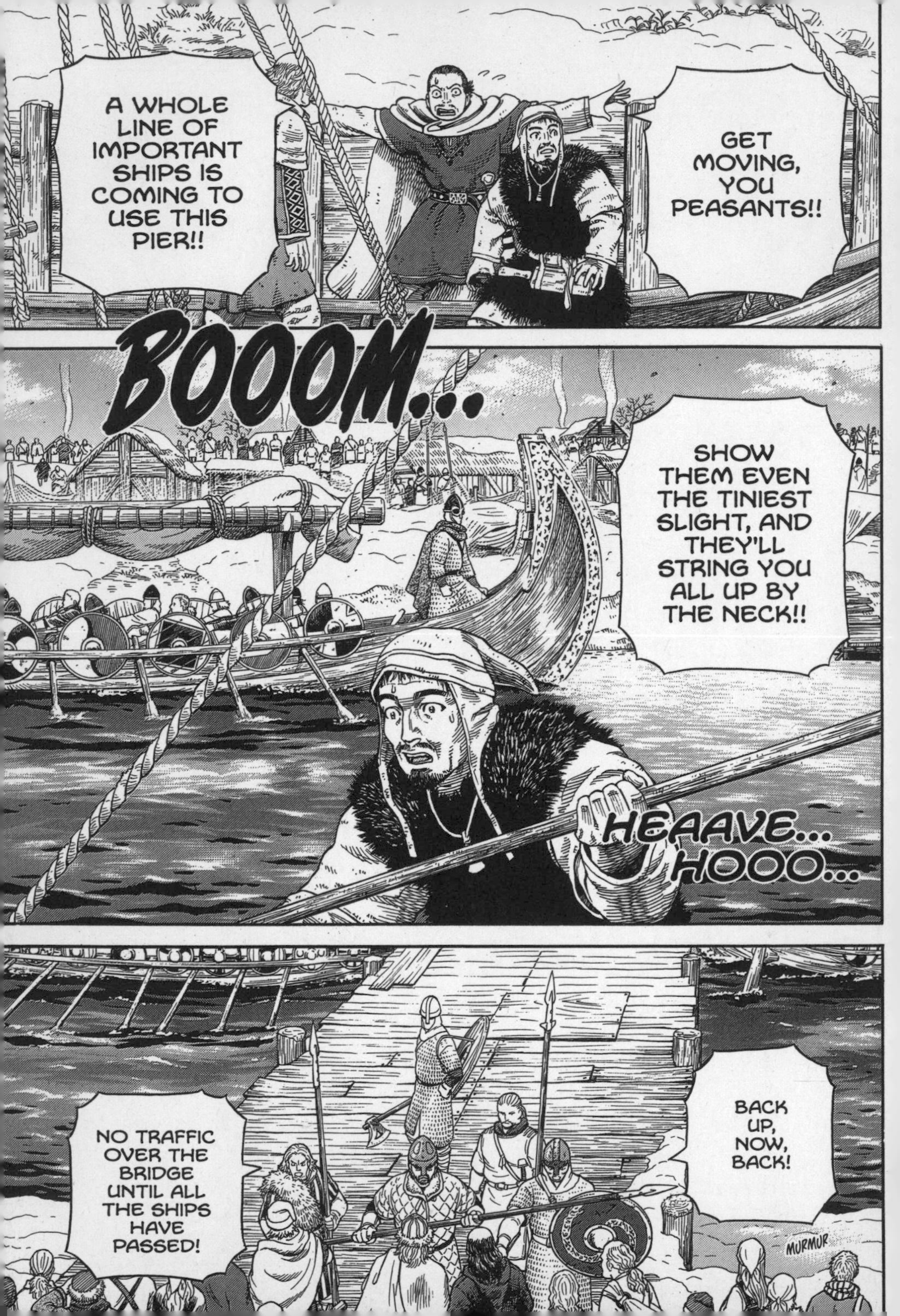
GET MOVING, YOU PEASANTS!!
A WHOLE LINE OF IMPORTANT SHIPS IS COMING TO USE THIS PIER!!
BOOOM...
SHOW THEM EVEN THE TINIEST SLIGHT, AND THEY'LL STRING YOU ALL UP BY THE NECK!!
HEAAVE... HOOO...
BACK UP, NOW, BACK!
NO TRAFFIC OVER THE BRIDGE UNTIL ALL THE SHIPS HAVE PASSED!
MURMUR

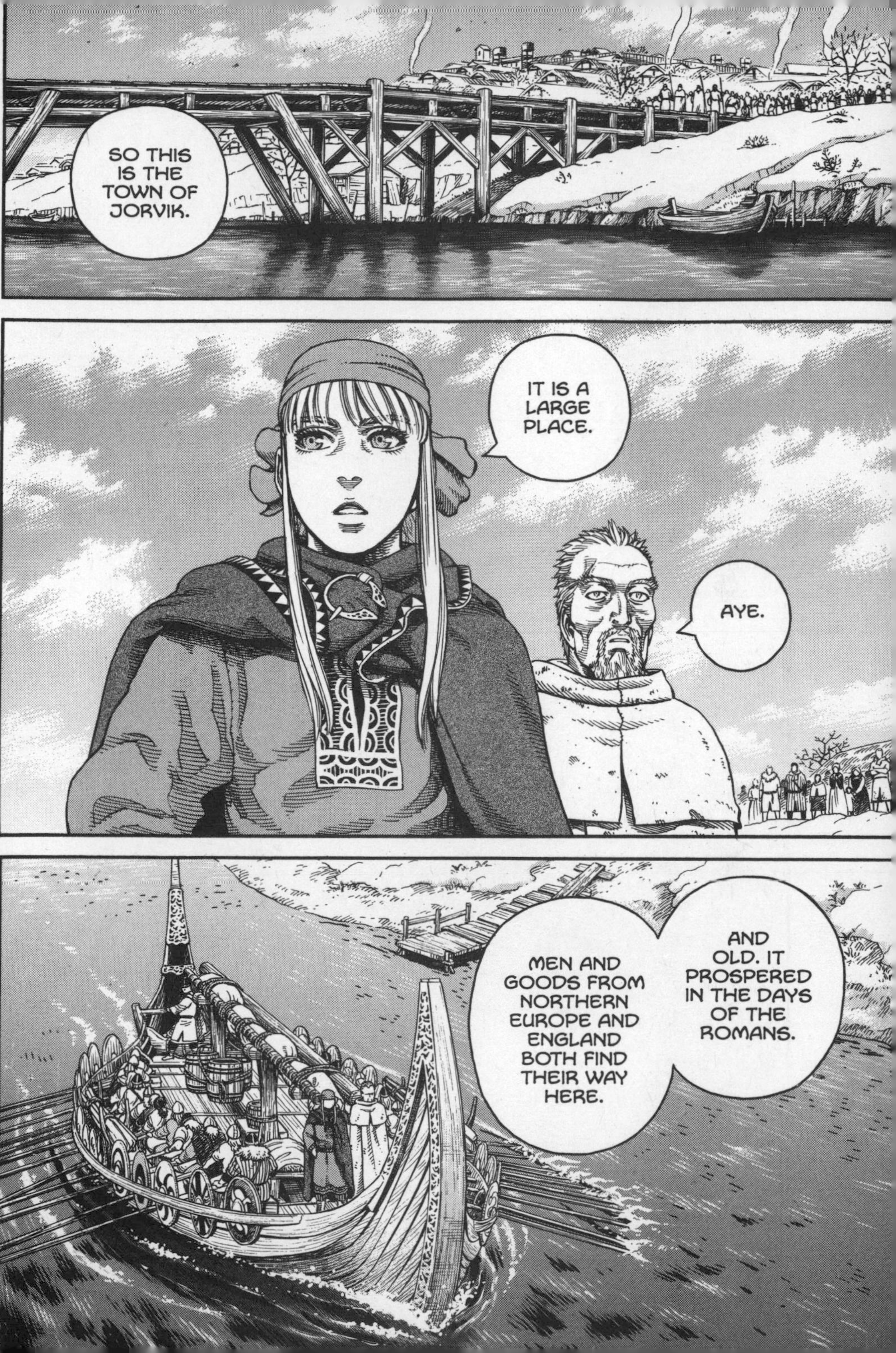
SO THIS IS THE TOWN OF JORVIK.
IT IS A LARGE PLACE.
AYE.
AND OLD. IT PROSPERED IN THE DAYS OF THE ROMANS.
MEN AND GOODS FROM NORTHERN EUROPE AND ENGLAND BOTH FIND THEIR WAY HERE.

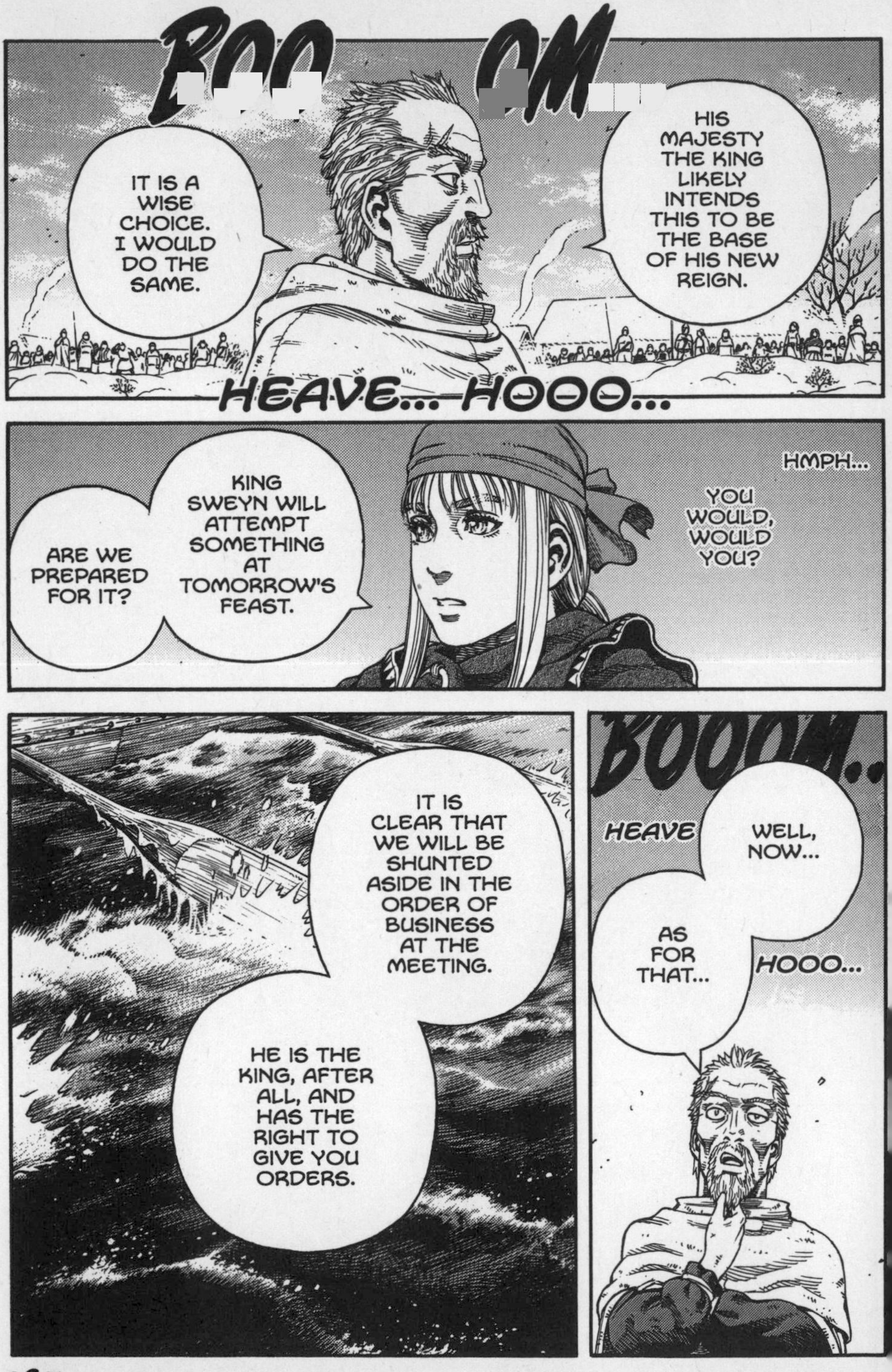
BOO OM
HIS MAJESTY THE KING LIKELY INTENDS THIS TO BE THE BASE OF HIS NEW REIGN.
IT IS A WISE CHOICE. I WOULD DO THE SAME.
HEAVE... HOOO...
HMPH...
YOU WOULD, WOULD YOU?
KING SWEYN WILL ATTEMPT SOMETHING AT TOMORROW'S FEAST.
ARE WE PREPARED FOR IT?
BOOOM...
HEAVE
WELL, NOW...
AS FOR THAT...
HOOO...
IT IS CLEAR THAT WE WILL BE SHUNTED ASIDE IN THE ORDER OF BUSINESS AT THE MEETING.
HE IS THE KING, AFTER ALL, AND HAS THE RIGHT TO GIVE YOU ORDERS.

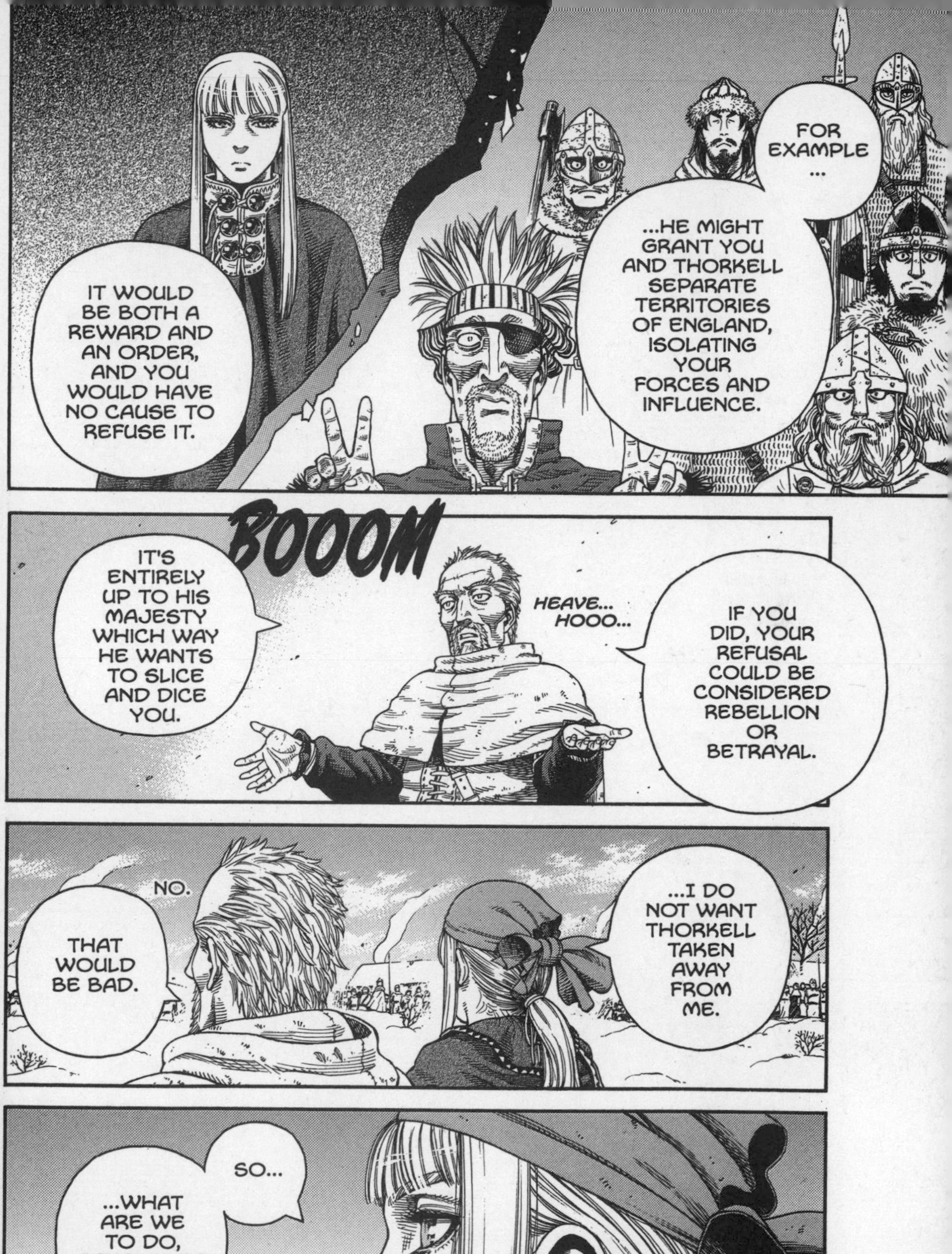
FOR EXAMPLE ...
...HE MIGHT GRANT YOU AND THORKELL SEPARATE TERRITORIES OF ENGLAND, ISOLATING YOUR FORCES AND INFLUENCE.
IT WOULD BE BOTH A REWARD AND AN ORDER, AND YOU WOULD HAVE NO CAUSE TO REFUSE IT.
BOOOM
IF YOU DID, YOUR REFUSAL COULD BE CONSIDERED REBELLION OR BETRAYAL.
HEAVE... HOOO...
IT'S ENTIRELY UP TO HIS MAJESTY WHICH WAY HE WANTS TO SLICE AND DICE YOU.
...I DO NOT WANT THORKELL TAKEN AWAY FROM ME.
NO.
THAT WOULD BE BAD.
SO...
...WHAT ARE WE TO DO, ASKELADD?

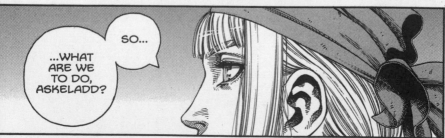

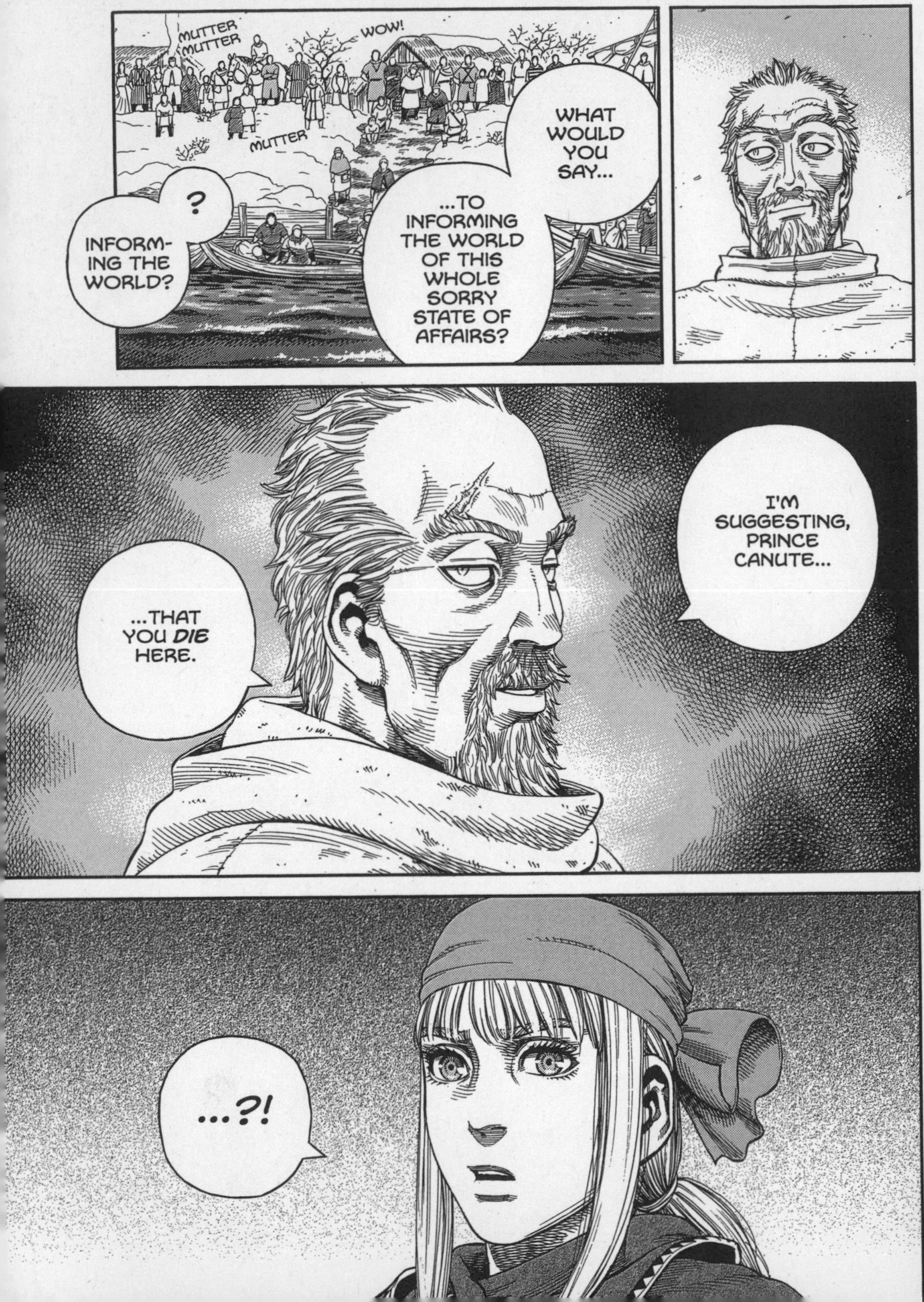
WOW!
MUTTER MUTTER
MUTTER
WHAT WOULD YOU SAY...
...TO INFORMING THE WORLD OF THIS WHOLE SORRY STATE OF AFFAIRS?
? INFORMING THE WORLD?
I'M SUGGESTING, PRINCE CANUTE...
...THAT YOU *DIE* HERE.
...?!

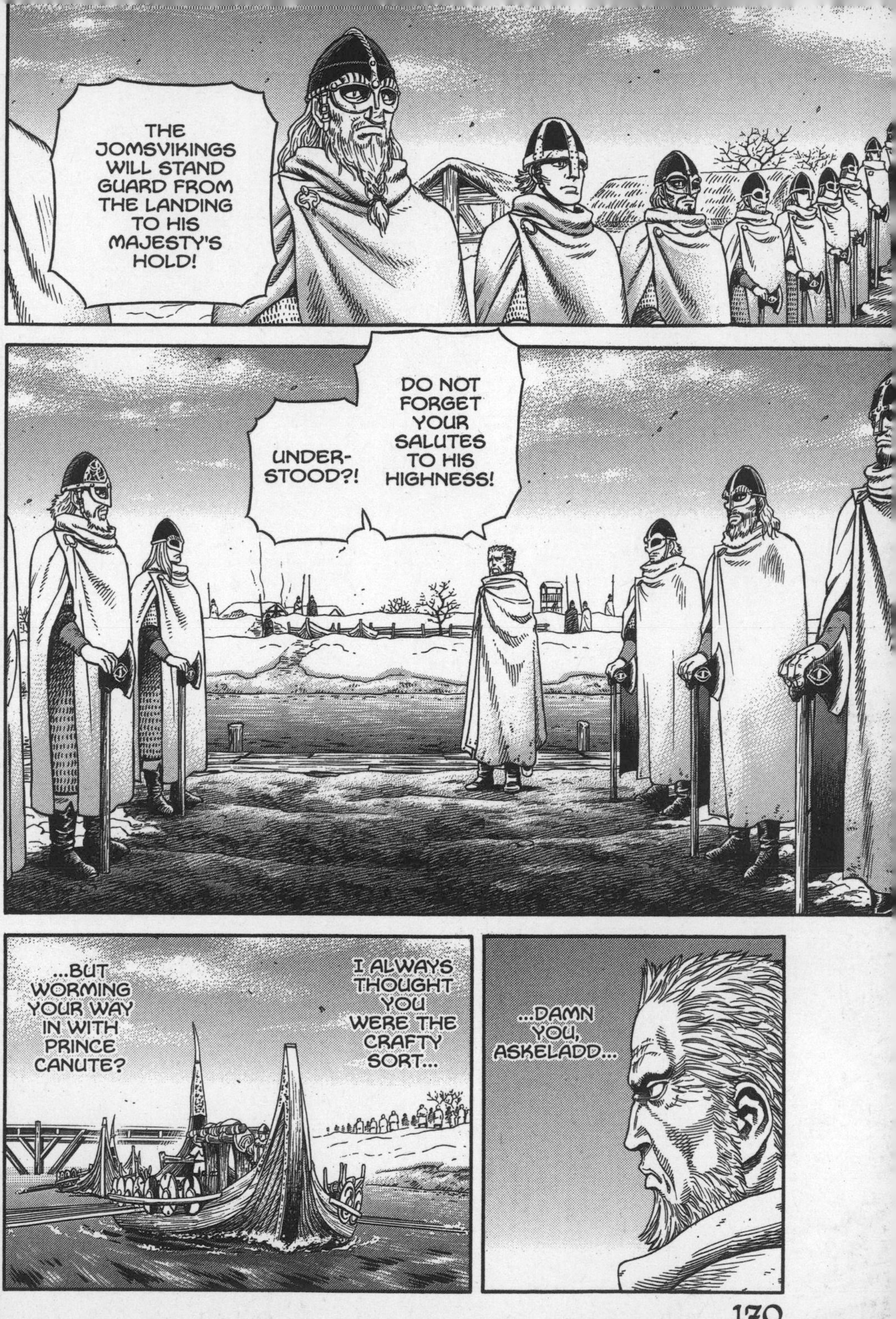
THE JOMSVIKINGS WILL STAND GUARD FROM THE LANDING TO HIS MAJESTY'S HOLD!
DO NOT FORGET YOUR SALUTES TO HIS HIGHNESS!
UNDER-STOOD?!
...DAMN YOU, ASKELADD...
I ALWAYS THOUGHT YOU WERE THE CRAFTY SORT...
...BUT WORMING YOUR WAY IN WITH PRINCE CANUTE?

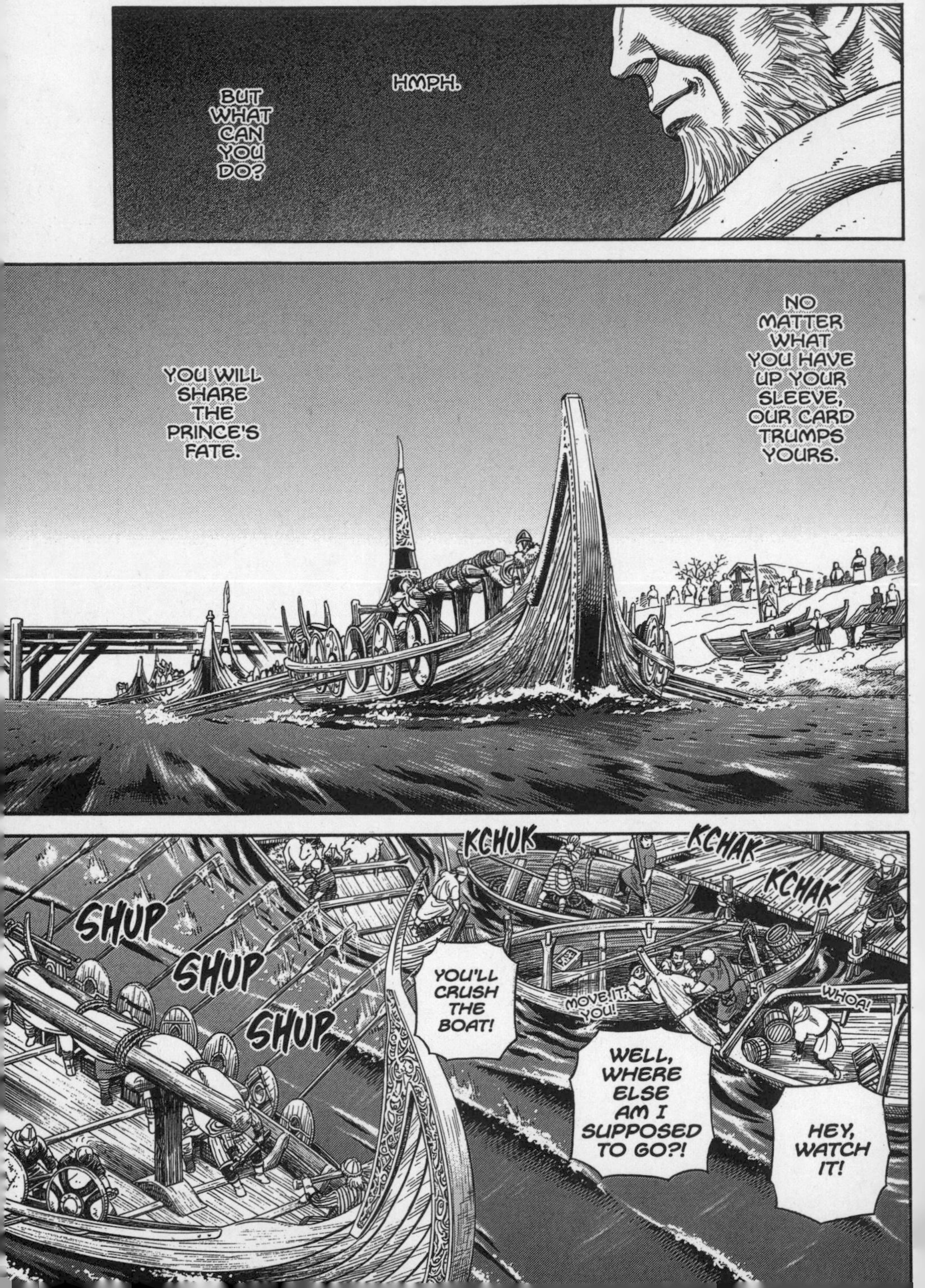
HMPH.
BUT WHAT CAN YOU DO?
NO MATTER WHAT YOU HAVE UP YOUR SLEEVE, OUR CARD TRUMPS YOURS.
YOU WILL SHARE THE PRINCE'S FATE.
KCHAK
KCHAK
KCHUK
WHOA!
MOVE IT, YOU!
YOU'LL CRUSH THE BOAT!
SHUP
SHUP
SHUP
HEY, WATCH IT!
WELL, WHERE ELSE AM I SUPPOSED TO GO?!

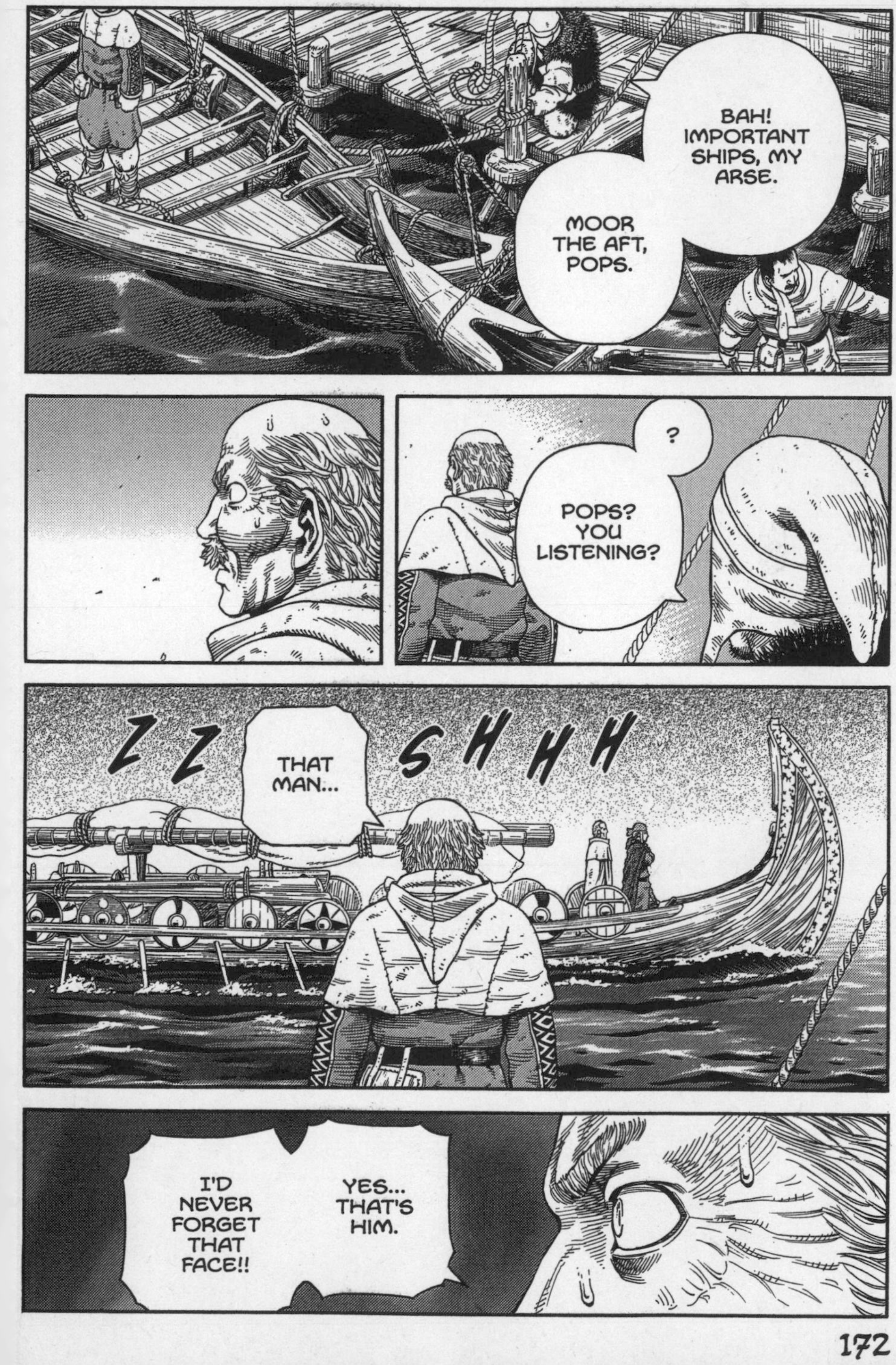
BAH! IMPORTANT SHIPS, MY ARSE.
MOOR THE AFT, POPS.
?
POPS? YOU LISTENING?
SHHH
THAT MAN...
ZZ
YES... THAT'S HIM.
I'D NEVER FORGET THAT FACE!!

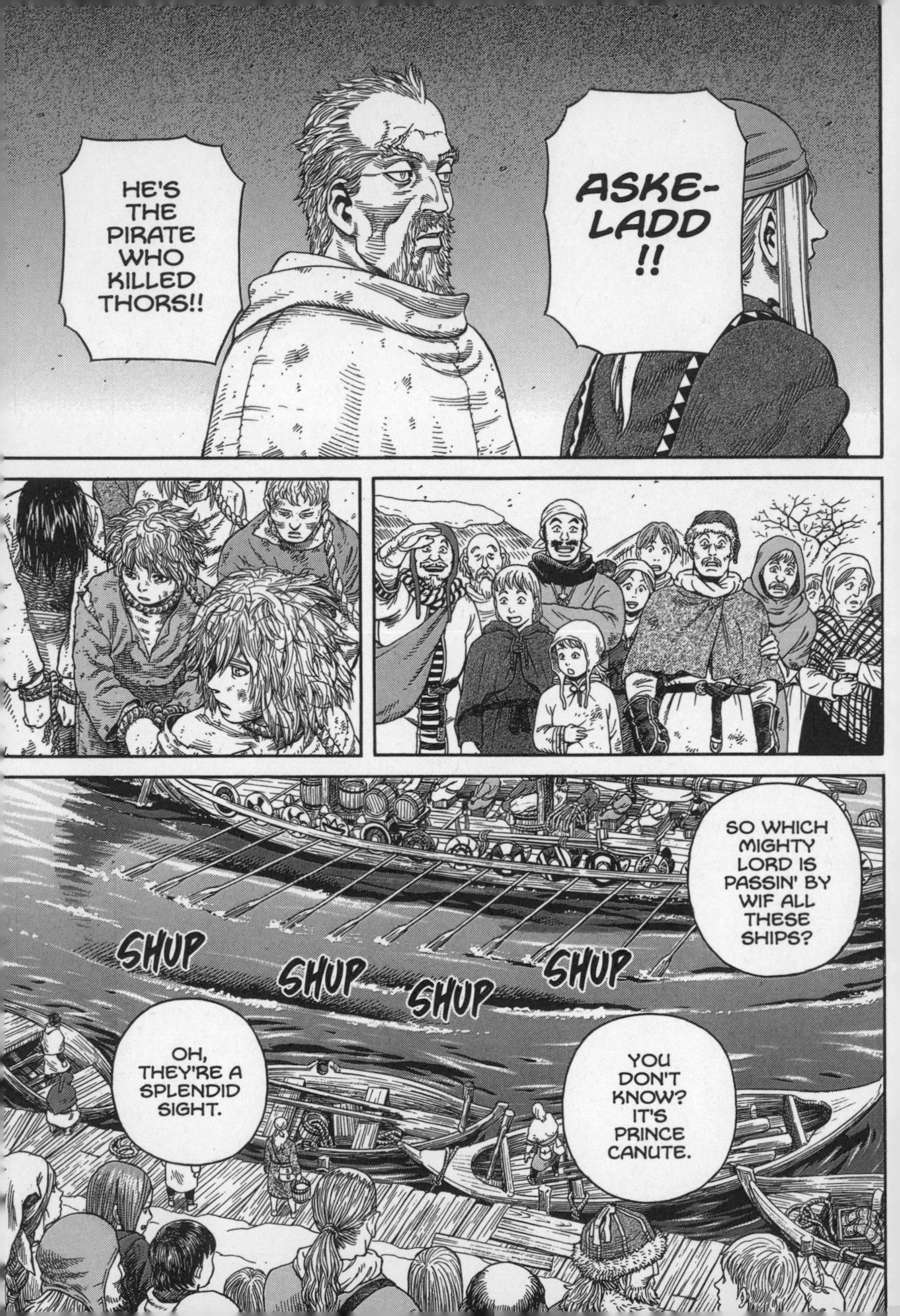

ASKE-LADD!!
HE'S THE PIRATE WHO KILLED THORS!!
SO WHICH MIGHTY LORD IS PASSIN' BY WIF ALL THESE SHIPS?
SHUP
SHUP
SHUP
SHUP
YOU DON'T KNOW? IT'S PRINCE CANUTE.
OH, THEY'RE A SPLENDID SIGHT.

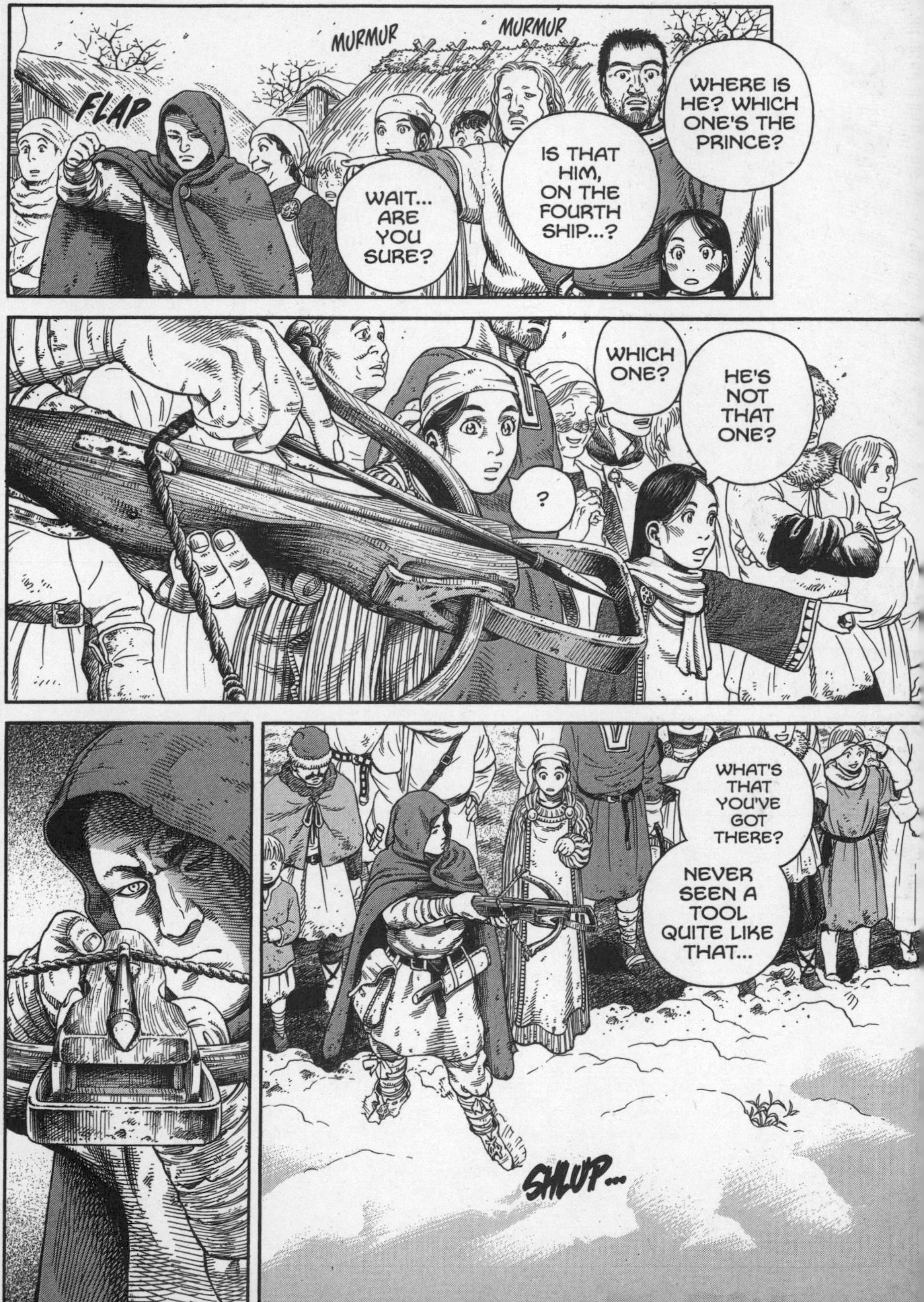
MURMUR
MURMUR
WHERE IS HE? WHICH ONE'S THE PRINCE?
IS THAT HIM, ON THE FOURTH SHIP...?
WAIT... ARE YOU SURE?
FLAP
HE'S NOT THAT ONE?
WHICH ONE?
?
WHAT'S THAT YOU'VE GOT THERE?
NEVER SEEN A TOOL QUITE LIKE THAT...
SHLUP...

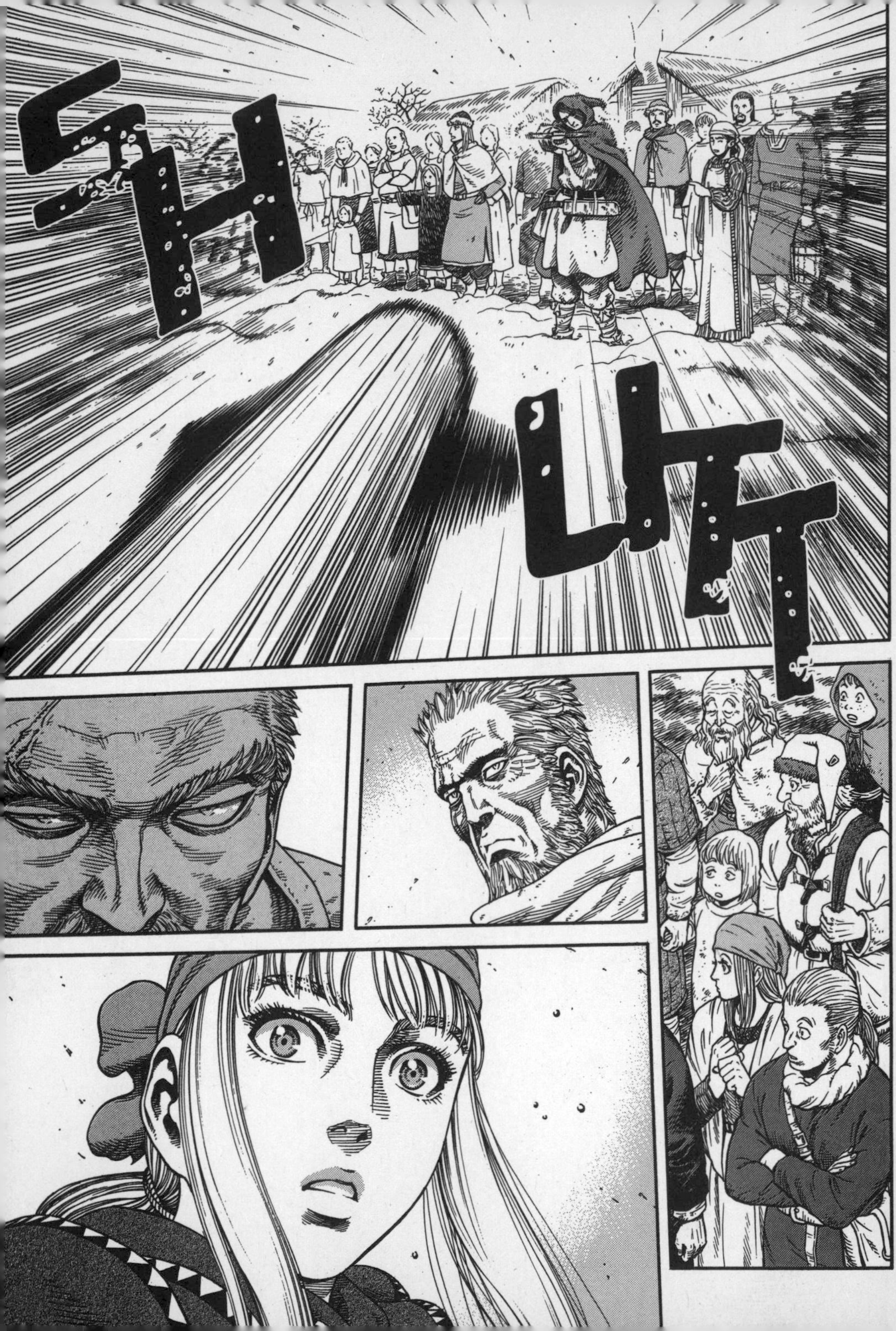
SHUFT

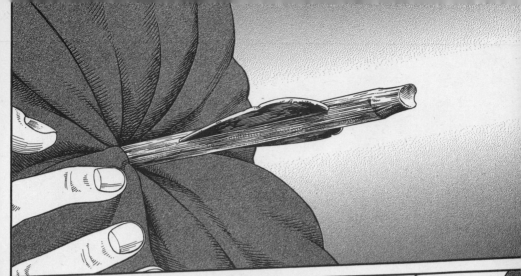

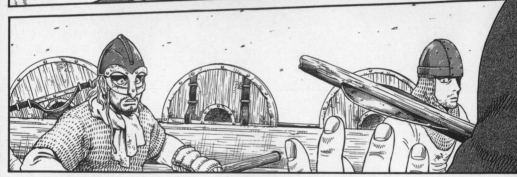

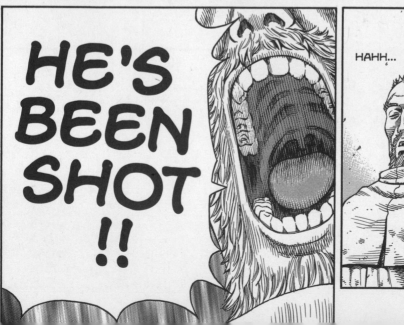

HE'S BEEN SHOT !!

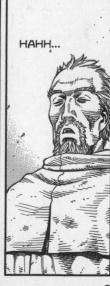

HAHH...

176

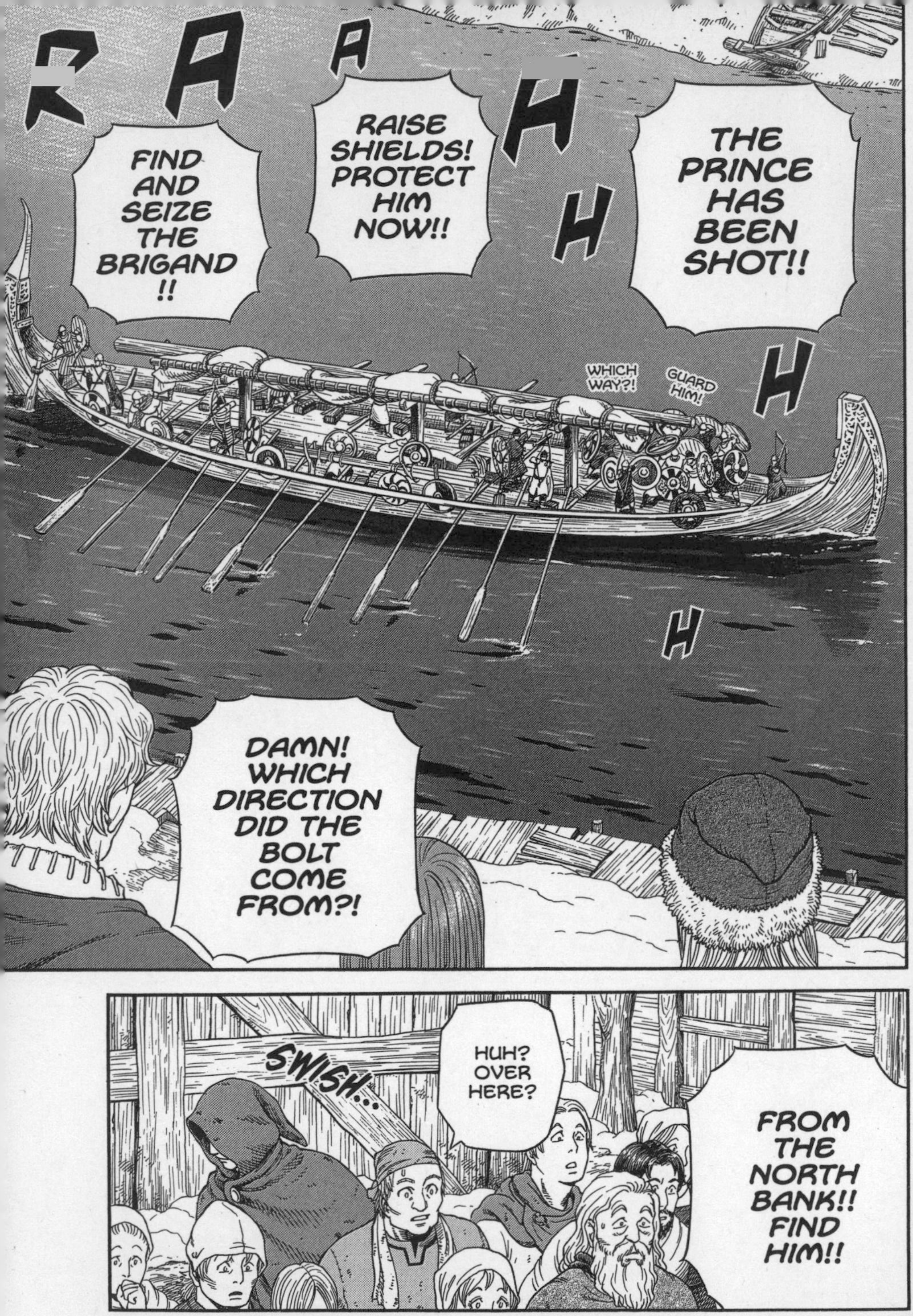
RAAAHHHH
THE PRINCE HAS BEEN SHOT!!
RAISE SHIELDS! PROTECT HIM NOW!!
FIND AND SEIZE THE BRIGAND!!
GUARD HIM!
WHICH WAY?!
DAMN! WHICH DIRECTION DID THE BOLT COME FROM?!
FROM THE NORTH BANK!! FIND HIM!!
HUH? OVER HERE?
SWISH...

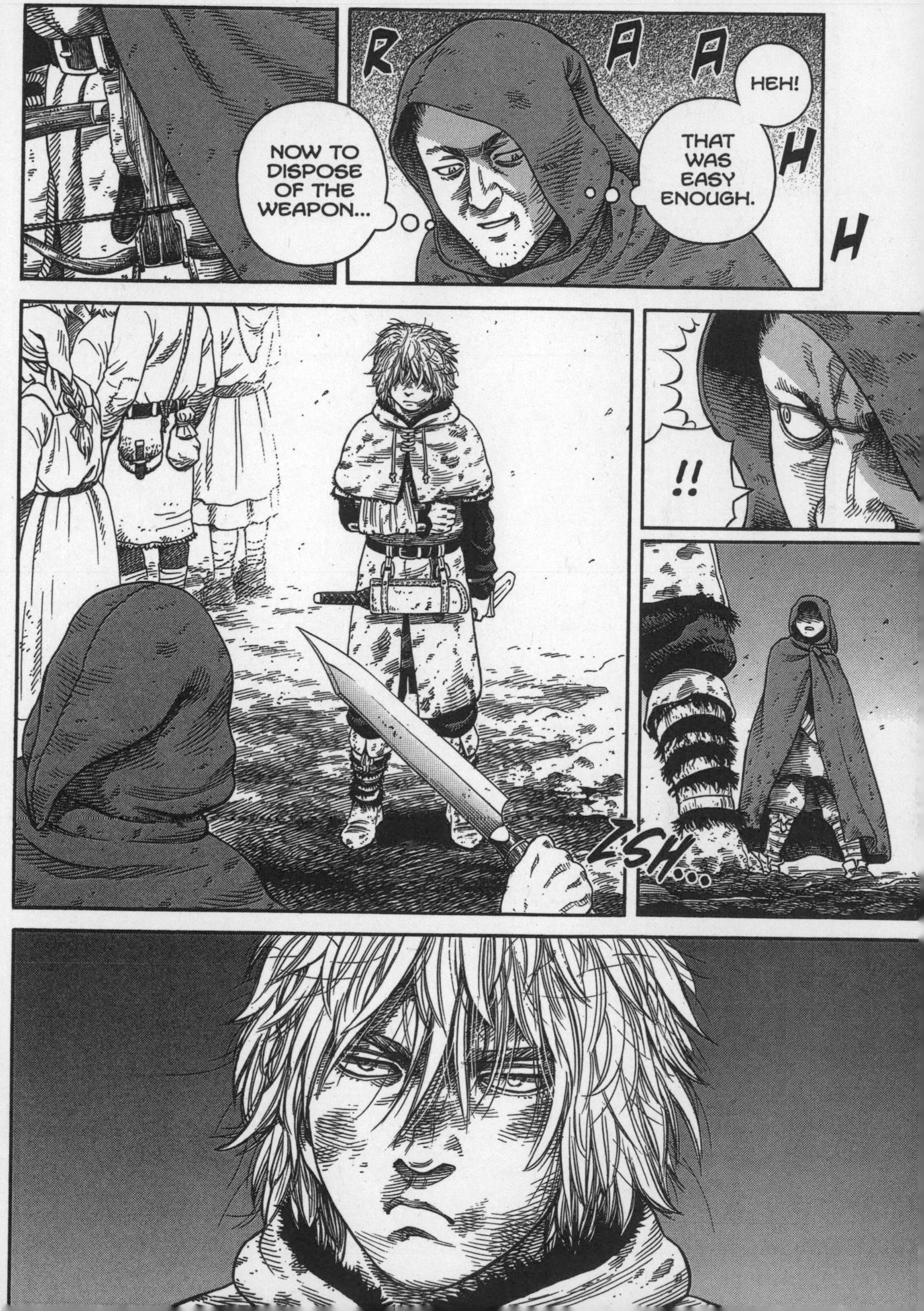
RAAAHH
HEH!
THAT WAS EASY ENOUGH.
NOW TO DISPOSE OF THE WEAPON...
!!
ZSH...

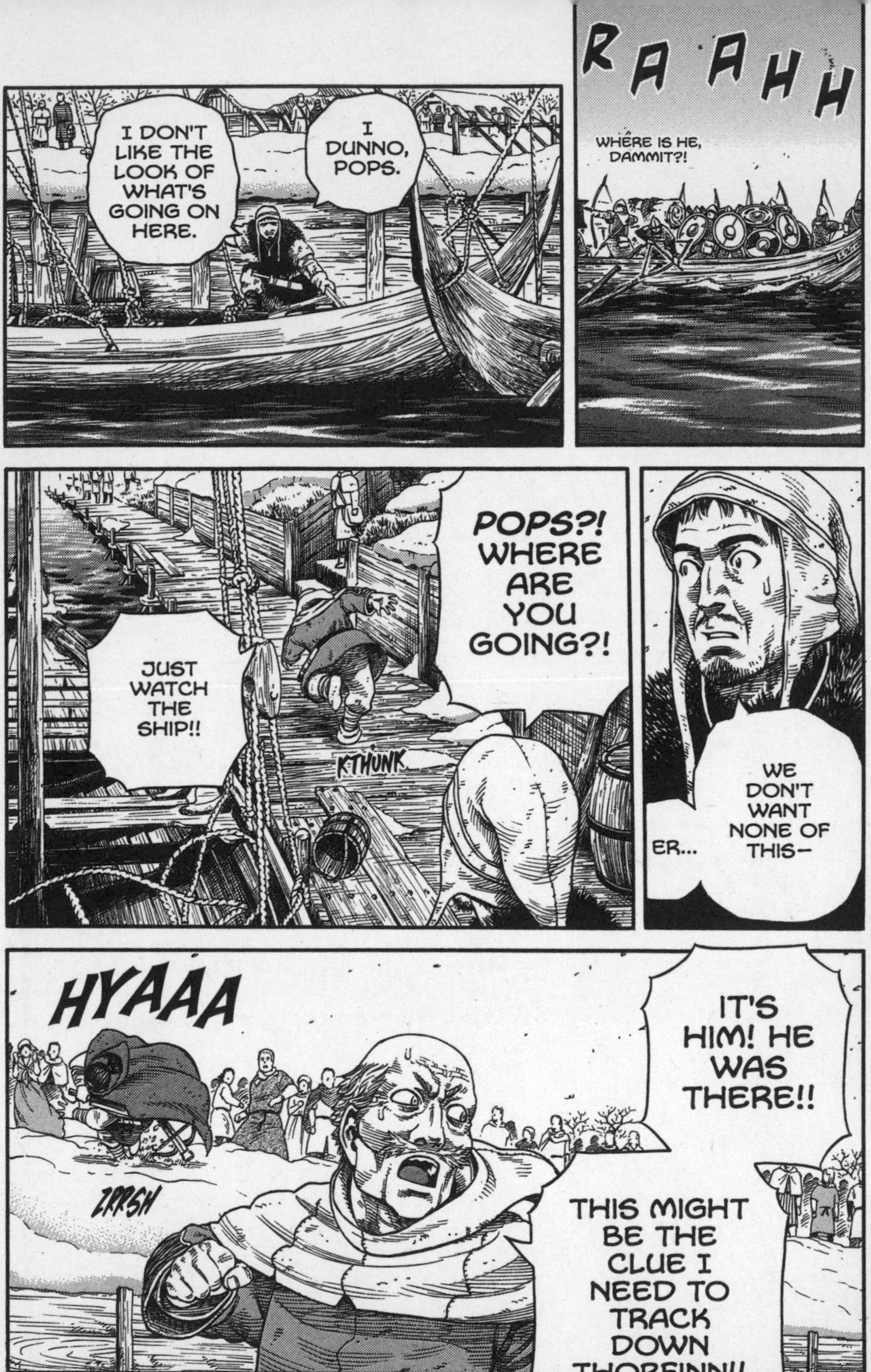

RAAHH
WHERE IS HE, DAMMIT?!
I DUNNO, POPS.
I DON'T LIKE THE LOOK OF WHAT'S GOING ON HERE.
WE DON'T WANT NONE OF THIS–
ER...
POPS?! WHERE ARE YOU GOING?!
JUST WATCH THE SHIP!!
K-THUNK
HYAAA
IT'S HIM! HE WAS THERE!!
ZRRSH
THIS MIGHT BE THE CLUE I NEED TO TRACK DOWN THORFINN!!

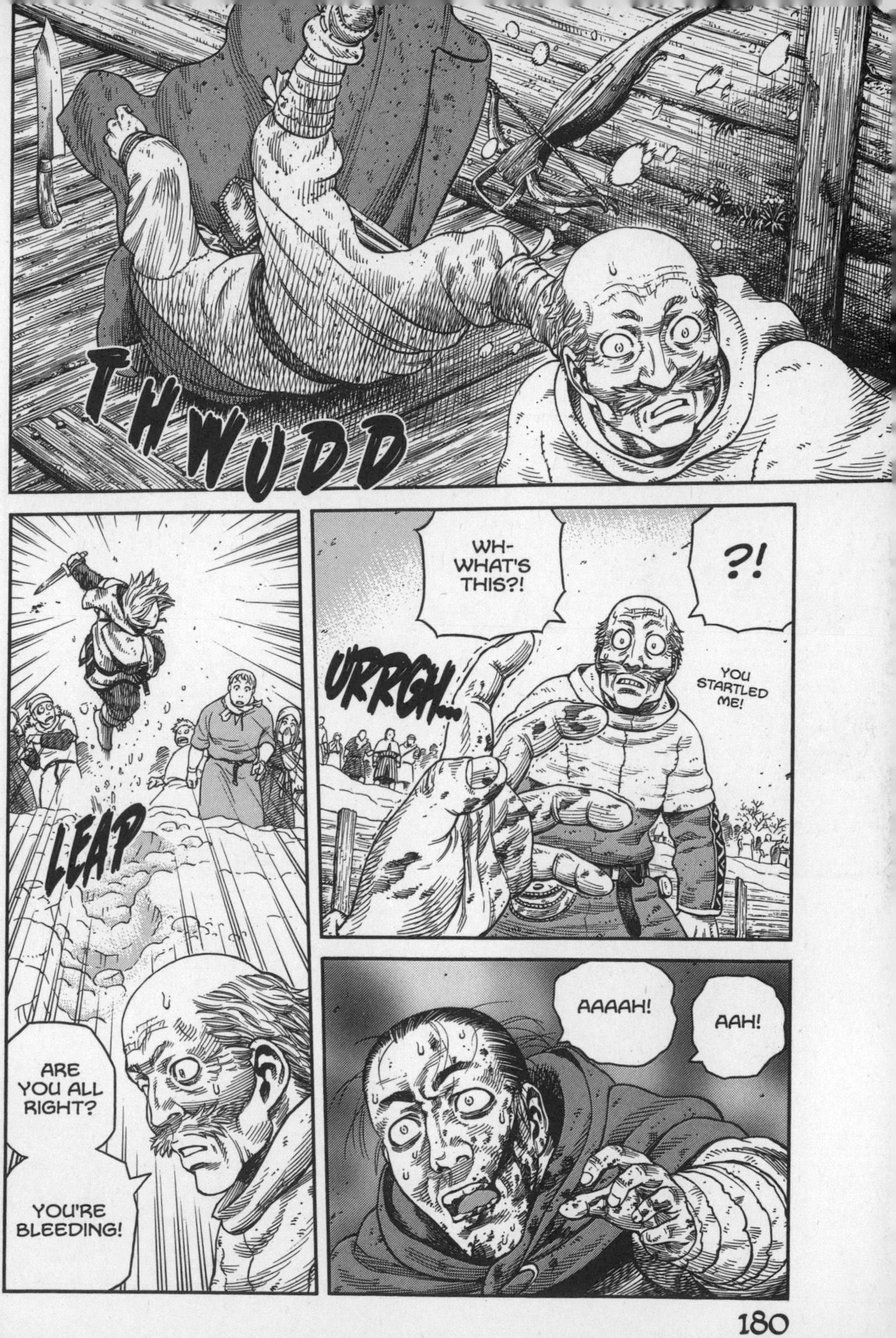
THWUDD
?!
WH- WHAT'S THIS?!
YOU STARTLED ME!
URRGH...
AAH!
AAAAH!
LEAP
ARE YOU ALL RIGHT?
YOU'RE BLEEDING!

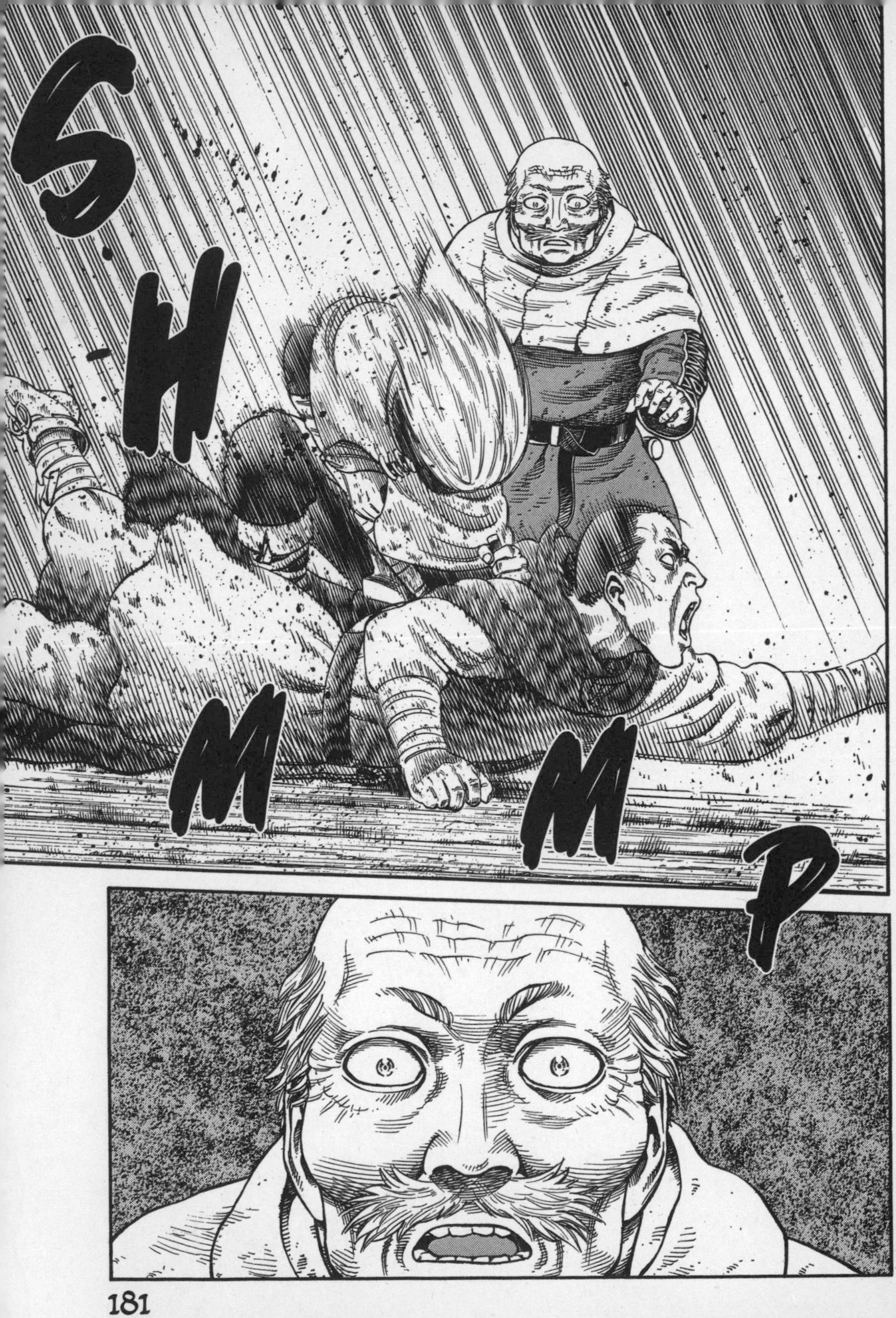
SHMMP

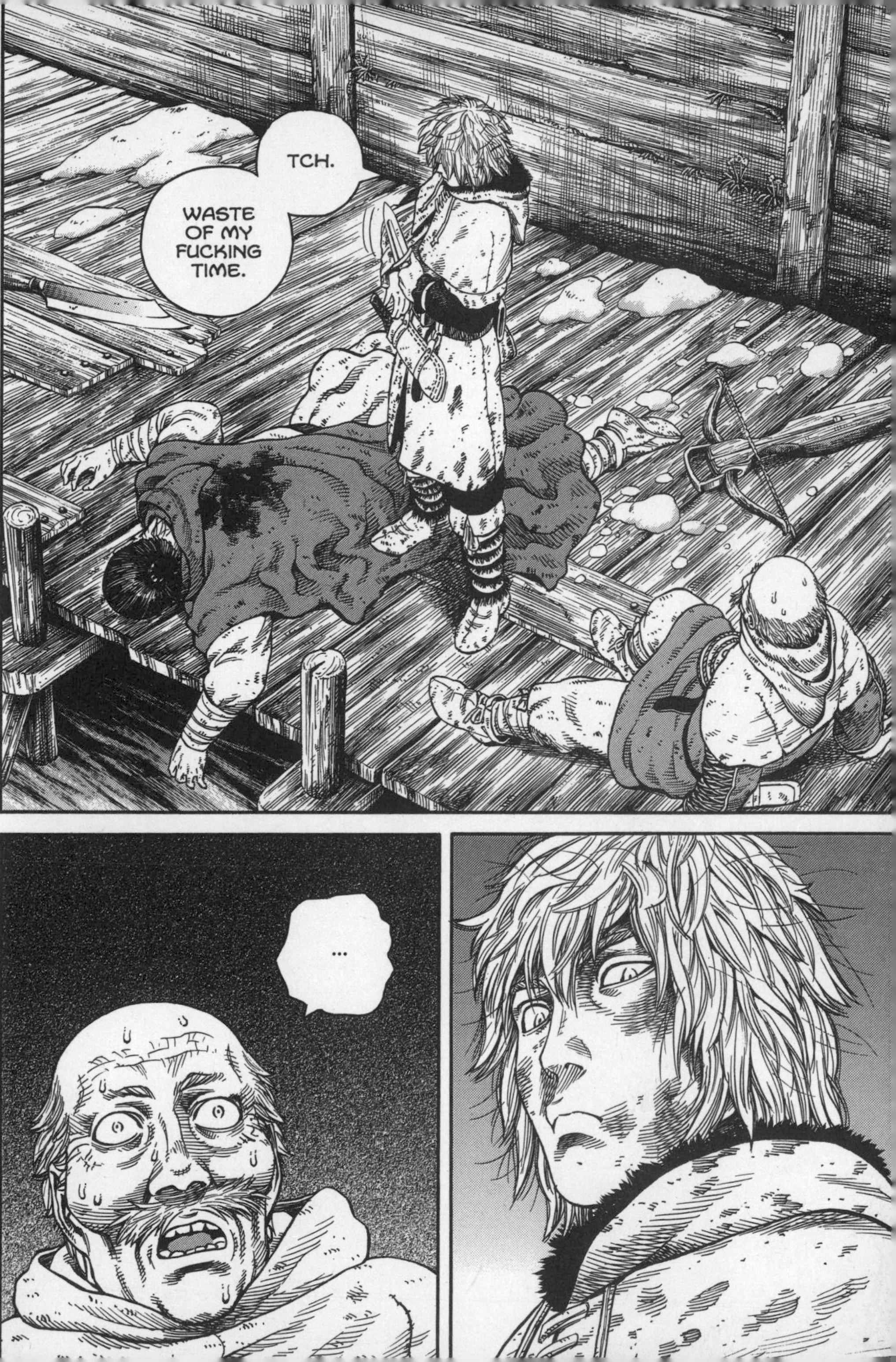
TCH.
WASTE OF MY FUCKING TIME.
...

CHAPTER 48 - END

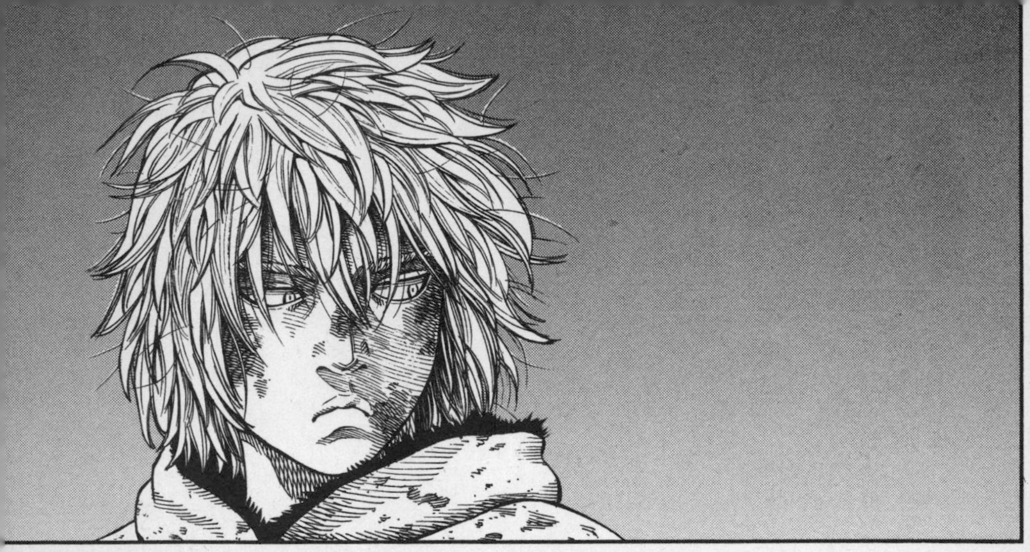

CHAPTER 49: KARLSEFNI

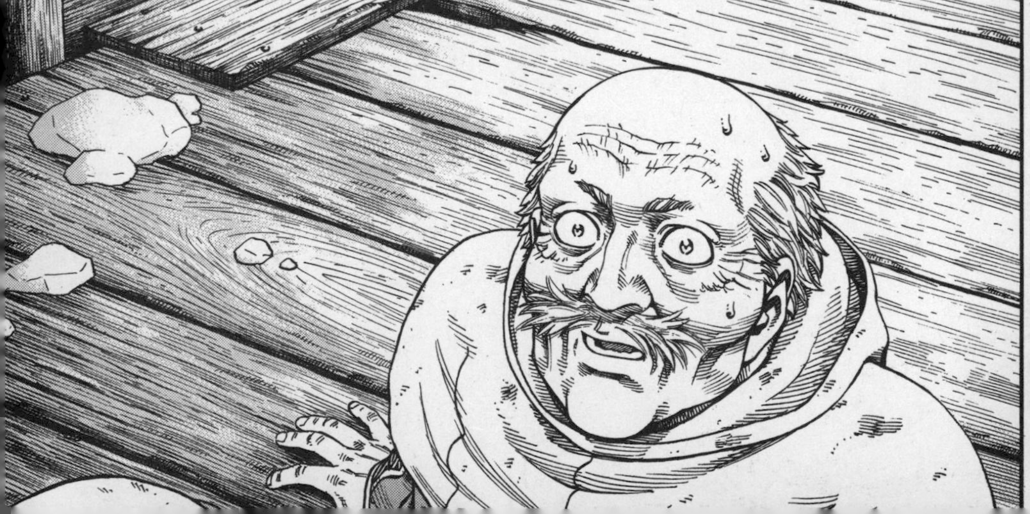

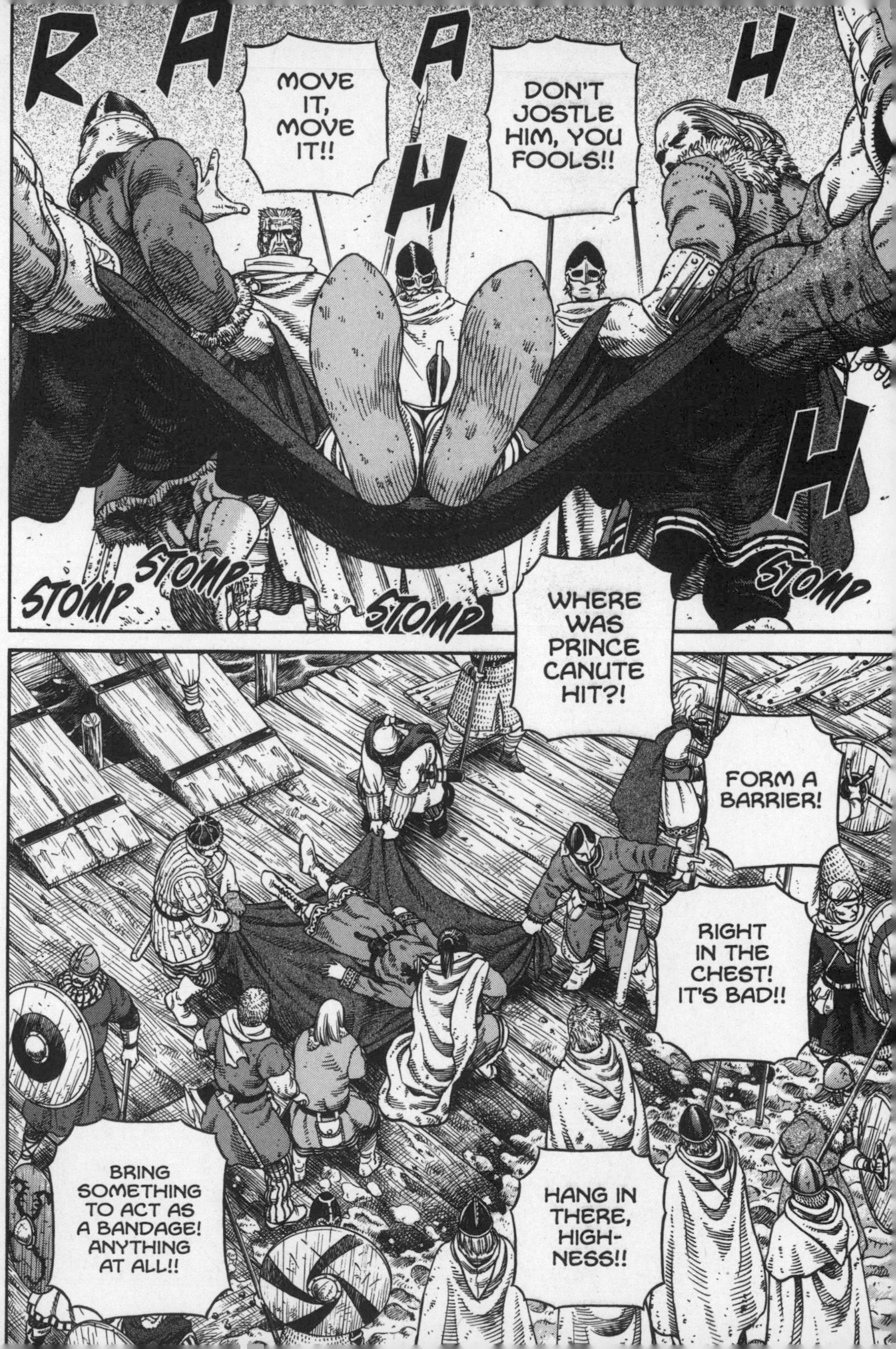

RAAHHH
DON'T JOSTLE HIM, YOU FOOLS!!
MOVE IT, MOVE IT!!
STOMP
STOMP
STOMP
STOMP
WHERE WAS PRINCE CANUTE HIT?!
FORM A BARRIER!
RIGHT IN THE CHEST! IT'S BAD!!
HANG IN THERE, HIGHNESS!!
BRING SOMETHING TO ACT AS A BANDAGE! ANYTHING AT ALL!!

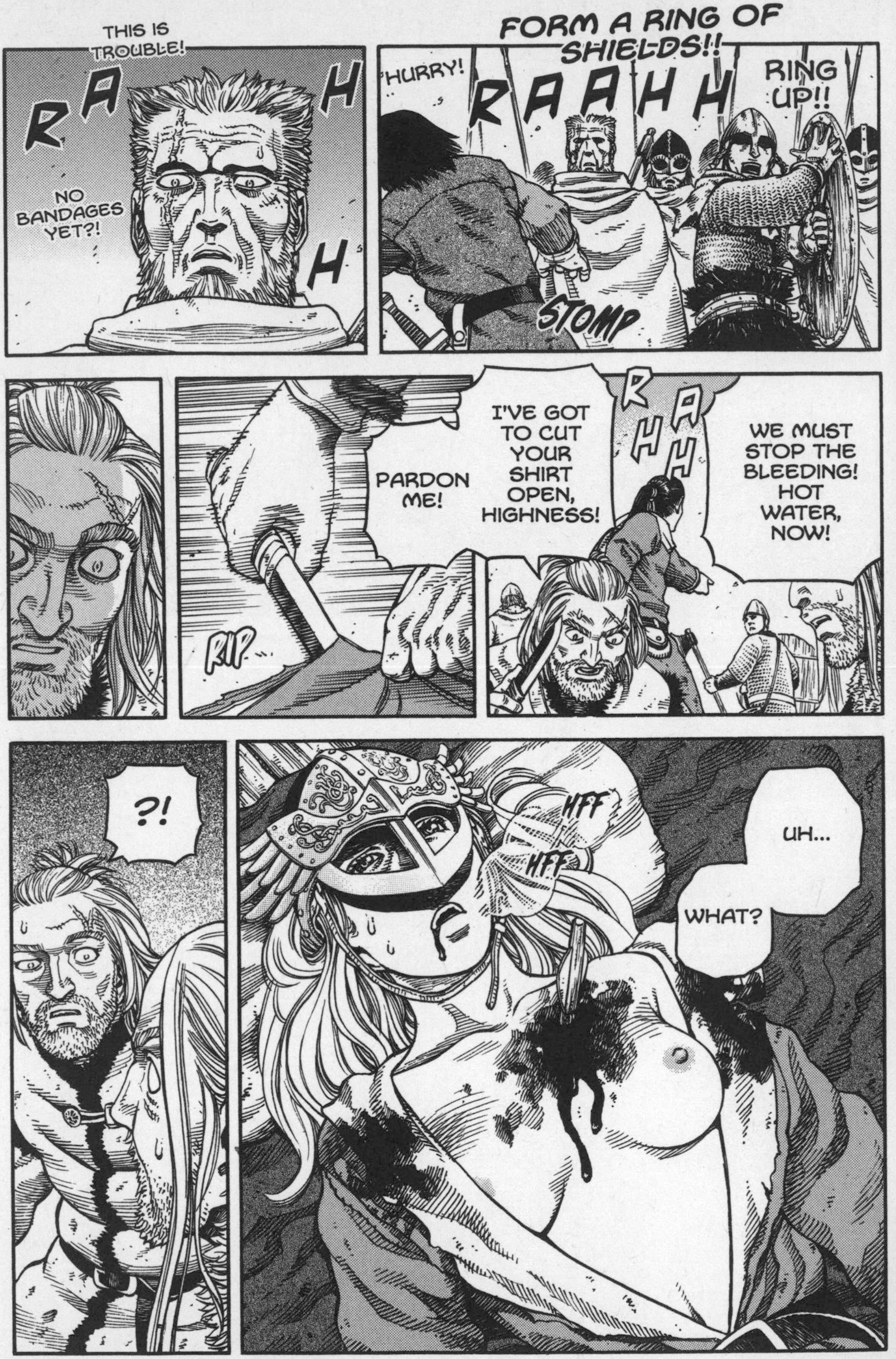
FORM A RING OF SHIELDS!!
RING UP!!
RAAHH
HURRY!
STOMP
THIS IS TROUBLE!
RAHH
NO BANDAGES YET?!
WE MUST STOP THE BLEEDING! HOT WATER, NOW!
RAHH
I'VE GOT TO CUT YOUR SHIRT OPEN, HIGHNESS!
PARDON ME!
RIP
HFF
HFF
UH...
WHAT?
?!

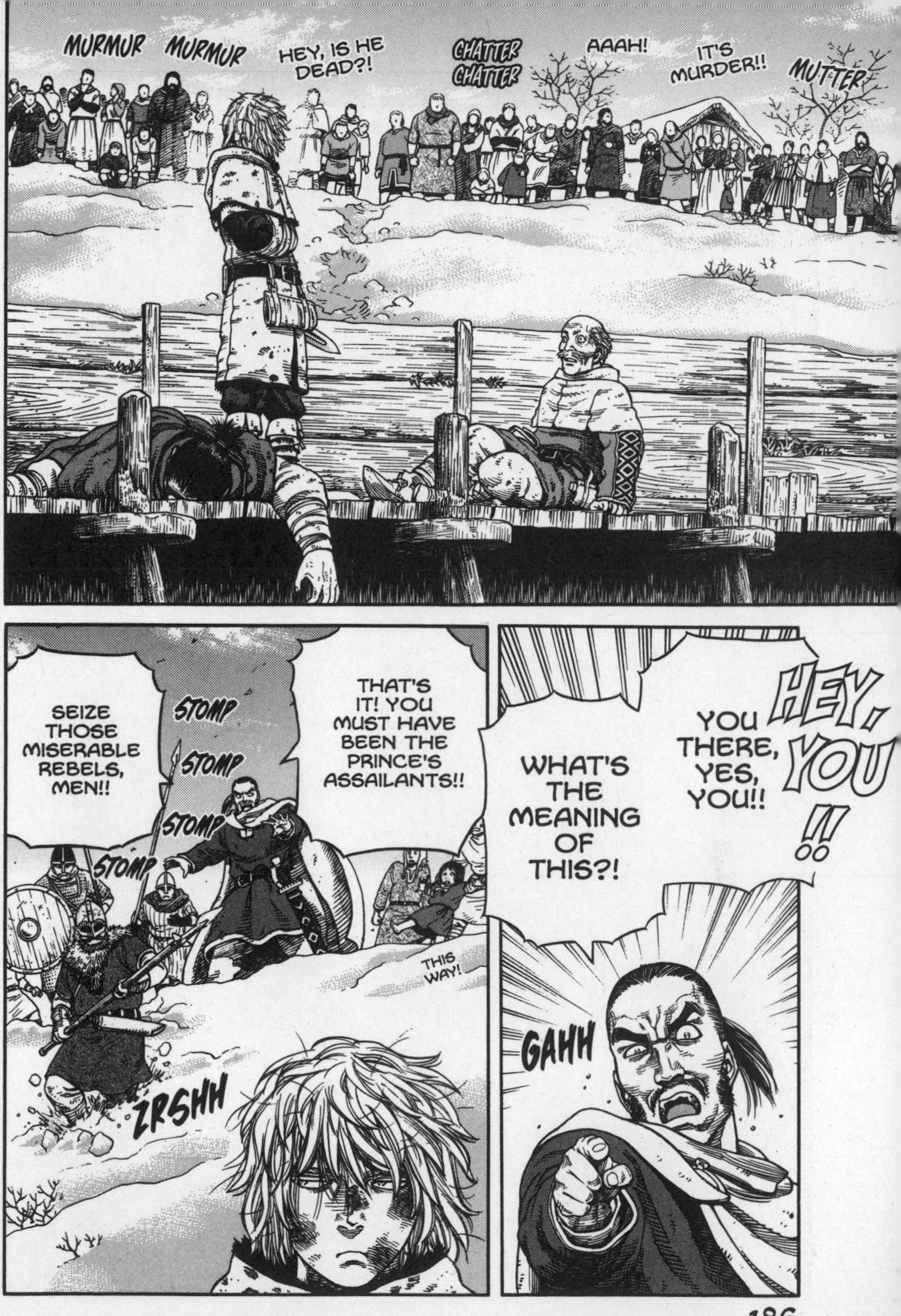
MUTTER
IT'S MURDER!!
AAAH!
CHATTER CHATTER
HEY, IS HE DEAD?!
MURMUR
MURMUR
HEY, YOU!!
YOU THERE, YES, YOU!!
WHAT'S THE MEANING OF THIS?!
GAHH
THAT'S IT! YOU MUST HAVE BEEN THE PRINCE'S ASSAILANTS!!
STOMP
STOMP
STOMP
STOMP
SEIZE THOSE MISERABLE REBELS, MEN!!
THIS WAY!
ZRSHH

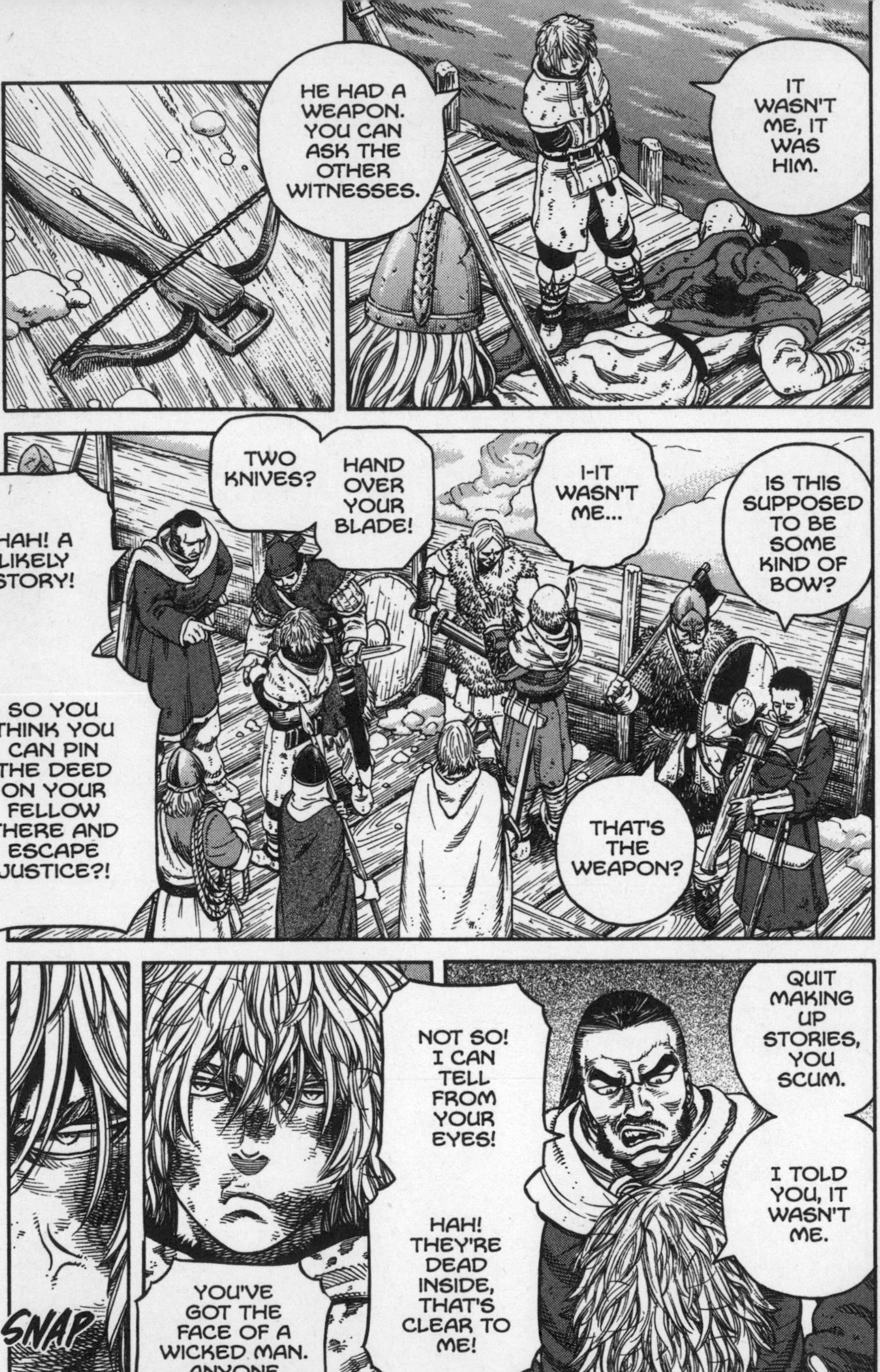
IT WASN'T ME, IT WAS HIM.
HE HAD A WEAPON. YOU CAN ASK THE OTHER WITNESSES.
IS THIS SUPPOSED TO BE SOME KIND OF BOW?
I-IT WASN'T ME...
HAND OVER YOUR BLADE!
TWO KNIVES?
THAT'S THE WEAPON?
HAH! A LIKELY STORY!
SO YOU THINK YOU CAN PIN THE DEED ON YOUR FELLOW THERE AND ESCAPE JUSTICE?!
QUIT MAKING UP STORIES, YOU SCUM.
I TOLD YOU, IT WASN'T ME.
NOT SO! I CAN TELL FROM YOUR EYES!
HAH! THEY'RE DEAD INSIDE, THAT'S CLEAR TO ME!
YOU'VE GOT THE FACE OF A WICKED MAN. ANYONE WOULD AGREE!!
SNAP

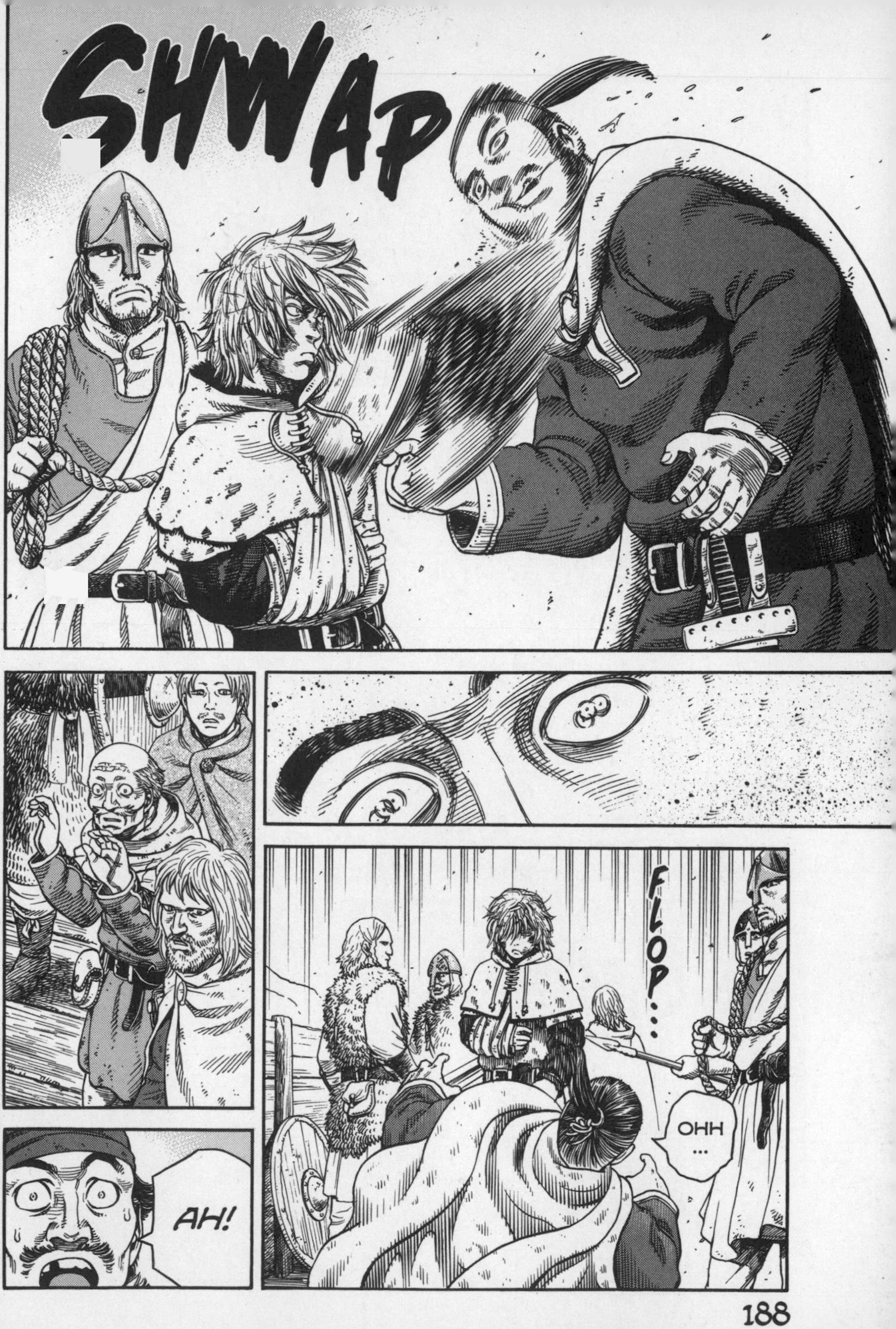
SHWAP
FLOP...
OHH ...
AH!

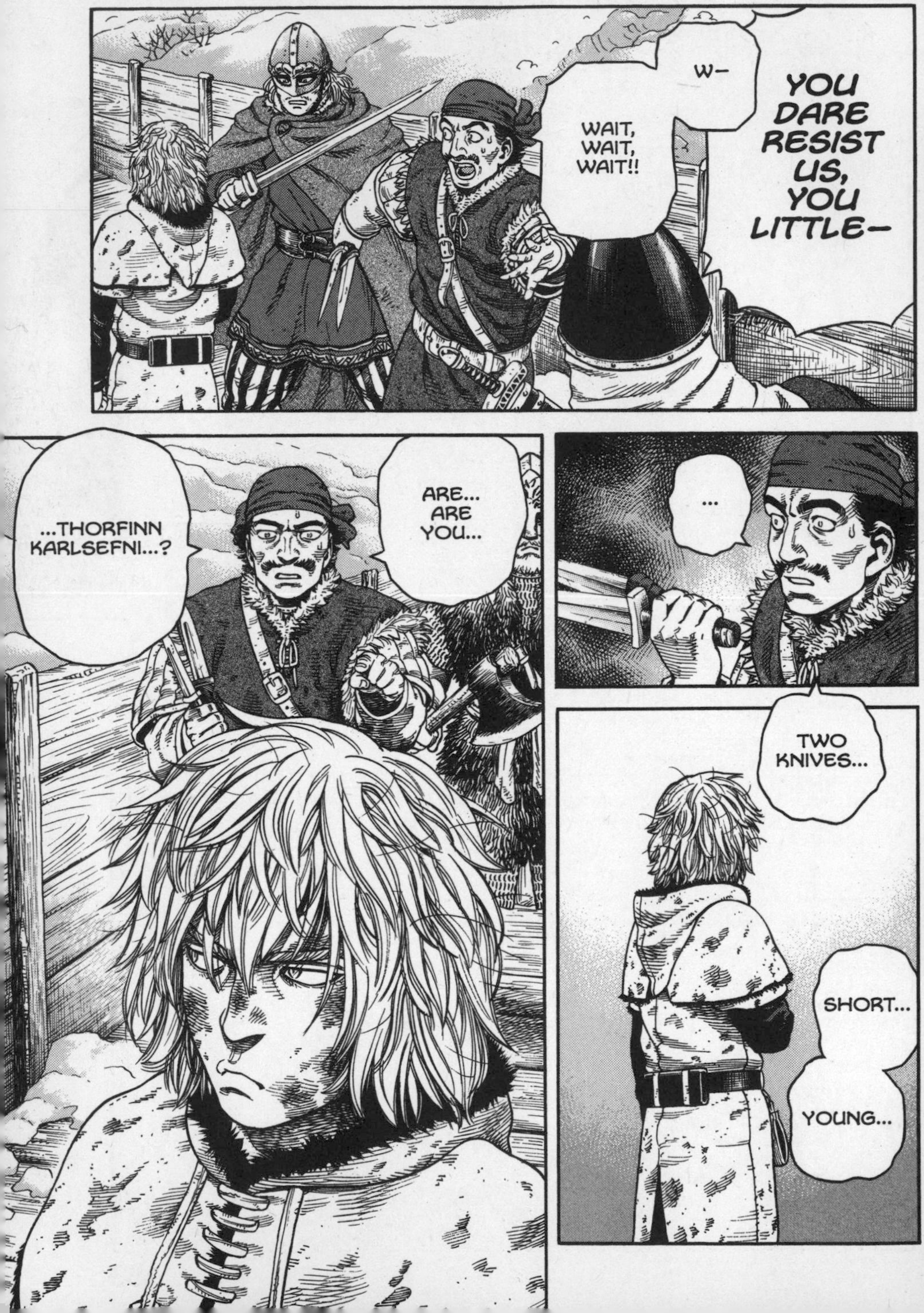
YOU DARE RESIST US, YOU LITTLE—
W—
WAIT, WAIT, WAIT!!
...
TWO KNIVES...
SHORT...
YOUNG...
ARE... ARE YOU...
...THORFINN KARLSEFNI...?

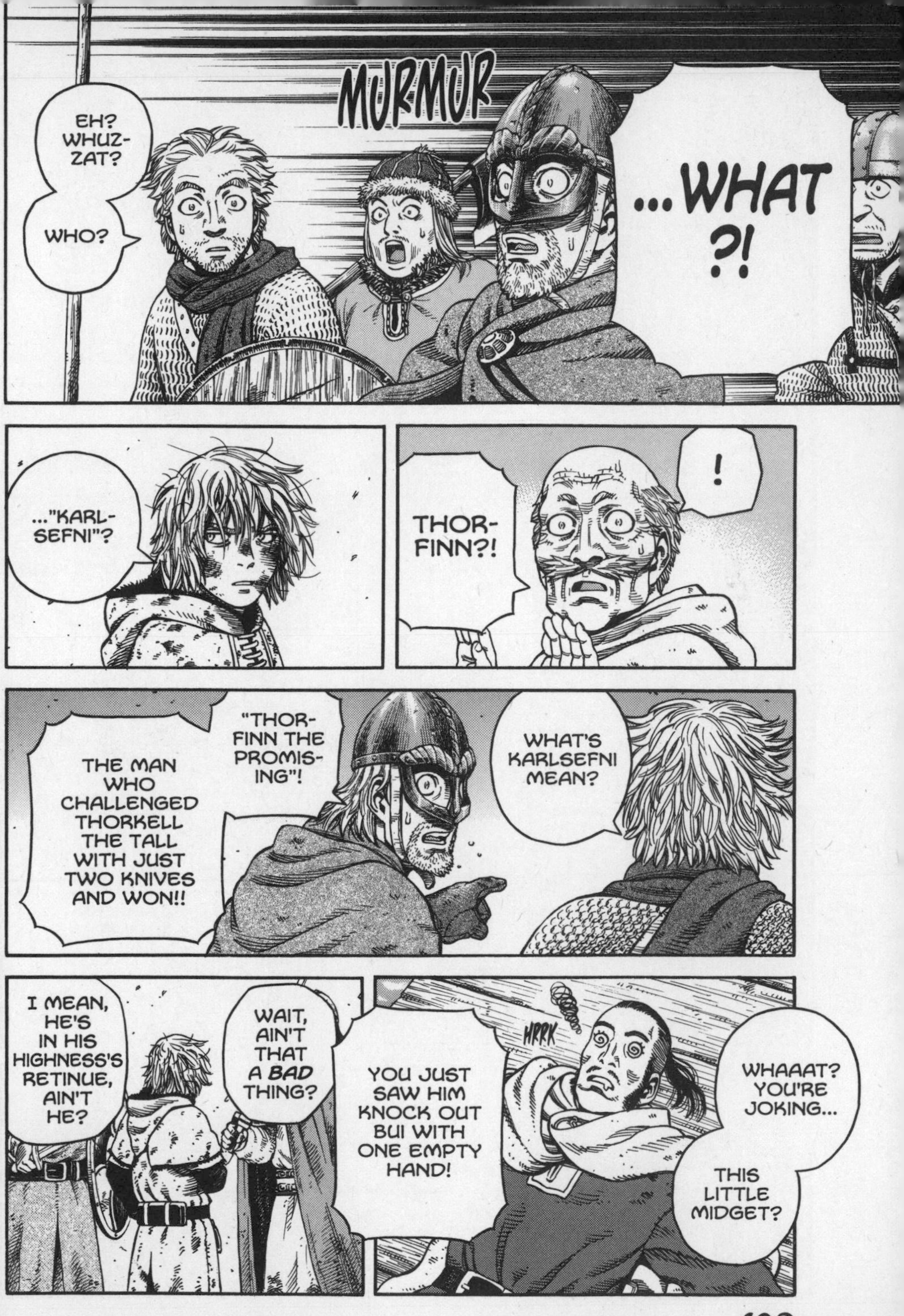
...WHAT ?!
MURMUR
EH? WHUZ-ZAT?
WHO?
!
THOR-FINN?!
..."KARL-SEFNI"?
WHAT'S KARLSEFNI MEAN?
"THOR-FINN THE PROMIS-ING"!
THE MAN WHO CHALLENGED THORKELL THE TALL WITH JUST TWO KNIVES AND WON!!
WHAAAT? YOU'RE JOKING...
THIS LITTLE MIDGET?
HRRK
YOU JUST SAW HIM KNOCK OUT BUI WITH ONE EMPTY HAND!
WAIT, AIN'T THAT A *BAD* THING?
I MEAN, HE'S IN HIS HIGHNESS'S RETINUE, AIN'T HE?

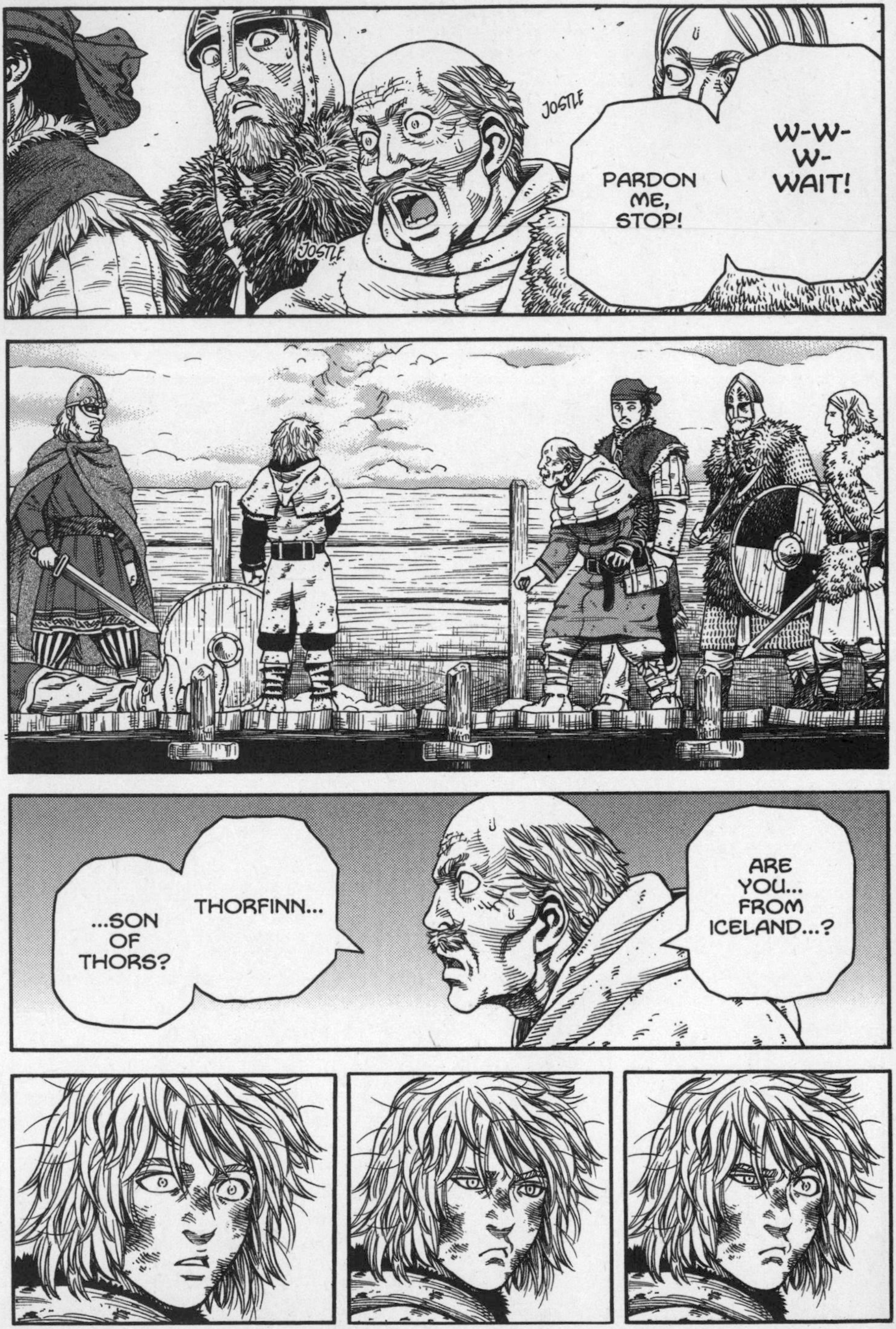
W-W-W-WAIT!
PARDON ME, STOP!
JOSTLE
JOSTLE
ARE YOU... FROM ICELAND...?
THORFINN...
...SON OF THORS?

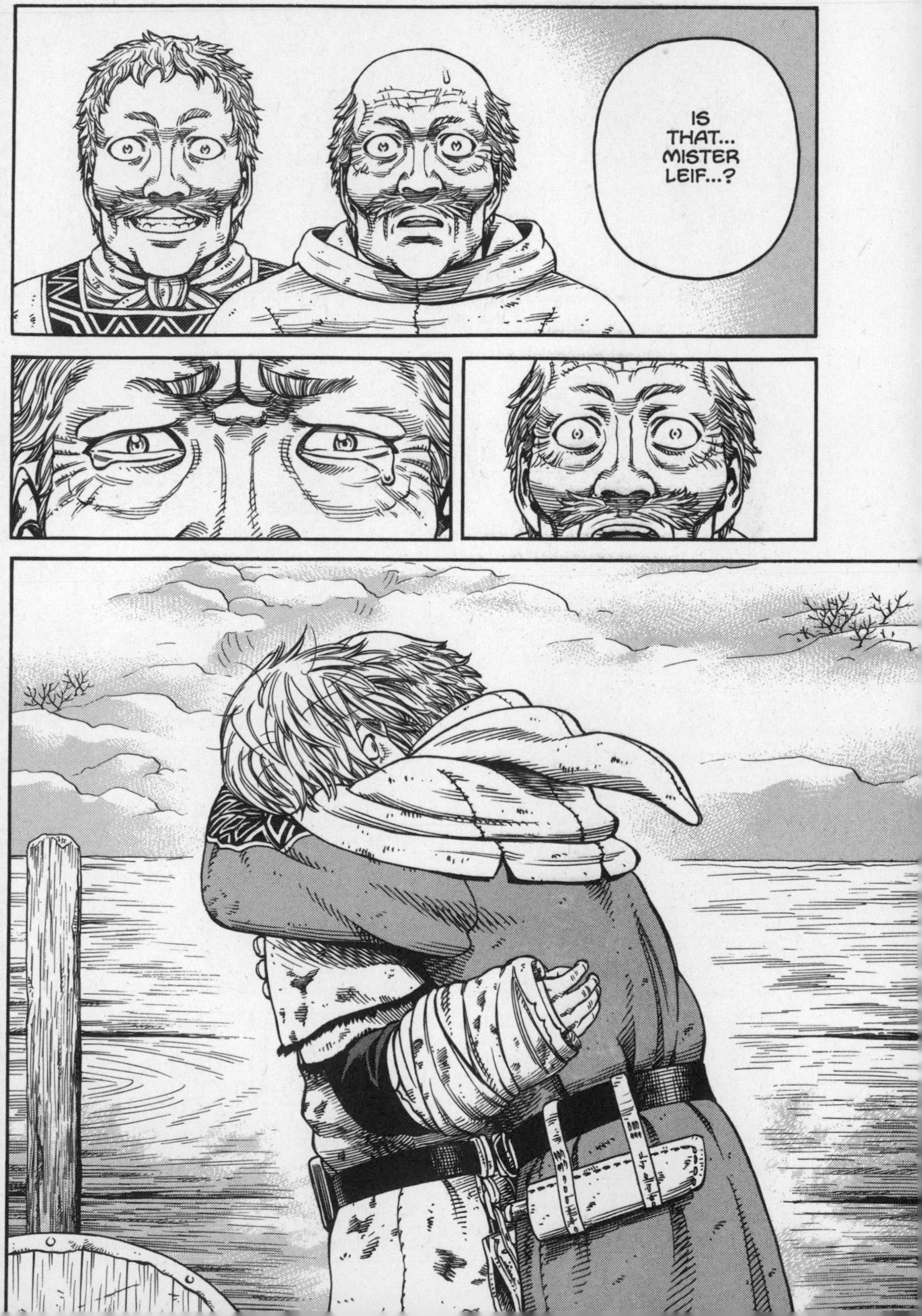
IS THAT... MISTER LEIF...?

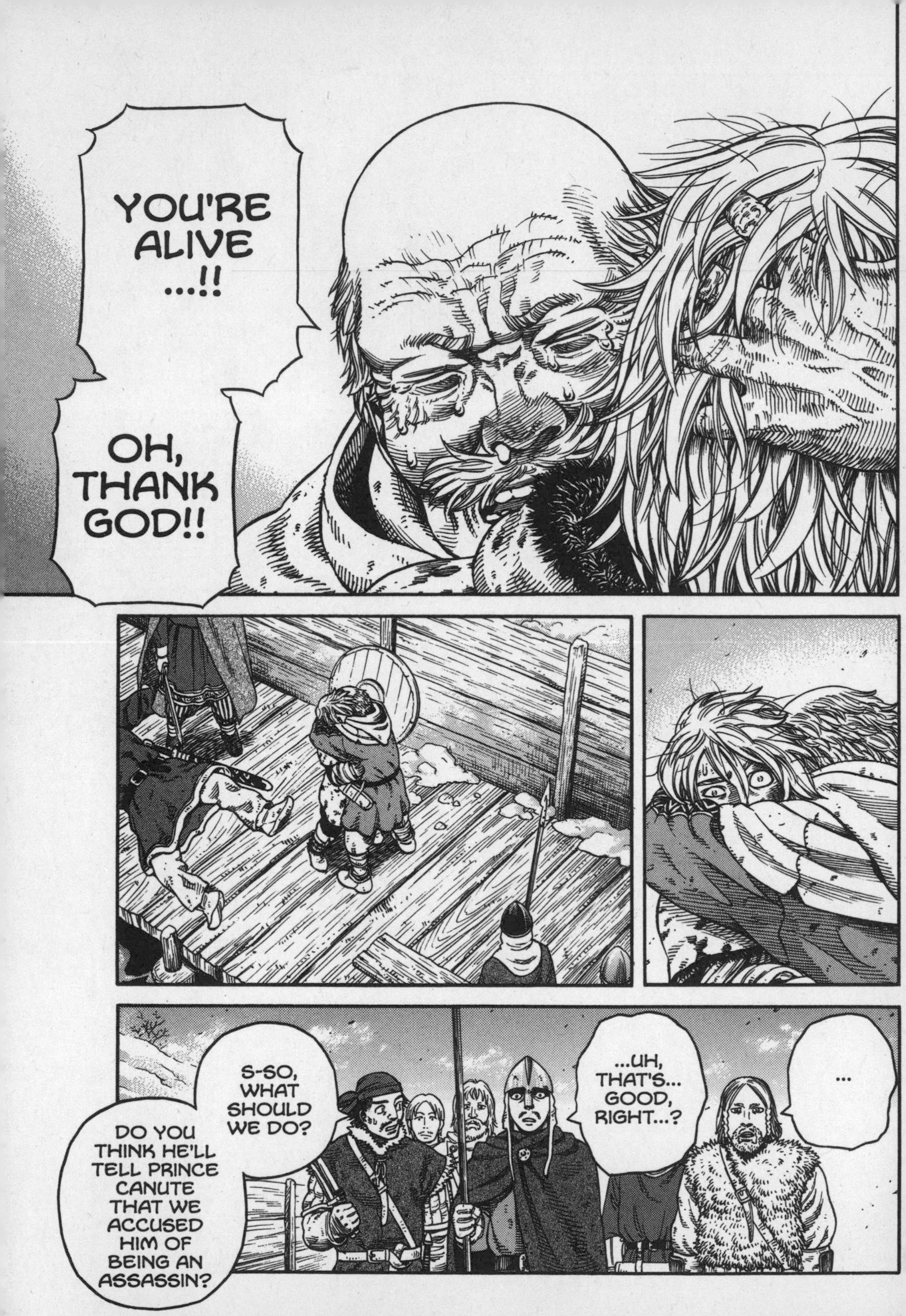
YOU'RE ALIVE ...!!
OH, THANK GOD!!
...
...UH, THAT'S... GOOD, RIGHT...?
S-SO, WHAT SHOULD WE DO?
DO YOU THINK HE'LL TELL PRINCE CANUTE THAT WE ACCUSED HIM OF BEING AN ASSASSIN?

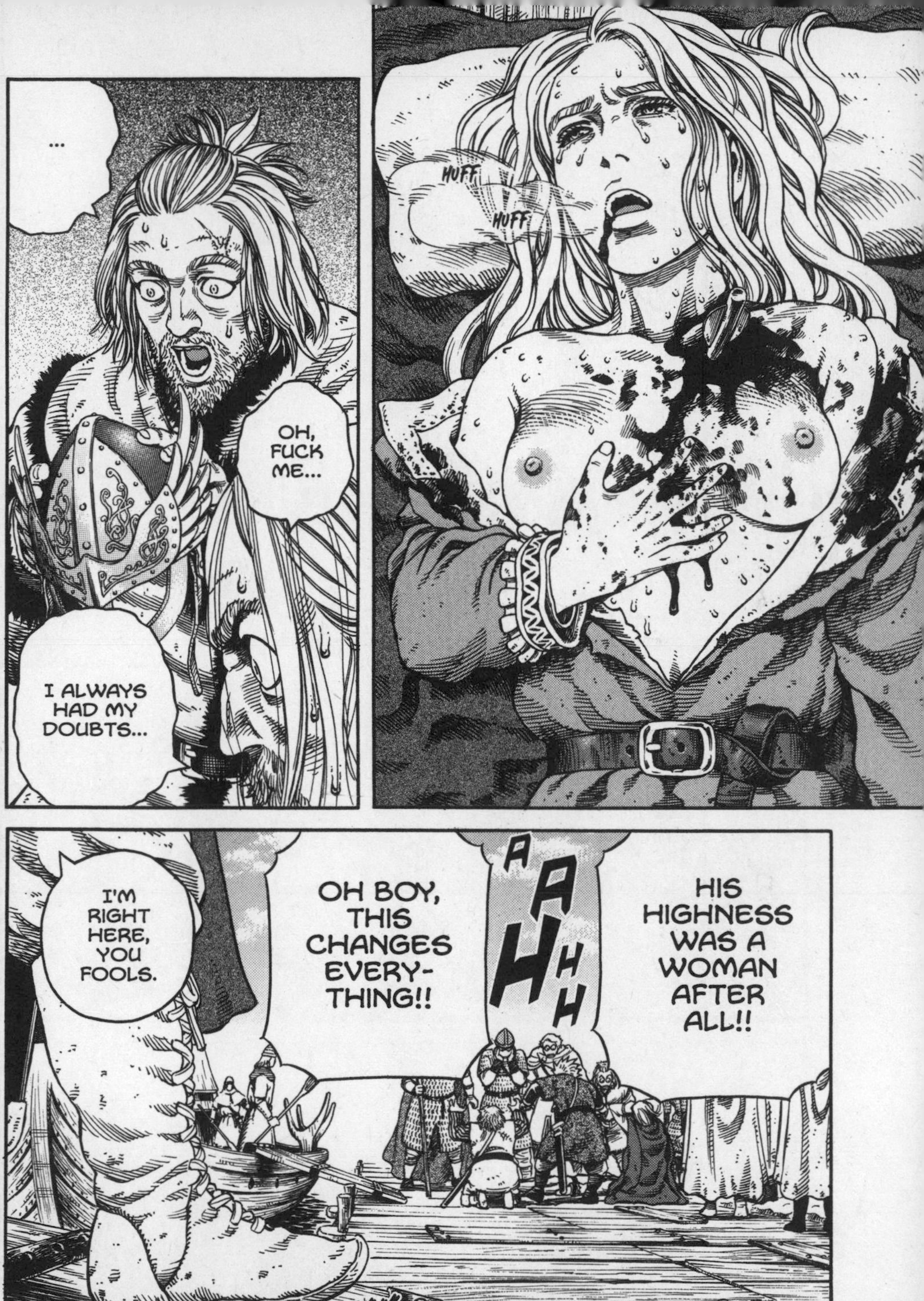
HUFF
HUFF
...
OH, FUCK ME...
I ALWAYS HAD MY DOUBTS...
HIS HIGHNESS WAS A WOMAN AFTER ALL!!
AAHHHH
OH BOY, THIS CHANGES EVERY-THING!!
I'M RIGHT HERE, YOU FOOLS.
CREAK

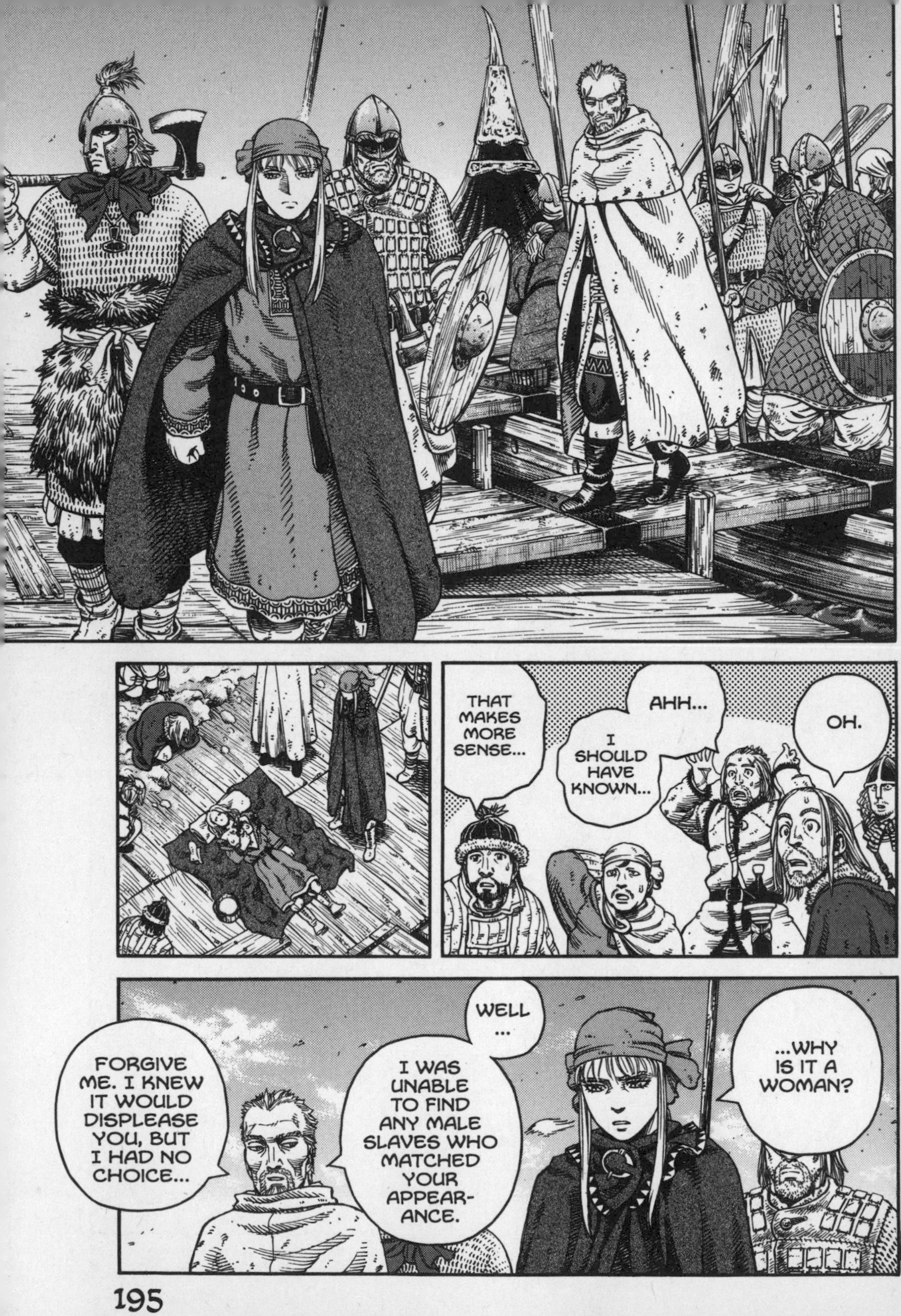
OH.
AHH... I SHOULD HAVE KNOWN...
THAT MAKES MORE SENSE...
...WHY IS IT A WOMAN?
WELL ...
I WAS UNABLE TO FIND ANY MALE SLAVES WHO MATCHED YOUR APPEARANCE.
FORGIVE ME. I KNEW IT WOULD DISPLEASE YOU, BUT I HAD NO CHOICE...

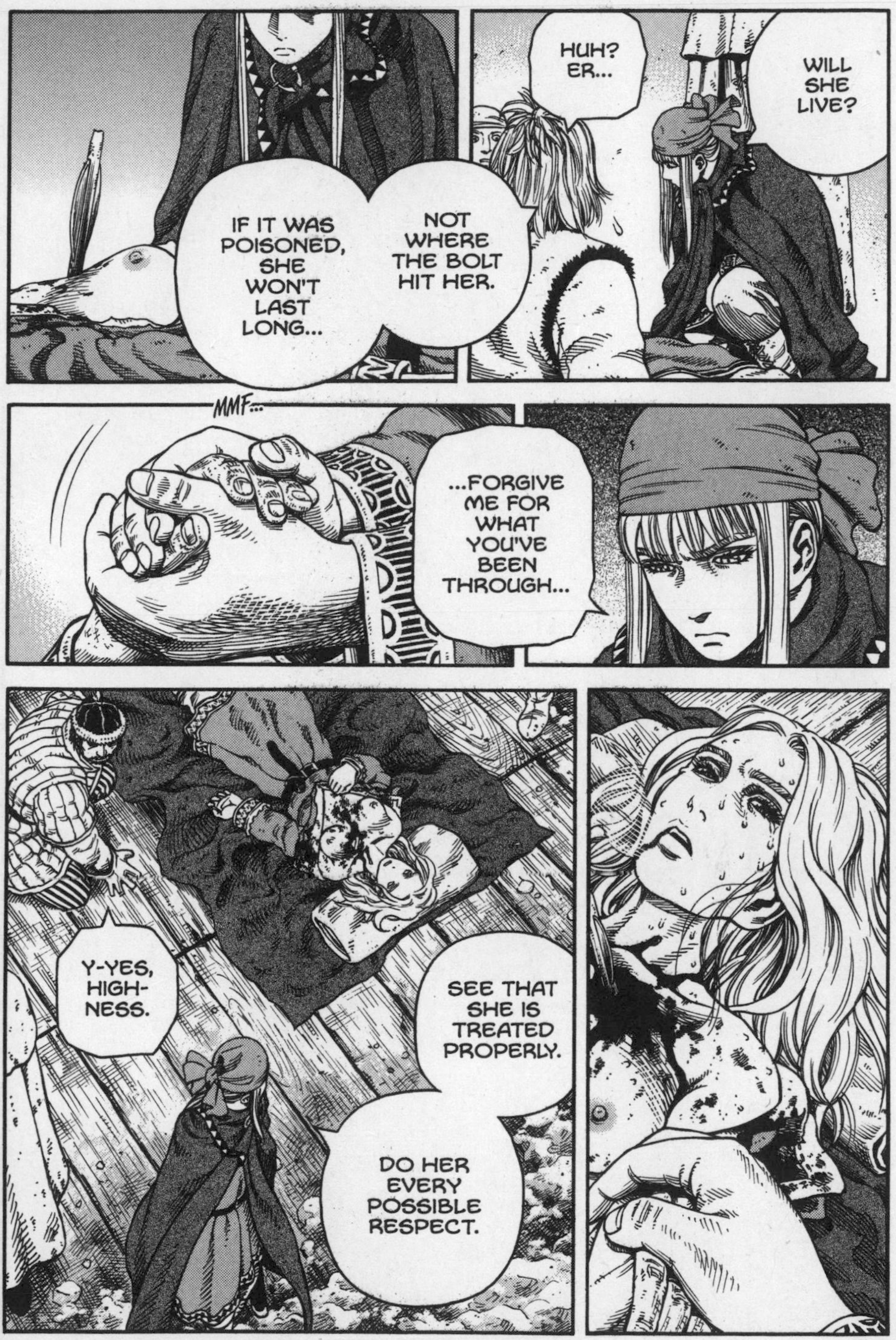
WILL SHE LIVE?
HUH? ER...
NOT WHERE THE BOLT HIT HER.
IF IT WAS POISONED, SHE WON'T LAST LONG...
...FORGIVE ME FOR WHAT YOU'VE BEEN THROUGH...
MMF...
SEE THAT SHE IS TREATED PROPERLY.
DO HER EVERY POSSIBLE RESPECT.
Y-YES, HIGHNESS.

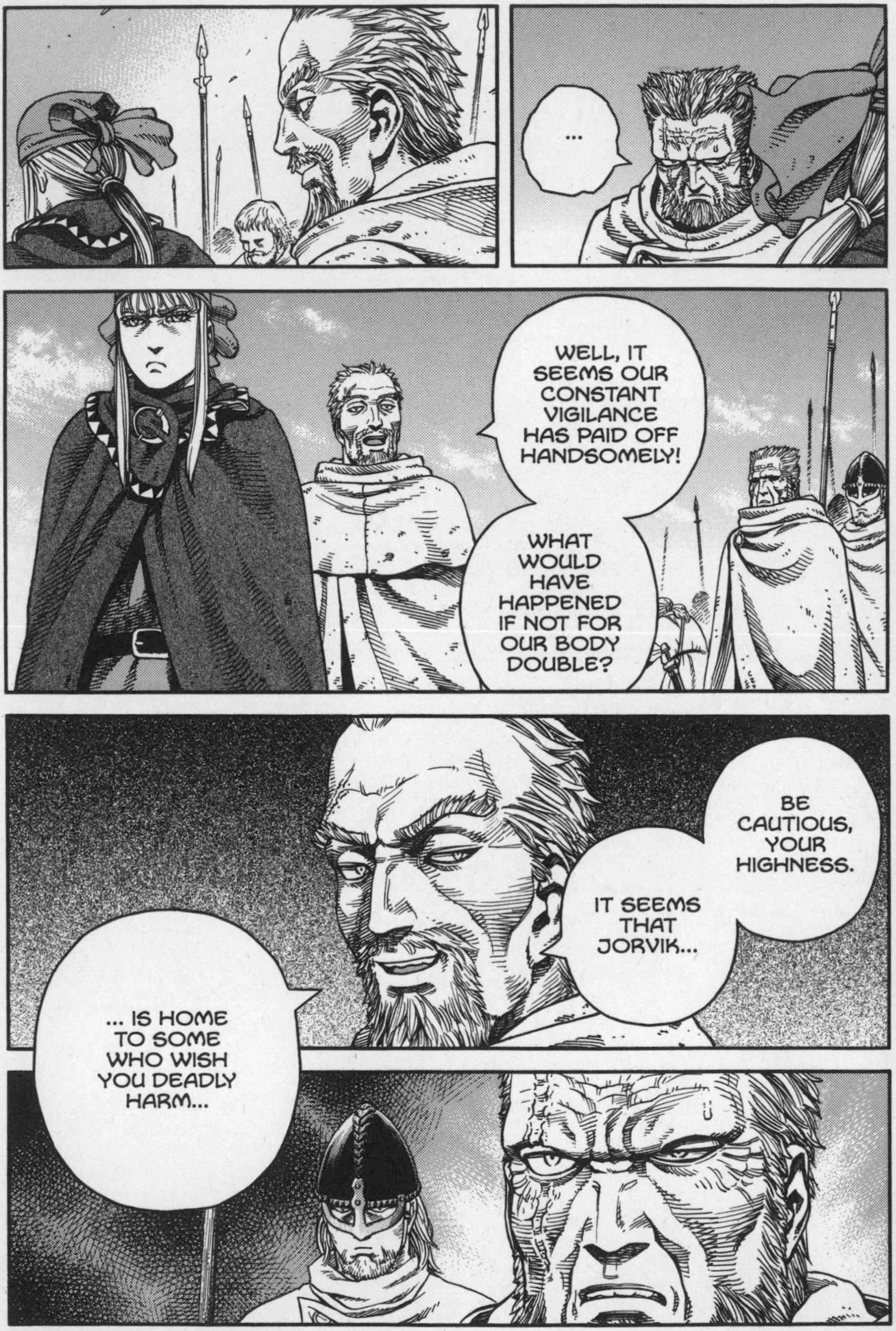
...
WELL, IT SEEMS OUR CONSTANT VIGILANCE HAS PAID OFF HANDSOMELY!
WHAT WOULD HAVE HAPPENED IF NOT FOR OUR BODY DOUBLE?
BE CAUTIOUS, YOUR HIGHNESS.
IT SEEMS THAT JORVIK...
... IS HOME TO SOME WHO WISH YOU DEADLY HARM...

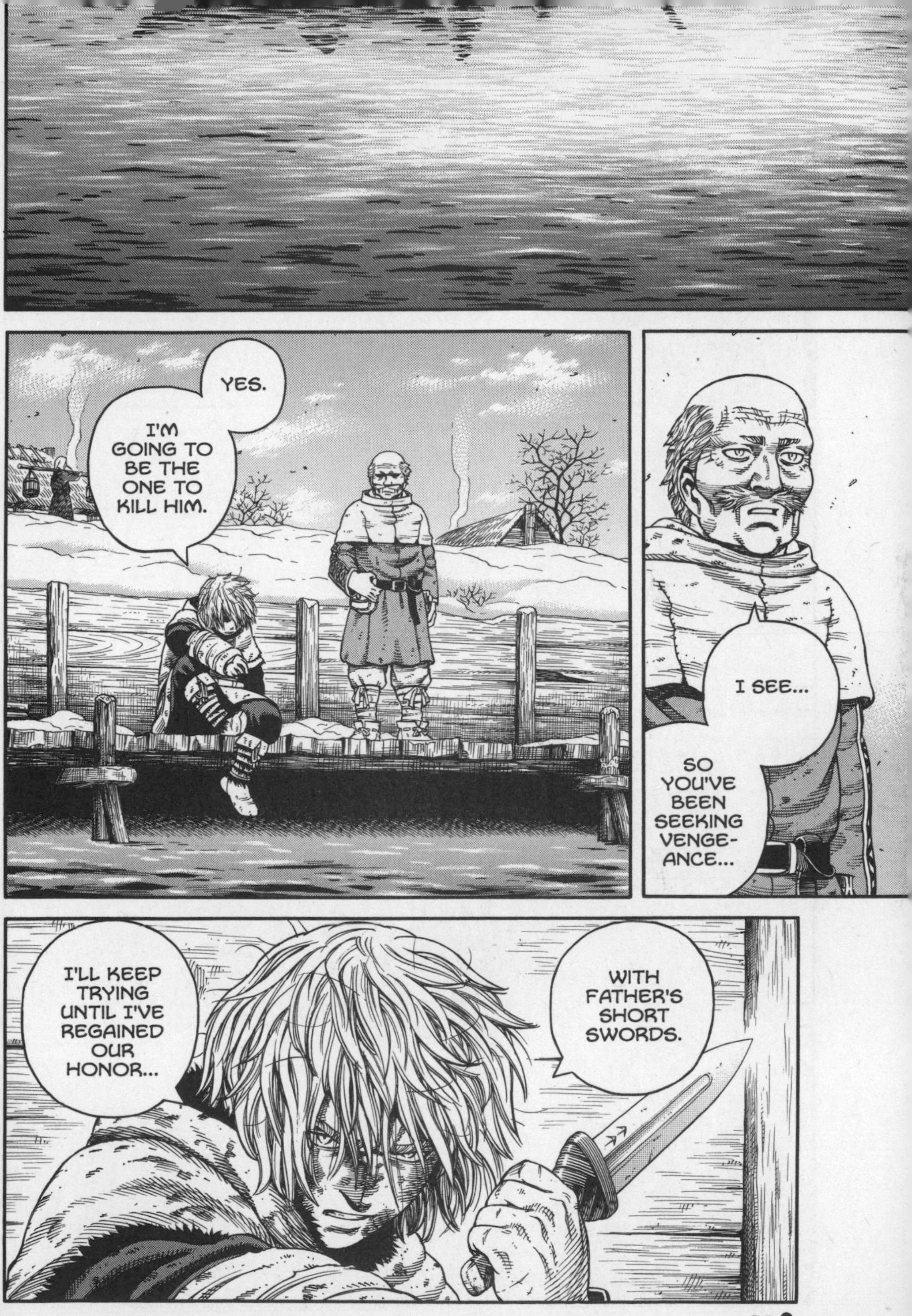
I SEE...
SO YOU'VE BEEN SEEKING VENGE-ANCE...
YES.
I'M GOING TO BE THE ONE TO KILL HIM.
WITH FATHER'S SHORT SWORDS.
I'LL KEEP TRYING UNTIL I'VE REGAINED OUR HONOR...

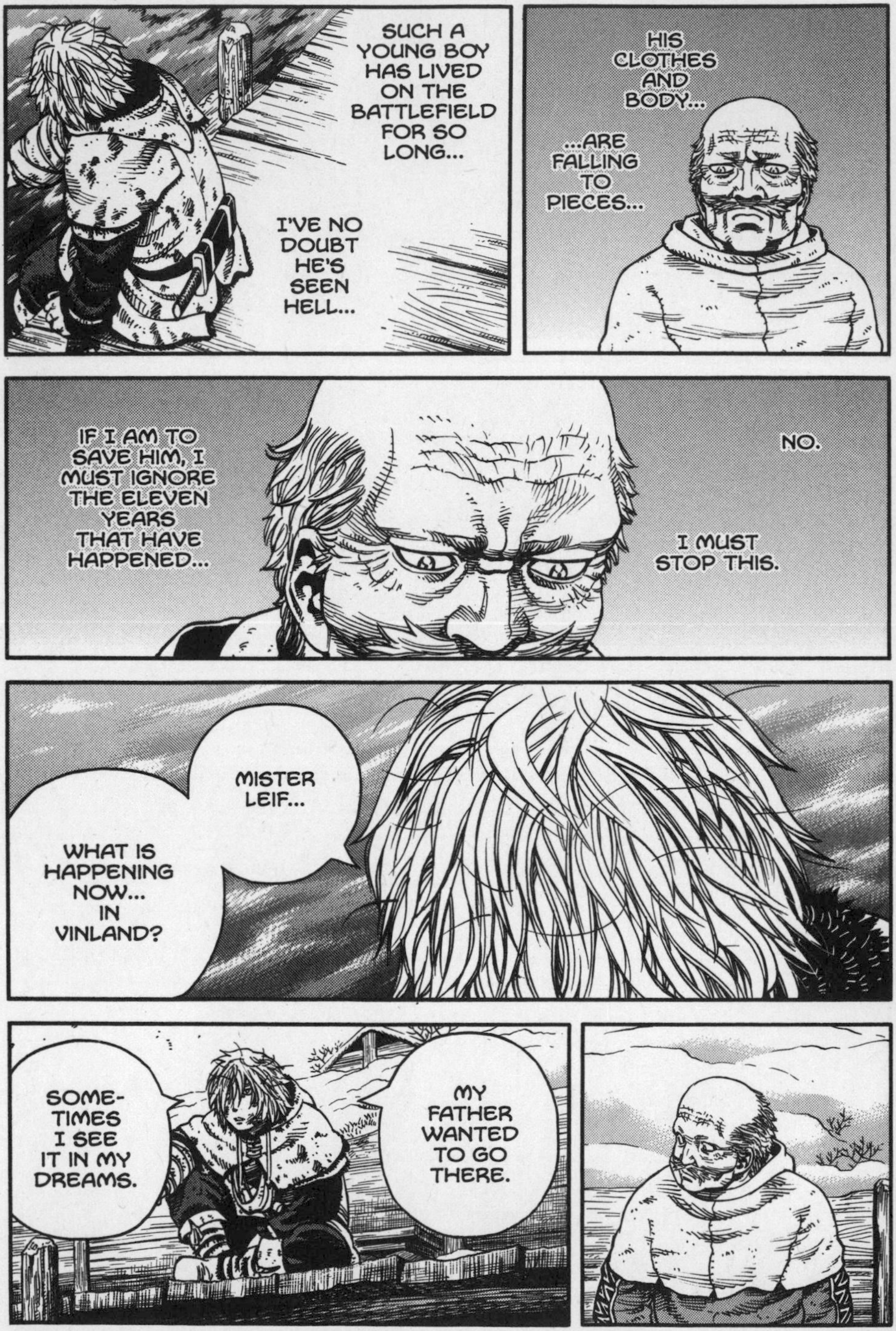
HIS CLOTHES AND BODY...
...ARE FALLING TO PIECES...
SUCH A YOUNG BOY HAS LIVED ON THE BATTLEFIELD FOR SO LONG...
I'VE NO DOUBT HE'S SEEN HELL...
NO.
I MUST STOP THIS.
IF I AM TO SAVE HIM, I MUST IGNORE THE ELEVEN YEARS THAT HAVE HAPPENED...
MISTER LEIF...
WHAT IS HAPPENING NOW... IN VINLAND?
MY FATHER WANTED TO GO THERE.
SOME-TIMES I SEE IT IN MY DREAMS.

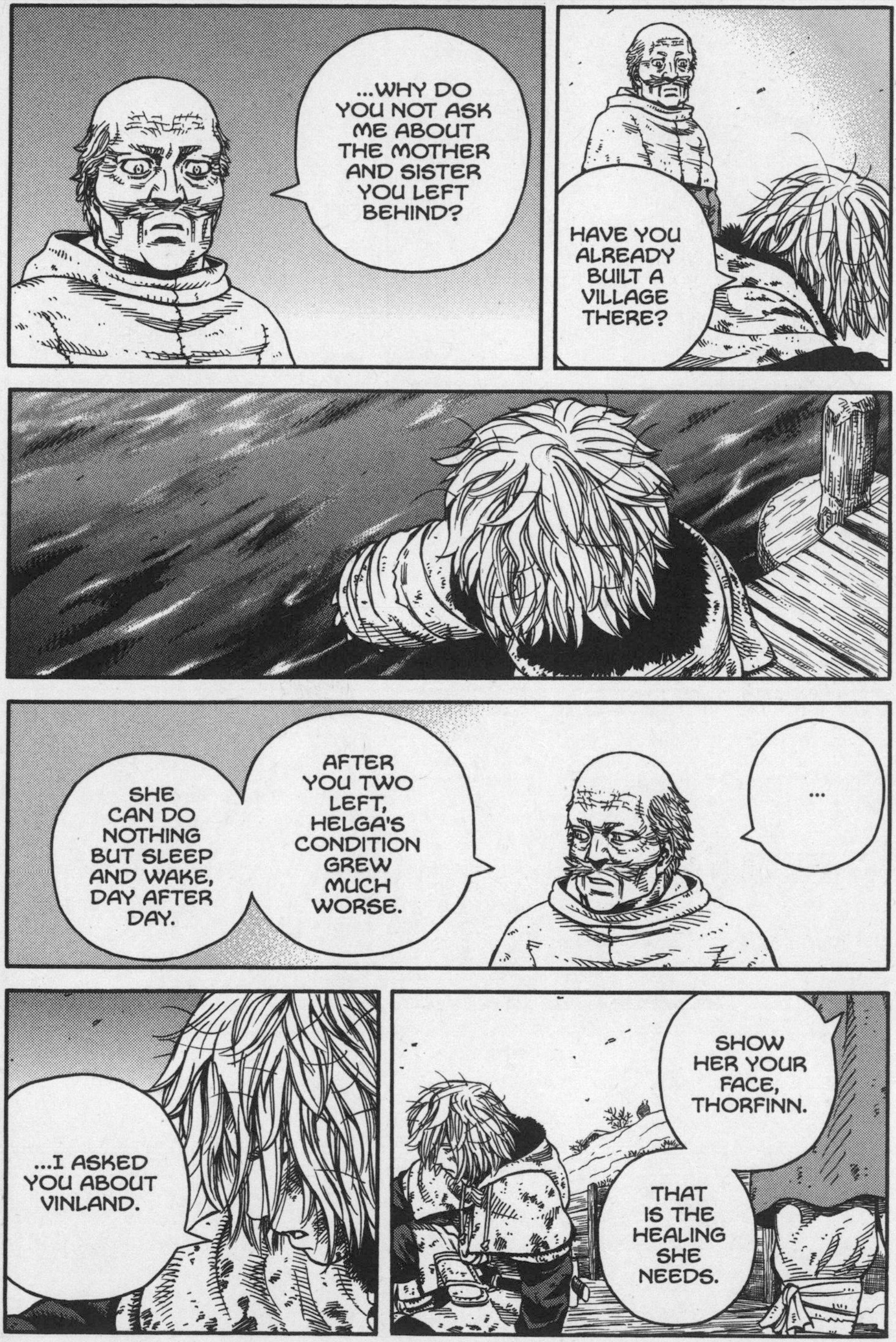
HAVE YOU ALREADY BUILT A VILLAGE THERE?
...WHY DO YOU NOT ASK ME ABOUT THE MOTHER AND SISTER YOU LEFT BEHIND?
...
AFTER YOU TWO LEFT, HELGA'S CONDITION GREW MUCH WORSE.
SHE CAN DO NOTHING BUT SLEEP AND WAKE, DAY AFTER DAY.
SHOW HER YOUR FACE, THORFINN.
THAT IS THE HEALING SHE NEEDS.
...I ASKED YOU ABOUT VINLAND.

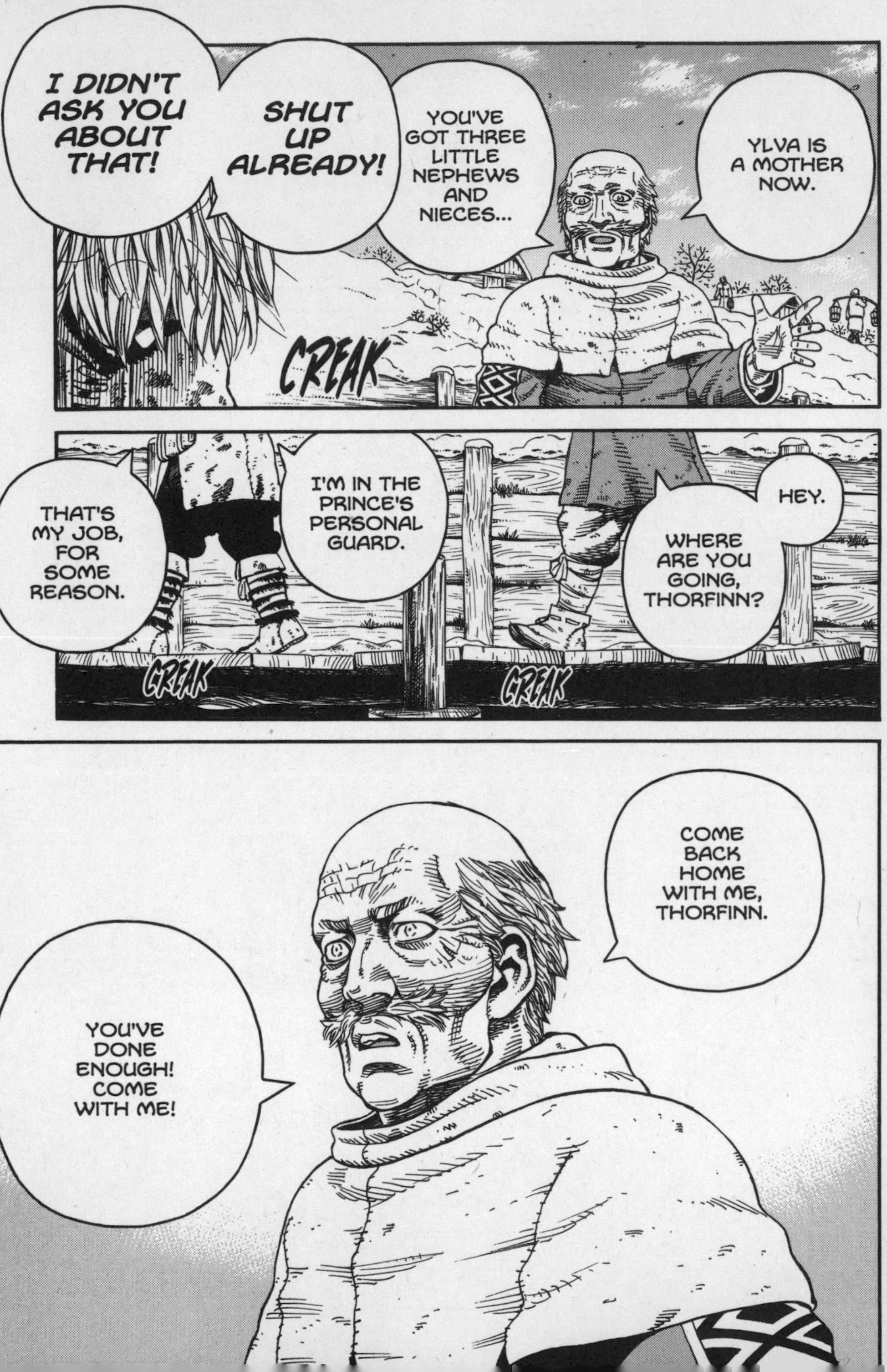
YLVA IS A MOTHER NOW.
YOU'VE GOT THREE LITTLE NEPHEWS AND NIECES...
SHUT UP ALREADY!
I DIDN'T ASK YOU ABOUT THAT!
CREAK
HEY.
WHERE ARE YOU GOING, THORFINN?
I'M IN THE PRINCE'S PERSONAL GUARD.
THAT'S MY JOB, FOR SOME REASON.
CREAK
CREAK
COME BACK HOME WITH ME, THORFINN.
YOU'VE DONE ENOUGH! COME WITH ME!

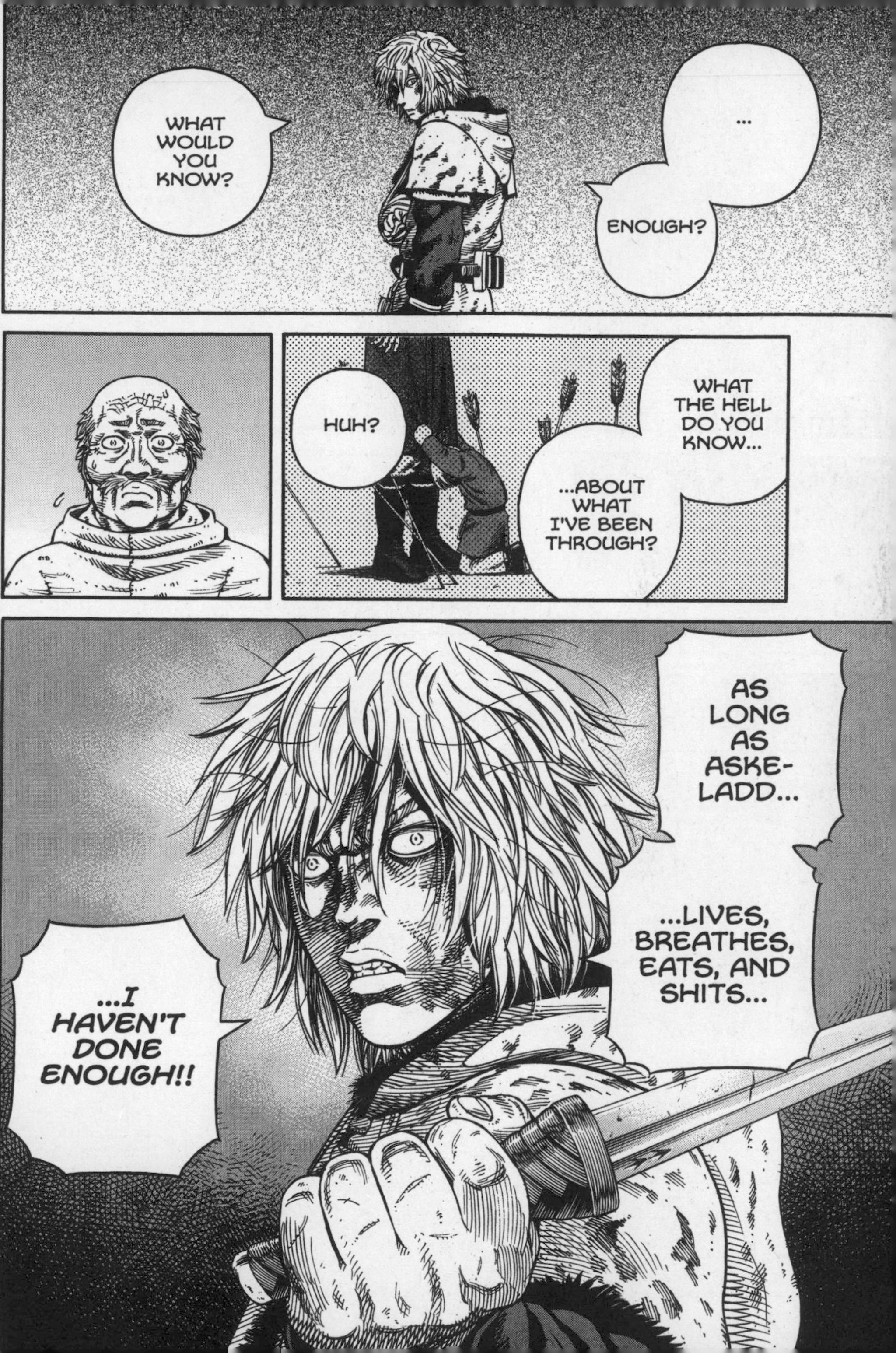
...
ENOUGH?
WHAT WOULD YOU KNOW?
WHAT THE HELL DO YOU KNOW...
...ABOUT WHAT I'VE BEEN THROUGH?
HUH?
AS LONG AS ASKE-LADD...
...LIVES, BREATHES, EATS, AND SHITS...
...I HAVEN'T DONE ENOUGH!!

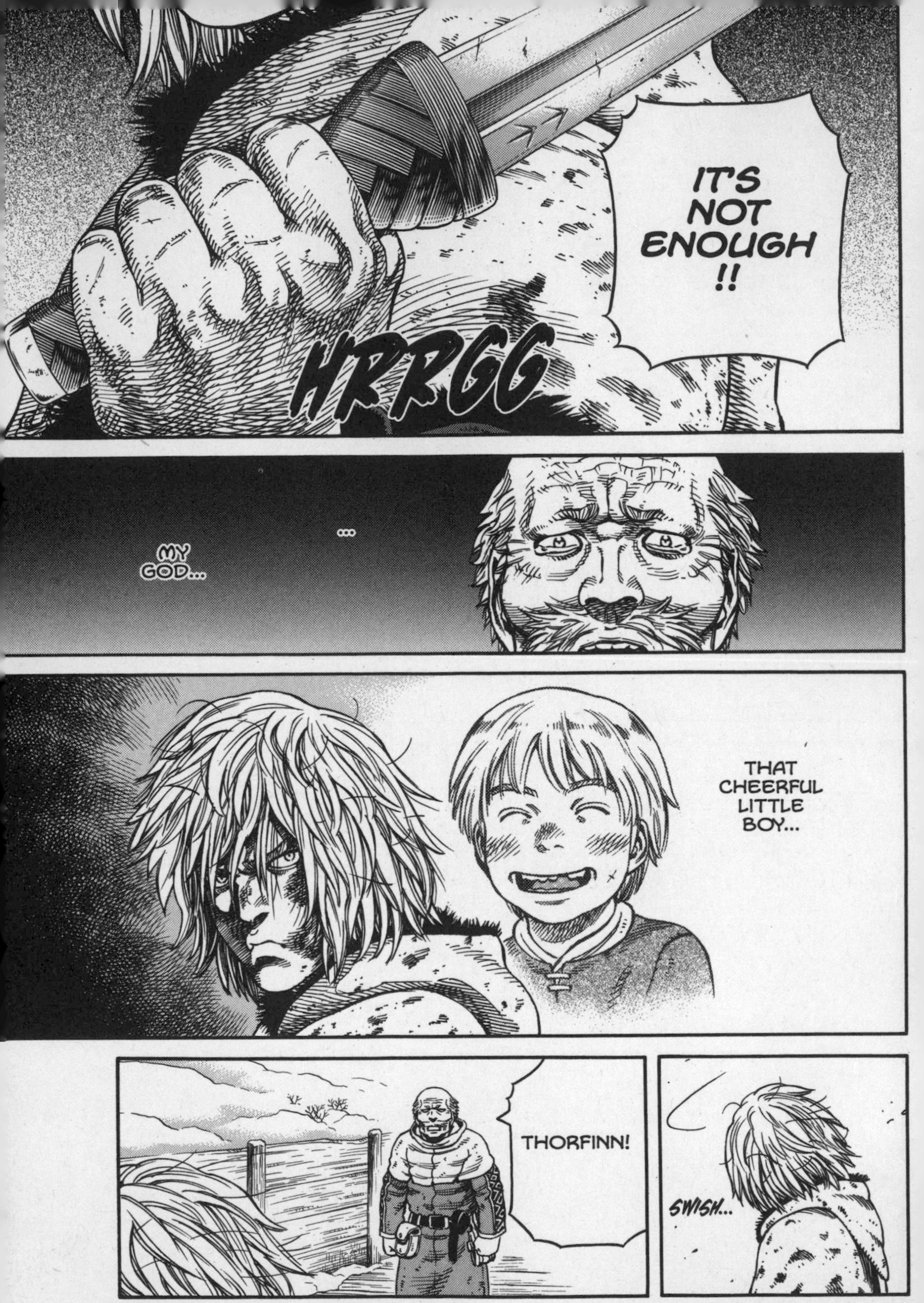
IT'S NOT ENOUGH!!
HRRGG
...
MY GOD...
THAT CHEERFUL LITTLE BOY...
SWISH...
THORFINN!

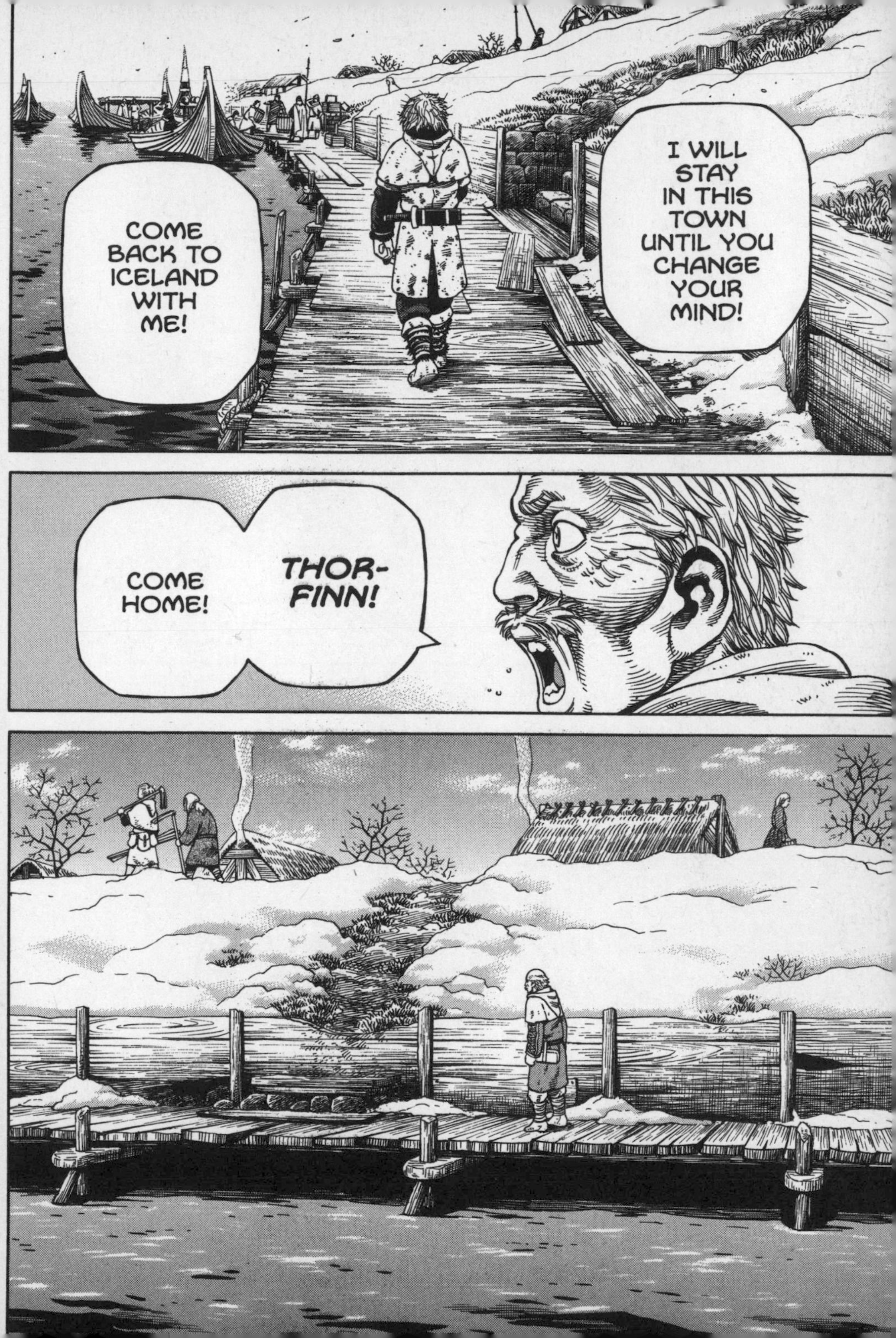
I WILL STAY IN THIS TOWN UNTIL YOU CHANGE YOUR MIND!
COME BACK TO ICELAND WITH ME!
THOR-FINN!
COME HOME!

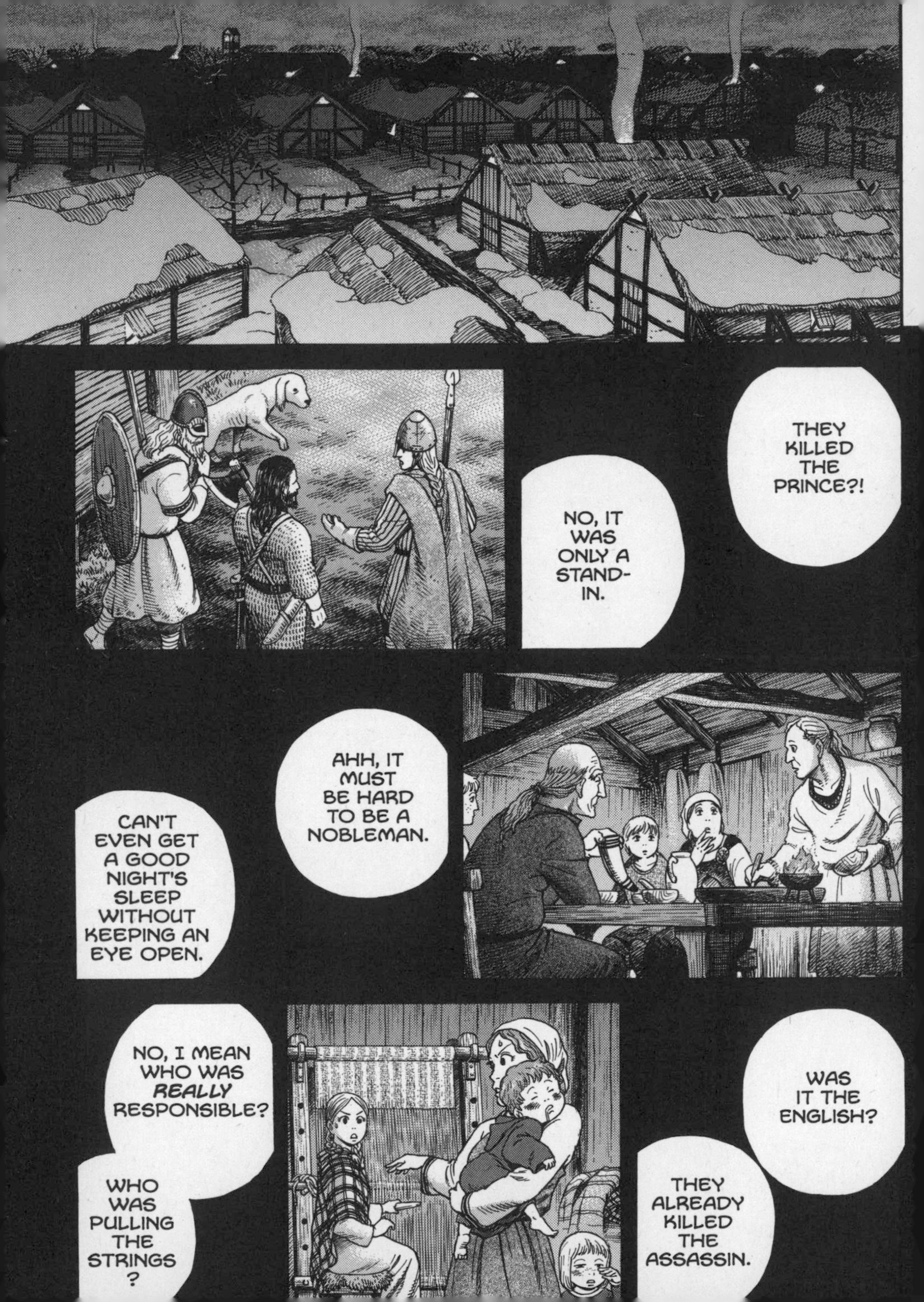
THEY KILLED THE PRINCE?!
NO, IT WAS ONLY A STAND-IN.
AHH, IT MUST BE HARD TO BE A NOBLEMAN.
CAN'T EVEN GET A GOOD NIGHT'S SLEEP WITHOUT KEEPING AN EYE OPEN.
WAS IT THE ENGLISH?
THEY ALREADY KILLED THE ASSASSIN.
NO, I MEAN WHO WAS *REALLY* RESPONSIBLE?
WHO WAS PULLING THE STRINGS?

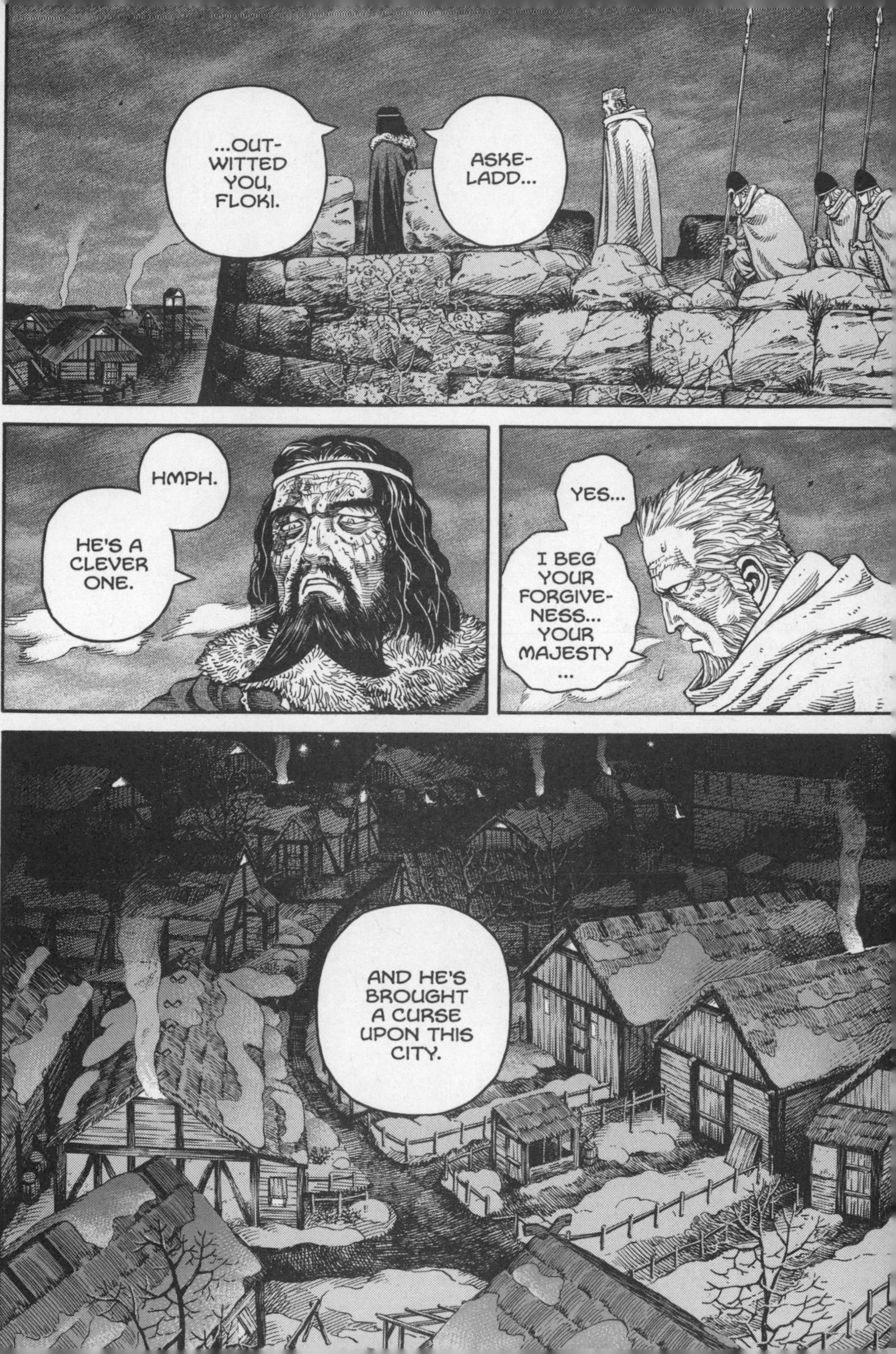
ASKE-LADD...
...OUT-WITTED YOU, FLOKI.
YES...
I BEG YOUR FORGIVE-NESS... YOUR MAJESTY ...
HMPH.
HE'S A CLEVER ONE.
AND HE'S BROUGHT A CURSE UPON THIS CITY.

CHAPTER 5 END

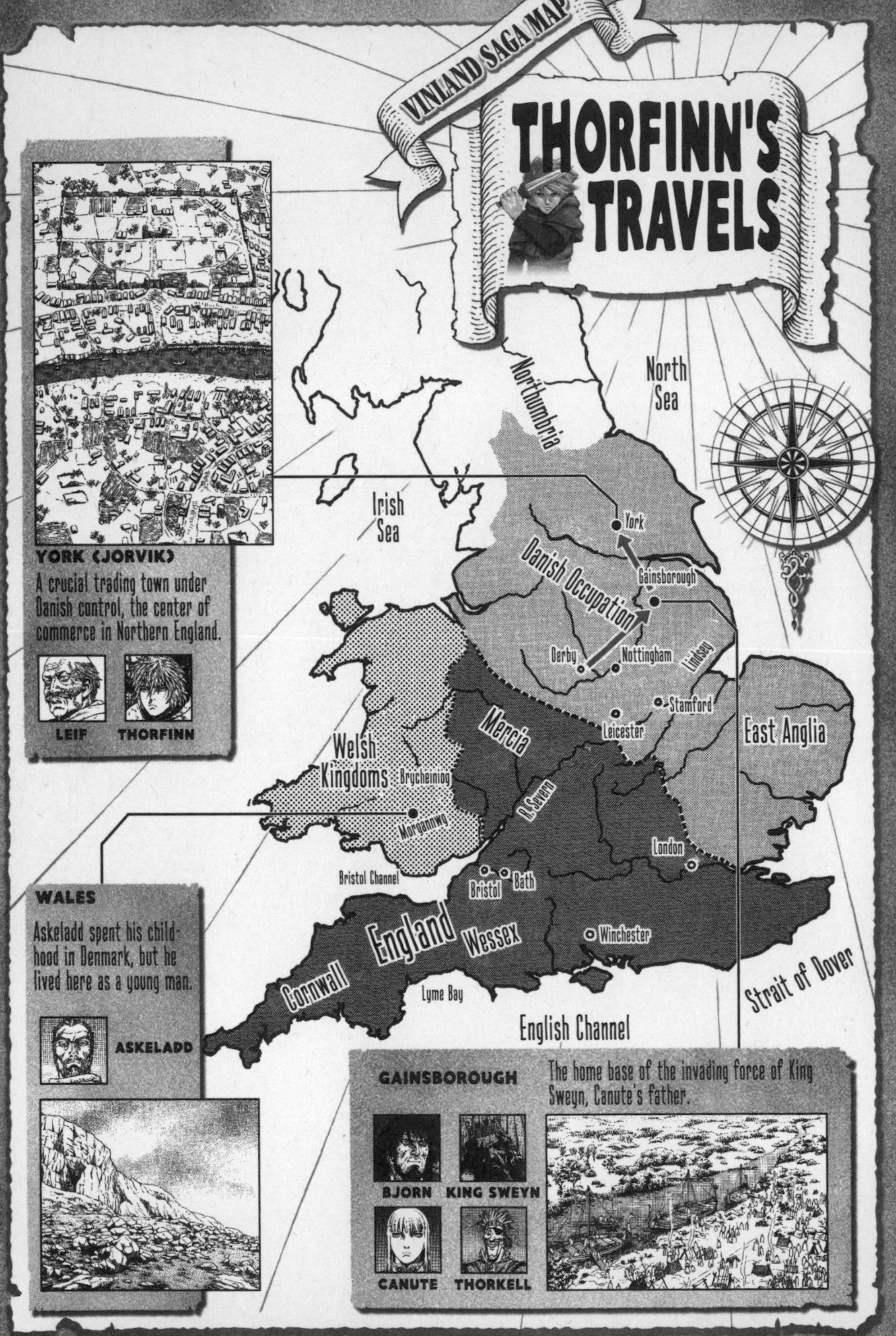
VINLAND SAGA MAP
THORFINN'S TRAVELS
YORK (JORVIK)
A crucial trading town under Danish control, the center of commerce in Northern England.
LEIF
THORFINN
Northumbria
North Sea
Irish Sea
York
Danish Occupation
Gainsborough
Derby
Nottingham
Lindsey
Stamford
Leicester
East Anglia
Mercia
Welsh Kingdoms
Brycheiniog
Morgannwg
R. Severn
London
Bristol Channel
Bristol
Bath
England
Wessex
Winchester
Cornwall
Lyme Bay
English Channel
Strait of Dover
WALES
Askeladd spent his childhood in Denmark, but he lived here as a young man.
ASKELADD
GAINSBOROUGH
The home base of the invading force of King Sweyn, Canute's father.
BJORN
KING SWEYN
CANUTE
THORKELL

SUPPLE-
MENTAL
DESIGNS

CANUTE

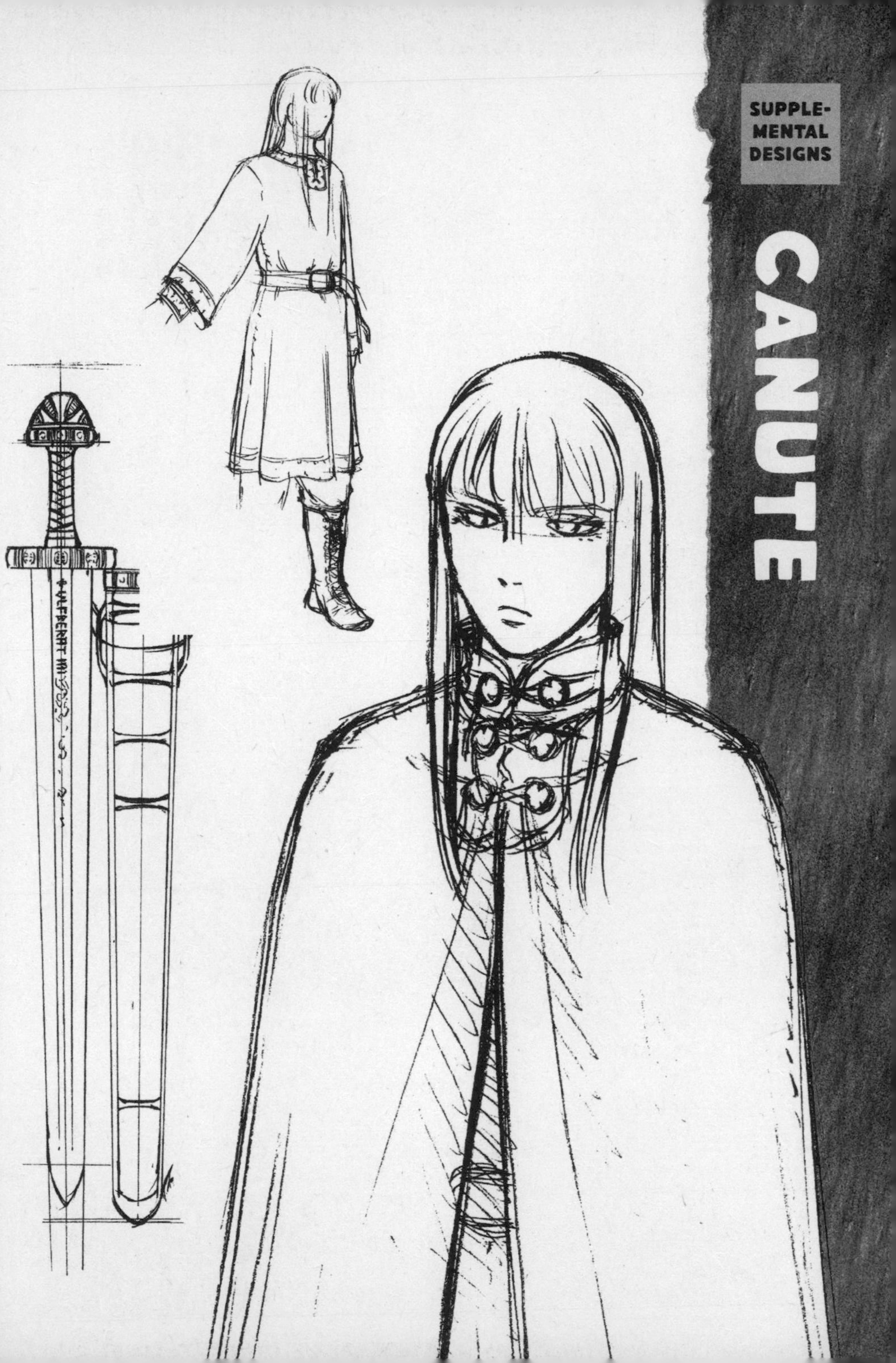

The Viking warriors hated being shamed more than anything else. Those who shrank away from violence and death, or did not answer insult with vengeance, were considered cowards. No warrior could survive being branded a coward. He would be excluded from Viking society. So they fought with their lives to protect their pride. I'm afraid of being hurt and dying. Honestly, I'd rather lose my pride than get into a fistfight. If it means being shunned, then so be it. I'd rather have it that way.

Pride above all: one facet of the Viking mindset that I truly hate.

MAKOTO YUKIMURA

VINLAND SAGA

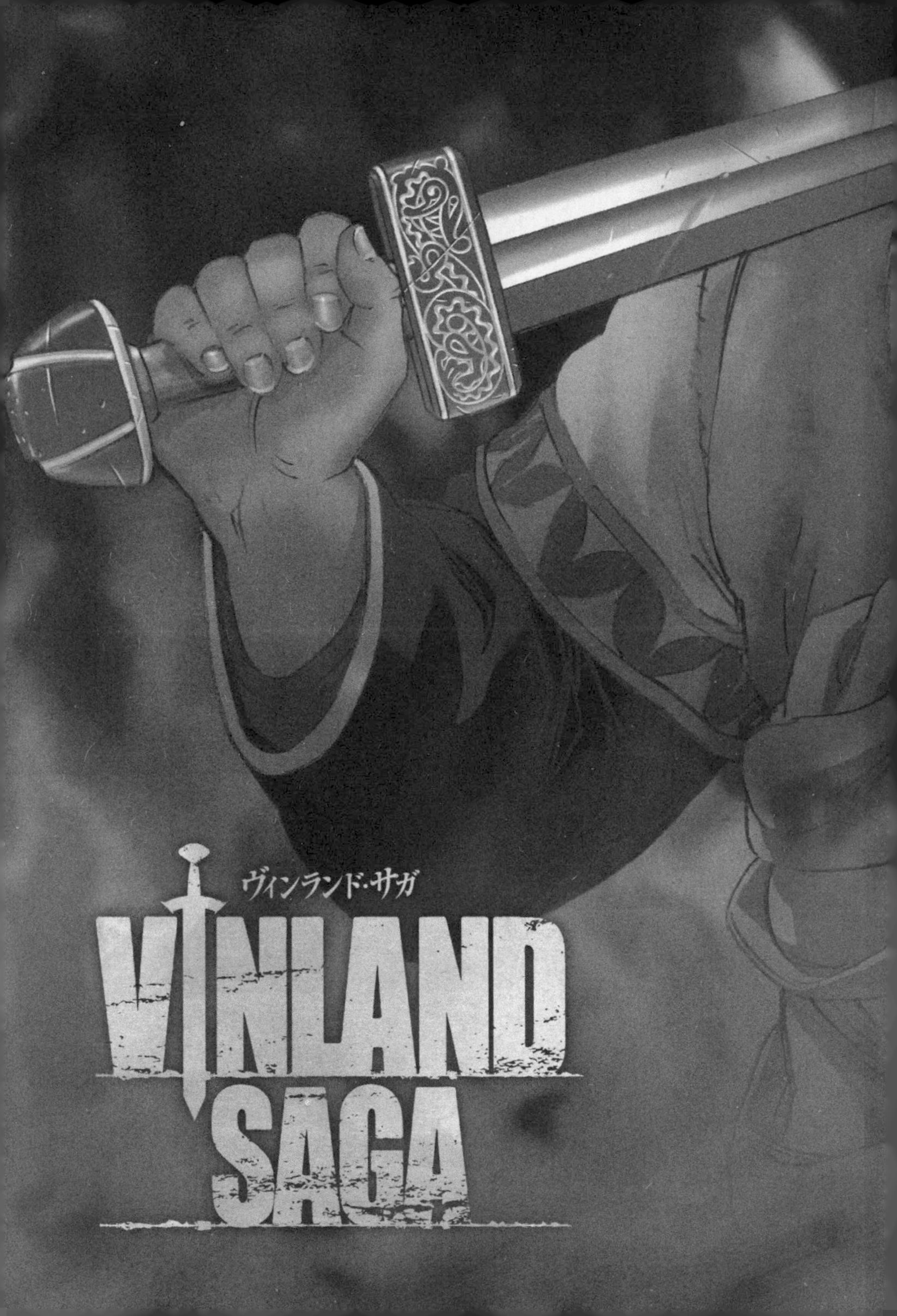
ヴィンランド・サガ
VINLAND SAGA

CHAPTER 50: PLOT

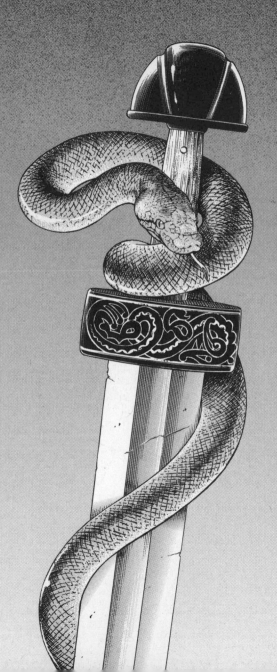

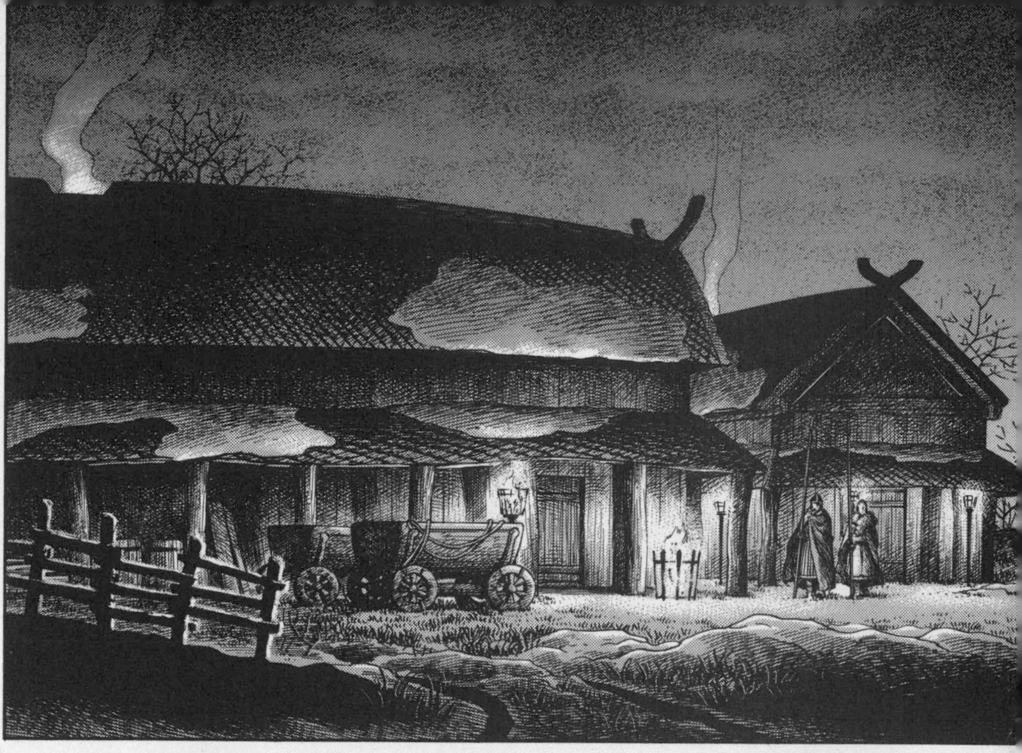
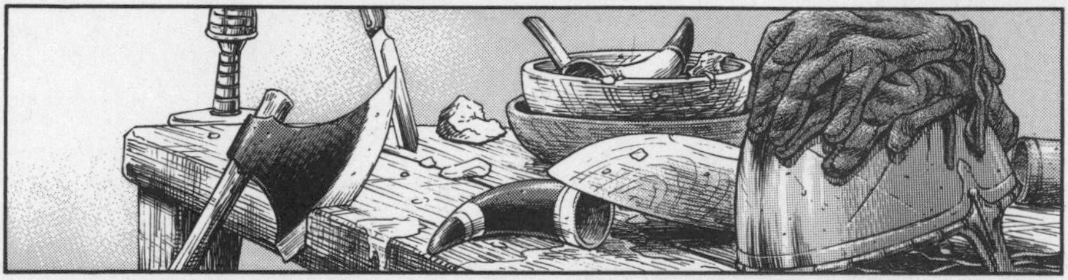
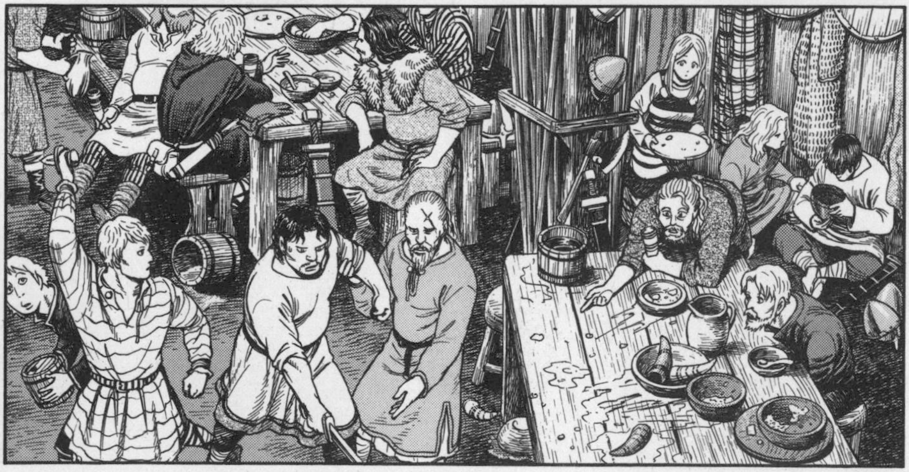

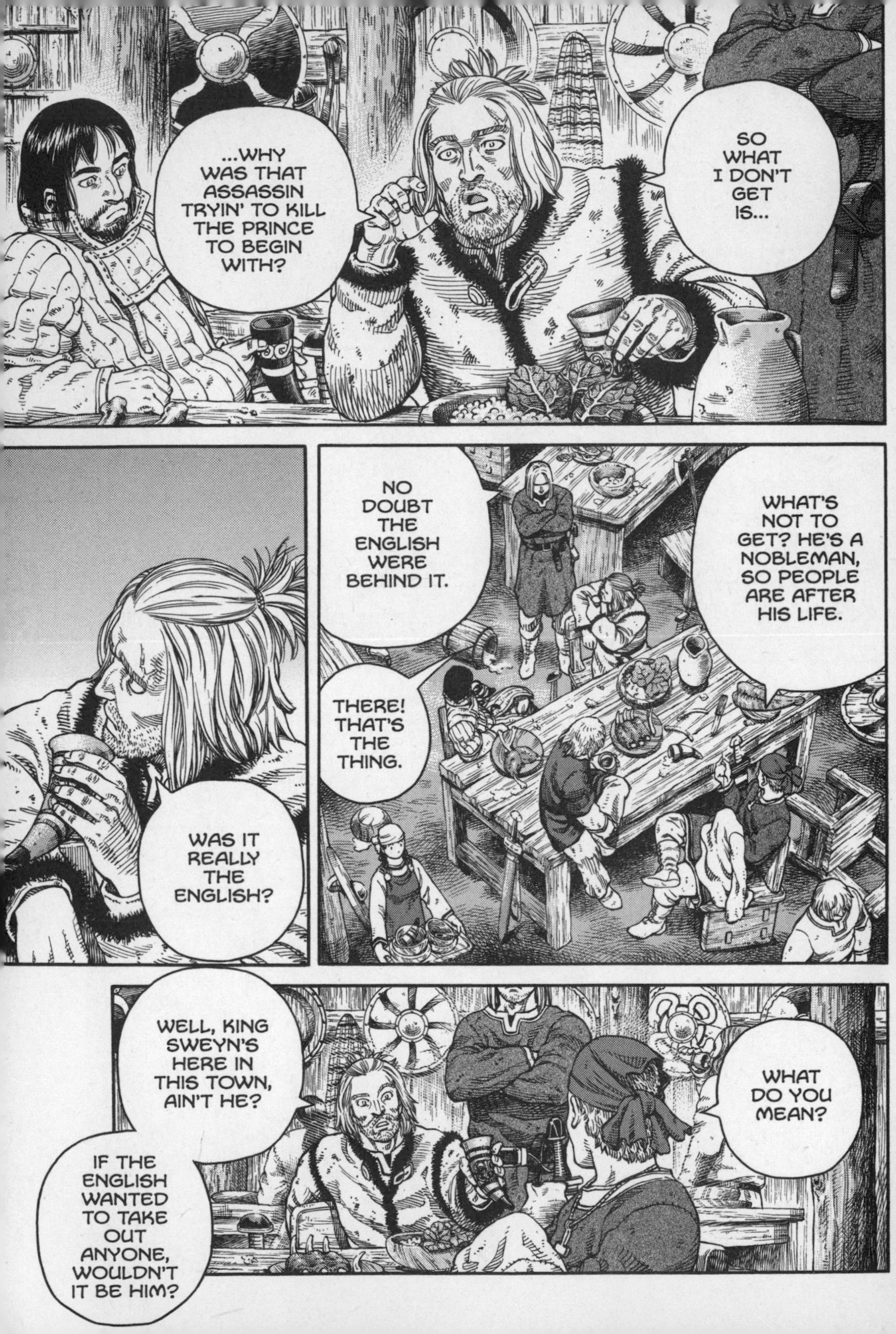
SO WHAT I DON'T GET IS...
...WHY WAS THAT ASSASSIN TRYIN' TO KILL THE PRINCE TO BEGIN WITH?
WHAT'S NOT TO GET? HE'S A NOBLEMAN, SO PEOPLE ARE AFTER HIS LIFE.
NO DOUBT THE ENGLISH WERE BEHIND IT.
THERE! THAT'S THE THING.
WAS IT REALLY THE ENGLISH?
WHAT DO YOU MEAN?
WELL, KING SWEYN'S HERE IN THIS TOWN, AIN'T HE?
IF THE ENGLISH WANTED TO TAKE OUT ANYONE, WOULDN'T IT BE HIM?

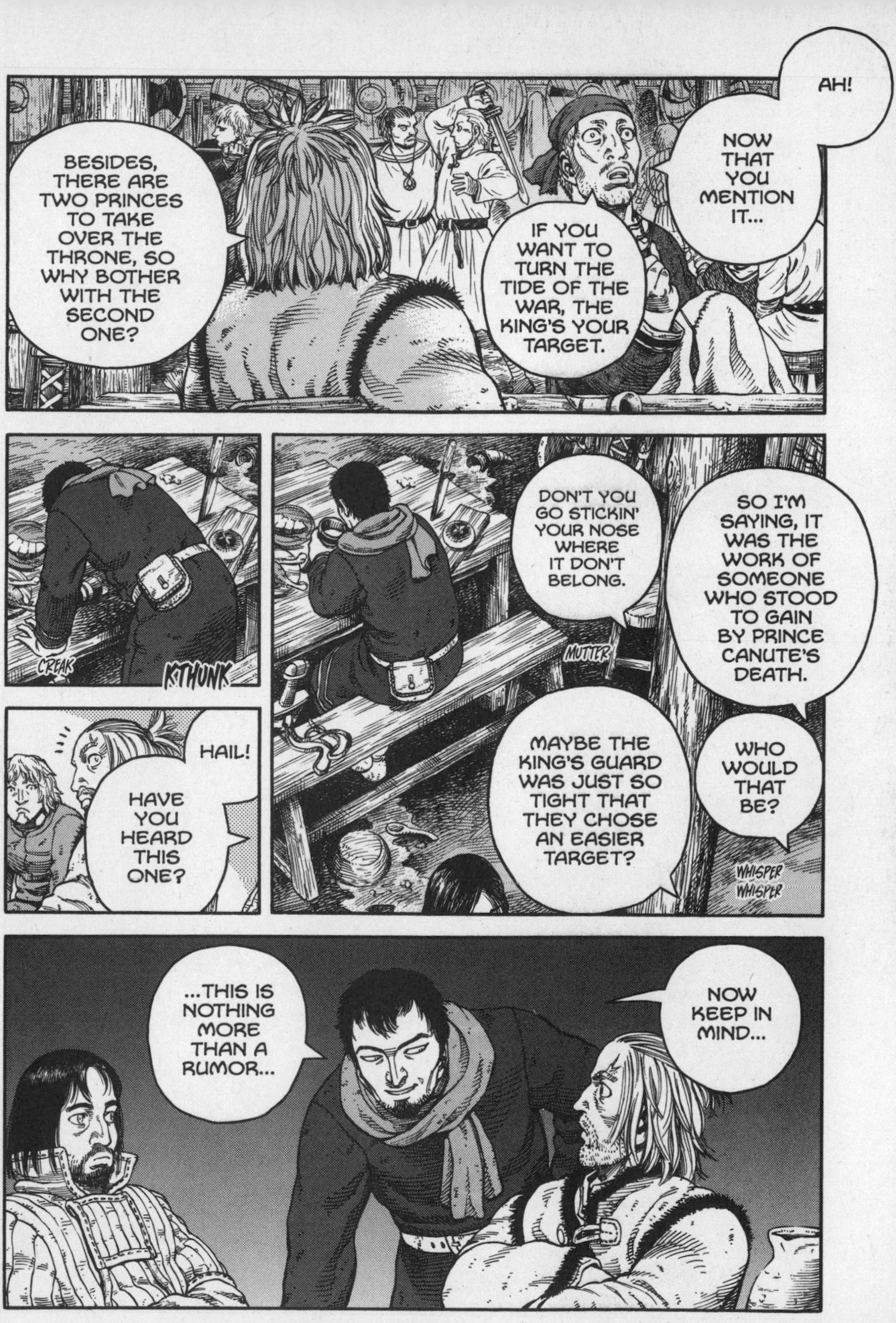
AH!
NOW THAT YOU MENTION IT...
IF YOU WANT TO TURN THE TIDE OF THE WAR, THE KING'S YOUR TARGET.
BESIDES, THERE ARE TWO PRINCES TO TAKE OVER THE THRONE, SO WHY BOTHER WITH THE SECOND ONE?
SO I'M SAYING, IT WAS THE WORK OF SOMEONE WHO STOOD TO GAIN BY PRINCE CANUTE'S DEATH.
DON'T YOU GO STICKIN' YOUR NOSE WHERE IT DON'T BELONG.
MUTTER
WHO WOULD THAT BE?
MAYBE THE KING'S GUARD WAS JUST SO TIGHT THAT THEY CHOSE AN EASIER TARGET?
WHISPER WHISPER
KTHUNK
CREAK
HAIL!
HAVE YOU HEARD THIS ONE?
NOW KEEP IN MIND...
...THIS IS NOTHING MORE THAN A RUMOR...

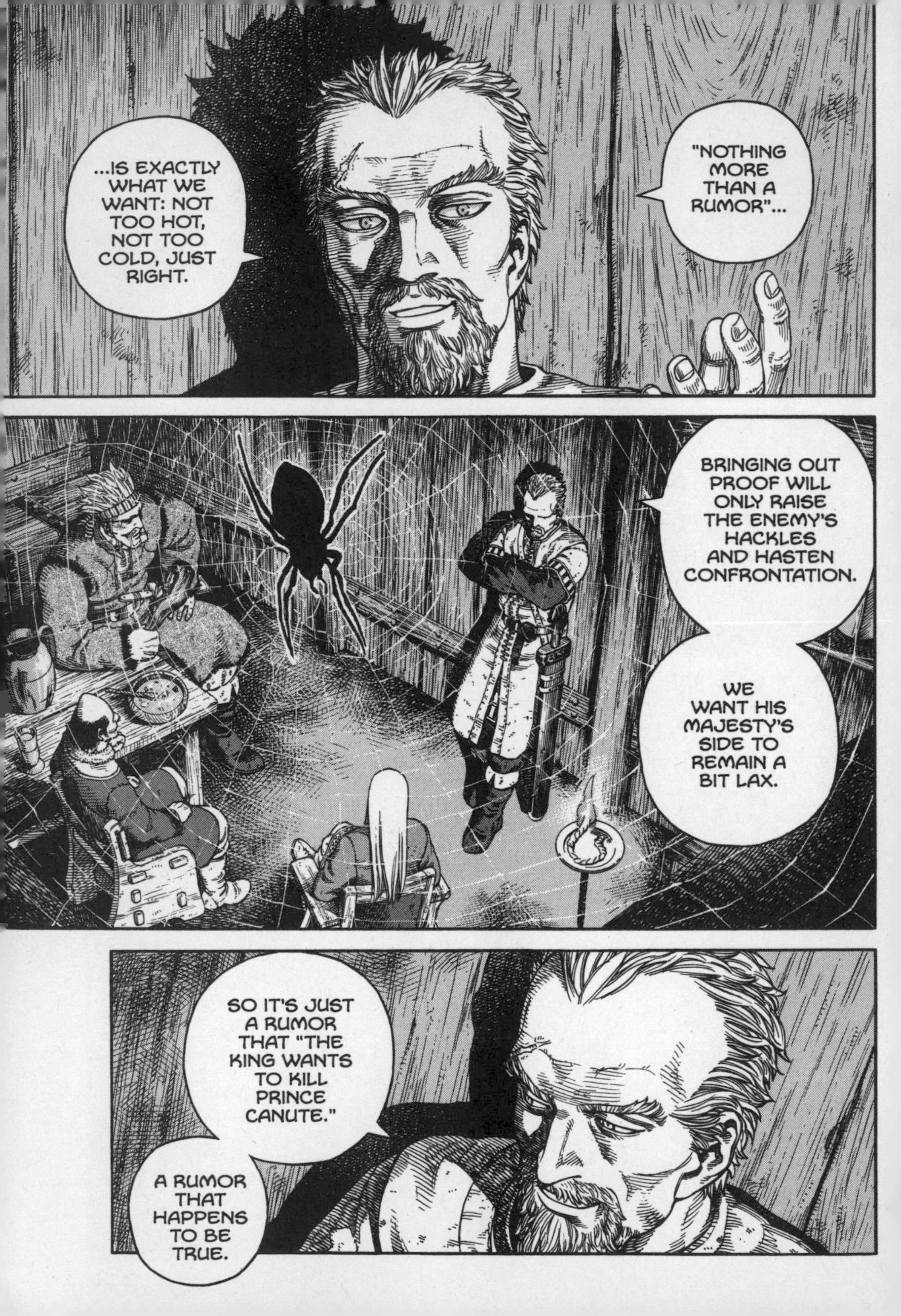
"NOTHING MORE THAN A RUMOR"...
...IS EXACTLY WHAT WE WANT: NOT TOO HOT, NOT TOO COLD, JUST RIGHT.
BRINGING OUT PROOF WILL ONLY RAISE THE ENEMY'S HACKLES AND HASTEN CONFRONTATION.
WE WANT HIS MAJESTY'S SIDE TO REMAIN A BIT LAX.
SO IT'S JUST A RUMOR THAT "THE KING WANTS TO KILL PRINCE CANUTE."
A RUMOR THAT HAPPENS TO BE TRUE.

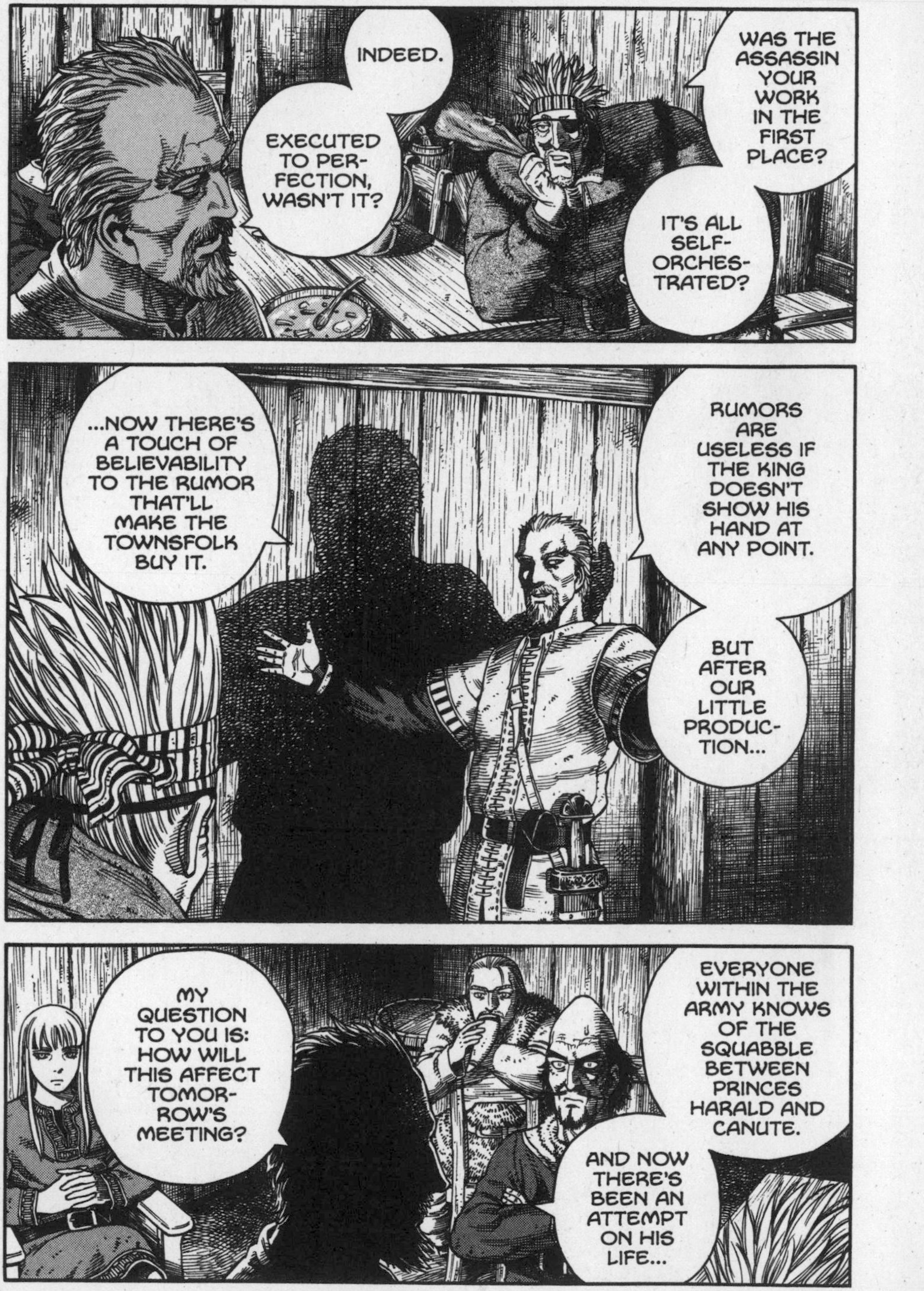
WAS THE ASSASSIN YOUR WORK IN THE FIRST PLACE?
IT'S ALL SELF-ORCHESTRATED?
INDEED.
EXECUTED TO PERFECTION, WASN'T IT?
RUMORS ARE USELESS IF THE KING DOESN'T SHOW HIS HAND AT ANY POINT.
BUT AFTER OUR LITTLE PRODUCTION...
...NOW THERE'S A TOUCH OF BELIEVABILITY TO THE RUMOR THAT'LL MAKE THE TOWNSFOLK BUY IT.
EVERYONE WITHIN THE ARMY KNOWS OF THE SQUABBLE BETWEEN PRINCES HARALD AND CANUTE.
AND NOW THERE'S BEEN AN ATTEMPT ON HIS LIFE...
MY QUESTION TO YOU IS: HOW WILL THIS AFFECT TOMORROW'S MEETING?

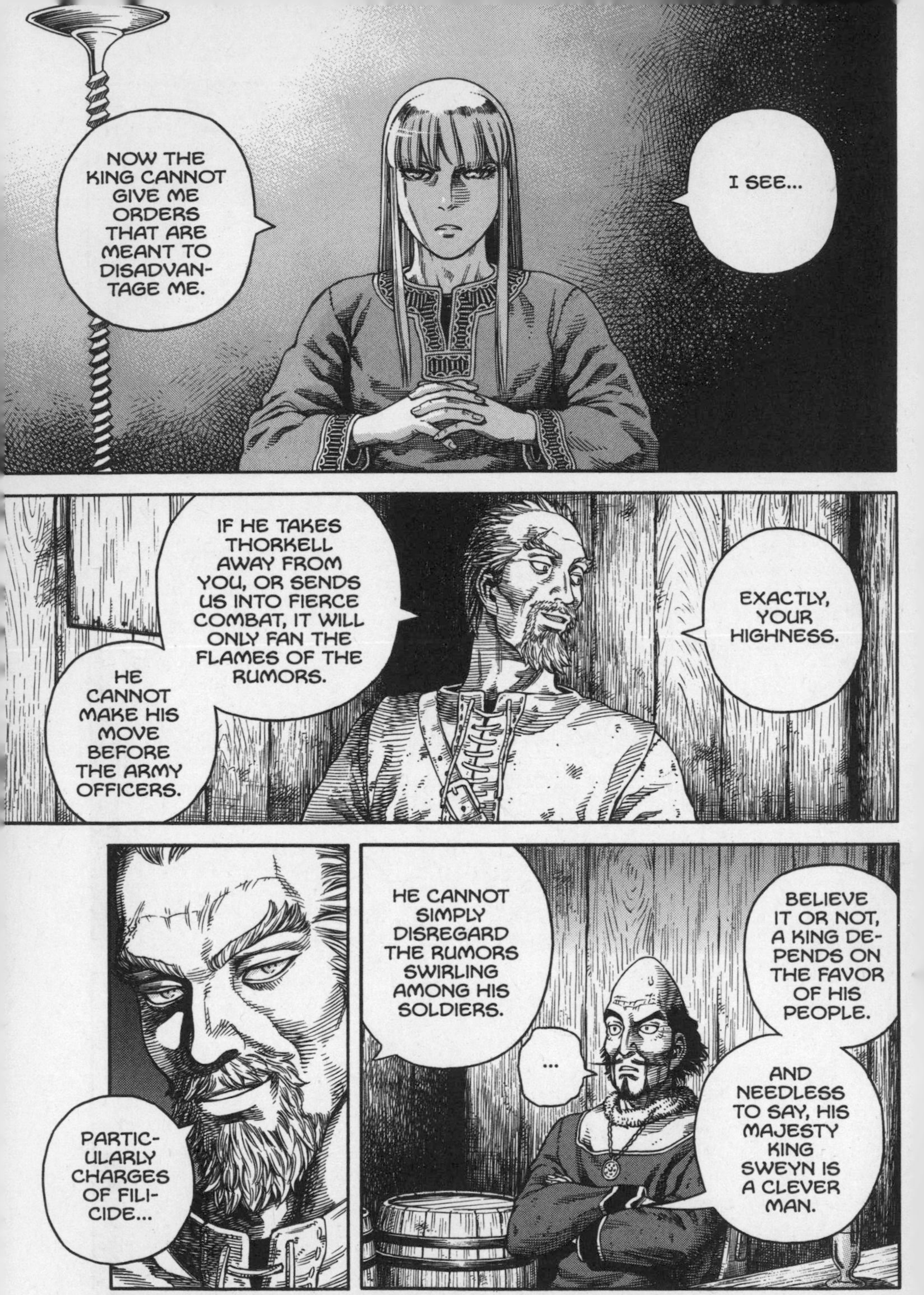

I SEE...
NOW THE KING CANNOT GIVE ME ORDERS THAT ARE MEANT TO DISADVANTAGE ME.
EXACTLY, YOUR HIGHNESS.
IF HE TAKES THORKELL AWAY FROM YOU, OR SENDS US INTO FIERCE COMBAT, IT WILL ONLY FAN THE FLAMES OF THE RUMORS.
HE CANNOT MAKE HIS MOVE BEFORE THE ARMY OFFICERS.
BELIEVE IT OR NOT, A KING DEPENDS ON THE FAVOR OF HIS PEOPLE.
HE CANNOT SIMPLY DISREGARD THE RUMORS SWIRLING AMONG HIS SOLDIERS.
AND NEEDLESS TO SAY, HIS MAJESTY KING SWEYN IS A CLEVER MAN.
...
PARTICULARLY CHARGES OF FILICIDE...

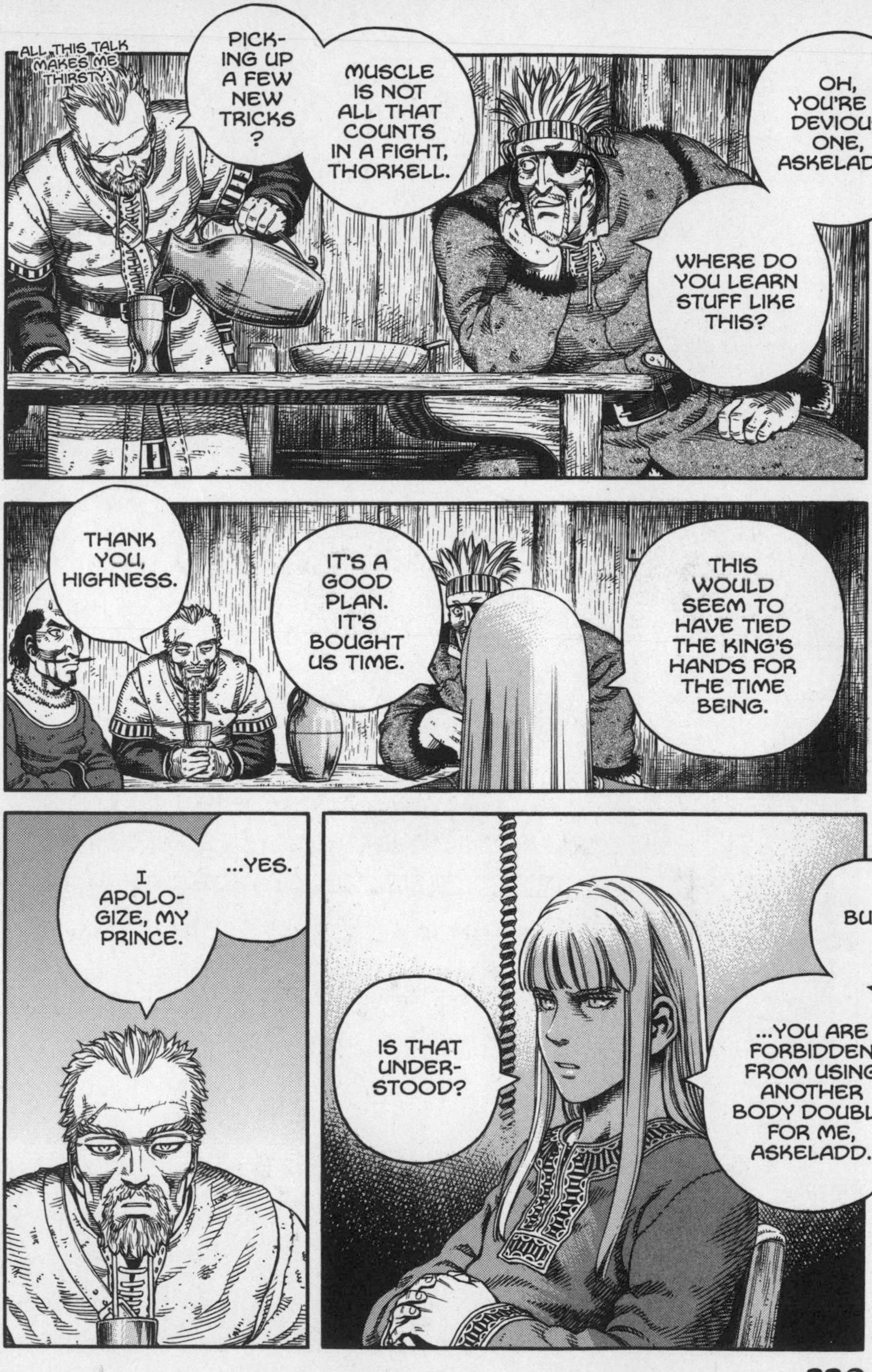
OH, YOU'RE A DEVIOUS ONE, ASKELADD.
WHERE DO YOU LEARN STUFF LIKE THIS?
MUSCLE IS NOT ALL THAT COUNTS IN A FIGHT, THORKELL.
PICK-ING UP A FEW NEW TRICKS ?
ALL THIS TALK MAKES ME THIRSTY.
THIS WOULD SEEM TO HAVE TIED THE KING'S HANDS FOR THE TIME BEING.
IT'S A GOOD PLAN. IT'S BOUGHT US TIME.
THANK YOU, HIGHNESS.
BUT...
...YOU ARE FORBIDDEN FROM USING ANOTHER BODY DOUBLE FOR ME, ASKELADD.
IS THAT UNDER-STOOD?
...YES.
I APOLO-GIZE, MY PRINCE.

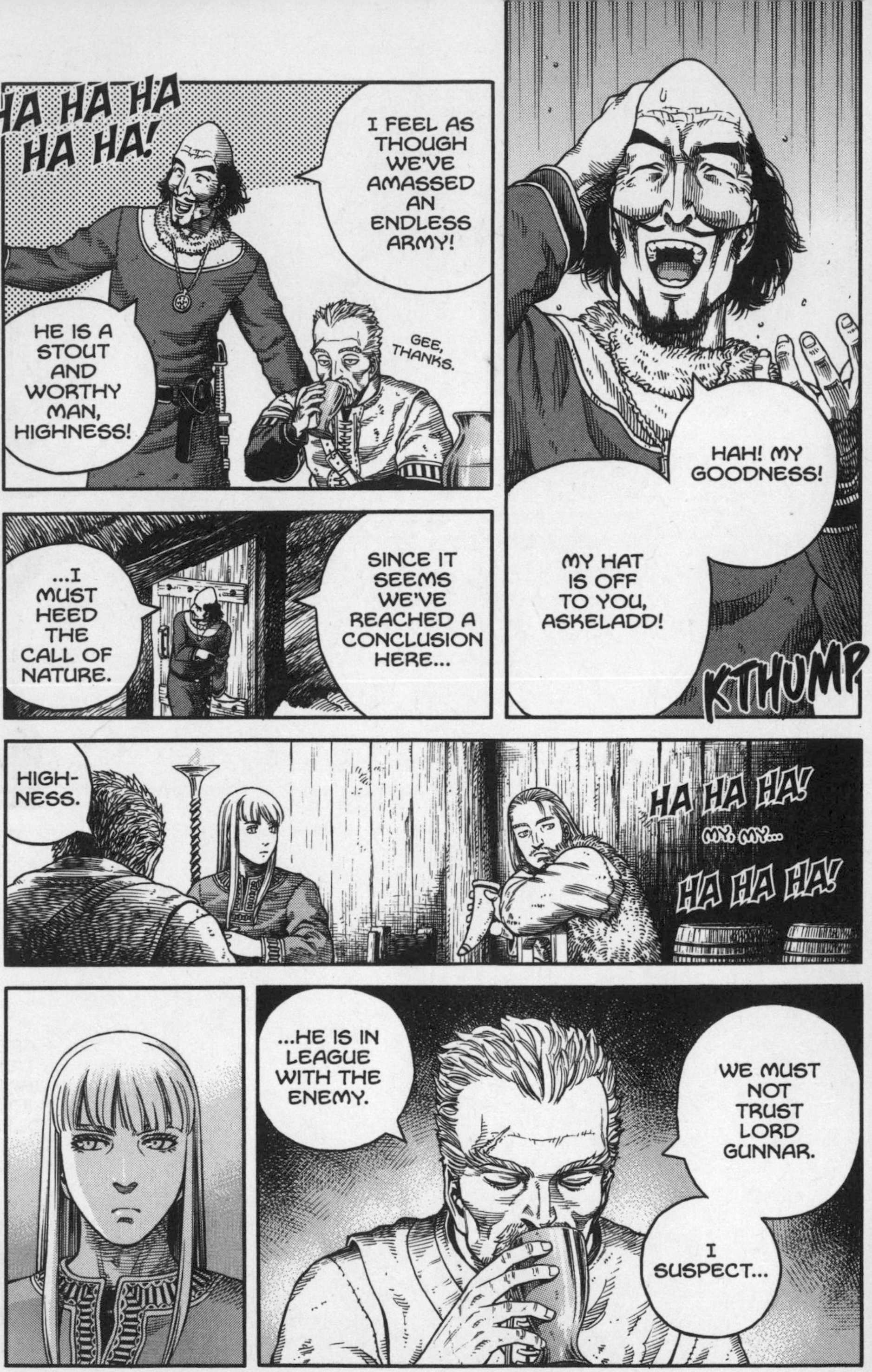
HAH! MY GOODNESS!
MY HAT IS OFF TO YOU, ASKELADD!
KTHUMP
I FEEL AS THOUGH WE'VE AMASSED AN ENDLESS ARMY!
HA HA HA HA HA!
HE IS A STOUT AND WORTHY MAN, HIGHNESS!
GEE, THANKS.
SINCE IT SEEMS WE'VE REACHED A CONCLUSION HERE...
...I MUST HEED THE CALL OF NATURE.
HA HA HA!
MY, MY...
HA HA HA!
HIGH-NESS.
WE MUST NOT TRUST LORD GUNNAR.
I SUSPECT...
...HE IS IN LEAGUE WITH THE ENEMY.

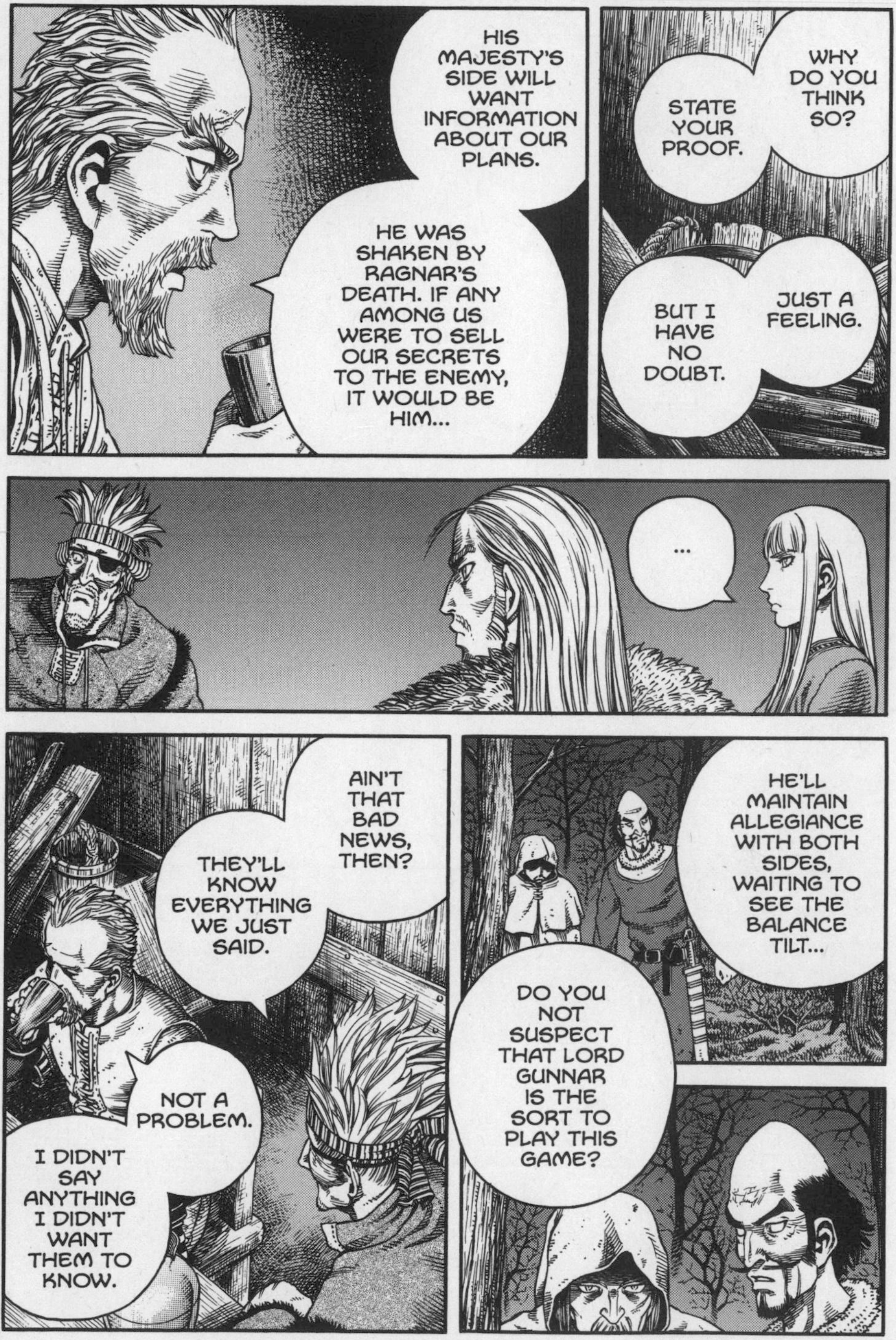
WHY DO YOU THINK SO?
STATE YOUR PROOF.
JUST A FEELING.
BUT I HAVE NO DOUBT.
HIS MAJESTY'S SIDE WILL WANT INFORMATION ABOUT OUR PLANS.
HE WAS SHAKEN BY RAGNAR'S DEATH. IF ANY AMONG US WERE TO SELL OUR SECRETS TO THE ENEMY, IT WOULD BE HIM...
...
HE'LL MAINTAIN ALLEGIANCE WITH BOTH SIDES, WAITING TO SEE THE BALANCE TILT...
DO YOU NOT SUSPECT THAT LORD GUNNAR IS THE SORT TO PLAY THIS GAME?
AIN'T THAT BAD NEWS, THEN?
THEY'LL KNOW EVERYTHING WE JUST SAID.
NOT A PROBLEM.
I DIDN'T SAY ANYTHING I DIDN'T WANT THEM TO KNOW.

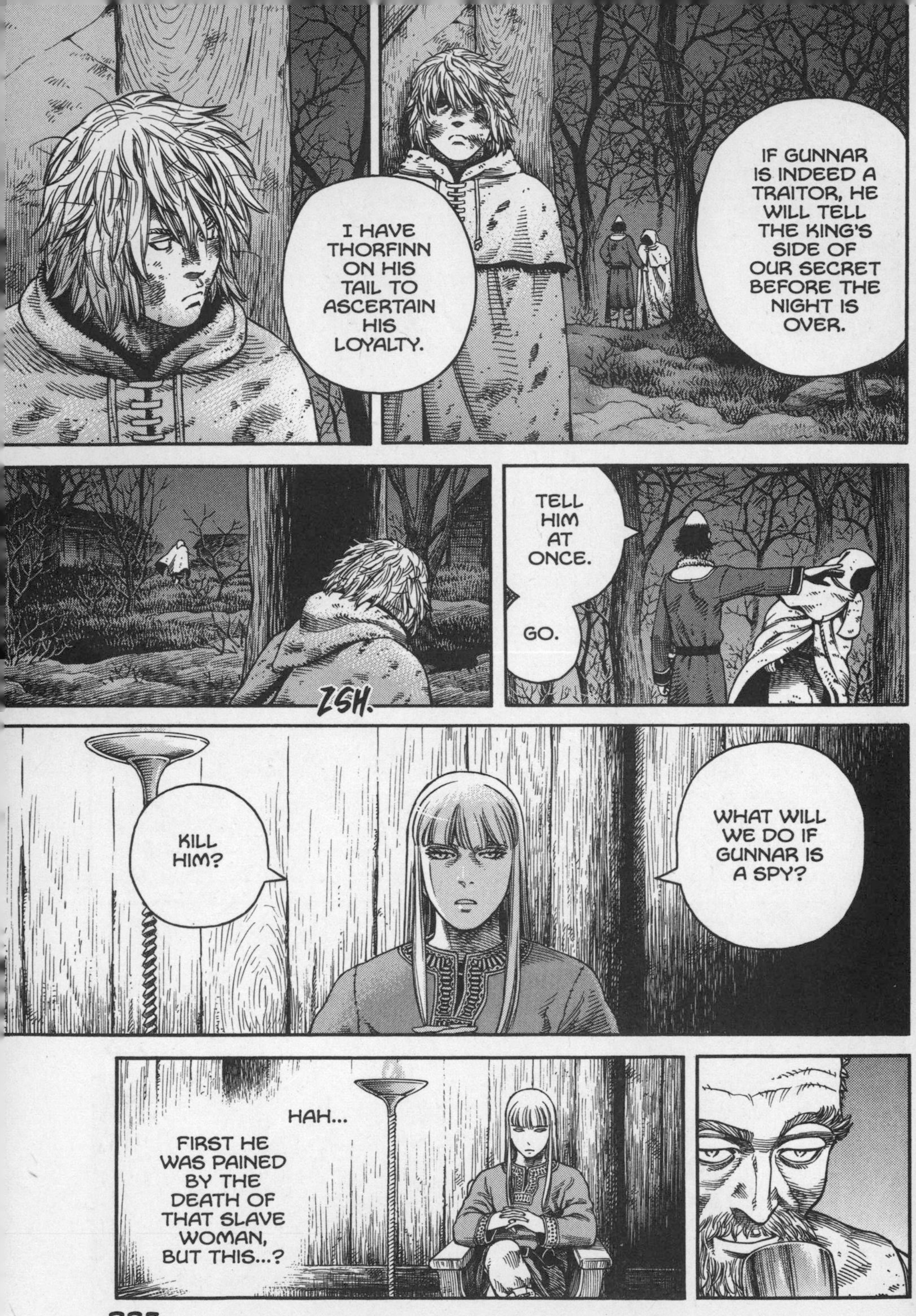

IF GUNNAR IS INDEED A TRAITOR, HE WILL TELL THE KING'S SIDE OF OUR SECRET BEFORE THE NIGHT IS OVER.
I HAVE THORFINN ON HIS TAIL TO ASCERTAIN HIS LOYALTY.
TELL HIM AT ONCE.
GO.
ZSH.
WHAT WILL WE DO IF GUNNAR IS A SPY?
KILL HIM?
HAH...
FIRST HE WAS PAINED BY THE DEATH OF THAT SLAVE WOMAN, BUT THIS...?

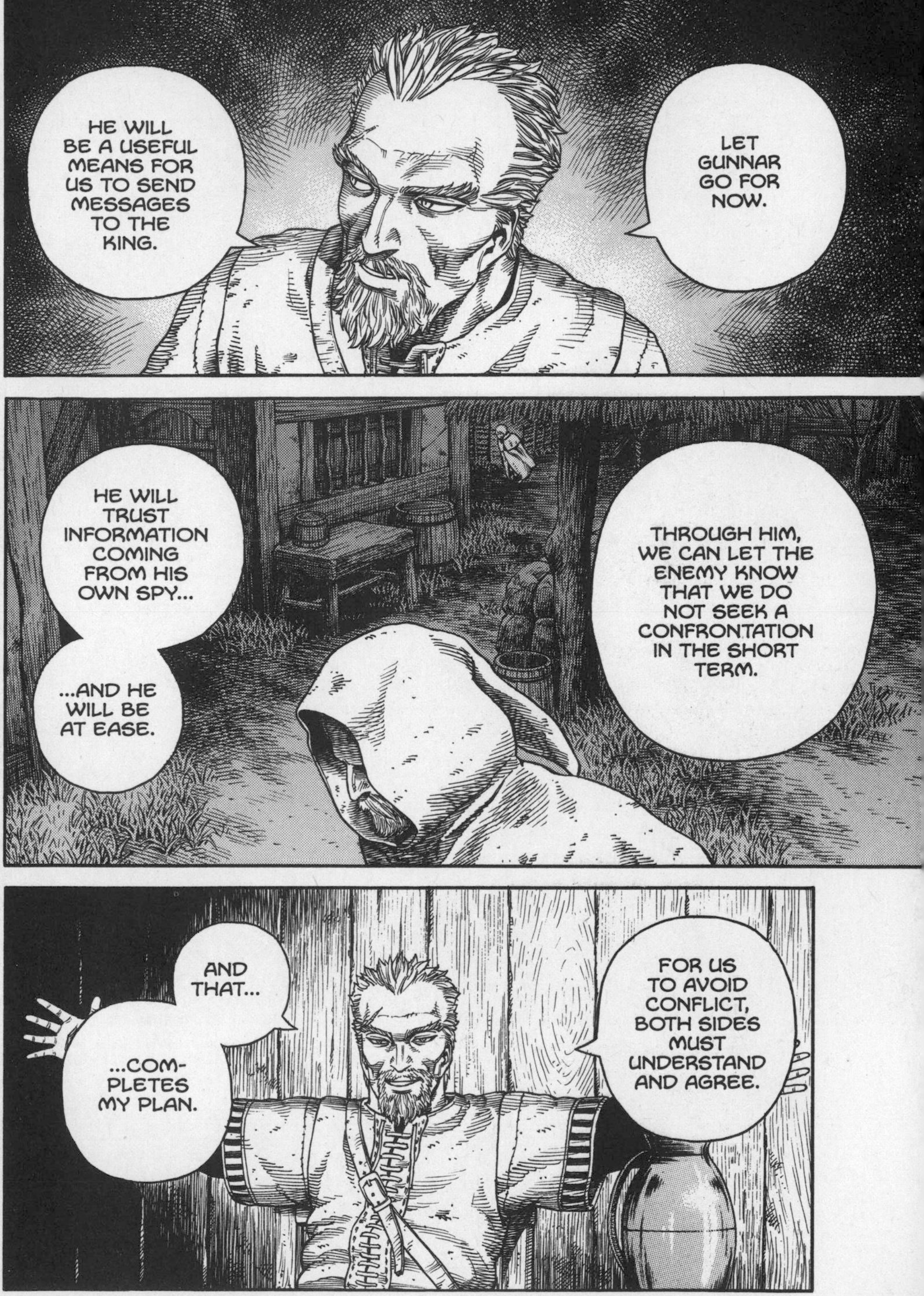
LET GUNNAR GO FOR NOW.
HE WILL BE A USEFUL MEANS FOR US TO SEND MESSAGES TO THE KING.
THROUGH HIM, WE CAN LET THE ENEMY KNOW THAT WE DO NOT SEEK A CONFRONTATION IN THE SHORT TERM.
HE WILL TRUST INFORMATION COMING FROM HIS OWN SPY...
...AND HE WILL BE AT EASE.
FOR US TO AVOID CONFLICT, BOTH SIDES MUST UNDERSTAND AND AGREE.
AND THAT...
...COM-
PLETES MY PLAN.

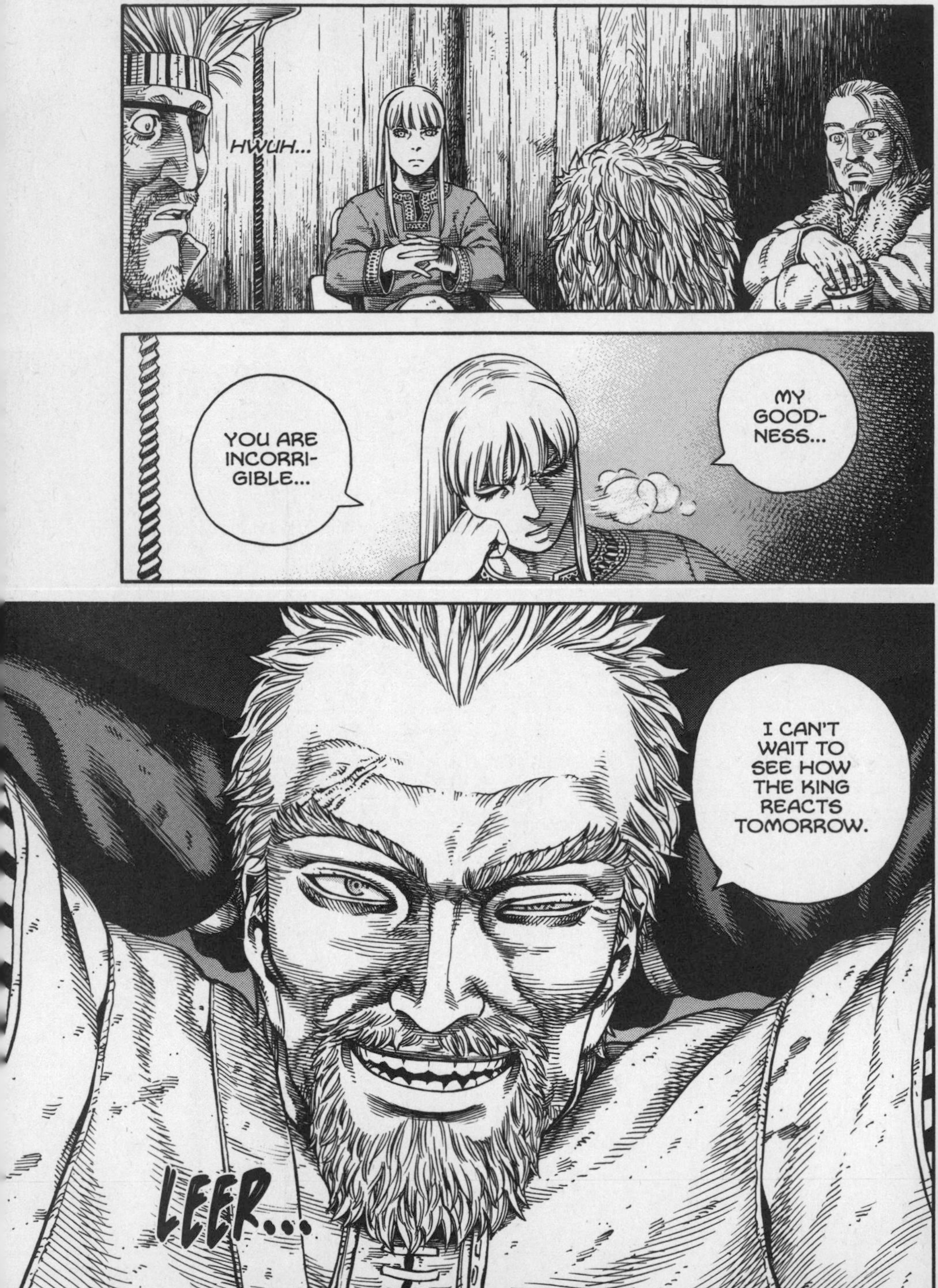
HWUH...
MY GOOD-NESS...
YOU ARE INCORRI-GIBLE...
I CAN'T WAIT TO SEE HOW THE KING REACTS TOMORROW.
LEER...

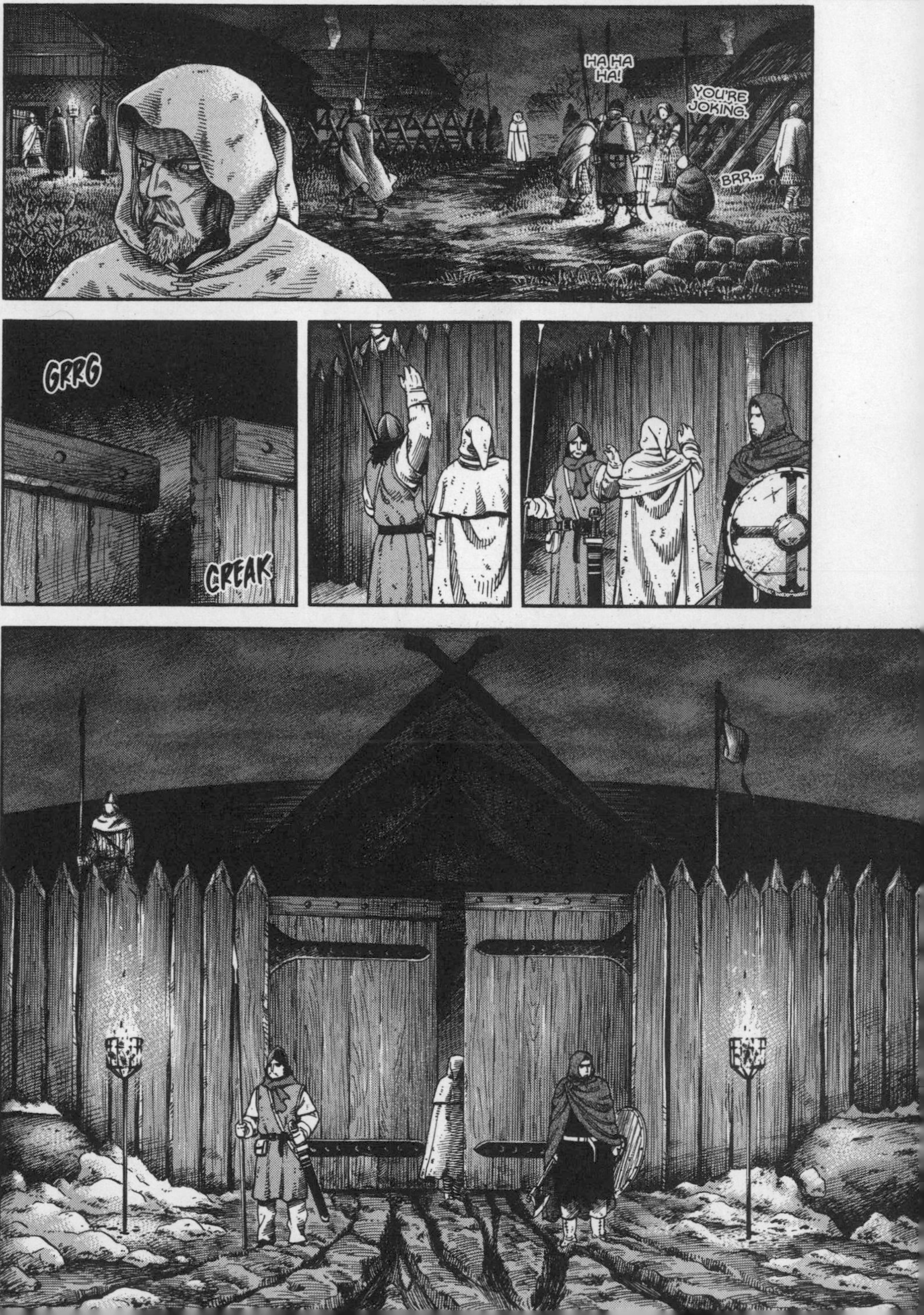
YOU'RE JOKING.
HA HA HA!
BRR...
GRRG
CREAK

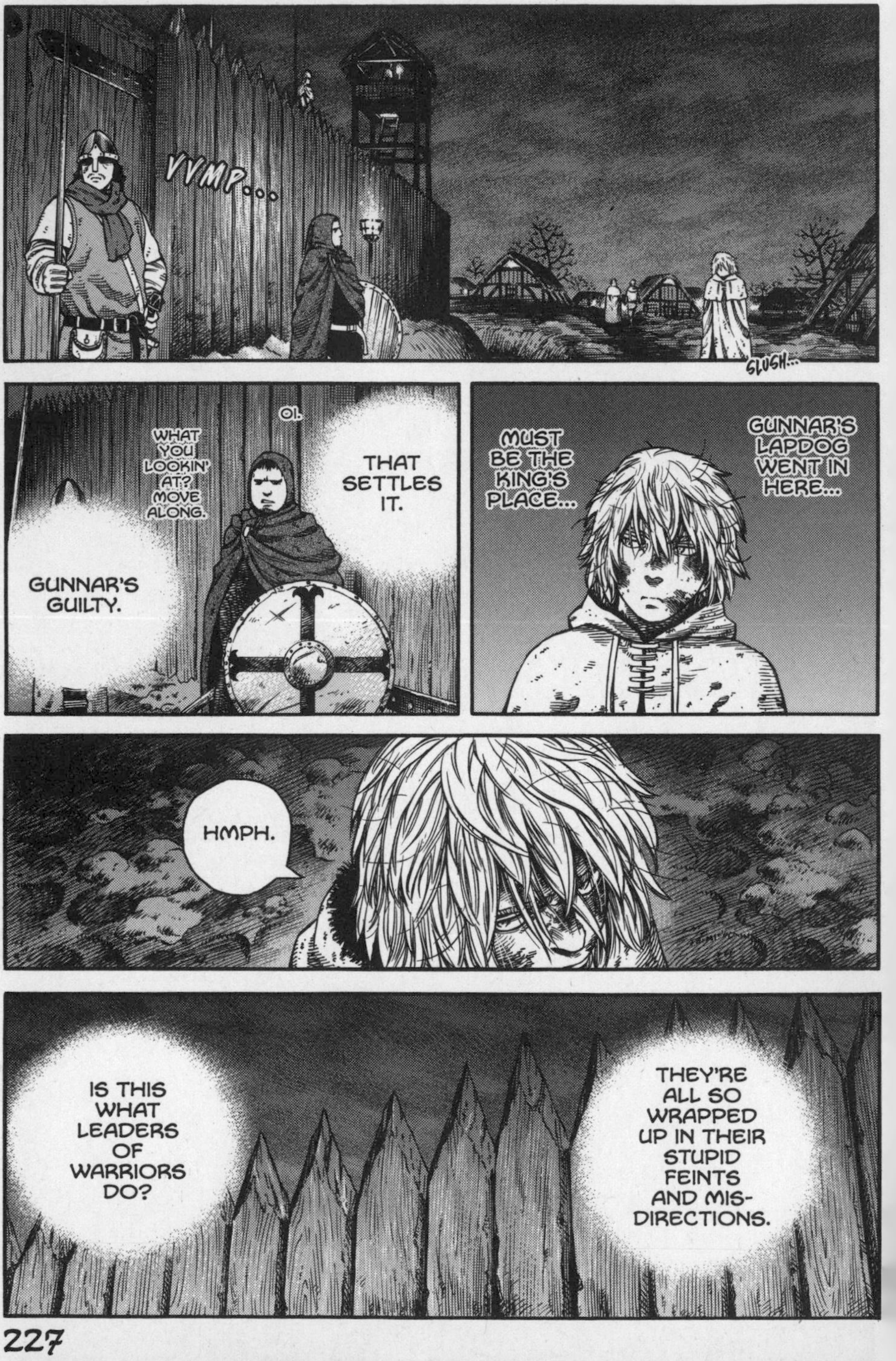
VVMP...
SLUSH...
GUNNAR'S LAPDOG WENT IN HERE...
MUST BE THE KING'S PLACE...
OI.
THAT SETTLES IT.
WHAT YOU LOOKIN' AT? MOVE ALONG.
GUNNAR'S GUILTY.
HMPH.
THEY'RE ALL SO WRAPPED UP IN THEIR STUPID FEINTS AND MIS-DIRECTIONS.
IS THIS WHAT LEADERS OF WARRIORS DO?

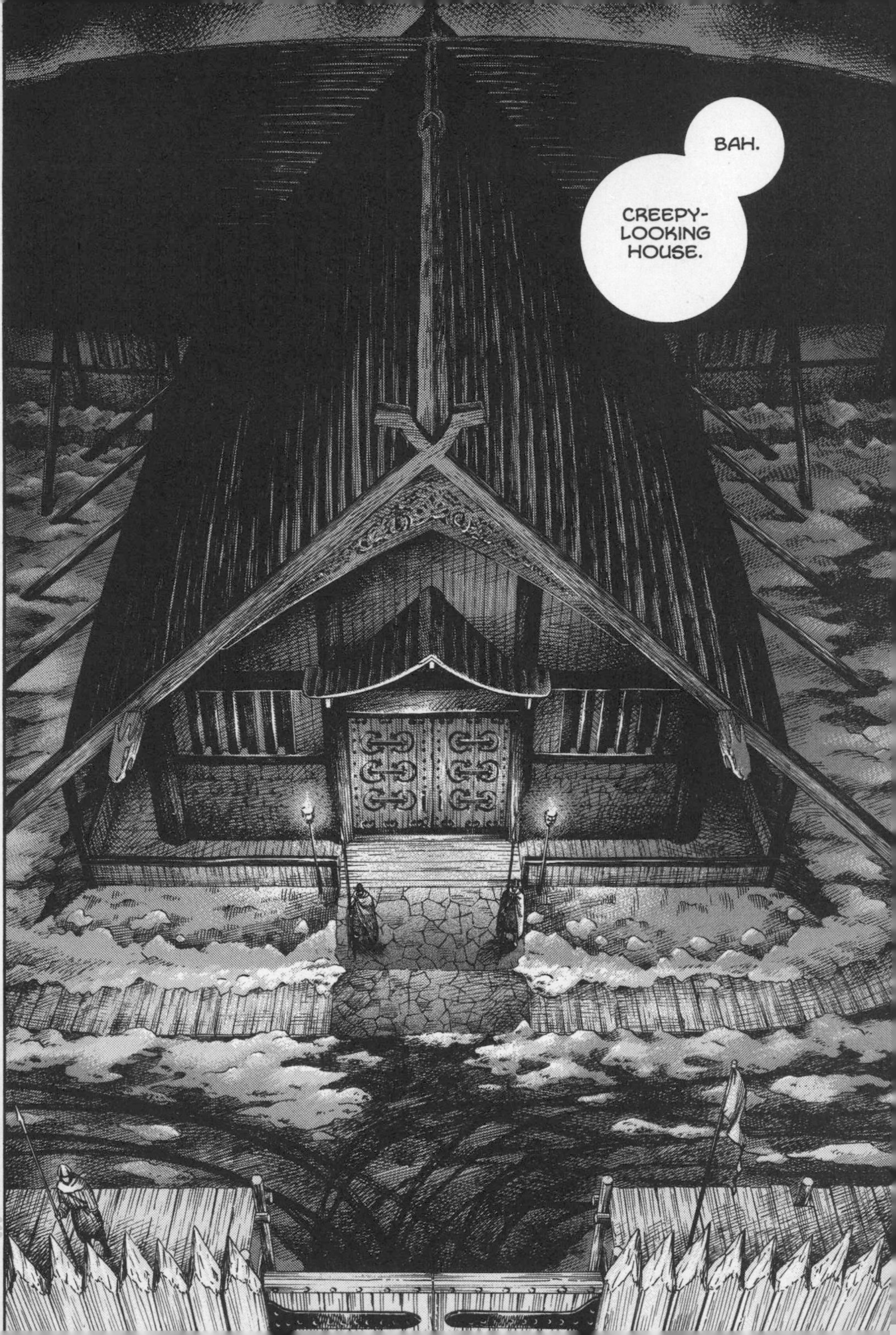
BAH.
CREEPY-LOOKING HOUSE.

CHAPTER 51: MISCALCULATION

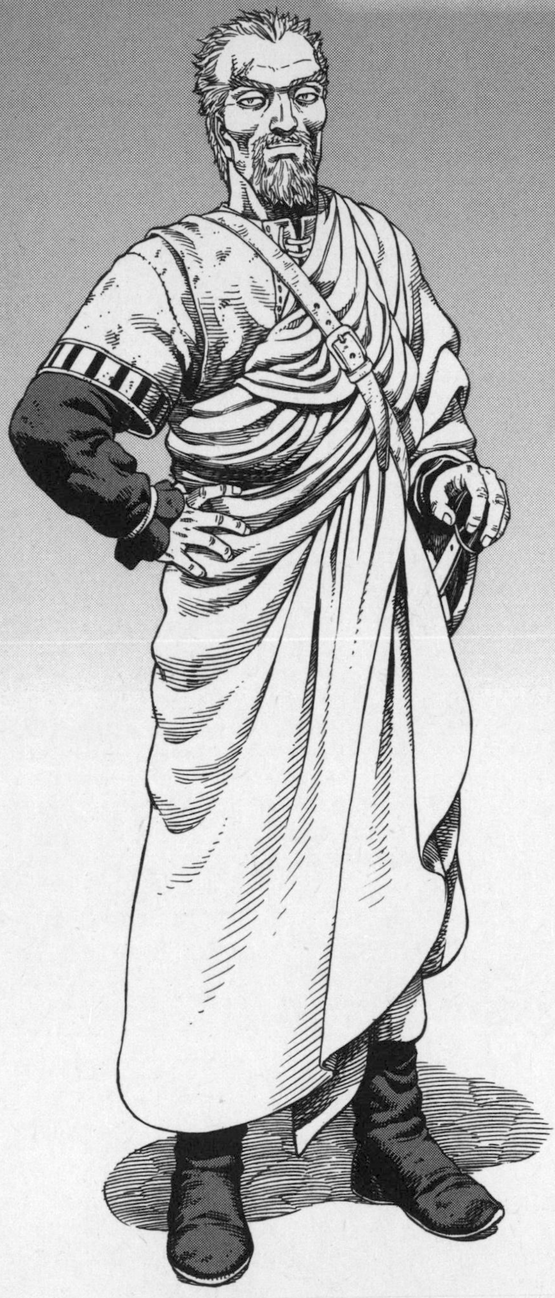

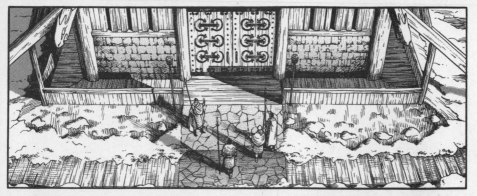

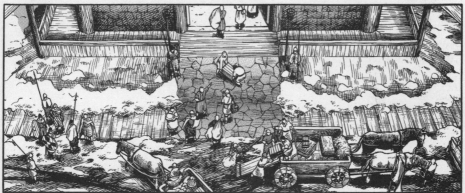

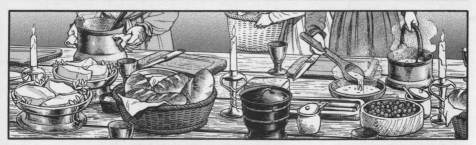

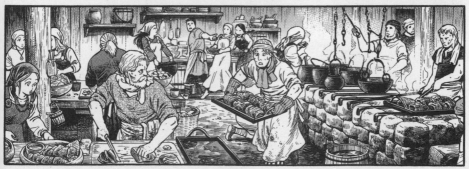

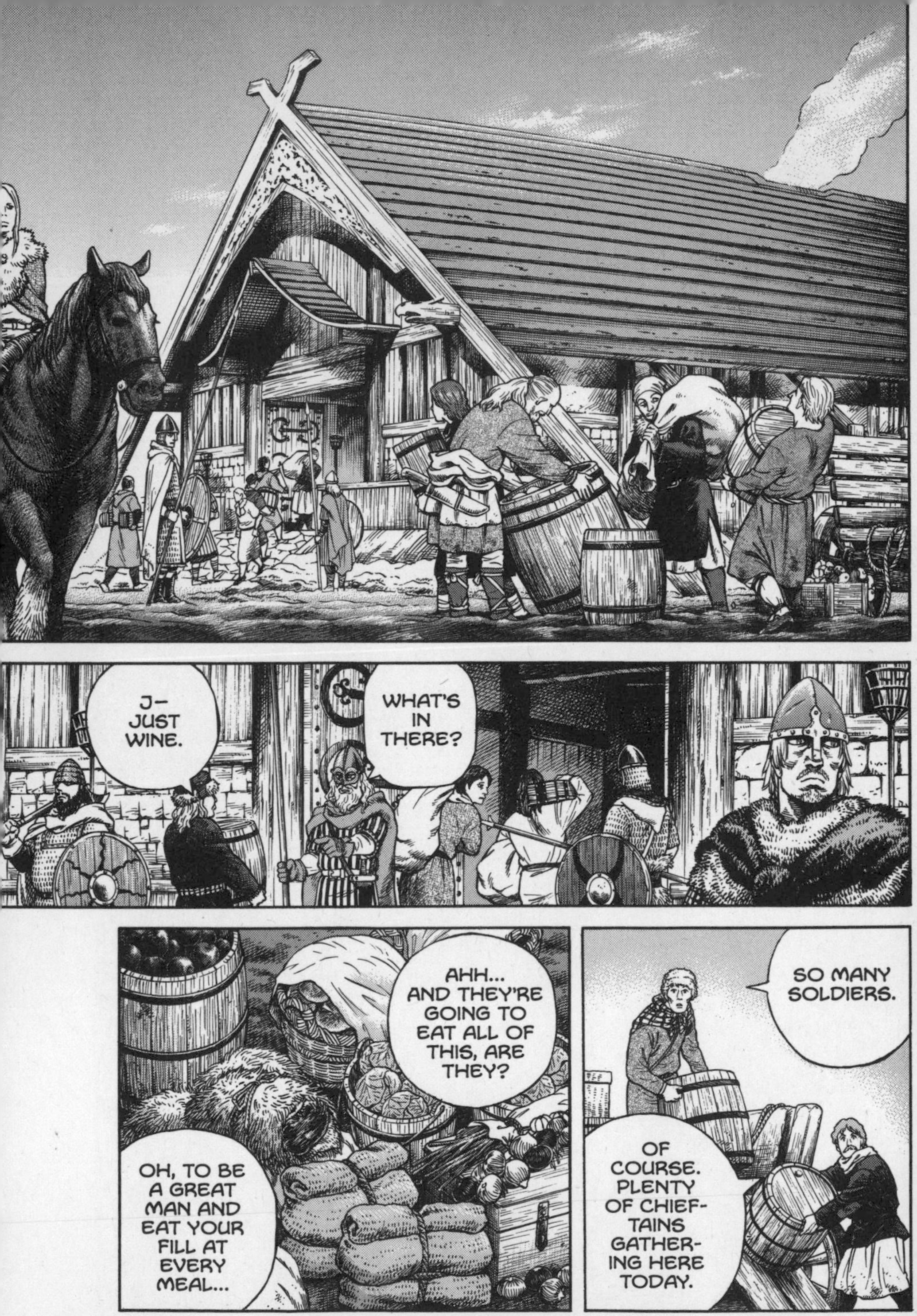
WHAT'S IN THERE?
J— JUST WINE.
SO MANY SOLDIERS.
OF COURSE. PLENTY OF CHIEF-TAINS GATHERING HERE TODAY.
AHH... AND THEY'RE GOING TO EAT ALL OF THIS, ARE THEY?
OH, TO BE A GREAT MAN AND EAT YOUR FILL AT EVERY MEAL...

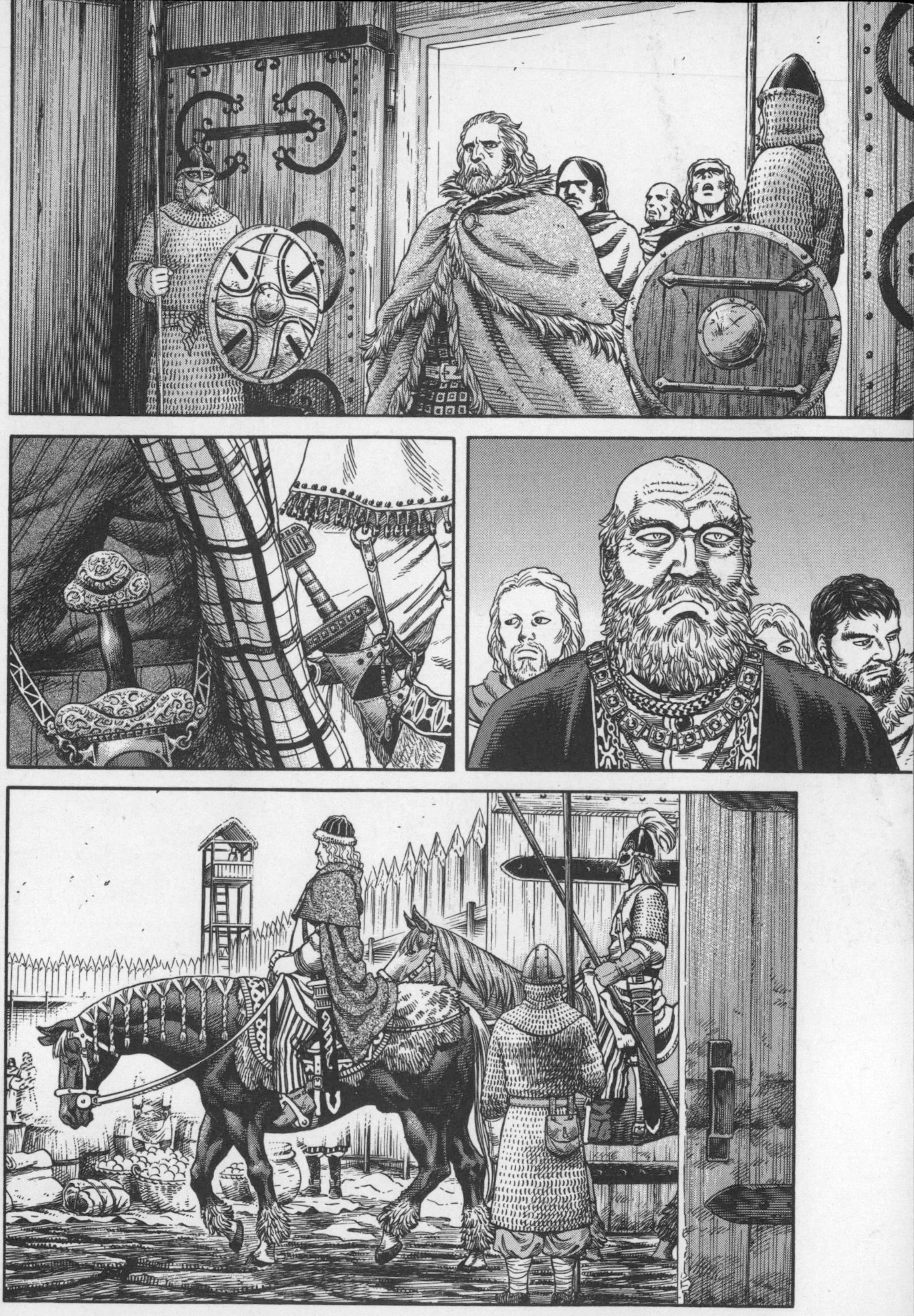

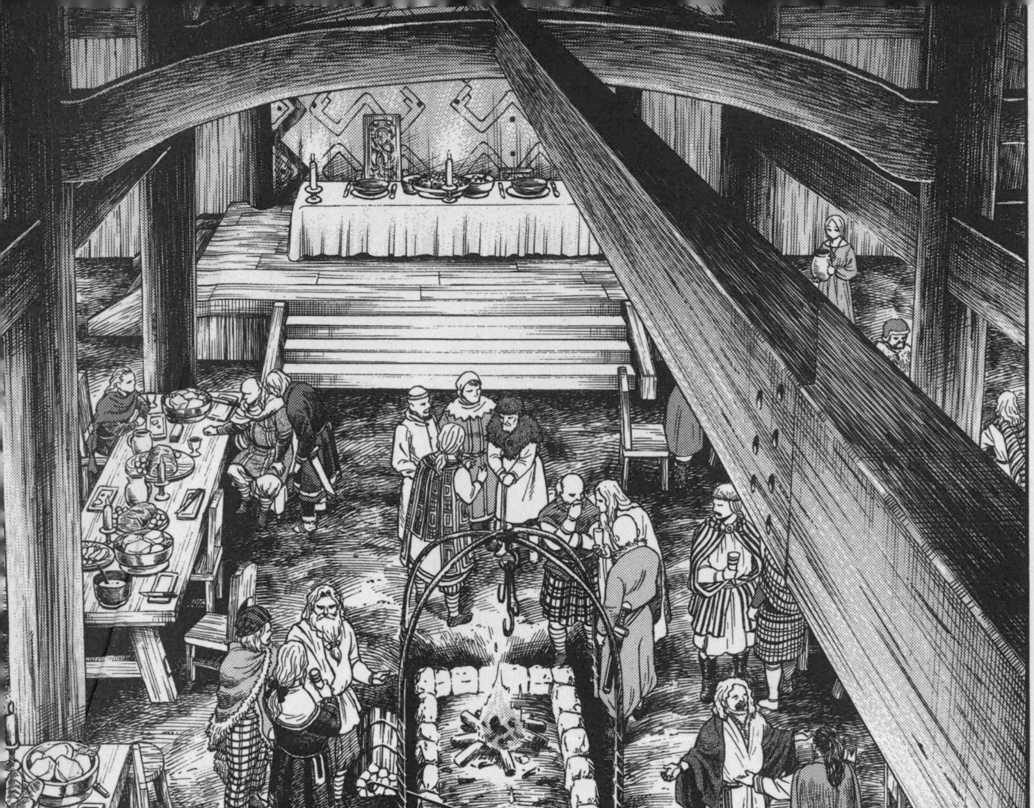

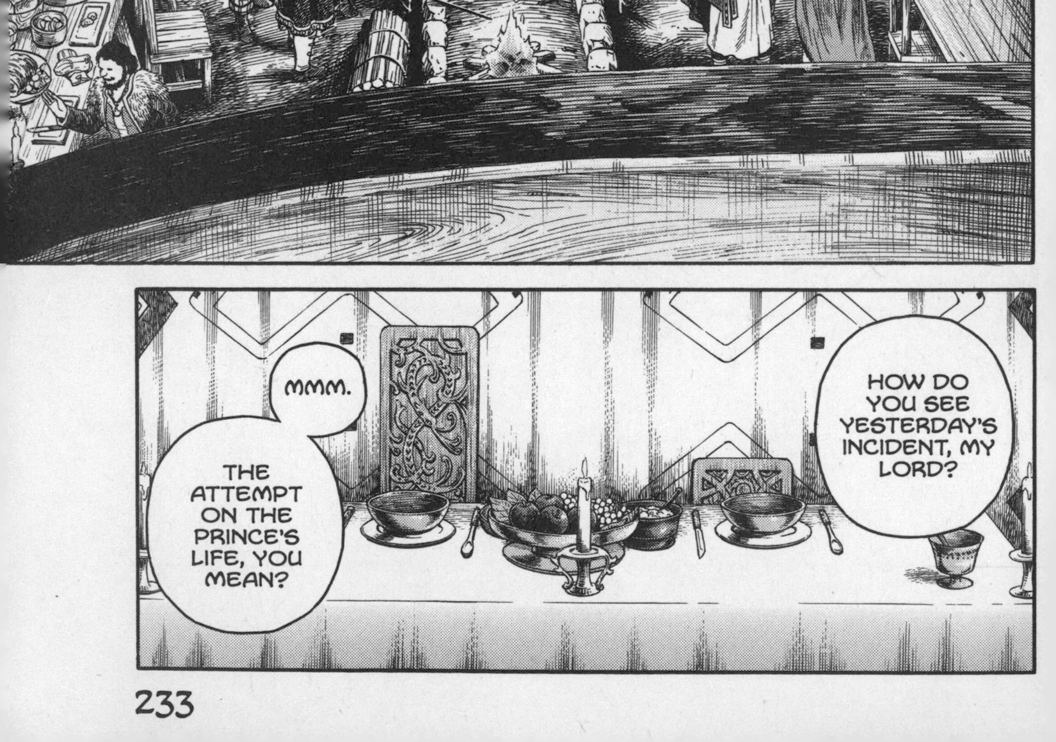
HOW DO YOU SEE YESTERDAY'S INCIDENT, MY LORD?
MMM.
THE ATTEMPT ON THE PRINCE'S LIFE, YOU MEAN?

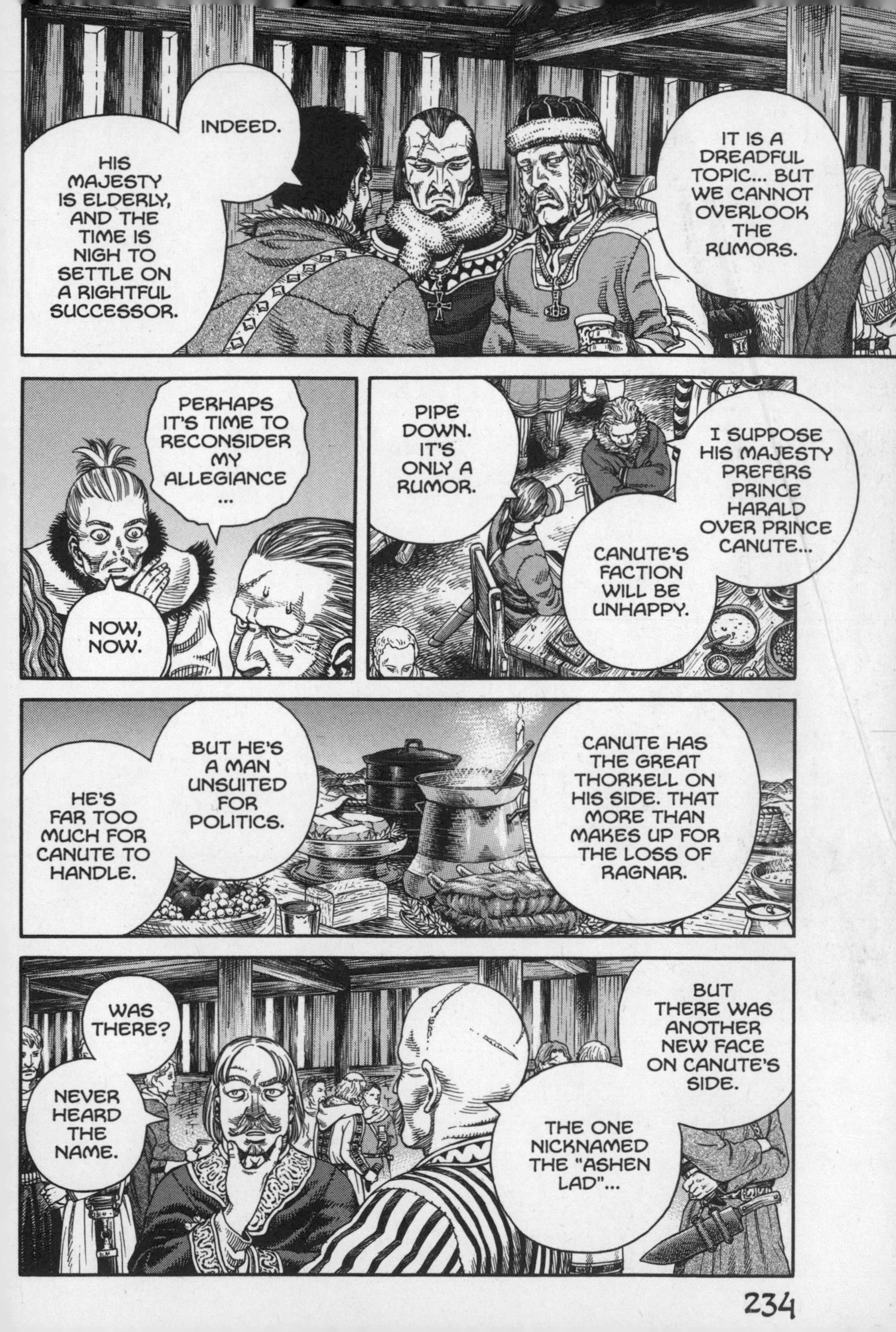
IT IS A DREADFUL TOPIC... BUT WE CANNOT OVERLOOK THE RUMORS.
INDEED.
HIS MAJESTY IS ELDERLY, AND THE TIME IS NIGH TO SETTLE ON A RIGHTFUL SUCCESSOR.
I SUPPOSE HIS MAJESTY PREFERS PRINCE HARALD OVER PRINCE CANUTE...
CANUTE'S FACTION WILL BE UNHAPPY.
PIPE DOWN. IT'S ONLY A RUMOR.
PERHAPS IT'S TIME TO RECONSIDER MY ALLEGIANCE...
NOW, NOW.
CANUTE HAS THE GREAT THORKELL ON HIS SIDE. THAT MORE THAN MAKES UP FOR THE LOSS OF RAGNAR.
BUT HE'S A MAN UNSUITED FOR POLITICS.
HE'S FAR TOO MUCH FOR CANUTE TO HANDLE.
BUT THERE WAS ANOTHER NEW FACE ON CANUTE'S SIDE.
THE ONE NICKNAMED THE "ASHEN LAD"...
WAS THERE?
NEVER HEARD THE NAME.

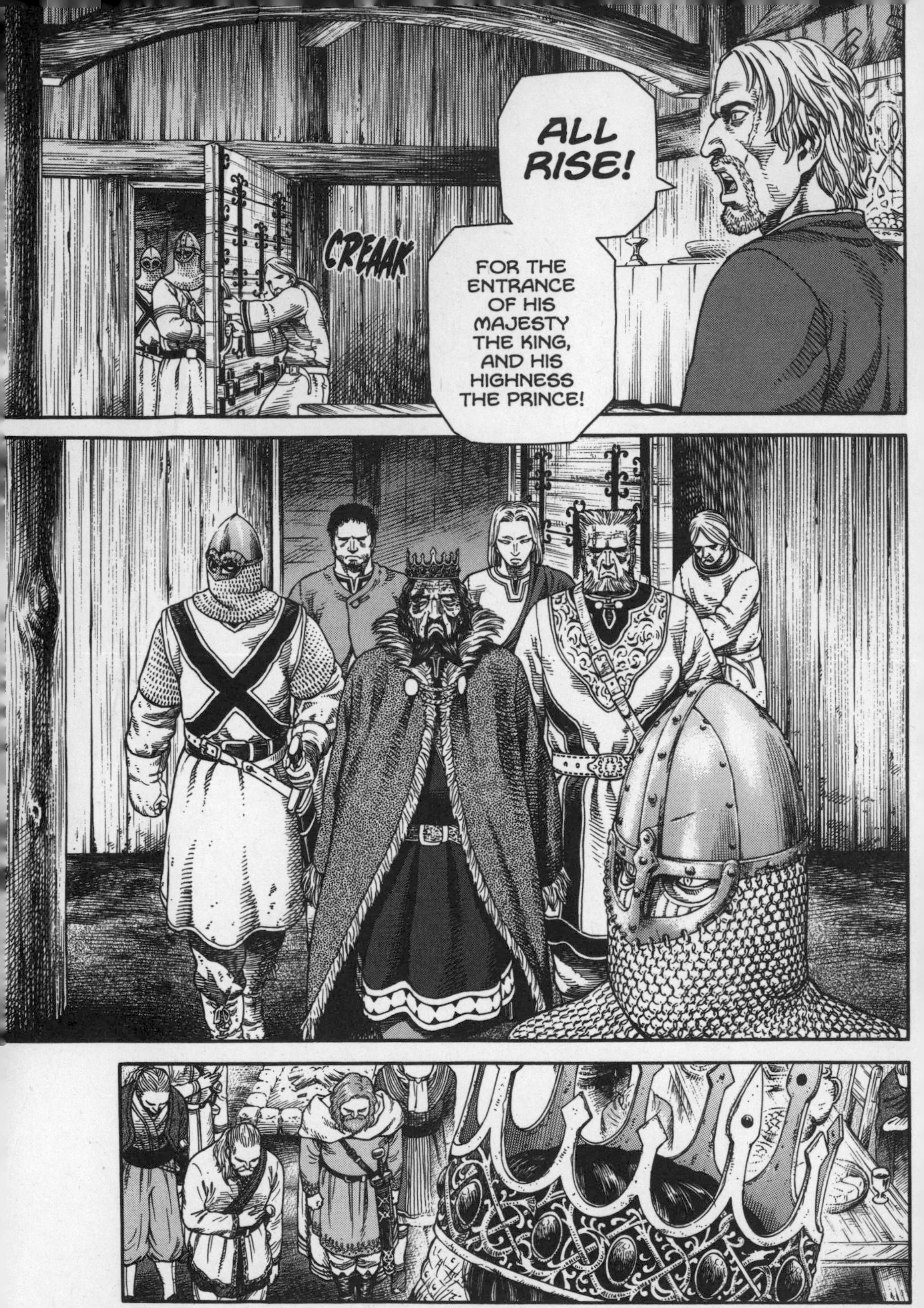
ALL RISE!
FOR THE ENTRANCE OF HIS MAJESTY THE KING, AND HIS HIGHNESS THE PRINCE!
CREAAK

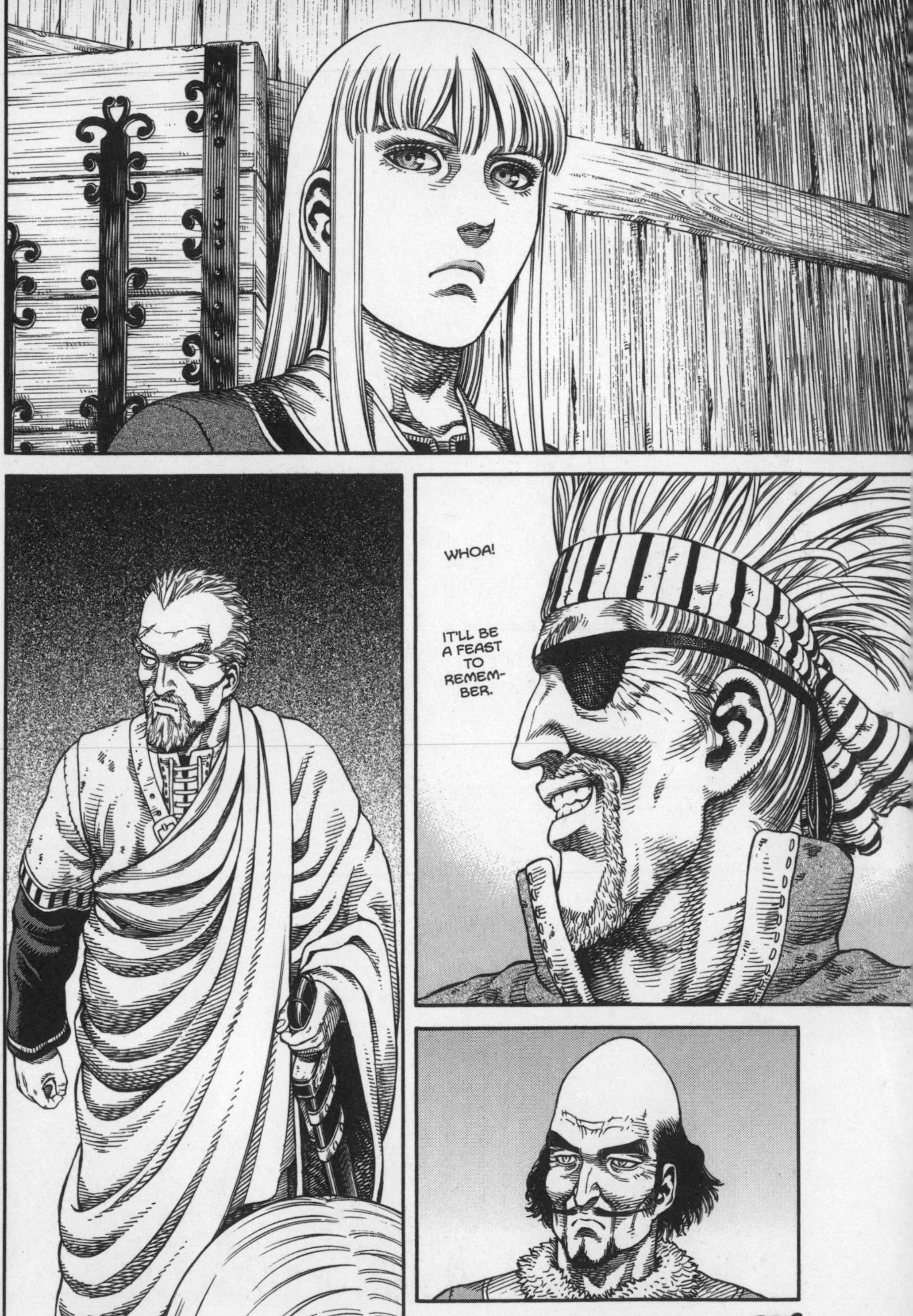
WHOA!
IT'LL BE A FEAST TO REMEMBER.

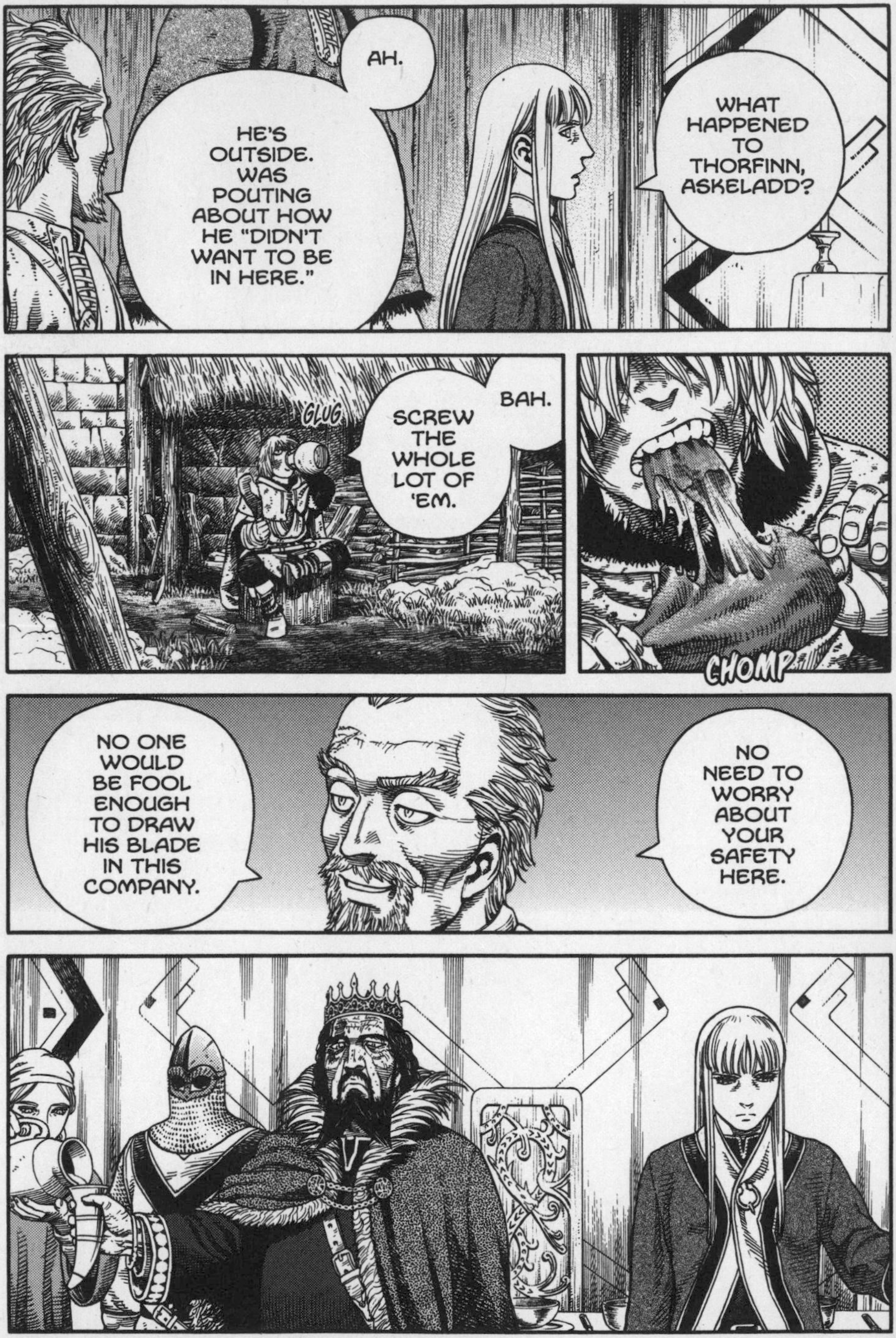

WHAT HAPPENED TO THORFINN, ASKELADD?
AH.
HE'S OUTSIDE. WAS POUTING ABOUT HOW HE "DIDN'T WANT TO BE IN HERE."
CHOMP
BAH.
SCREW THE WHOLE LOT OF 'EM.
GLUG
NO NEED TO WORRY ABOUT YOUR SAFETY HERE.
NO ONE WOULD BE FOOL ENOUGH TO DRAW HIS BLADE IN THIS COMPANY.

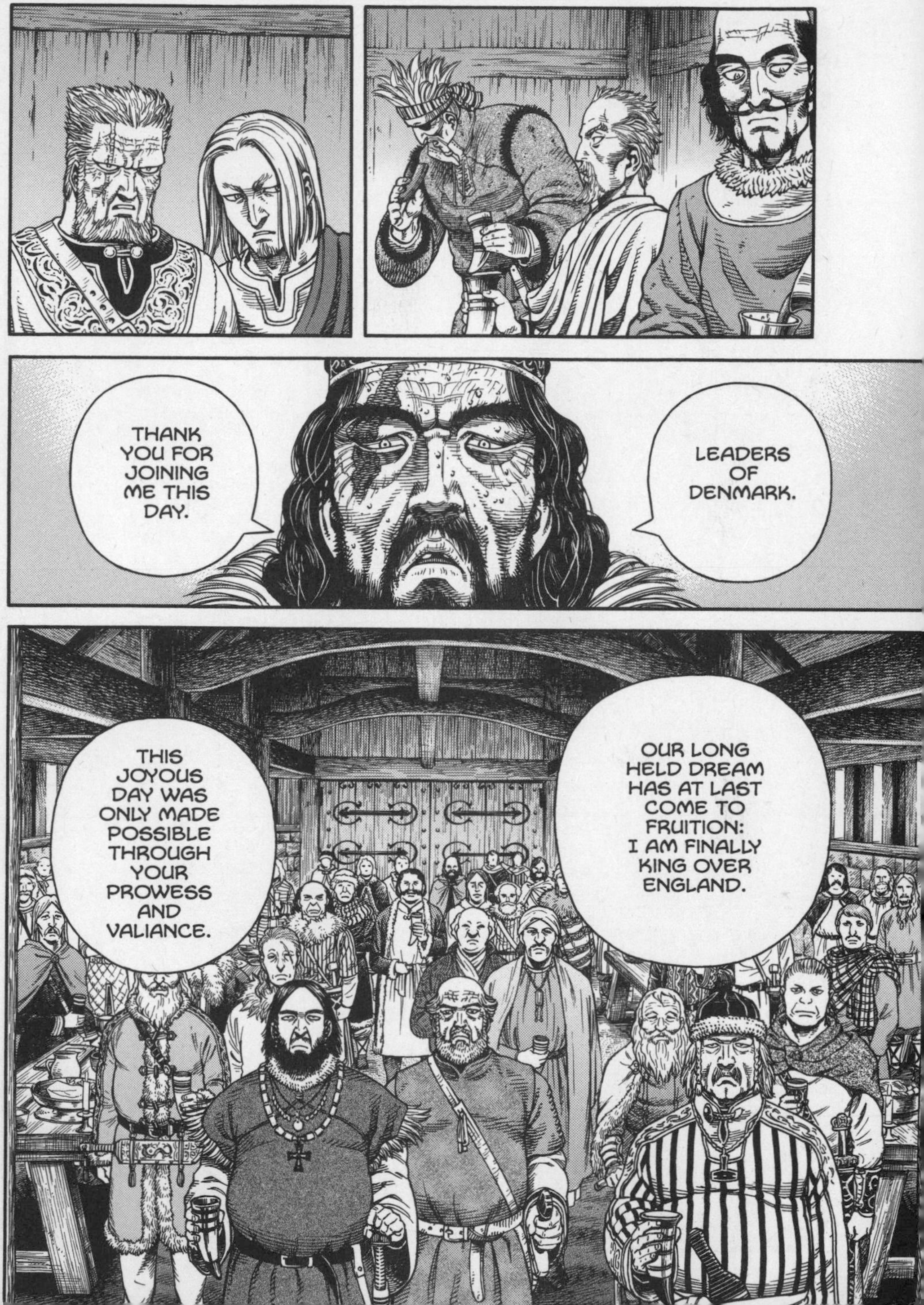
LEADERS OF DENMARK.
THANK YOU FOR JOINING ME THIS DAY.
OUR LONG HELD DREAM HAS AT LAST COME TO FRUITION: I AM FINALLY KING OVER ENGLAND.
THIS JOYOUS DAY WAS ONLY MADE POSSIBLE THROUGH YOUR PROWESS AND VALIANCE.

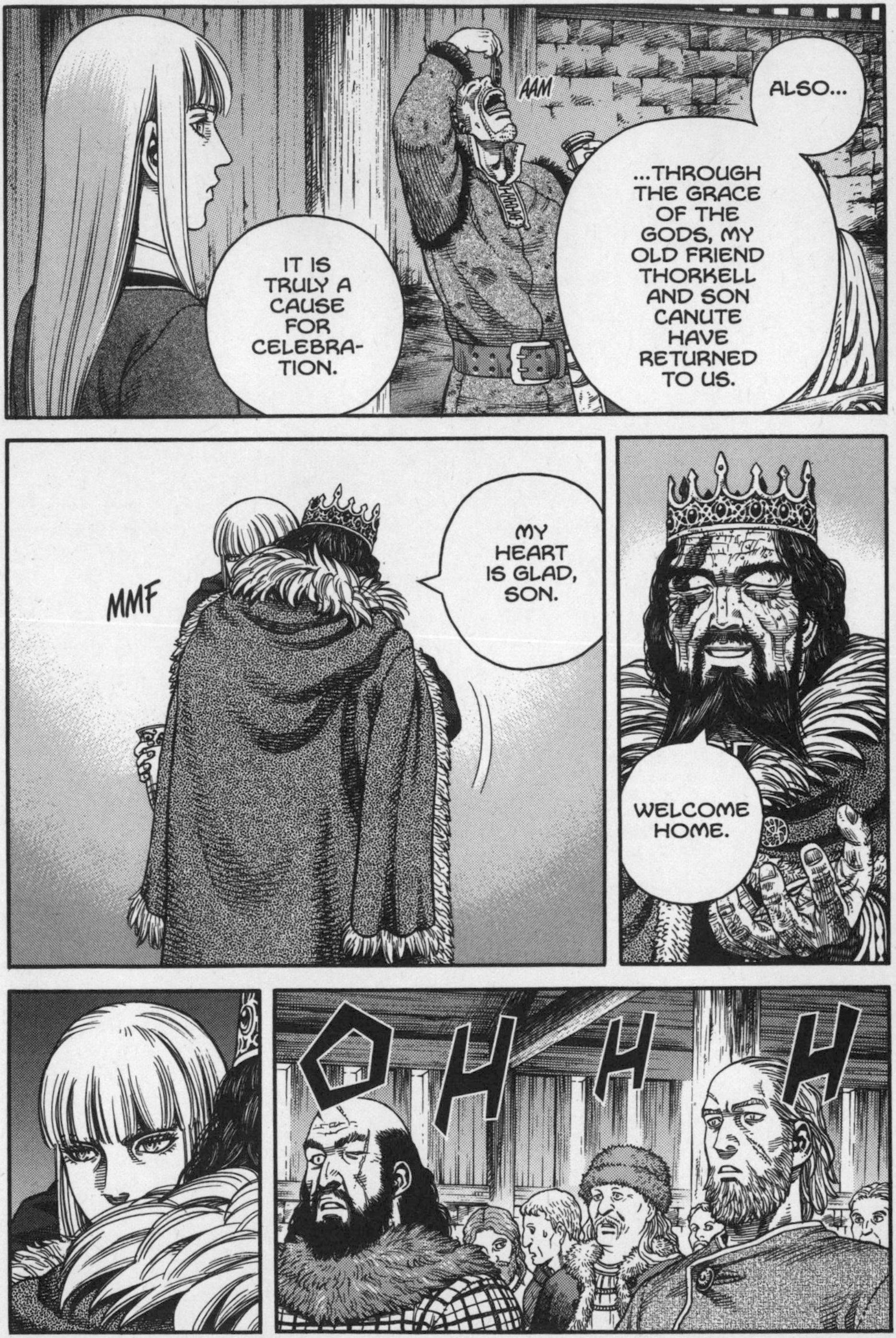
ALSO...
...THROUGH THE GRACE OF THE GODS, MY OLD FRIEND THORKELL AND SON CANUTE HAVE RETURNED TO US.
AAM
IT IS TRULY A CAUSE FOR CELEBRATION.
WELCOME HOME.
MY HEART IS GLAD, SON.
MMF
OHHH

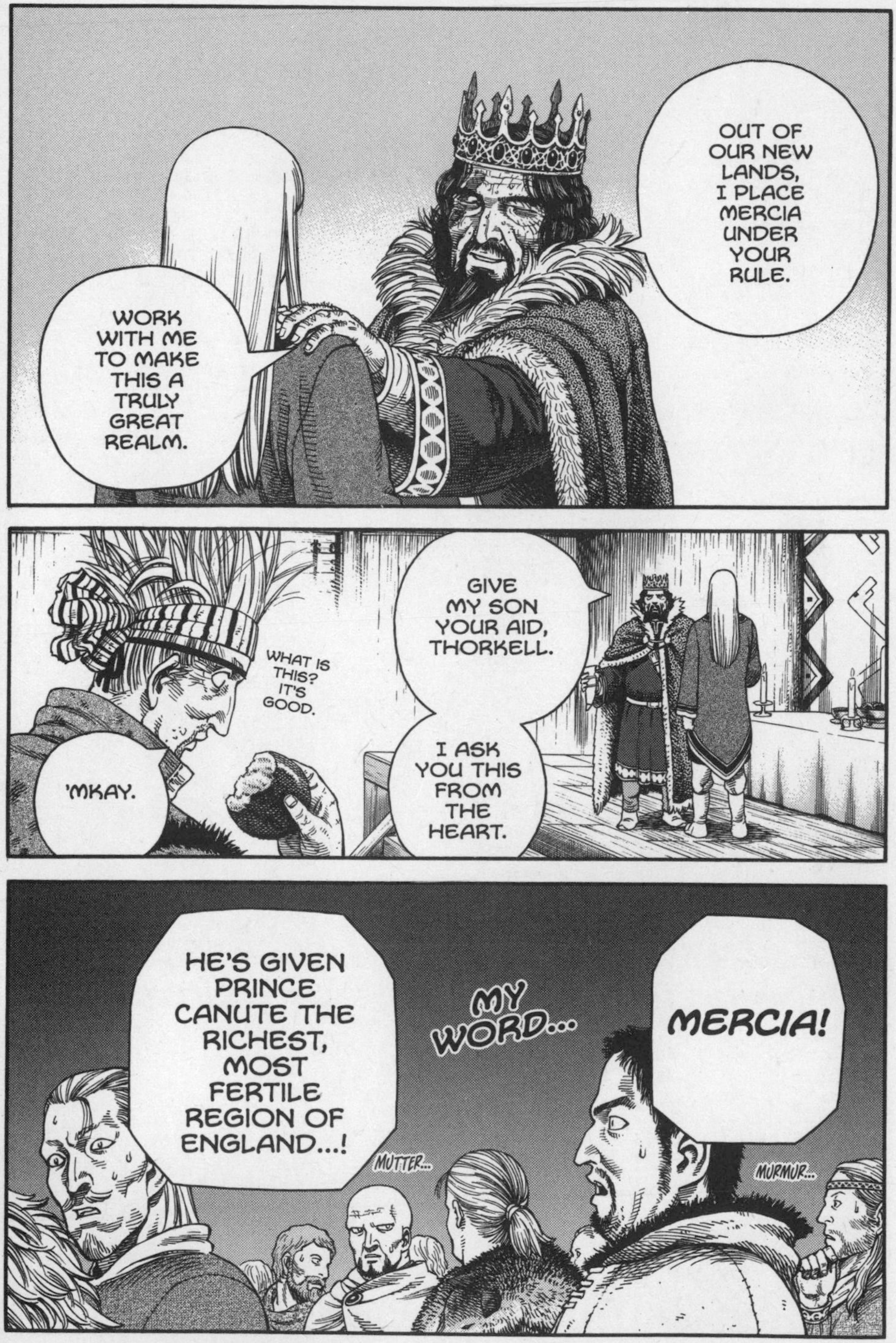
OUT OF OUR NEW LANDS, I PLACE MERCIA UNDER YOUR RULE.
WORK WITH ME TO MAKE THIS A TRULY GREAT REALM.
GIVE MY SON YOUR AID, THORKELL.
I ASK YOU THIS FROM THE HEART.
WHAT IS THIS? IT'S GOOD.
'MKAY.
MERCIA!
MURMUR...
MY WORD...
HE'S GIVEN PRINCE CANUTE THE RICHEST, MOST FERTILE REGION OF ENGLAND...!
MUTTER...

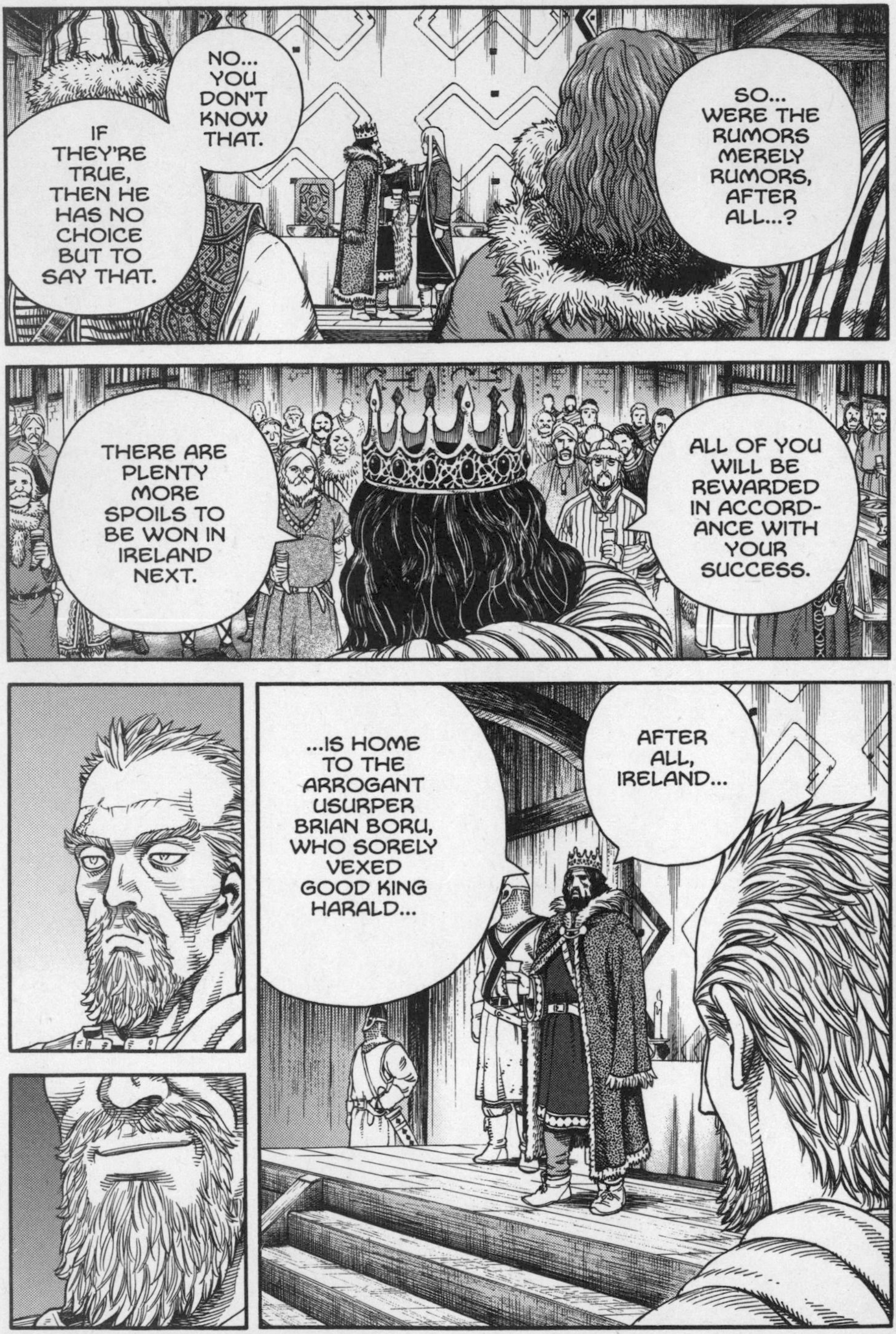
SO... WERE THE RUMORS MERELY RUMORS, AFTER ALL...?
NO... YOU DON'T KNOW THAT.
IF THEY'RE TRUE, THEN HE HAS NO CHOICE BUT TO SAY THAT.
ALL OF YOU WILL BE REWARDED IN ACCORDANCE WITH YOUR SUCCESS.
THERE ARE PLENTY MORE SPOILS TO BE WON IN IRELAND NEXT.
AFTER ALL, IRELAND...
...IS HOME TO THE ARROGANT USURPER BRIAN BORU, WHO SORELY VEXED GOOD KING HARALD...

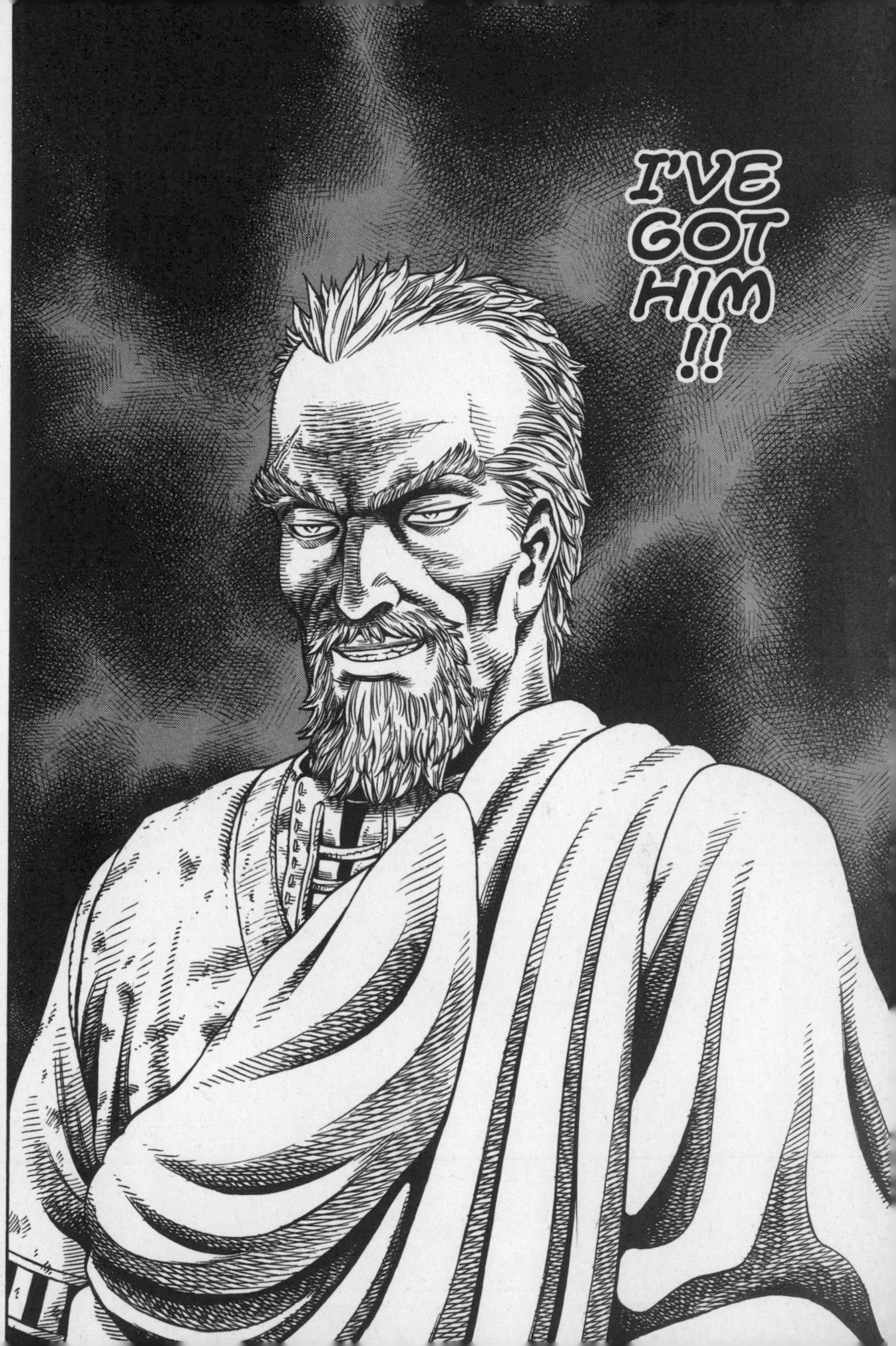
I'VE GOT HIM !!

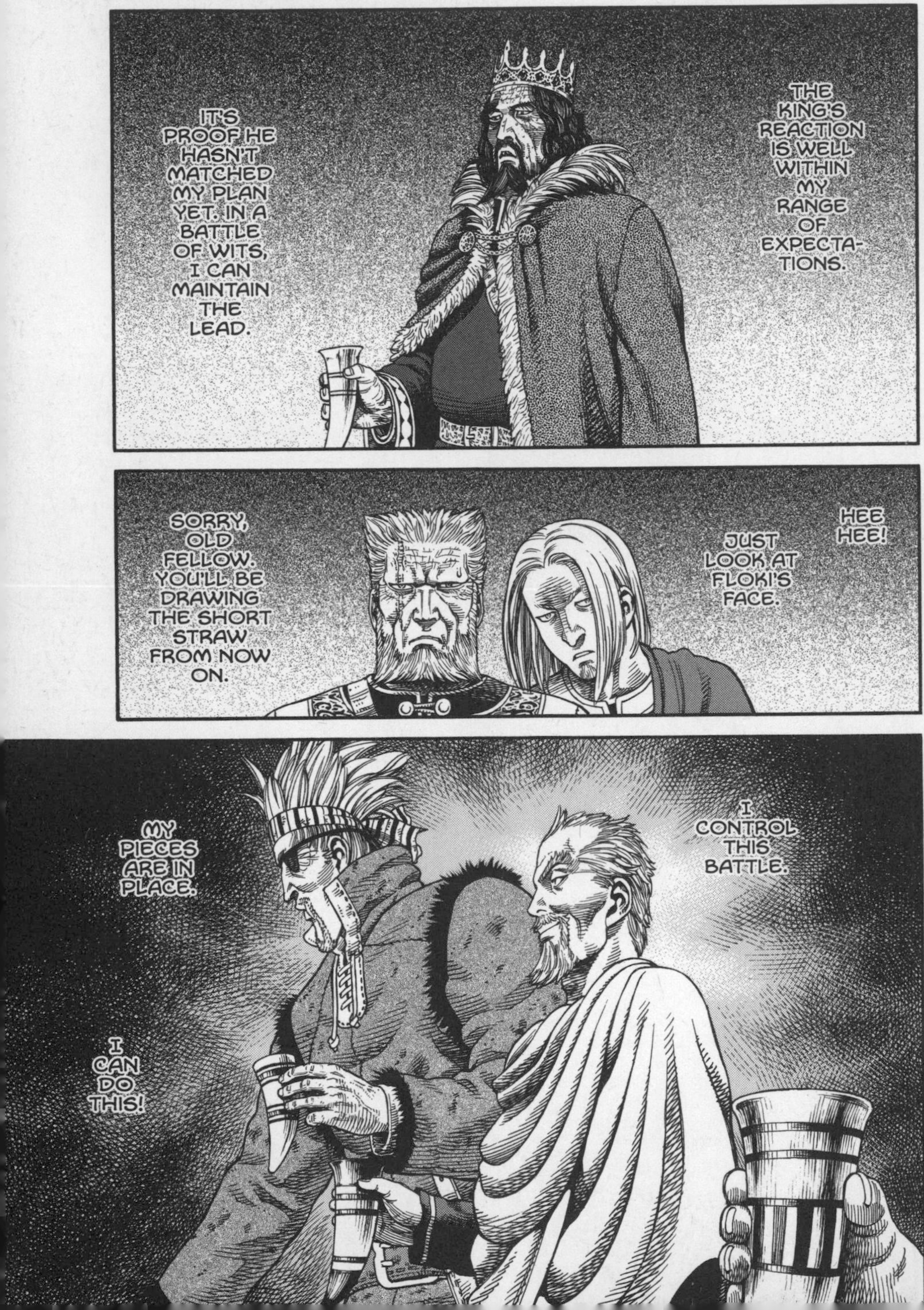
THE KING'S REACTION IS WELL WITHIN MY RANGE OF EXPECTATIONS.
IT'S PROOF HE HASN'T MATCHED MY PLAN YET. IN A BATTLE OF WITS, I CAN MAINTAIN THE LEAD.
HEE HEE!
JUST LOOK AT FLOKI'S FACE.
SORRY, OLD FELLOW. YOU'LL BE DRAWING THE SHORT STRAW FROM NOW ON.
I CONTROL THIS BATTLE.
MY PIECES ARE IN PLACE.
I CAN DO THIS!

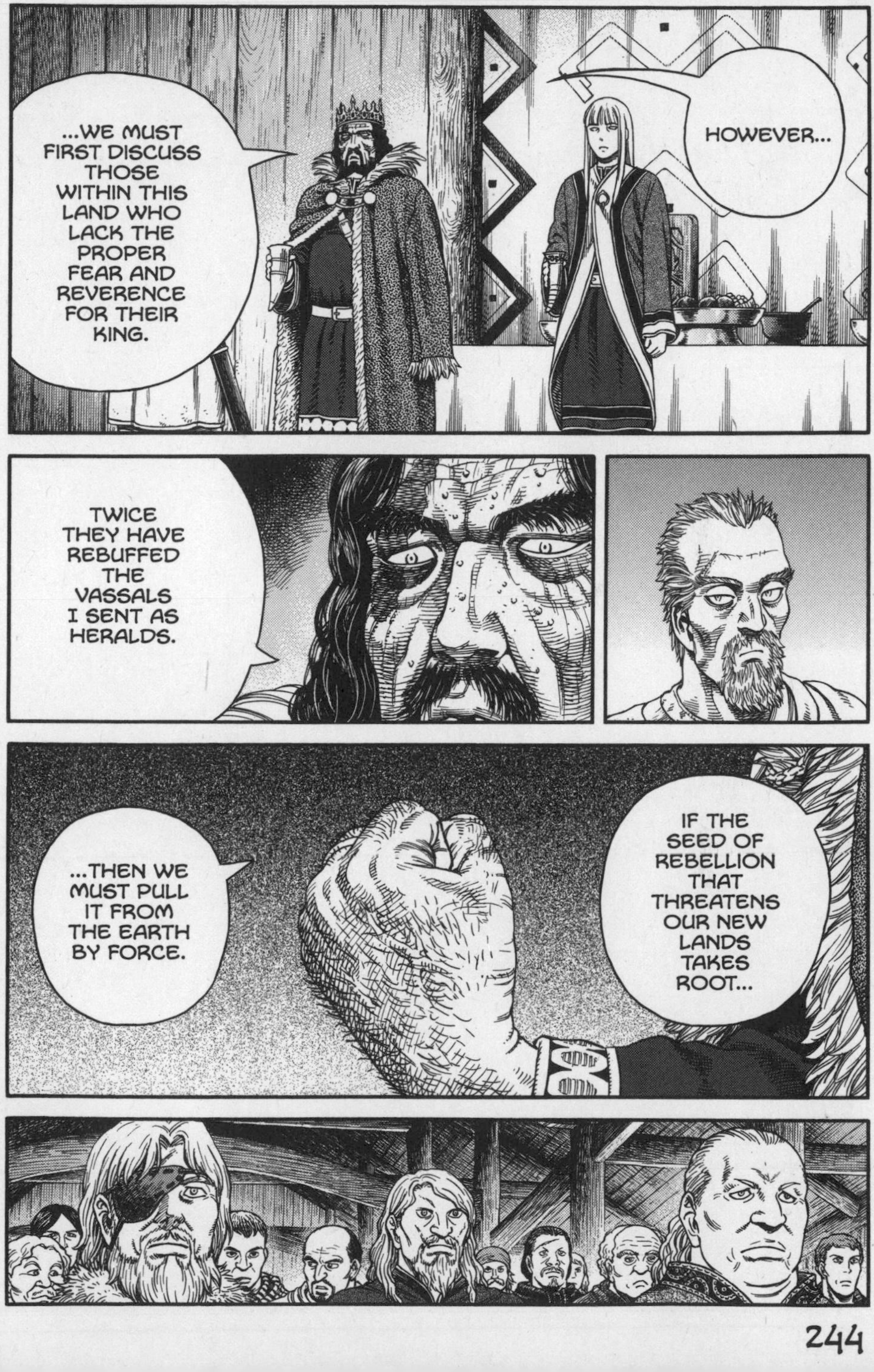
HOWEVER...
...WE MUST FIRST DISCUSS THOSE WITHIN THIS LAND WHO LACK THE PROPER FEAR AND REVERENCE FOR THEIR KING.
TWICE THEY HAVE REBUFFED THE VASSALS I SENT AS HERALDS.
IF THE SEED OF REBELLION THAT THREATENS OUR NEW LANDS TAKES ROOT...
...THEN WE MUST PULL IT FROM THE EARTH BY FORCE.

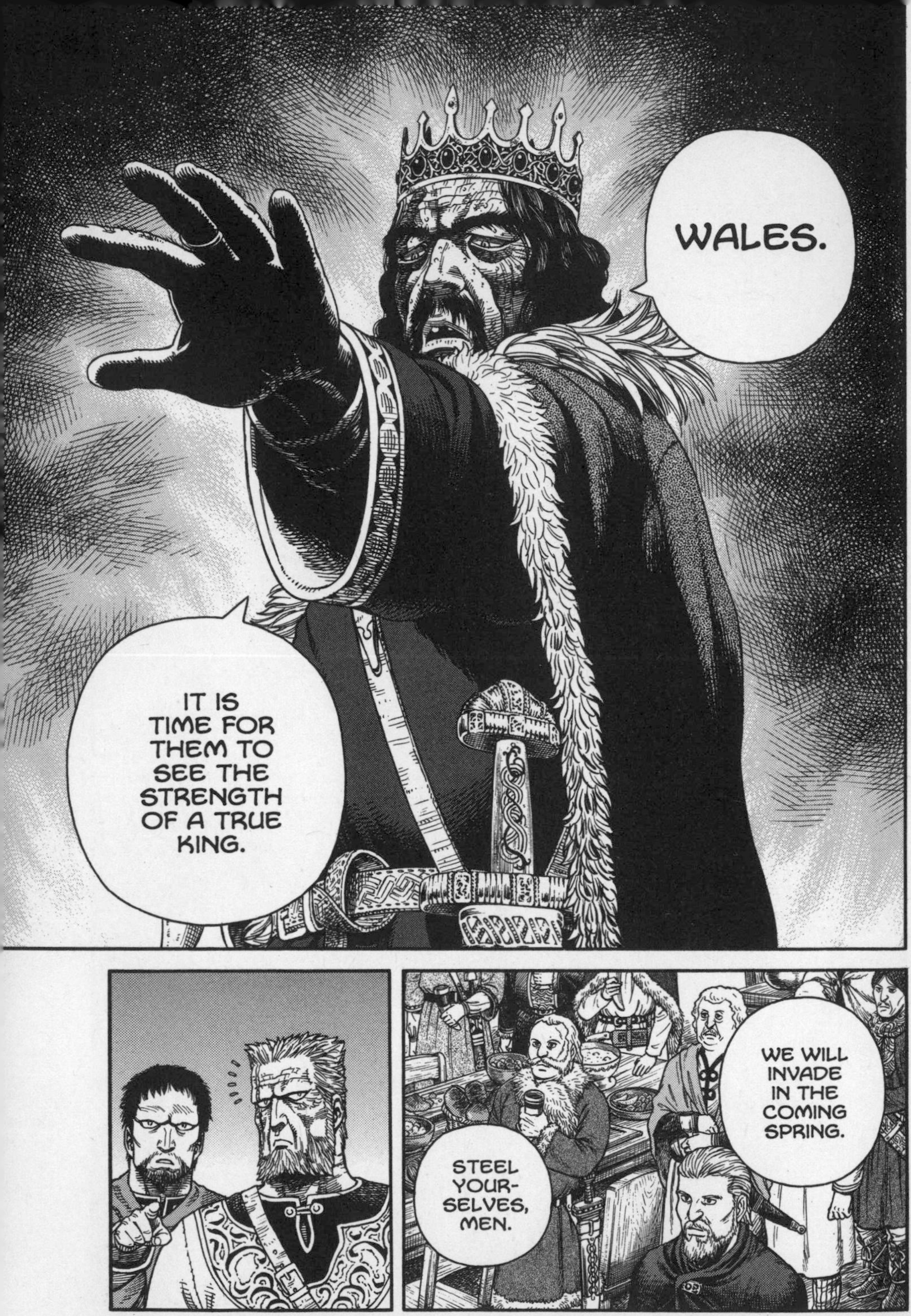
WALES.
IT IS TIME FOR THEM TO SEE THE STRENGTH OF A TRUE KING.
WE WILL INVADE IN THE COMING SPRING.
STEEL YOUR-SELVES, MEN.

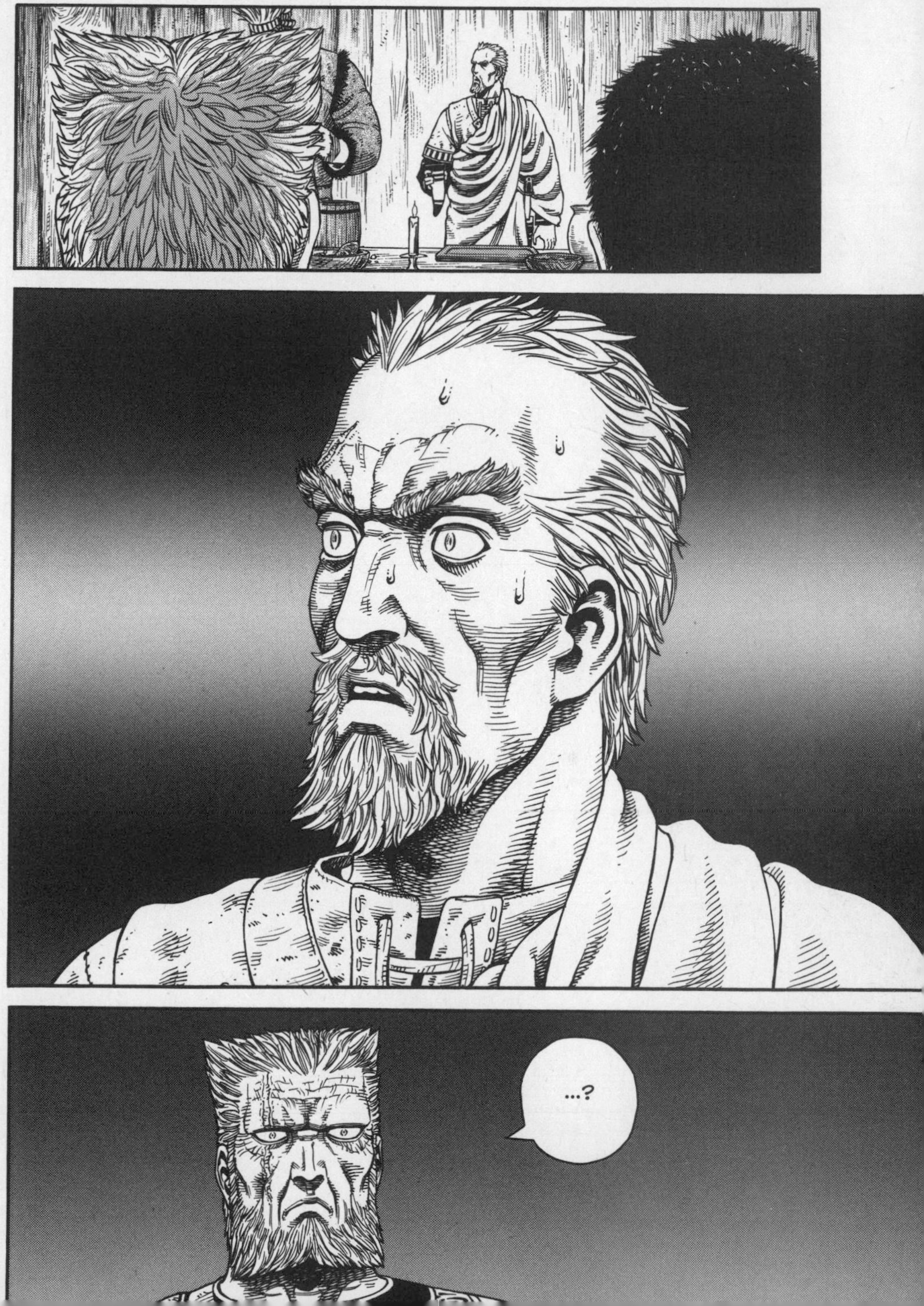
...?

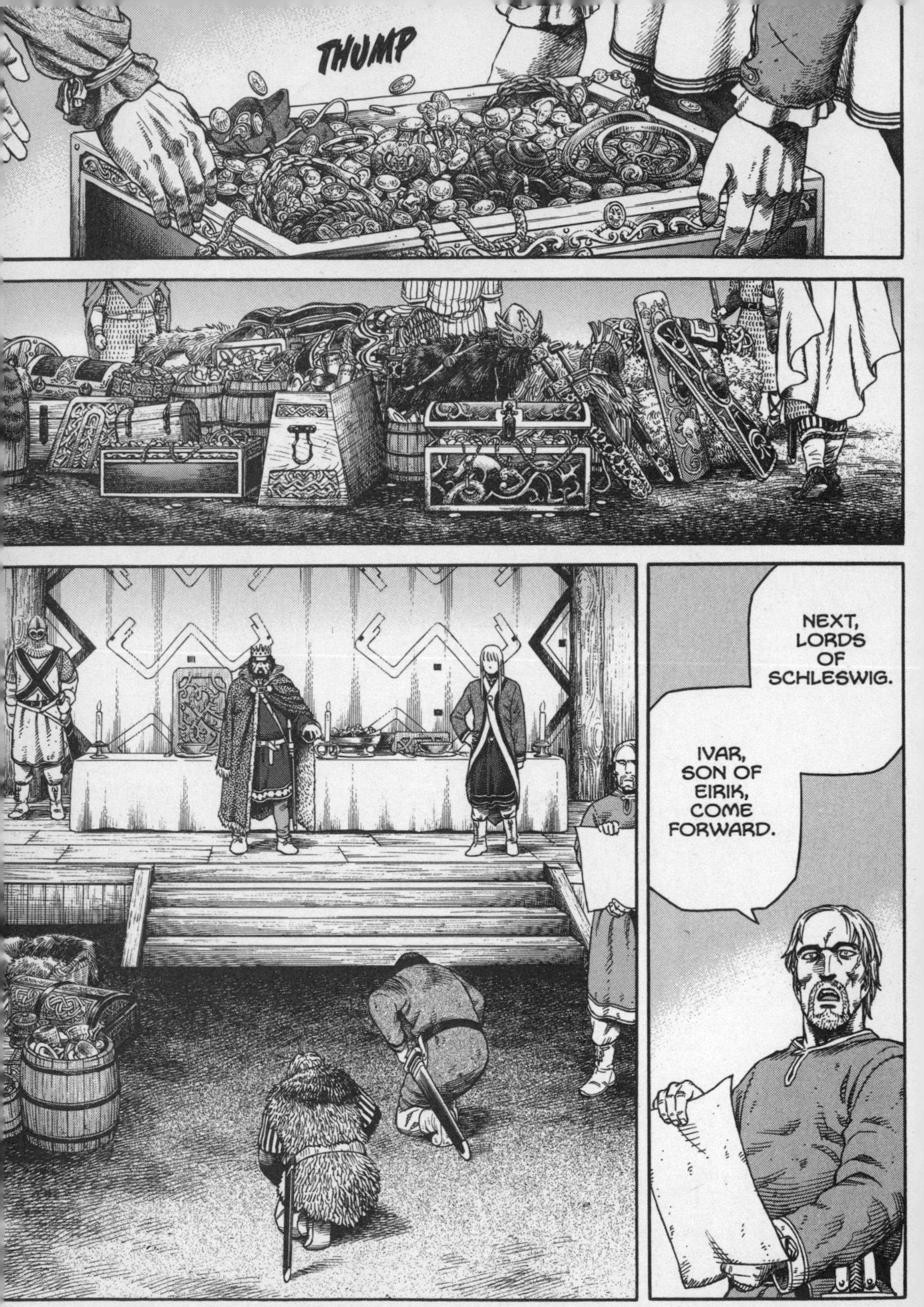
THUMP
NEXT, LORDS OF SCHLESWIG.
IVAR, SON OF EIRIK, COME FORWARD.

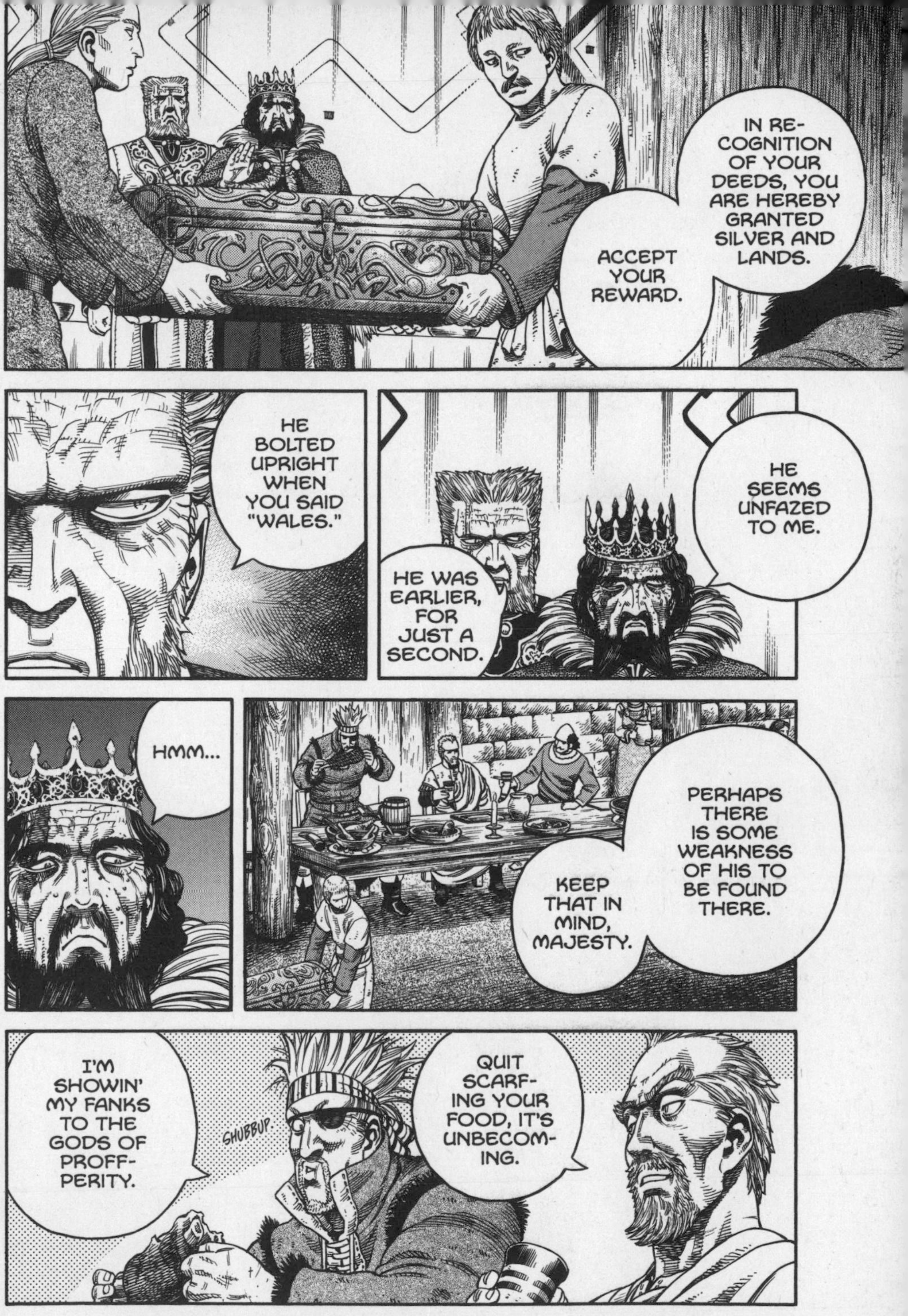
IN RECOGNITION OF YOUR DEEDS, YOU ARE HEREBY GRANTED SILVER AND LANDS.
ACCEPT YOUR REWARD.
HE SEEMS UNFAZED TO ME.
HE WAS EARLIER, FOR JUST A SECOND.
HE BOLTED UPRIGHT WHEN YOU SAID "WALES."
PERHAPS THERE IS SOME WEAKNESS OF HIS TO BE FOUND THERE.
KEEP THAT IN MIND, MAJESTY.
HMM...
QUIT SCARFING YOUR FOOD, IT'S UNBECOMING.
SHUBBUP
I'M SHOWIN' MY FANKS TO THE GODS OF PROFFPERITY.

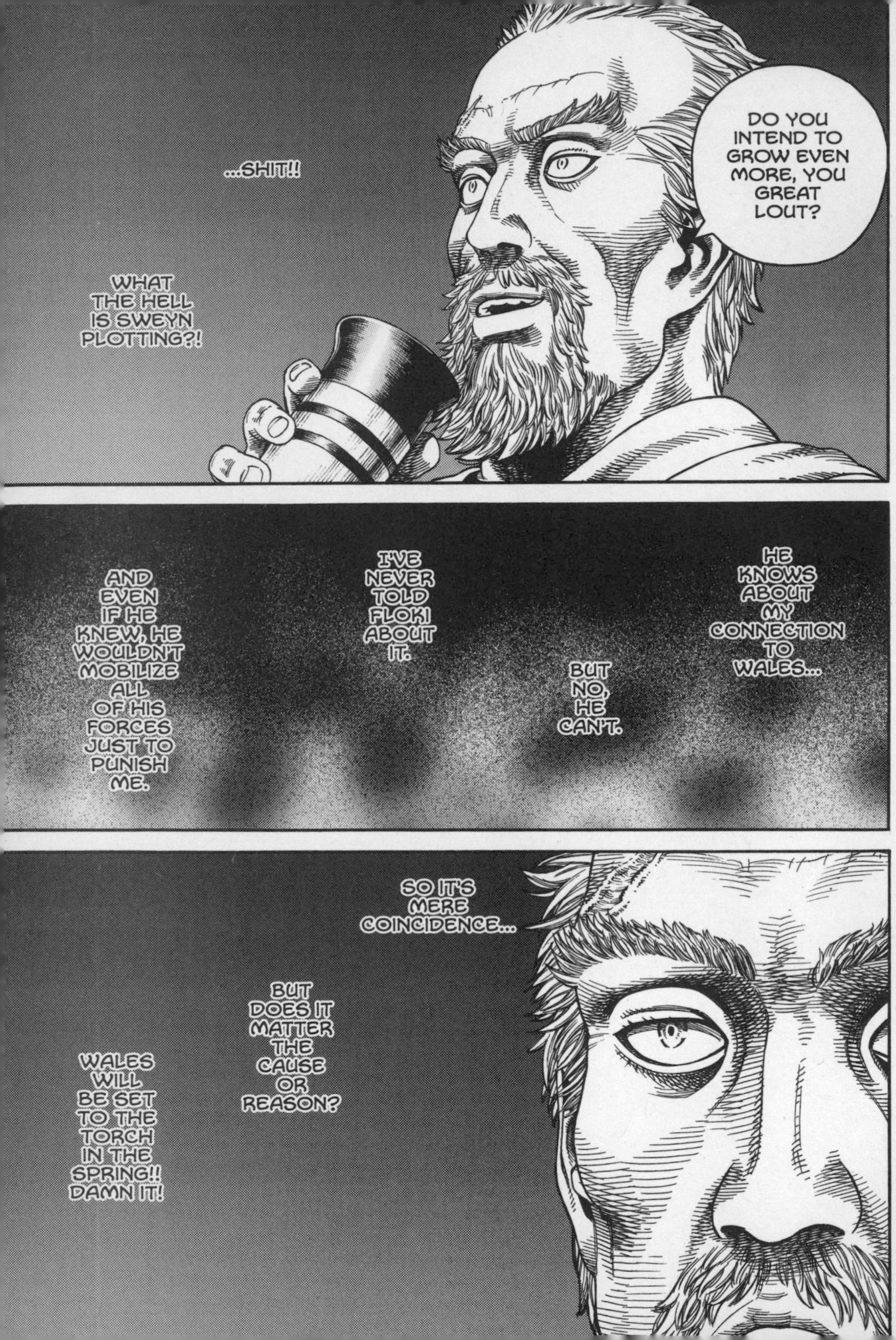
DO YOU INTEND TO GROW EVEN MORE, YOU GREAT LOUT?
...SHIT!!
WHAT THE HELL IS SWEYN PLOTTING?!
HE KNOWS ABOUT MY CONNECTION TO WALES...
BUT NO, HE CAN'T.
I'VE NEVER TOLD FLOKI ABOUT IT.
AND EVEN IF HE KNEW, HE WOULDN'T MOBILIZE ALL OF HIS FORCES JUST TO PUNISH ME.
SO IT'S MERE COINCIDENCE...
BUT DOES IT MATTER THE CAUSE OR REASON?
WALES WILL BE SET TO THE TORCH IN THE SPRING!! DAMN IT!

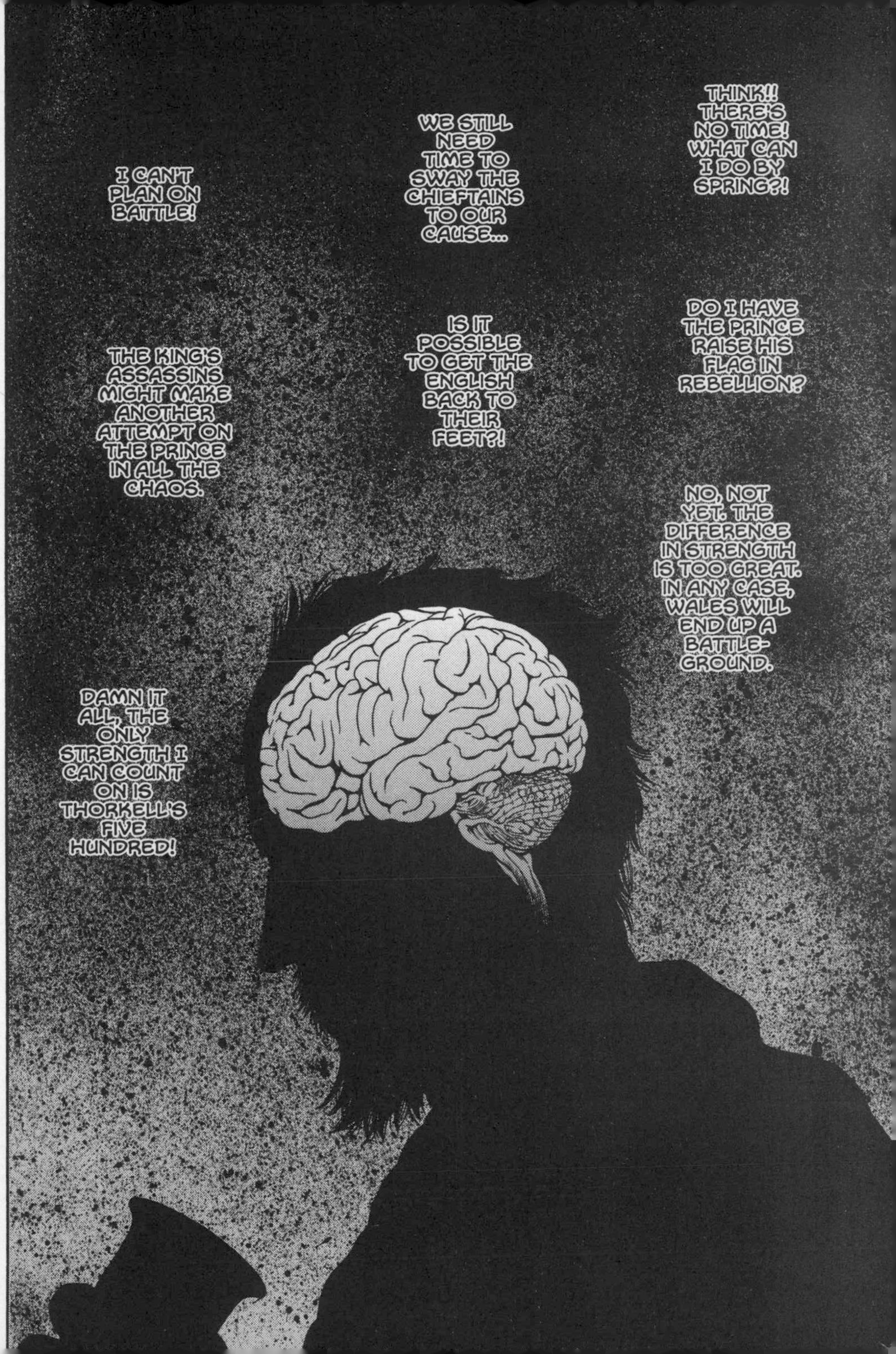
THINK!! THERE'S NO TIME! WHAT CAN I DO BY SPRING?!
WE STILL NEED TIME TO SWAY THE CHIEFTAINS TO OUR CAUSE...
I CAN'T PLAN ON BATTLE!
DO I HAVE THE PRINCE RAISE HIS FLAG IN REBELLION?
IS IT POSSIBLE TO GET THE ENGLISH BACK TO THEIR FEET?!
THE KING'S ASSASSINS MIGHT MAKE ANOTHER ATTEMPT ON THE PRINCE IN ALL THE CHAOS.
NO, NOT YET. THE DIFFERENCE IN STRENGTH IS TOO GREAT. IN ANY CASE, WALES WILL END UP A BATTLE-GROUND.
DAMN IT ALL, THE ONLY STRENGTH I CAN COUNT ON IS THORKELL'S FIVE HUNDRED!

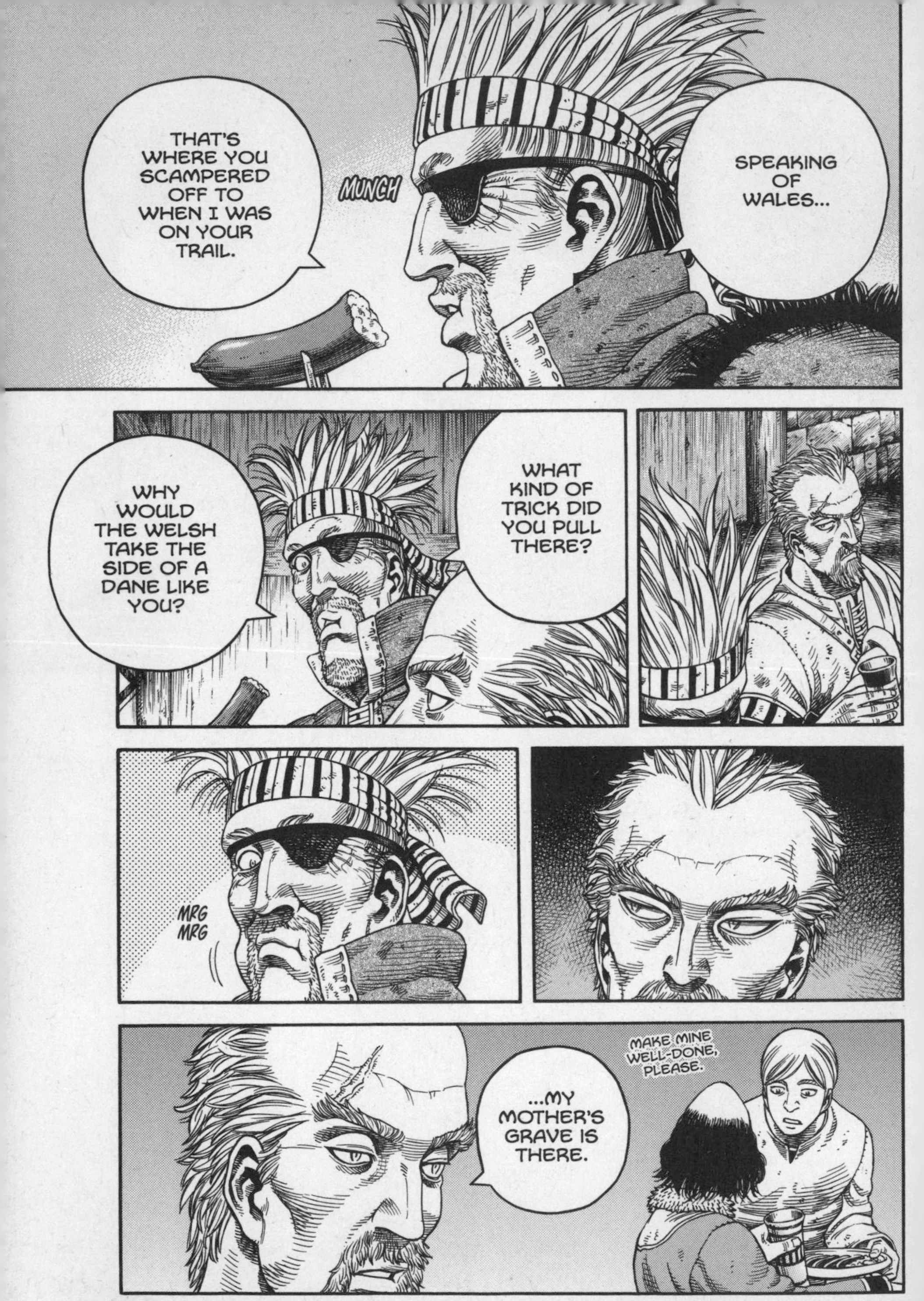
SPEAKING OF WALES...
MUNCH
THAT'S WHERE YOU SCAMPERED OFF TO WHEN I WAS ON YOUR TRAIL.
WHAT KIND OF TRICK DID YOU PULL THERE?
WHY WOULD THE WELSH TAKE THE SIDE OF A DANE LIKE YOU?
MRG MRG
MAKE MINE WELL-DONE, PLEASE.
...MY MOTHER'S GRAVE IS THERE.

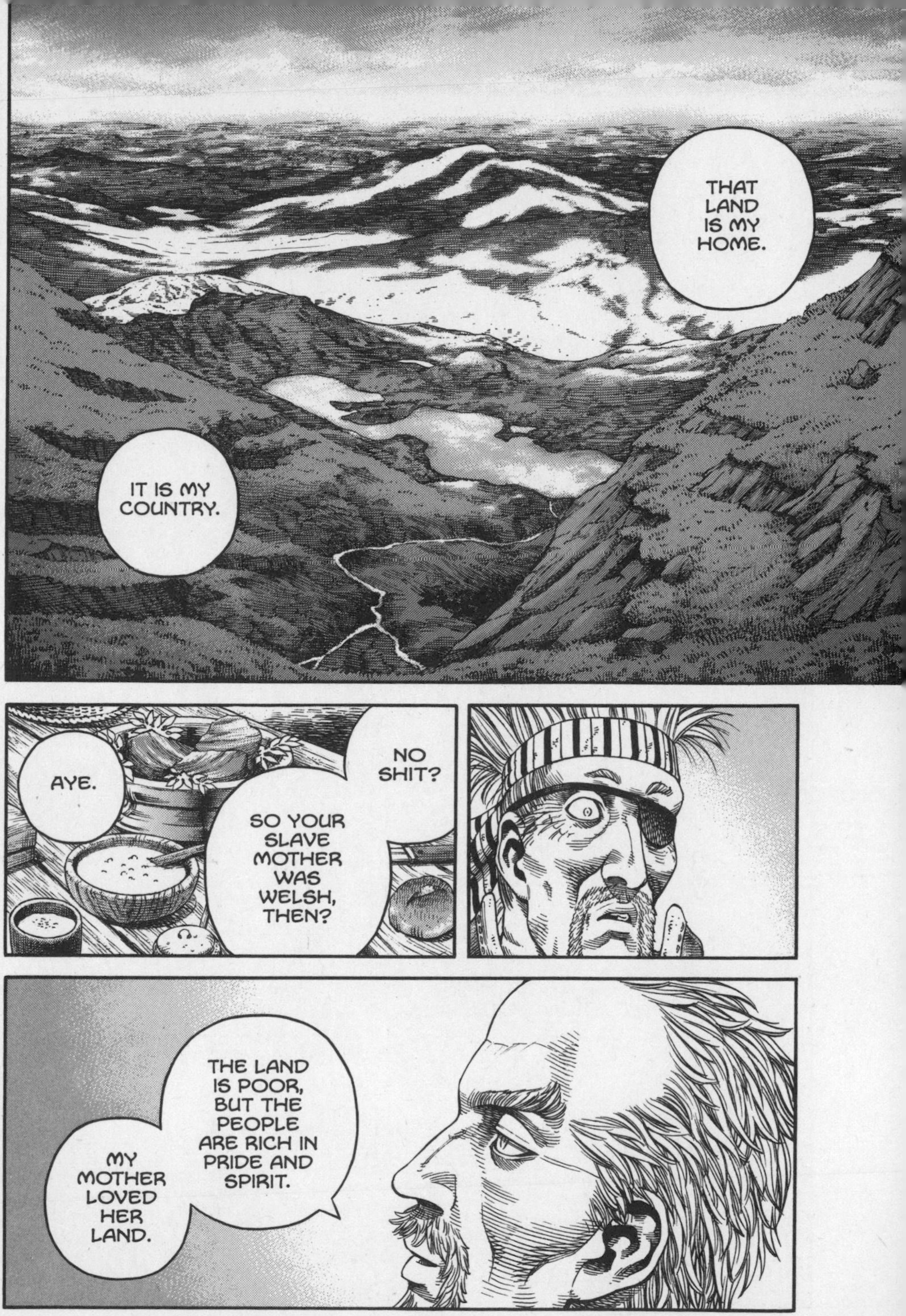
THAT LAND IS MY HOME.
IT IS MY COUNTRY.
NO SHIT?
SO YOUR SLAVE MOTHER WAS WELSH, THEN?
AYE.
THE LAND IS POOR, BUT THE PEOPLE ARE RICH IN PRIDE AND SPIRIT.
MY MOTHER LOVED HER LAND.

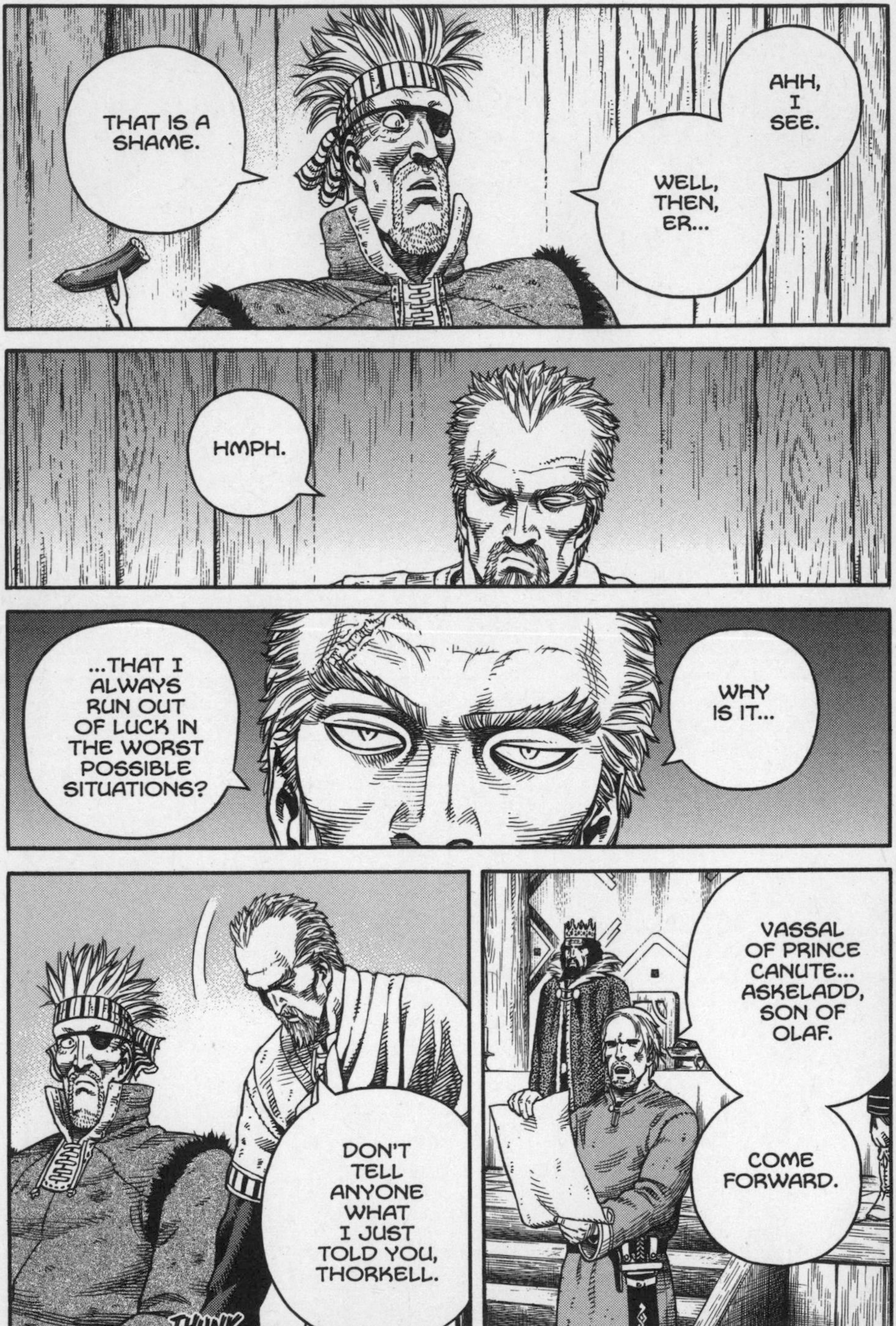
AHH, I SEE.
WELL, THEN, ER...
THAT IS A SHAME.
HMPH.
WHY IS IT...
...THAT I ALWAYS RUN OUT OF LUCK IN THE WORST POSSIBLE SITUATIONS?
VASSAL OF PRINCE CANUTE... ASKELADD, SON OF OLAF.
COME FORWARD.
DON'T TELL ANYONE WHAT I JUST TOLD YOU, THORKELL.
THUNK

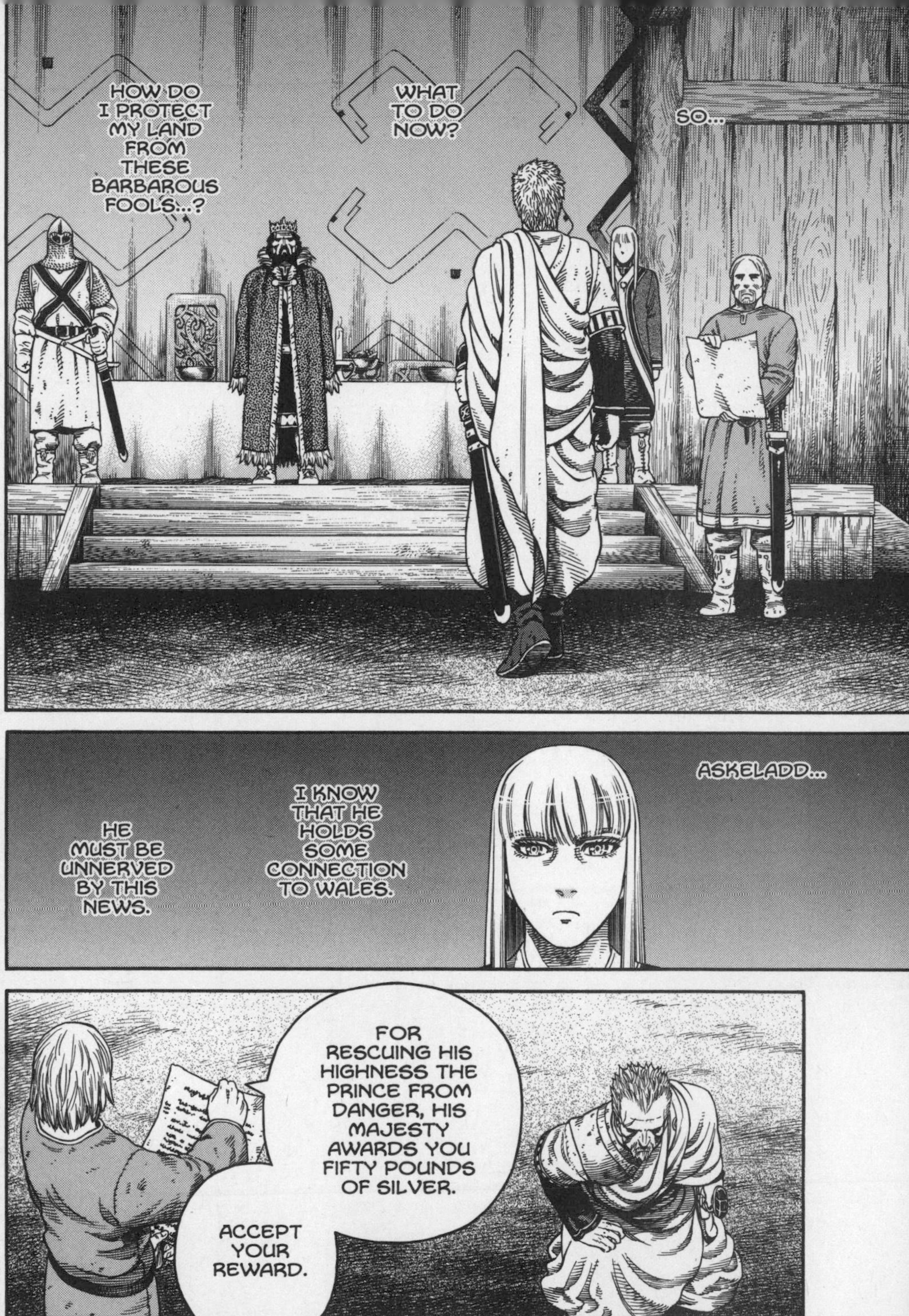
SO...
WHAT TO DO NOW?
HOW DO I PROTECT MY LAND FROM THESE BARBAROUS FOOLS...?
ASKELADD...
I KNOW THAT HE HOLDS SOME CONNECTION TO WALES.
HE MUST BE UNNERVED BY THIS NEWS.
FOR RESCUING HIS HIGHNESS THE PRINCE FROM DANGER, HIS MAJESTY AWARDS YOU FIFTY POUNDS OF SILVER.
ACCEPT YOUR REWARD.

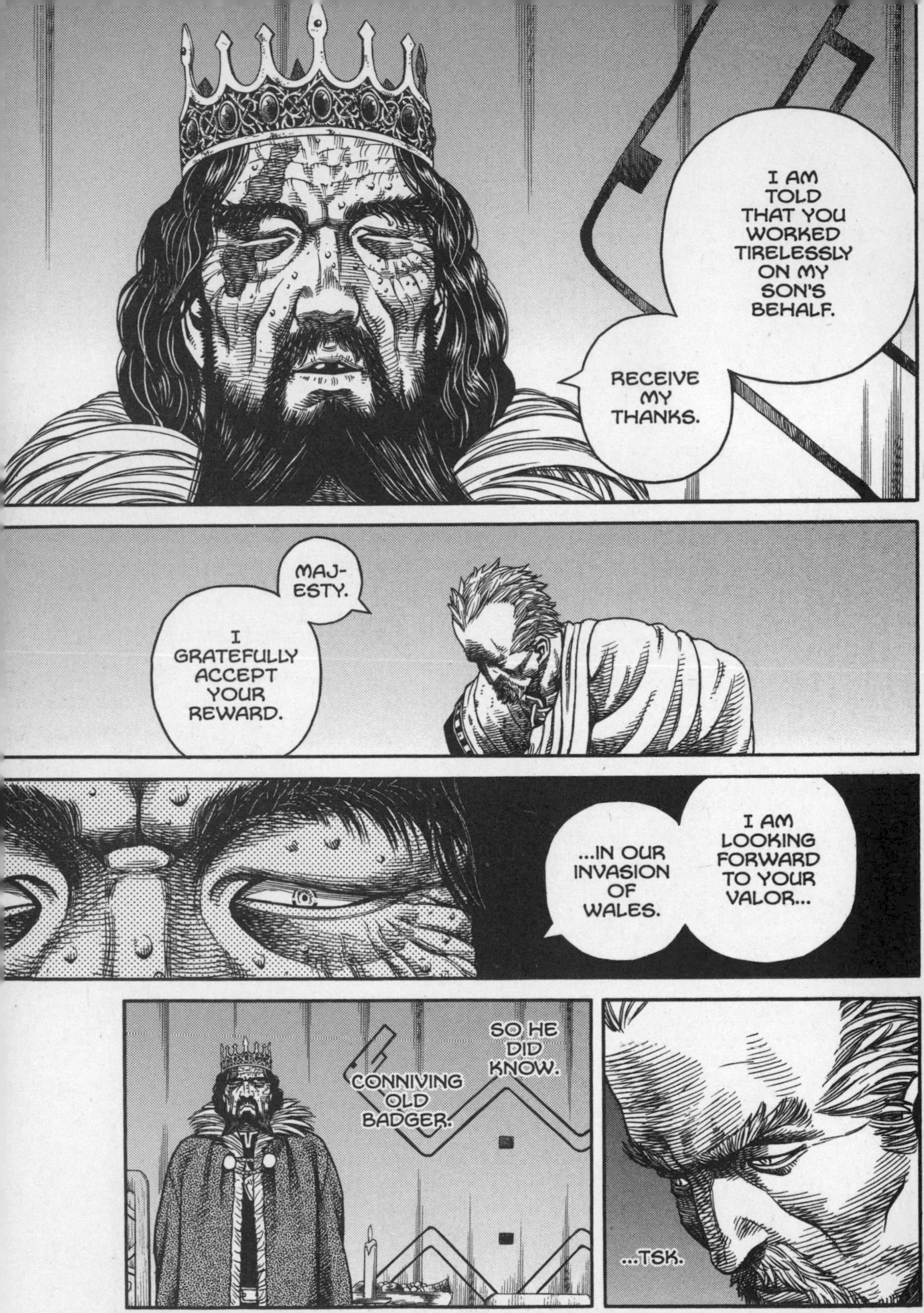
I AM TOLD THAT YOU WORKED TIRELESSLY ON MY SON'S BEHALF.
RECEIVE MY THANKS.
MAJ-ESTY.
I GRATEFULLY ACCEPT YOUR REWARD.
I AM LOOKING FORWARD TO YOUR VALOR...
...IN OUR INVASION OF WALES.
...TSK.
SO HE DID KNOW.
CONNIVING OLD BADGER.

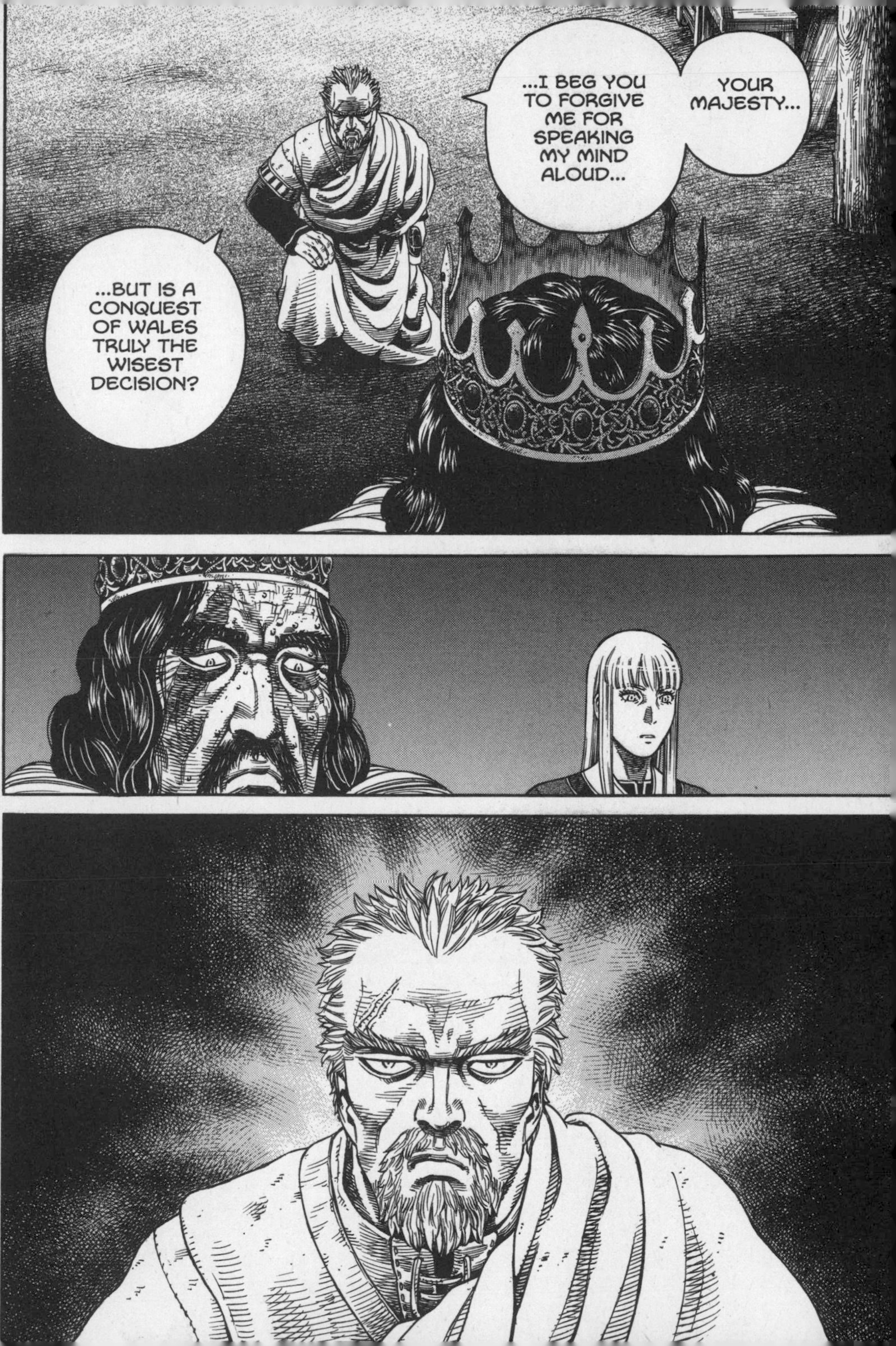
YOUR MAJESTY...
...I BEG YOU TO FORGIVE ME FOR SPEAKING MY MIND ALOUD...
...BUT IS A CONQUEST OF WALES TRULY THE WISEST DECISION?

CHAPTER 52: THE HERO RETURNS

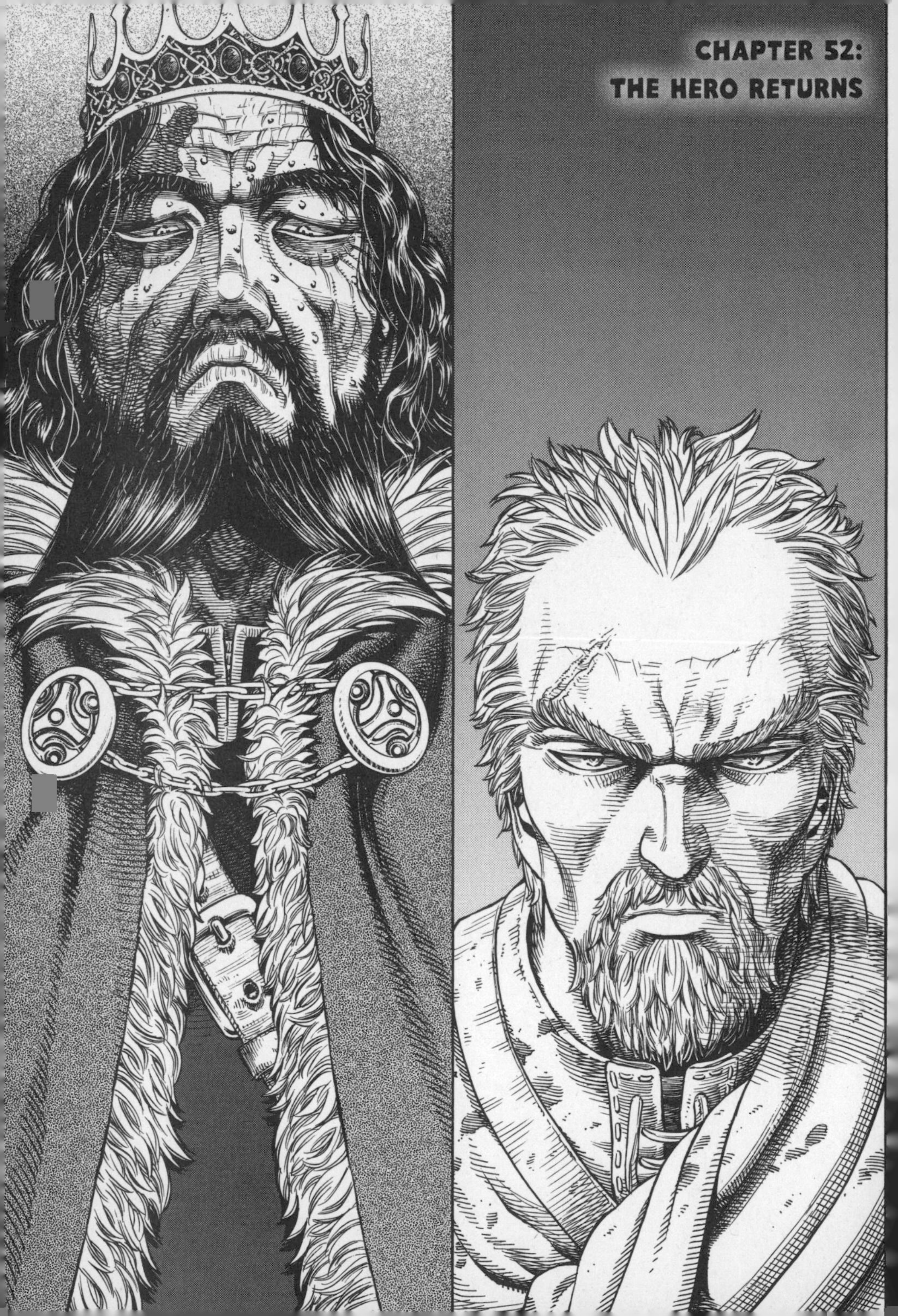

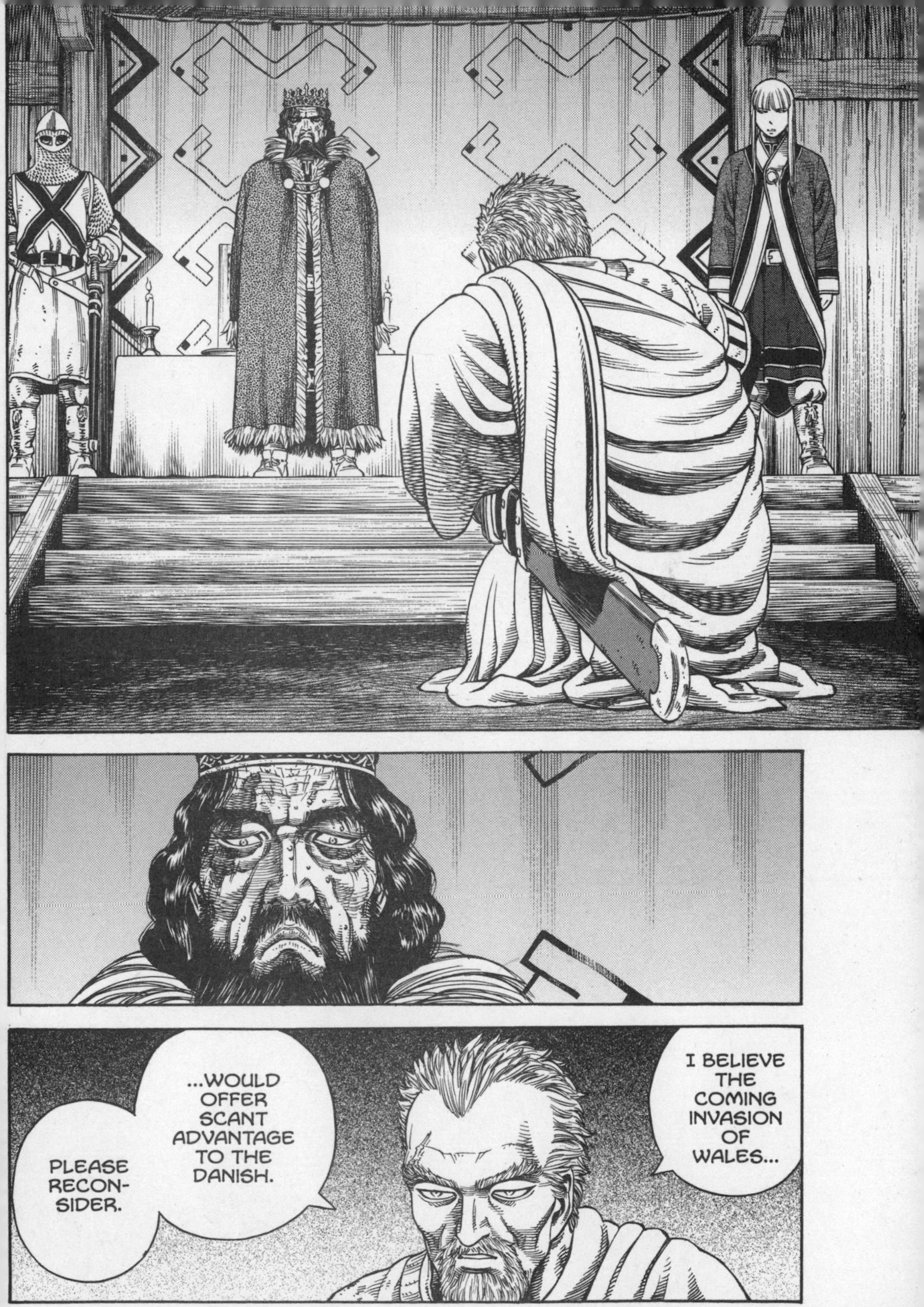
I BELIEVE THE COMING INVASION OF WALES...
...WOULD OFFER SCANT ADVANTAGE TO THE DANISH.
PLEASE RECON-SIDER.

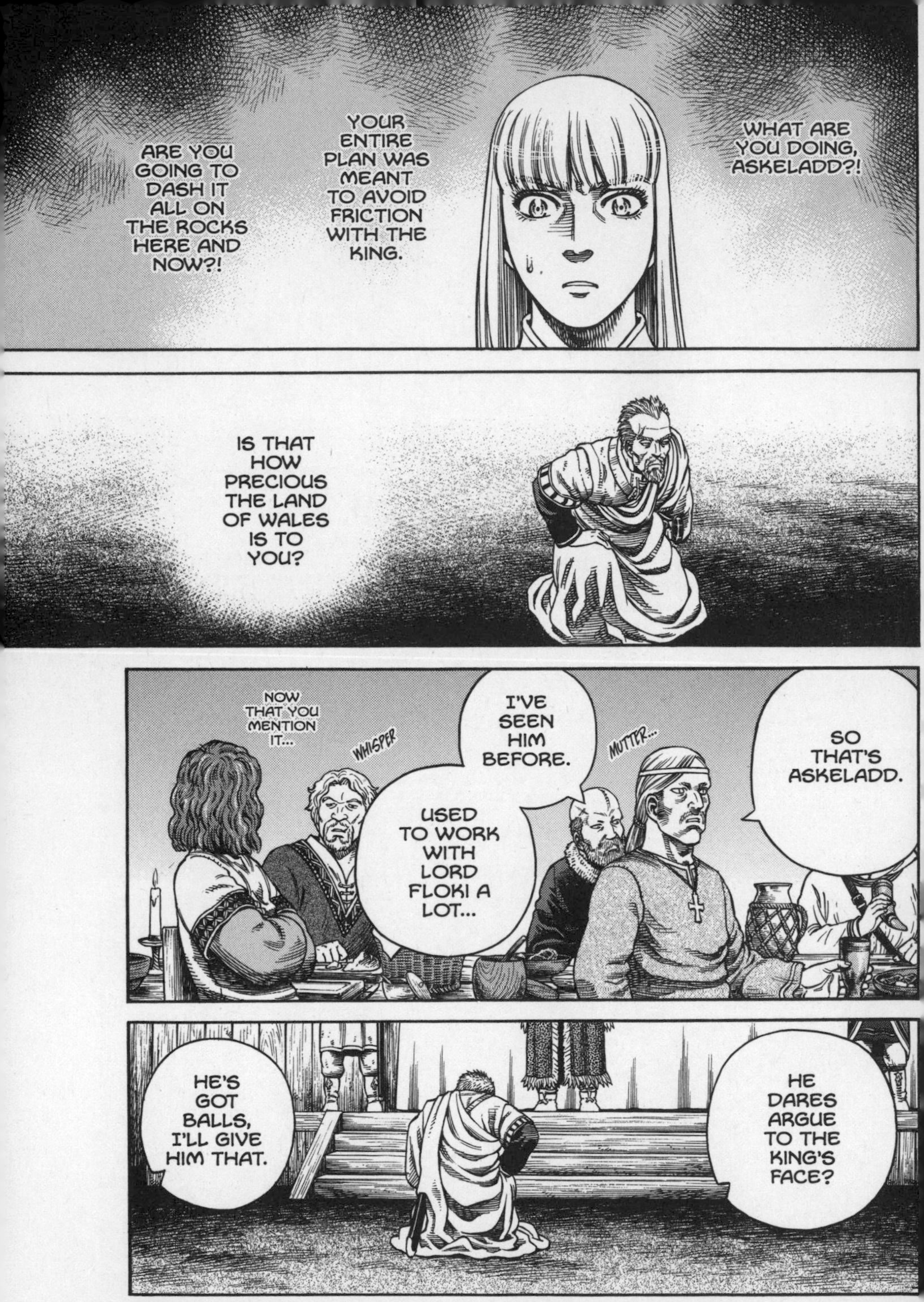
WHAT ARE YOU DOING, ASKELADD?!
YOUR ENTIRE PLAN WAS MEANT TO AVOID FRICTION WITH THE KING.
ARE YOU GOING TO DASH IT ALL ON THE ROCKS HERE AND NOW?!
IS THAT HOW PRECIOUS THE LAND OF WALES IS TO YOU?
SO THAT'S ASKELADD.
MUTTER...
I'VE SEEN HIM BEFORE.
USED TO WORK WITH LORD FLOKI A LOT...
WHISPER
NOW THAT YOU MENTION IT...
HE DARES ARGUE TO THE KING'S FACE?
HE'S GOT BALLS, I'LL GIVE HIM THAT.

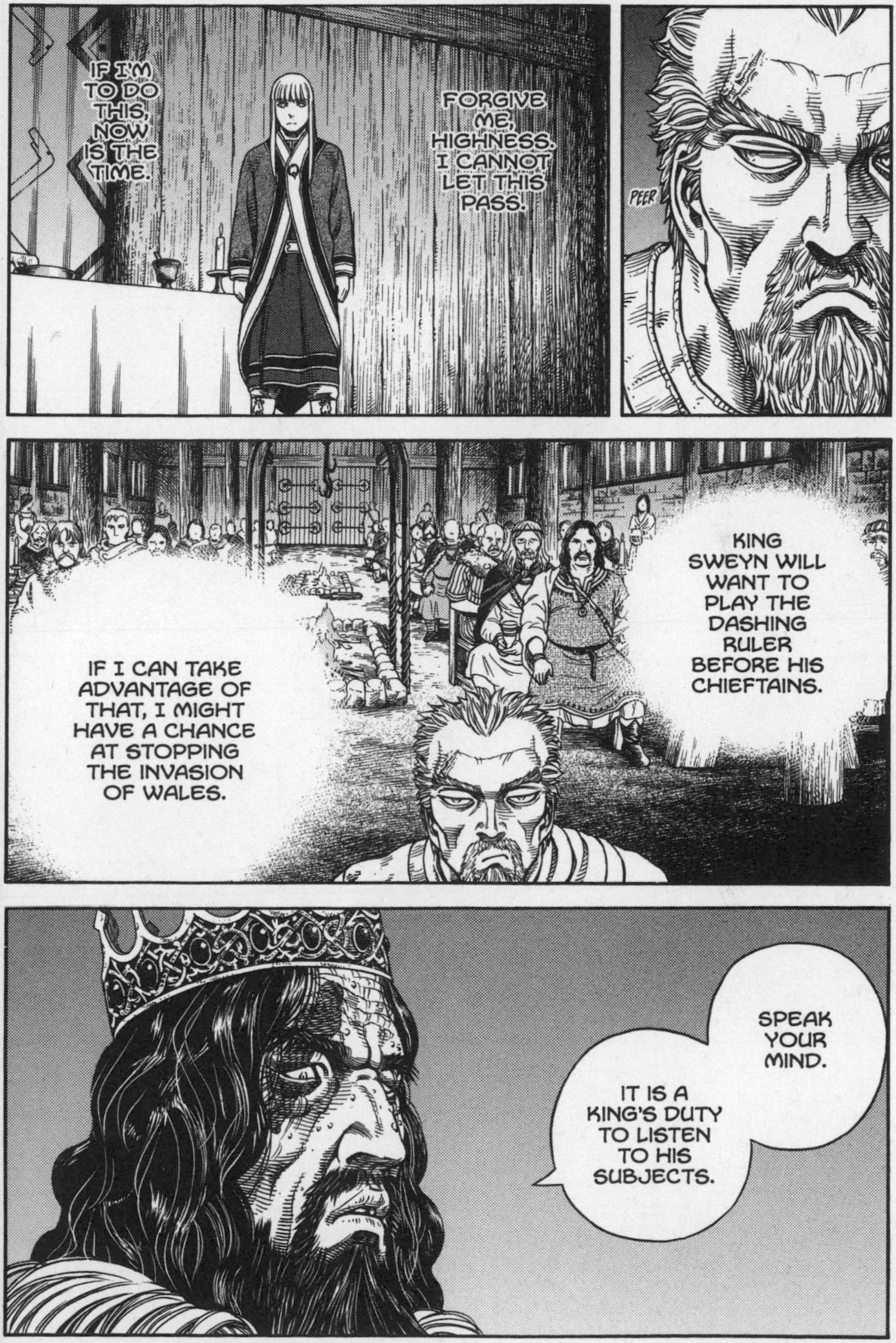
PEER
FORGIVE ME, HIGHNESS. I CANNOT LET THIS PASS.
IF I'M TO DO THIS, NOW IS THE TIME.
KING SWEYN WILL WANT TO PLAY THE DASHING RULER BEFORE HIS CHIEFTAINS.
IF I CAN TAKE ADVANTAGE OF THAT, I MIGHT HAVE A CHANCE AT STOPPING THE INVASION OF WALES.
SPEAK YOUR MIND.
IT IS A KING'S DUTY TO LISTEN TO HIS SUBJECTS.

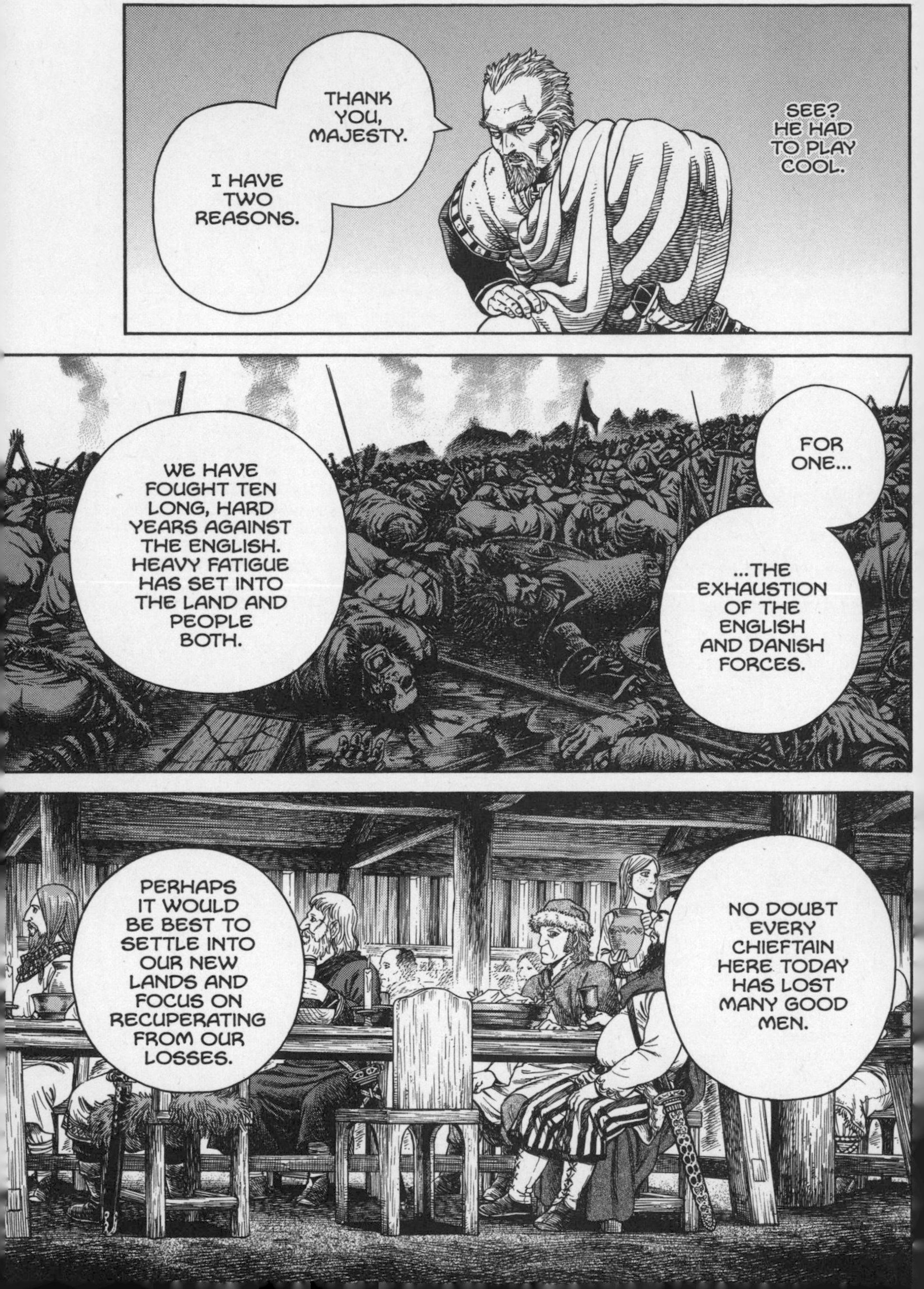
SEE? HE HAD TO PLAY COOL.
THANK YOU, MAJESTY.
I HAVE TWO REASONS.
FOR ONE...
...THE EXHAUSTION OF THE ENGLISH AND DANISH FORCES.
WE HAVE FOUGHT TEN LONG, HARD YEARS AGAINST THE ENGLISH. HEAVY FATIGUE HAS SET INTO THE LAND AND PEOPLE BOTH.
NO DOUBT EVERY CHIEFTAIN HERE TODAY HAS LOST MANY GOOD MEN.
PERHAPS IT WOULD BE BEST TO SETTLE INTO OUR NEW LANDS AND FOCUS ON RECUPERATING FROM OUR LOSSES.

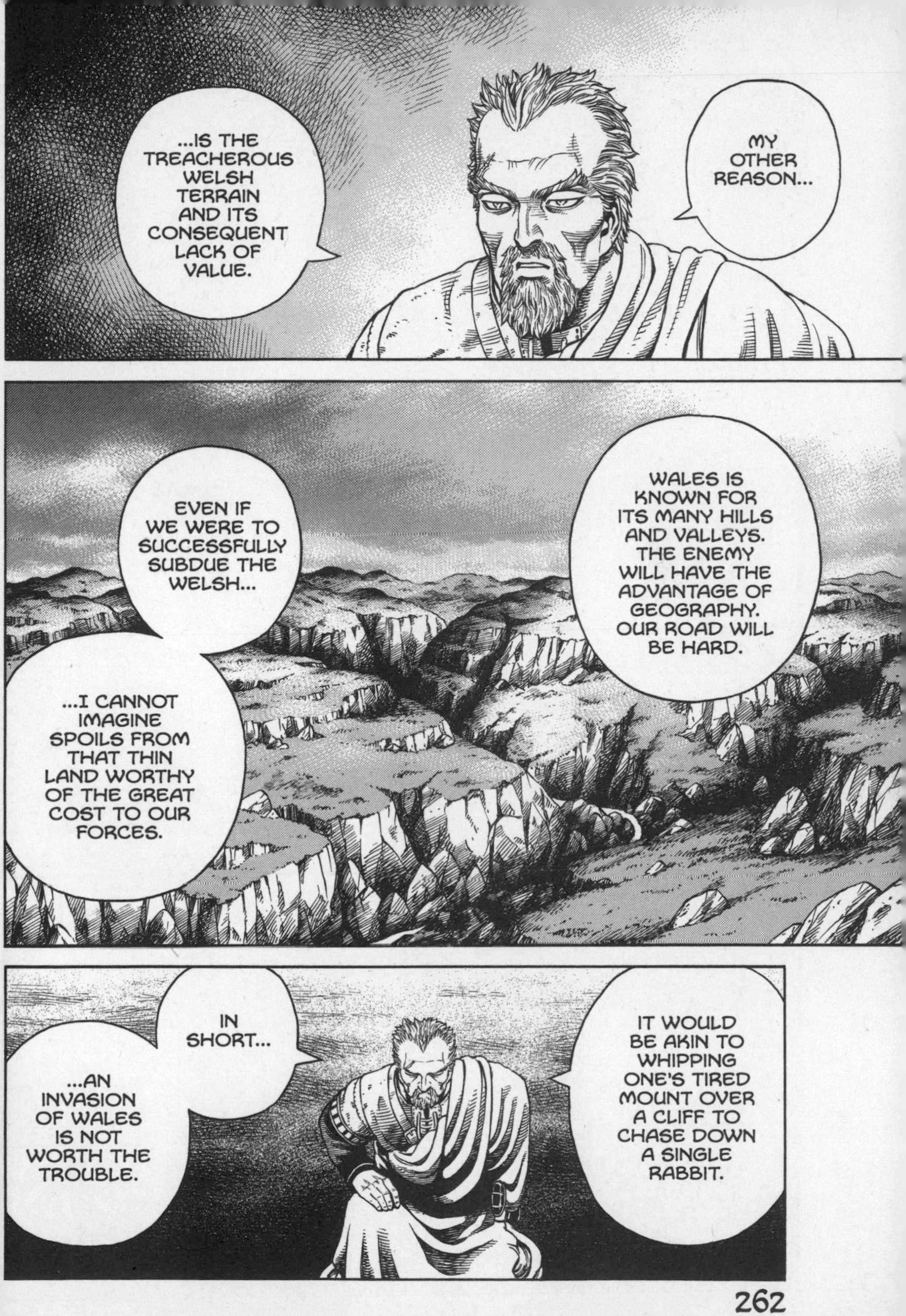
MY OTHER REASON...
...IS THE TREACHEROUS WELSH TERRAIN AND ITS CONSEQUENT LACK OF VALUE.
WALES IS KNOWN FOR ITS MANY HILLS AND VALLEYS. THE ENEMY WILL HAVE THE ADVANTAGE OF GEOGRAPHY. OUR ROAD WILL BE HARD.
EVEN IF WE WERE TO SUCCESSFULLY SUBDUE THE WELSH...
...I CANNOT IMAGINE SPOILS FROM THAT THIN LAND WORTHY OF THE GREAT COST TO OUR FORCES.
IT WOULD BE AKIN TO WHIPPING ONE'S TIRED MOUNT OVER A CLIFF TO CHASE DOWN A SINGLE RABBIT.
IN SHORT...
...AN INVASION OF WALES IS NOT WORTH THE TROUBLE.

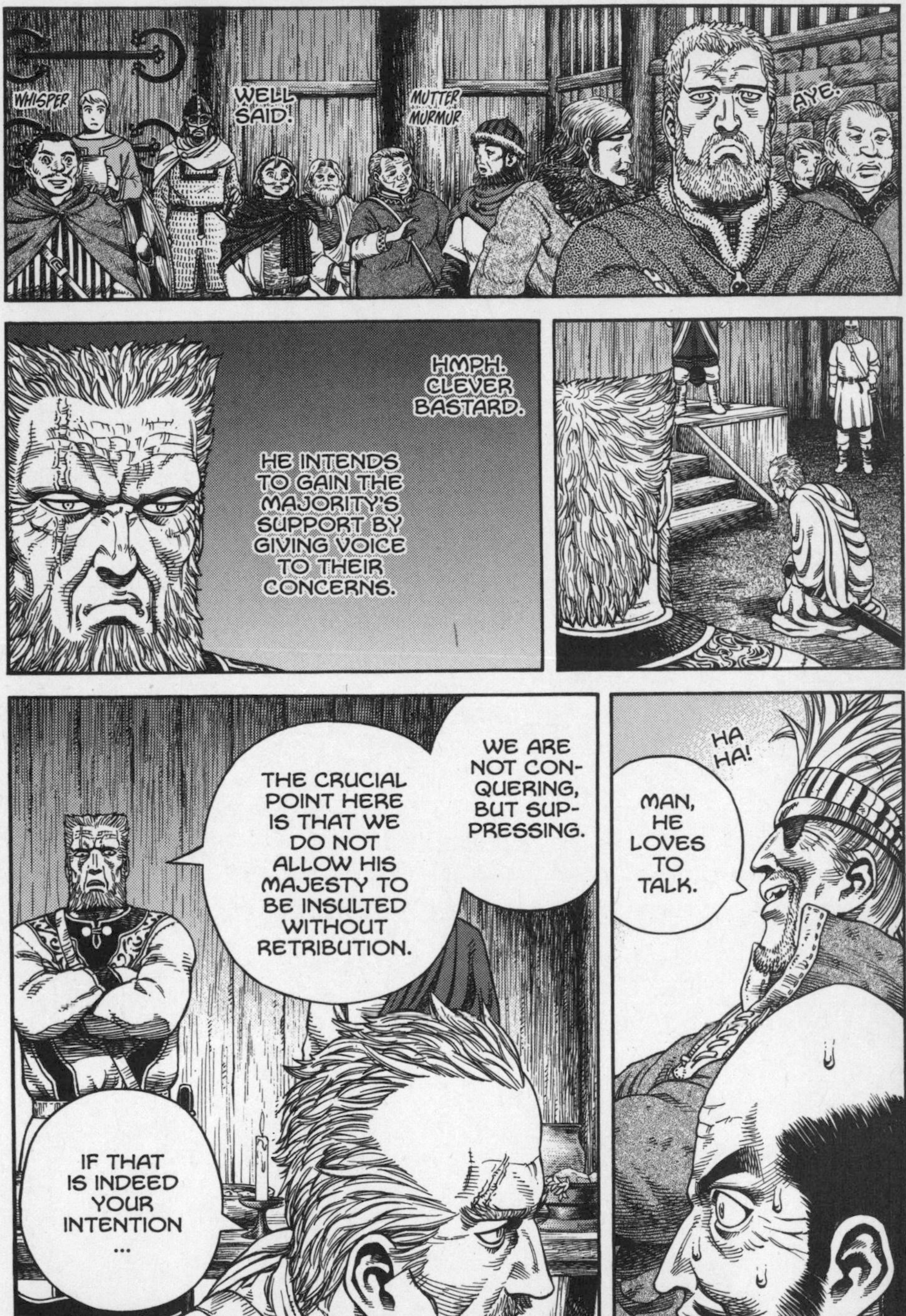
AYE.
MUTTER MURMUR
WELL SAID!
WHISPER
HMPH. CLEVER BASTARD.
HE INTENDS TO GAIN THE MAJORITY'S SUPPORT BY GIVING VOICE TO THEIR CONCERNS.
HA HA!
MAN, HE LOVES TO TALK.
WE ARE NOT CONQUERING, BUT SUPPRESSING.
THE CRUCIAL POINT HERE IS THAT WE DO NOT ALLOW HIS MAJESTY TO BE INSULTED WITHOUT RETRIBUTION.
IF THAT IS INDEED YOUR INTENTION ...

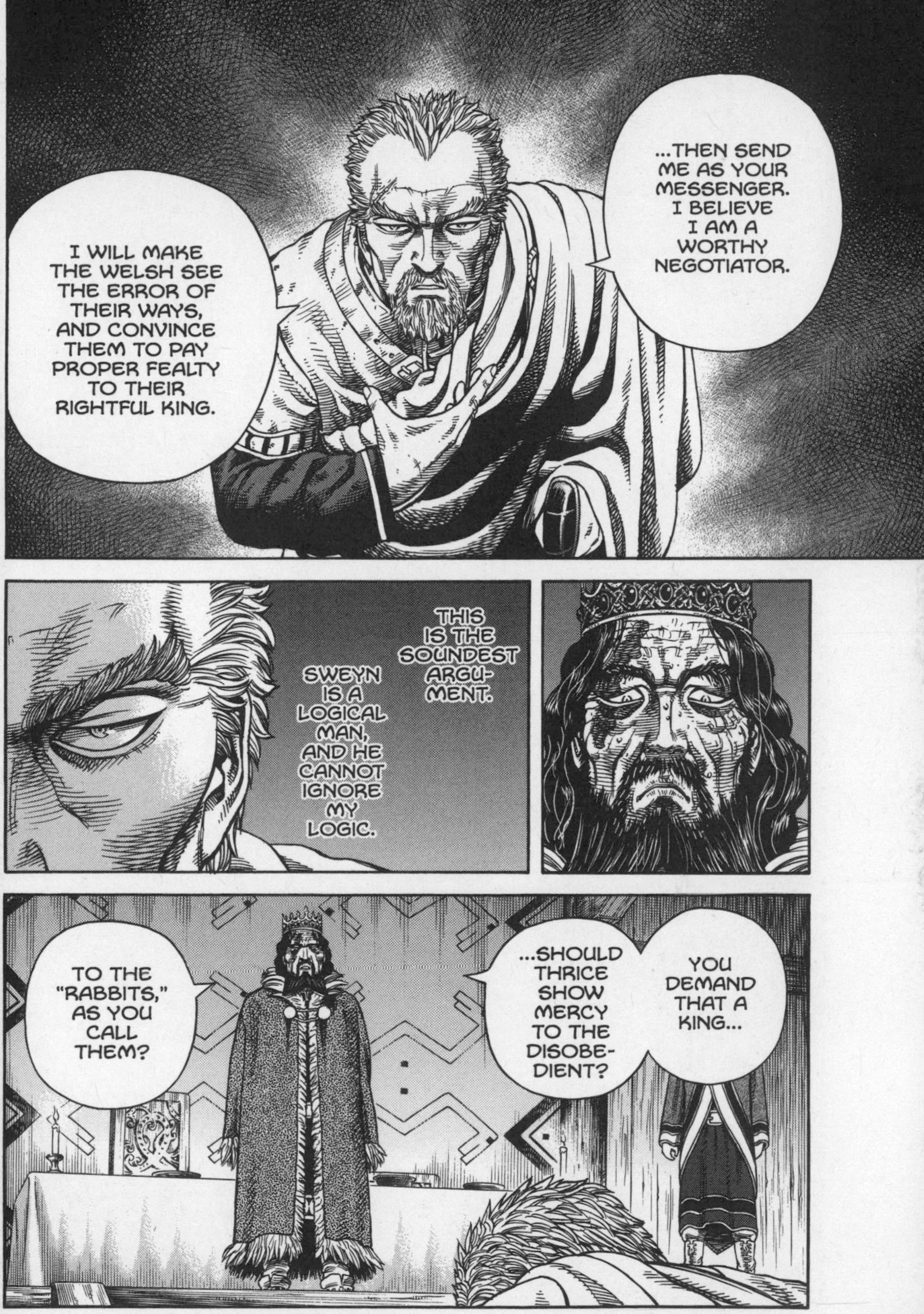
...THEN SEND ME AS YOUR MESSENGER. I BELIEVE I AM A WORTHY NEGOTIATOR.
I WILL MAKE THE WELSH SEE THE ERROR OF THEIR WAYS, AND CONVINCE THEM TO PAY PROPER FEALTY TO THEIR RIGHTFUL KING.
THIS IS THE SOUNDEST ARGU-MENT.
SWEYN IS A LOGICAL MAN, AND HE CANNOT IGNORE MY LOGIC.
YOU DEMAND THAT A KING...
...SHOULD THRICE SHOW MERCY TO THE DISOBE-DIENT?
TO THE "RABBITS," AS YOU CALL THEM?

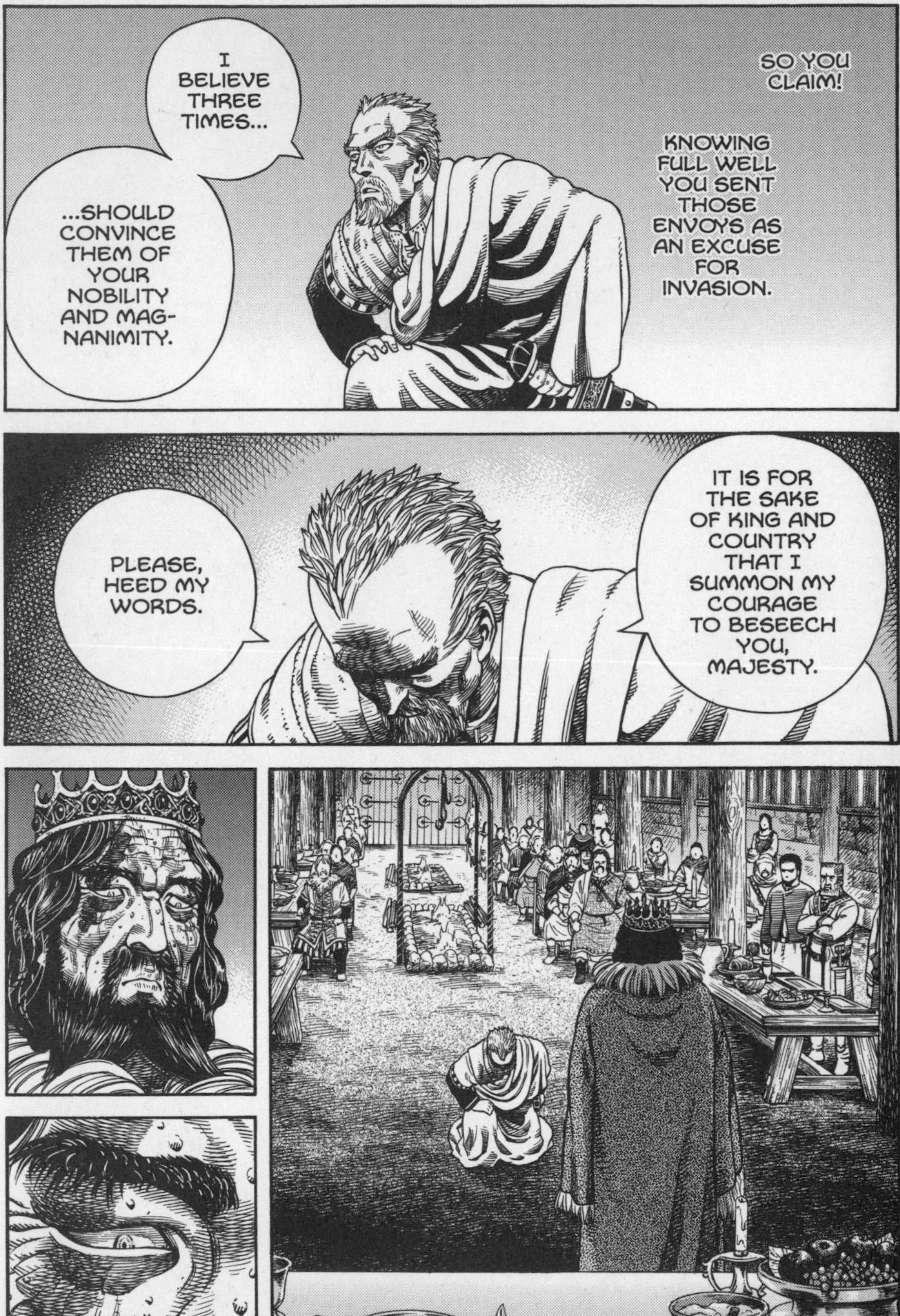
SO YOU CLAIM!
KNOWING FULL WELL YOU SENT THOSE ENVOYS AS AN EXCUSE FOR INVASION.
I BELIEVE THREE TIMES...
...SHOULD CONVINCE THEM OF YOUR NOBILITY AND MAG-NANIMITY.
IT IS FOR THE SAKE OF KING AND COUNTRY THAT I SUMMON MY COURAGE TO BESEECH YOU, MAJESTY.
PLEASE, HEED MY WORDS.

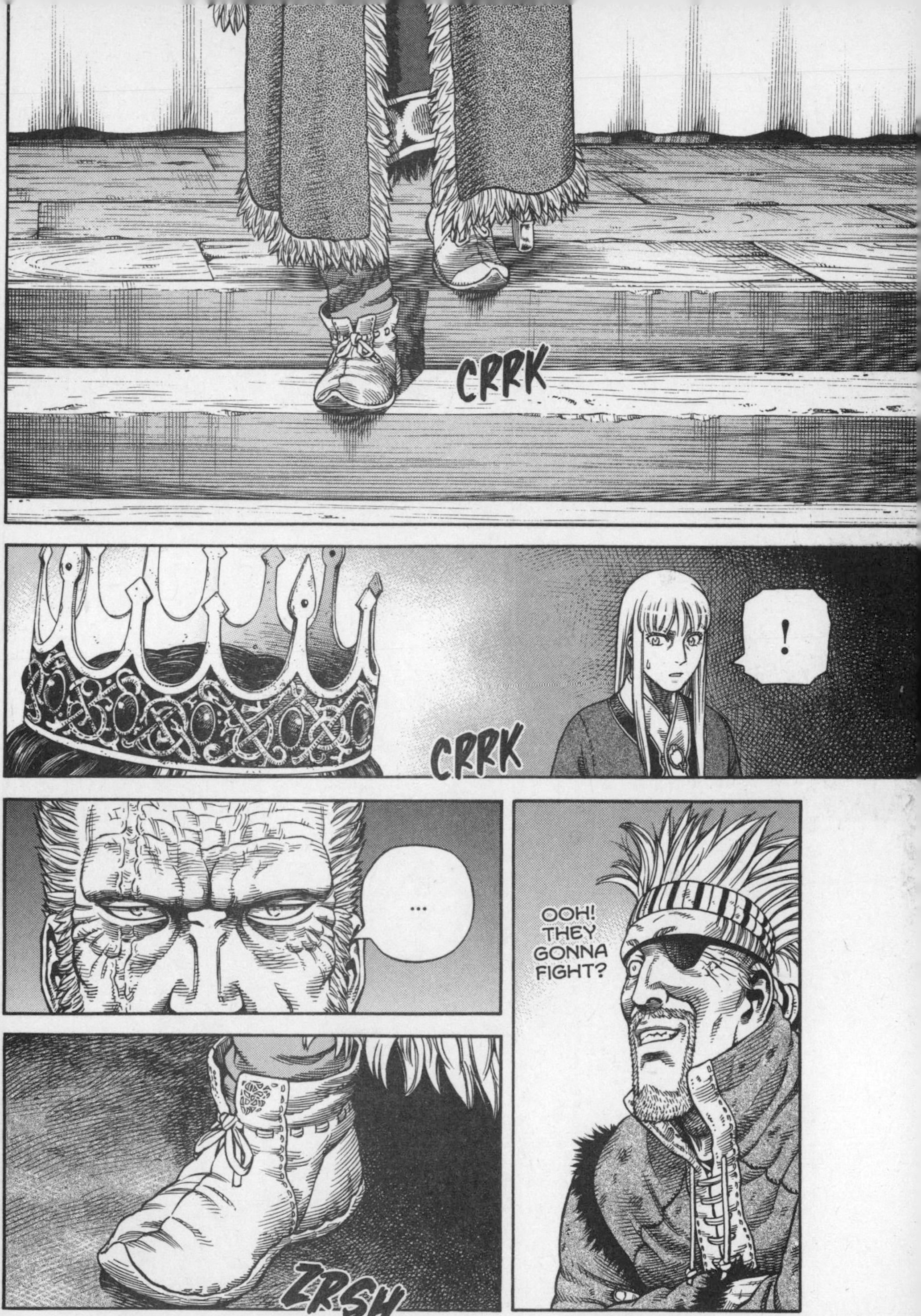
CRRK
!
CRRK
OOH! THEY GONNA FIGHT?
...
ZRSH

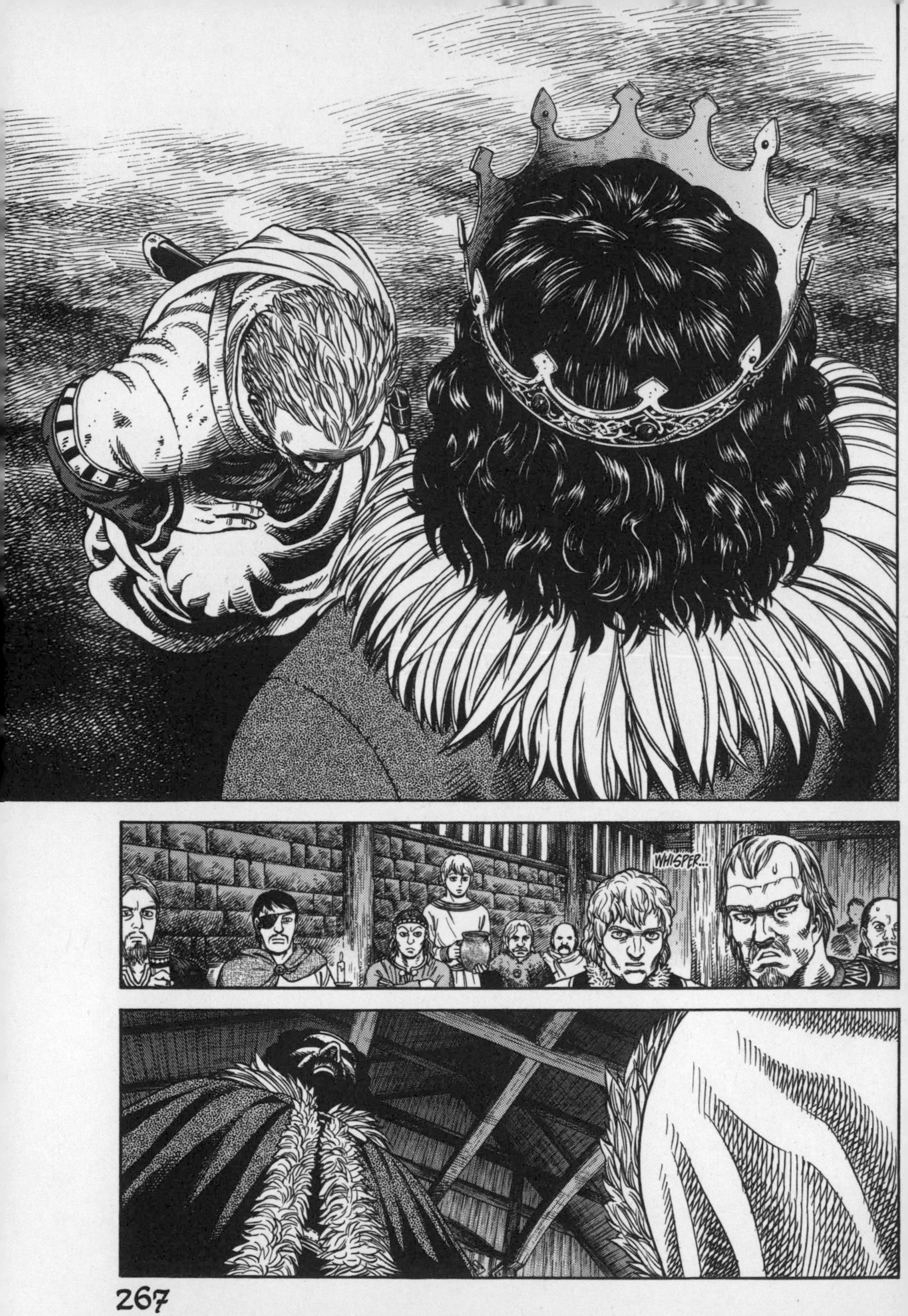
WHISPER...

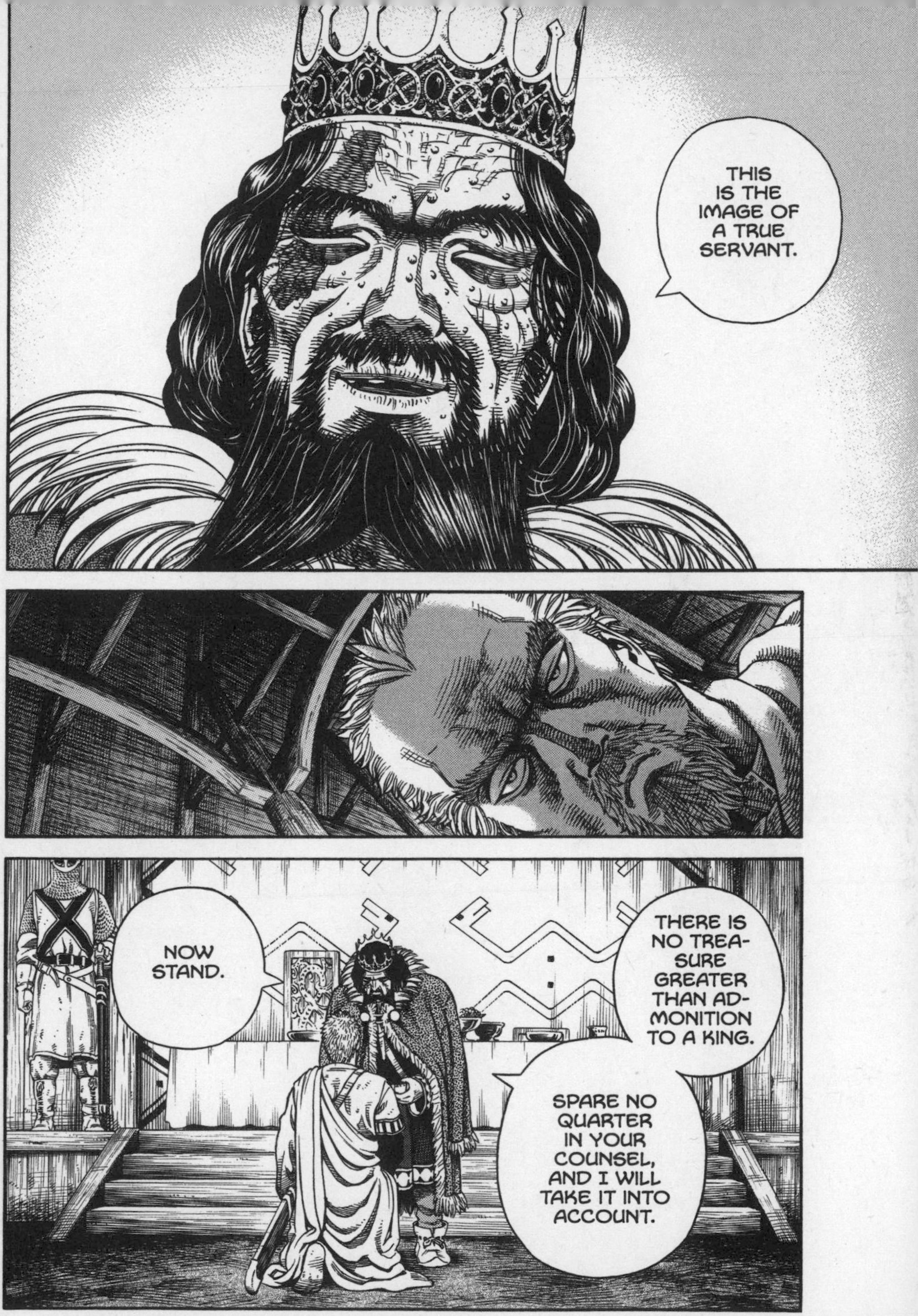
THIS IS THE IMAGE OF A TRUE SERVANT.
THERE IS NO TREASURE GREATER THAN ADMONITION TO A KING.
SPARE NO QUARTER IN YOUR COUNSEL, AND I WILL TAKE IT INTO ACCOUNT.
NOW STAND.

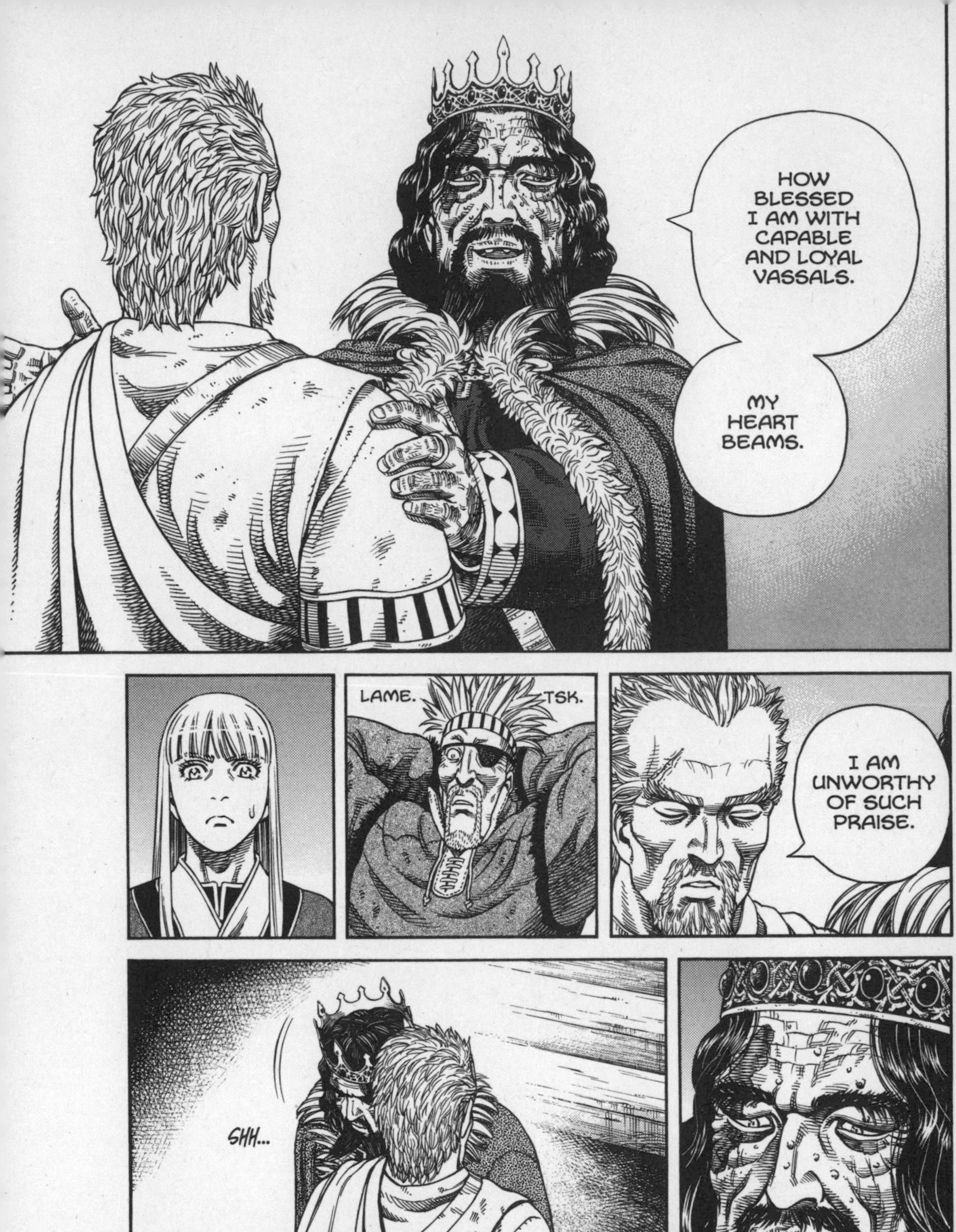
HOW BLESSED I AM WITH CAPABLE AND LOYAL VASSALS.
MY HEART BEAMS.
I AM UNWORTHY OF SUCH PRAISE.
TSK.
LAME.
SHH...

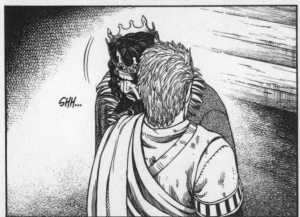

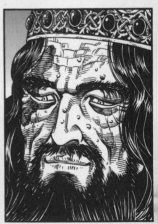

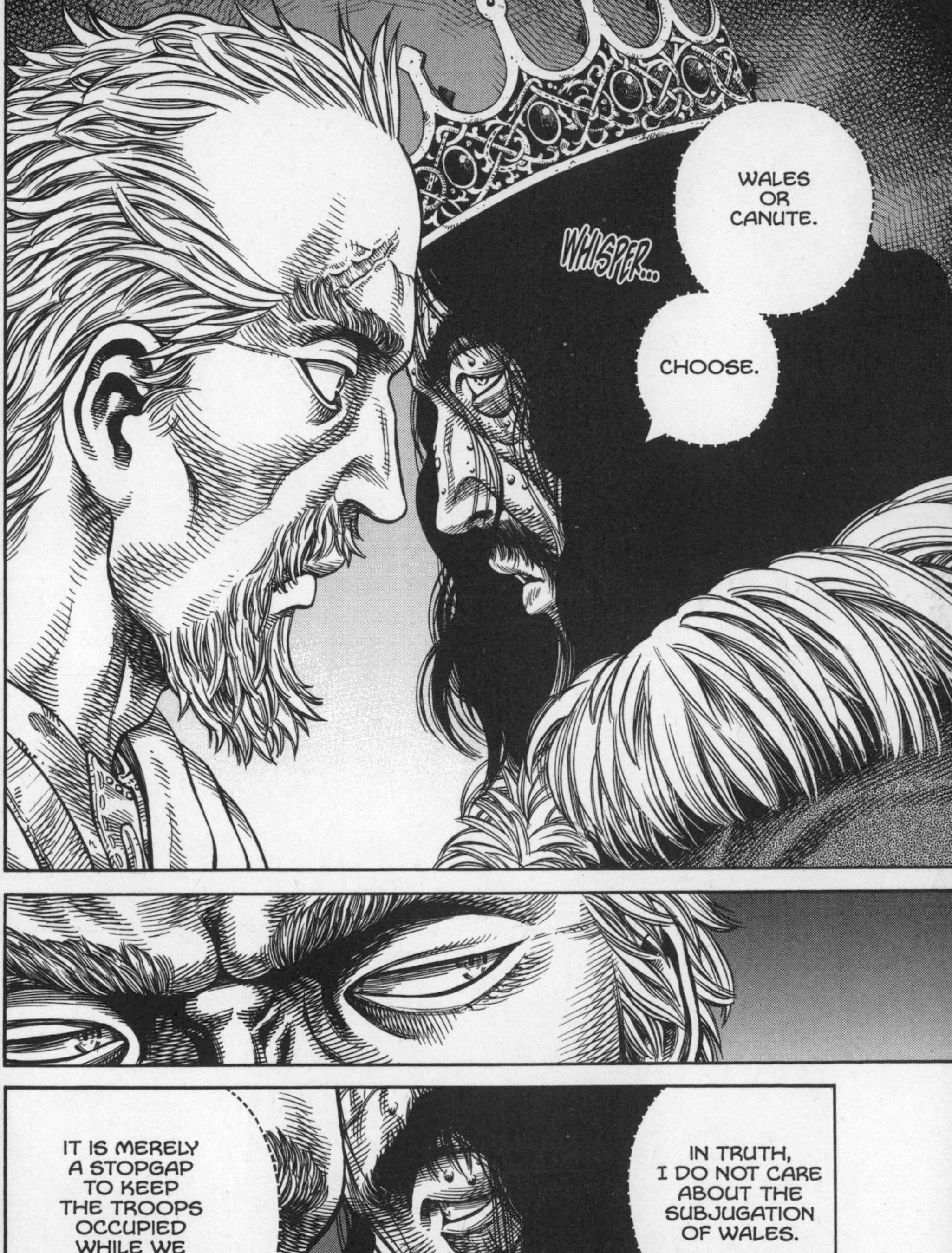
WALES OR CANUTE.
WHISPER...
CHOOSE.
IN TRUTH, I DO NOT CARE ABOUT THE SUBJUGATION OF WALES.
IT IS MERELY A STOPGAP TO KEEP THE TROOPS OCCUPIED WHILE WE PREPARE FOR IRELAND.

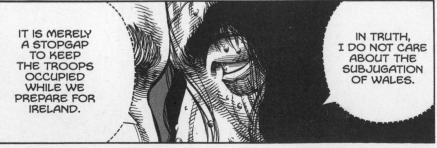

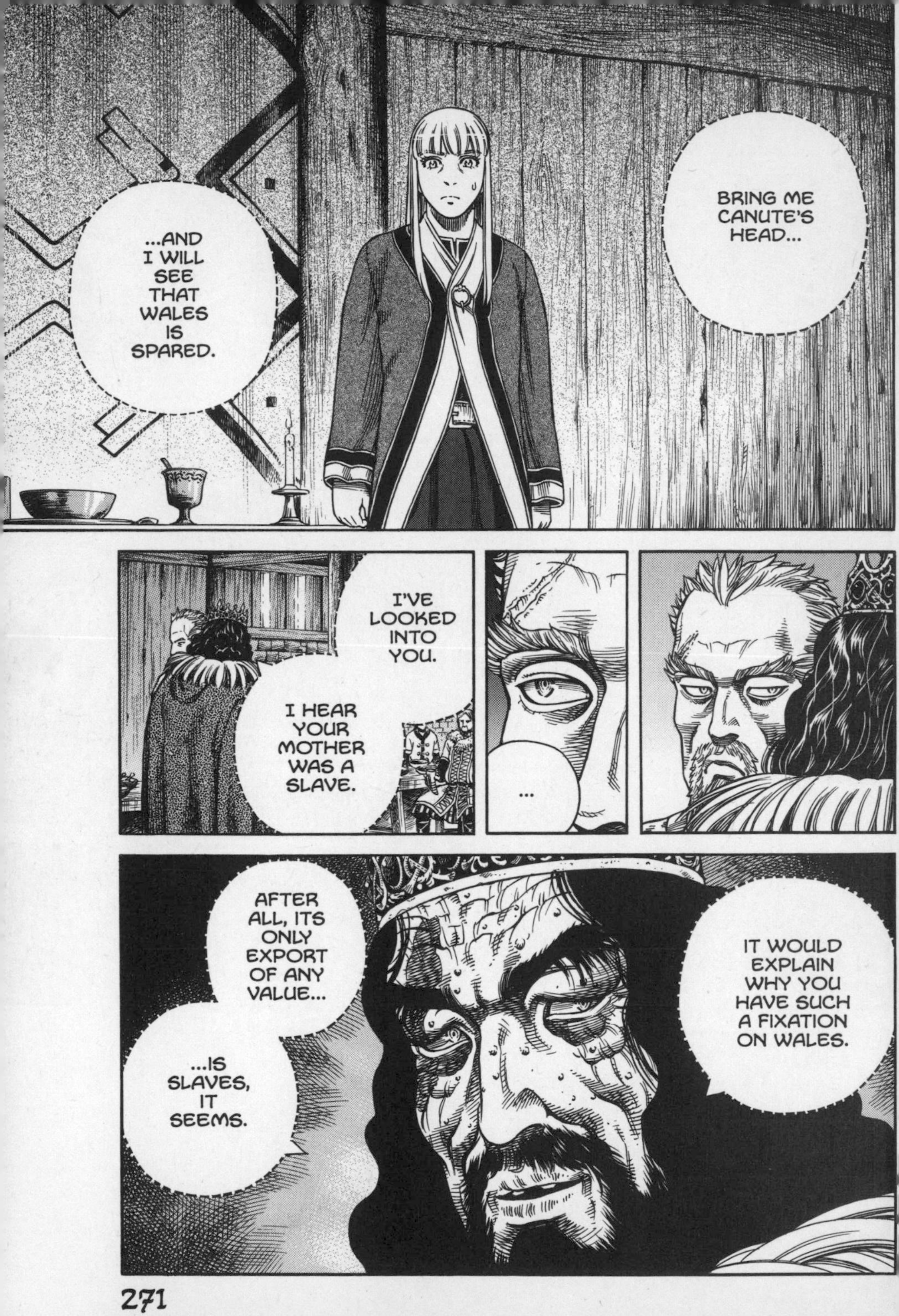
BRING ME CANUTE'S HEAD...
...AND I WILL SEE THAT WALES IS SPARED.
...
I'VE LOOKED INTO YOU.
I HEAR YOUR MOTHER WAS A SLAVE.
IT WOULD EXPLAIN WHY YOU HAVE SUCH A FIXATION ON WALES.
AFTER ALL, ITS ONLY EXPORT OF ANY VALUE...
...IS SLAVES, IT SEEMS.

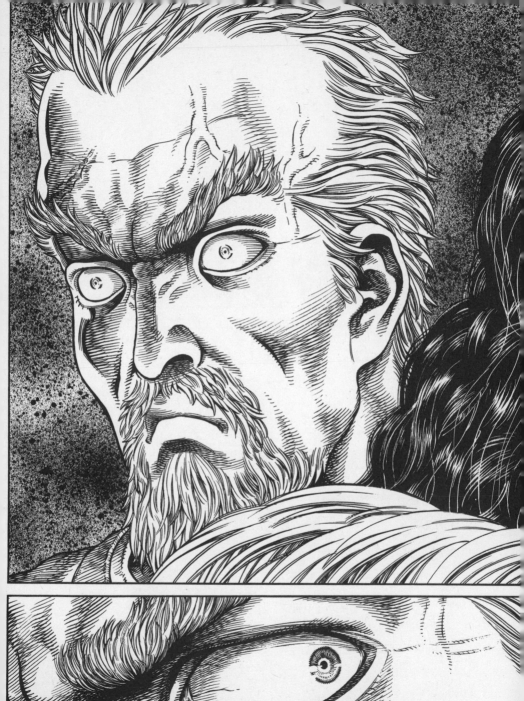
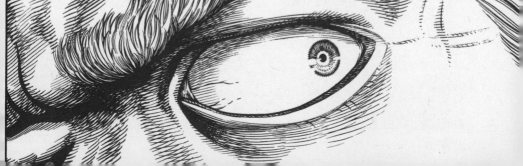

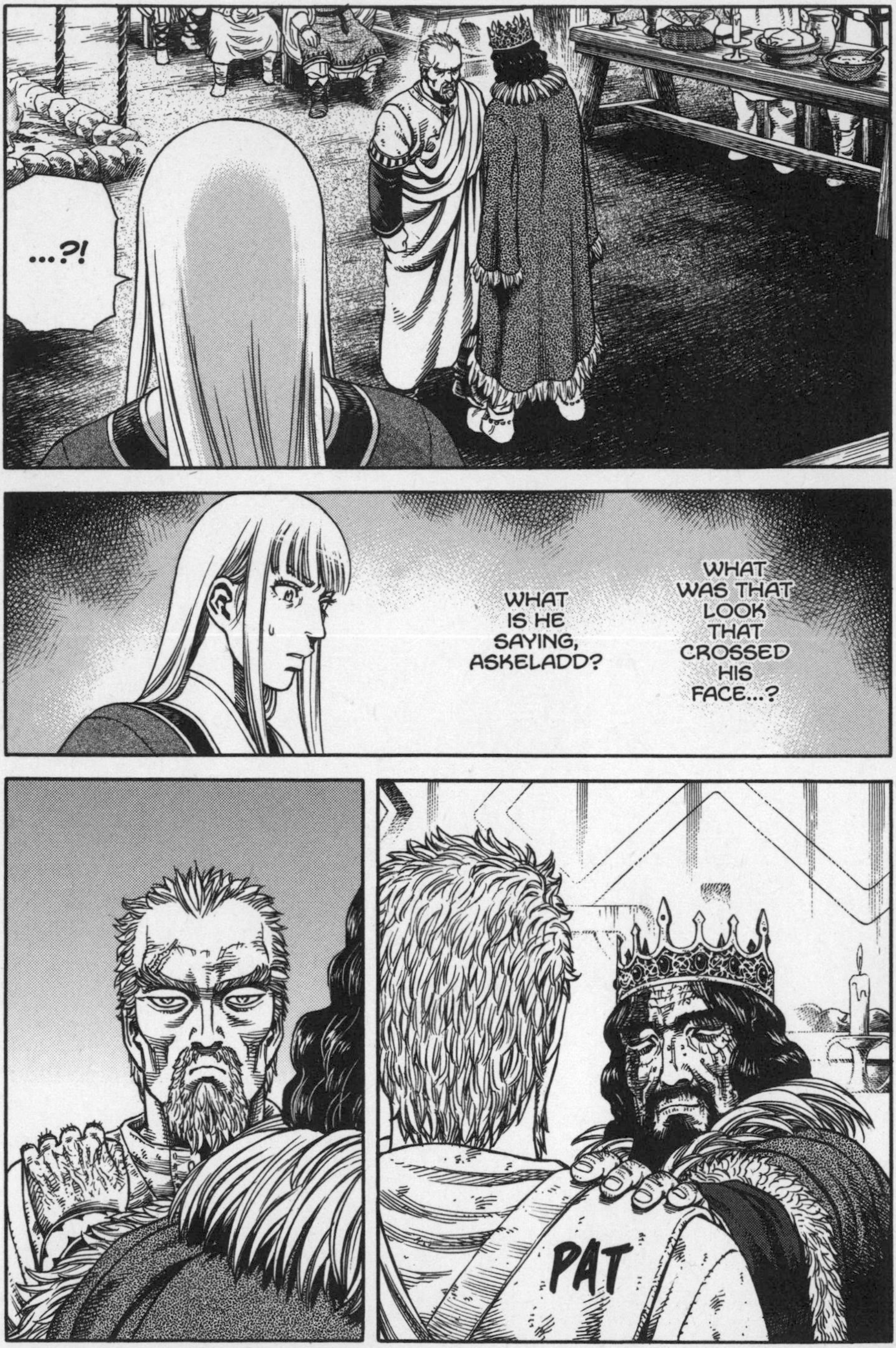
...?!
WHAT WAS THAT LOOK THAT CROSSED HIS FACE...?
WHAT IS HE SAYING, ASKELADD?
PAT

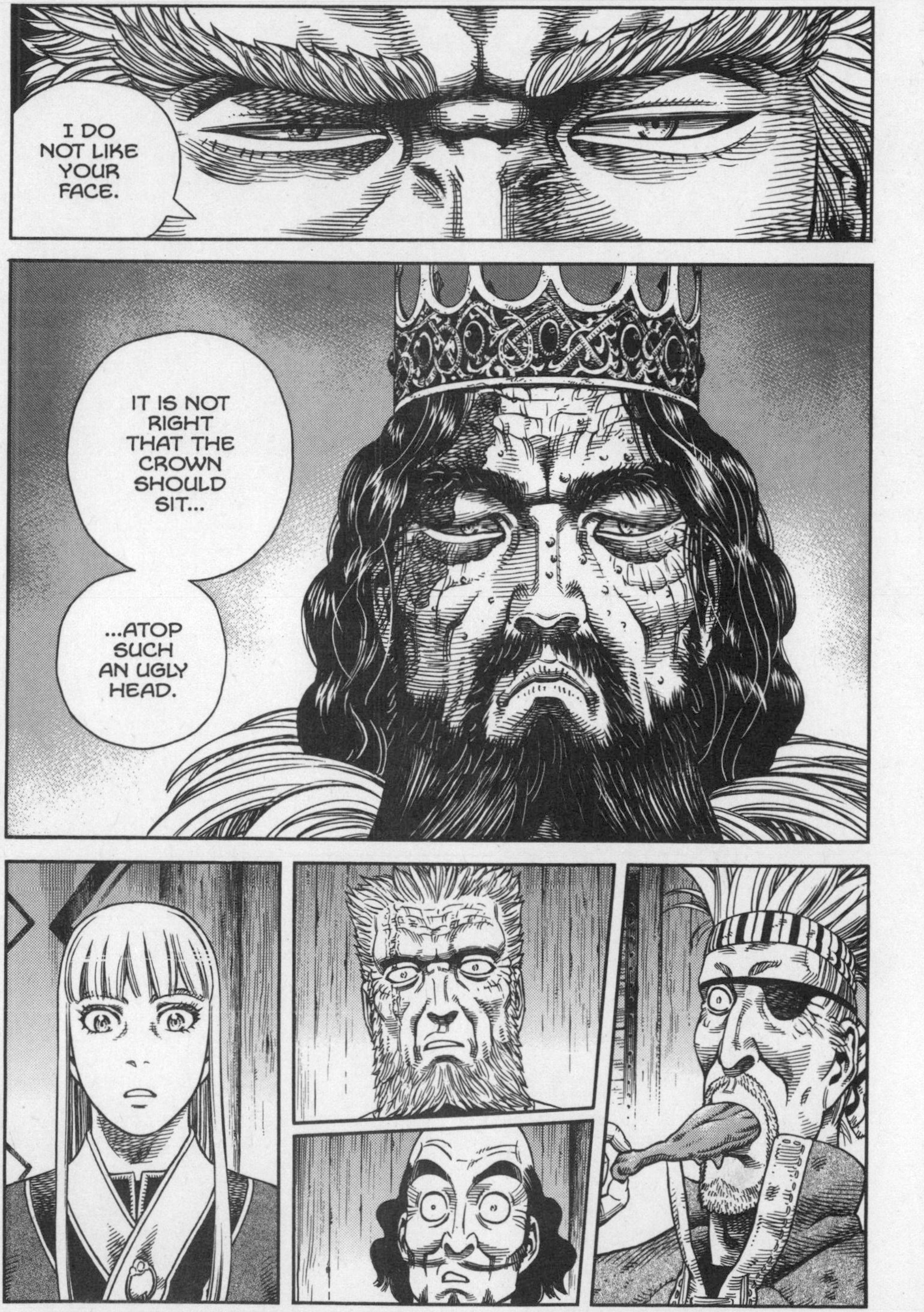
I DO NOT LIKE YOUR FACE.
IT IS NOT RIGHT THAT THE CROWN SHOULD SIT...
...ATOP SUCH AN UGLY HEAD.

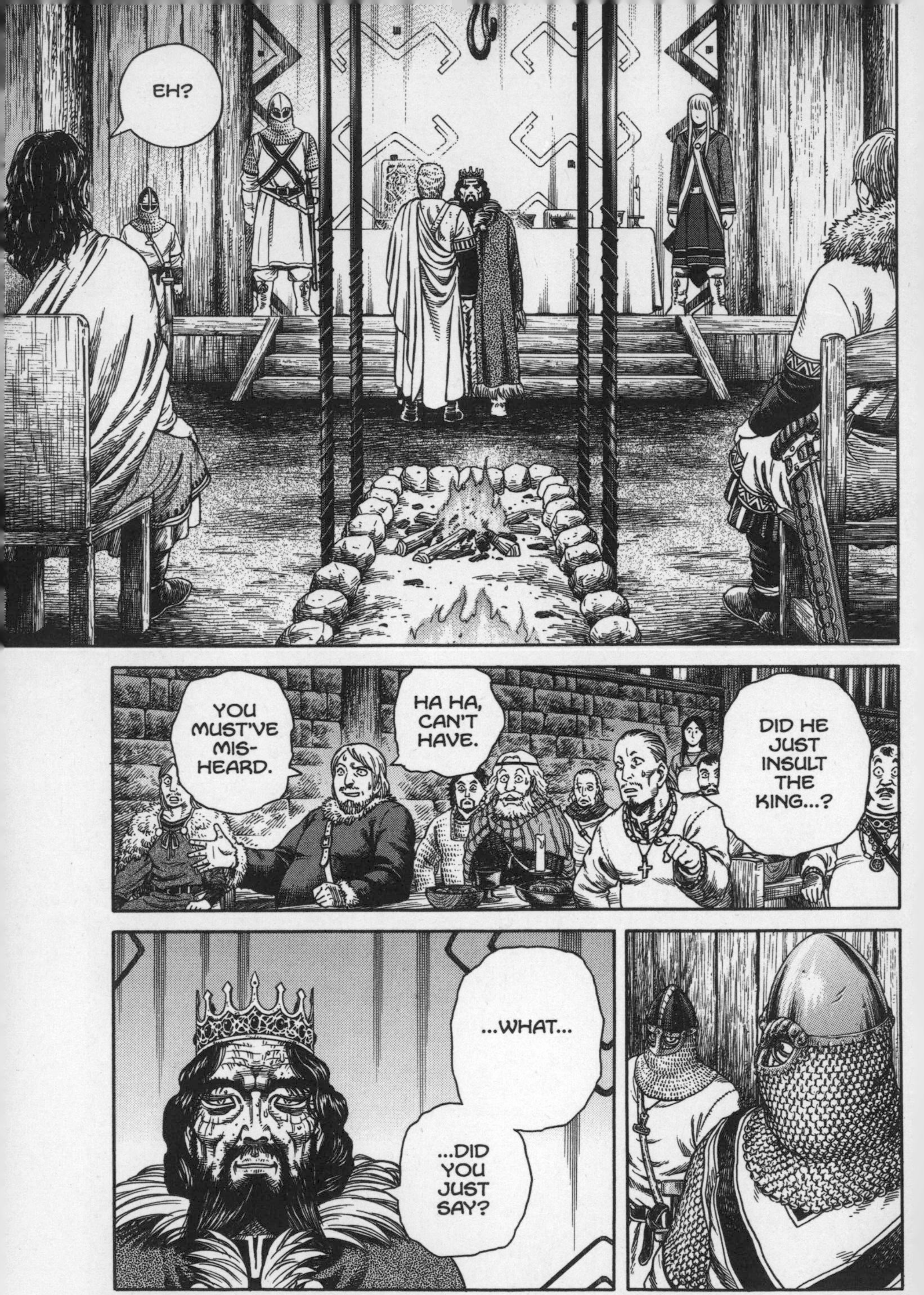
EH?
DID HE JUST INSULT THE KING...?
HA HA, CAN'T HAVE.
YOU MUST'VE MIS-HEARD.
...WHAT...
...DID YOU JUST SAY?

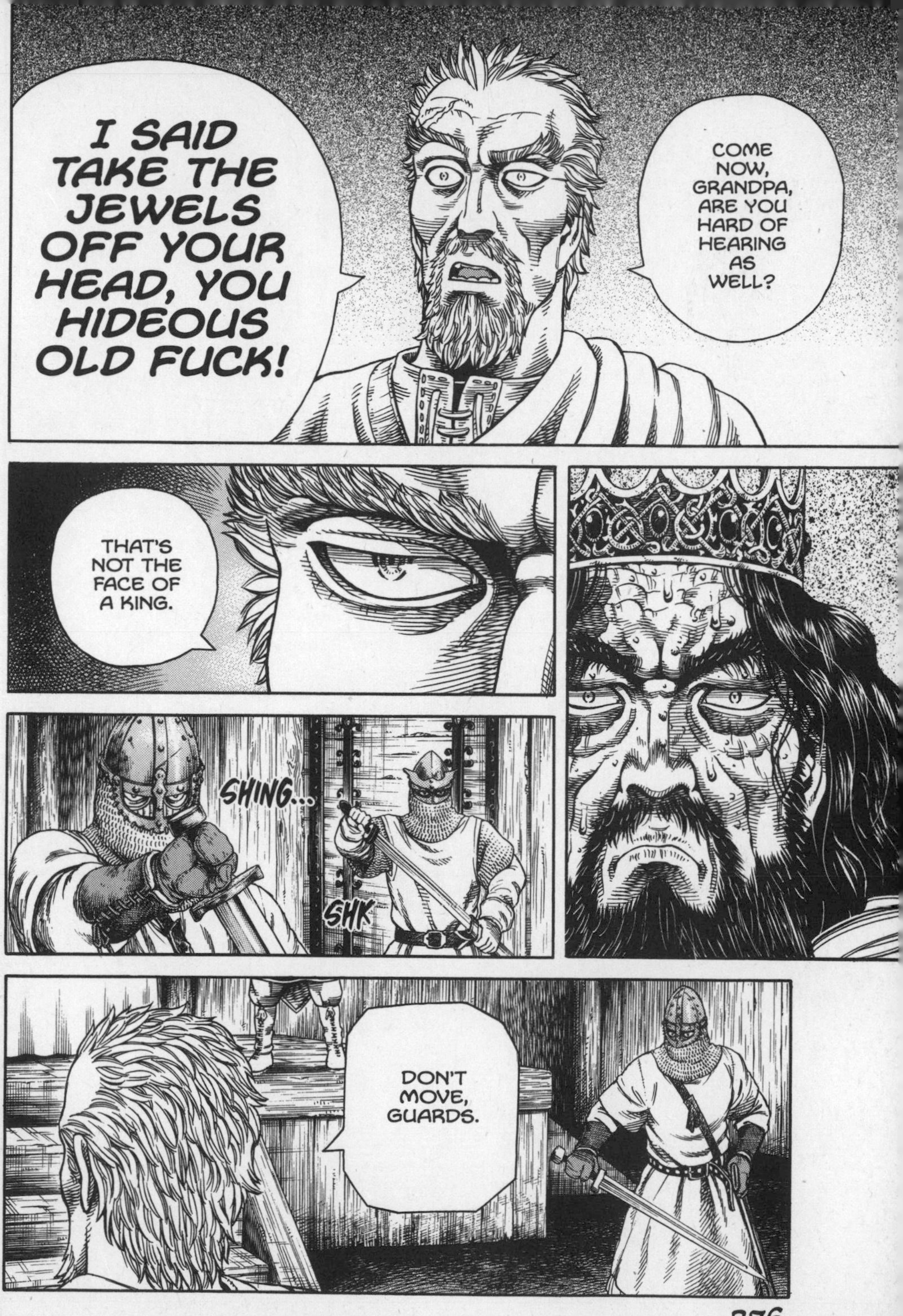
COME NOW, GRANDPA, ARE YOU HARD OF HEARING AS WELL?
I SAID TAKE THE JEWELS OFF YOUR HEAD, YOU HIDEOUS OLD FUCK!
THAT'S NOT THE FACE OF A KING.
SHING...
SHK
DON'T MOVE, GUARDS.

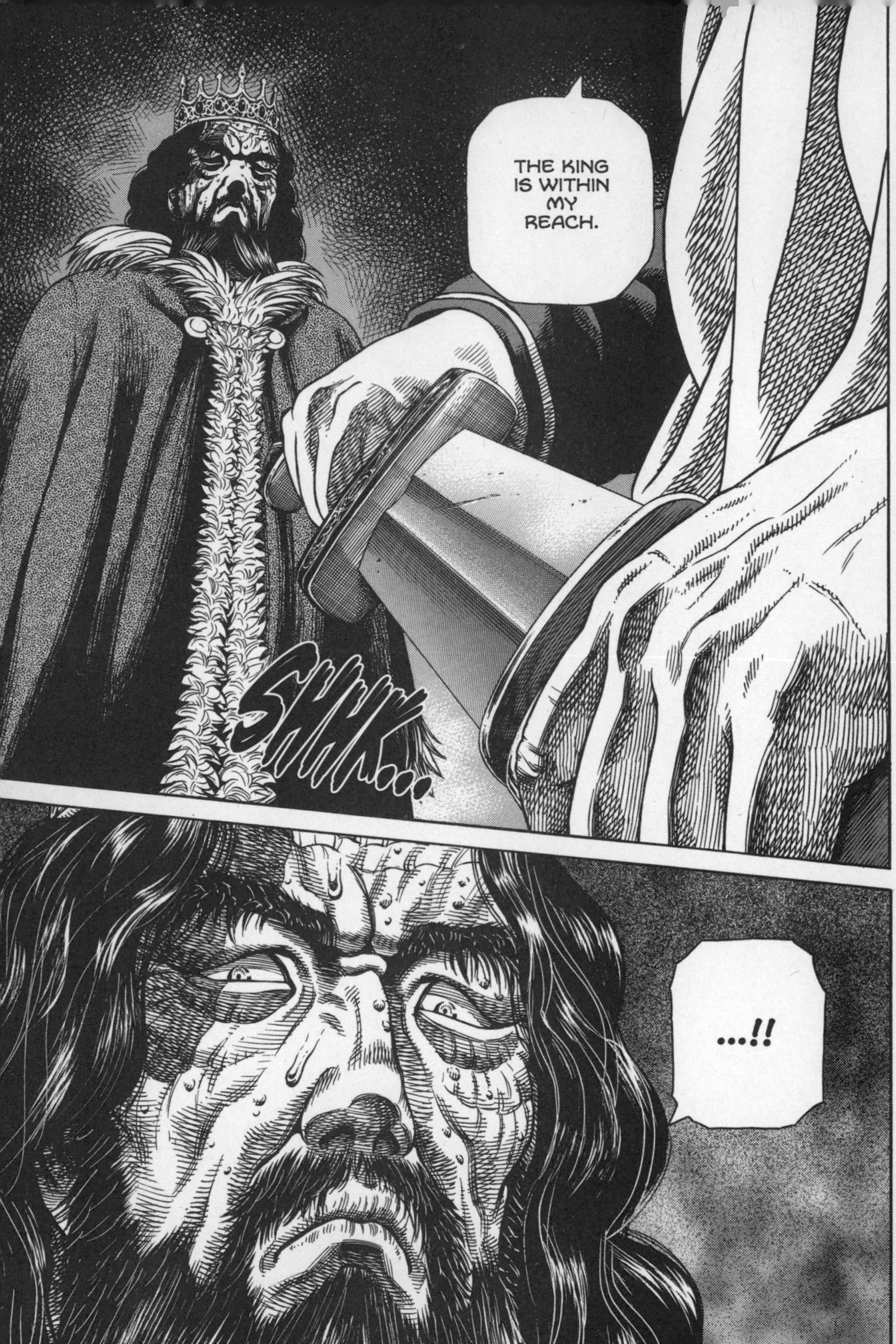
THE KING IS WITHIN MY REACH.
SHHK...
...!!

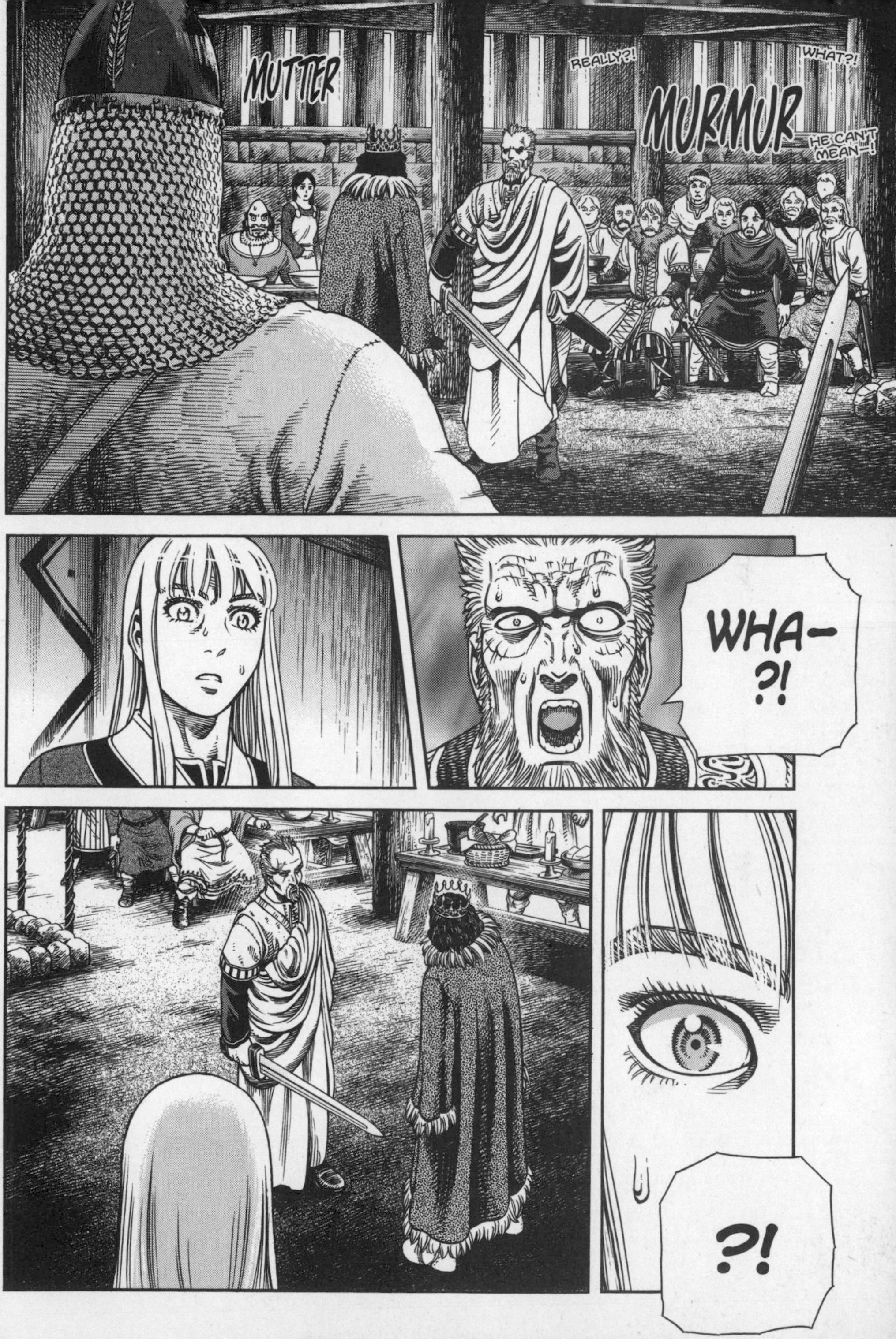
WHAT?!
HE CAN'T MEAN—!
MURMUR
REALLY?!
MUTTER
WHA- ?!
?!

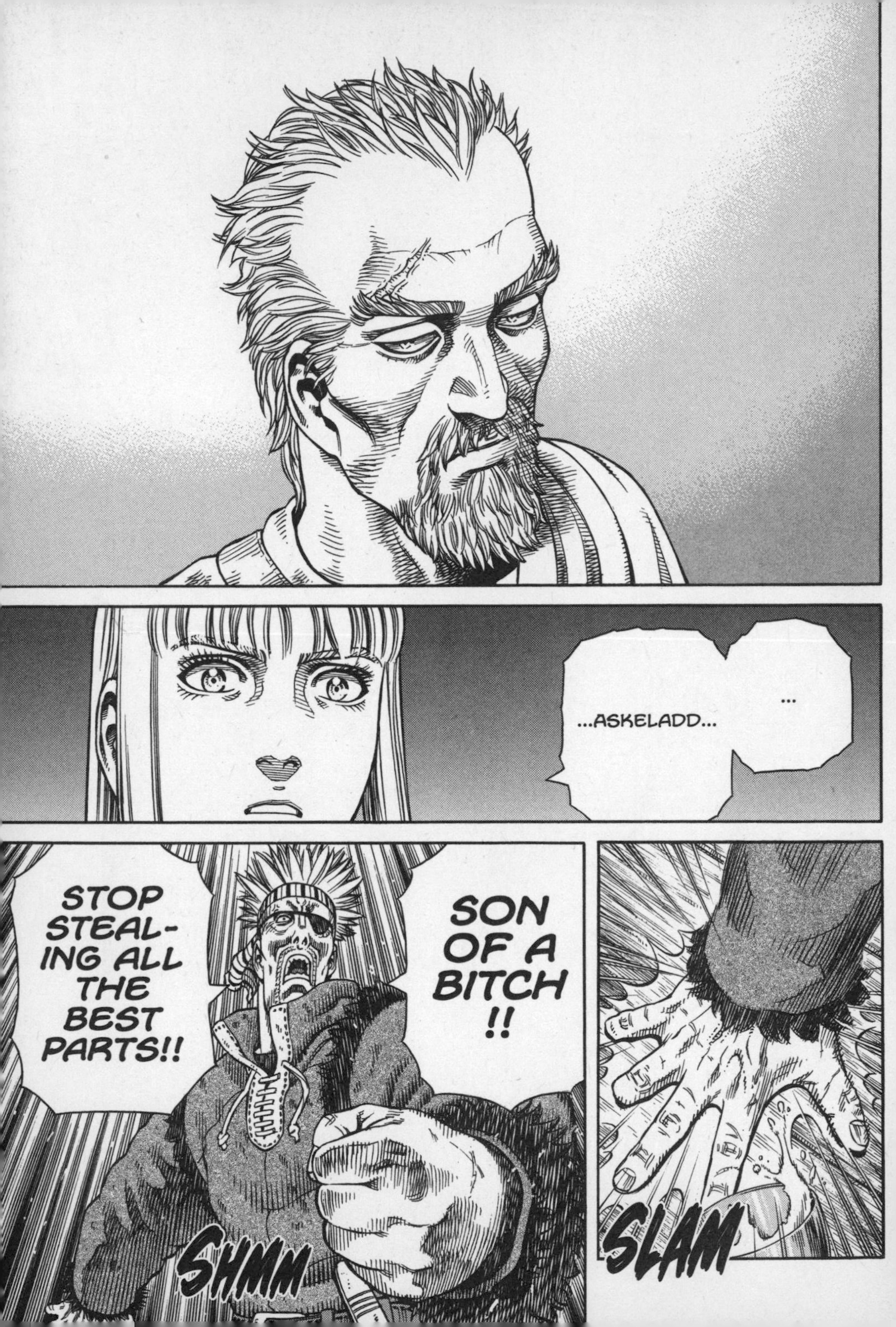
...
...ASKELADD...
SLAM
SON OF A BITCH !!
STOP STEAL-ING ALL THE BEST PARTS!!
SHMM

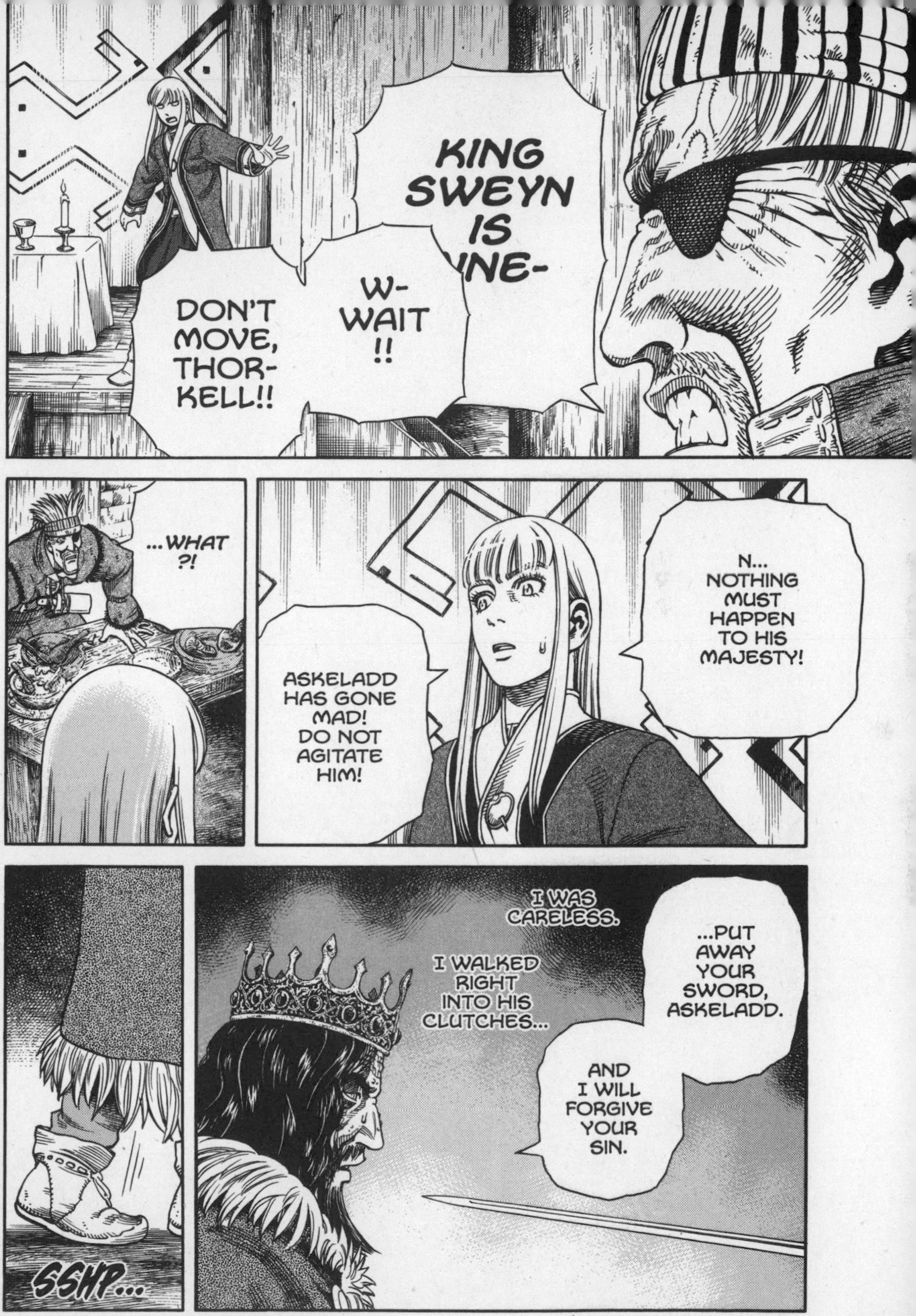

KING SWEYN IS
W-WAIT!!
DON'T MOVE, THORKELL!!
N... NOTHING MUST HAPPEN TO HIS MAJESTY!
ASKELADD HAS GONE MAD! DO NOT AGITATE HIM!
...WHAT?!
I WAS CARELESS.
I WALKED RIGHT INTO HIS CLUTCHES...
...PUT AWAY YOUR SWORD, ASKELADD.
AND I WILL FORGIVE YOUR SIN.
SSHP...

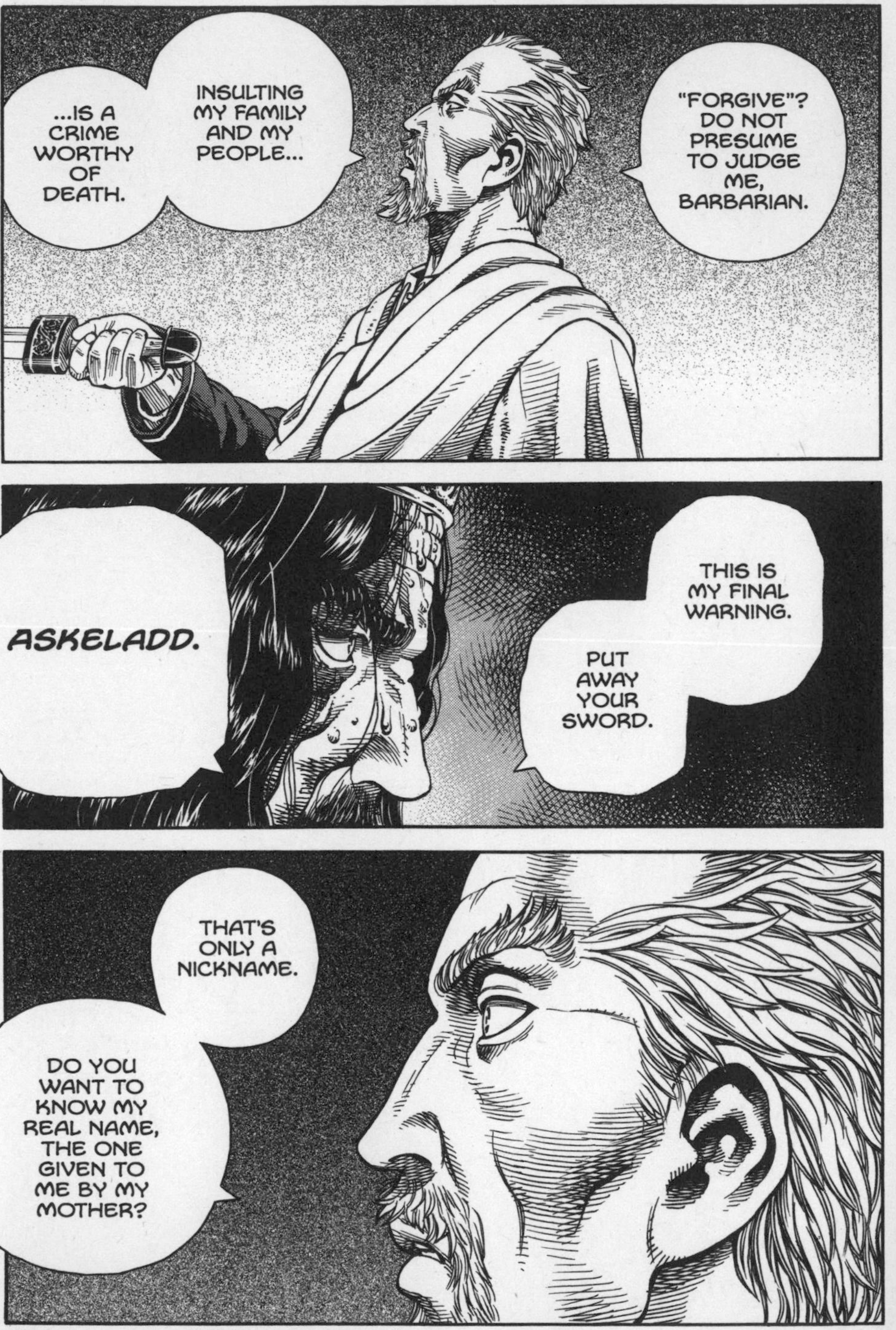
"FORGIVE"? DO NOT PRESUME TO JUDGE ME, BARBARIAN.
INSULTING MY FAMILY AND MY PEOPLE...
...IS A CRIME WORTHY OF DEATH.
THIS IS MY FINAL WARNING.
PUT AWAY YOUR SWORD.
ASKELADD.
THAT'S ONLY A NICKNAME.
DO YOU WANT TO KNOW MY REAL NAME, THE ONE GIVEN TO ME BY MY MOTHER?

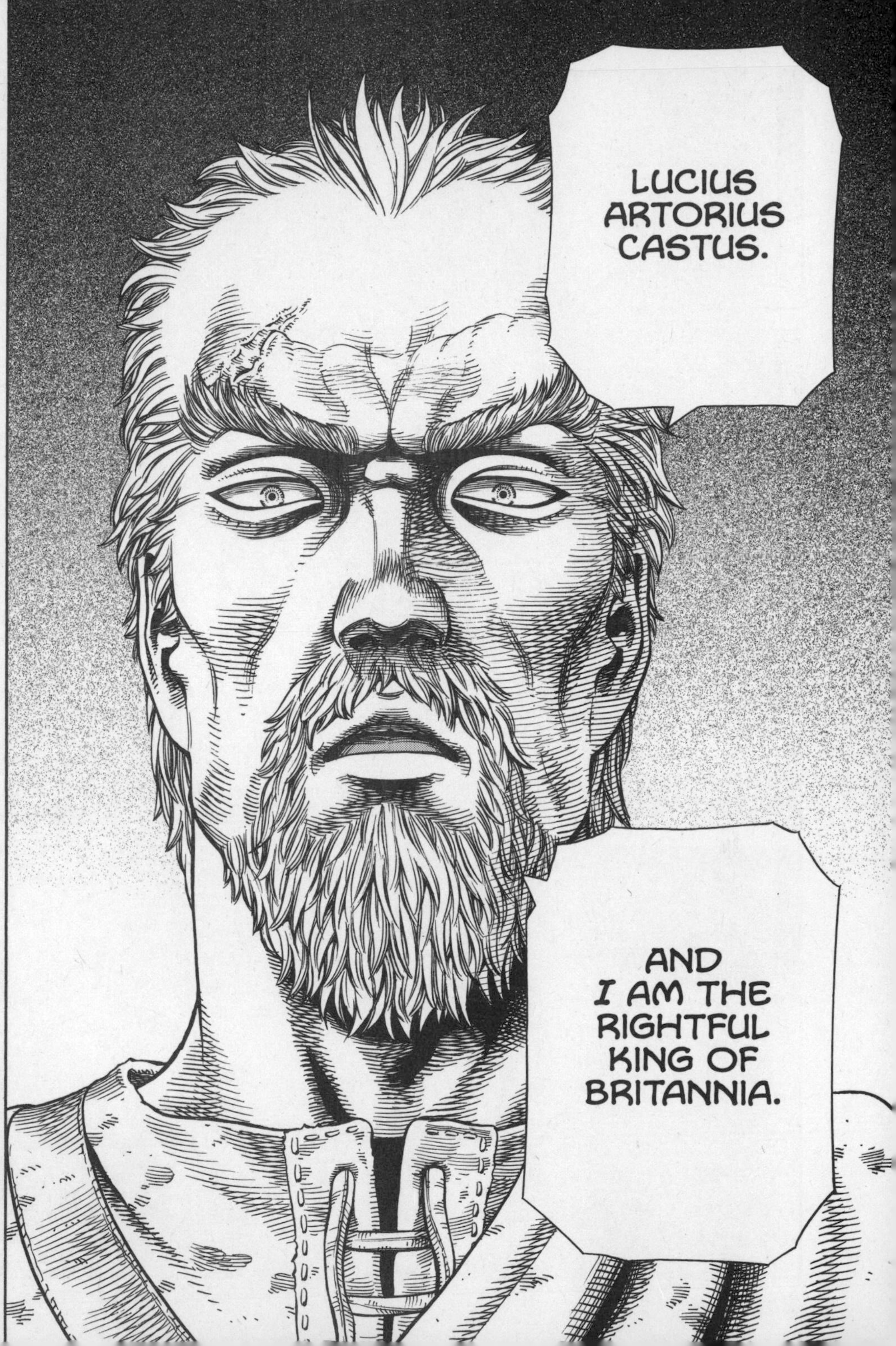
LUCIUS ARTORIUS CASTUS.
AND I AM THE RIGHTFUL KING OF BRITANNIA.

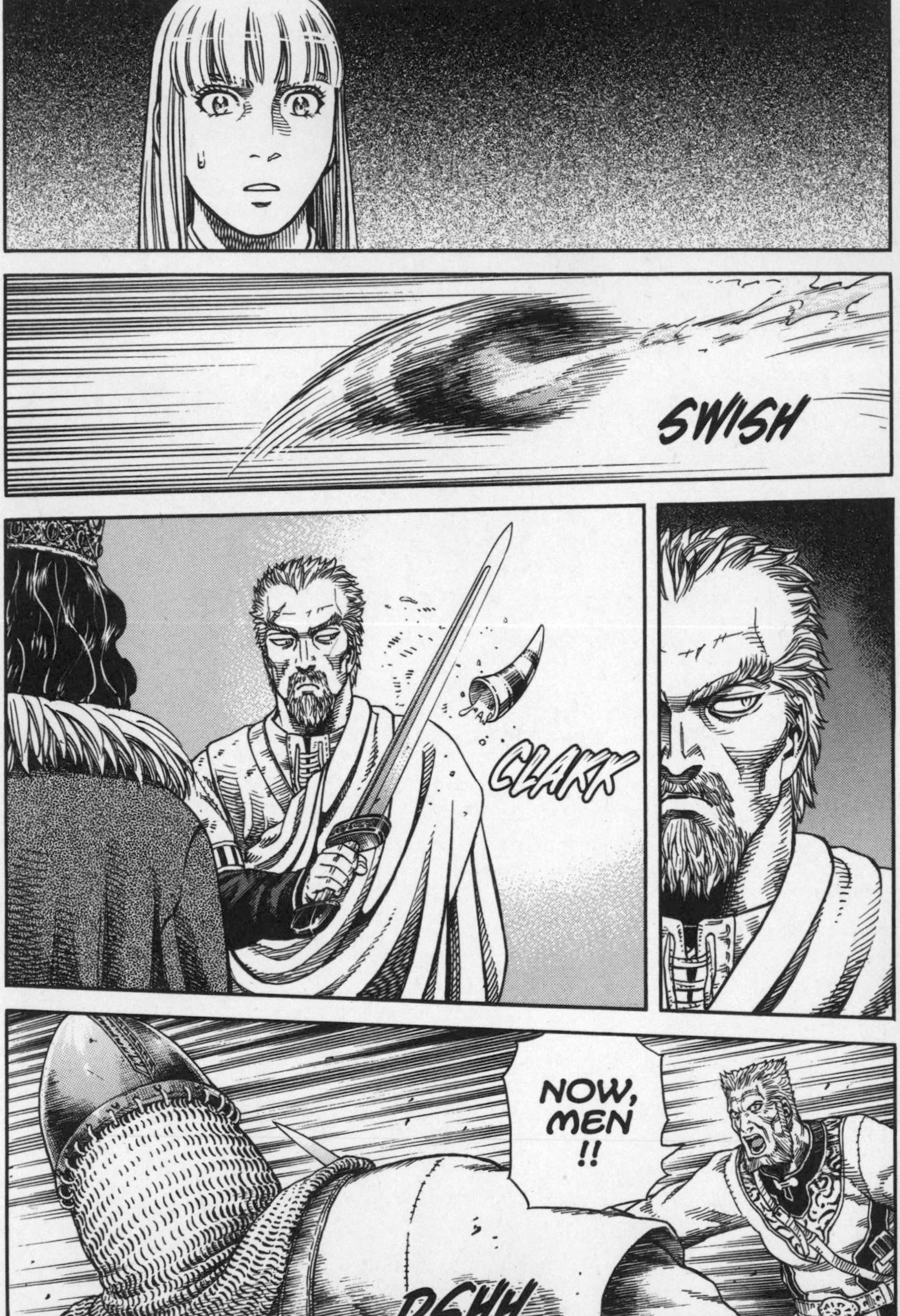
SWISH
CLAKK
NOW, MEN !!
DSHH

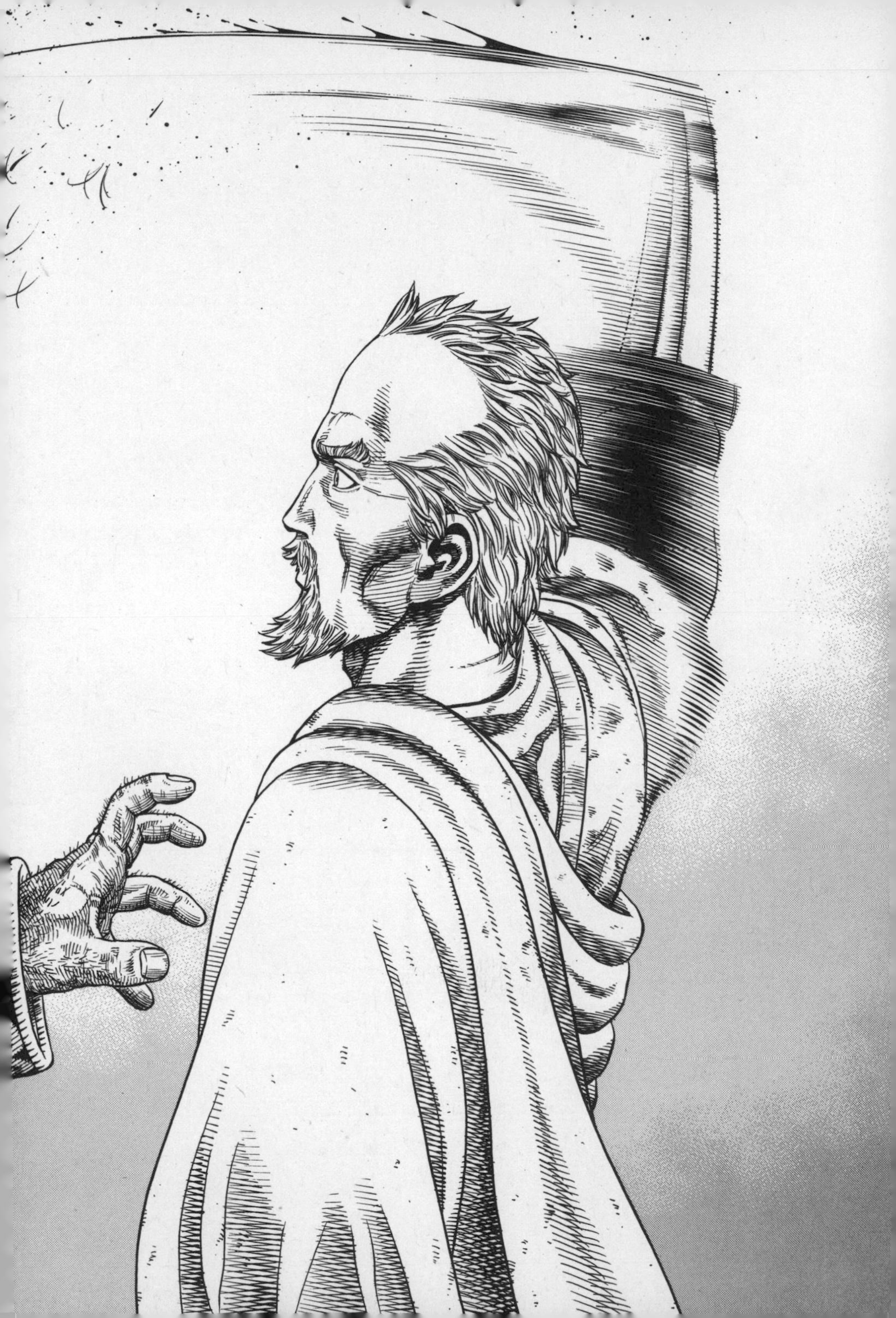

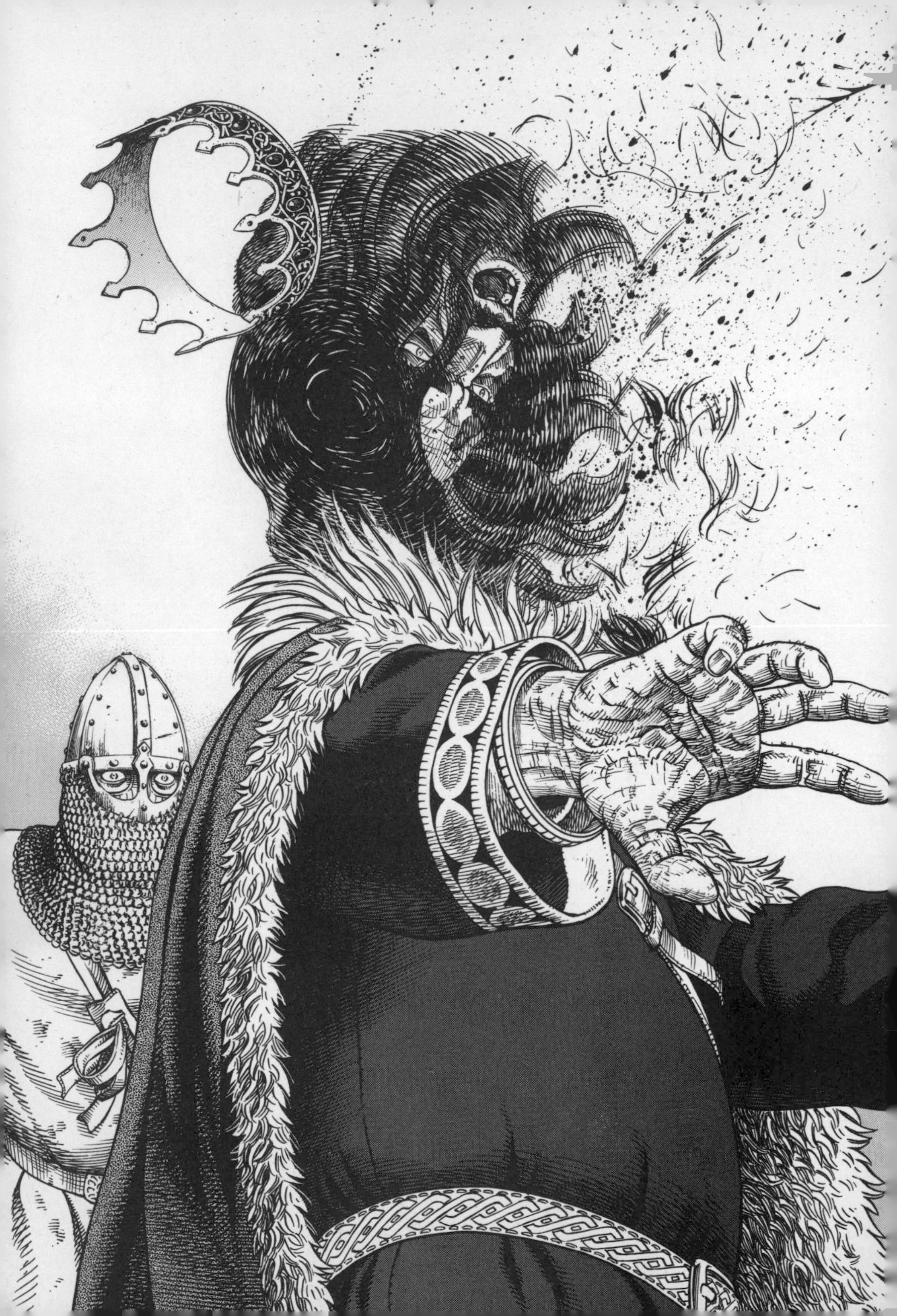

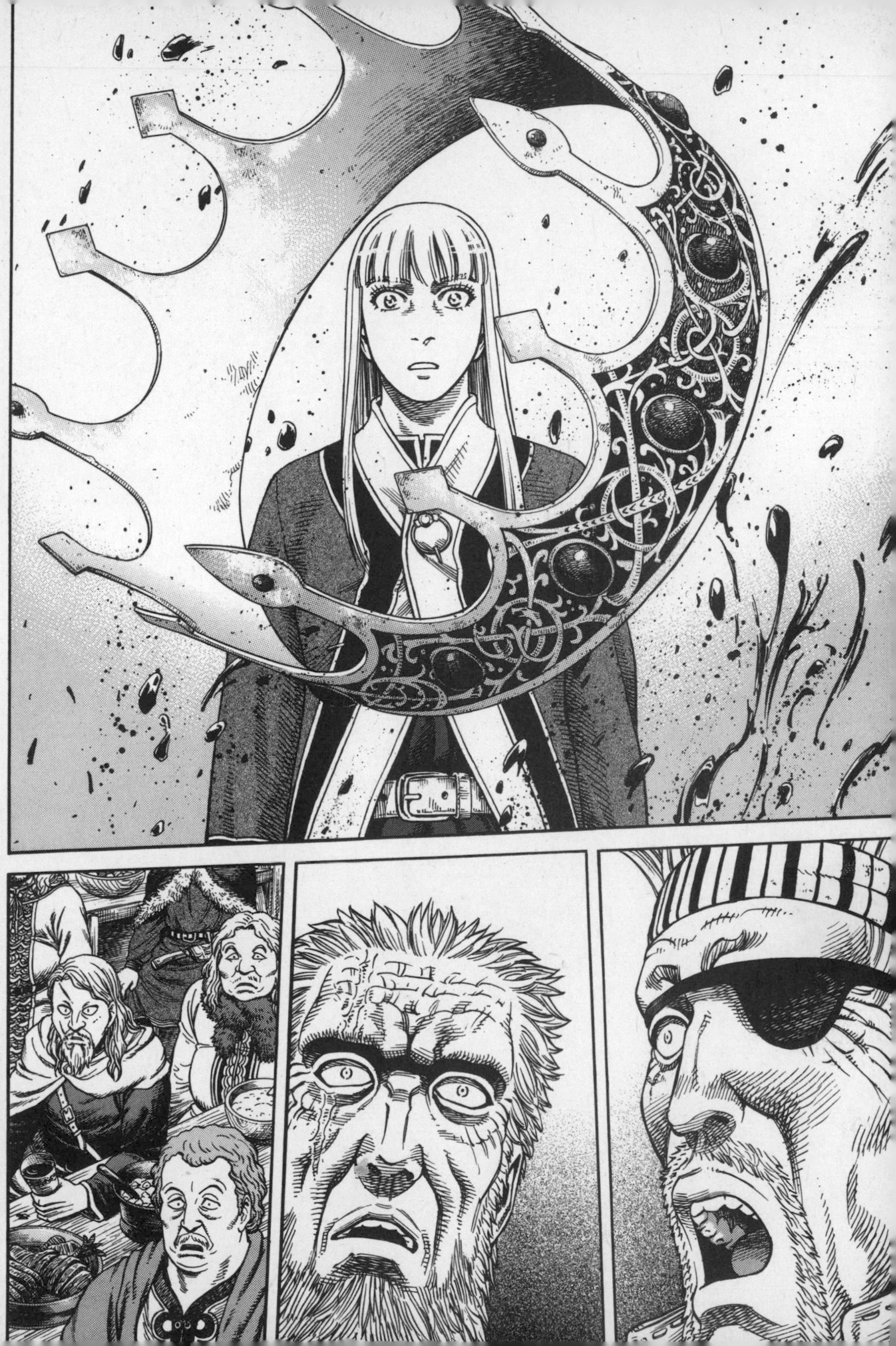

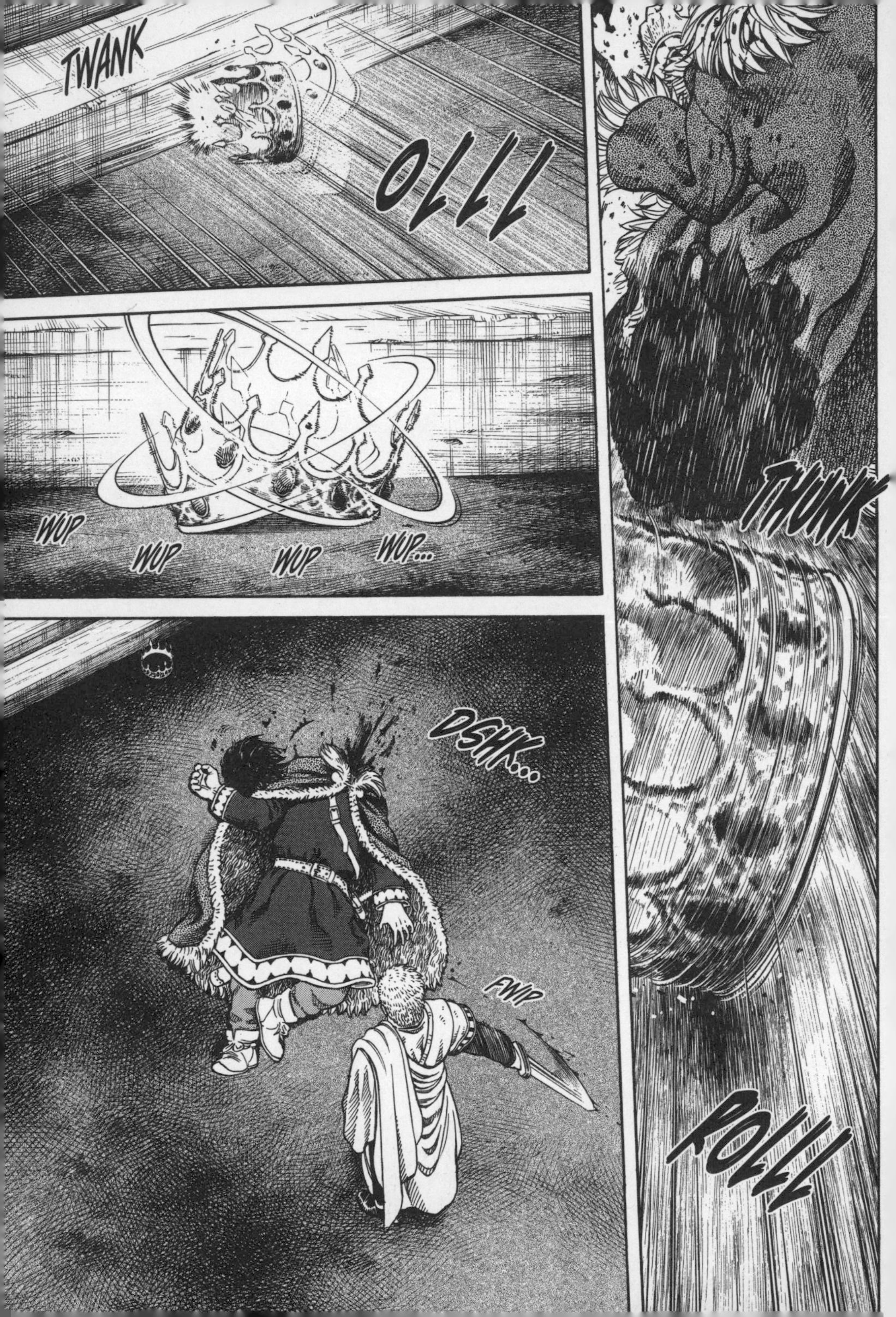
THUNK
ROLL
TWANK
WUP
WUP
WUP
WUP...
DSHK...
FWIP

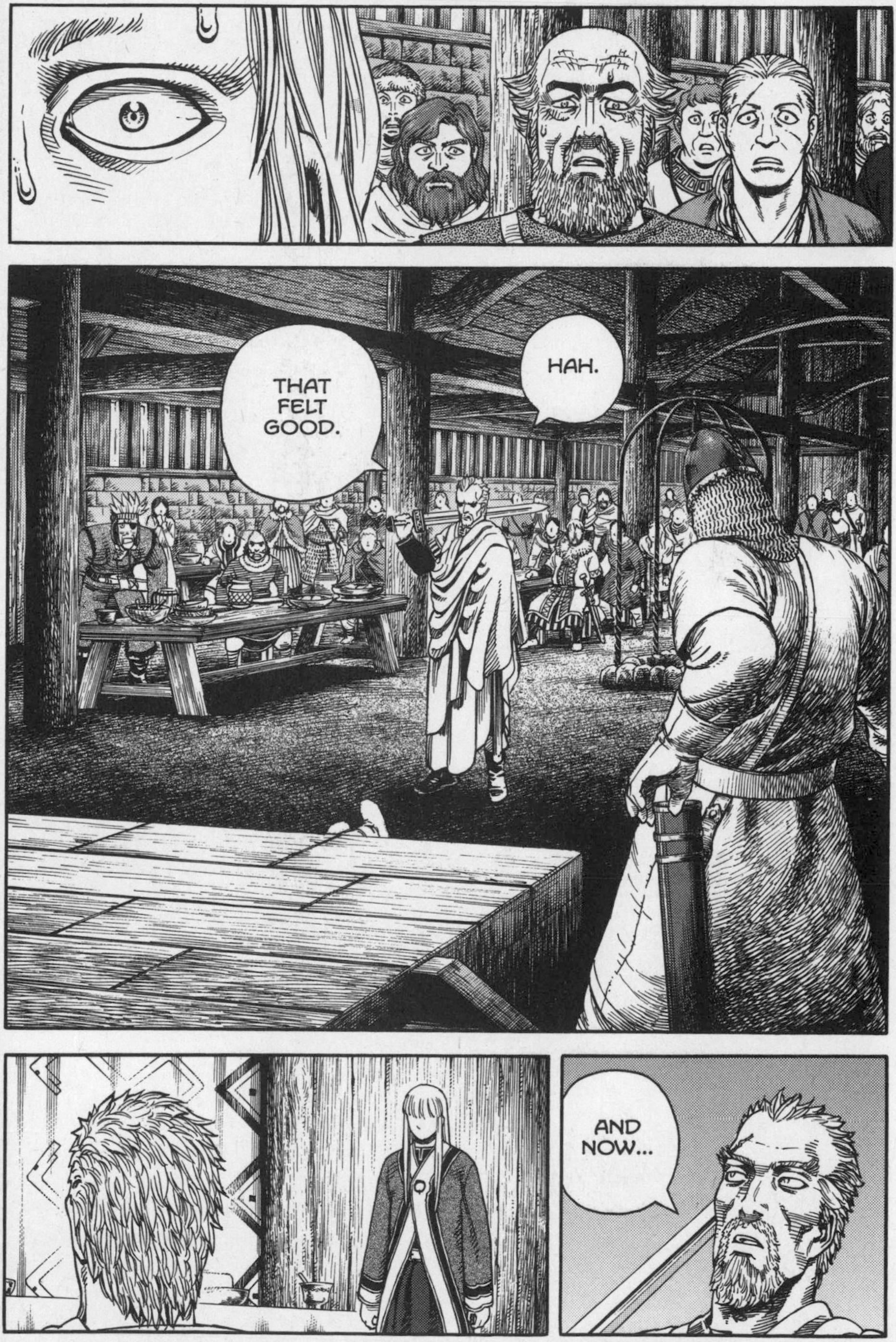
HAH.
THAT FELT GOOD.
AND NOW...

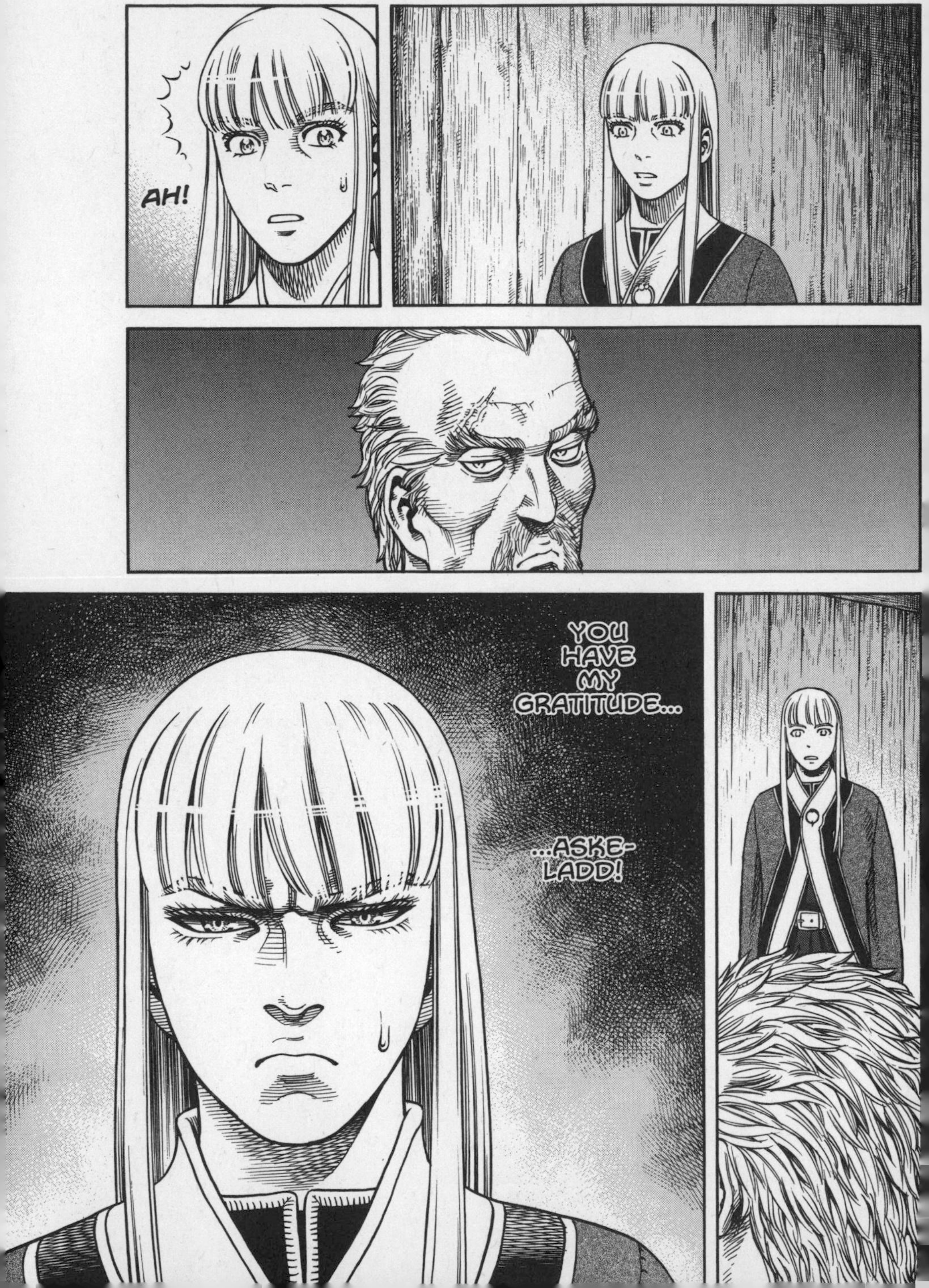
AH!
YOU HAVE MY GRATITUDE...
...ASKE-LADD!

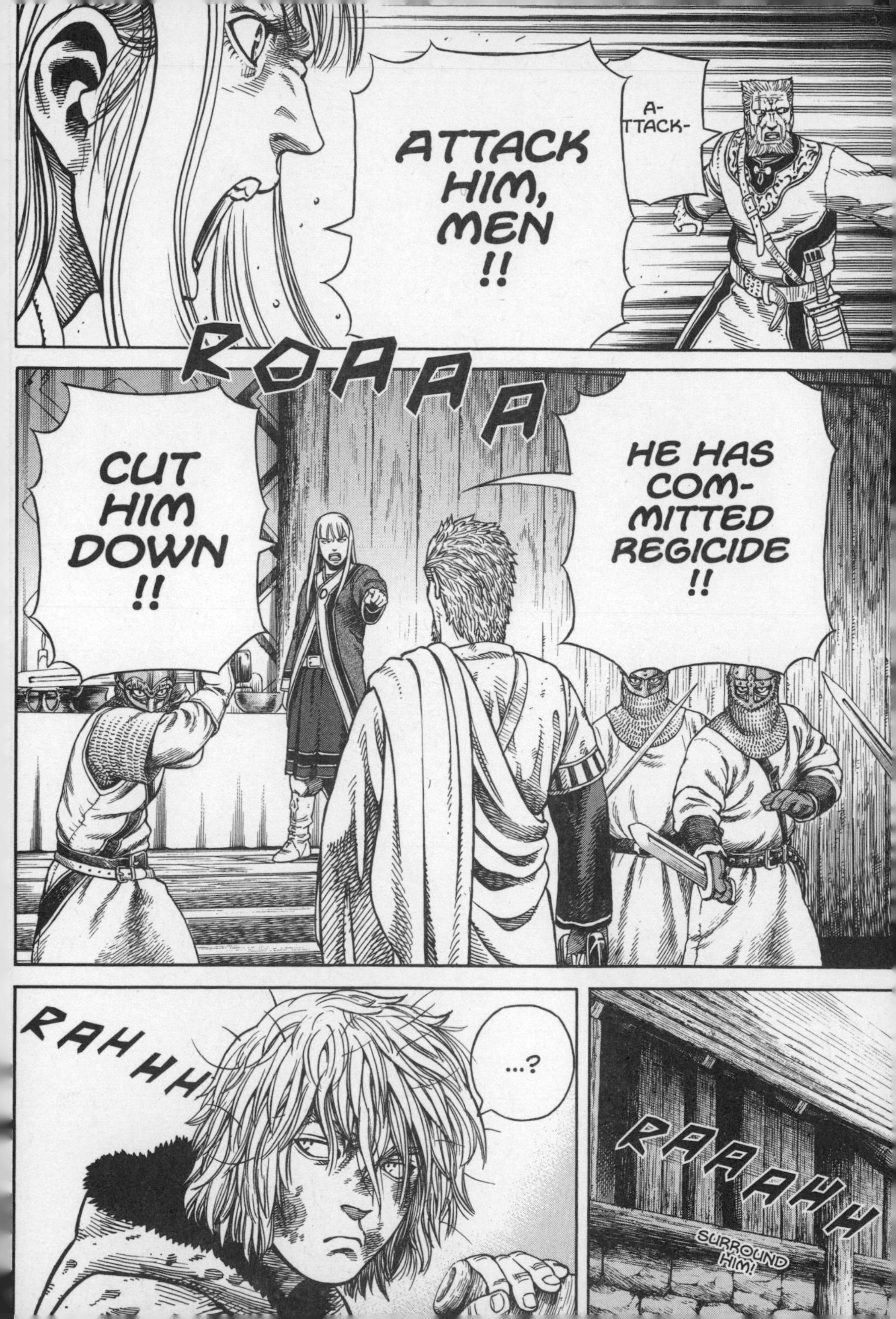
A- TTACK-
ATTACK HIM, MEN !!
ROAAAA
HE HAS COM- MITTED REGICIDE !!
CUT HIM DOWN !!
RAAAAHH
SURROUND HIM!
RAHHHH
...?

CHAPTER 53: THE FURY OF BRITANNIA'S KING

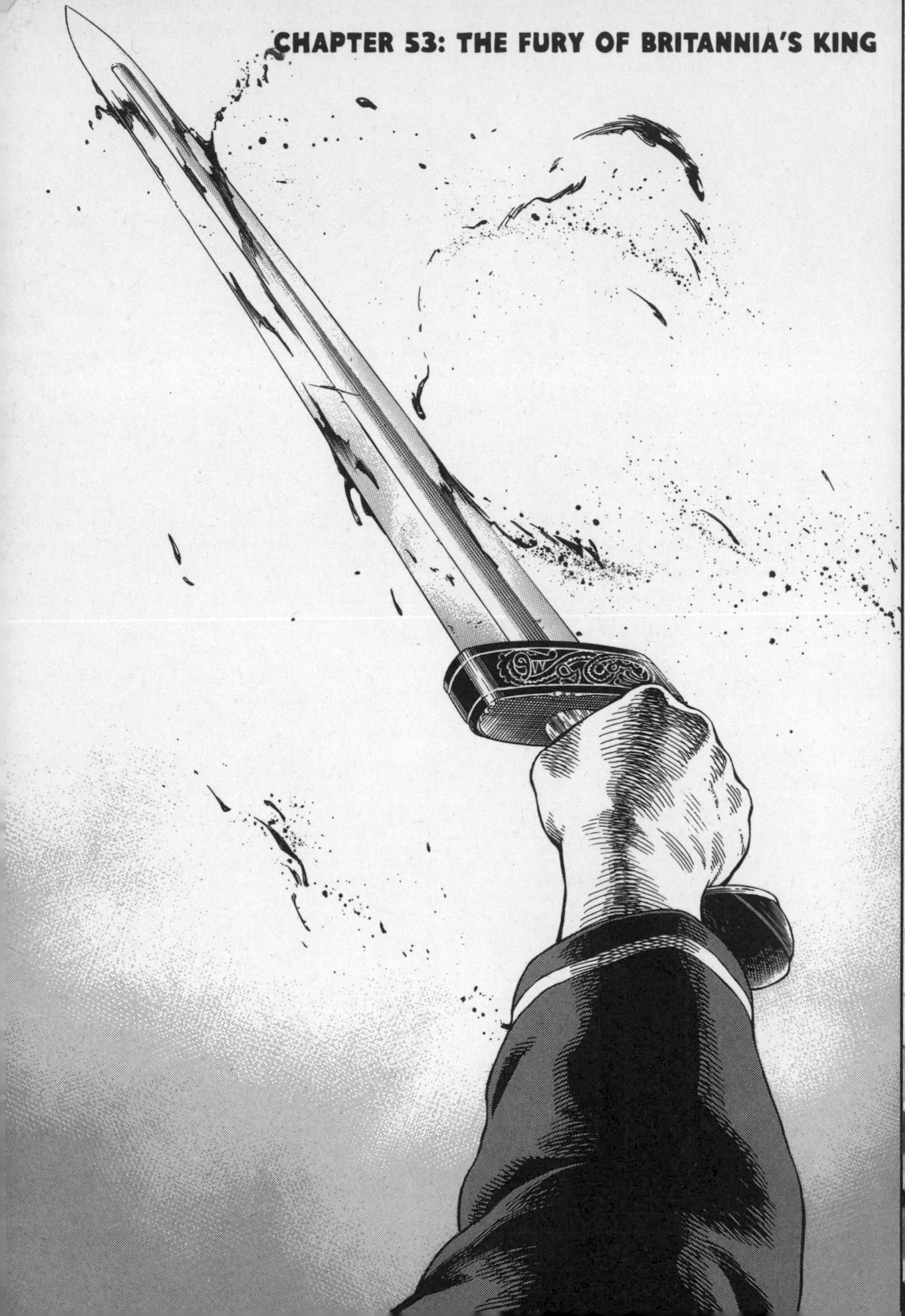

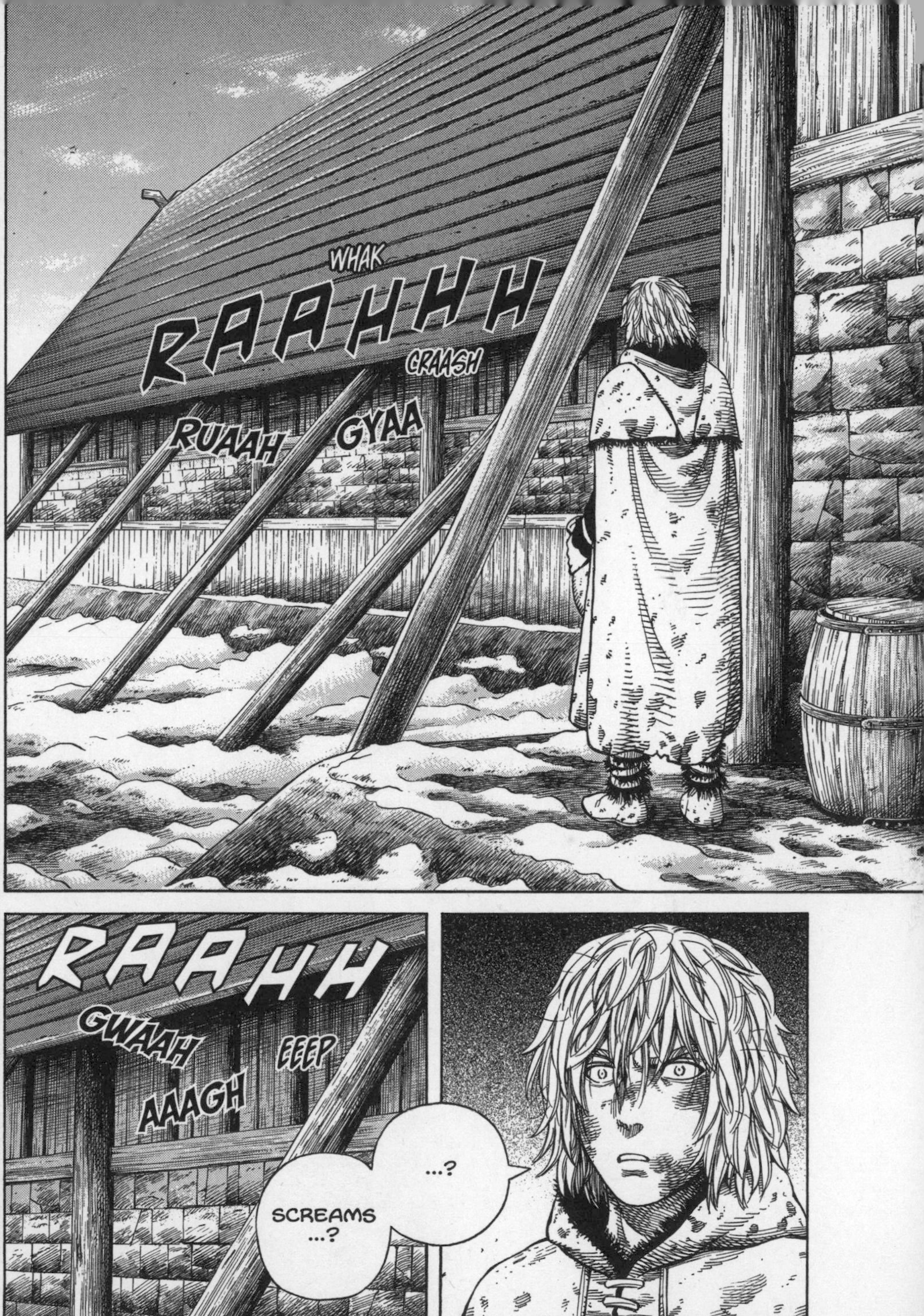
WHAK
RAAHHH
CRAASH
RUAAH
GYAA
...?
SCREAMS ...?
RAAHH
GWAAH
EEEP
AAAGH

STOMP

STOMP

WHAM

HURRY!

STOMP STOMP STOMP

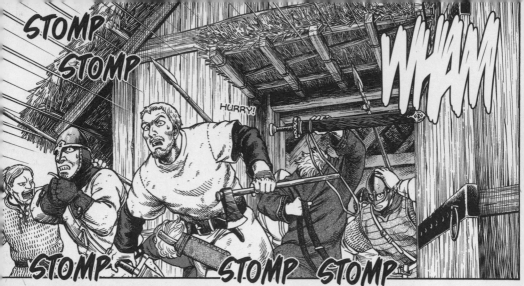

DSH DSH

DSH

RUN, RUN, RUN!!

YOU TAKE THE SECRET ENTRANCE!! THE REST, COME TO THE FRONT!!

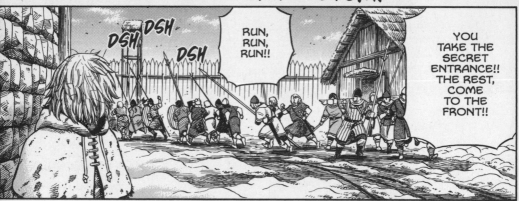

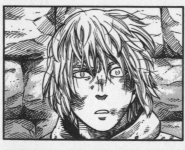

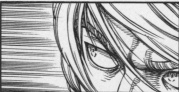

DSH

DSH

HE'S A HARDENED WARRIOR, I HEAR! DON'T GET SLOPPY!!

DSH

DSH

DSH

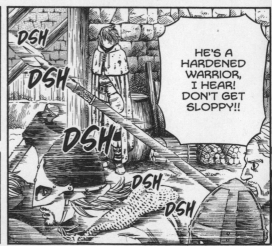

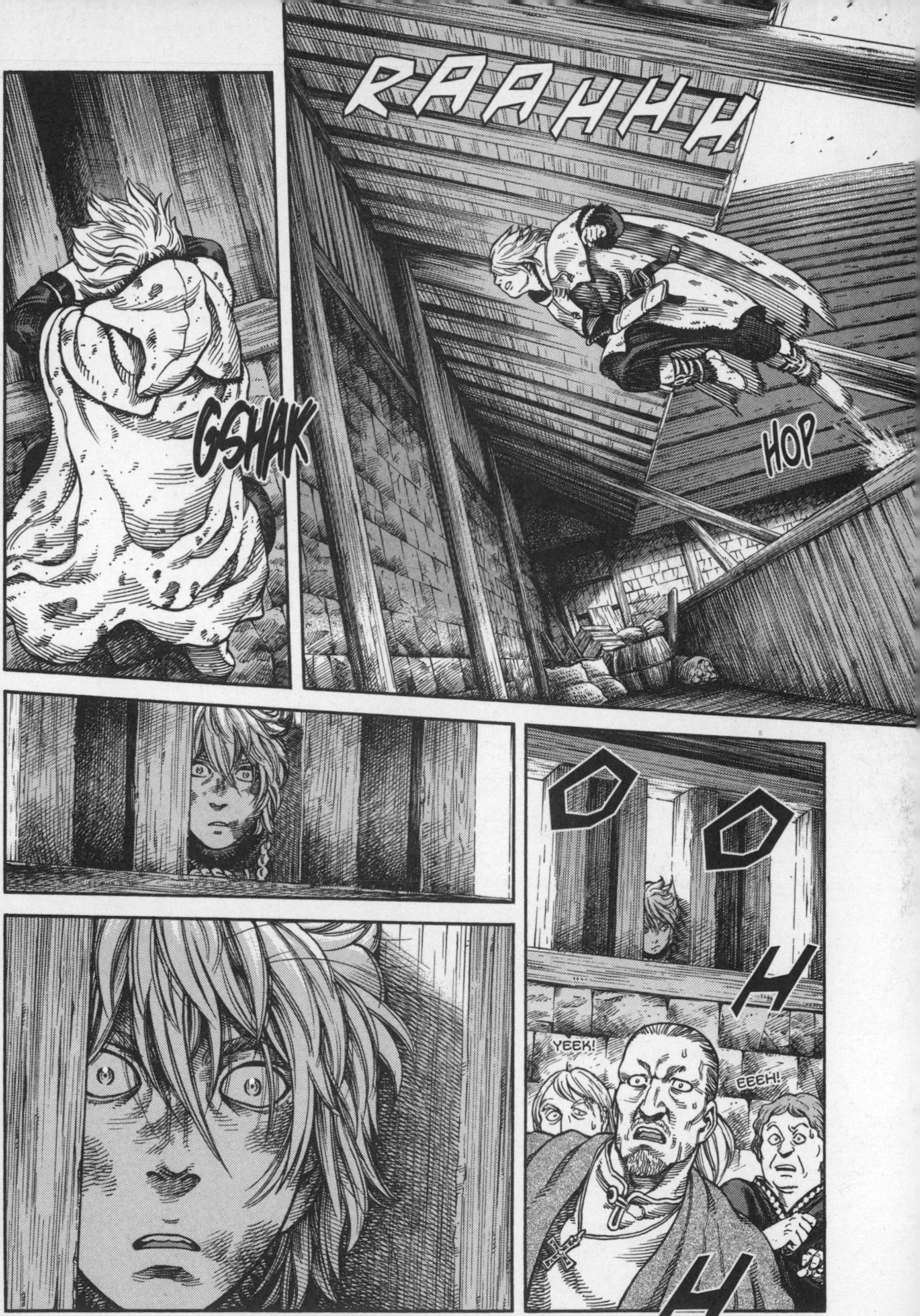
RAAHHH
HOP
GSHAK
OOHH
YEEK!
EEEH!

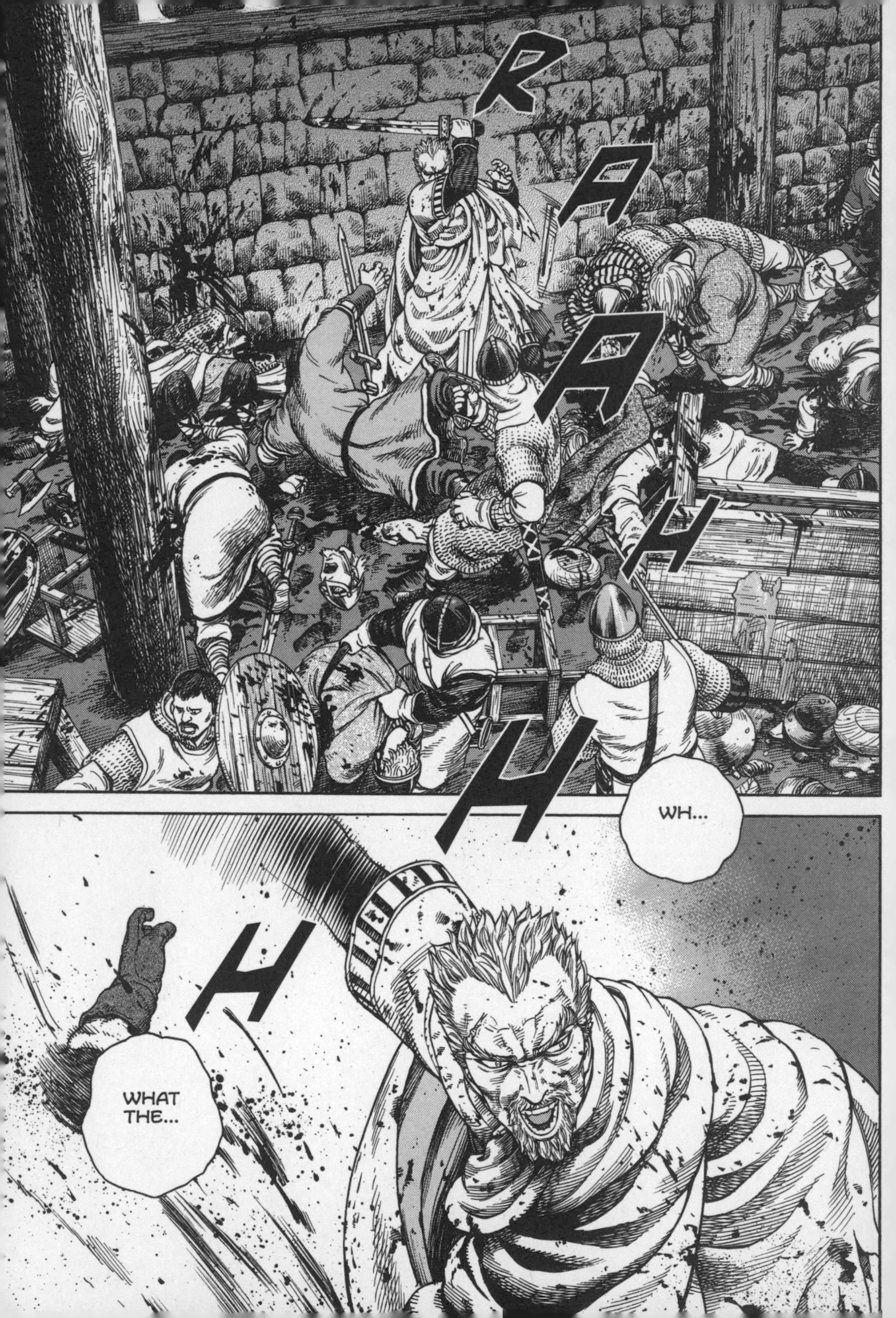
RAAHHH
WH...
WHAT THE...

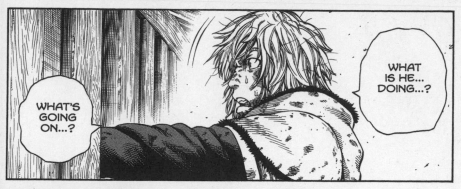

WHAT IS HE... DOING...?

WHAT'S GOING ON...?

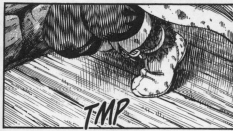

TMP

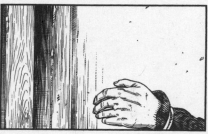

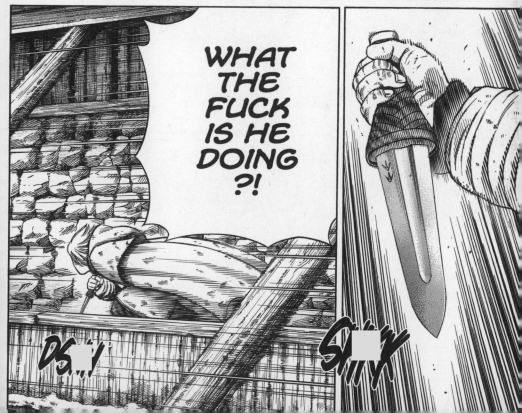

WHAT THE FUCK IS HE DOING ?!

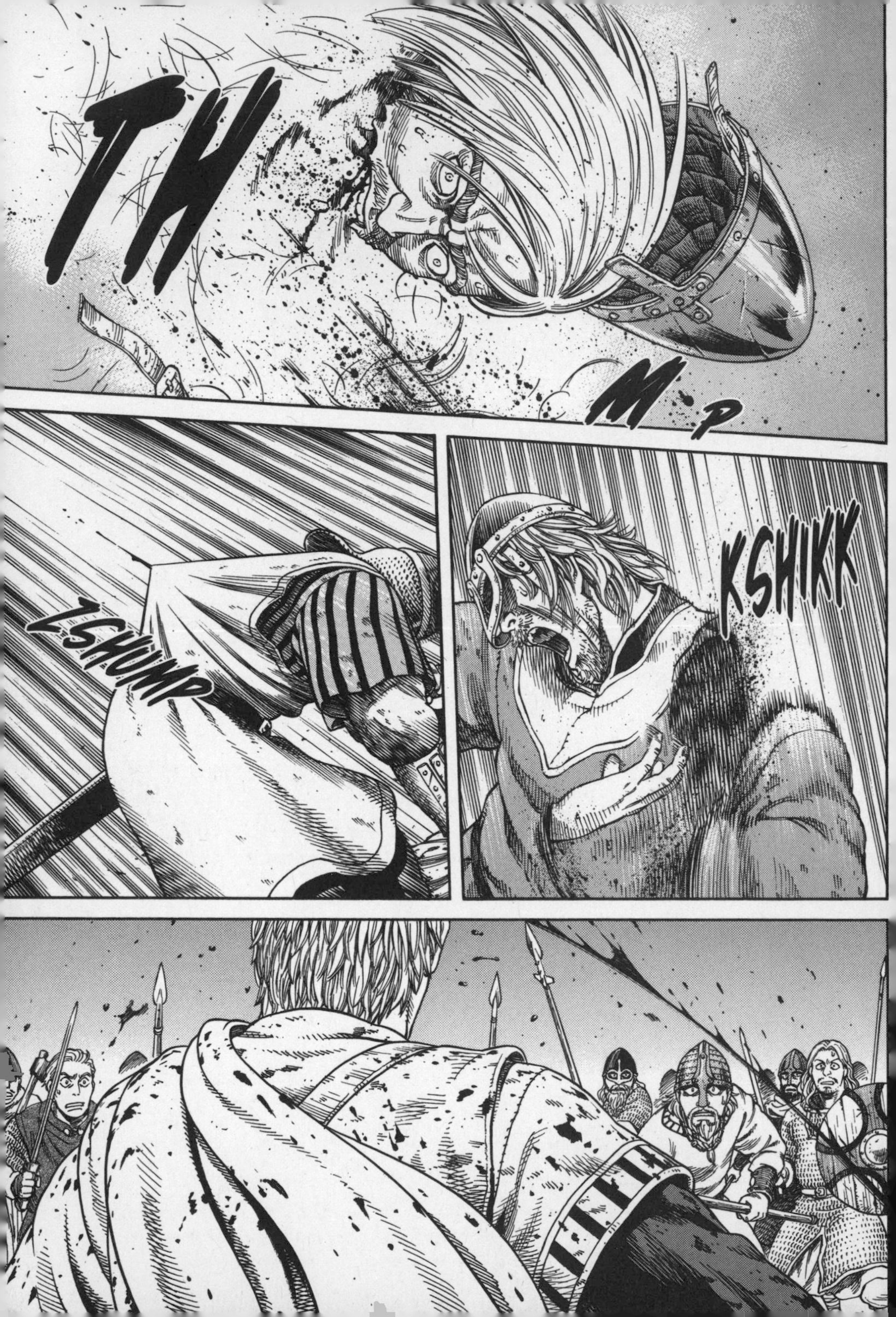
TH
MP
KSHIKK
ZSHUMP

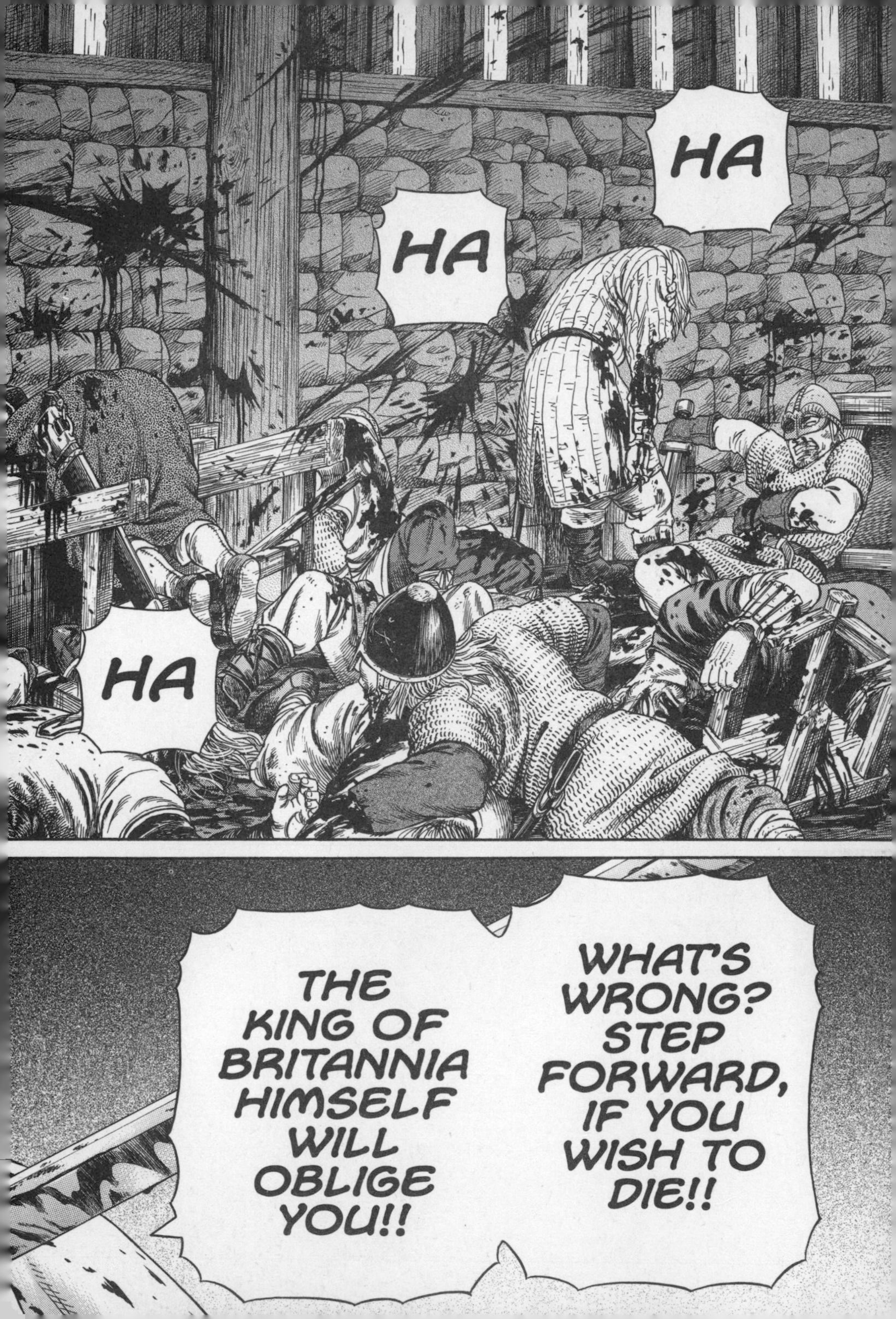
HA
HA
HA
WHAT'S WRONG? STEP FORWARD, IF YOU WISH TO DIE!!
THE KING OF BRITANNIA HIMSELF WILL OBLIGE YOU!!

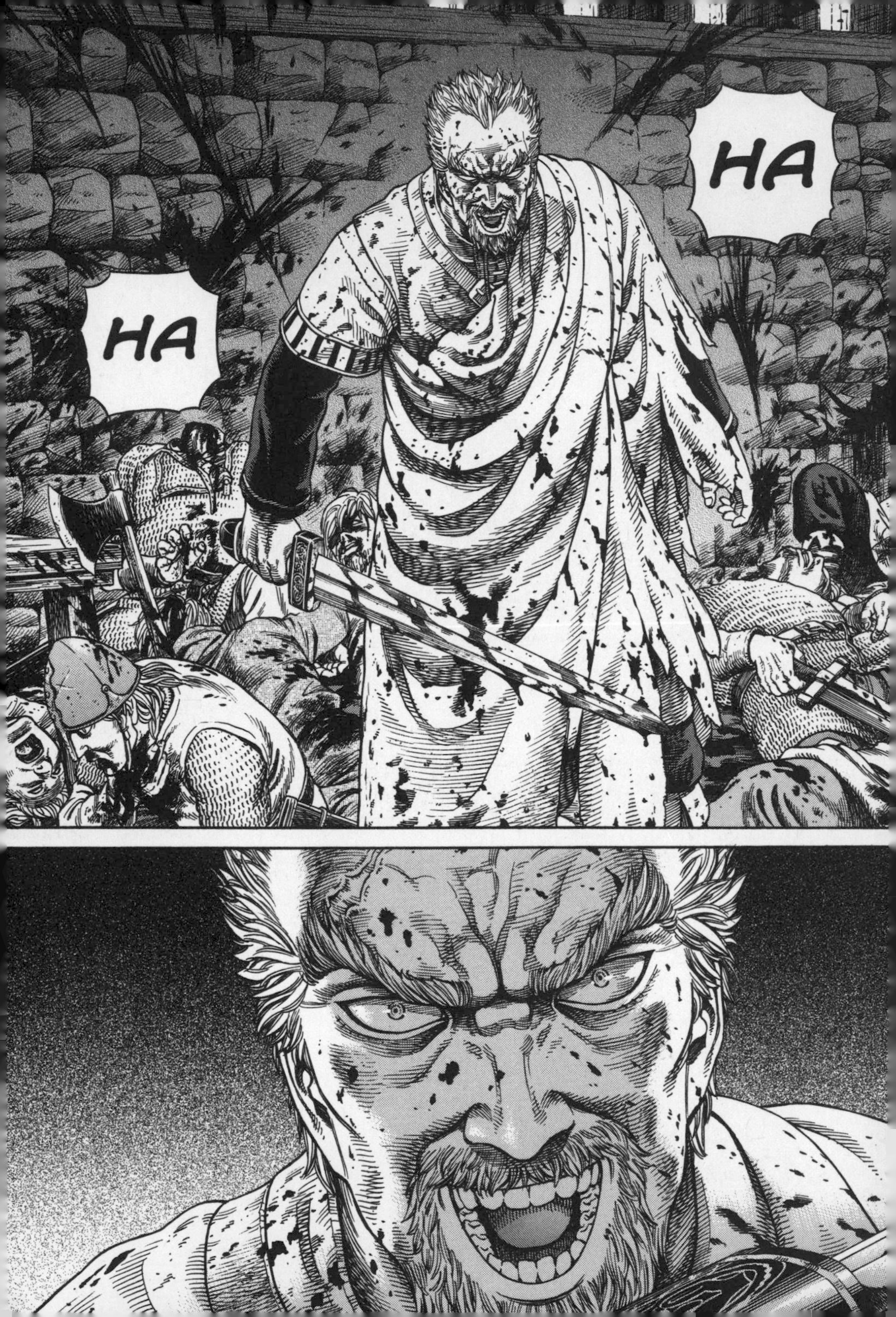
HA
HA

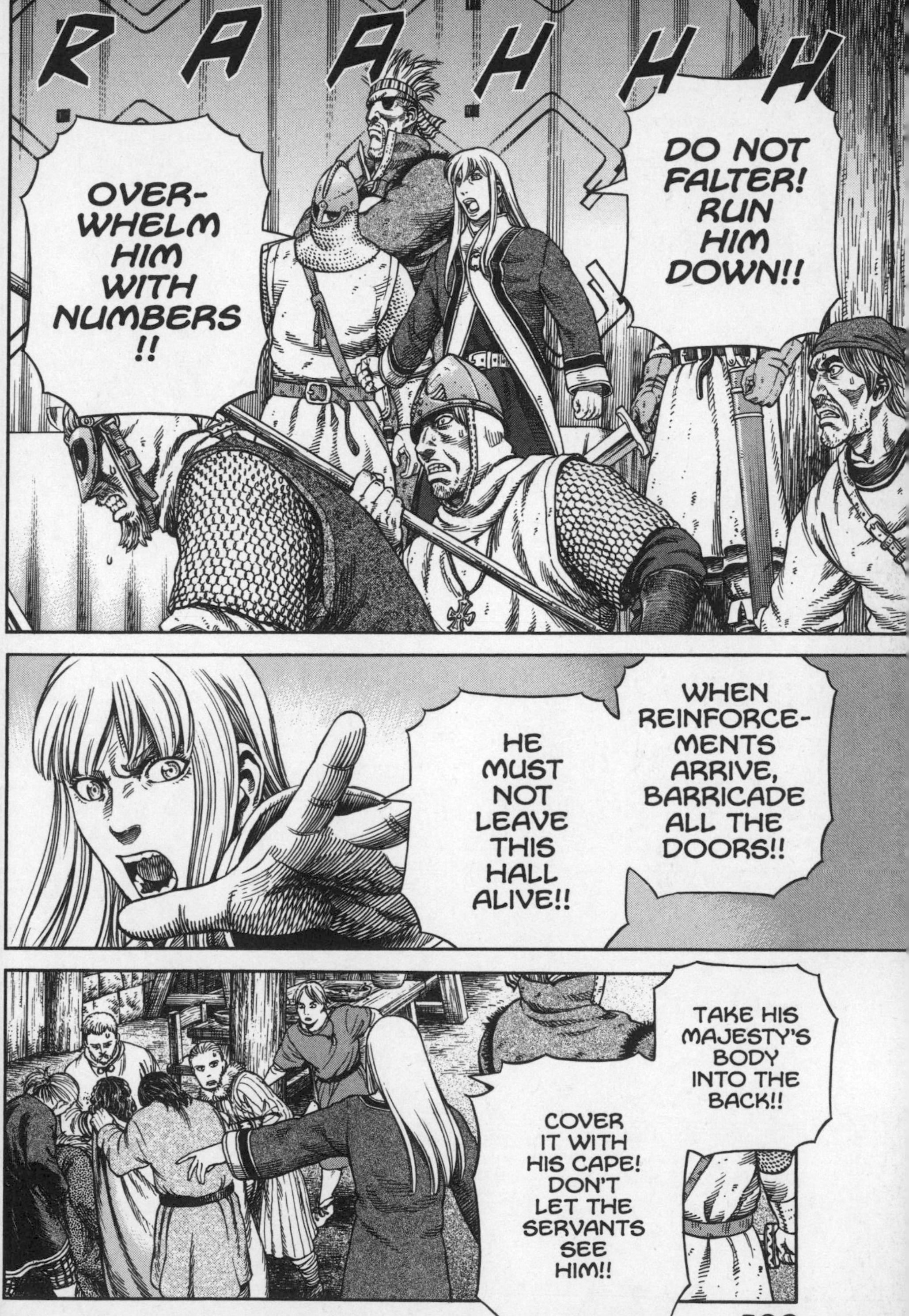
RAAHHH
DO NOT FALTER! RUN HIM DOWN!!
OVER-WHELM HIM WITH NUMBERS!!
WHEN REINFORCE-MENTS ARRIVE, BARRICADE ALL THE DOORS!!
HE MUST NOT LEAVE THIS HALL ALIVE!!
TAKE HIS MAJESTY'S BODY INTO THE BACK!!
COVER IT WITH HIS CAPE! DON'T LET THE SERVANTS SEE HIM!!

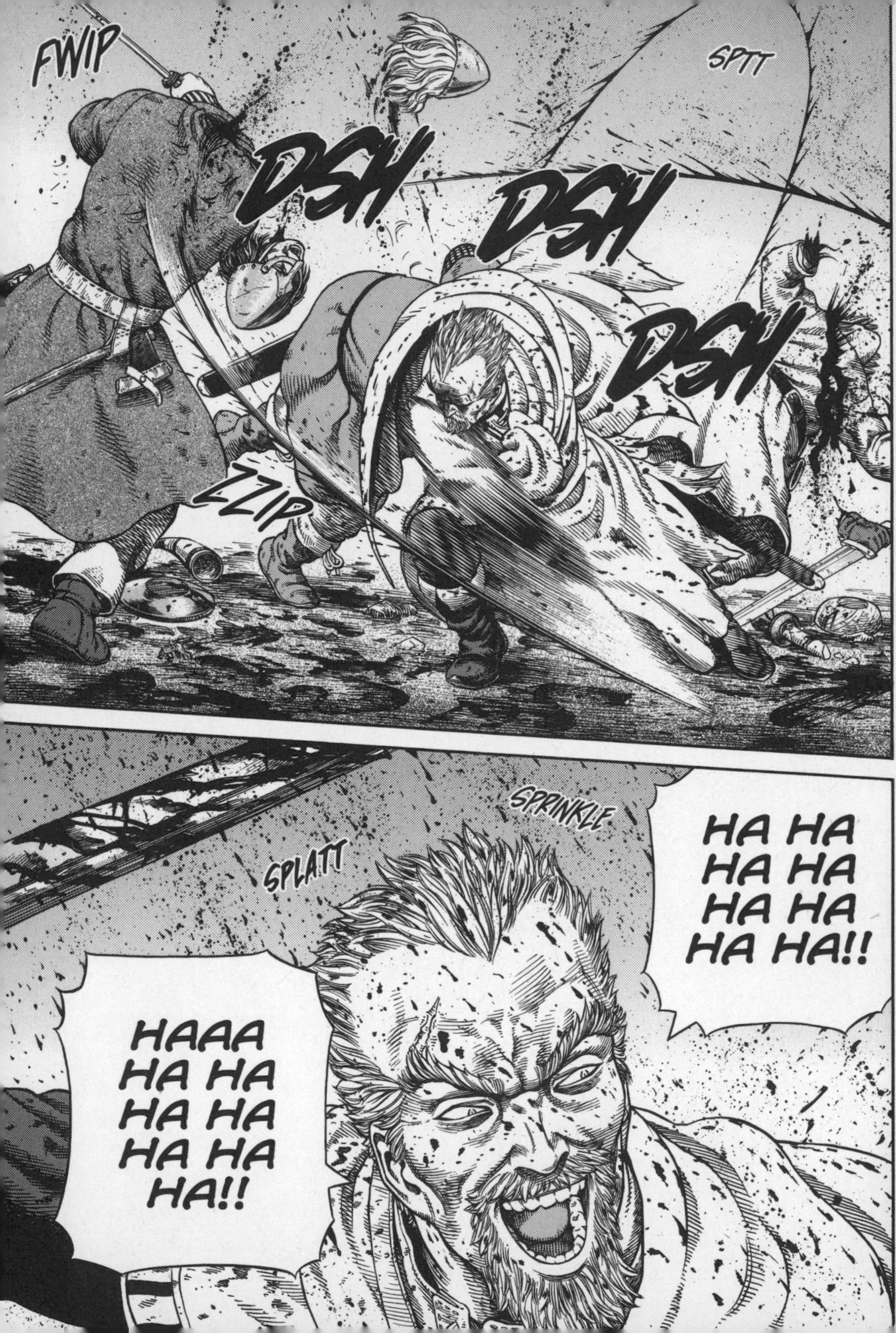
SPTT
FWIP
DSH
DSH
DSH
ZZIP
HA HA HA HA HA HA HA HA!!
SPRINKLE
SPLATT
HAAA HA HA HA HA HA HA HA!!

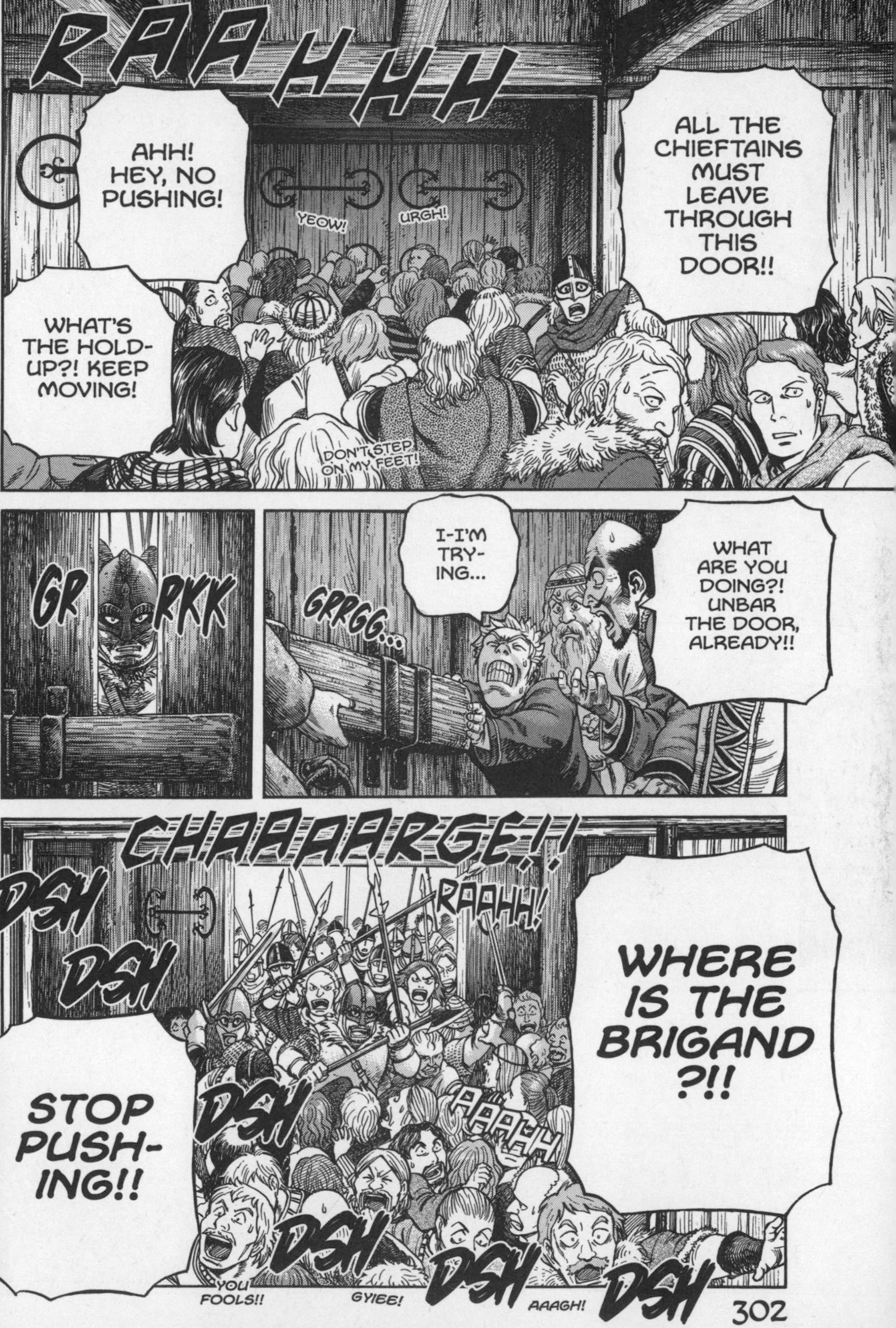
RAAHHHH
ALL THE CHIEFTAINS MUST LEAVE THROUGH THIS DOOR!!
AHH! HEY, NO PUSHING!
URGH!
YEOW!
WHAT'S THE HOLD-UP?! KEEP MOVING!
DON'T STEP ON MY FEET!
WHAT ARE YOU DOING?! UNBAR THE DOOR, ALREADY!!
I-I'M TRY-ING...
GRRGG...
GRRKK
CHAAAAARGE!!
WHERE IS THE BRIGAND?!!
RAAHH!
DSH
DSH
AAAHHH
STOP PUSH-ING!!
DSH
DSH
DSH
DSH
YOU FOOLS!!
GYIEE!
AAAGH!

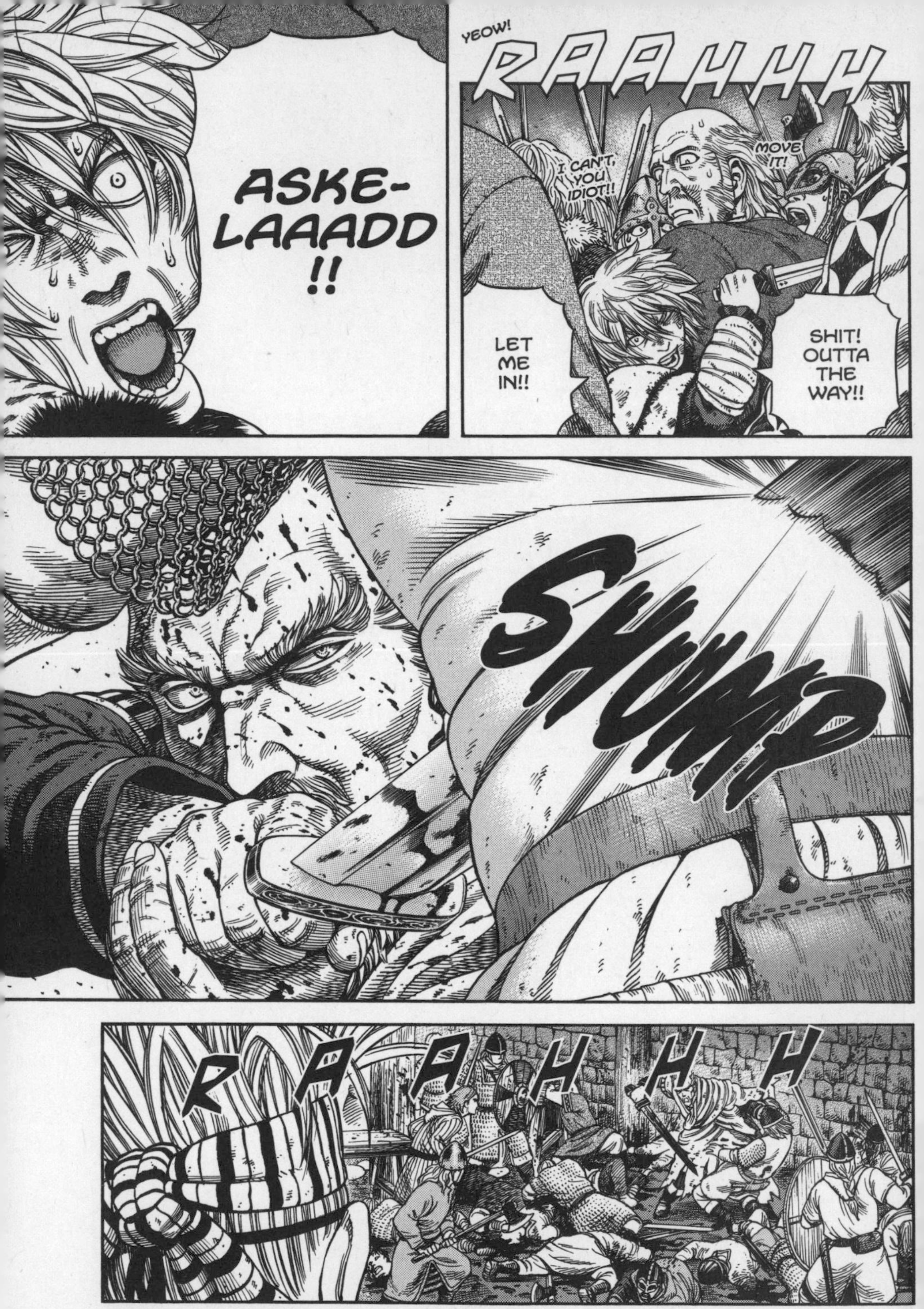
YEOW!
RAAHHH
MOVE IT!
I CAN'T, YOU IDIOT!!
SHIT! OUTTA THE WAY!!
LET ME IN!!
ASKE-LAAADD!!
SHUMP
RAAHHH

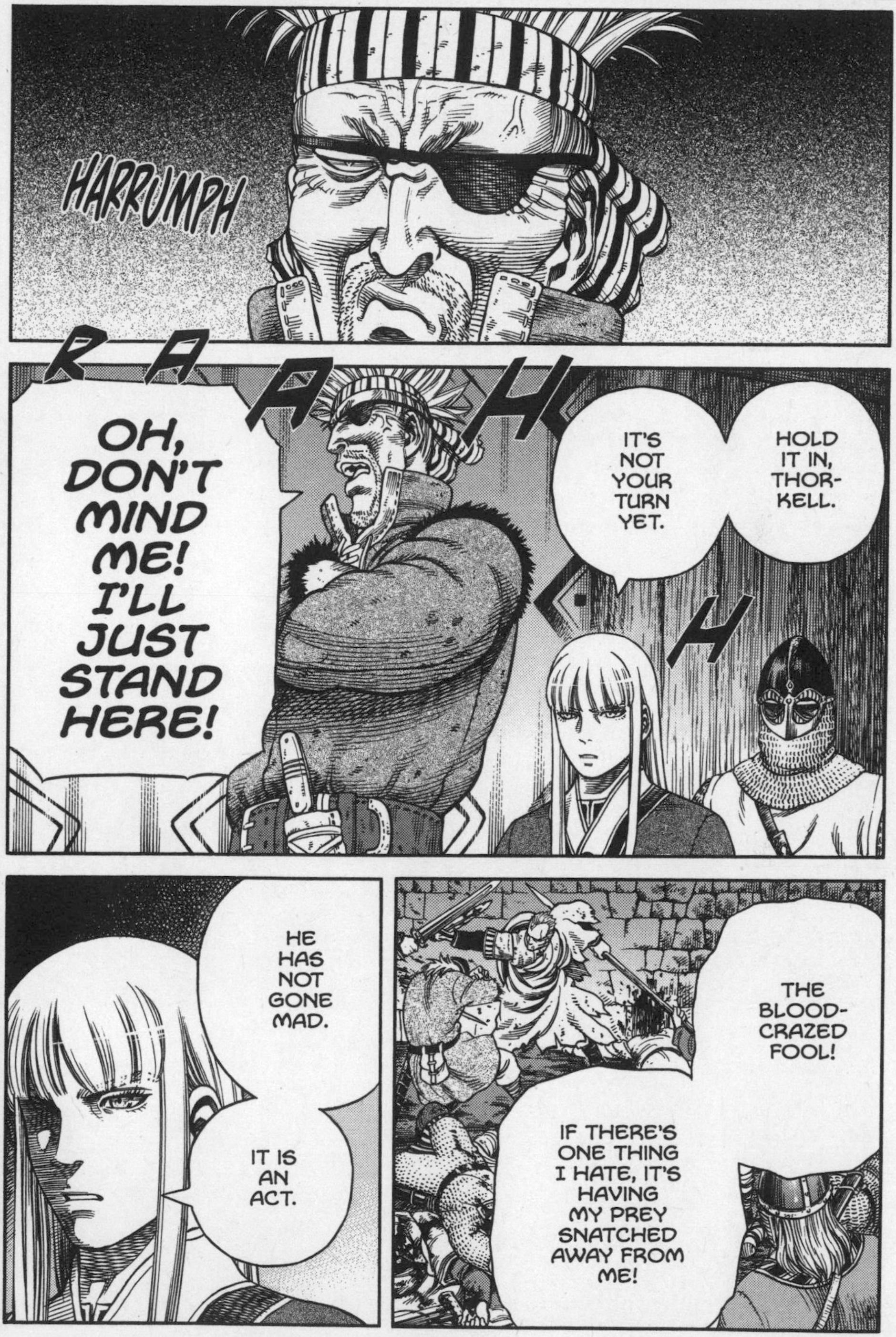
HARRUMPH
HOLD IT IN, THORKELL.
IT'S NOT YOUR TURN YET.
RAAHH
OH, DON'T MIND ME! I'LL JUST STAND HERE!
THE BLOOD-CRAZED FOOL!
IF THERE'S ONE THING I HATE, IT'S HAVING MY PREY SNATCHED AWAY FROM ME!
HE HAS NOT GONE MAD.
IT IS AN ACT.

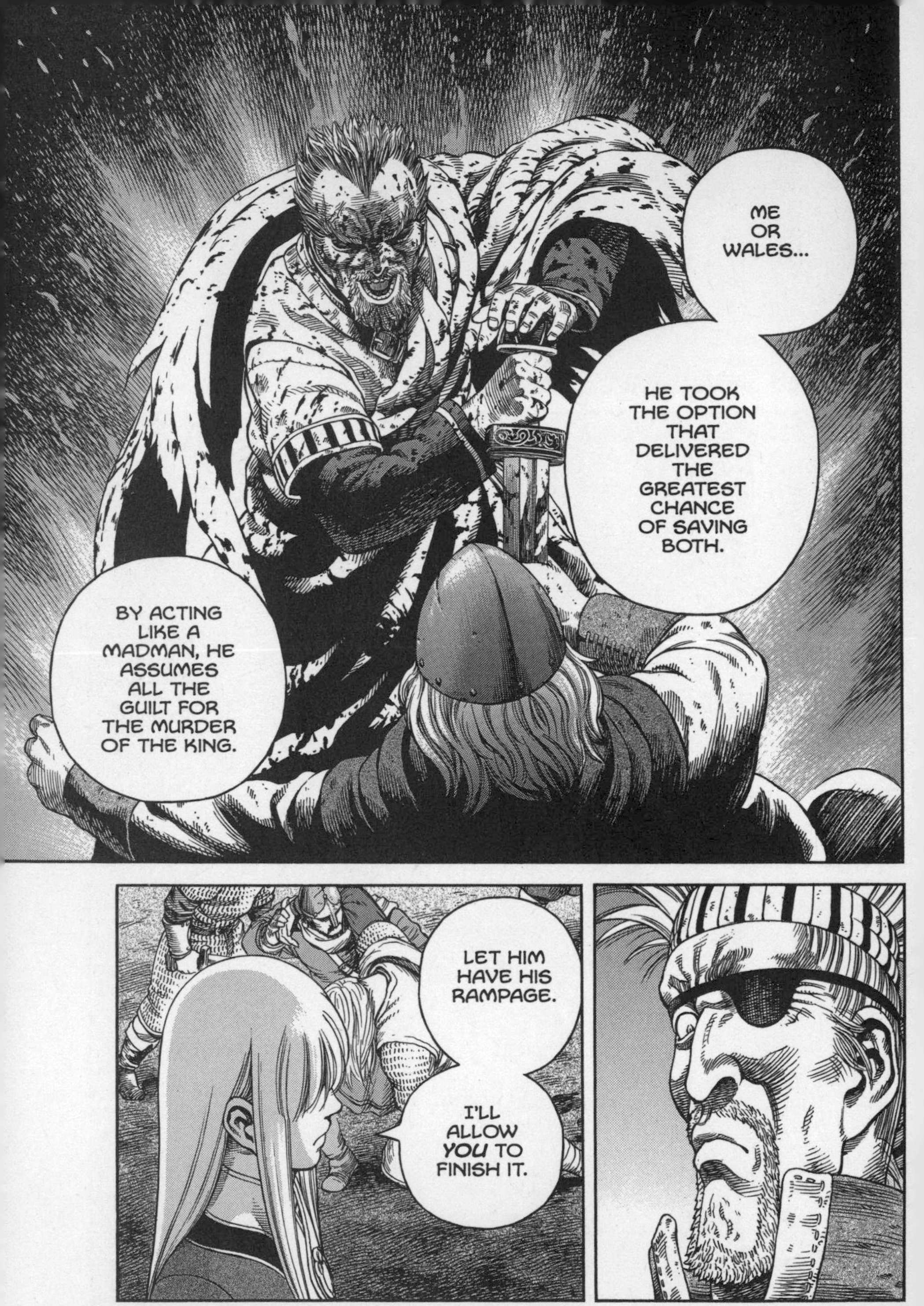
ME OR WALES...
HE TOOK THE OPTION THAT DELIVERED THE GREATEST CHANCE OF SAVING BOTH.
BY ACTING LIKE A MADMAN, HE ASSUMES ALL THE GUILT FOR THE MURDER OF THE KING.
LET HIM HAVE HIS RAMPAGE.
I'LL ALLOW *YOU* TO FINISH IT.

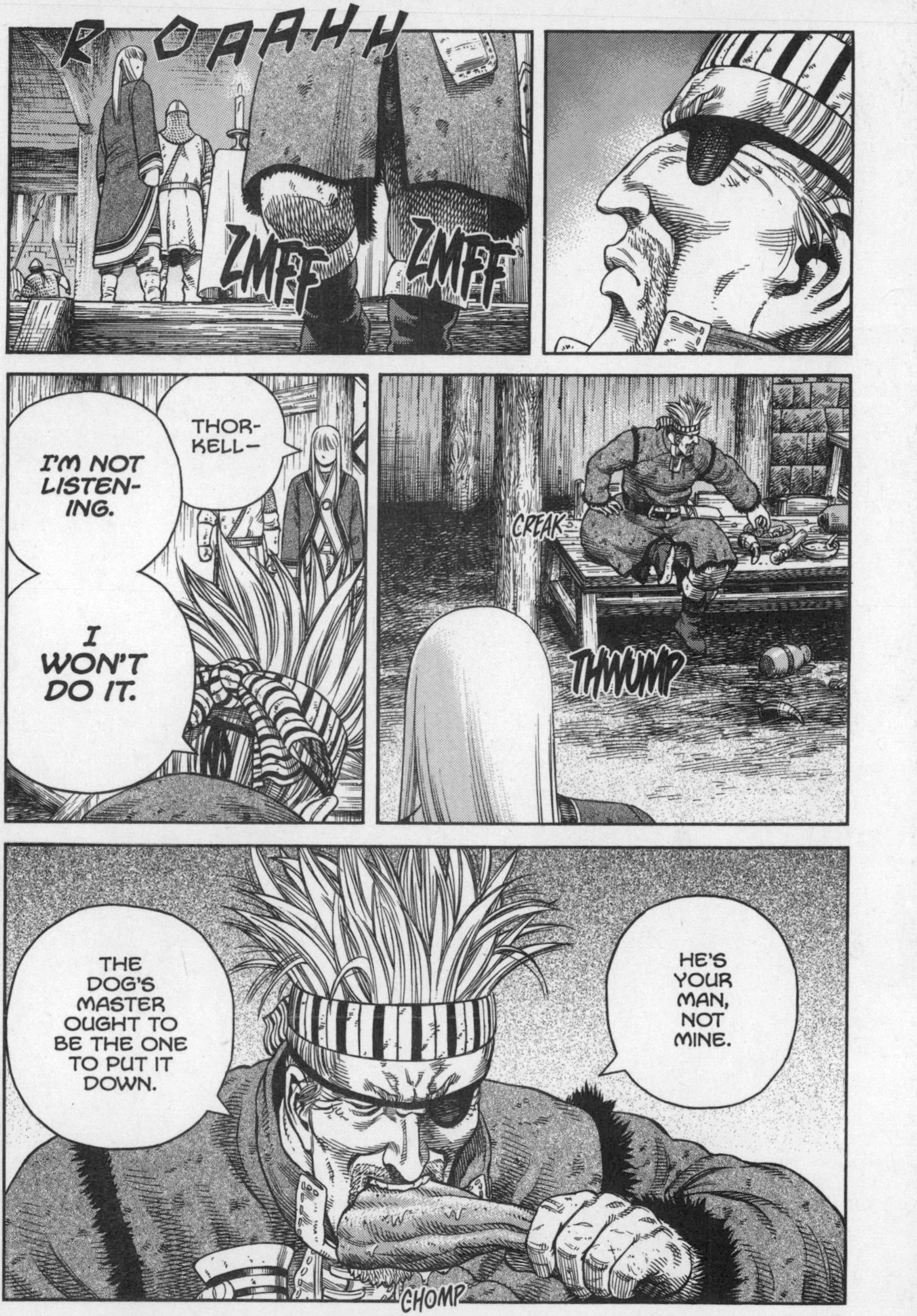
ROAAHH
ZMFF
ZMFF
CREAK
THWUMP
THOR-KELL—
I'M NOT LISTENING.
I WON'T DO IT.
HE'S YOUR MAN, NOT MINE.
THE DOG'S MASTER OUGHT TO BE THE ONE TO PUT IT DOWN.
CHOMP

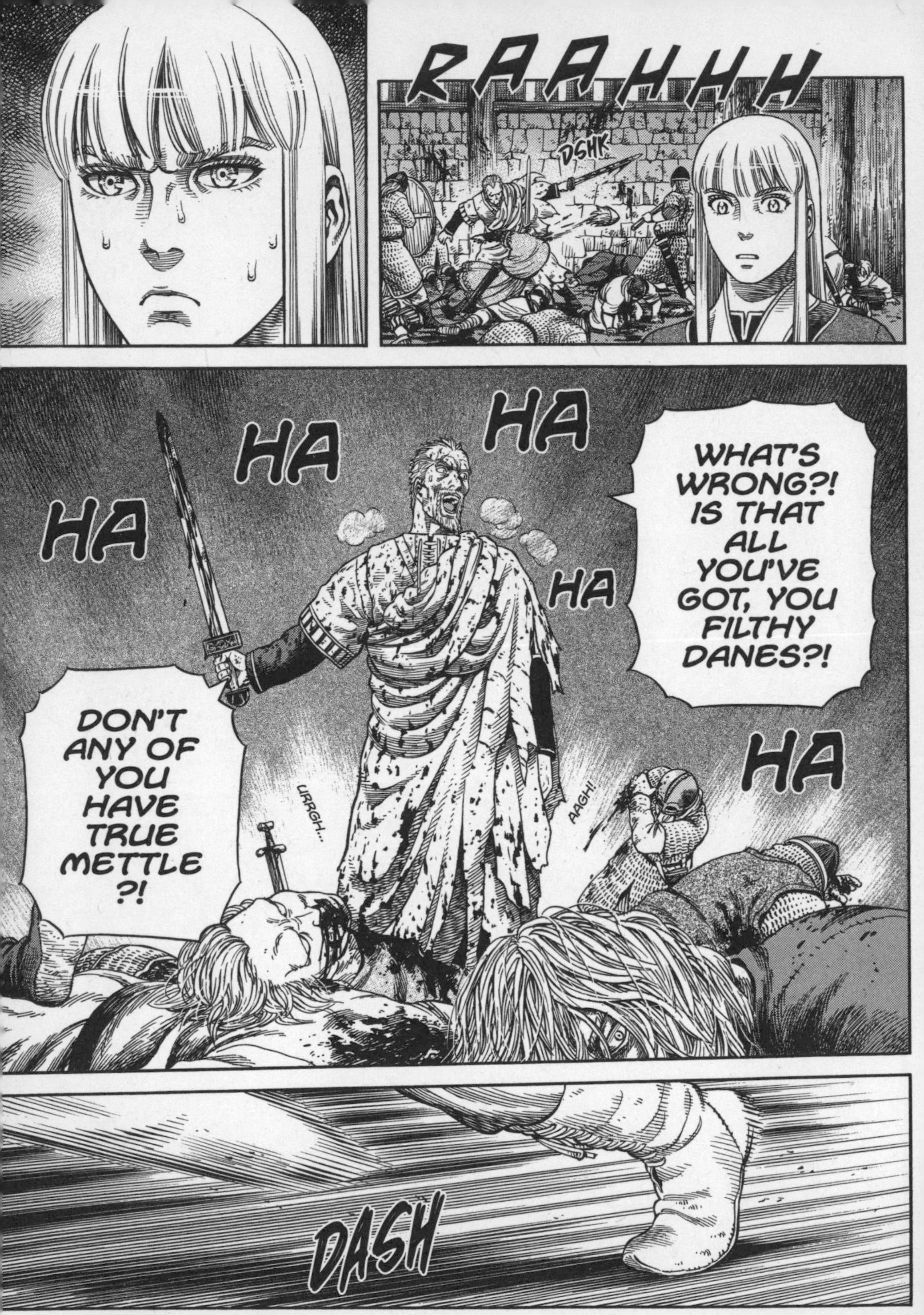
RAAHHH
DSHK
HA
WHAT'S WRONG?! IS THAT ALL YOU'VE GOT, YOU FILTHY DANES?!
HA
HA
HA
HA
HA
AAGH!
URRGH...
DON'T ANY OF YOU HAVE TRUE METTLE ?!
DASH

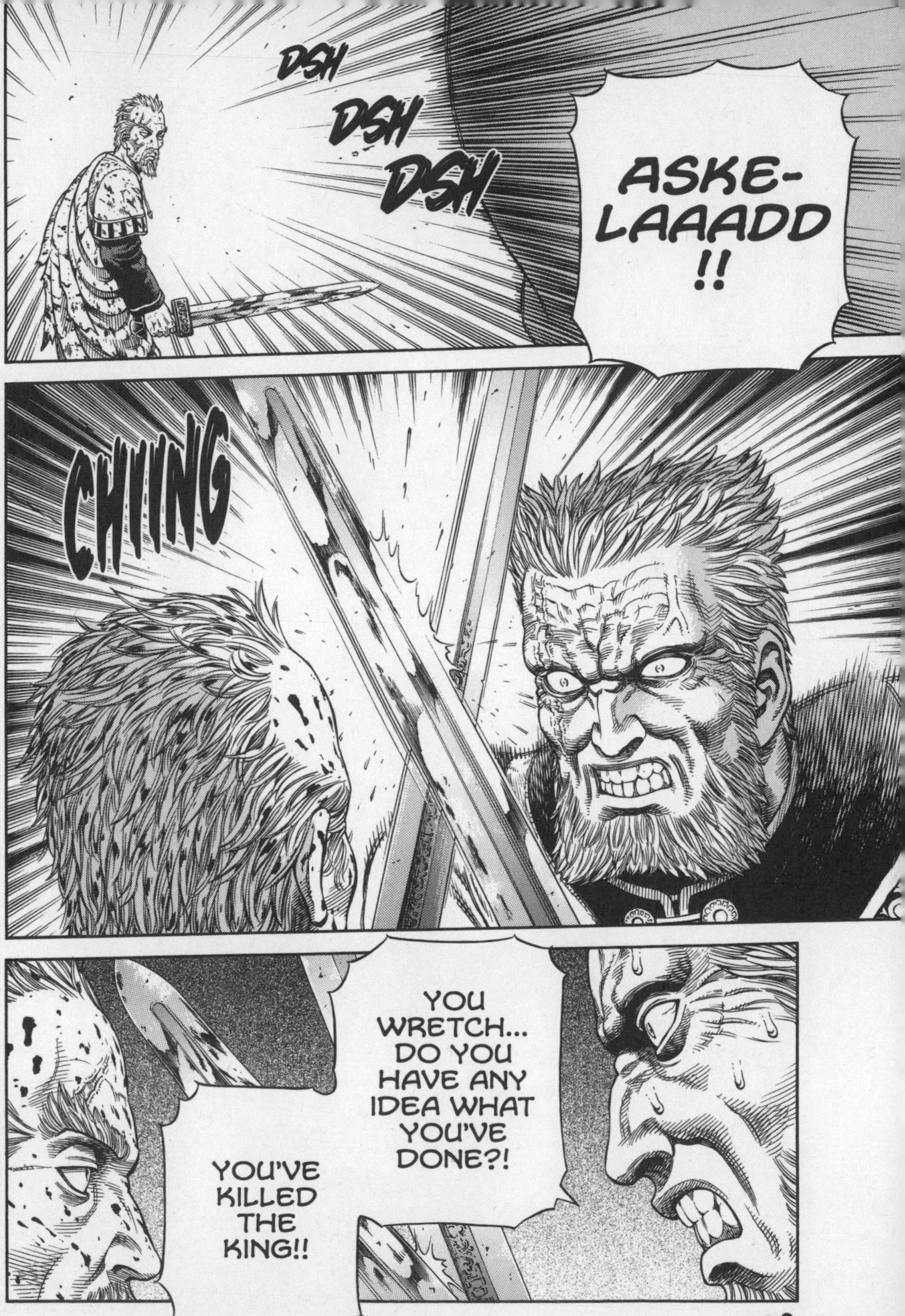
ASKE-LAAADD!!
DSH
DSH
DSH
CHIING
YOU WRETCH... DO YOU HAVE ANY IDEA WHAT YOU'VE DONE?!
YOU'VE KILLED THE KING!!

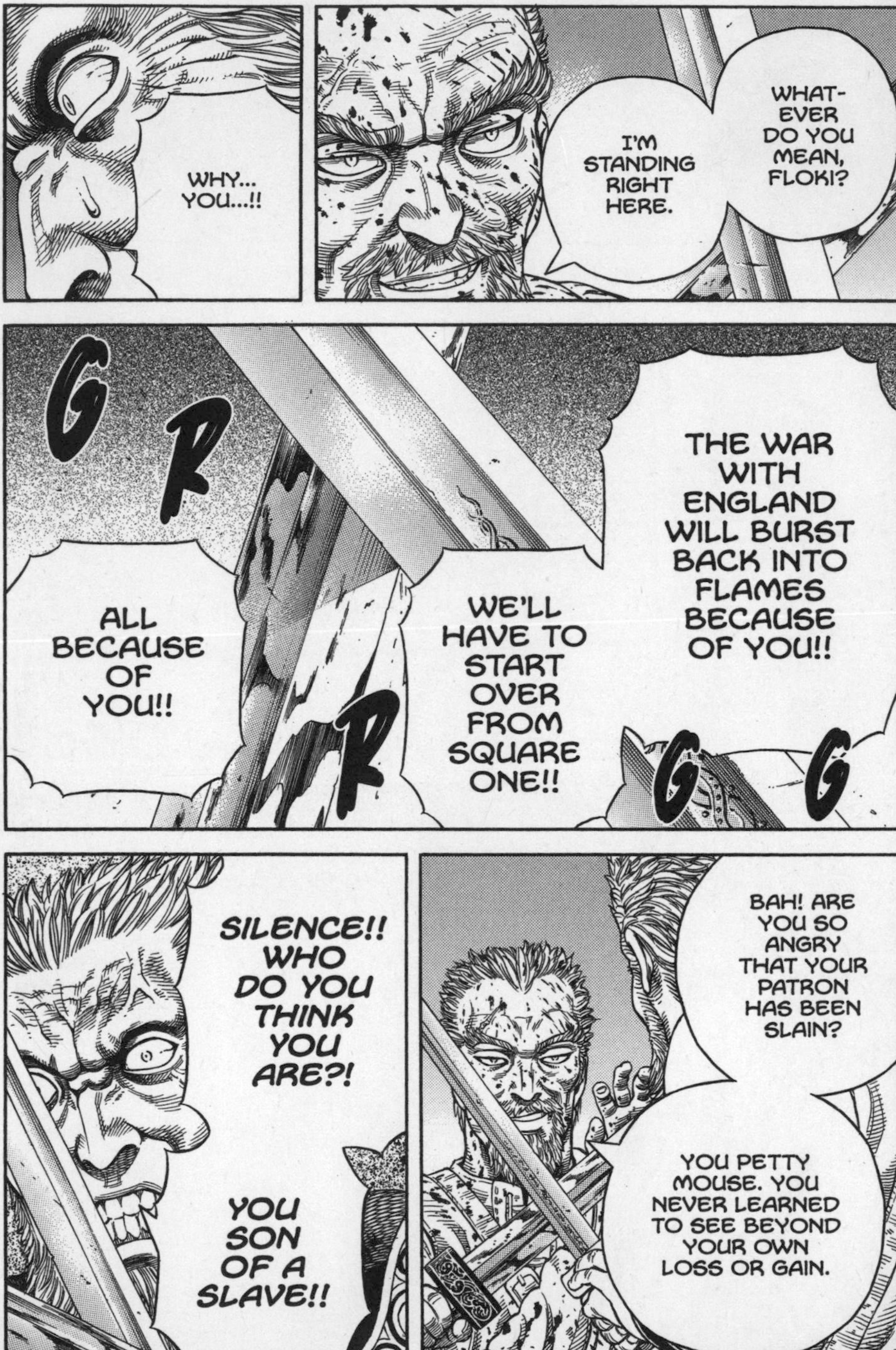
WHAT-EVER DO YOU MEAN, FLOKI?
I'M STANDING RIGHT HERE.
WHY... YOU...!!
THE WAR WITH ENGLAND WILL BURST BACK INTO FLAMES BECAUSE OF YOU!!
WE'LL HAVE TO START OVER FROM SQUARE ONE!!
ALL BECAUSE OF YOU!!
G R R G G
BAH! ARE YOU SO ANGRY THAT YOUR PATRON HAS BEEN SLAIN?
YOU PETTY MOUSE. YOU NEVER LEARNED TO SEE BEYOND YOUR OWN LOSS OR GAIN.
SILENCE!! WHO DO YOU THINK YOU ARE?!
YOU SON OF A SLAVE!!

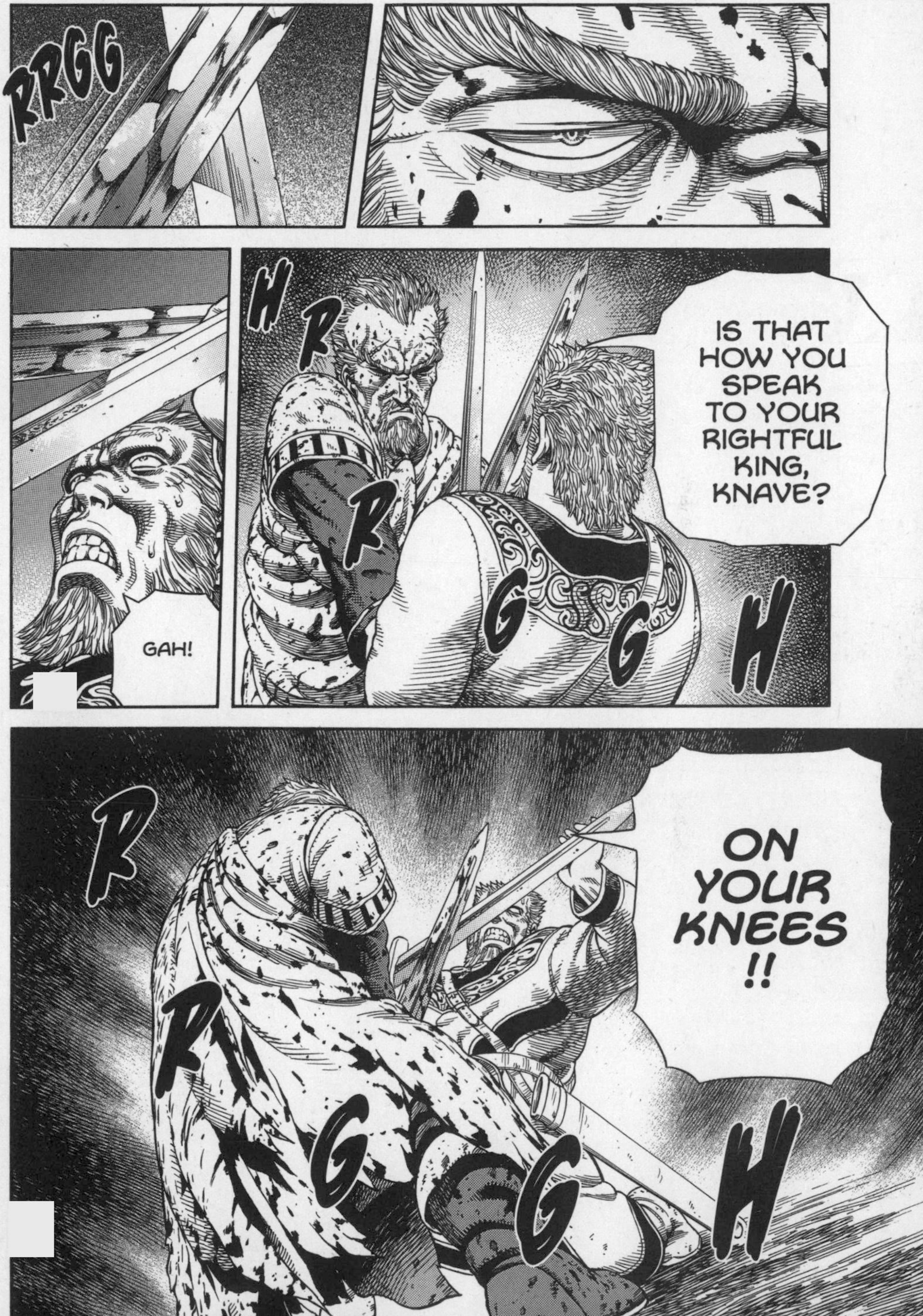
RRGG
HRRGGH
IS THAT HOW YOU SPEAK TO YOUR RIGHTFUL KING, KNAVE?
GAH!
ON YOUR KNEES !!
RRGGH

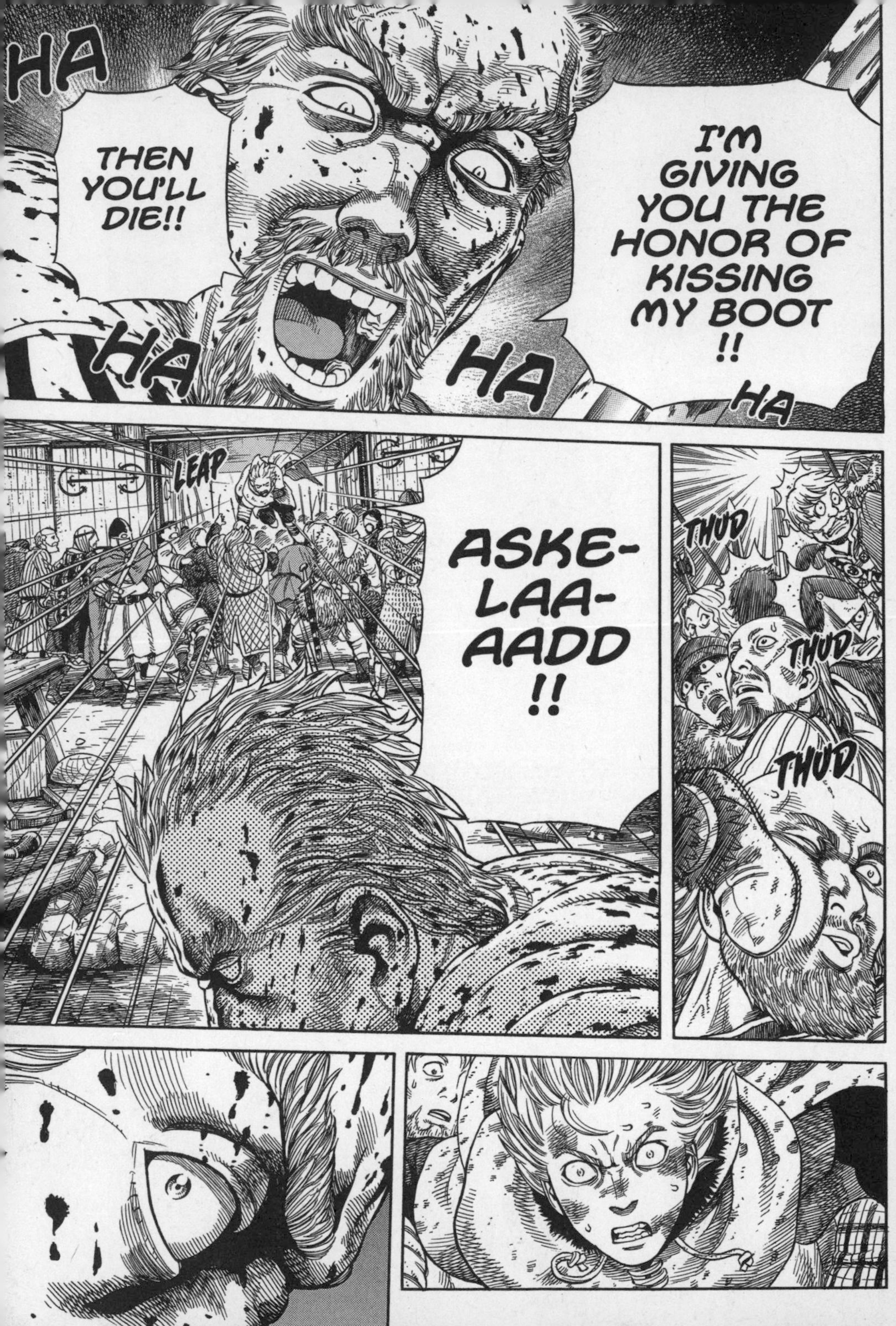
I'M GIVING YOU THE HONOR OF KISSING MY BOOT !!
HA
THEN YOU'LL DIE!!
HA
HA
HA
THUD
THUD
THUD
ASKE-LAA-AADD !!
LEAP

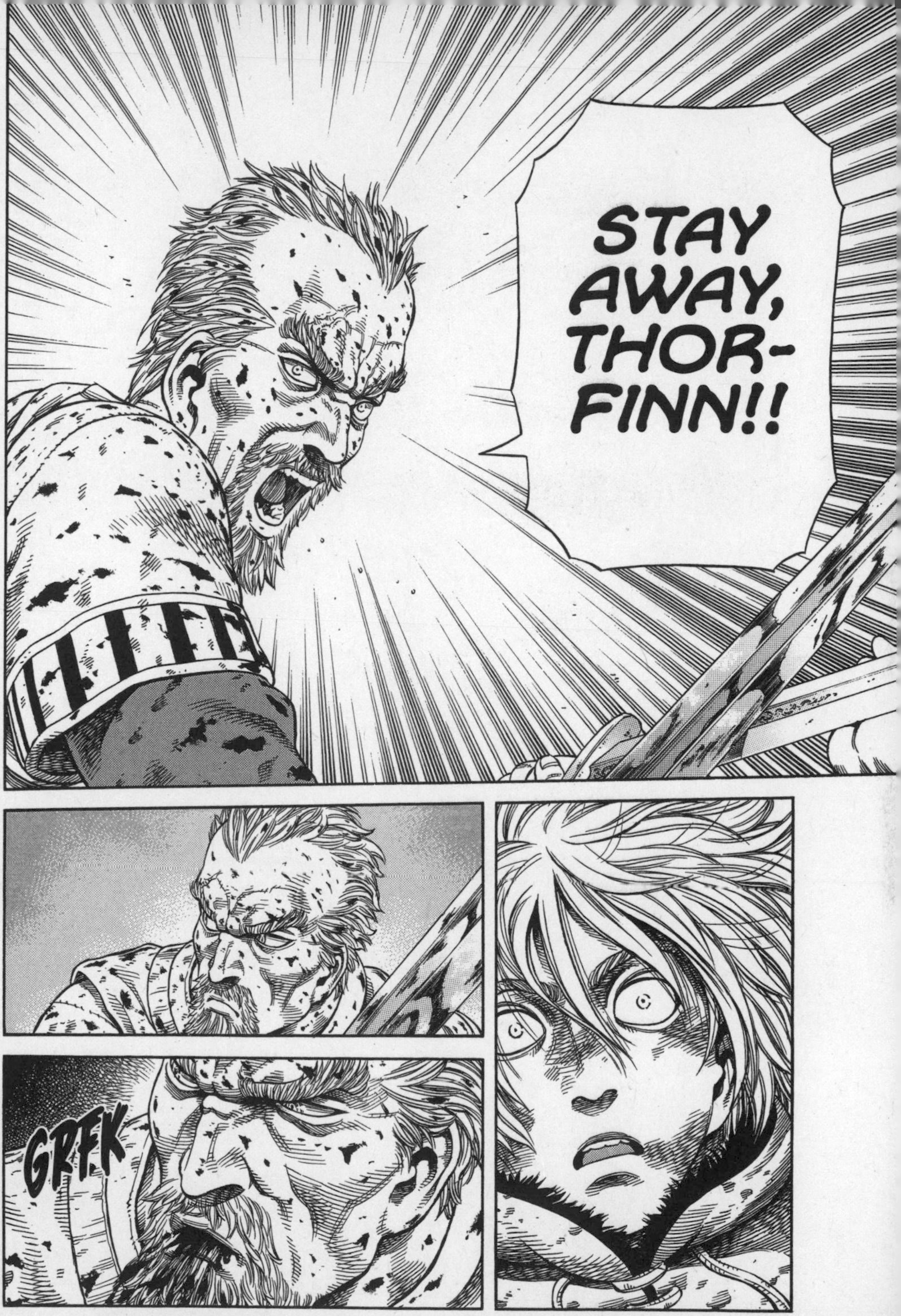
STAY AWAY, THOR-FINN!!
GRFK

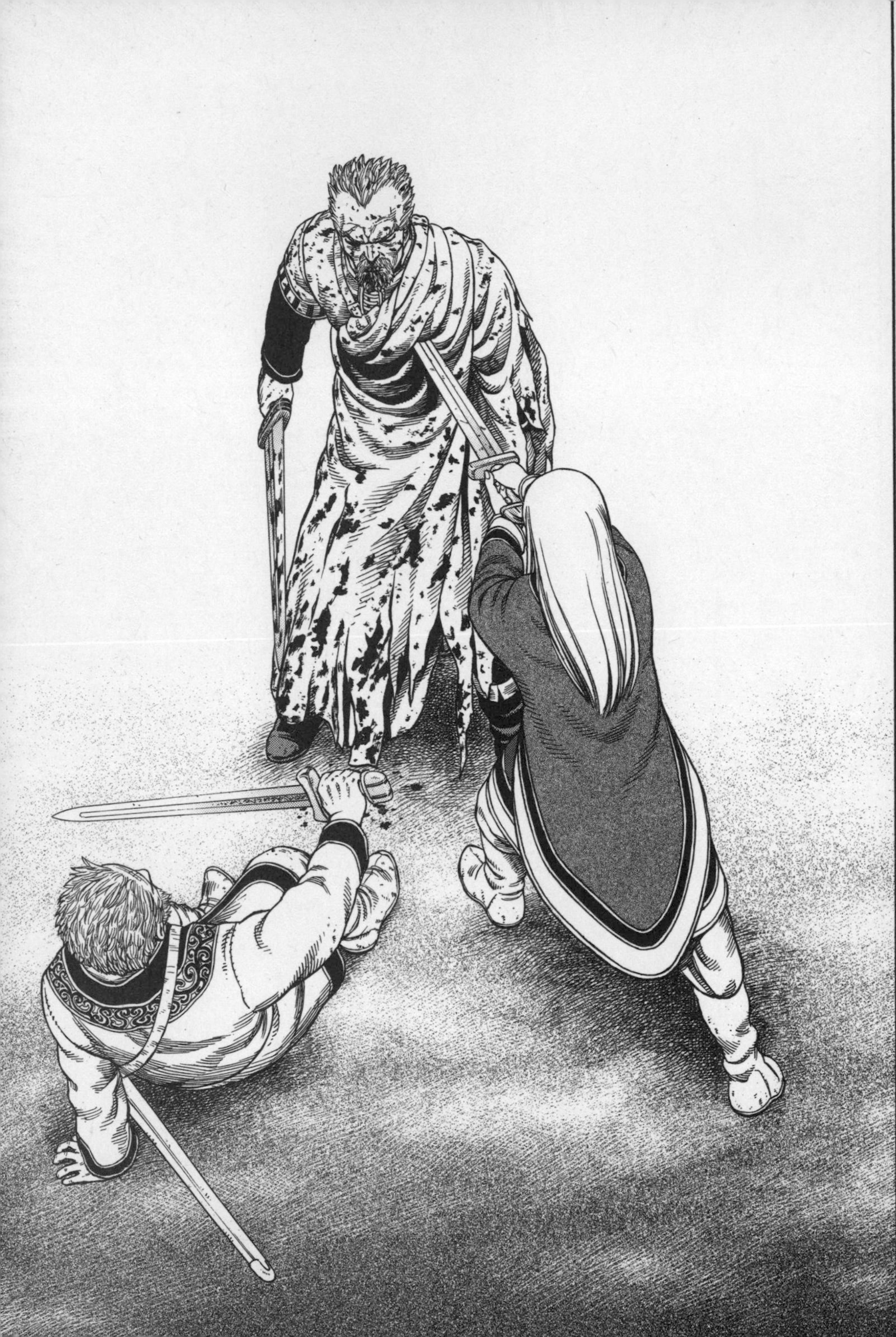

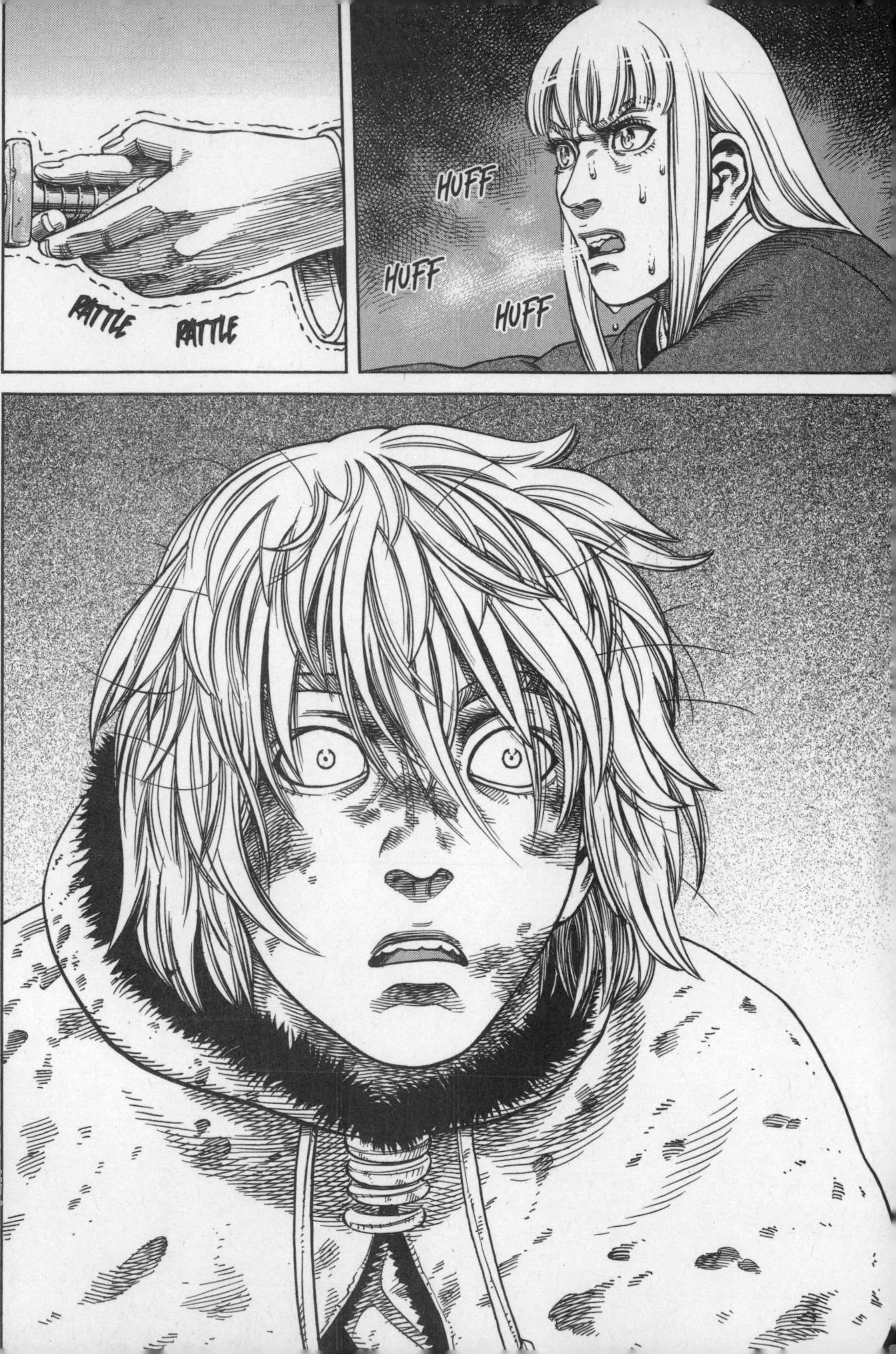
HUFF
HUFF
HUFF
RATTLE
RATTLE

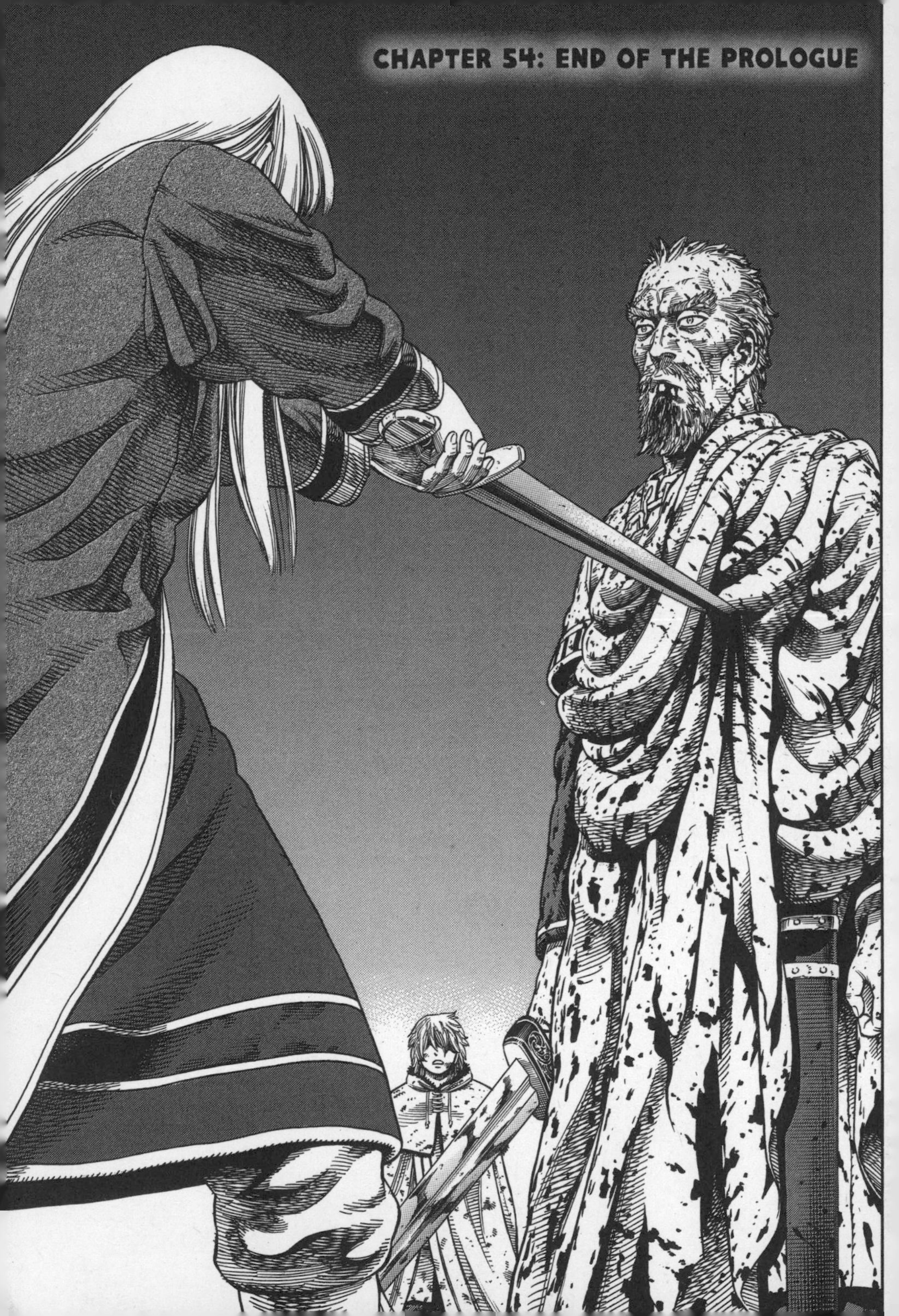
CHAPTER 54: END OF THE PROLOGUE

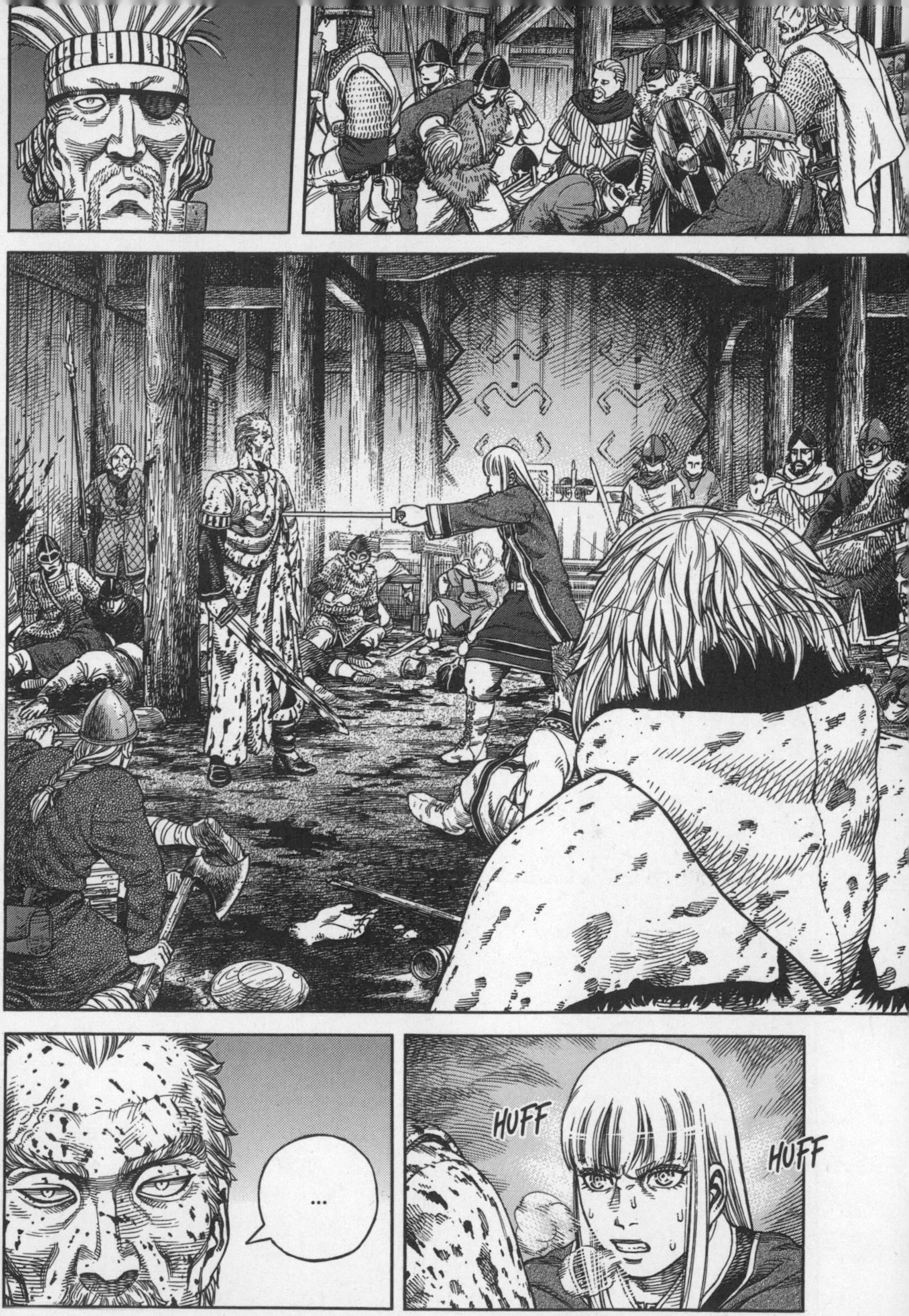
HUFF
HUFF
...

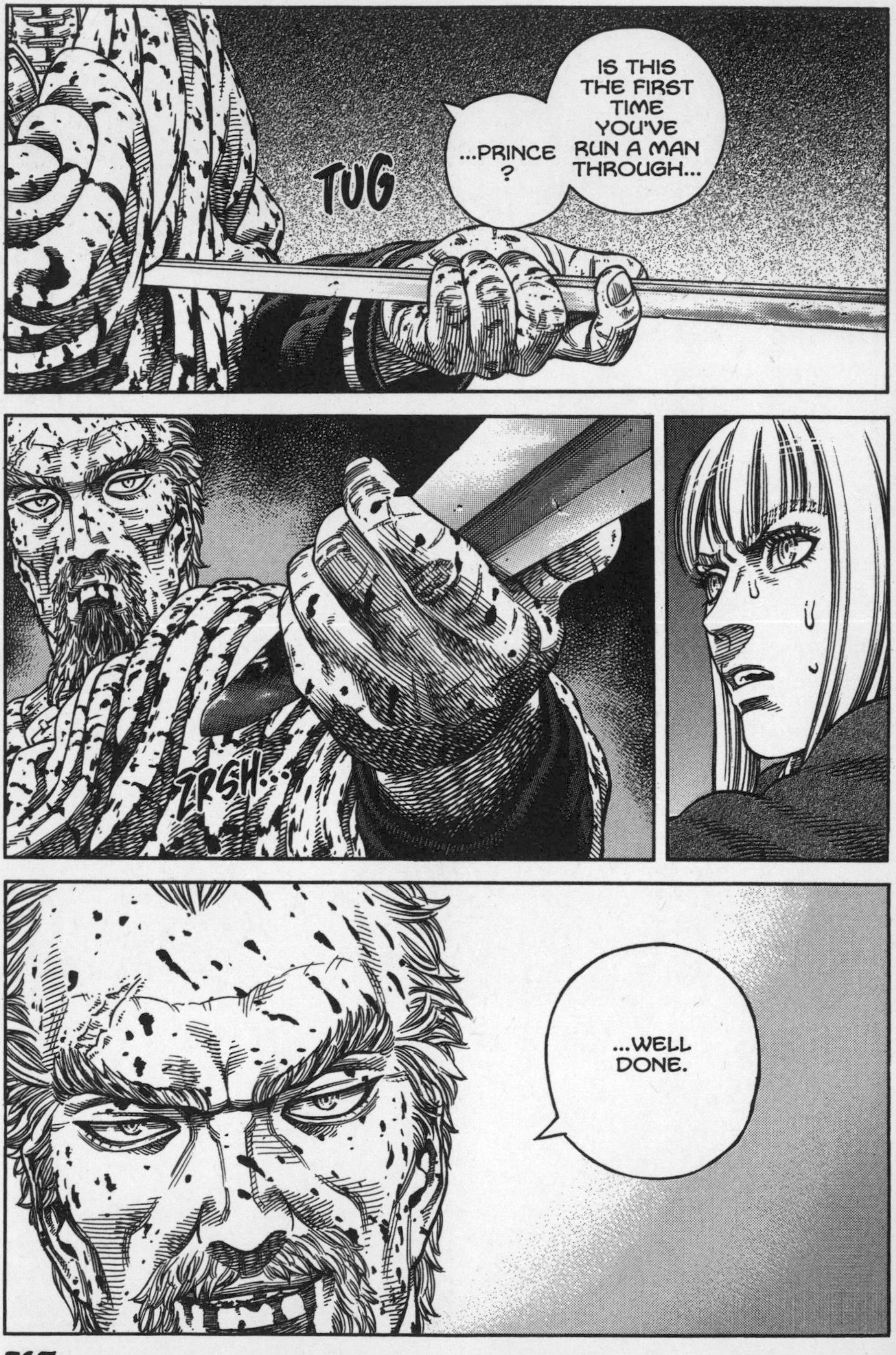
IS THIS THE FIRST TIME YOU'VE RUN A MAN THROUGH... ...PRINCE?
TUG
ZRSH...
...WELL DONE.

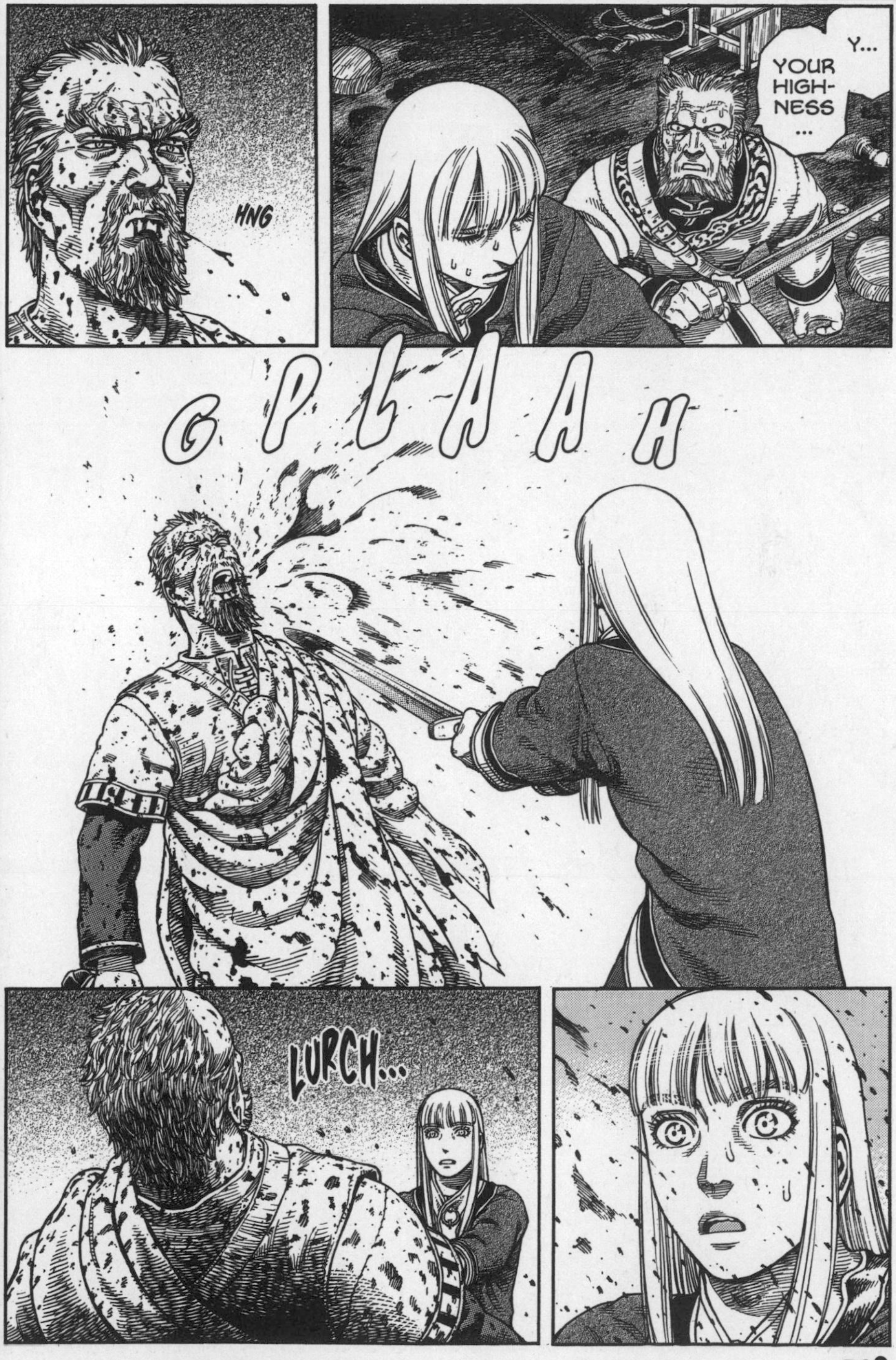
Y... YOUR HIGH-NESS ...
HNG
GPLAAH
LURCH...

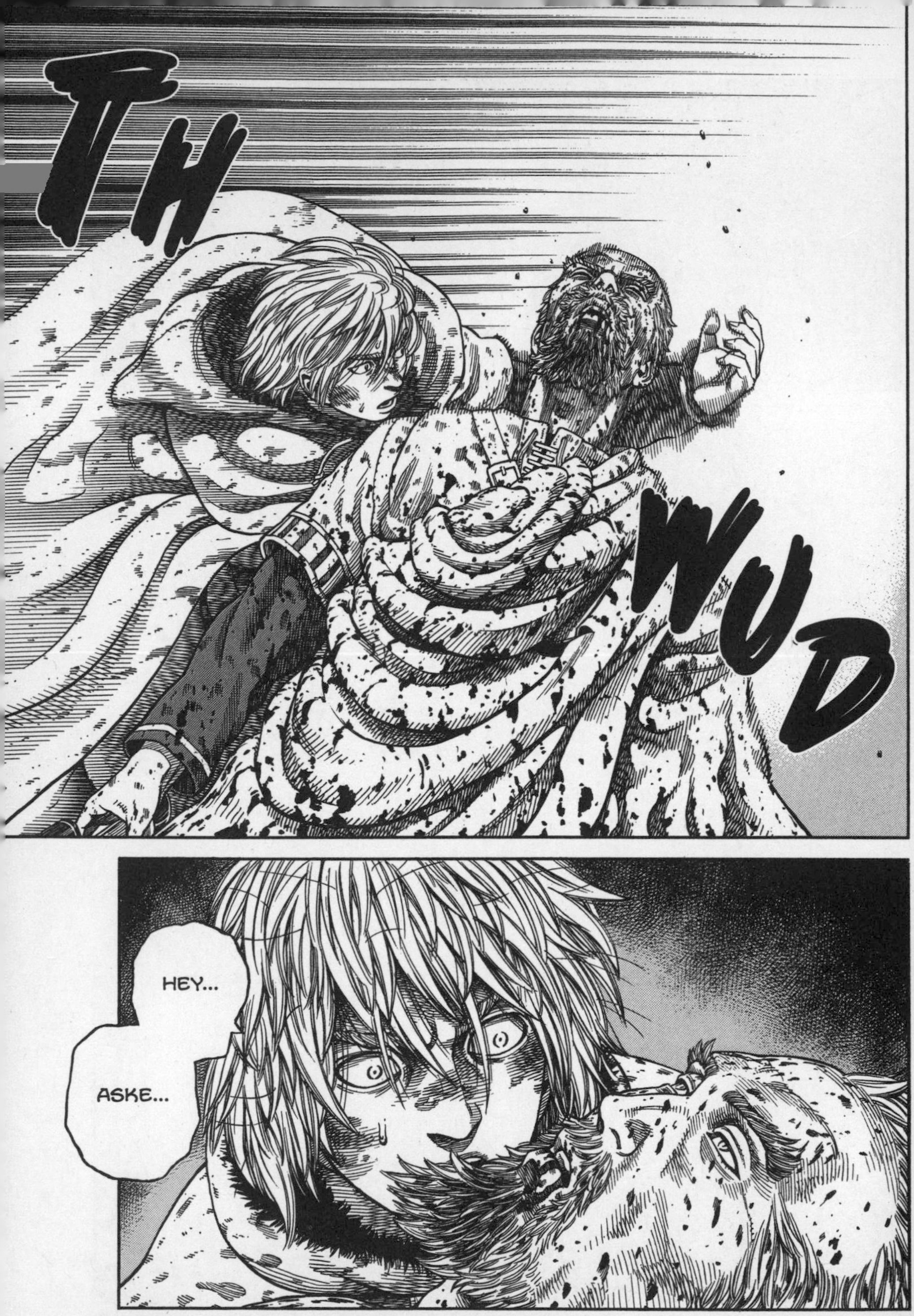
THWUD
HEY...
ASKE...

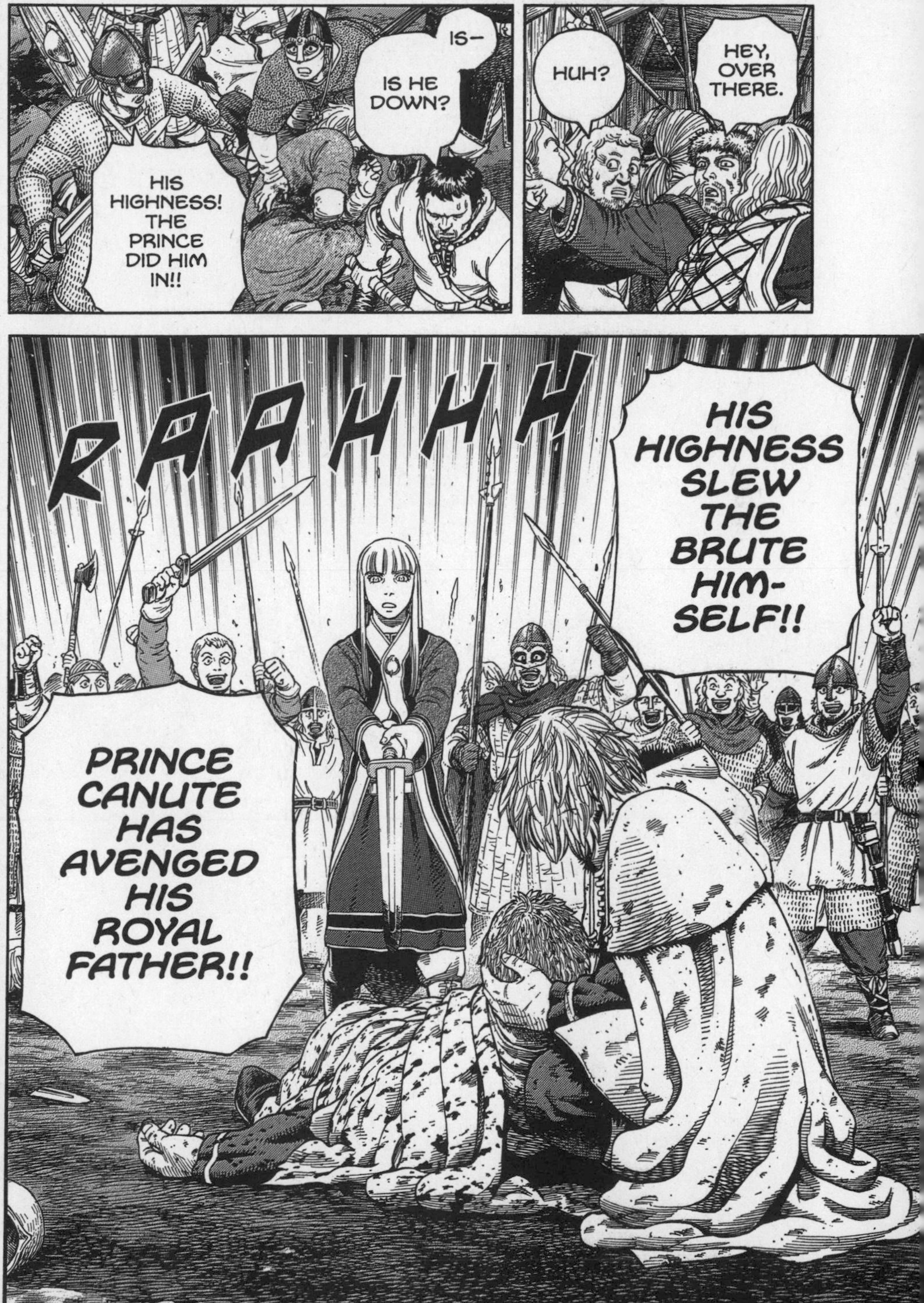
HEY, OVER THERE.
HUH?
IS—
IS HE DOWN?
HIS HIGHNESS! THE PRINCE DID HIM IN!!
RAAHHH
HIS HIGHNESS SLEW THE BRUTE HIM-SELF!!
PRINCE CANUTE HAS AVENGED HIS ROYAL FATHER!!

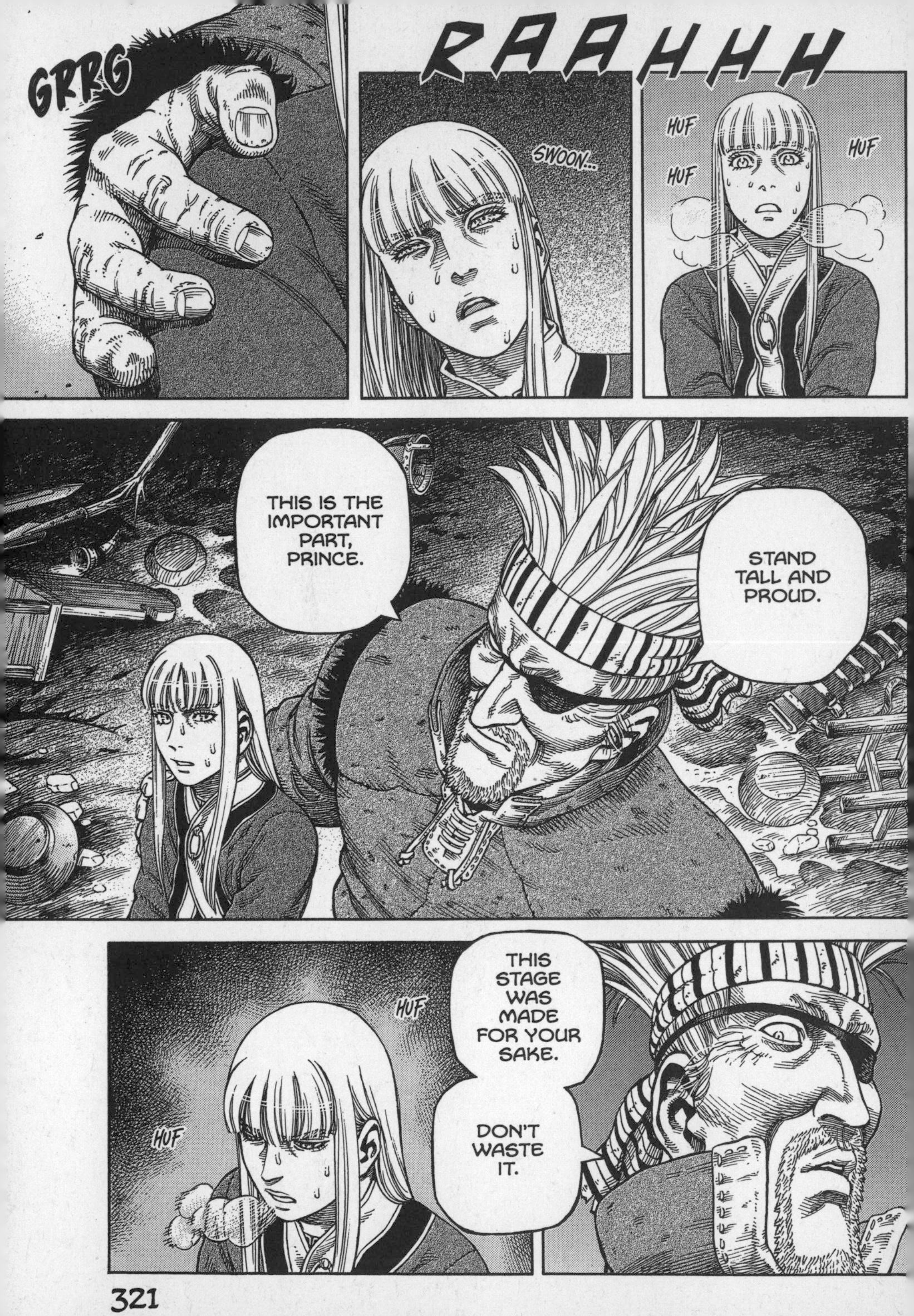
RAAHHH
HUF
HUF
HUF
SWOON...
GRRG
THIS IS THE IMPORTANT PART, PRINCE.
STAND TALL AND PROUD.
THIS STAGE WAS MADE FOR YOUR SAKE.
DON'T WASTE IT.
HUF
HUF

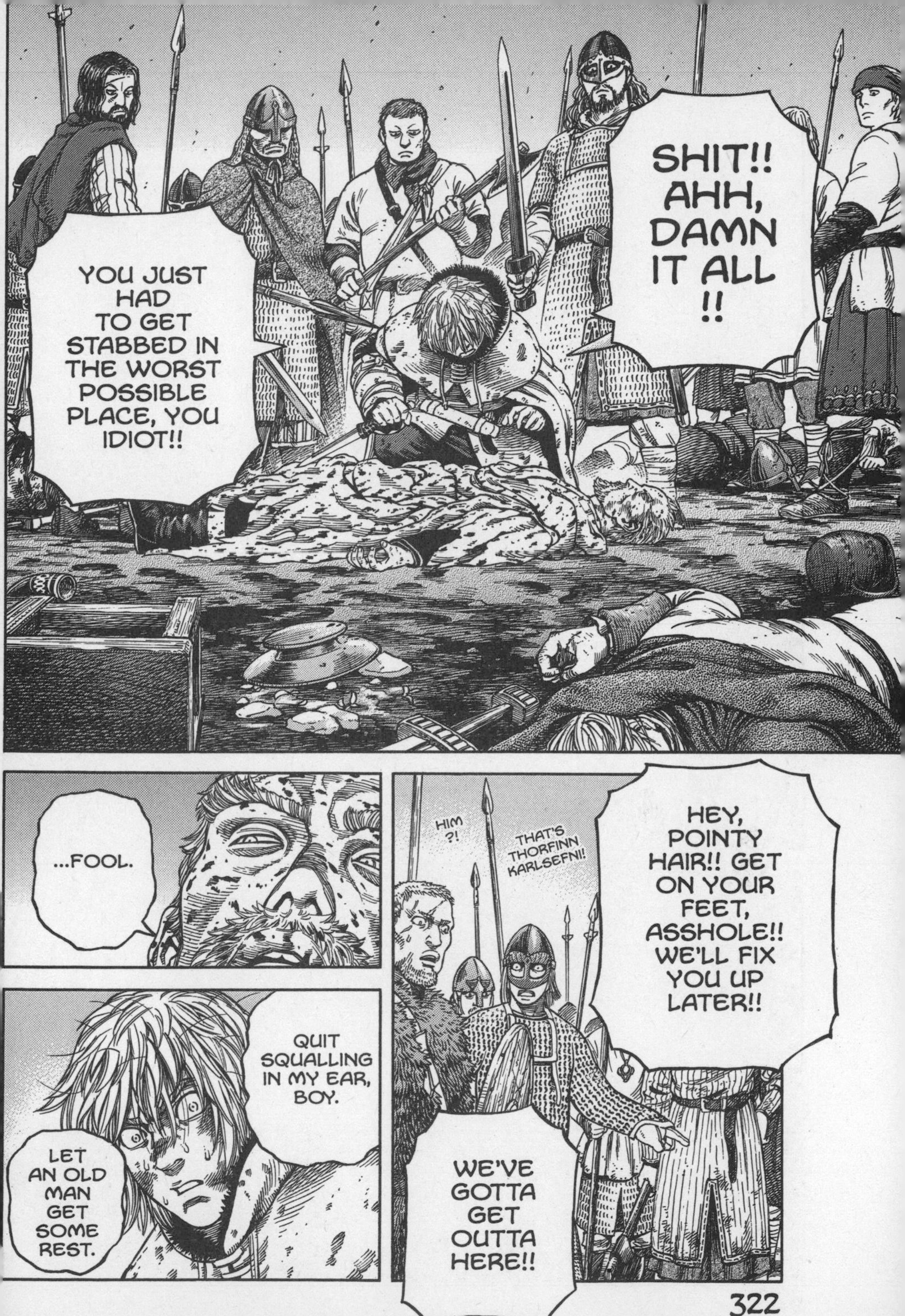
SHIT!! AHH, DAMN IT ALL !!
YOU JUST HAD TO GET STABBED IN THE WORST POSSIBLE PLACE, YOU IDIOT!!
HEY, POINTY HAIR!! GET ON YOUR FEET, ASSHOLE!! WE'LL FIX YOU UP LATER!!
THAT'S THORFINN KARLSEFNI!
HIM ?!
WE'VE GOTTA GET OUTTA HERE!!
...FOOL.
QUIT SQUALLING IN MY EAR, BOY.
LET AN OLD MAN GET SOME REST.

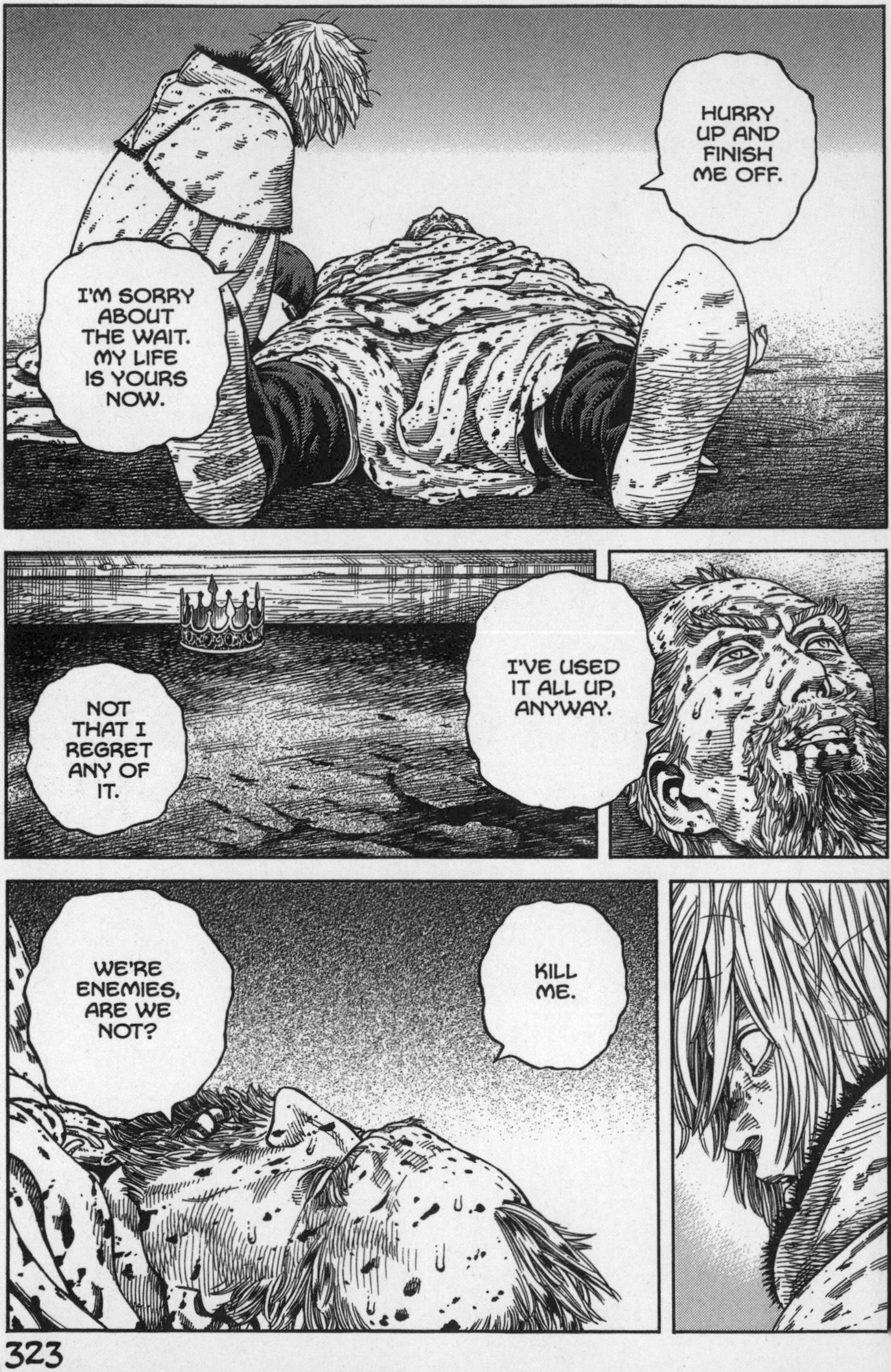
HURRY UP AND FINISH ME OFF.
I'M SORRY ABOUT THE WAIT. MY LIFE IS YOURS NOW.
I'VE USED IT ALL UP, ANYWAY.
NOT THAT I REGRET ANY OF IT.
KILL ME.
WE'RE ENEMIES, ARE WE NOT?

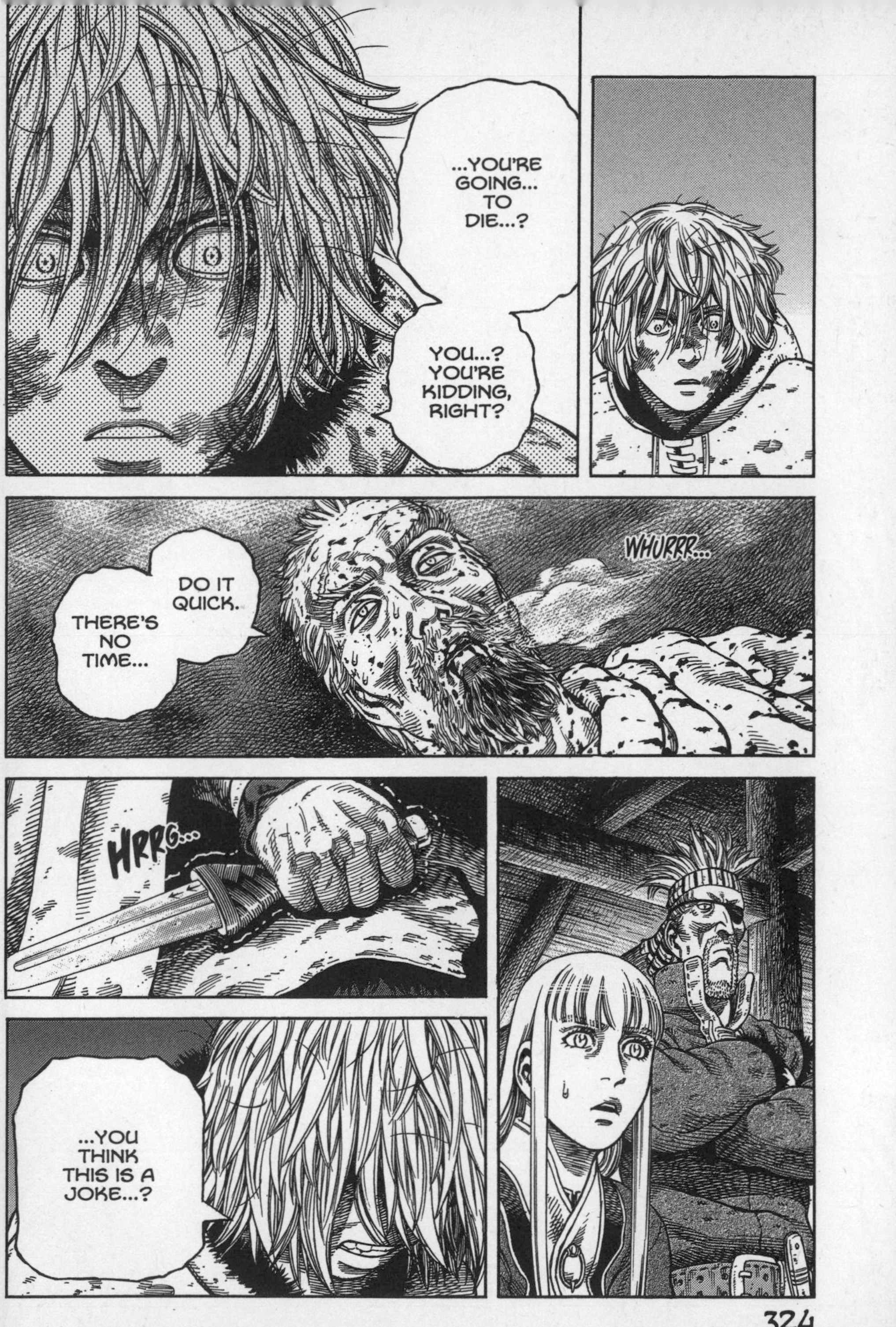
...YOU'RE GOING... TO DIE...?
YOU...? YOU'RE KIDDING, RIGHT?
WHURRR...
DO IT QUICK.
THERE'S NO TIME...
HRRG...
...YOU THINK THIS IS A JOKE...?

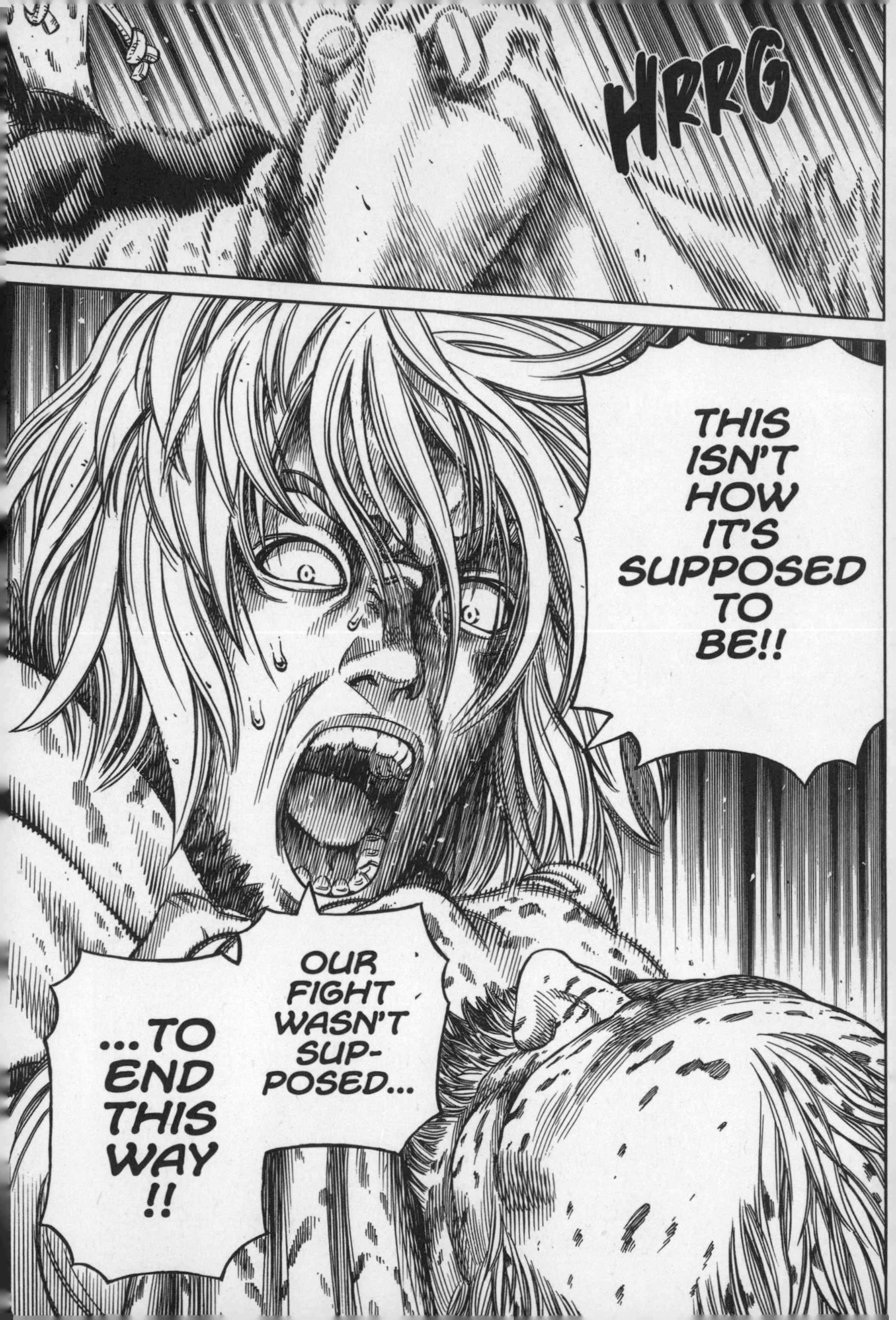
HRRG
THIS ISN'T HOW IT'S SUPPOSED TO BE!!
OUR FIGHT WASN'T SUP-POSED...
...TO END THIS WAY!!

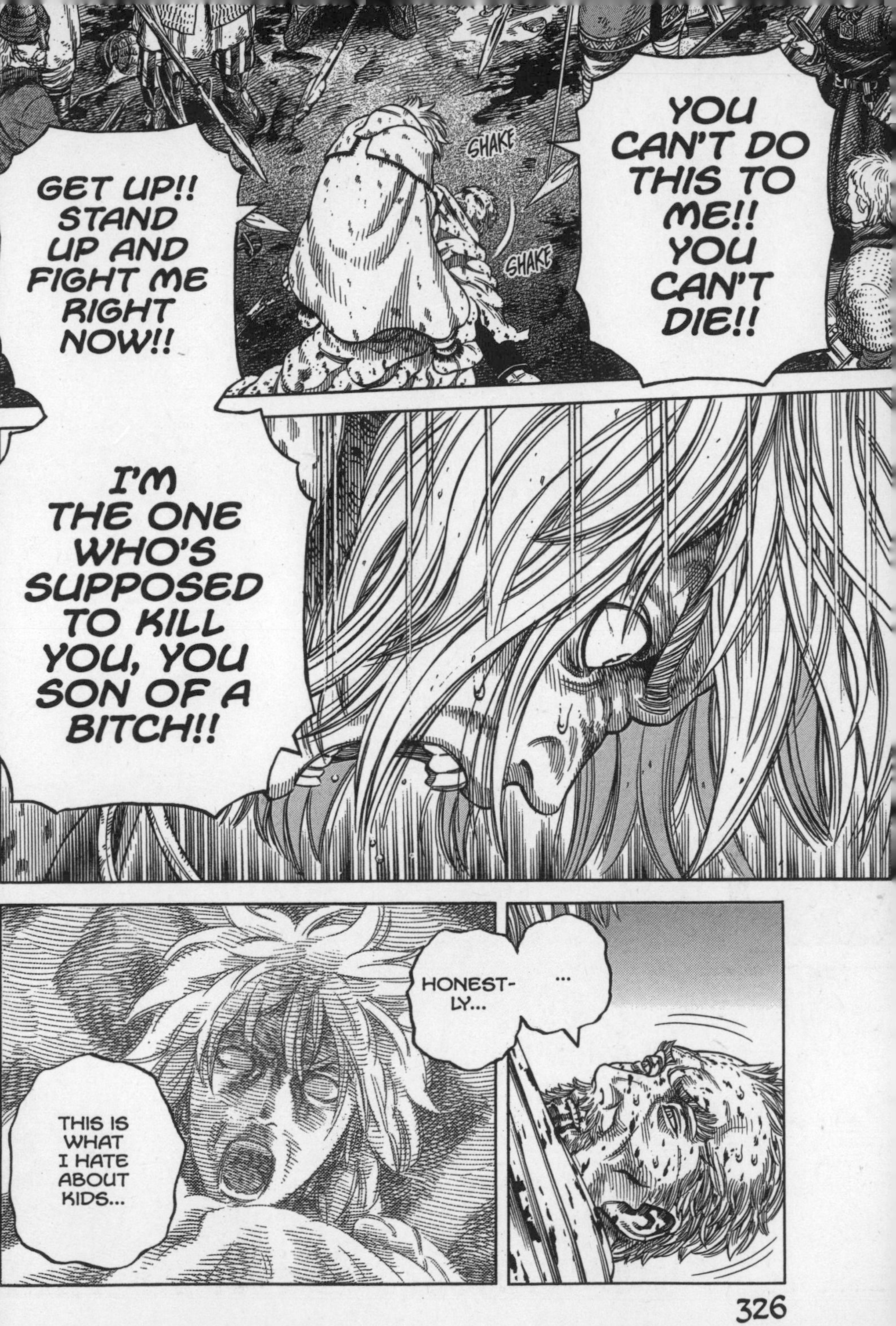
YOU CAN'T DO THIS TO ME!! YOU CAN'T DIE!!
SHAKE
SHAKE
GET UP!! STAND UP AND FIGHT ME RIGHT NOW!!
I'M THE ONE WHO'S SUPPOSED TO KILL YOU, YOU SON OF A BITCH!!
...
HONEST-LY...
THIS IS WHAT I HATE ABOUT KIDS...

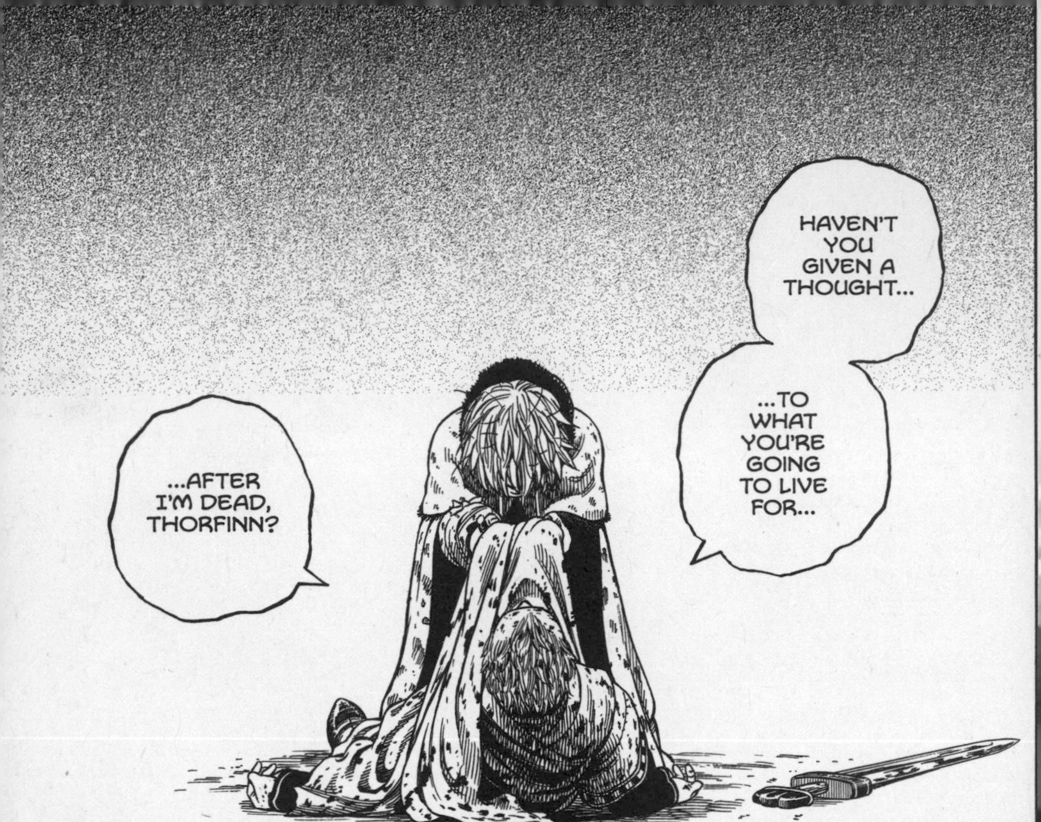
HAVEN'T YOU GIVEN A THOUGHT...
...TO WHAT YOU'RE GOING TO LIVE FOR...
...AFTER I'M DEAD, THORFINN?

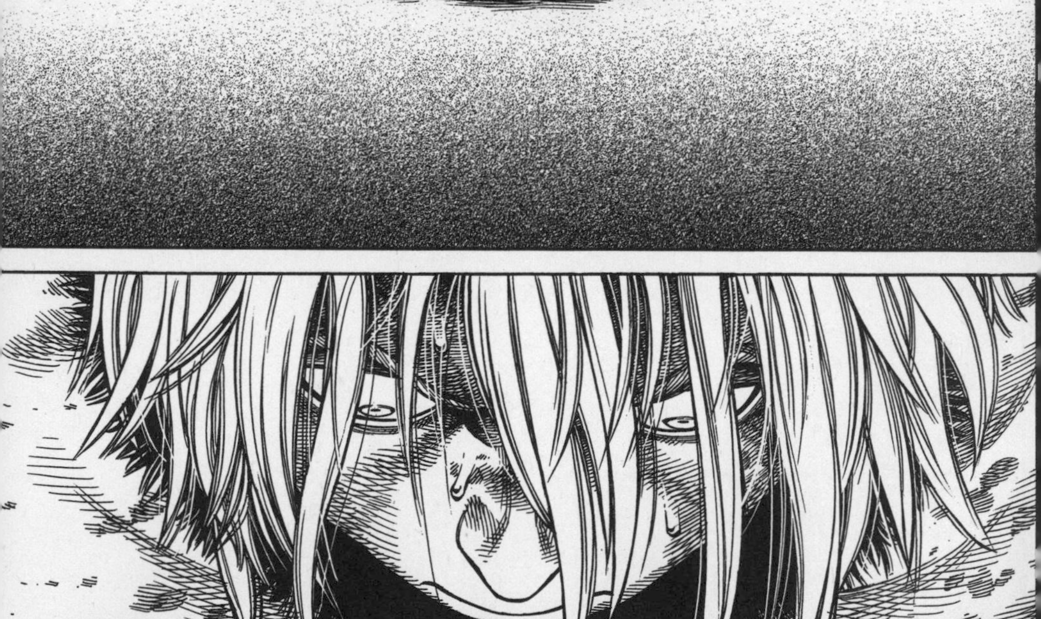

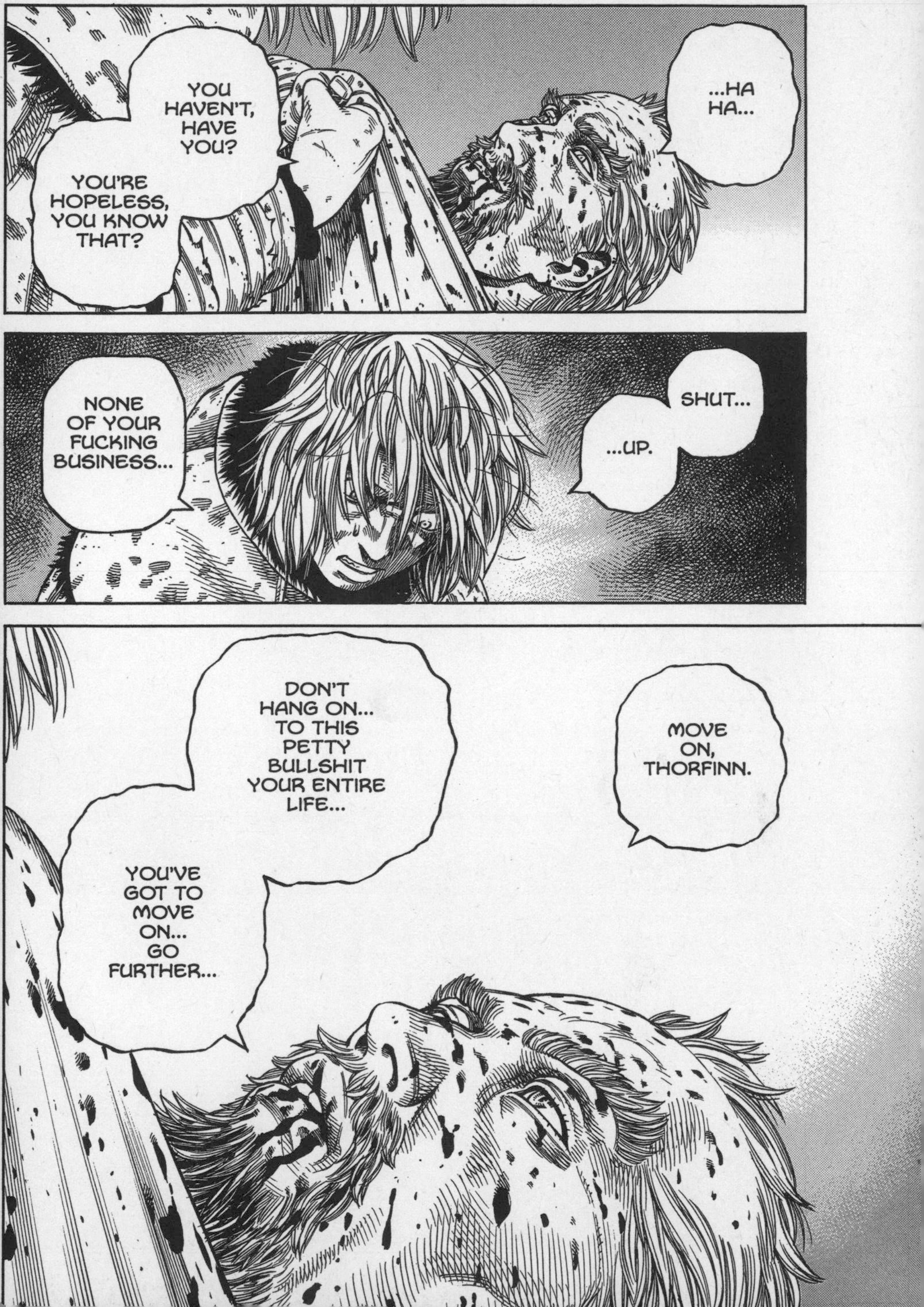
...HA HA...
YOU HAVEN'T, HAVE YOU?
YOU'RE HOPELESS, YOU KNOW THAT?
SHUT...
...UP.
NONE OF YOUR FUCKING BUSINESS...
MOVE ON, THORFINN.
DON'T HANG ON... TO THIS PETTY BULLSHIT YOUR ENTIRE LIFE...
YOU'VE GOT TO MOVE ON... GO FURTHER...

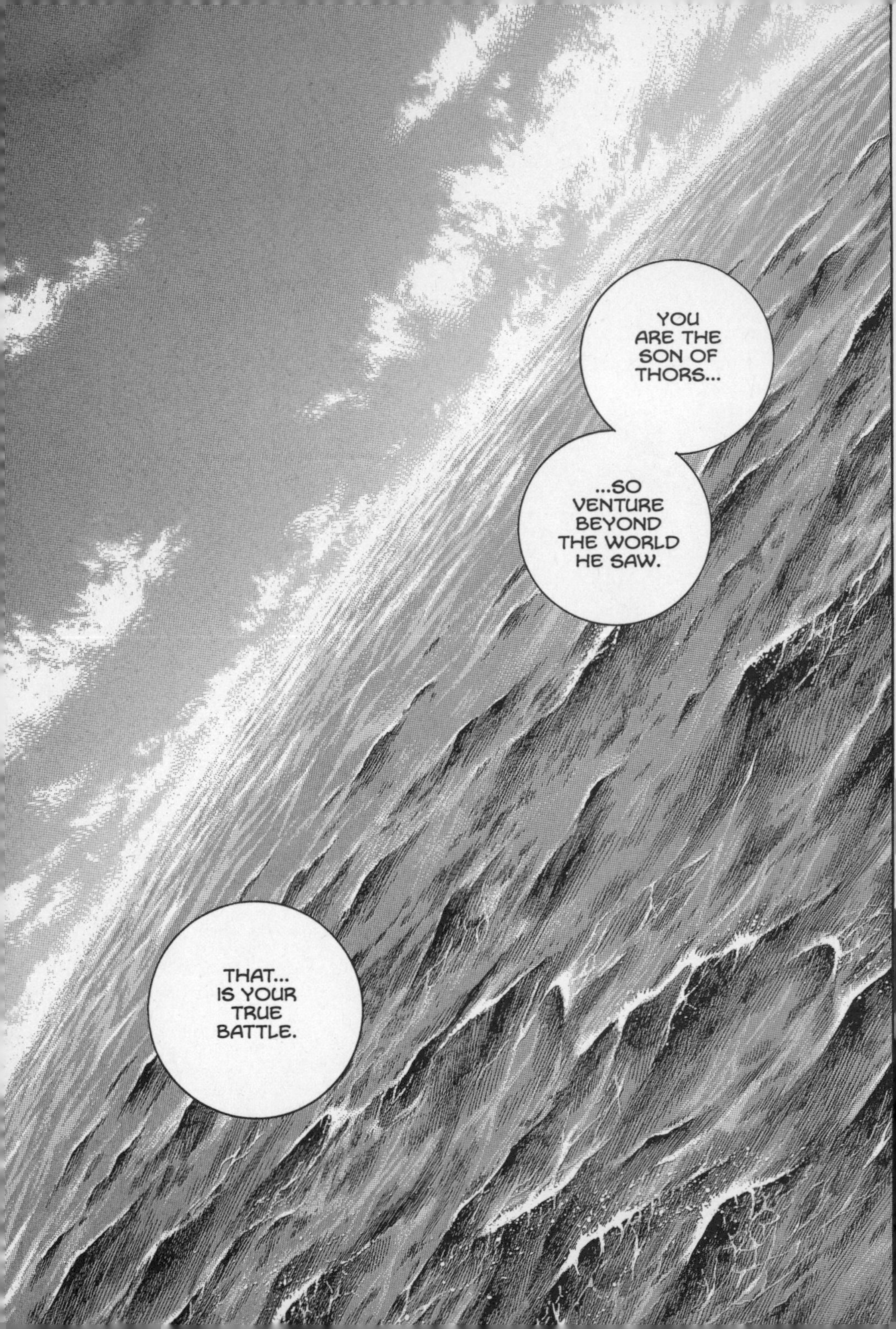
YOU ARE THE SON OF THORS...
...SO VENTURE BEYOND THE WORLD HE SAW.
THAT... IS YOUR TRUE BATTLE.

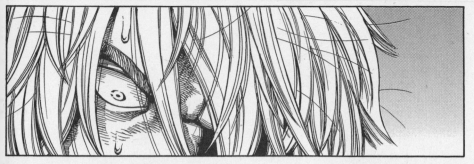

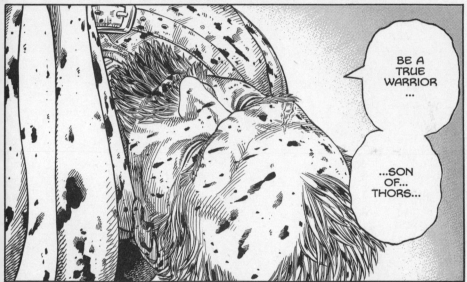

BE A
TRUE
WARRIOR
...

...SON
OF...
THORS...

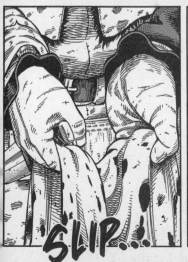

SLIP....

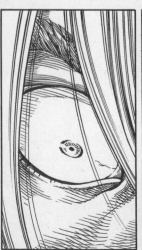

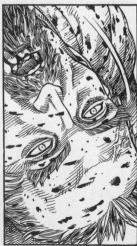

330

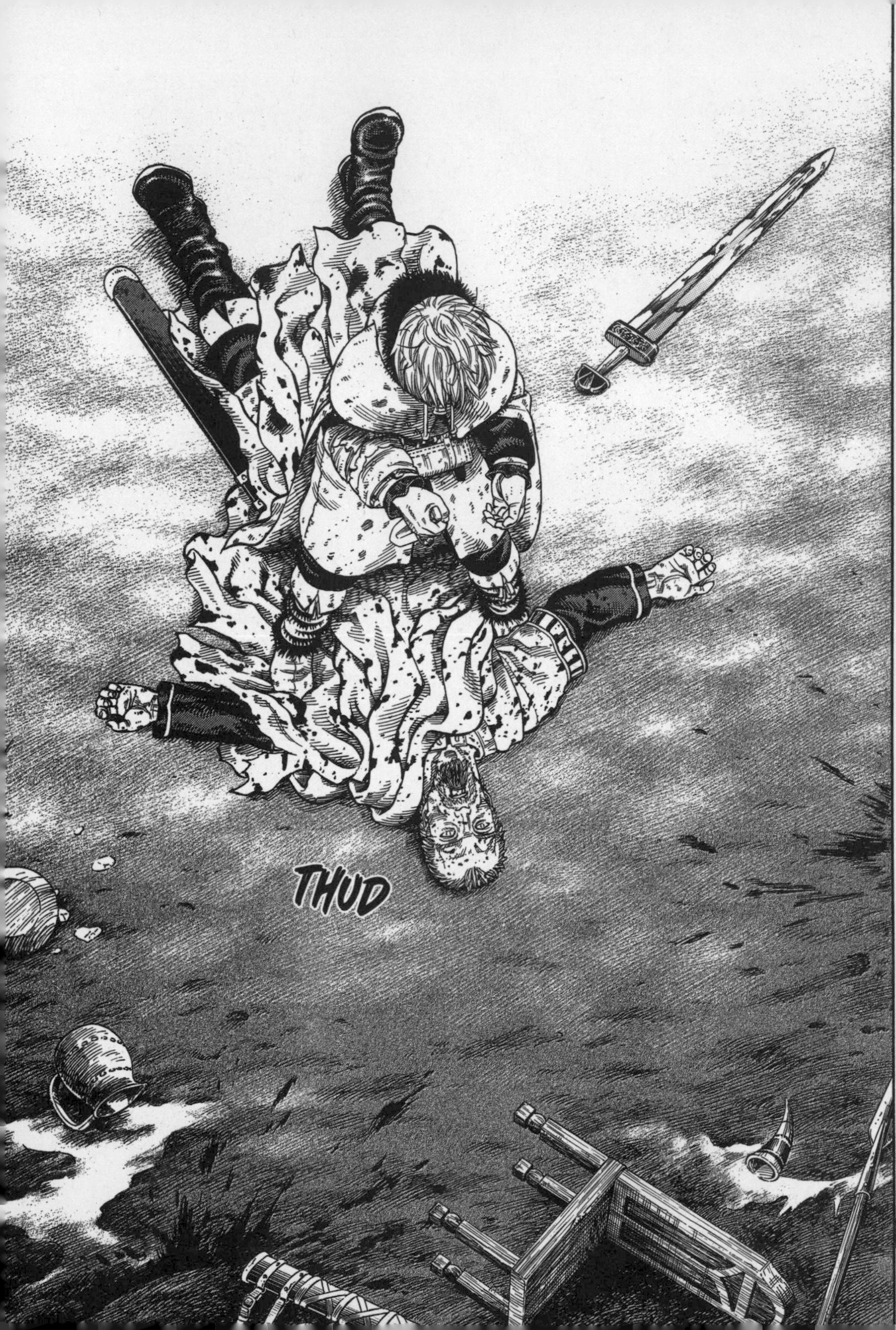
THUD

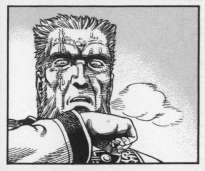

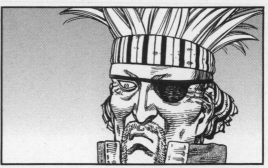

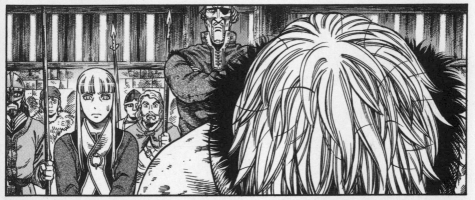

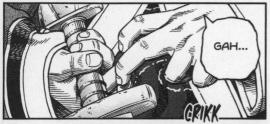

GAH...

GRIKK

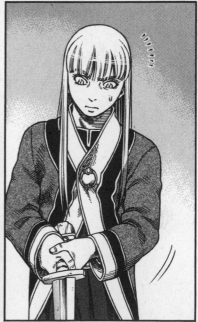

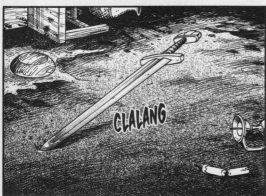

CLALANG

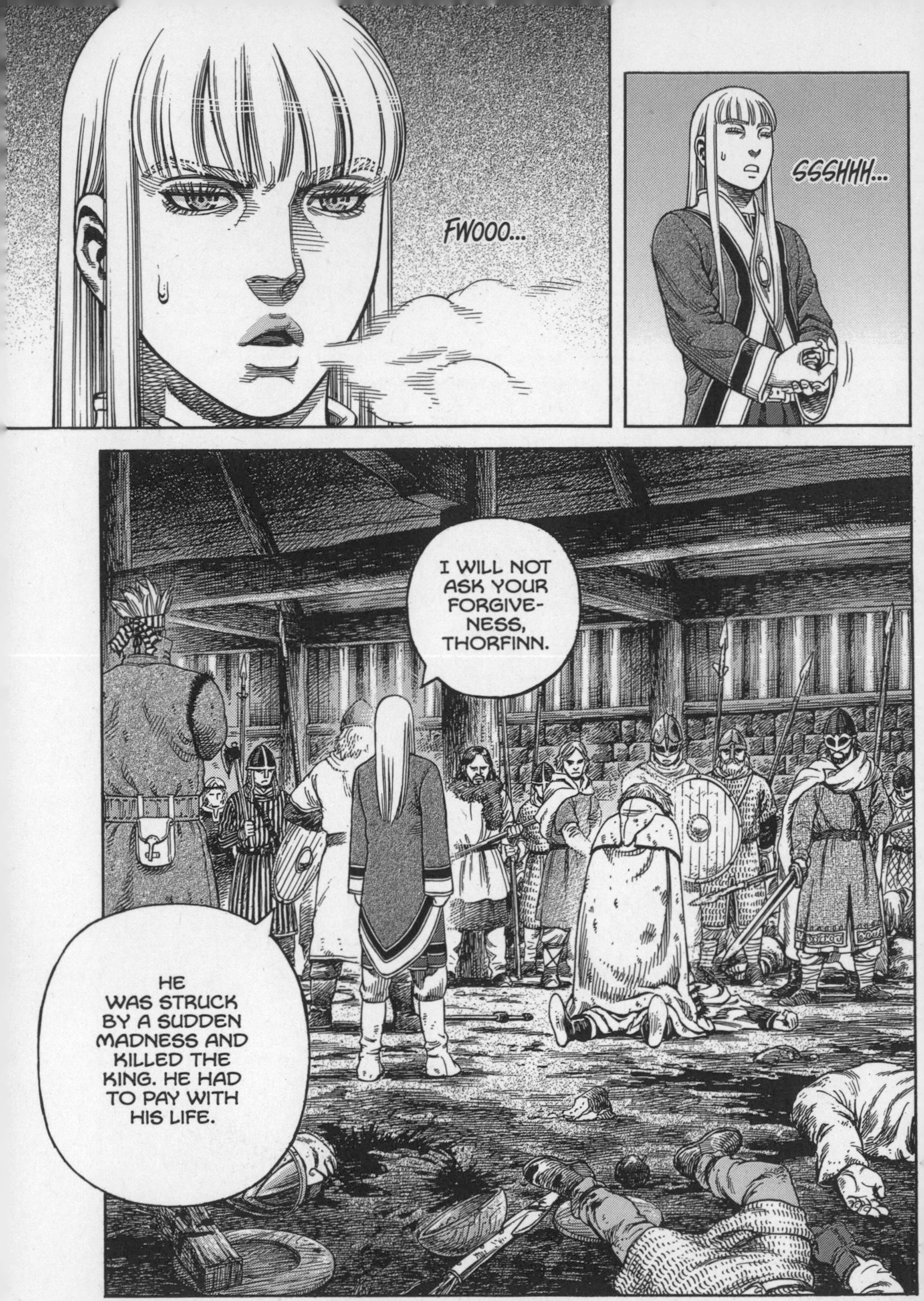
SSSHHH...
FWOOO...
I WILL NOT ASK YOUR FORGIVE-NESS, THORFINN.
HE WAS STRUCK BY A SUDDEN MADNESS AND KILLED THE KING. HE HAD TO PAY WITH HIS LIFE.

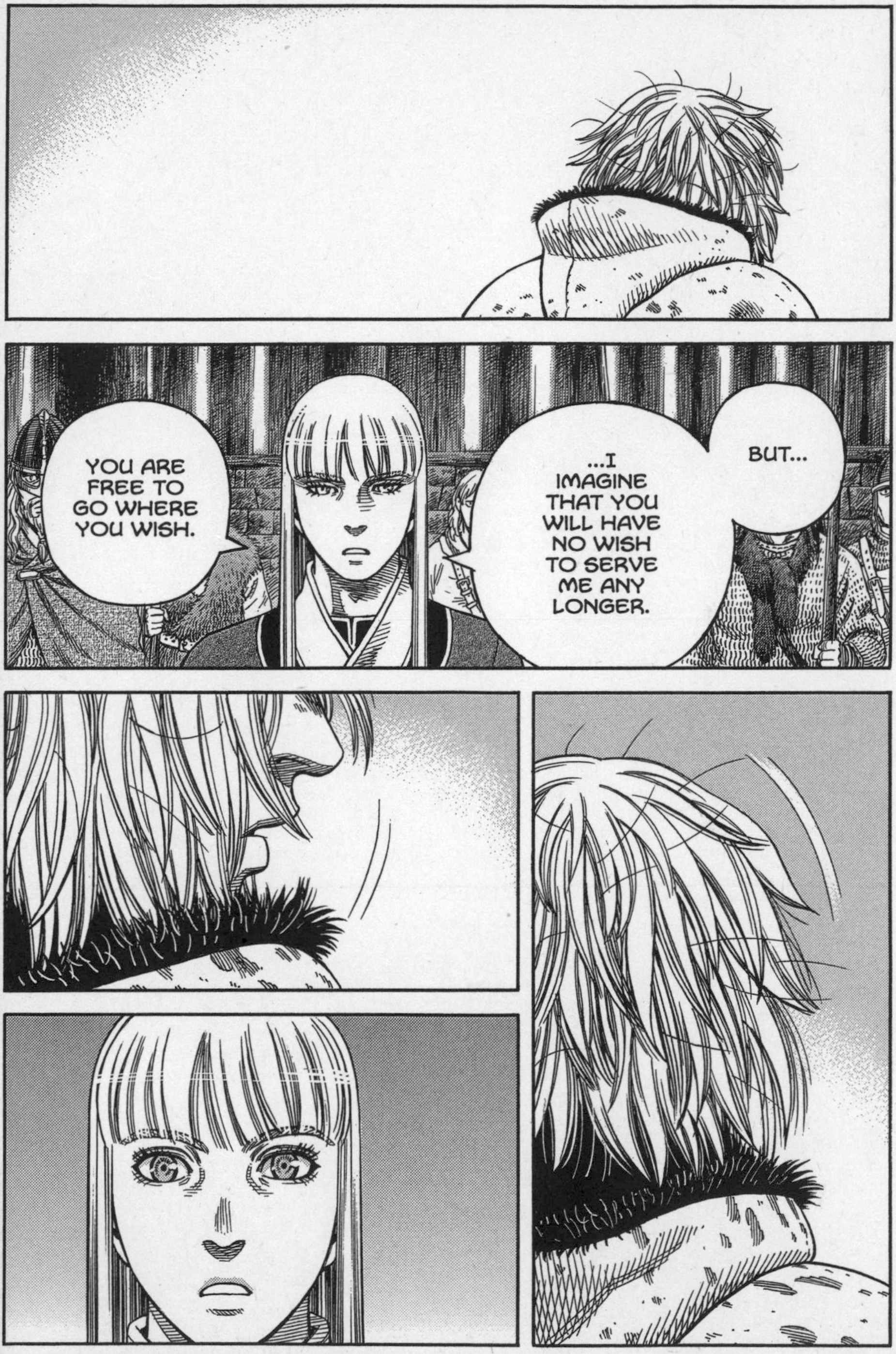
BUT...
...I IMAGINE THAT YOU WILL HAVE NO WISH TO SERVE ME ANY LONGER.
YOU ARE FREE TO GO WHERE YOU WISH.

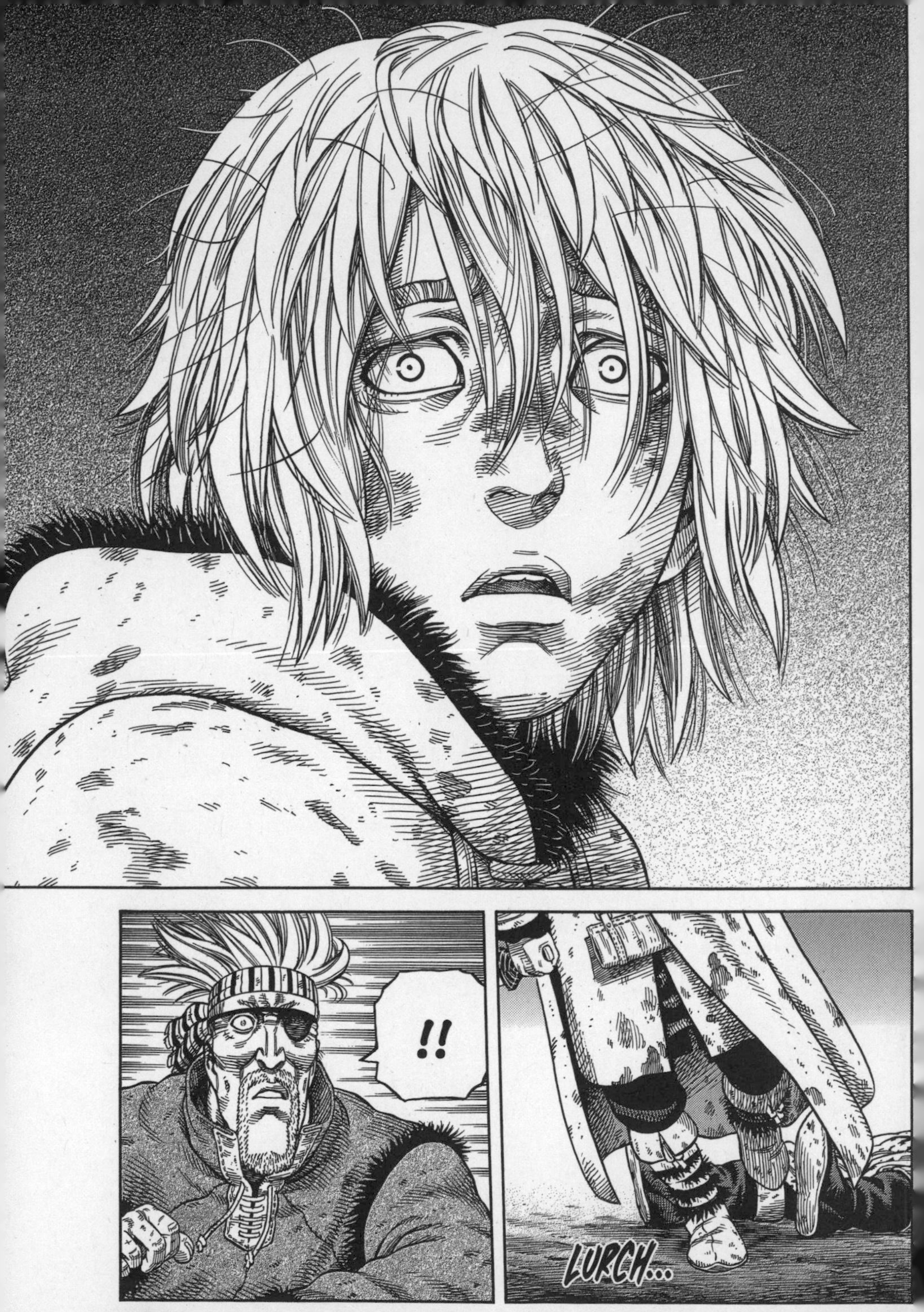

LURCH...
!!

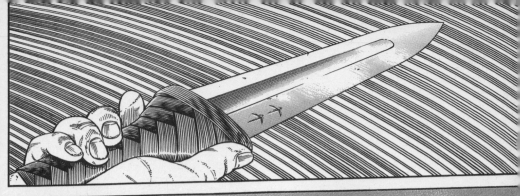

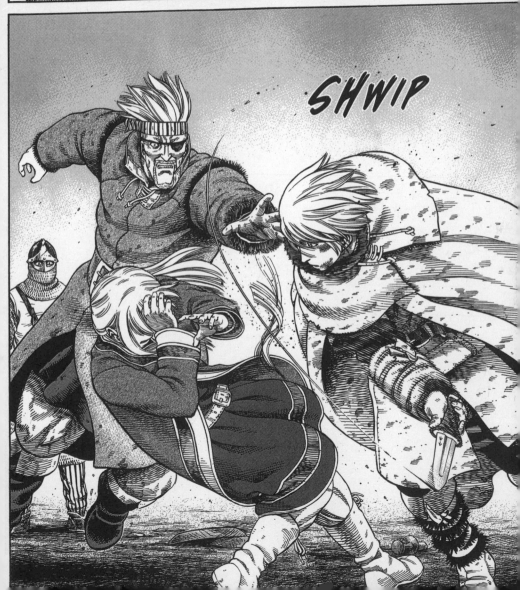

SHWIP

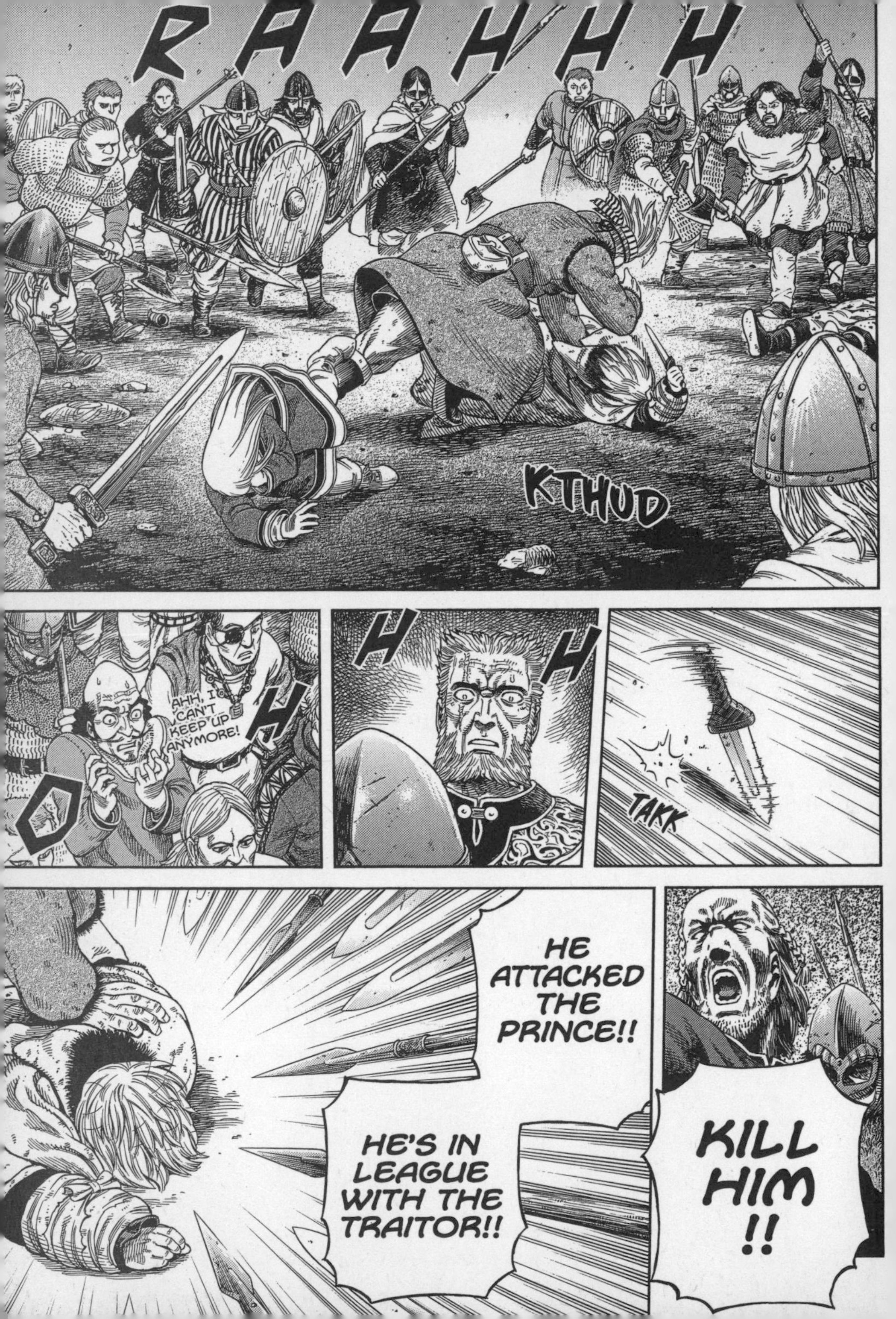
RAAHHH
KTHUD
TAKK
H H
AHH, I CAN'T KEEP UP ANYMORE!
H
KILL HIM!!
HE ATTACKED THE PRINCE!!
HE'S IN LEAGUE WITH THE TRAITOR!!

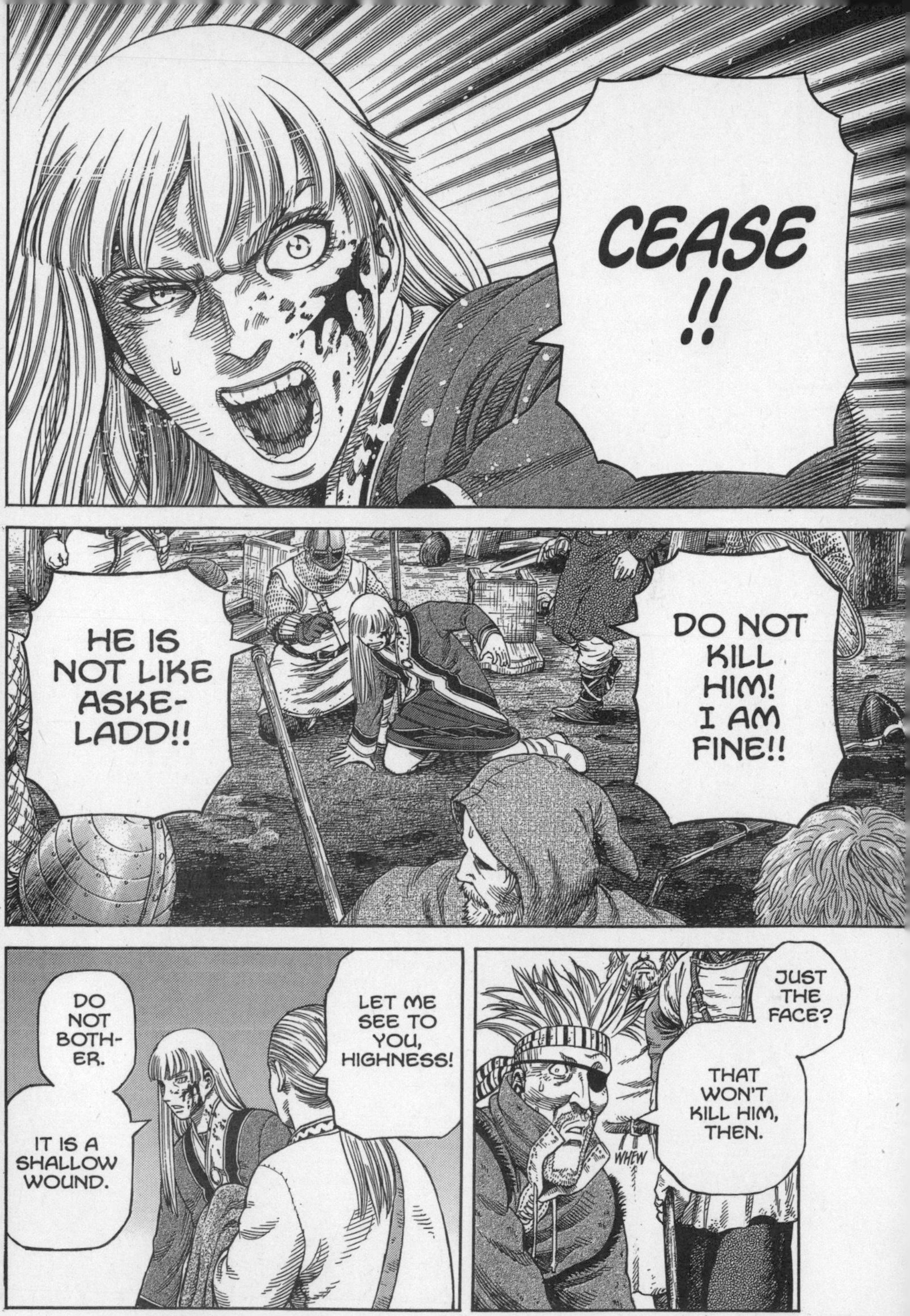
CEASE !!
DO NOT KILL HIM! I AM FINE!!
HE IS NOT LIKE ASKE-LADD!!
JUST THE FACE?
THAT WON'T KILL HIM, THEN.
WHEW
LET ME SEE TO YOU, HIGHNESS!
DO NOT BOTH-ER.
IT IS A SHALLOW WOUND.

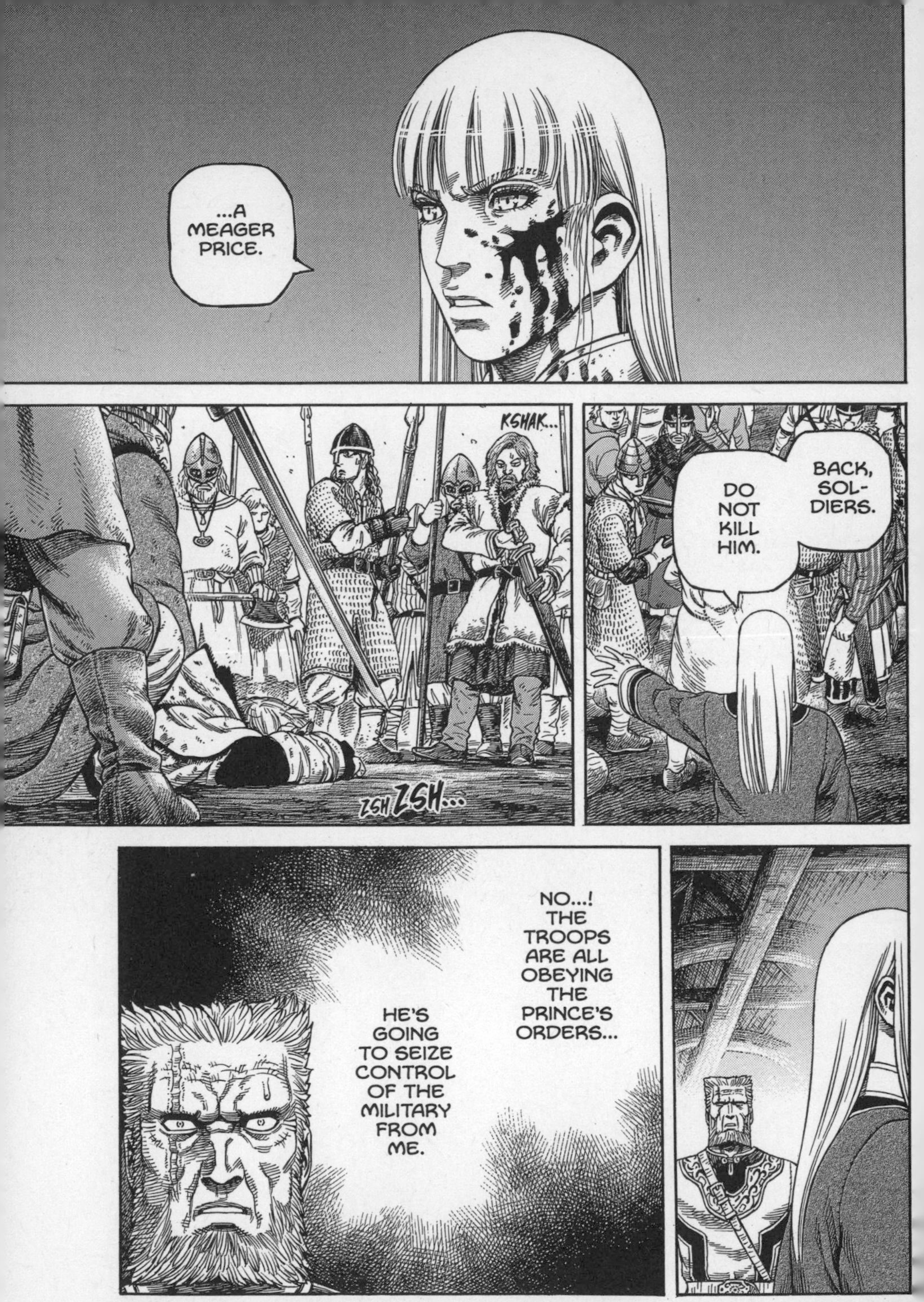
...A MEAGER PRICE.
BACK, SOLDIERS.
DO NOT KILL HIM.
KSHAK...
ZSH ZSH...
NO...! THE TROOPS ARE ALL OBEYING THE PRINCE'S ORDERS...
HE'S GOING TO SEIZE CONTROL OF THE MILITARY FROM ME.

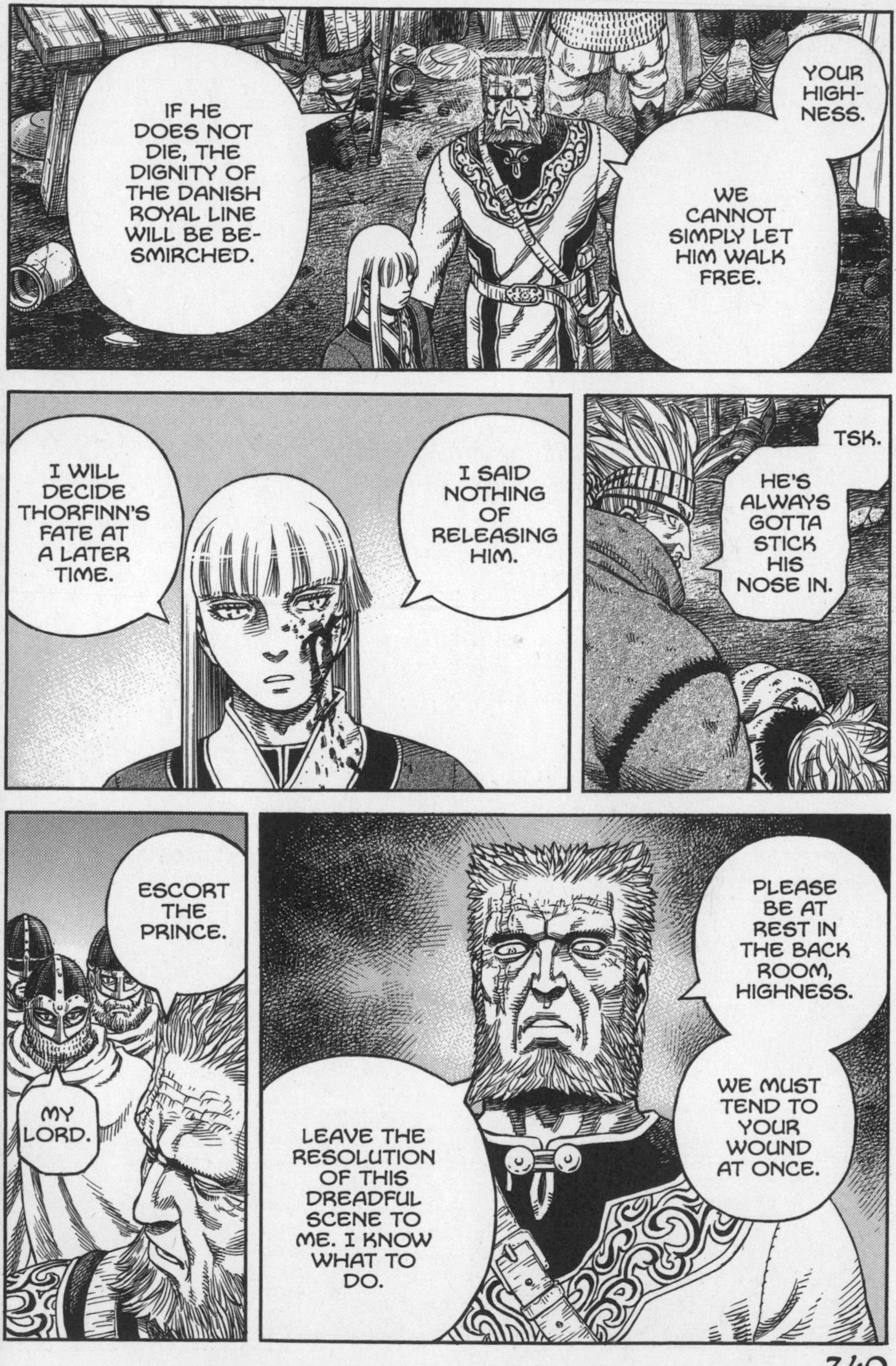
YOUR HIGHNESS.
WE CANNOT SIMPLY LET HIM WALK FREE.
IF HE DOES NOT DIE, THE DIGNITY OF THE DANISH ROYAL LINE WILL BE BE-SMIRCHED.
TSK.
HE'S ALWAYS GOTTA STICK HIS NOSE IN.
I SAID NOTHING OF RELEASING HIM.
I WILL DECIDE THORFINN'S FATE AT A LATER TIME.
PLEASE BE AT REST IN THE BACK ROOM, HIGHNESS.
WE MUST TEND TO YOUR WOUND AT ONCE.
LEAVE THE RESOLUTION OF THIS DREADFUL SCENE TO ME. I KNOW WHAT TO DO.
ESCORT THE PRINCE.
MY LORD.

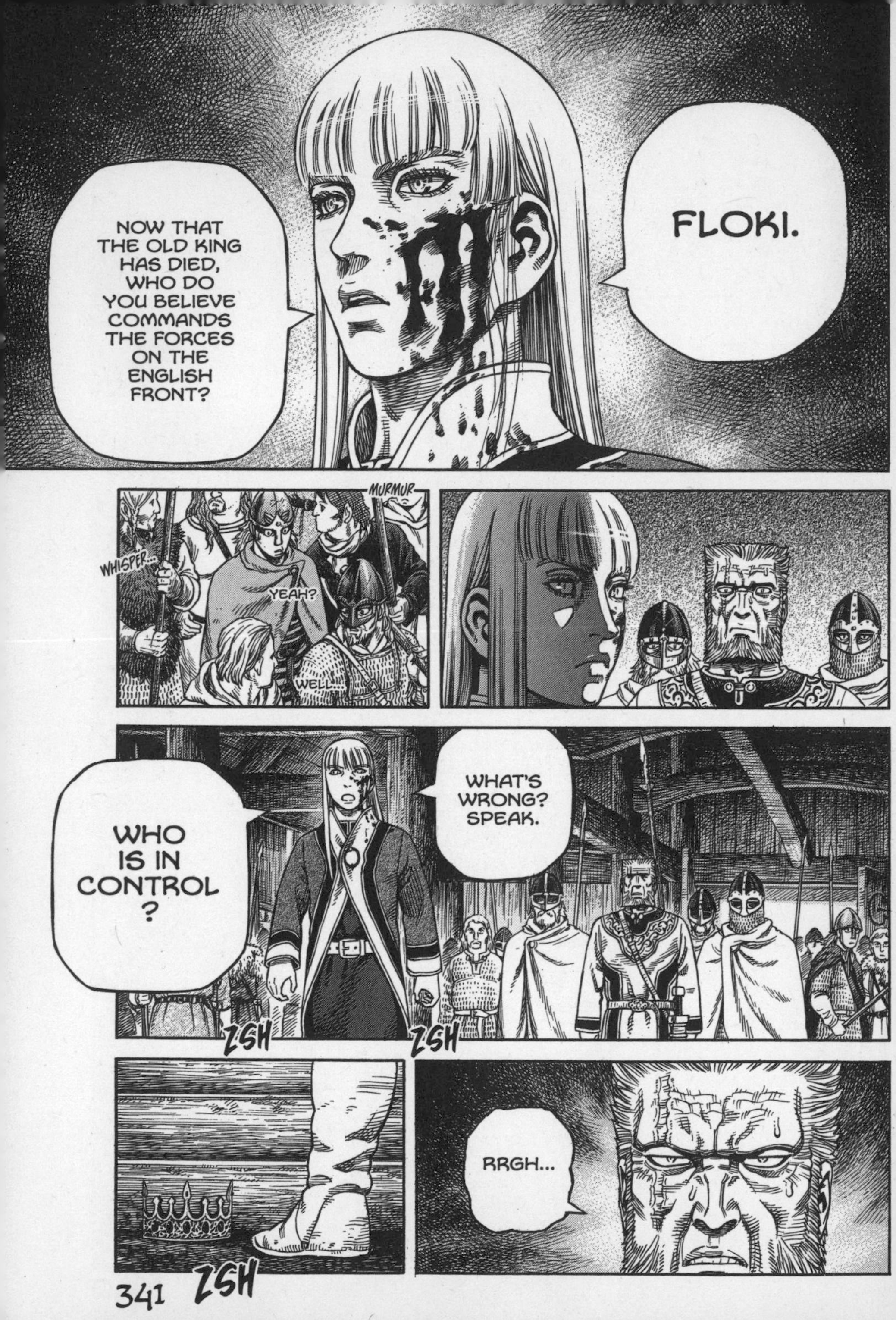
FLOKI.
NOW THAT THE OLD KING HAS DIED, WHO DO YOU BELIEVE COMMANDS THE FORCES ON THE ENGLISH FRONT?
MURMUR
WHISPER...
YEAH?
WELL...
WHAT'S WRONG? SPEAK.
WHO IS IN CONTROL ?
ZSH
ZSH
RRGH...
ZSH

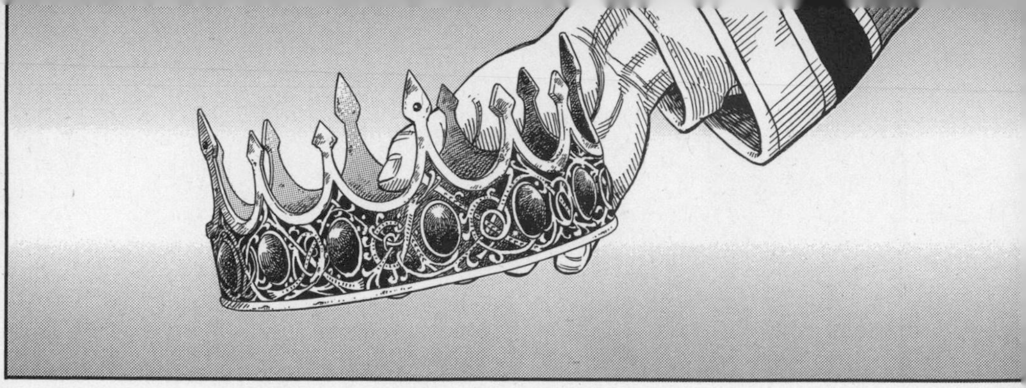
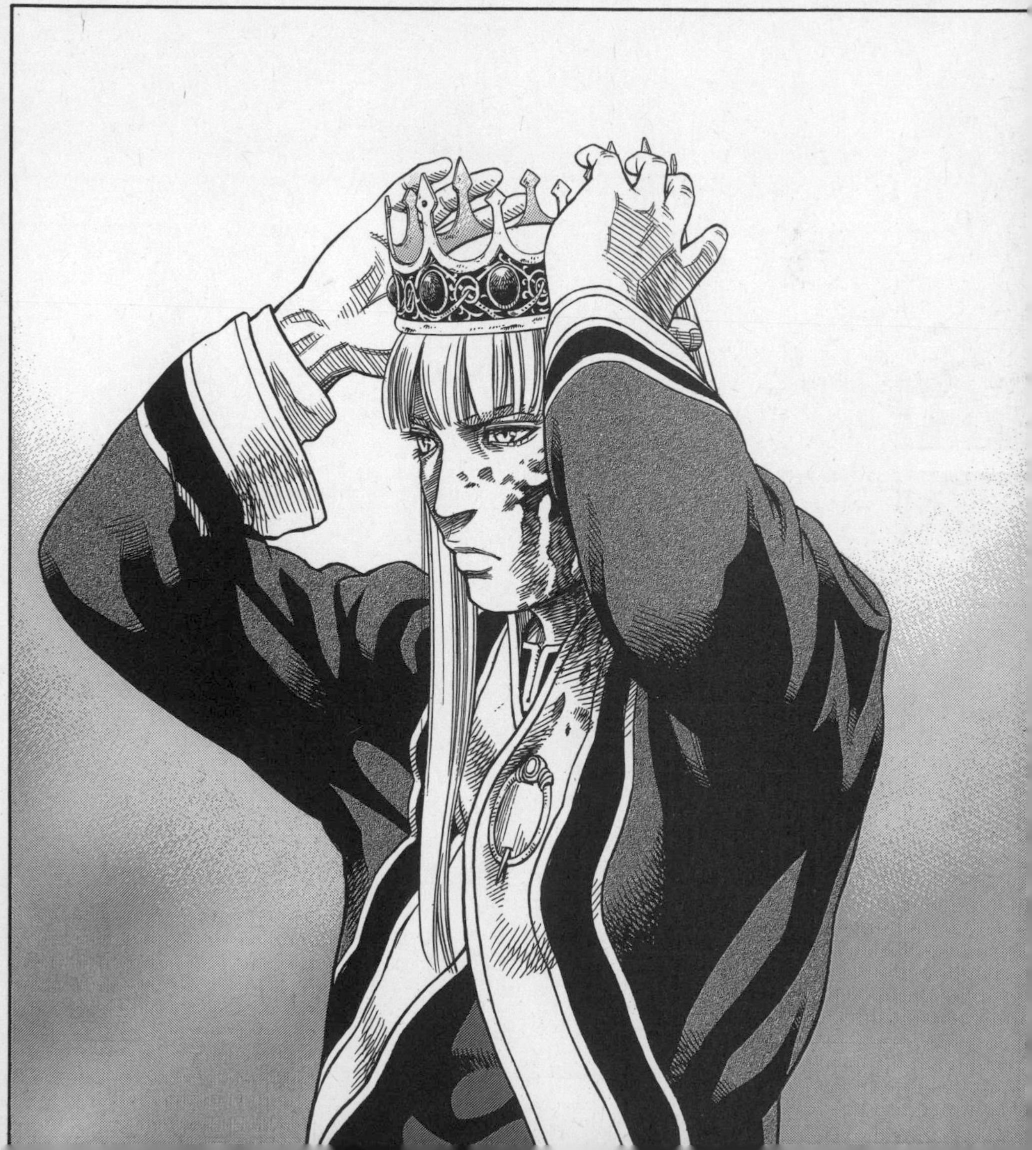

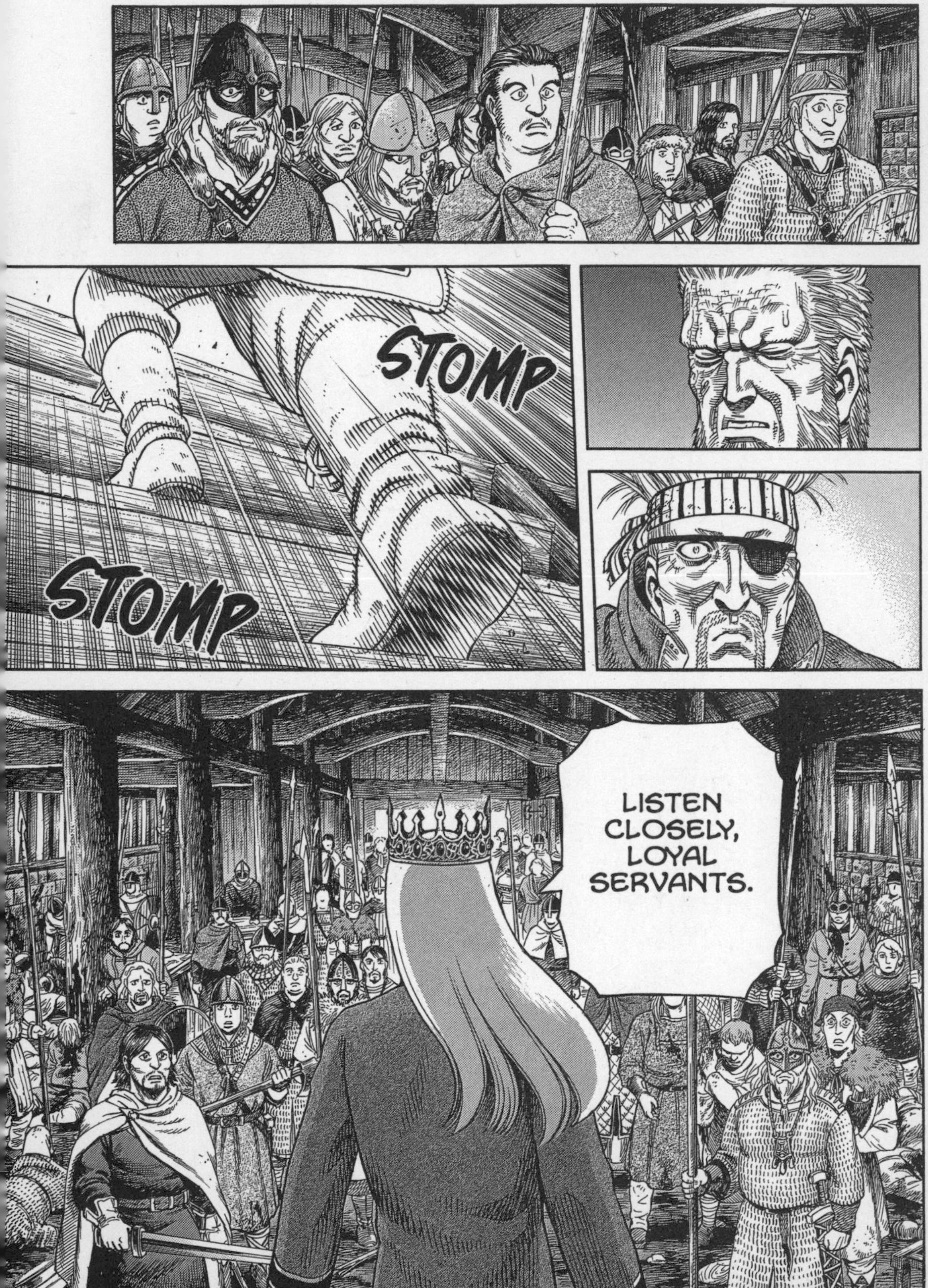
STOMP
STOMP
LISTEN CLOSELY, LOYAL SERVANTS.

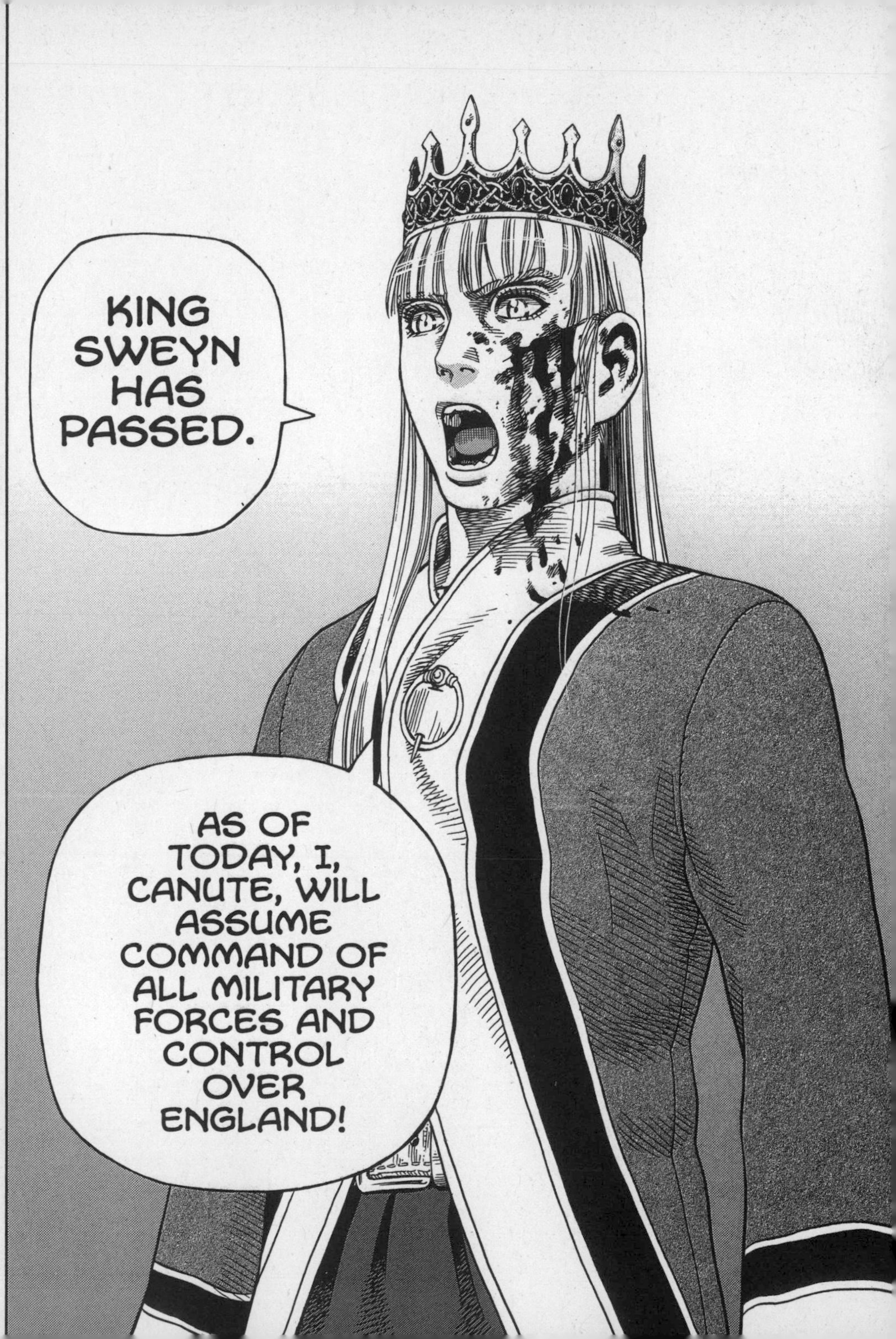
KING SWEYN HAS PASSED.
AS OF TODAY, I, CANUTE, WILL ASSUME COMMAND OF ALL MILITARY FORCES AND CONTROL OVER ENGLAND!

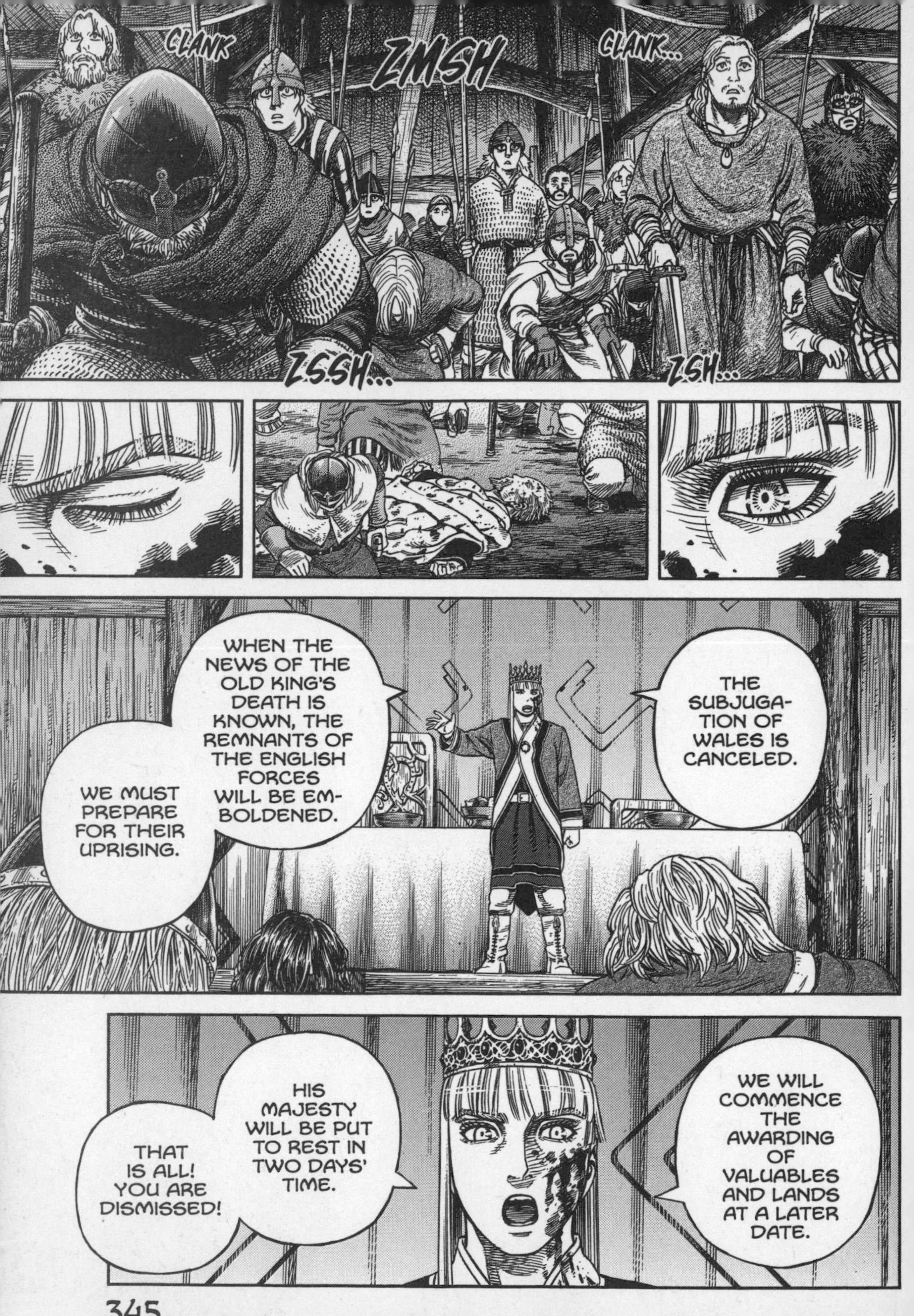
CLANK...
ZMSH
CLANK
ZSH...
ZSSH...
THE SUBJUGATION OF WALES IS CANCELED.
WHEN THE NEWS OF THE OLD KING'S DEATH IS KNOWN, THE REMNANTS OF THE ENGLISH FORCES WILL BE EMBOLDENED.
WE MUST PREPARE FOR THEIR UPRISING.
WE WILL COMMENCE THE AWARDING OF VALUABLES AND LANDS AT A LATER DATE.
HIS MAJESTY WILL BE PUT TO REST IN TWO DAYS' TIME.
THAT IS ALL! YOU ARE DISMISSED!

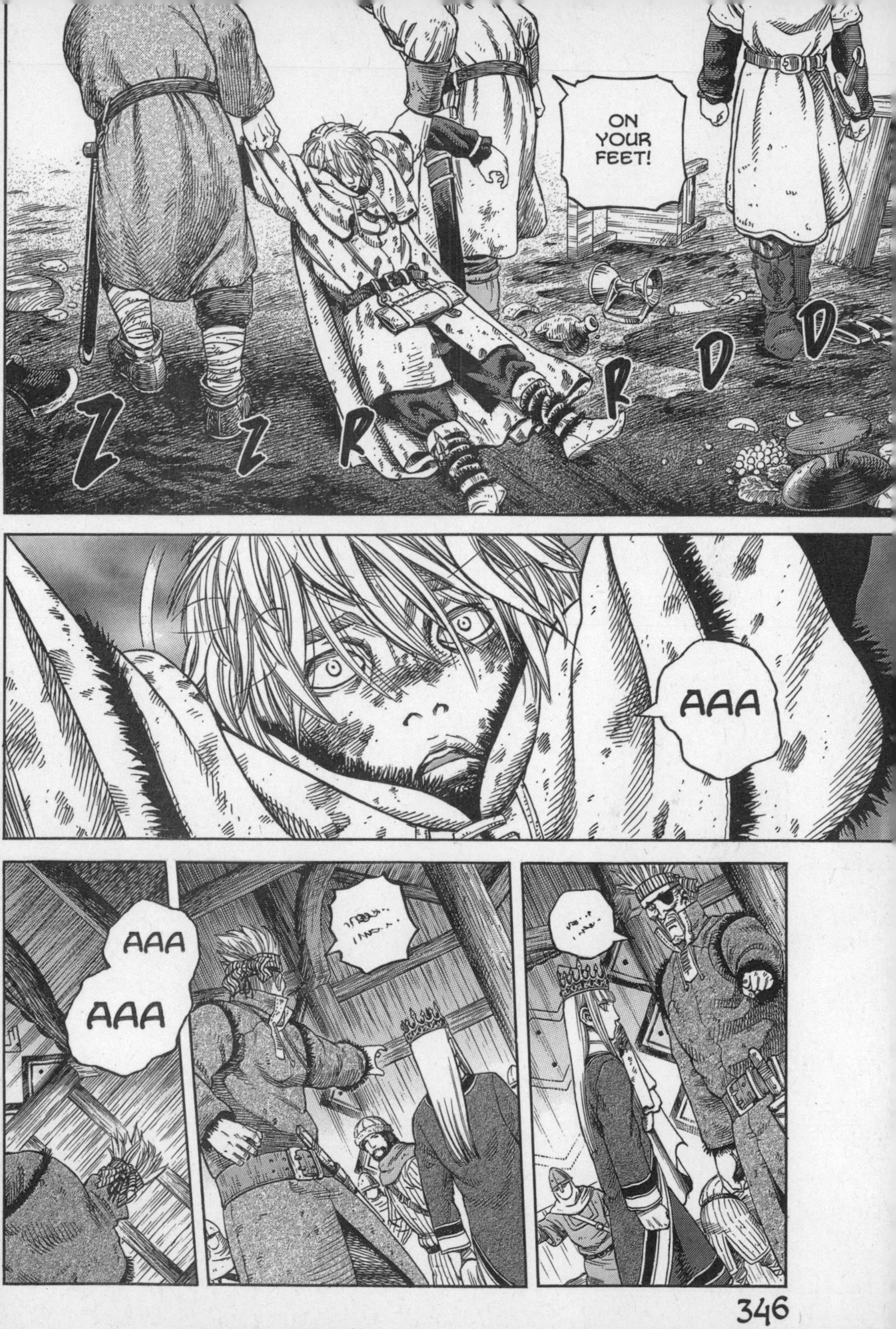
ON YOUR FEET!
ZZRRDD
AAA
AAA
AAA

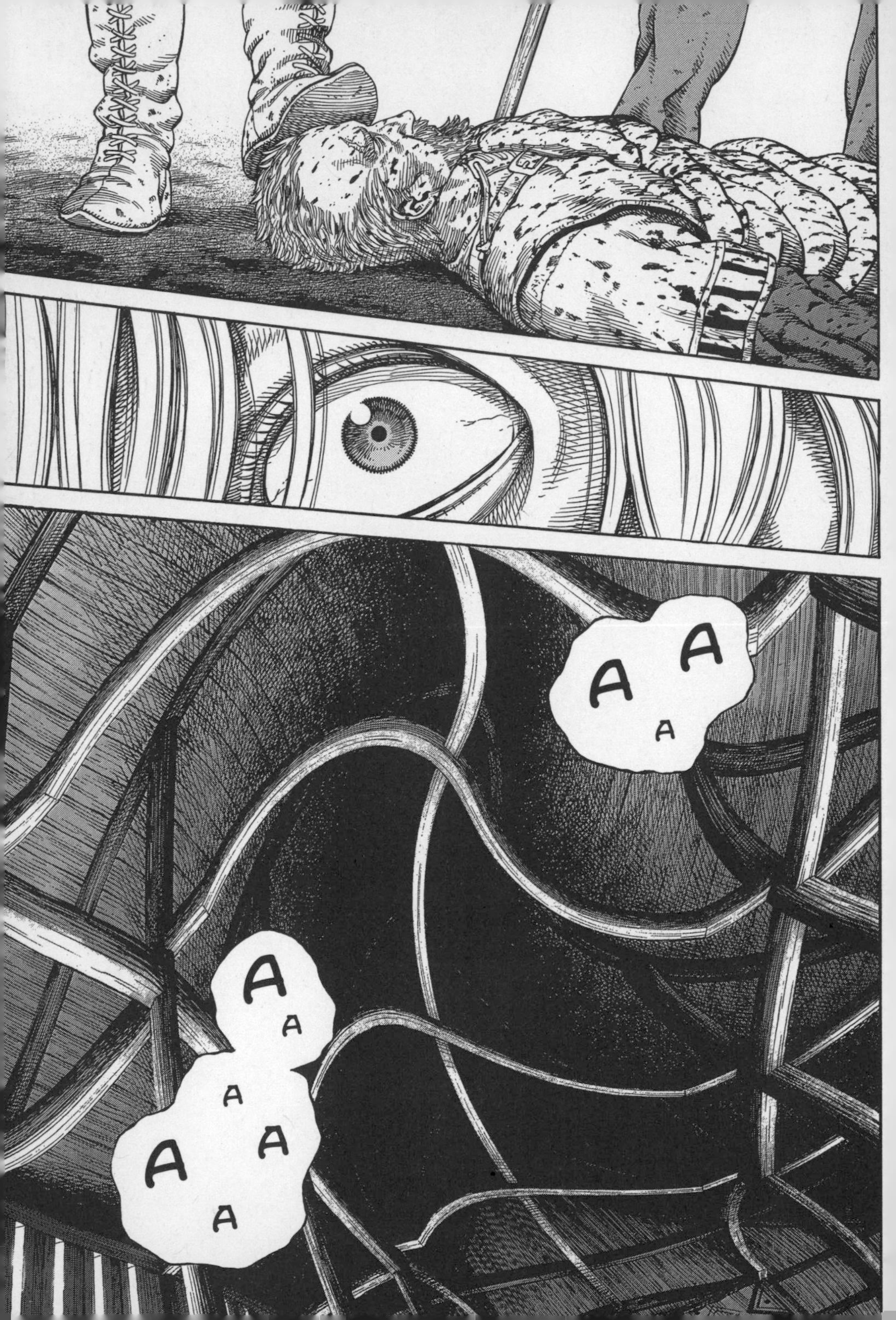
AAA
AA
AAAA

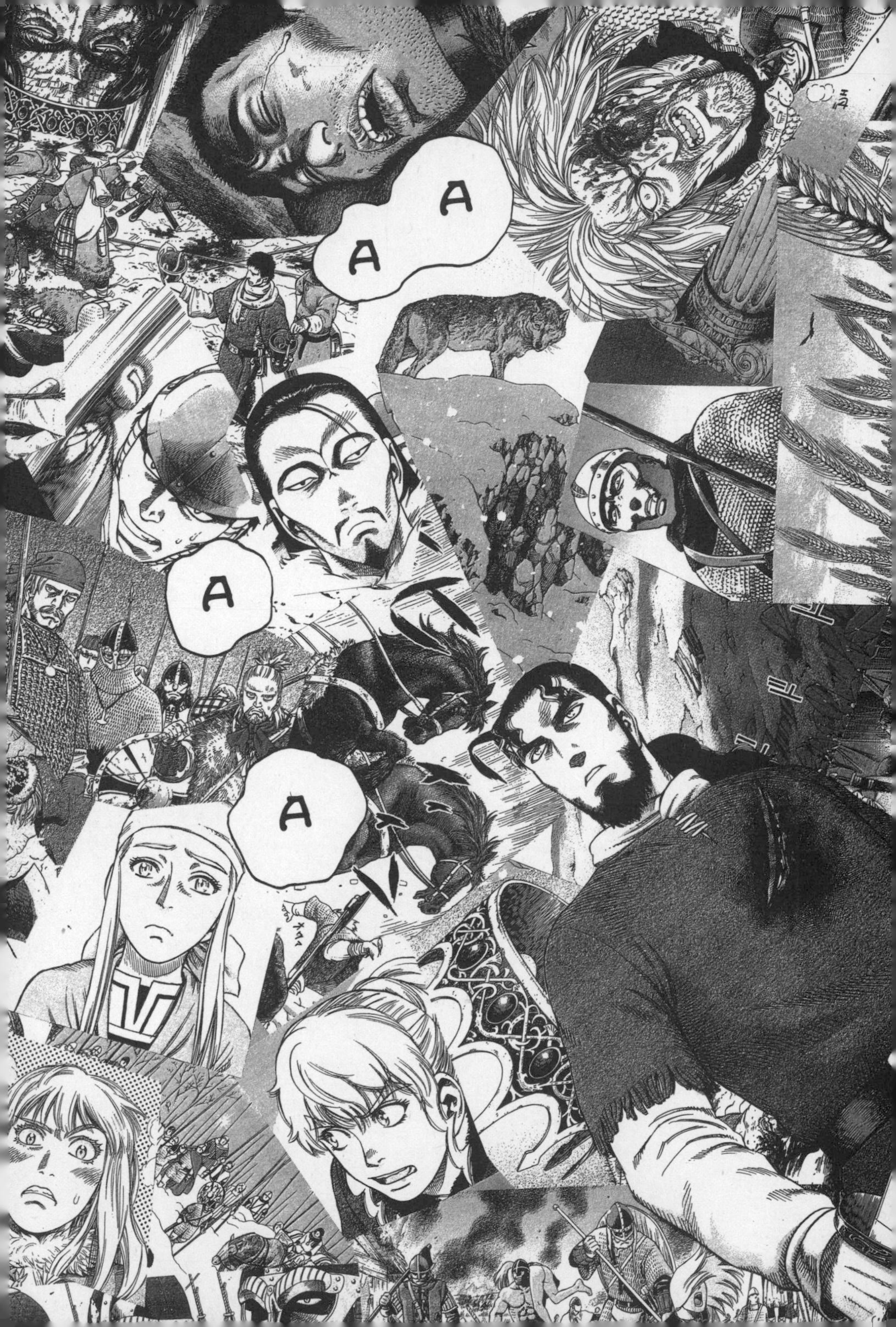
A A
A
A

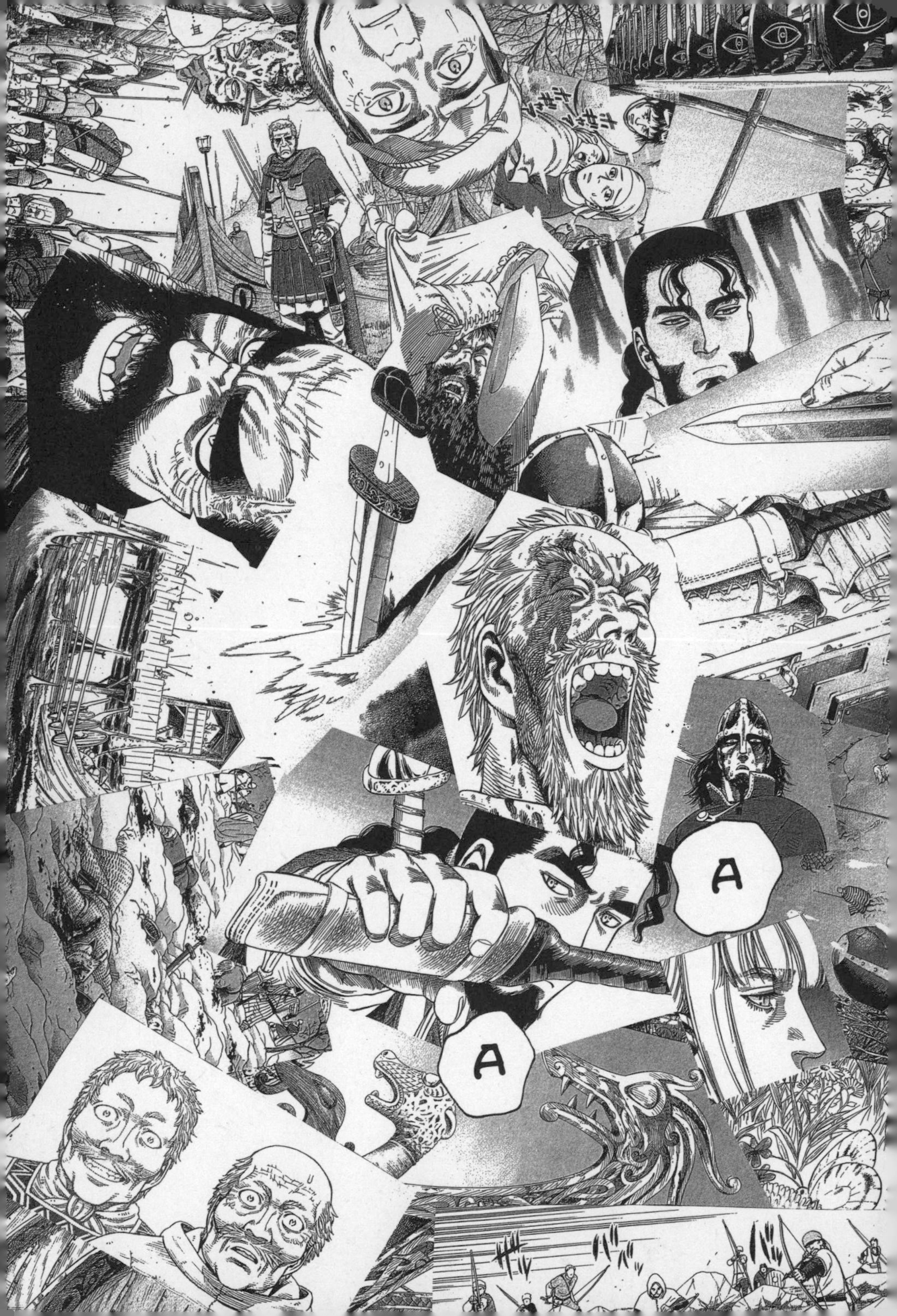
A
A

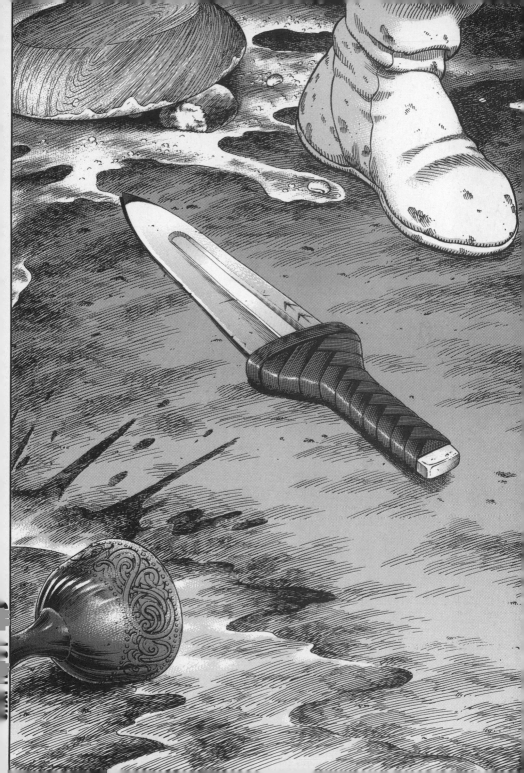

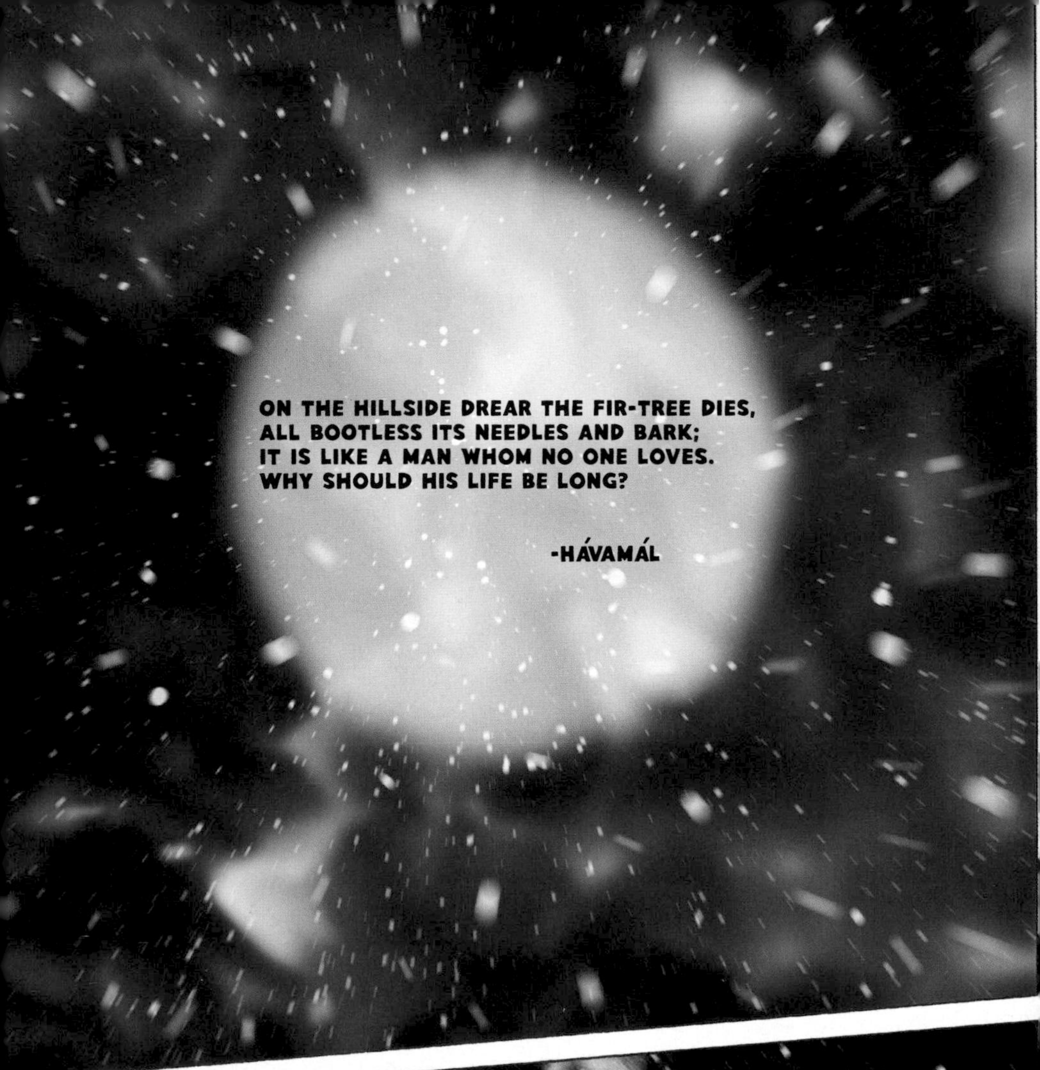
ON THE HILLSIDE DREAR THE FIR-TREE DIES,
ALL BOOTLESS ITS NEEDLES AND BARK;
IT IS LIKE A MAN WHOM NO ONE LOVES.
WHY SHOULD HIS LIFE BE LONG?
-HÁVAMÁL

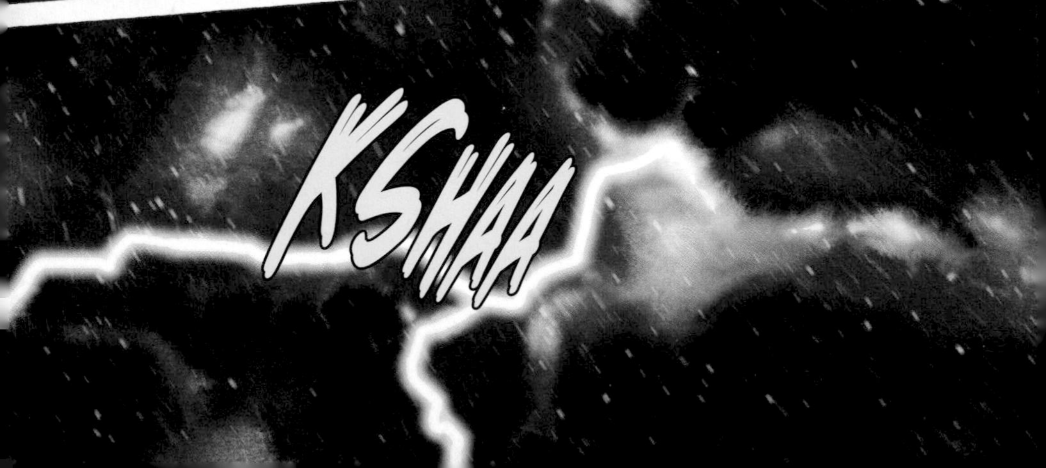
KSHAA

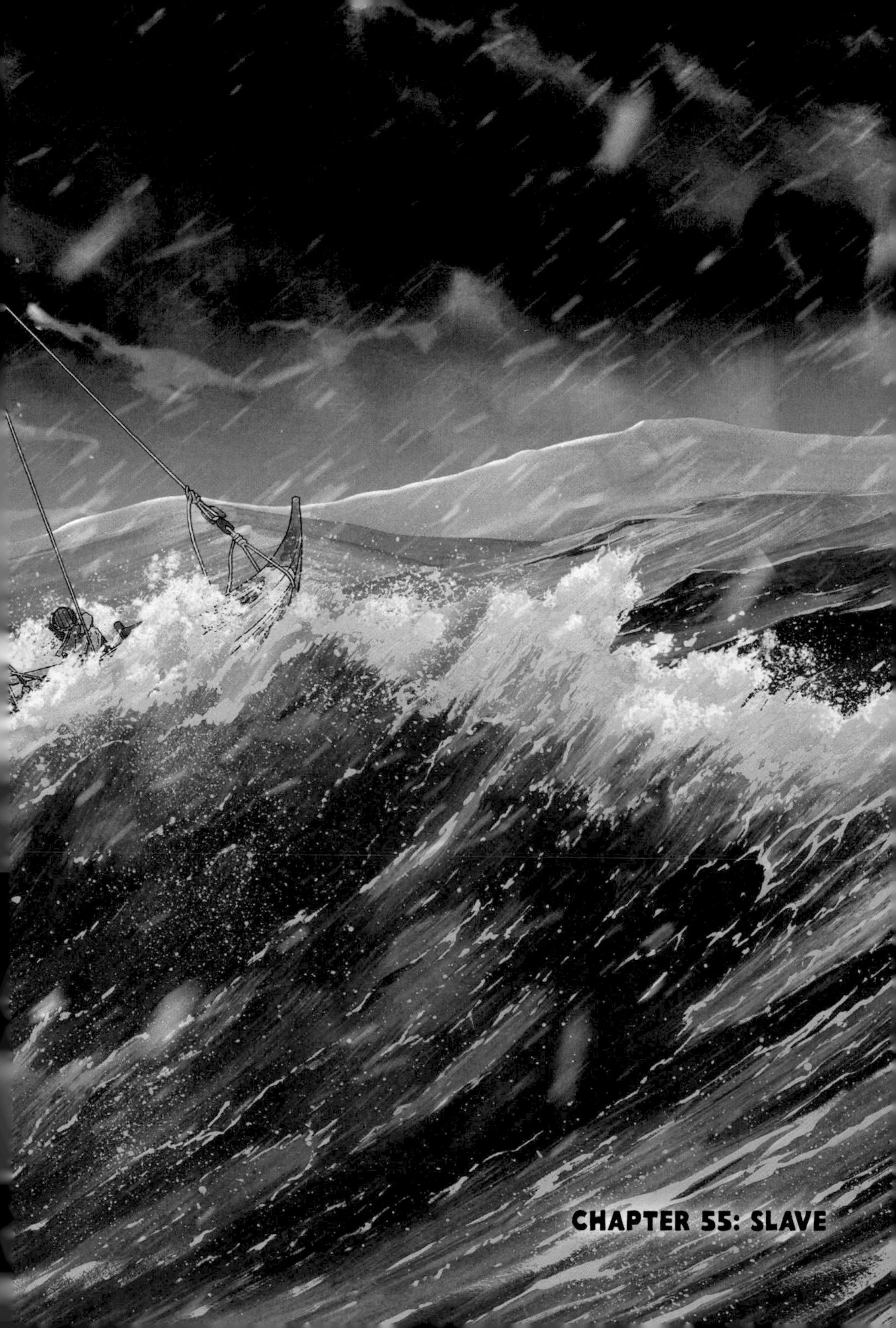
CHAPTER 55: SLAVE

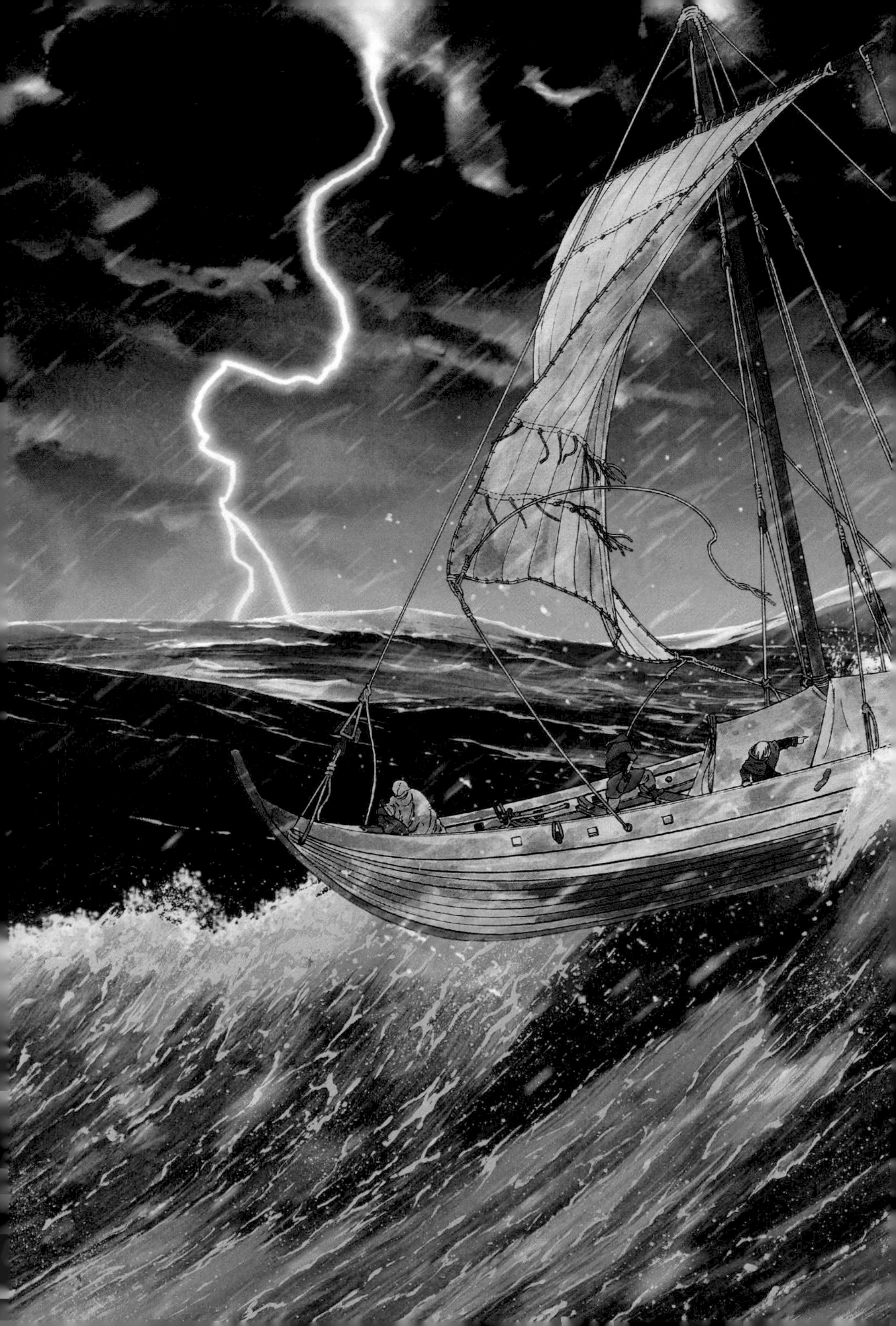

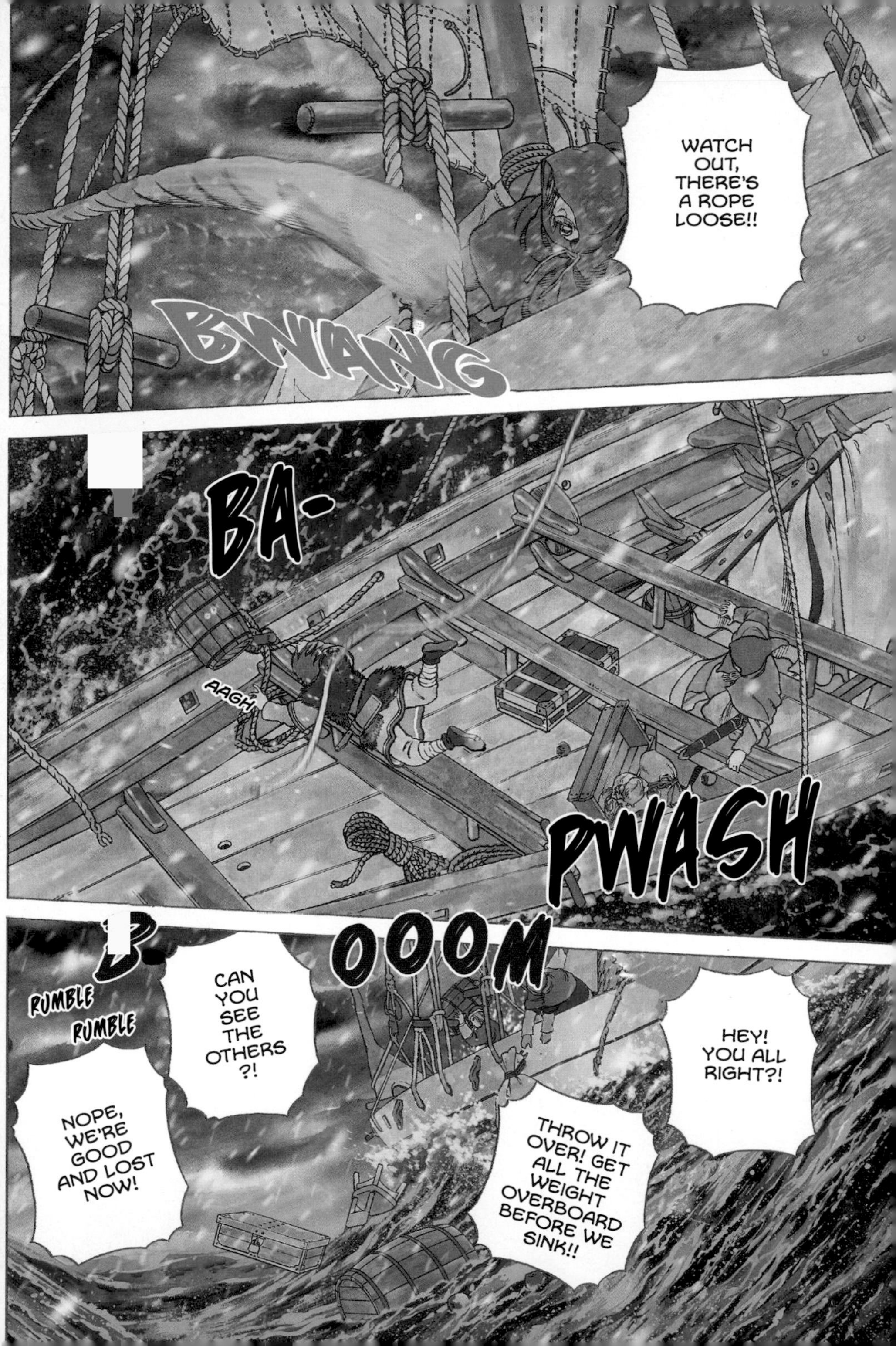
WATCH OUT, THERE'S A ROPE LOOSE!!
BWANG
BA-
AAGH
PWASH
BOOOM
HEY! YOU ALL RIGHT?!
THROW IT OVER! GET ALL THE WEIGHT OVERBOARD BEFORE WE SINK!!
CAN YOU SEE THE OTHERS?!
NOPE, WE'RE GOOD AND LOST NOW!
RUMBLE RUMBLE

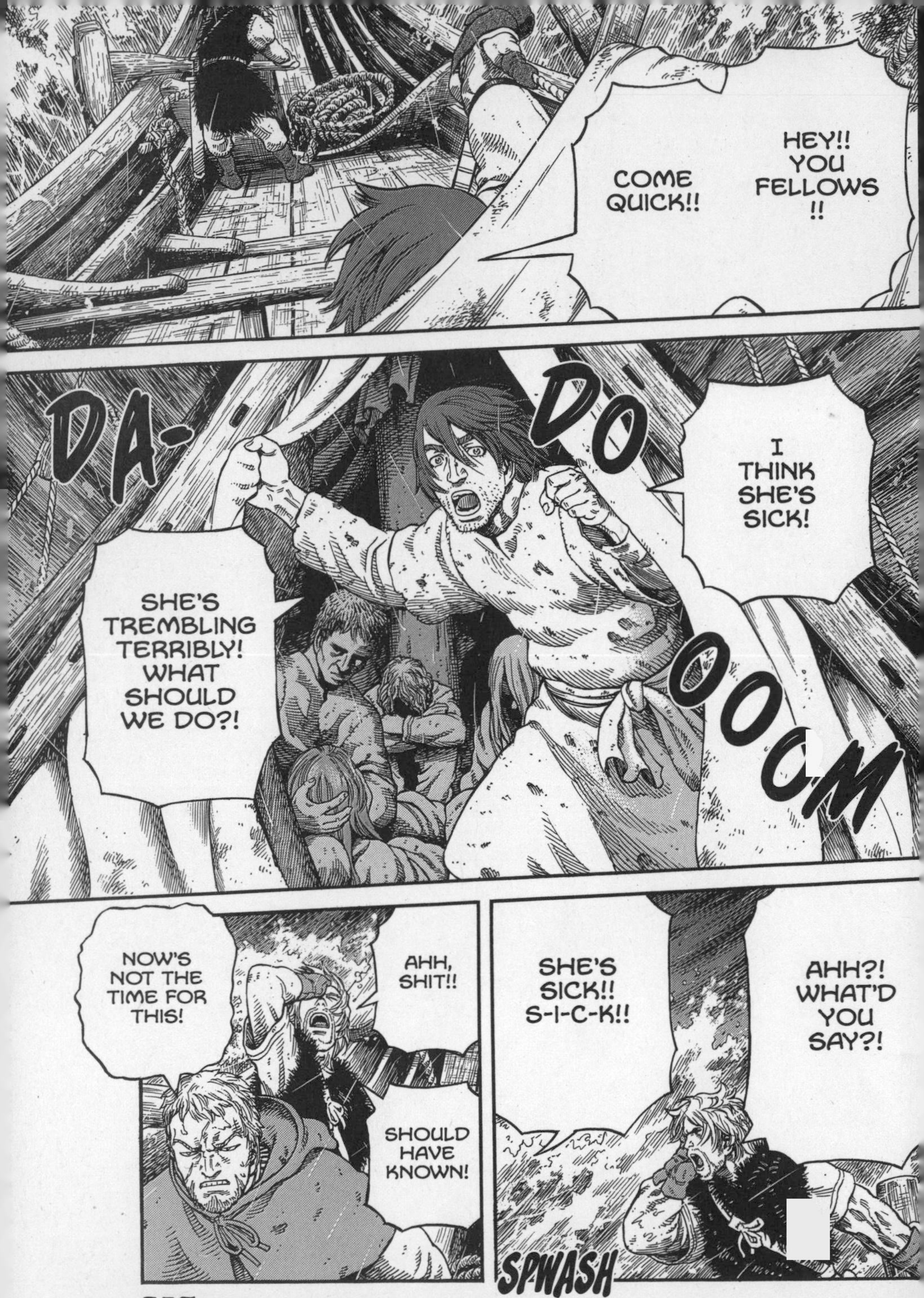
HEY!! YOU FELLOWS !!
COME QUICK!!
I THINK SHE'S SICK!
DA-DOOOOM
SHE'S TREMBLING TERRIBLY! WHAT SHOULD WE DO?!
AHH?! WHAT'D YOU SAY?!
SHE'S SICK!! S-I-C-K!!
SPWASH
AHH, SHIT!!
NOW'S NOT THE TIME FOR THIS!
SHOULD HAVE KNOWN!

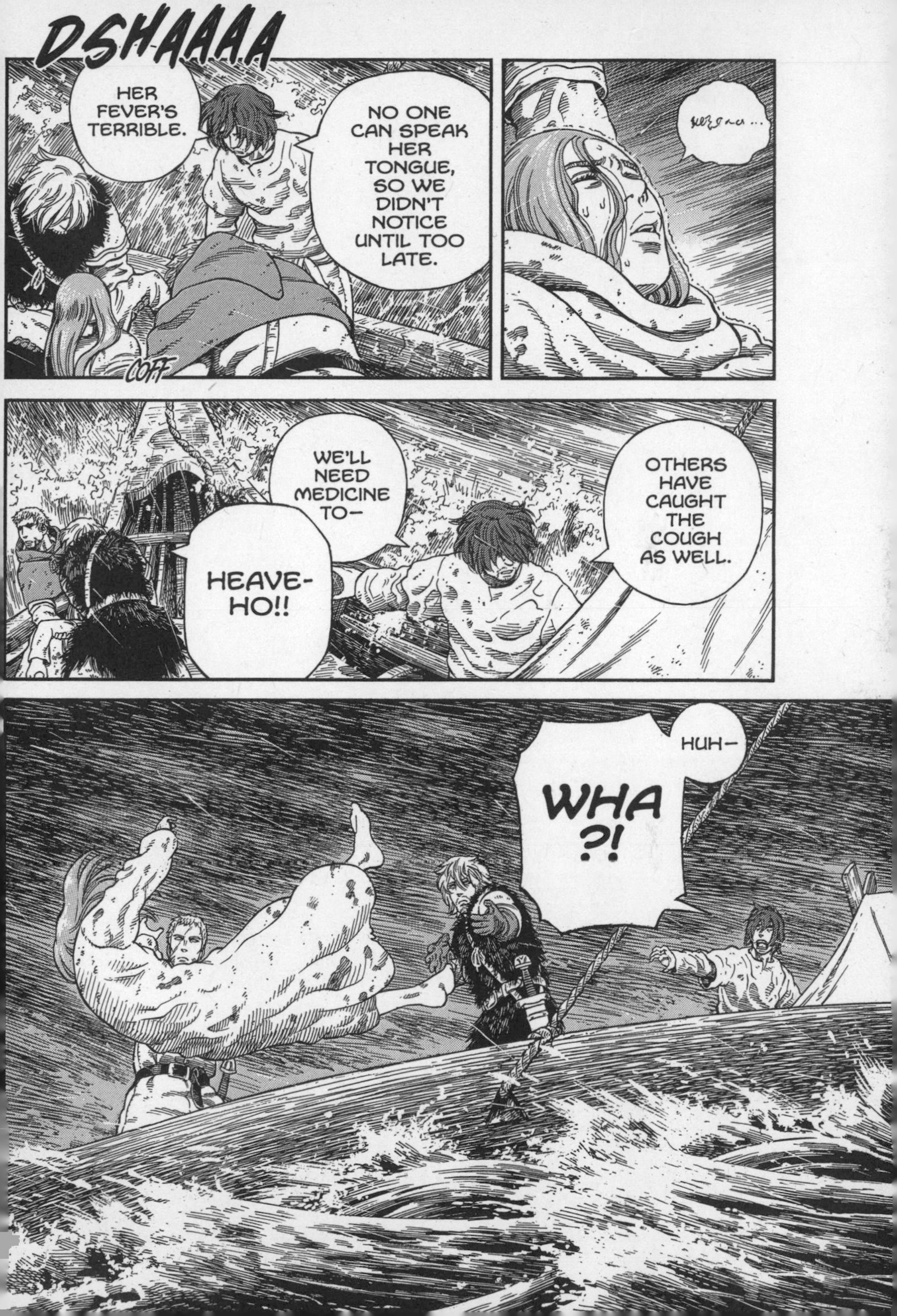
NO ONE CAN SPEAK HER TONGUE, SO WE DIDN'T NOTICE UNTIL TOO LATE.
DSHAAAA
HER FEVER'S TERRIBLE.
COFF
OTHERS HAVE CAUGHT THE COUGH AS WELL.
WE'LL NEED MEDICINE TO—
HEAVE-HO!!
HUH—
WHA ?!

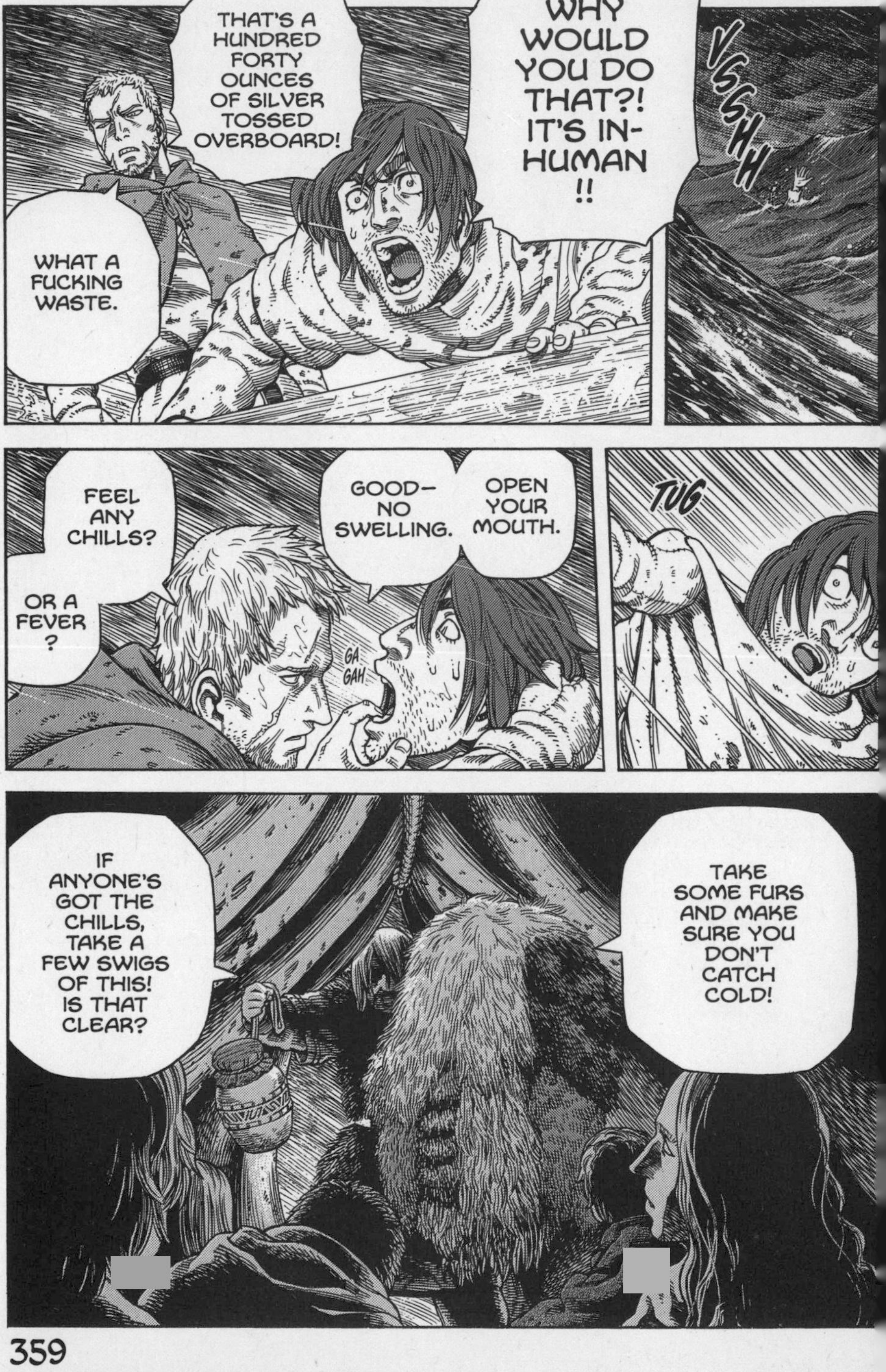
VSSHH
WHY WOULD YOU DO THAT?! IT'S IN-HUMAN !!
THAT'S A HUNDRED FORTY OUNCES OF SILVER TOSSED OVERBOARD!
WHAT A FUCKING WASTE.
TUG
OPEN YOUR MOUTH.
GOOD— NO SWELLING.
GA GAH
FEEL ANY CHILLS?
OR A FEVER ?
TAKE SOME FURS AND MAKE SURE YOU DON'T CATCH COLD!
IF ANYONE'S GOT THE CHILLS, TAKE A FEW SWIGS OF THIS! IS THAT CLEAR?

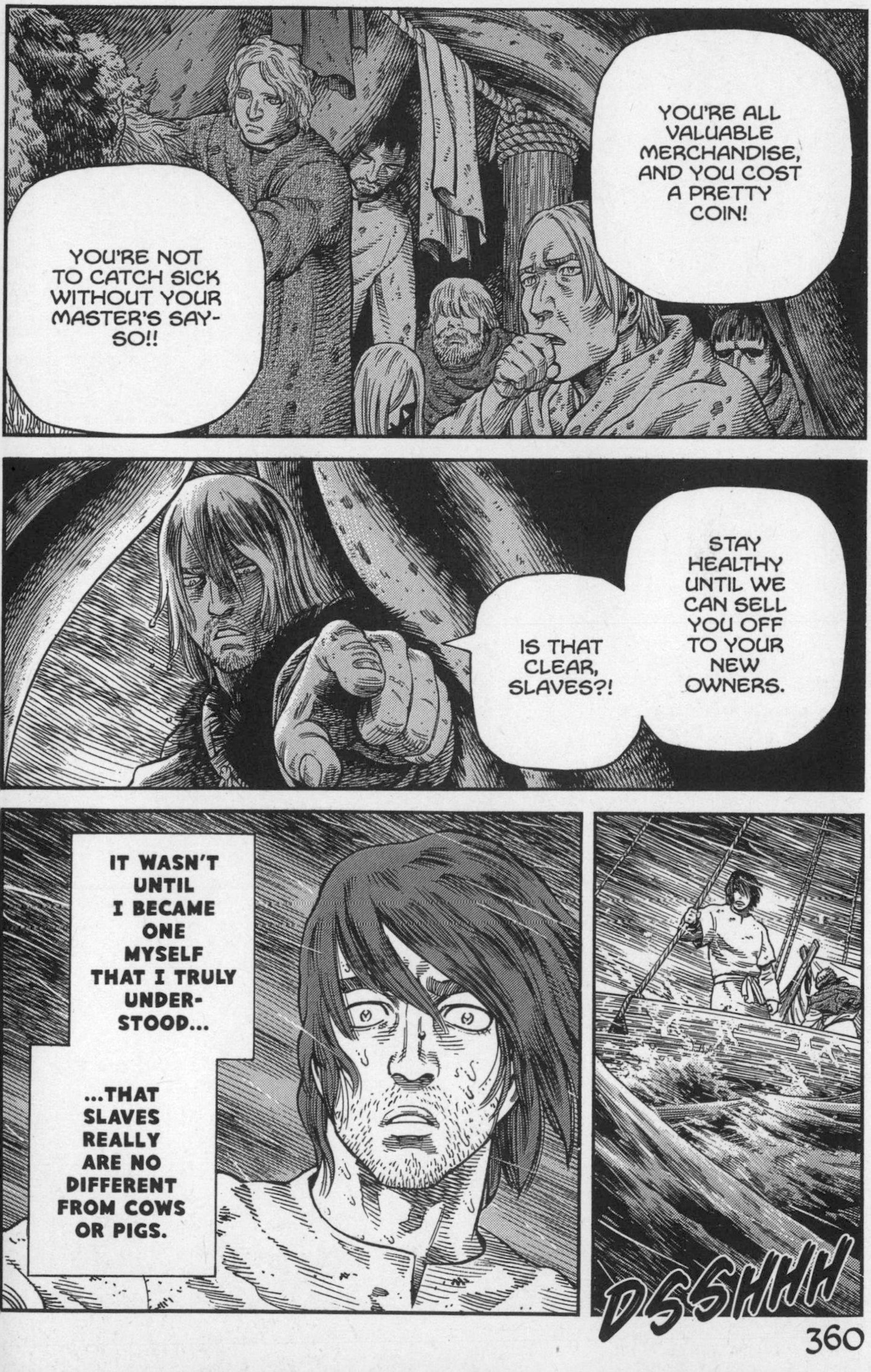
YOU'RE ALL VALUABLE MERCHANDISE, AND YOU COST A PRETTY COIN!
YOU'RE NOT TO CATCH SICK WITHOUT YOUR MASTER'S SAY-SO!!
STAY HEALTHY UNTIL WE CAN SELL YOU OFF TO YOUR NEW OWNERS.
IS THAT CLEAR, SLAVES?!
DSSHHH
IT WASN'T UNTIL I BECAME ONE MYSELF THAT I TRULY UNDER-STOOD...
...THAT SLAVES REALLY ARE NO DIFFERENT FROM COWS OR PIGS.

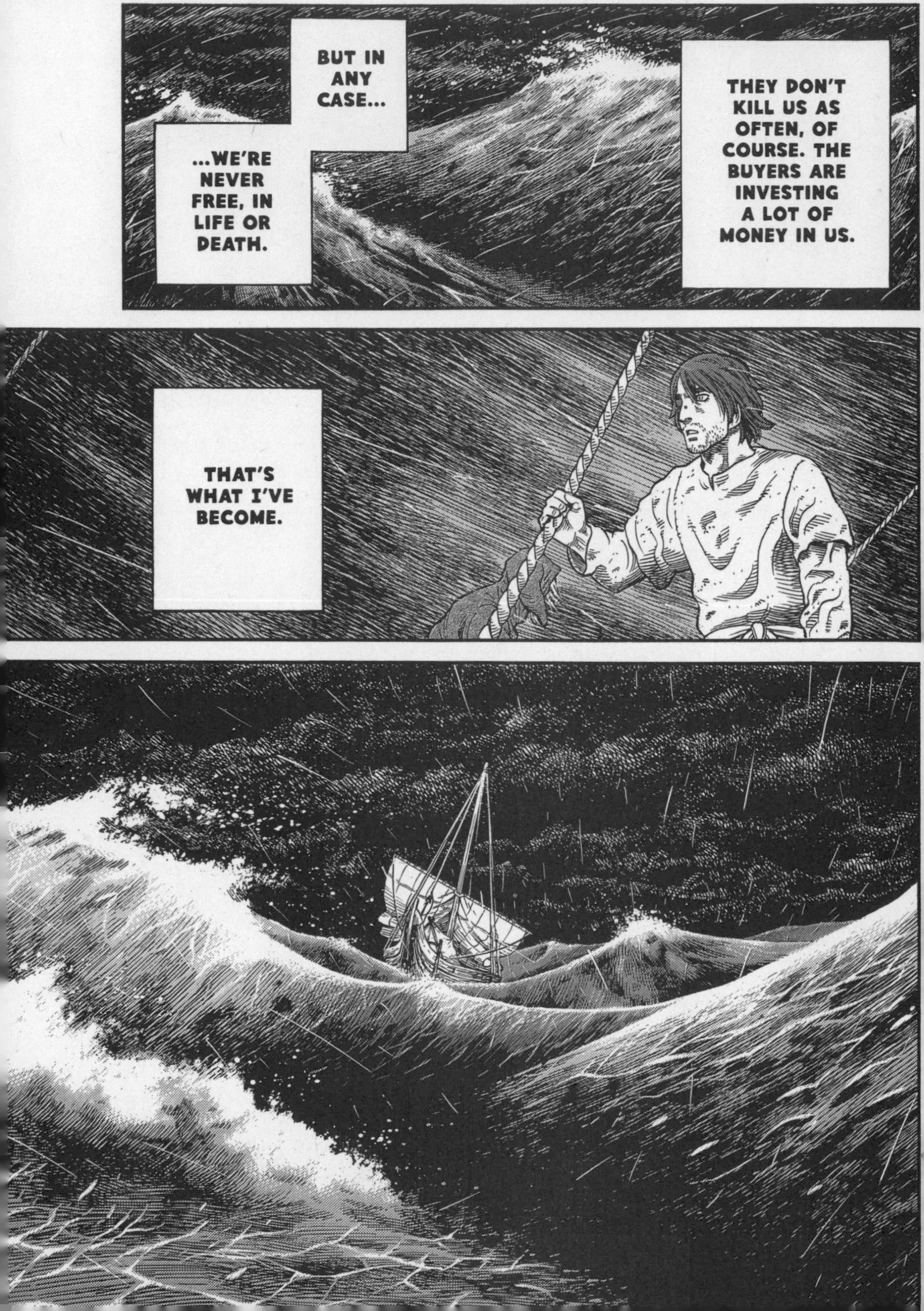
THEY DON'T KILL US AS OFTEN, OF COURSE. THE BUYERS ARE INVESTING A LOT OF MONEY IN US.
BUT IN ANY CASE...
...WE'RE NEVER FREE, IN LIFE OR DEATH.
THAT'S WHAT I'VE BECOME.

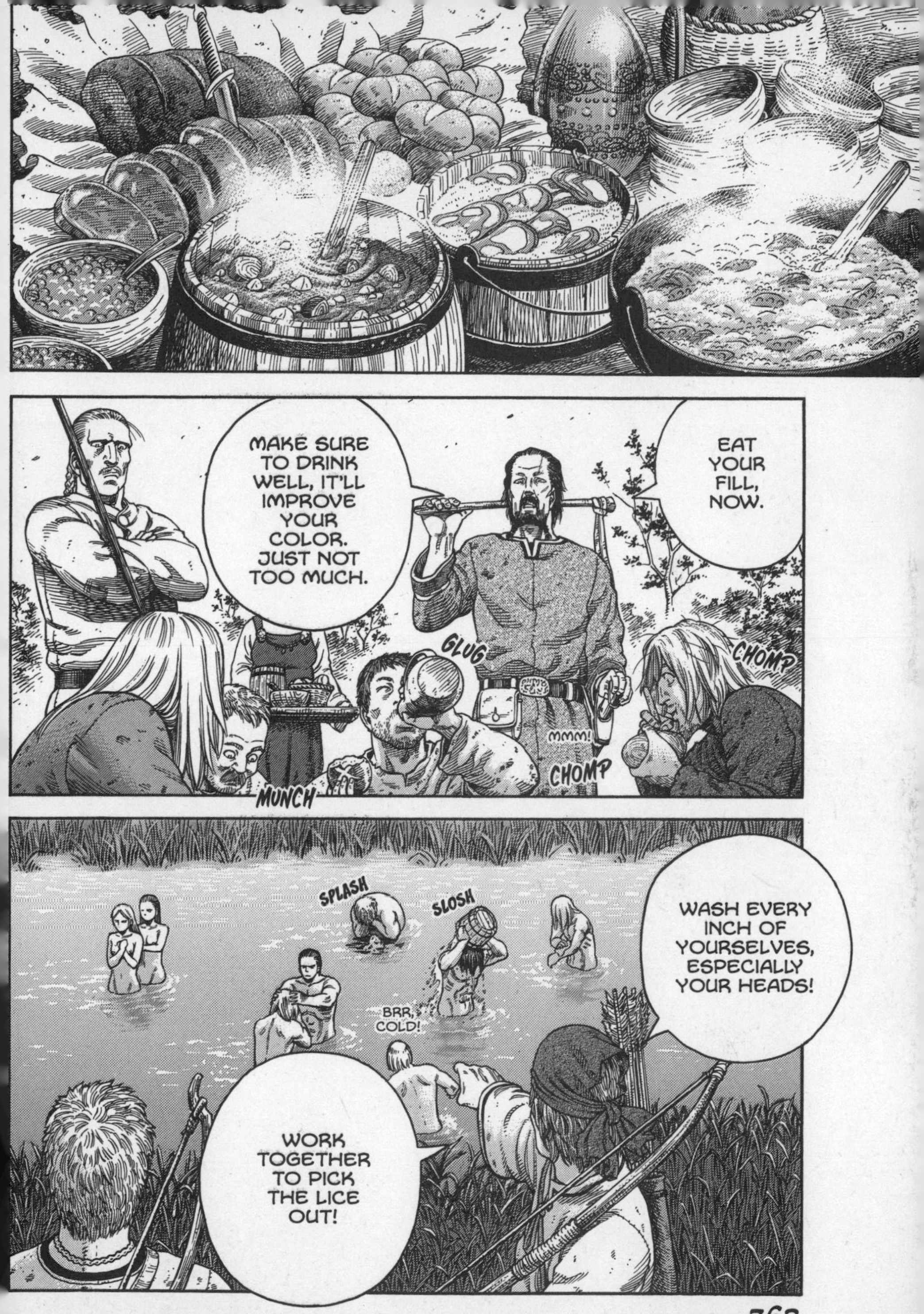
EAT YOUR FILL, NOW.
MAKE SURE TO DRINK WELL, IT'LL IMPROVE YOUR COLOR. JUST NOT TOO MUCH.
CHOMP
GLUG
MMM!
CHOMP
MUNCH
WASH EVERY INCH OF YOURSELVES, ESPECIALLY YOUR HEADS!
SLOSH
SPLASH
BRR, COLD!
WORK TOGETHER TO PICK THE LICE OUT!

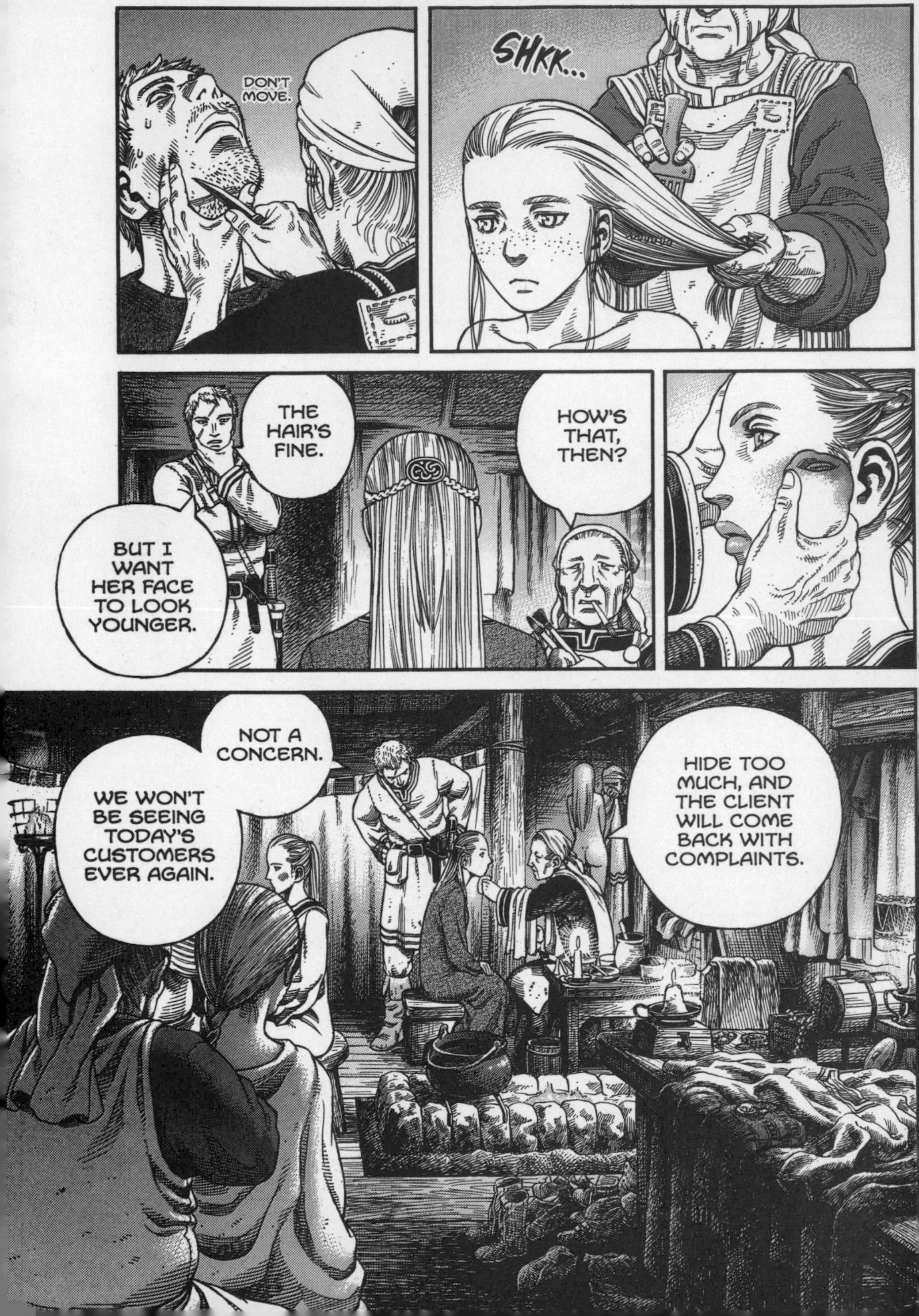
SHKK...
DON'T MOVE.
HOW'S THAT, THEN?
THE HAIR'S FINE.
BUT I WANT HER FACE TO LOOK YOUNGER.
HIDE TOO MUCH, AND THE CLIENT WILL COME BACK WITH COMPLAINTS.
NOT A CONCERN.
WE WON'T BE SEEING TODAY'S CUSTOMERS EVER AGAIN.

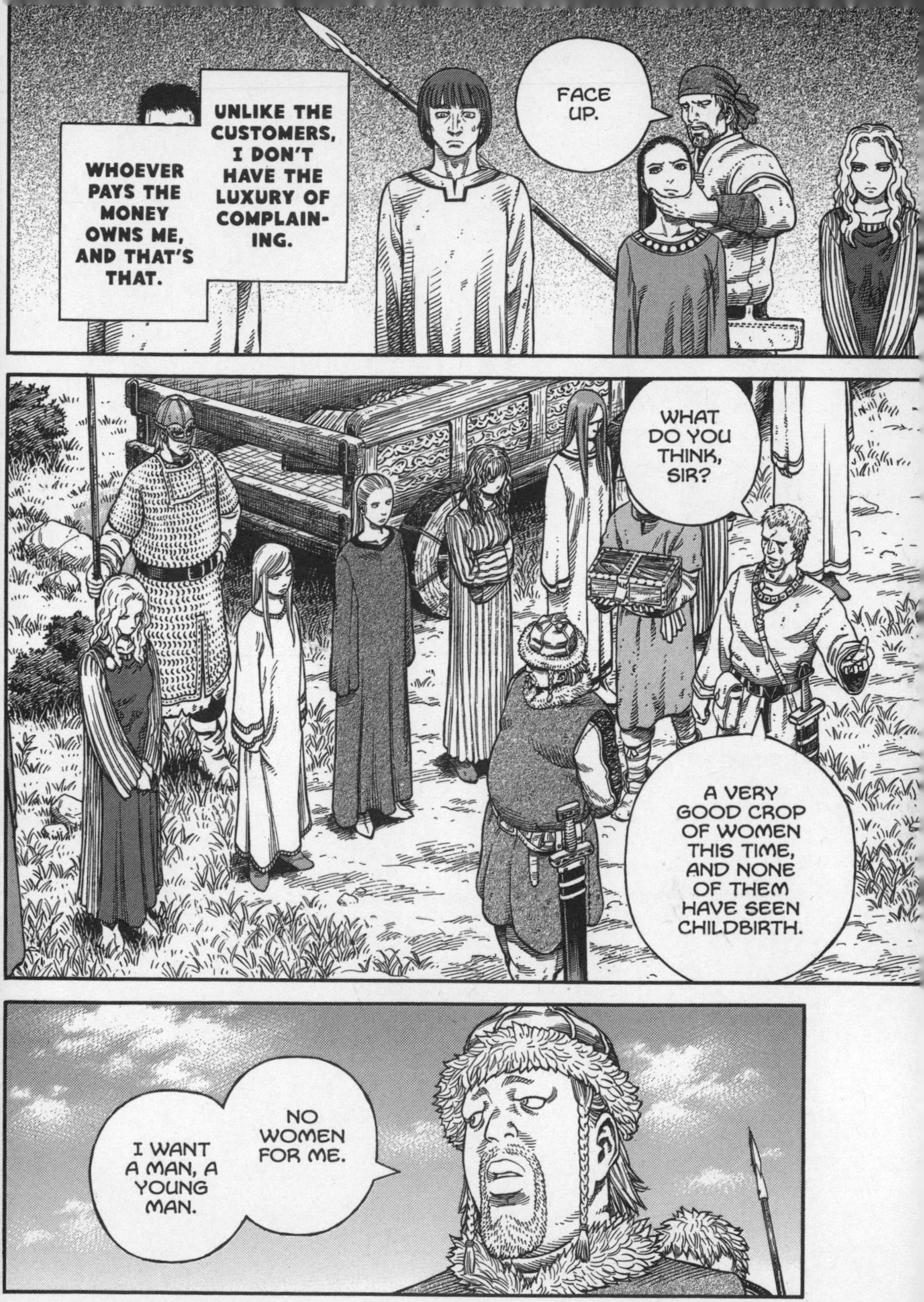
FACE UP.
UNLIKE THE CUSTOMERS, I DON'T HAVE THE LUXURY OF COMPLAIN-ING.
WHOEVER PAYS THE MONEY OWNS ME, AND THAT'S THAT.
WHAT DO YOU THINK, SIR?
A VERY GOOD CROP OF WOMEN THIS TIME, AND NONE OF THEM HAVE SEEN CHILDBIRTH.
NO WOMEN FOR ME.
I WANT A MAN, A YOUNG MAN.

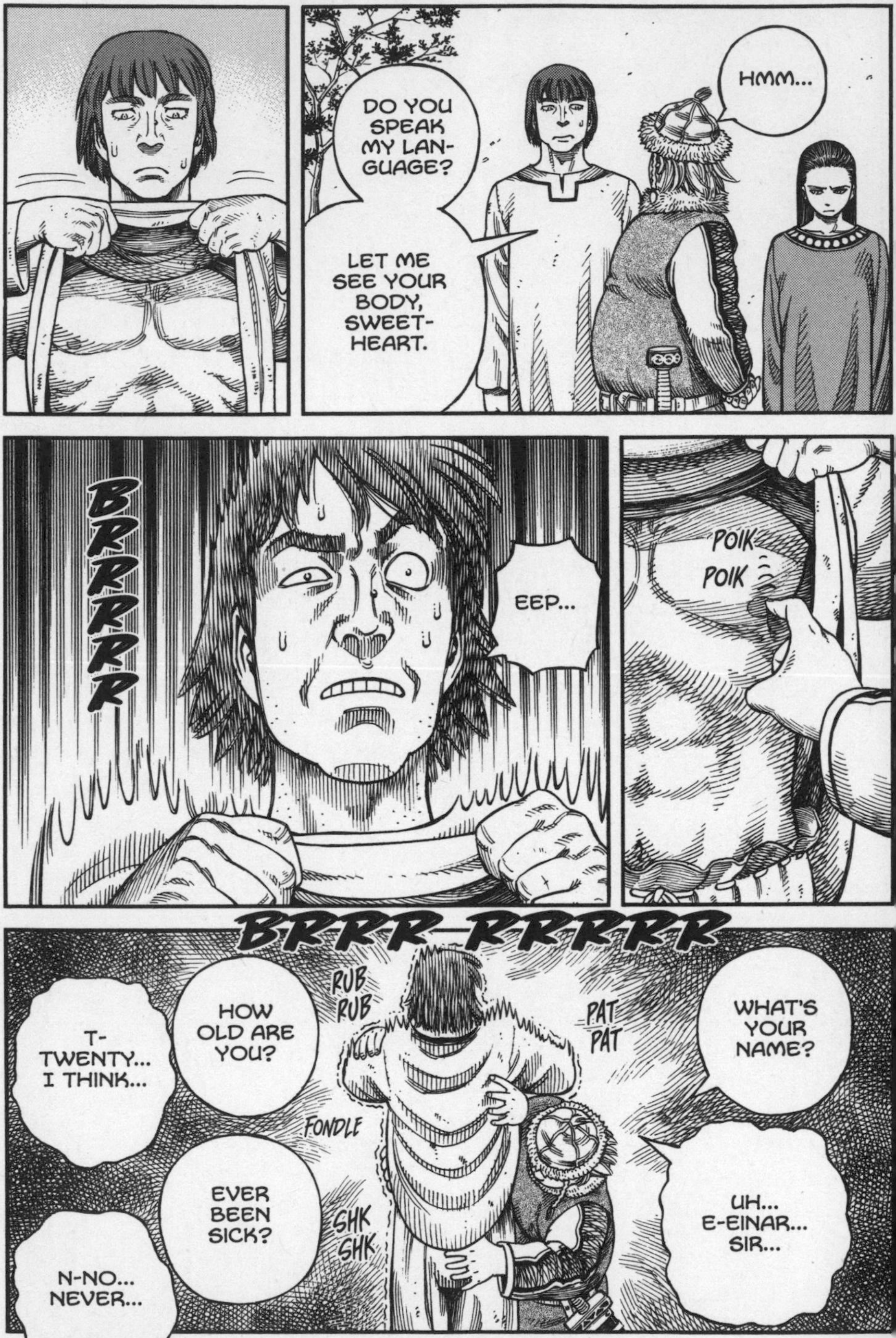
HMM...
DO YOU SPEAK MY LAN-GUAGE?
LET ME SEE YOUR BODY, SWEET-HEART.
POIK POIK
EEP...
BRRRRRR
BRRRR-RRRRRR
WHAT'S YOUR NAME?
UH... E-EINAR... SIR...
PAT PAT
RUB RUB
HOW OLD ARE YOU?
T-TWENTY... I THINK...
FONDLE
EVER BEEN SICK?
SHK SHK
N-NO... NEVER...

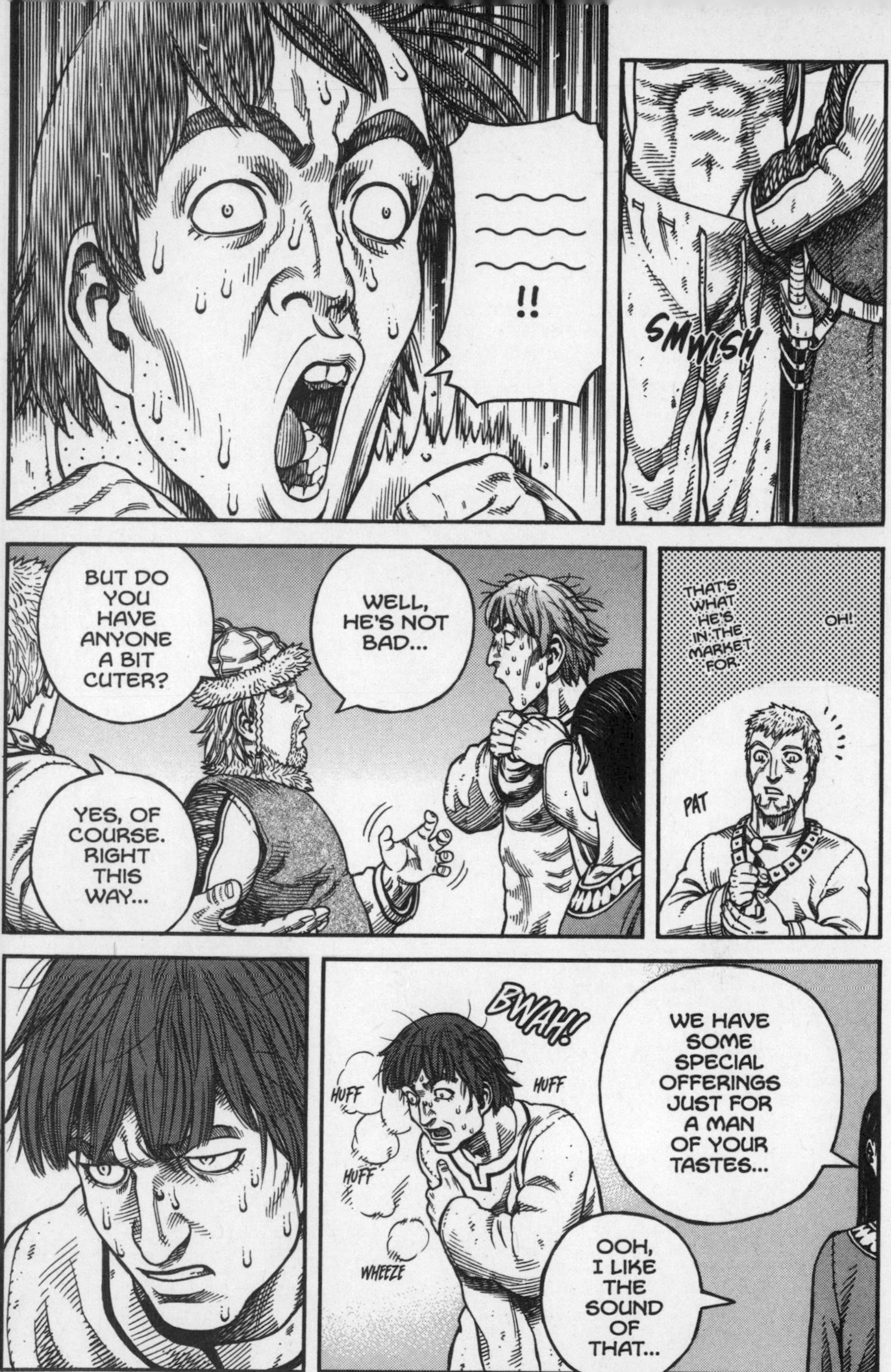
SMWISH
!!
THAT'S WHAT HE'S IN THE MARKET FOR.
OH!
PAT
WELL, HE'S NOT BAD...
BUT DO YOU HAVE ANYONE A BIT CUTER?
YES, OF COURSE. RIGHT THIS WAY...
WE HAVE SOME SPECIAL OFFERINGS JUST FOR A MAN OF YOUR TASTES...
BWAH!
HUFF
HUFF
HUFF
OOH, I LIKE THE SOUND OF THAT...
WHEEZE

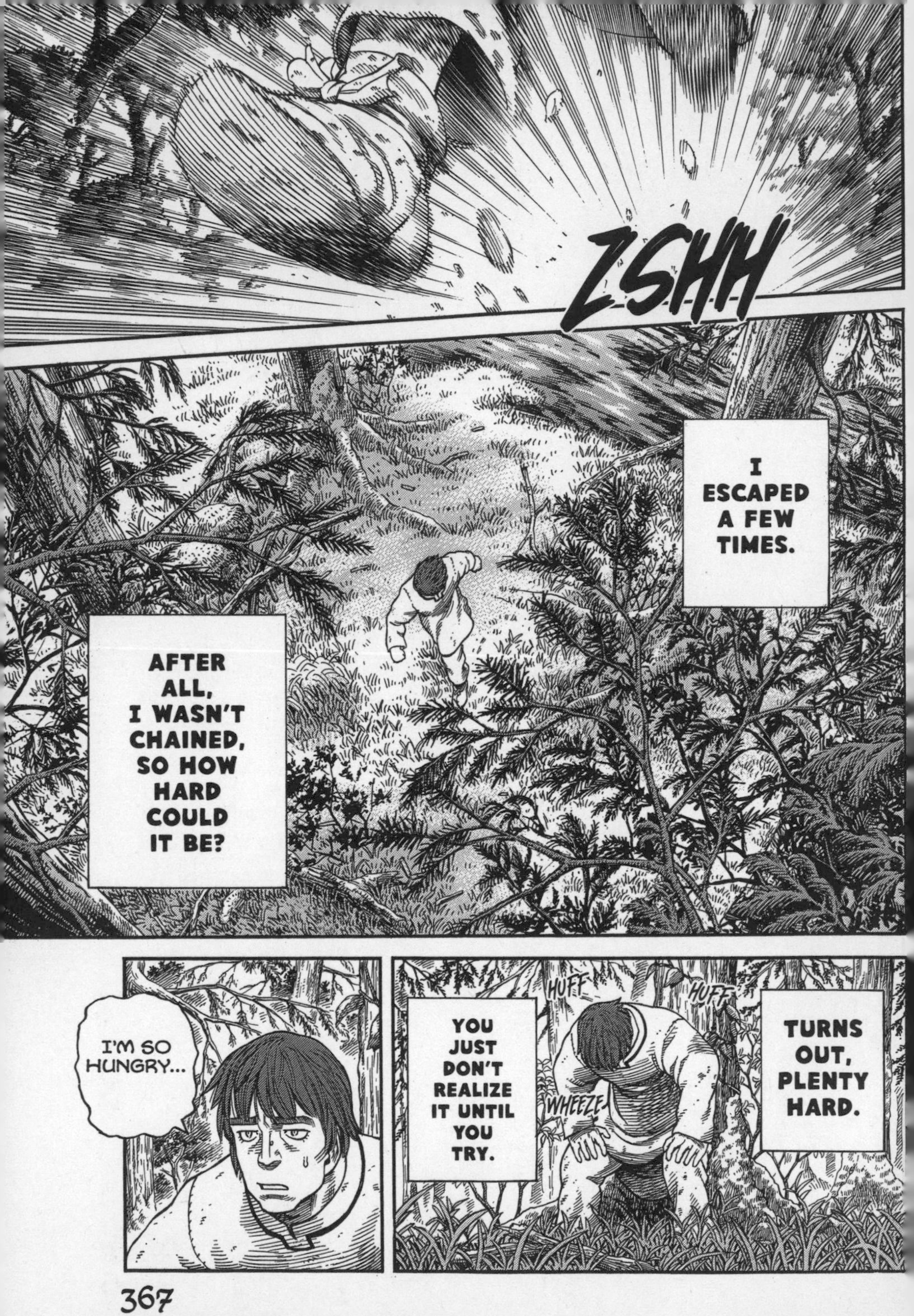
ZSHH
I ESCAPED A FEW TIMES.
AFTER ALL, I WASN'T CHAINED, SO HOW HARD COULD IT BE?
HUFF
HUFF
TURNS OUT, PLENTY HARD.
YOU JUST DON'T REALIZE IT UNTIL YOU TRY.
WHEEZE
I'M SO HUNGRY...

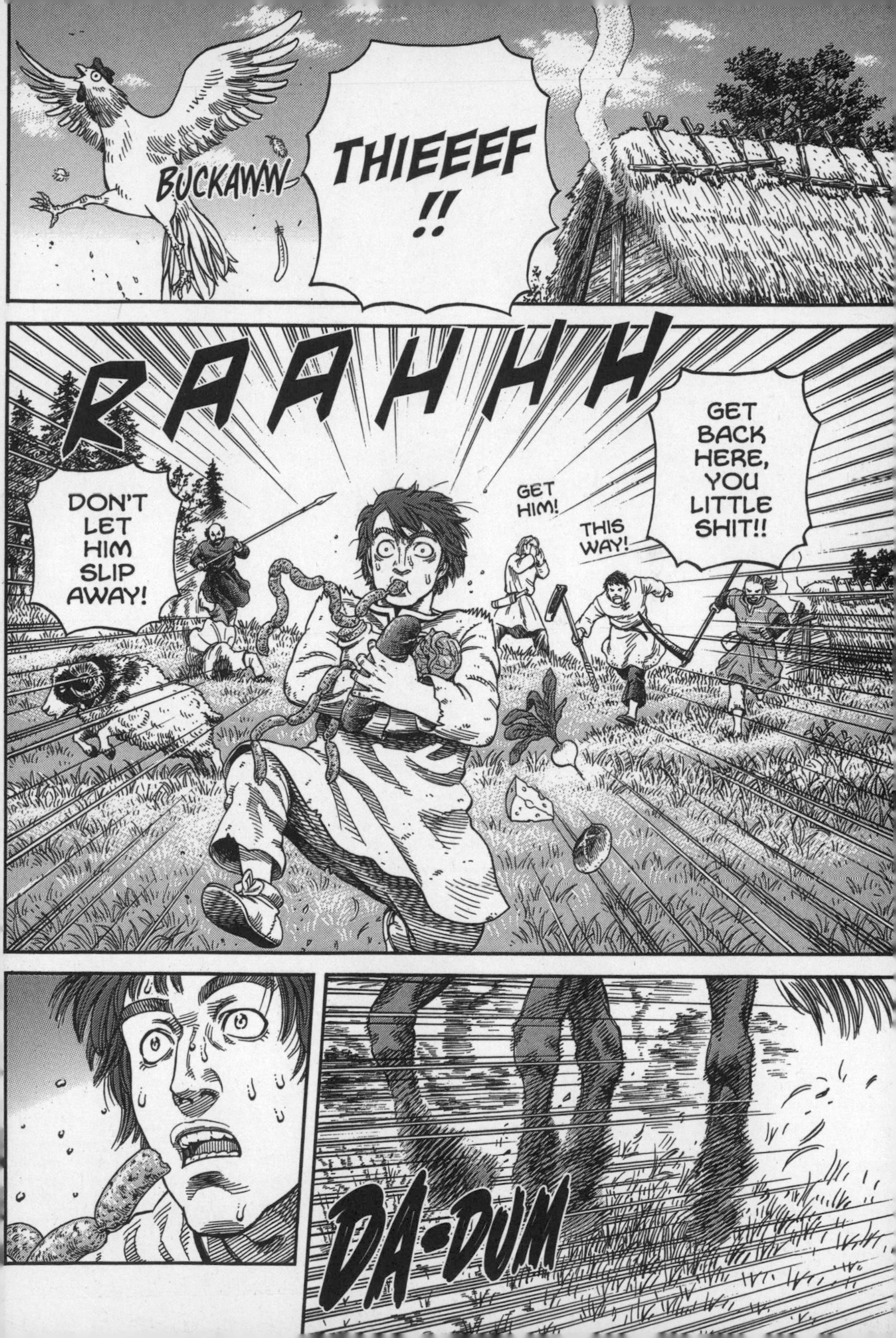
THIEEEF !!
BUCKAWW
RAAHHH
GET BACK HERE, YOU LITTLE SHIT!!
THIS WAY!
GET HIM!
DON'T LET HIM SLIP AWAY!
DA-DUM

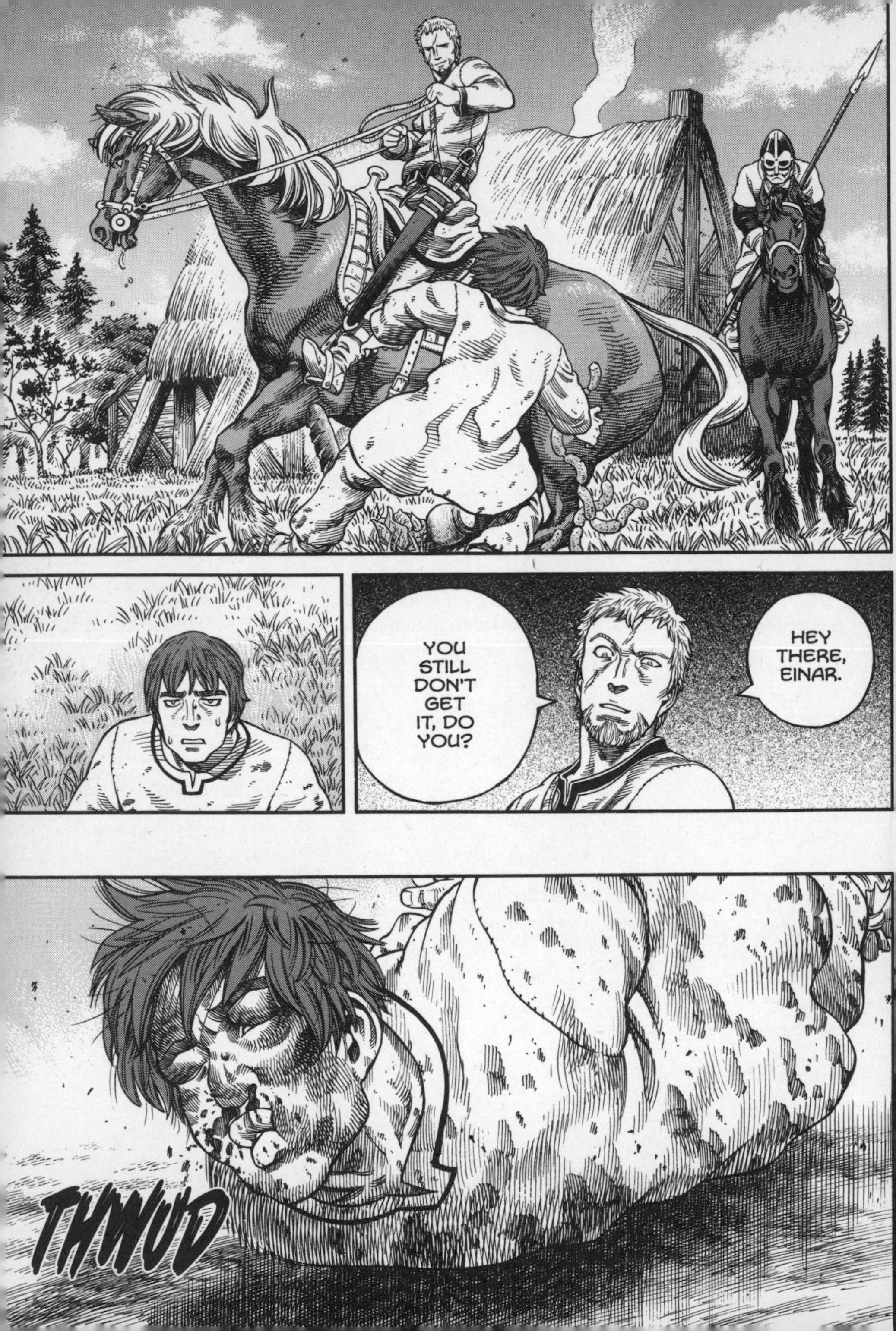
HEY THERE, EINAR.
YOU STILL DON'T GET IT, DO YOU?
THWUD

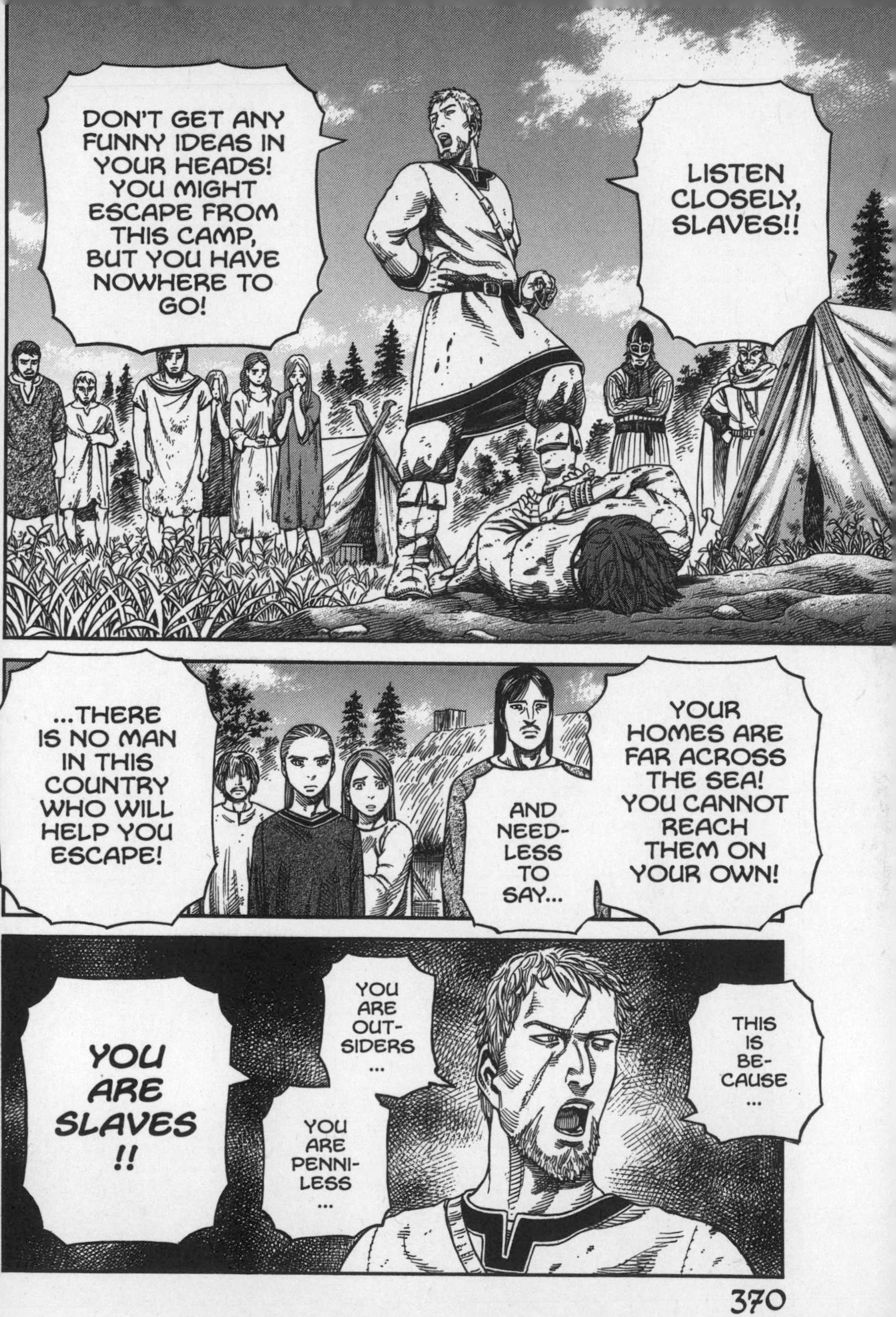
LISTEN CLOSELY, SLAVES!!
DON'T GET ANY FUNNY IDEAS IN YOUR HEADS! YOU MIGHT ESCAPE FROM THIS CAMP, BUT YOU HAVE NOWHERE TO GO!
YOUR HOMES ARE FAR ACROSS THE SEA! YOU CANNOT REACH THEM ON YOUR OWN!
AND NEED-LESS TO SAY...
...THERE IS NO MAN IN THIS COUNTRY WHO WILL HELP YOU ESCAPE!
THIS IS BE-CAUSE ...
YOU ARE OUT-SIDERS ...
YOU ARE PENNI-LESS ...
YOU ARE SLAVES !!

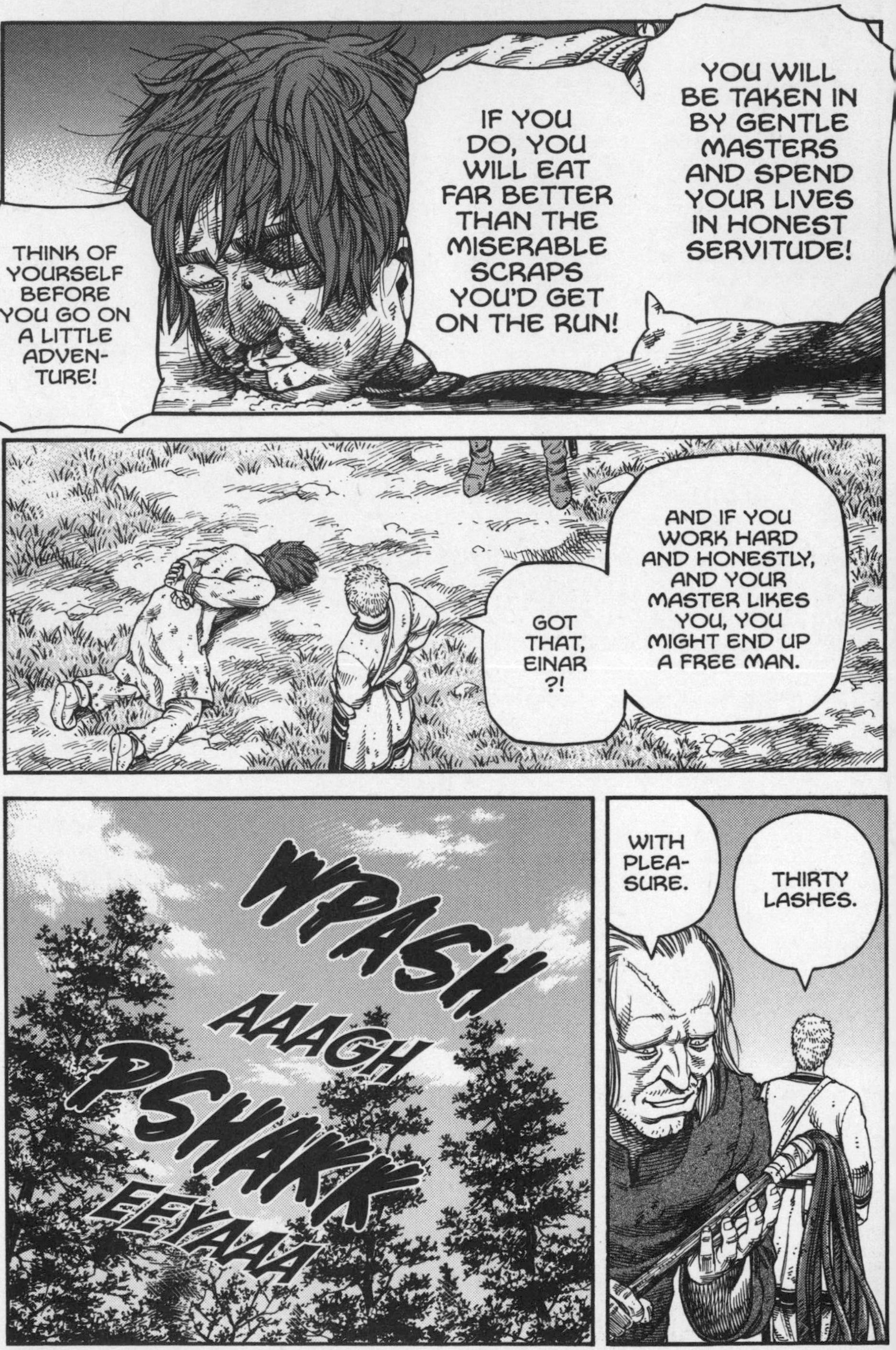
YOU WILL BE TAKEN IN BY GENTLE MASTERS AND SPEND YOUR LIVES IN HONEST SERVITUDE!
IF YOU DO, YOU WILL EAT FAR BETTER THAN THE MISERABLE SCRAPS YOU'D GET ON THE RUN!
THINK OF YOURSELF BEFORE YOU GO ON A LITTLE ADVEN-TURE!
AND IF YOU WORK HARD AND HONESTLY, AND YOUR MASTER LIKES YOU, YOU MIGHT END UP A FREE MAN.
GOT THAT, EINAR ?!
THIRTY LASHES.
WITH PLEA-SURE.
WPASH
AAAGH
PSHAKK
EEYAAA

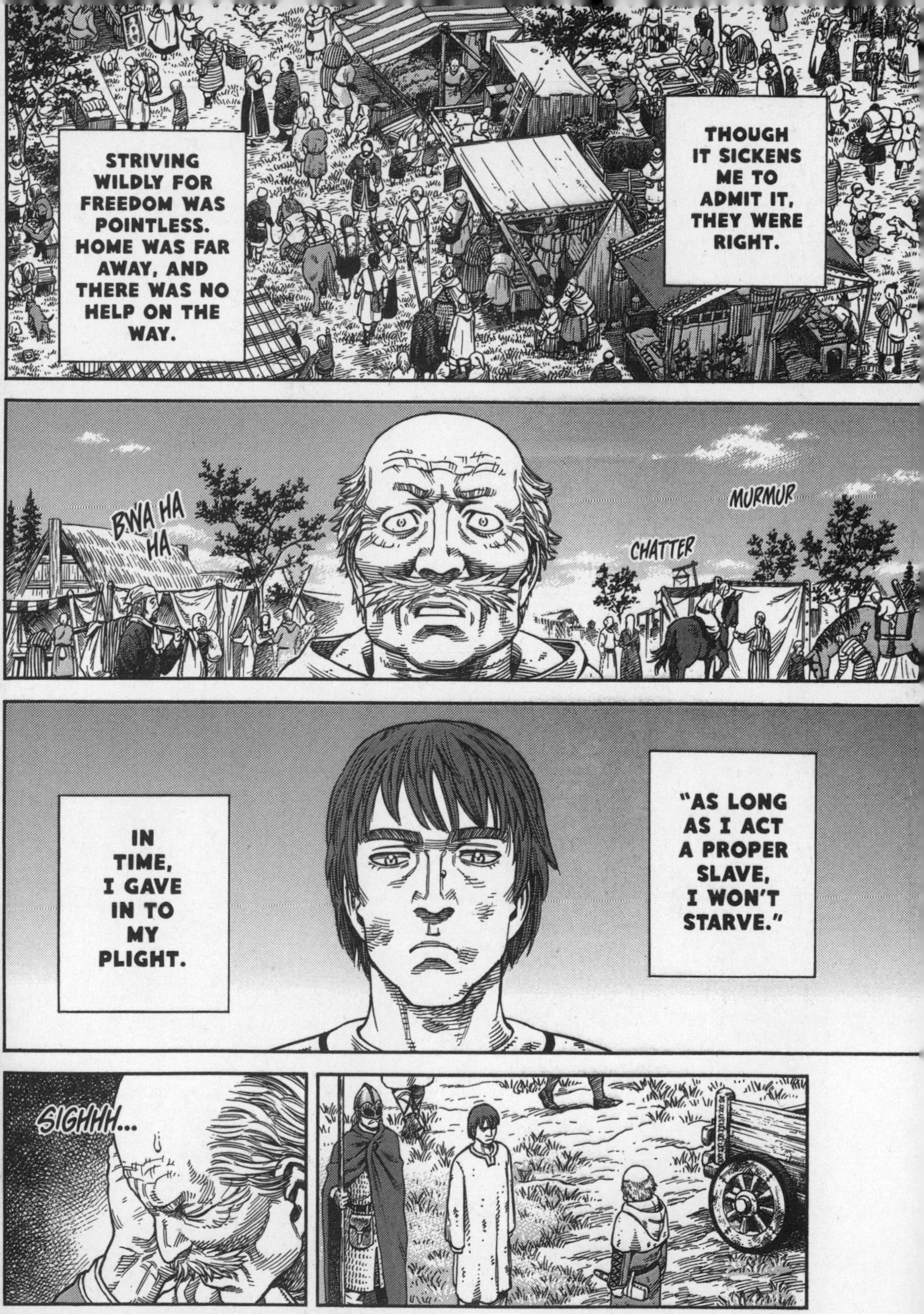
THOUGH IT SICKENS ME TO ADMIT IT, THEY WERE RIGHT.
STRIVING WILDLY FOR FREEDOM WAS POINTLESS. HOME WAS FAR AWAY, AND THERE WAS NO HELP ON THE WAY.
MURMUR
CHATTER
BWA HA HA
"AS LONG AS I ACT A PROPER SLAVE, I WON'T STARVE."
IN TIME, I GAVE IN TO MY PLIGHT.
SIGHHH...

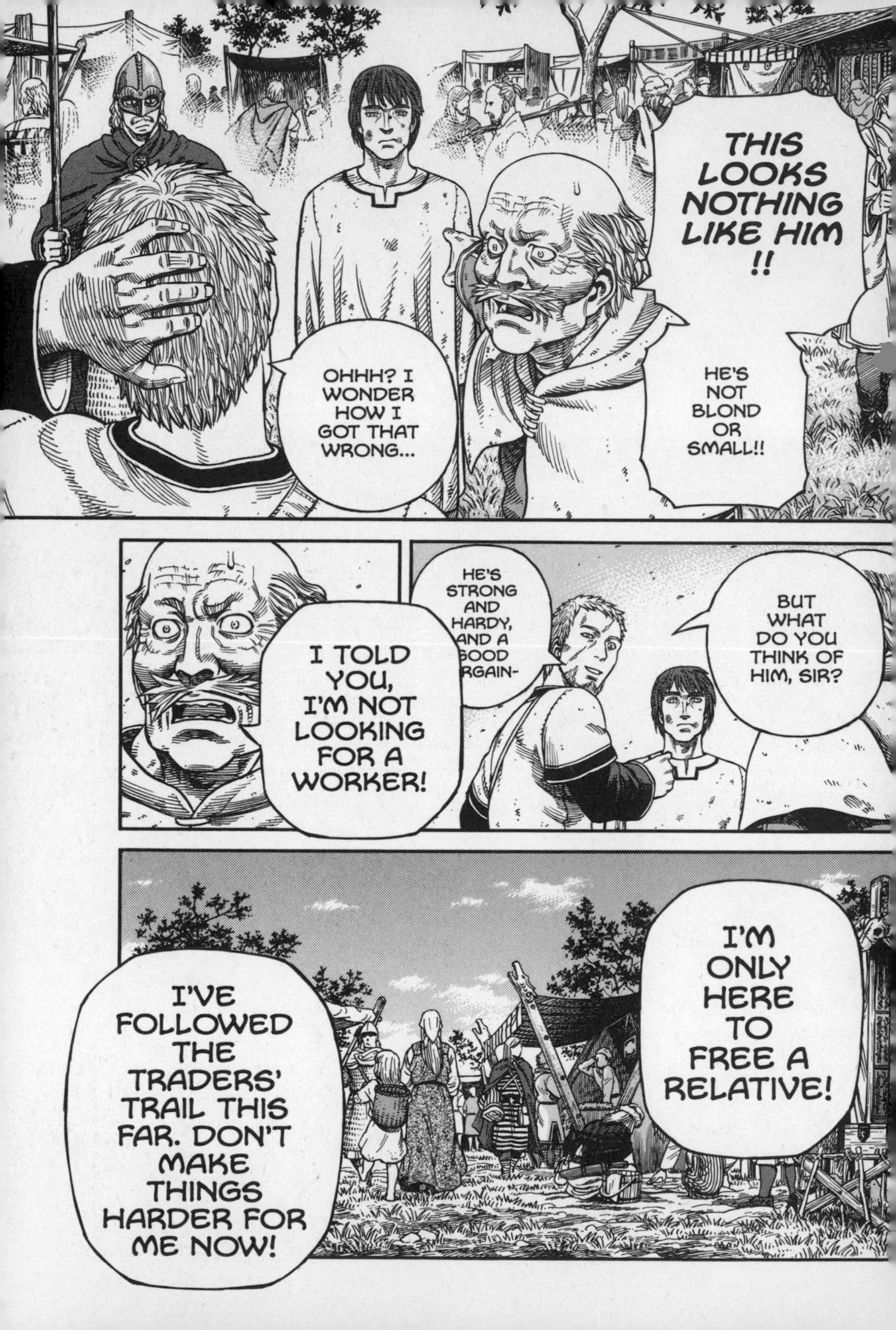
THIS LOOKS NOTHING LIKE HIM !!
HE'S NOT BLOND OR SMALL!!
OHHH? I WONDER HOW I GOT THAT WRONG...
BUT WHAT DO YOU THINK OF HIM, SIR?
HE'S STRONG AND HARDY, AND A GOOD RGAIN-
I TOLD YOU, I'M NOT LOOKING FOR A WORKER!
I'M ONLY HERE TO FREE A RELATIVE!
I'VE FOLLOWED THE TRADERS' TRAIL THIS FAR. DON'T MAKE THINGS HARDER FOR ME NOW!

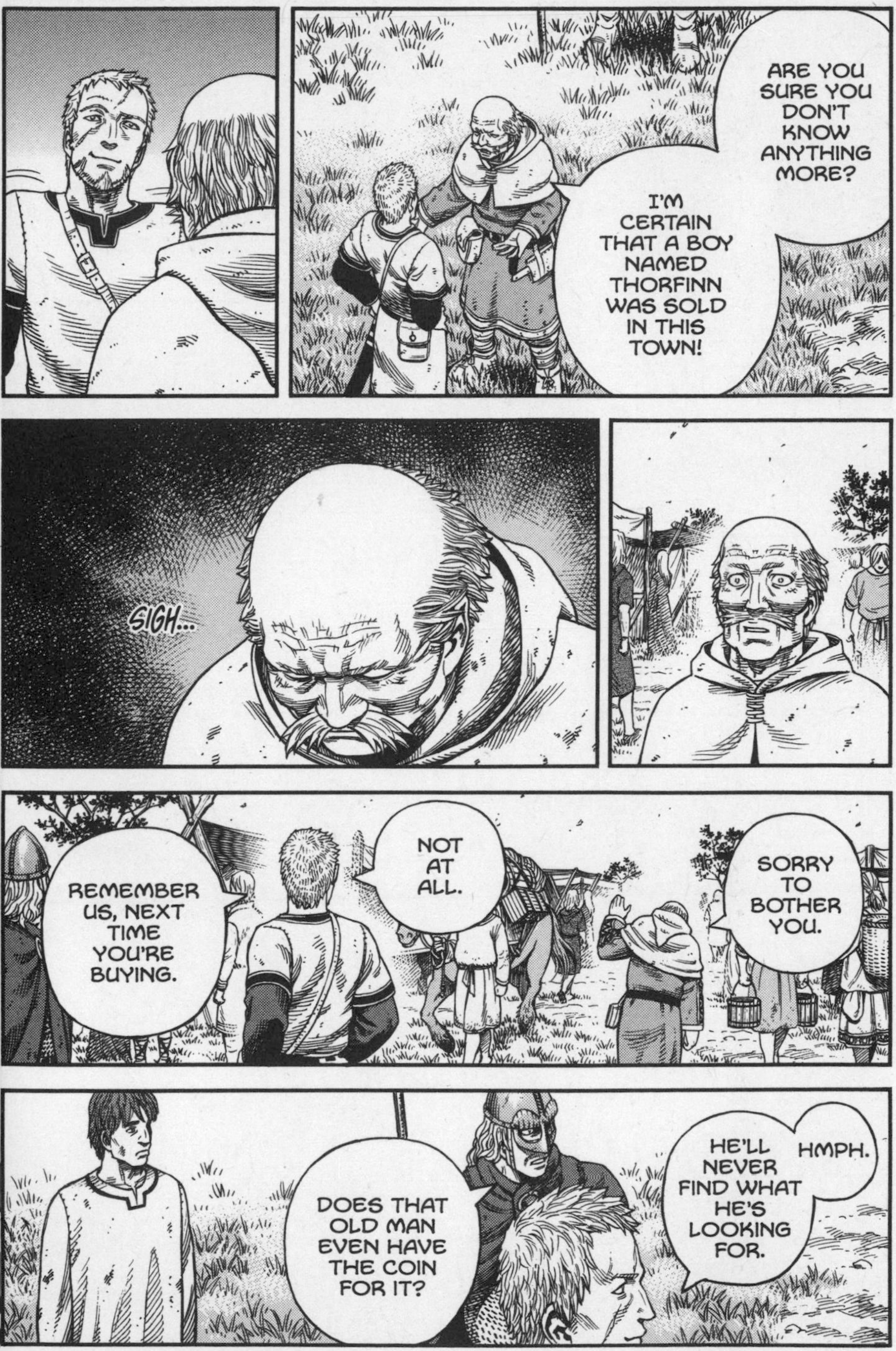
ARE YOU SURE YOU DON'T KNOW ANYTHING MORE?
I'M CERTAIN THAT A BOY NAMED THORFINN WAS SOLD IN THIS TOWN!
SIGH...
SORRY TO BOTHER YOU.
NOT AT ALL.
REMEMBER US, NEXT TIME YOU'RE BUYING.
HMPH.
HE'LL NEVER FIND WHAT HE'S LOOKING FOR.
DOES THAT OLD MAN EVEN HAVE THE COIN FOR IT?

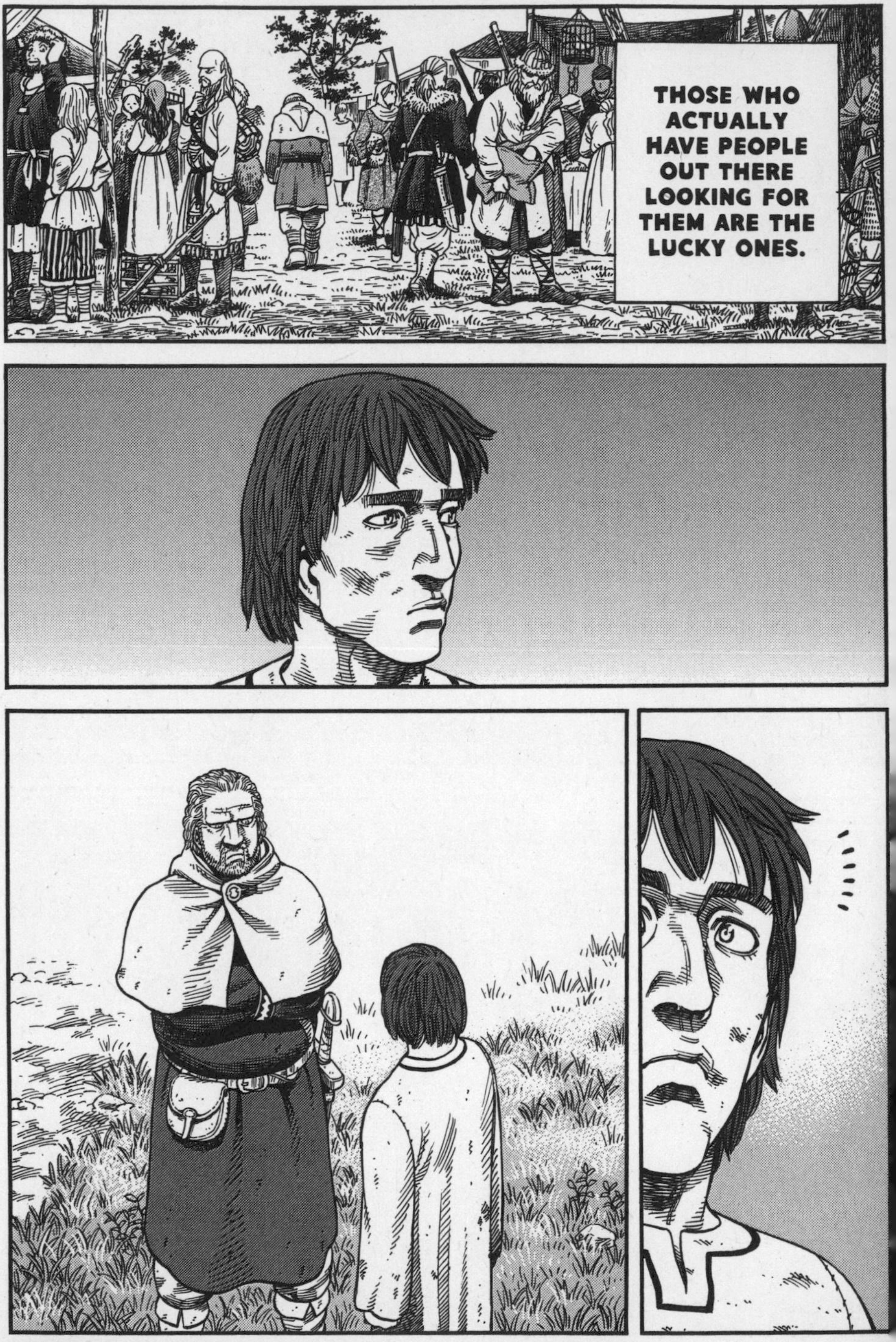
THOSE WHO ACTUALLY HAVE PEOPLE OUT THERE LOOKING FOR THEM ARE THE LUCKY ONES.

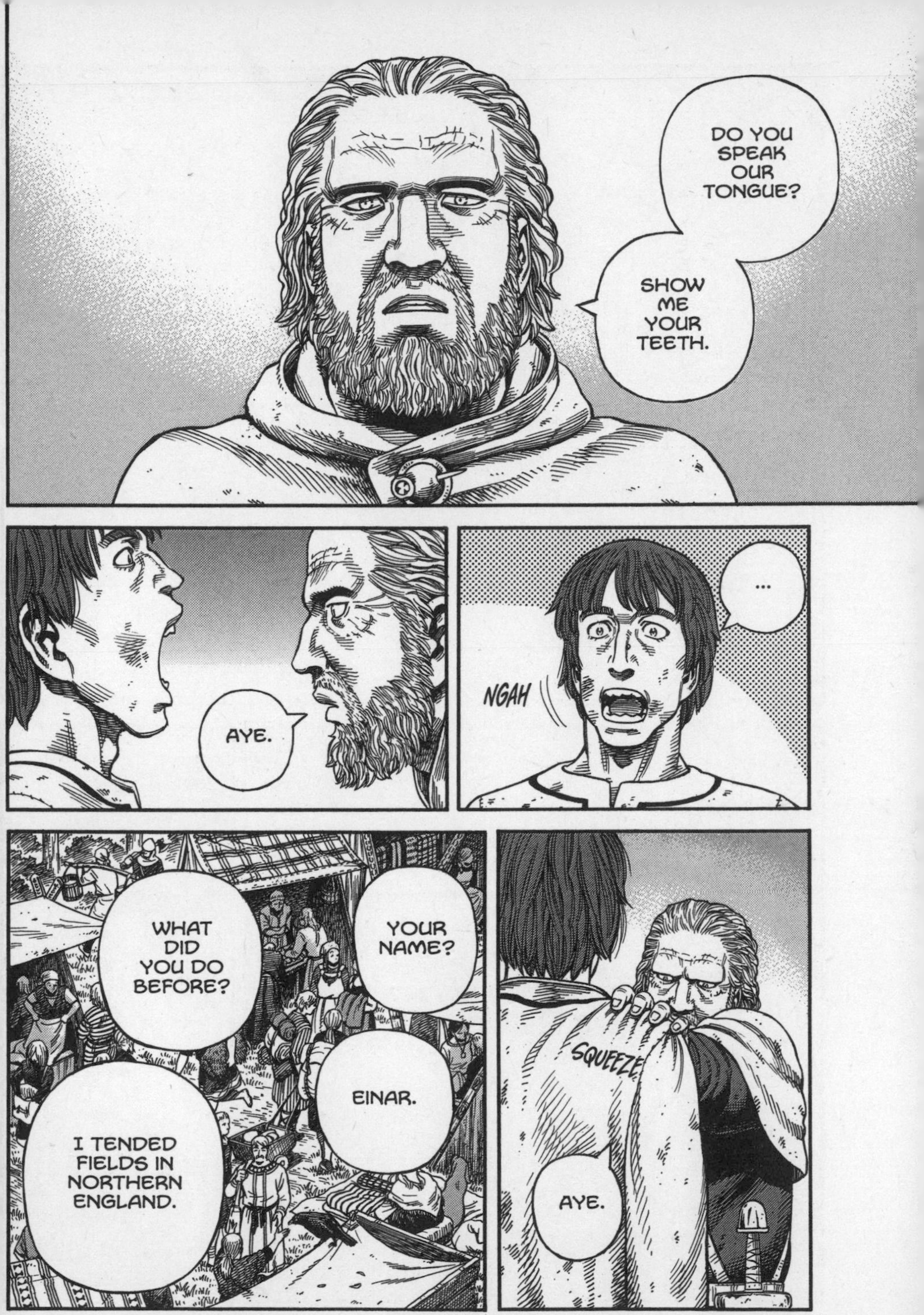
DO YOU SPEAK OUR TONGUE?
SHOW ME YOUR TEETH.
...
NGAH
AYE.
SQUEEZE
AYE.
YOUR NAME?
EINAR.
WHAT DID YOU DO BEFORE?
I TENDED FIELDS IN NORTHERN ENGLAND.

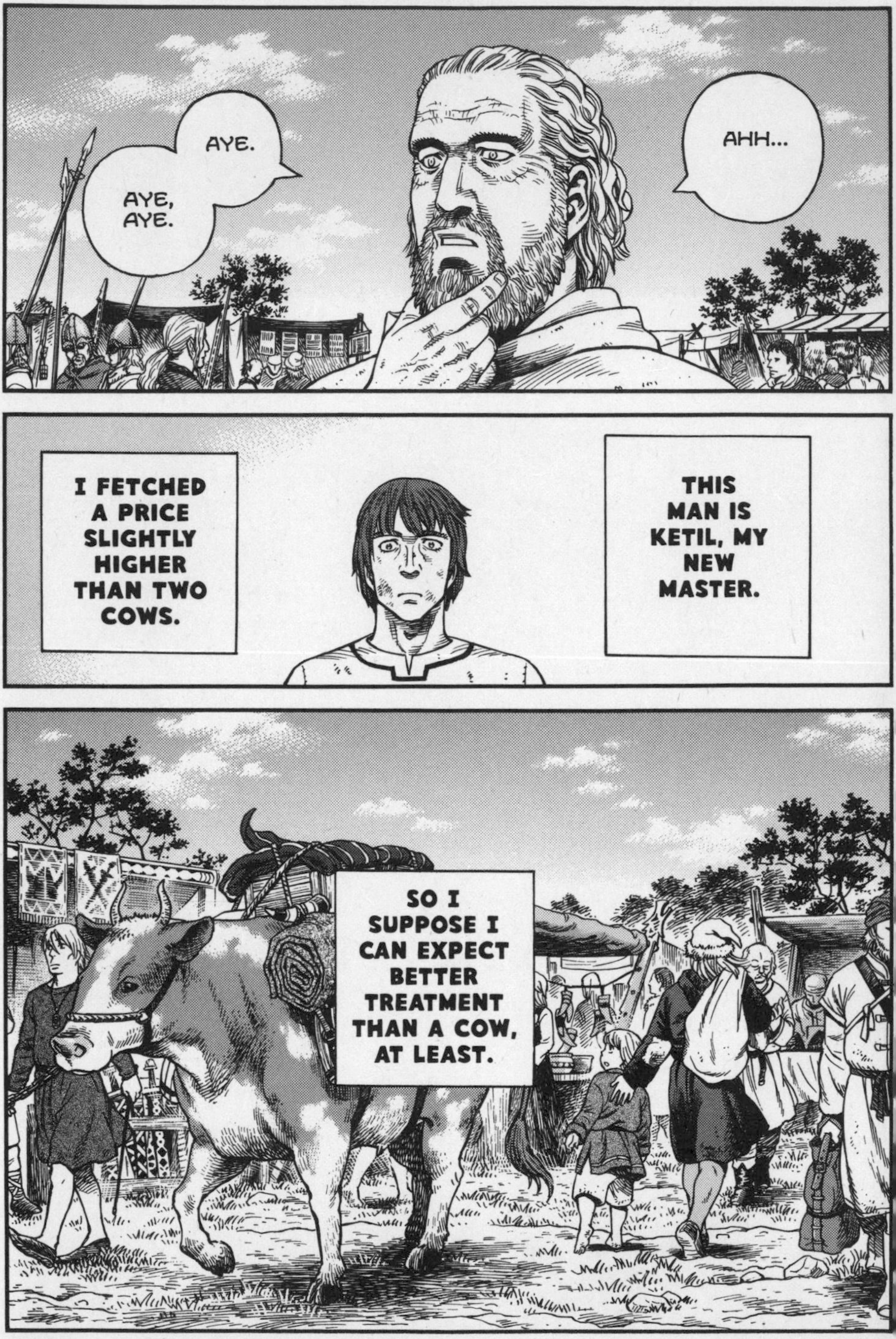
AHH...
AYE.
AYE, AYE.
THIS MAN IS KETIL, MY NEW MASTER.
I FETCHED A PRICE SLIGHTLY HIGHER THAN TWO COWS.
SO I SUPPOSE I CAN EXPECT BETTER TREATMENT THAN A COW, AT LEAST.

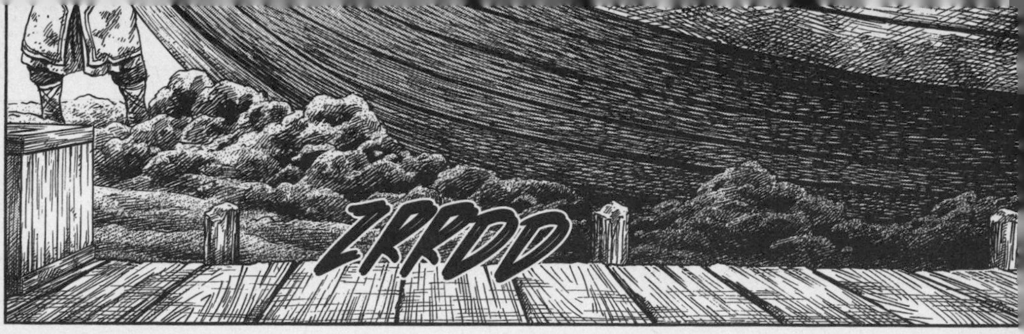
ZRRDD

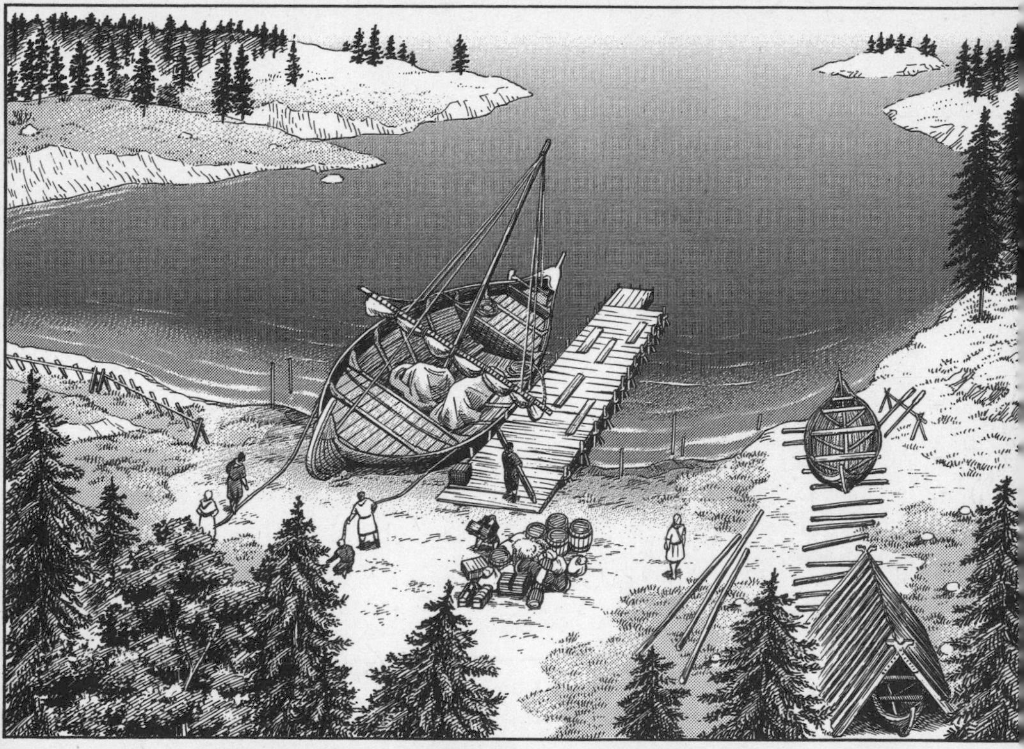

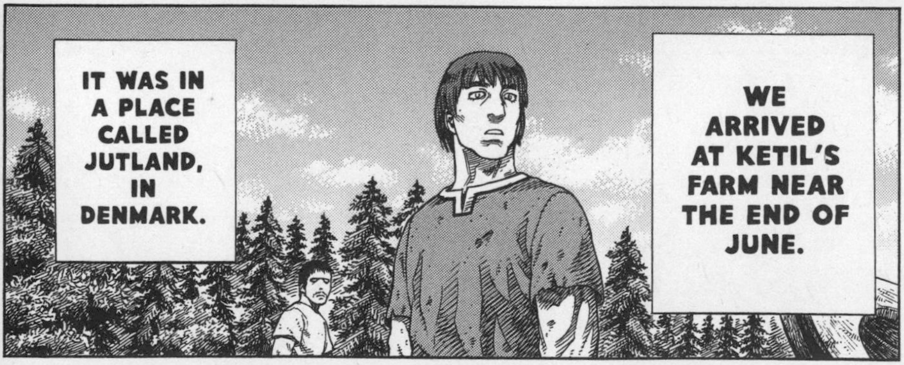
WE ARRIVED AT KETIL'S FARM NEAR THE END OF JUNE.
IT WAS IN A PLACE CALLED JUTLAND, IN DENMARK.

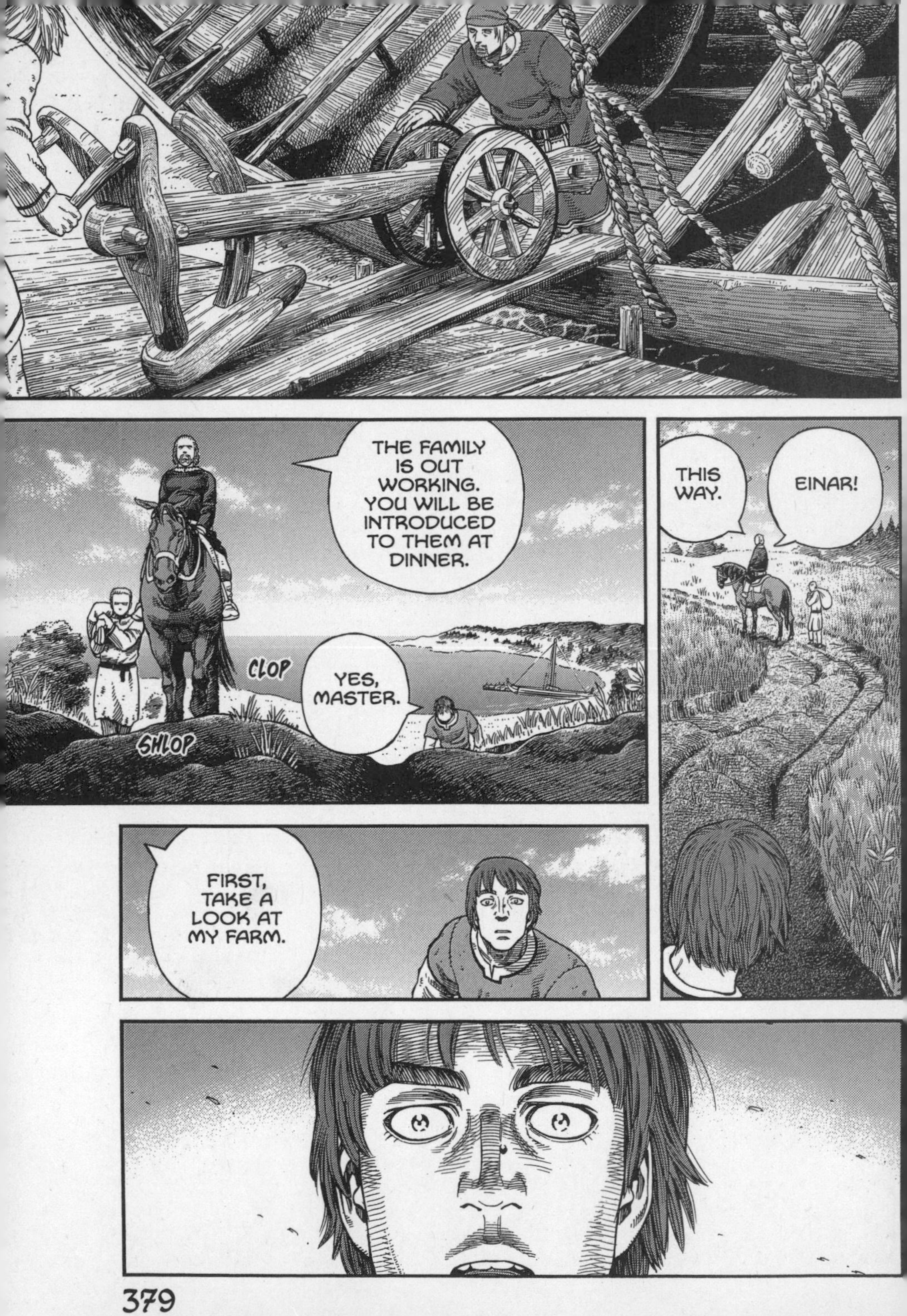
EINAR!
THIS WAY.
THE FAMILY IS OUT WORKING. YOU WILL BE INTRODUCED TO THEM AT DINNER.
YES, MASTER.
CLOP
SHLOP
FIRST, TAKE A LOOK AT MY FARM.

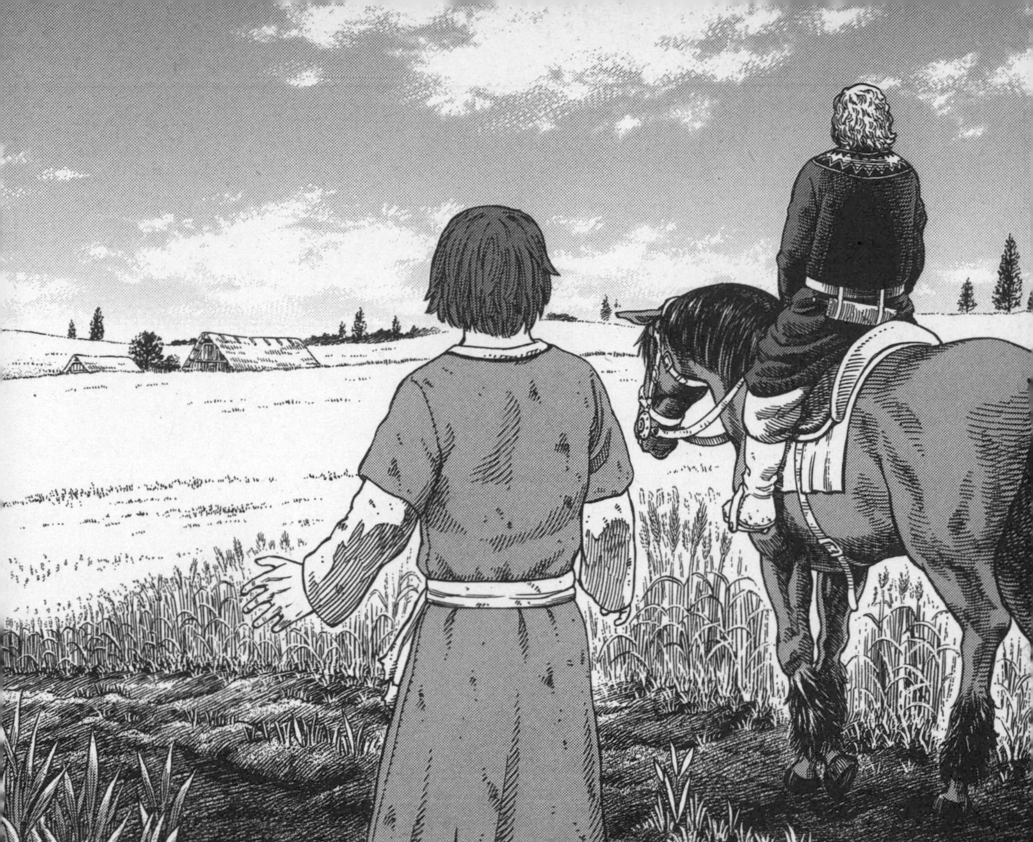

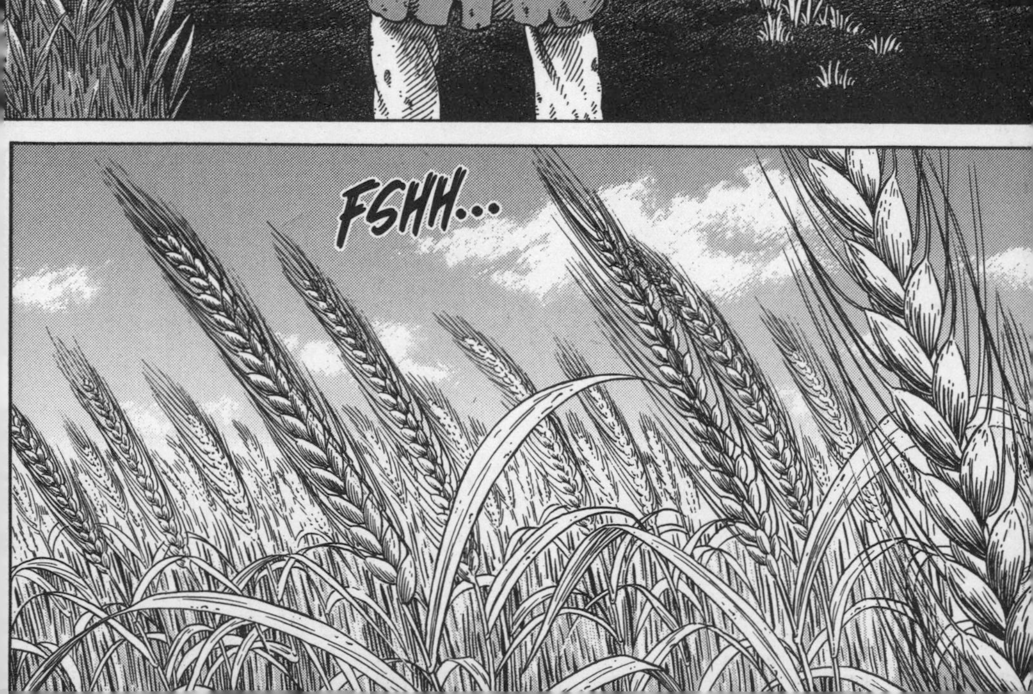
FSHH...

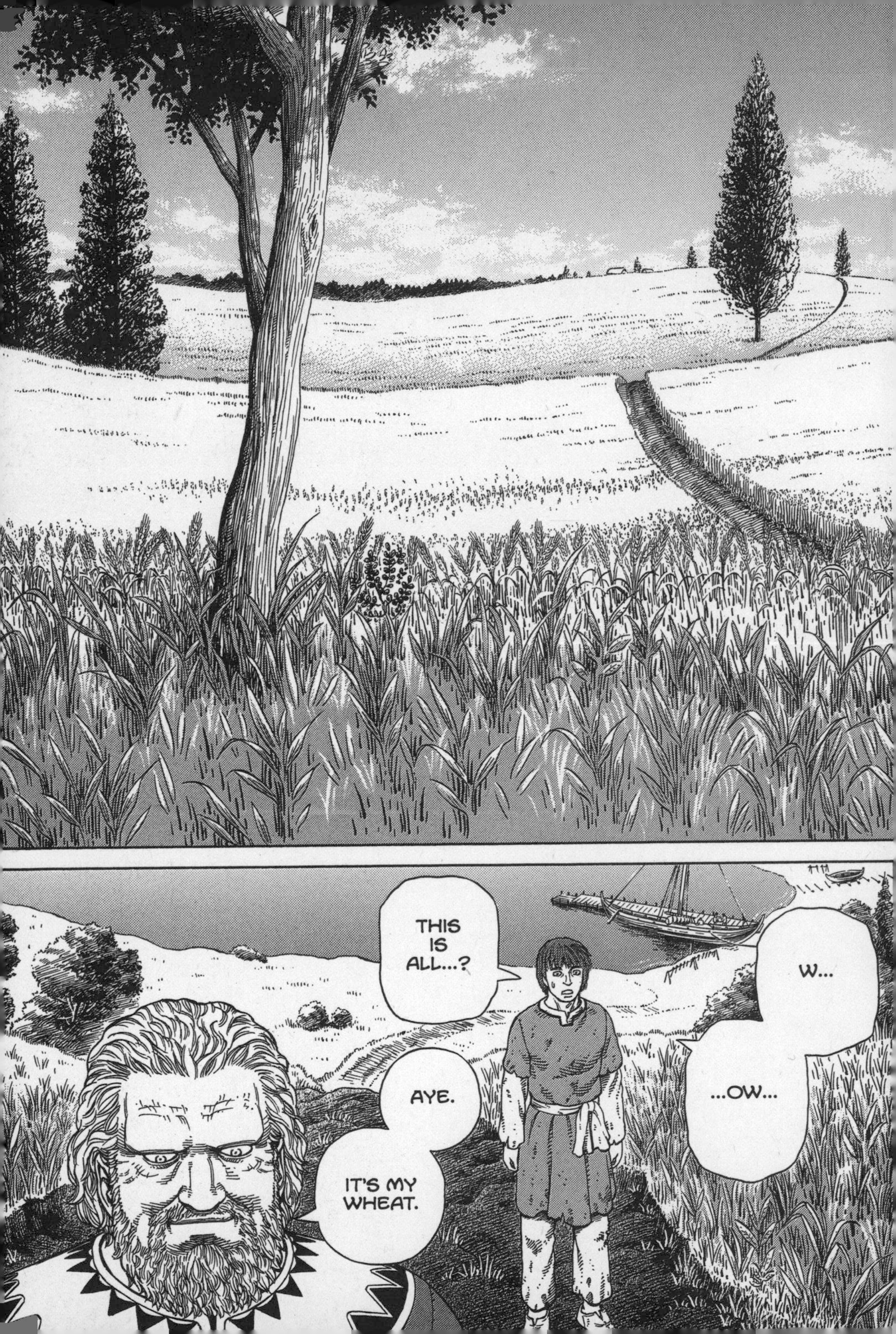
W...
...OW...
THIS IS ALL...?
AYE.
IT'S MY WHEAT.

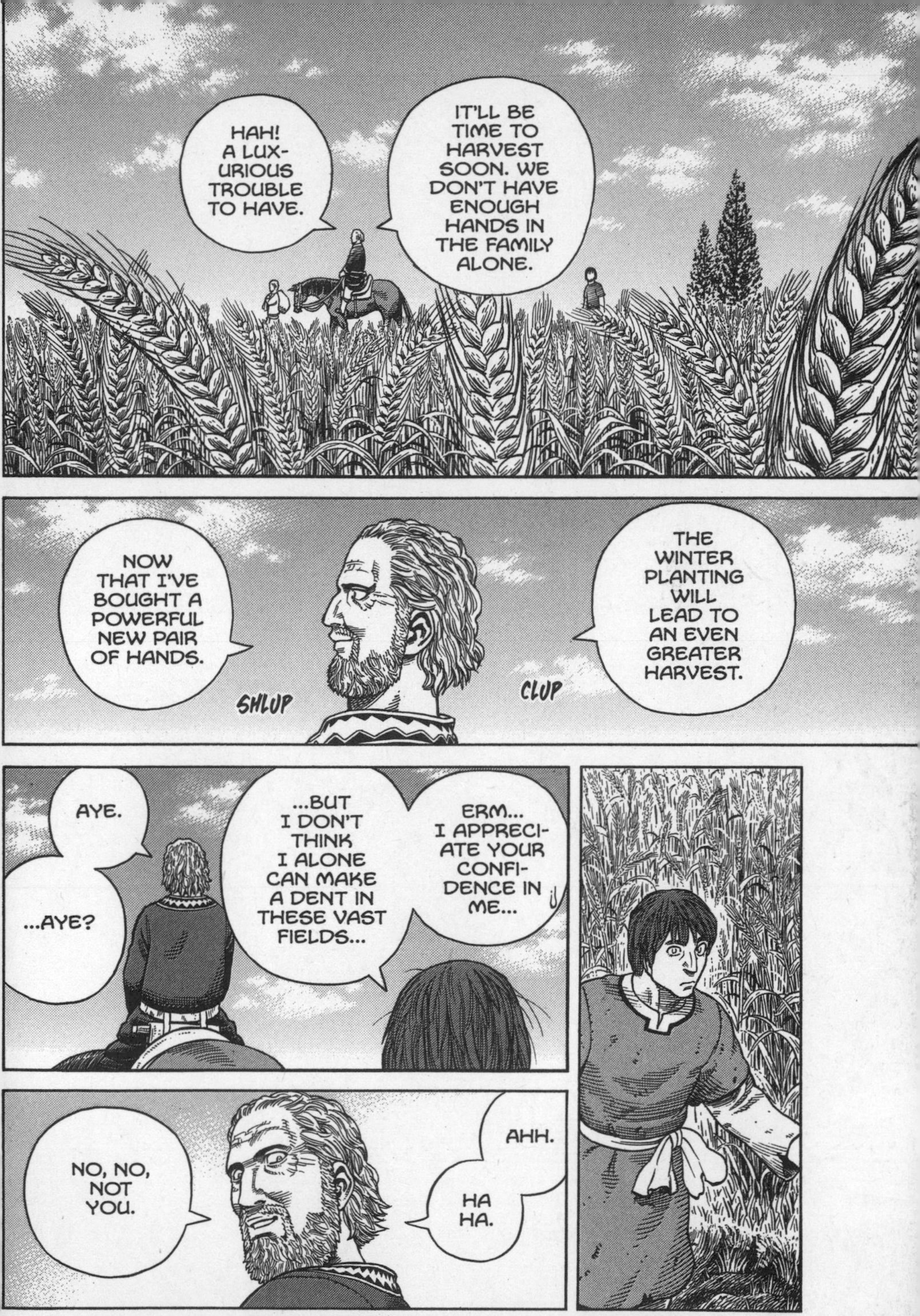
IT'LL BE TIME TO HARVEST SOON. WE DON'T HAVE ENOUGH HANDS IN THE FAMILY ALONE.
HAH! A LUX-URIOUS TROUBLE TO HAVE.
THE WINTER PLANTING WILL LEAD TO AN EVEN GREATER HARVEST.
CLUP
NOW THAT I'VE BOUGHT A POWERFUL NEW PAIR OF HANDS.
SHLUP
ERM... I APPRECI-ATE YOUR CONFI-DENCE IN ME...
...BUT I DON'T THINK I ALONE CAN MAKE A DENT IN THESE VAST FIELDS...
AYE.
...AYE?
AHH.
HA HA.
NO, NO, NOT YOU.

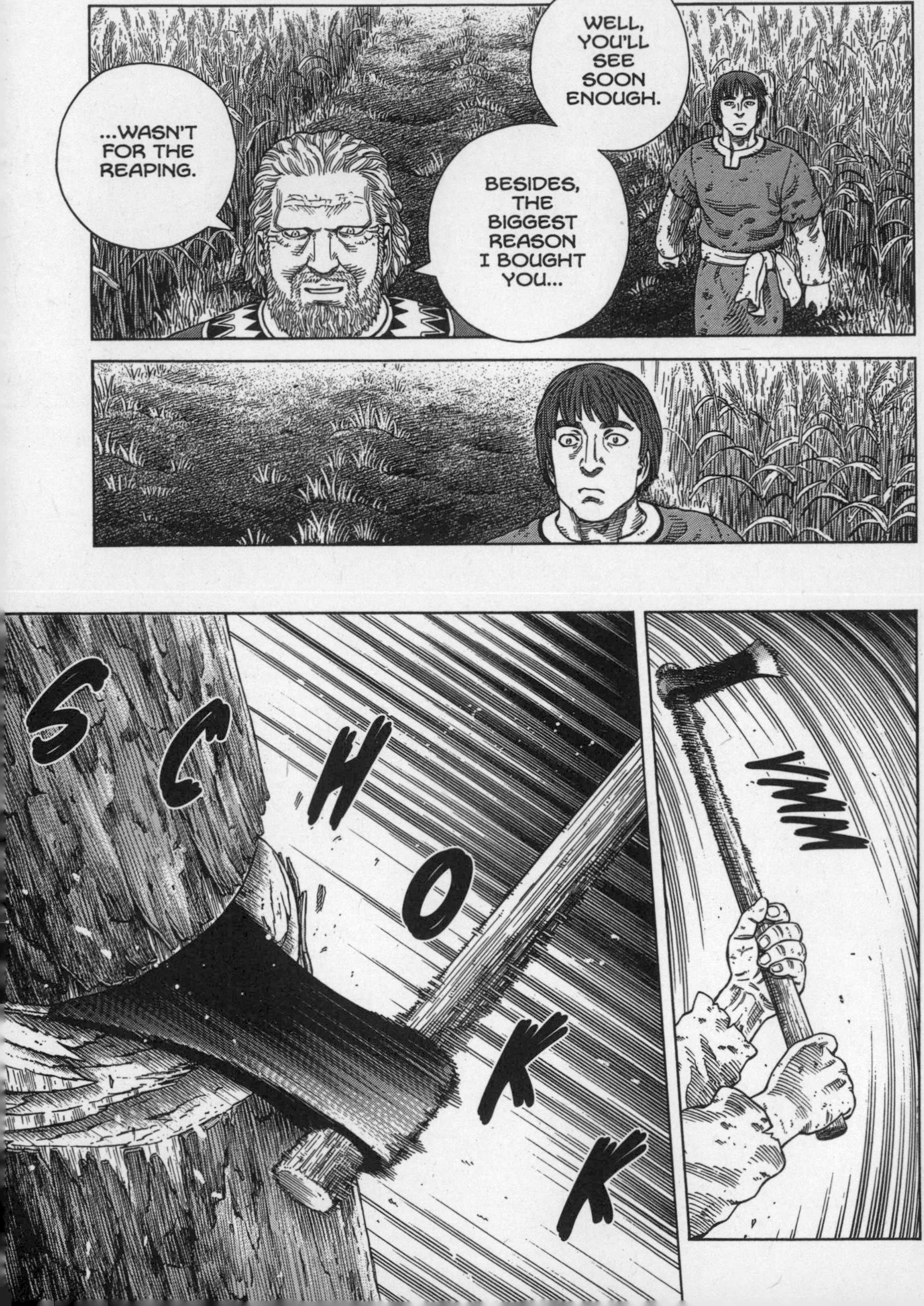
BESIDES, THE BIGGEST REASON I BOUGHT YOU...
...WASN'T FOR THE REAPING.
WELL, YOU'LL SEE SOON ENOUGH.
VMM
SCHOKK

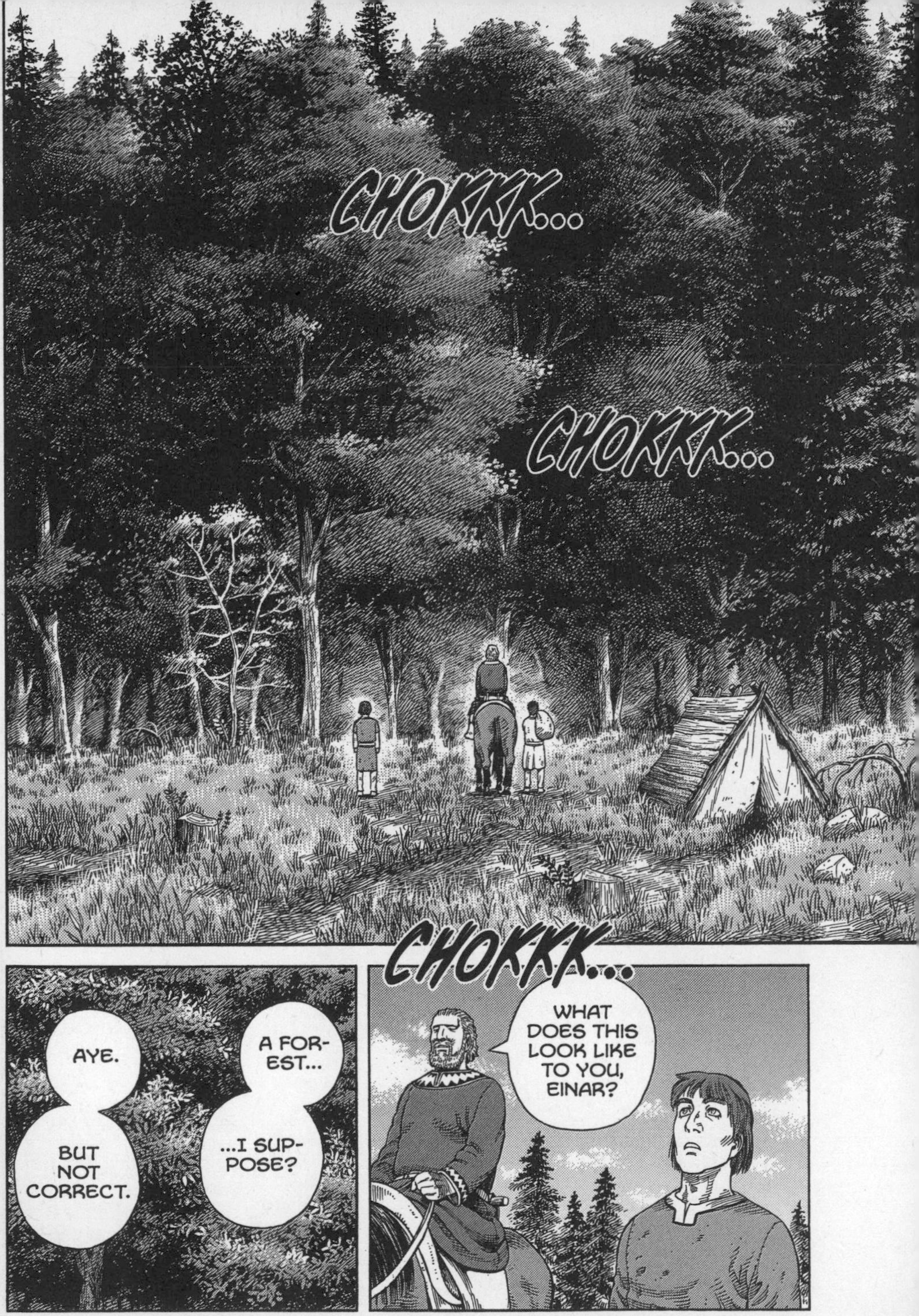

CHOKKK...
CHOKKK...
CHOKKK...
WHAT DOES THIS LOOK LIKE TO YOU, EINAR?
A FOR-EST...
...I SUP-POSE?
AYE.
BUT NOT CORRECT.

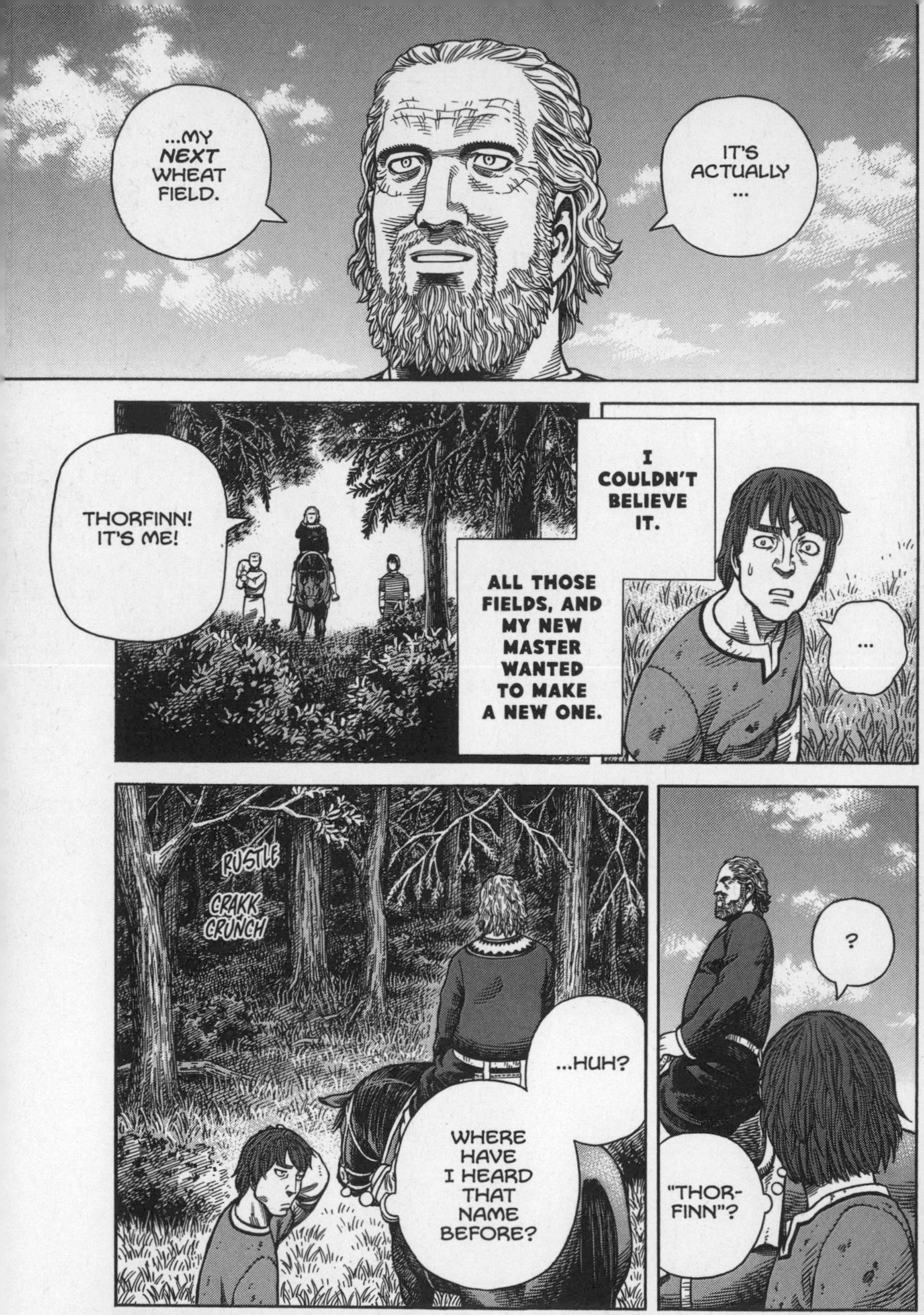
IT'S ACTUALLY ...
...MY *NEXT* WHEAT FIELD.
I COULDN'T BELIEVE IT.
ALL THOSE FIELDS, AND MY NEW MASTER WANTED TO MAKE A NEW ONE.
...
THORFINN! IT'S ME!
?
"THOR-FINN"?
RUSTLE
CRAKK CRUNCH
...HUH?
WHERE HAVE I HEARD THAT NAME BEFORE?

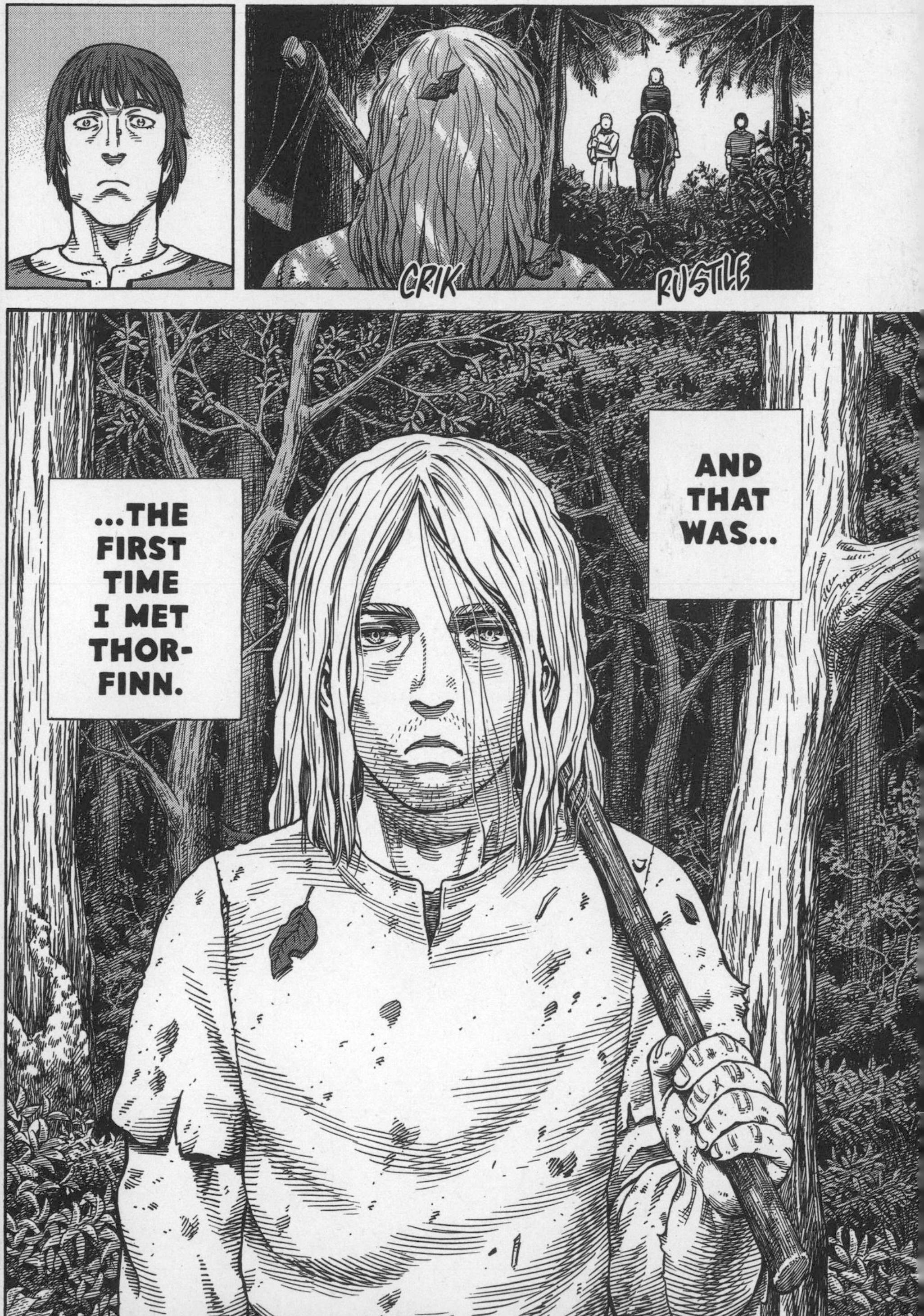
RUSTLE
CRIK
AND THAT WAS...
...THE FIRST TIME I MET THORFINN.

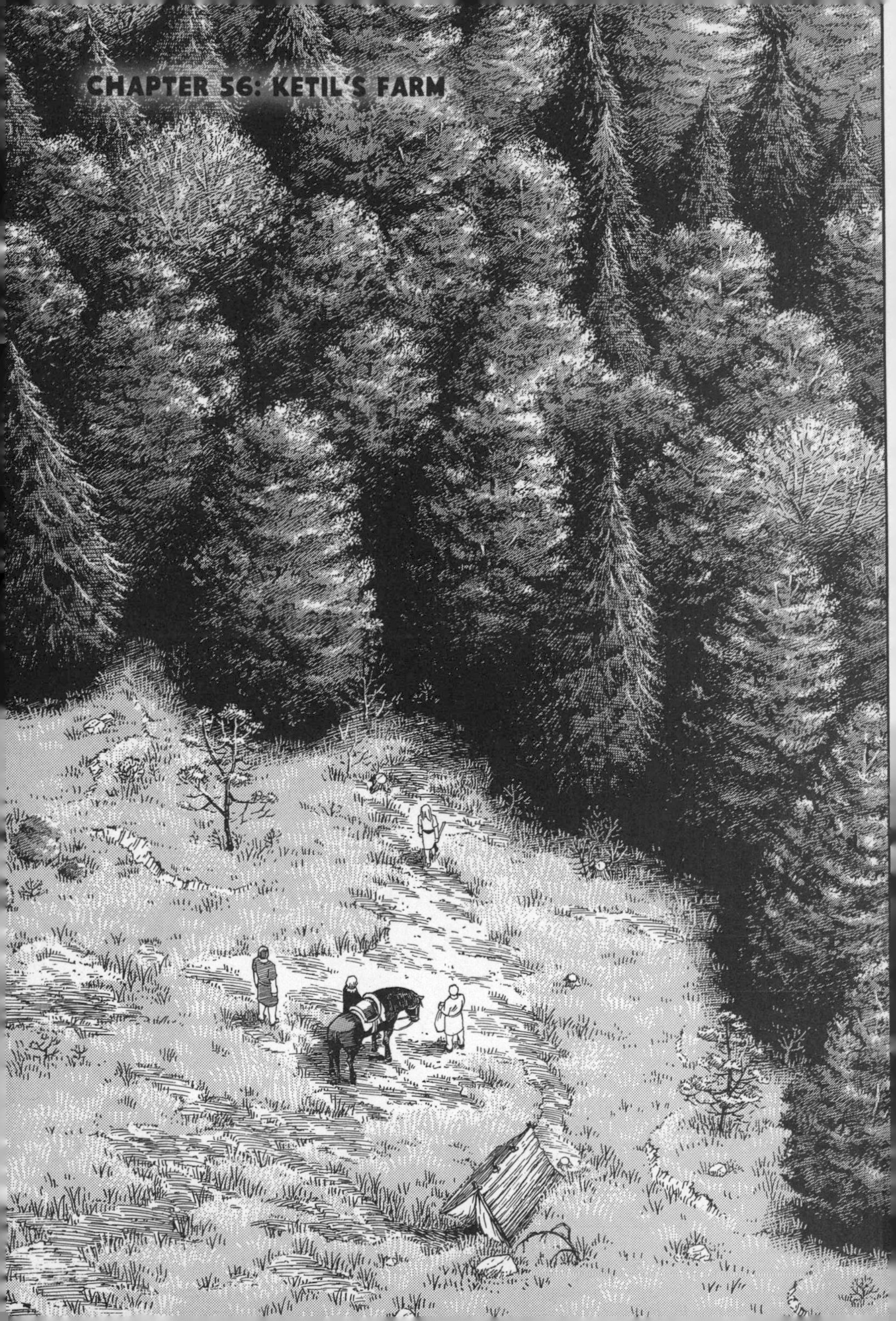
CHAPTER 56: KETIL'S FARM

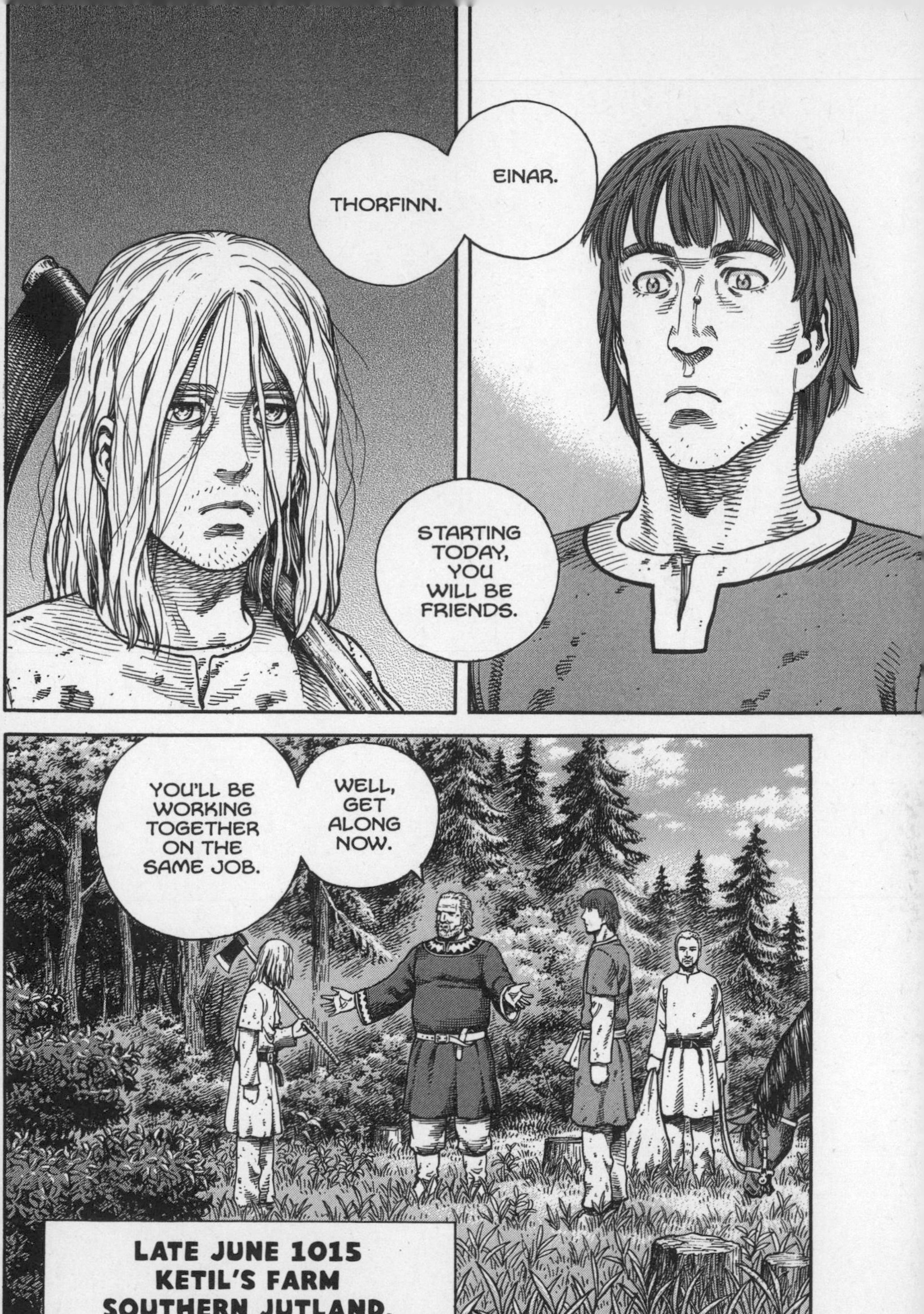
EINAR.
THORFINN.
STARTING TODAY, YOU WILL BE FRIENDS.
WELL, GET ALONG NOW.
YOU'LL BE WORKING TOGETHER ON THE SAME JOB.
LATE JUNE 1015
KETIL'S FARM
SOUTHERN JUTLAND, DENMARK

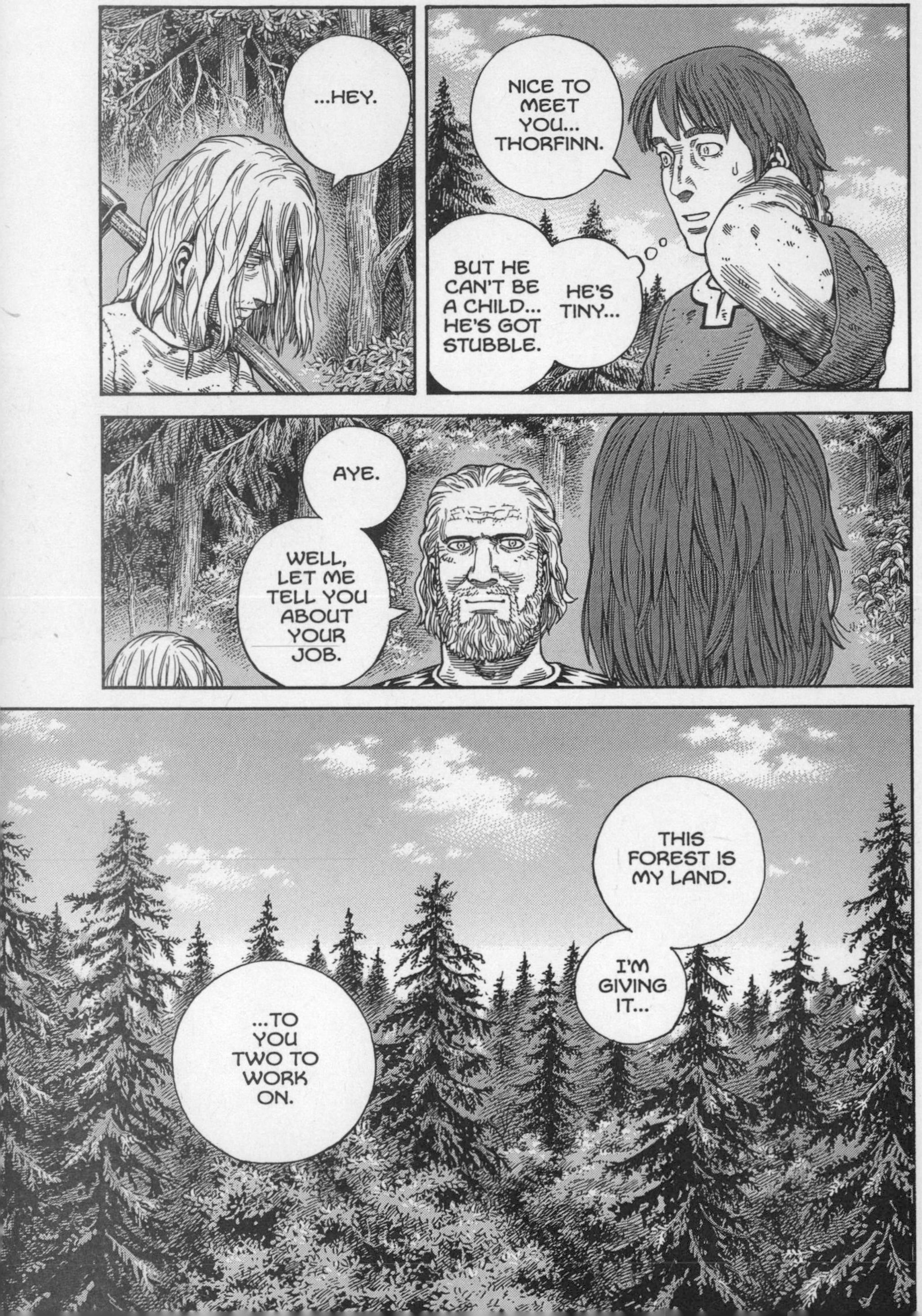
NICE TO MEET YOU... THORFINN.
HE'S TINY...
BUT HE CAN'T BE A CHILD... HE'S GOT STUBBLE.
...HEY.
AYE.
WELL, LET ME TELL YOU ABOUT YOUR JOB.
THIS FOREST IS MY LAND.
I'M GIVING IT...
...TO YOU TWO TO WORK ON.

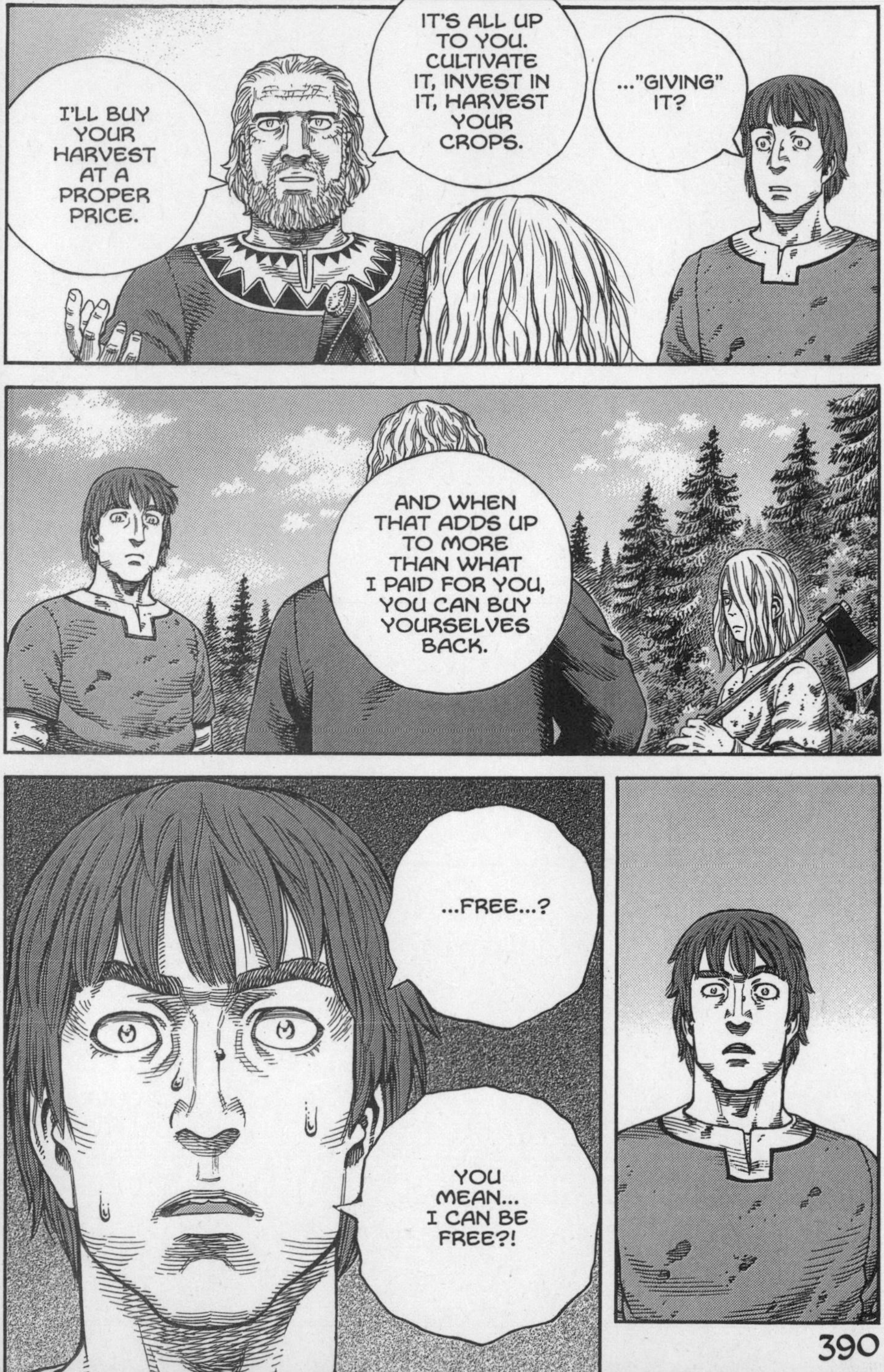
..."GIVING" IT?
IT'S ALL UP TO YOU. CULTIVATE IT, INVEST IN IT, HARVEST YOUR CROPS.
I'LL BUY YOUR HARVEST AT A PROPER PRICE.
AND WHEN THAT ADDS UP TO MORE THAN WHAT I PAID FOR YOU, YOU CAN BUY YOURSELVES BACK.
...FREE...?
YOU MEAN... I CAN BE FREE?!

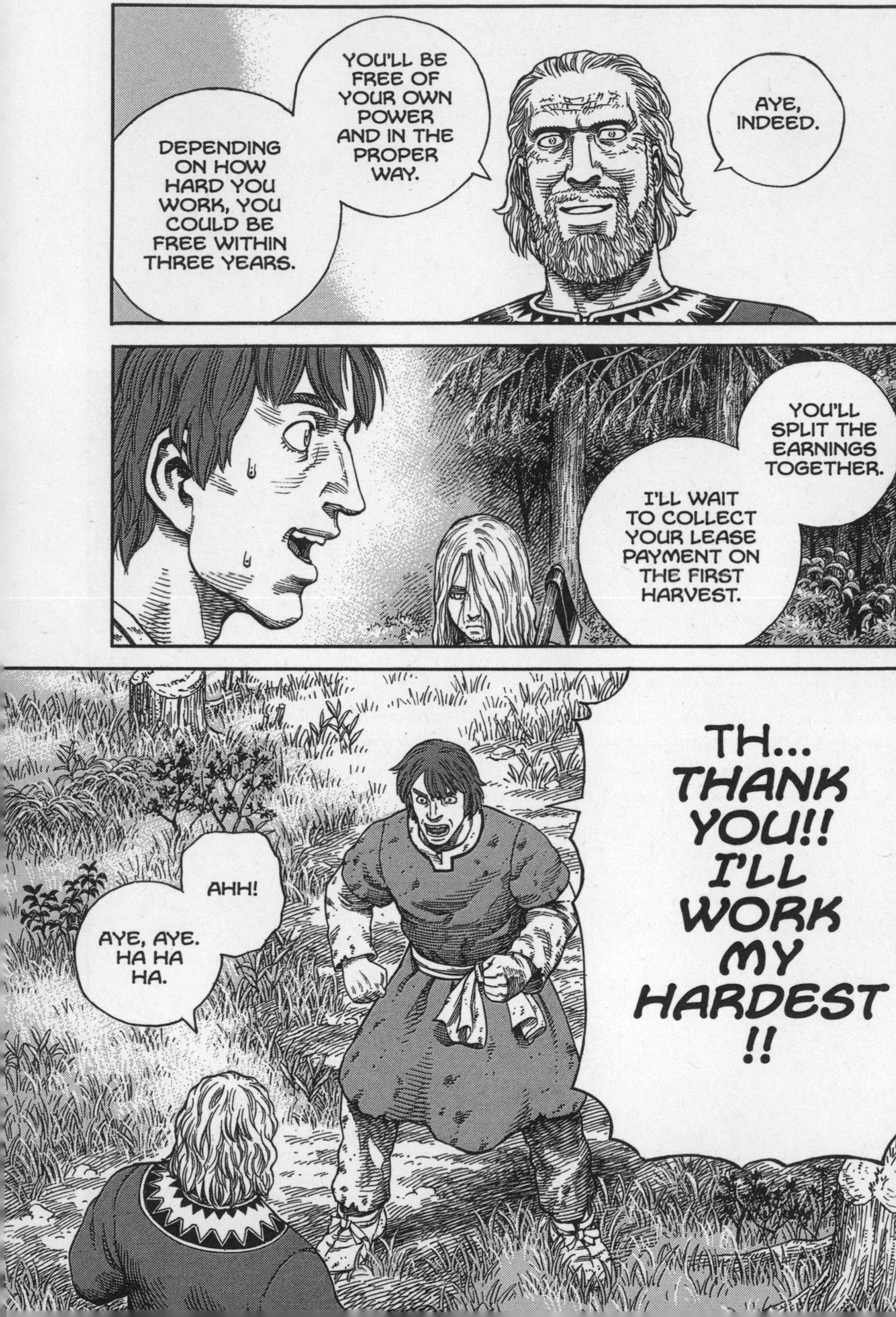
AYE, INDEED.
YOU'LL BE FREE OF YOUR OWN POWER AND IN THE PROPER WAY.
DEPENDING ON HOW HARD YOU WORK, YOU COULD BE FREE WITHIN THREE YEARS.
YOU'LL SPLIT THE EARNINGS TOGETHER.
I'LL WAIT TO COLLECT YOUR LEASE PAYMENT ON THE FIRST HARVEST.
TH... *THANK YOU!! I'LL WORK MY HARDEST!!*
AHH!
AYE, AYE. HA HA HA.

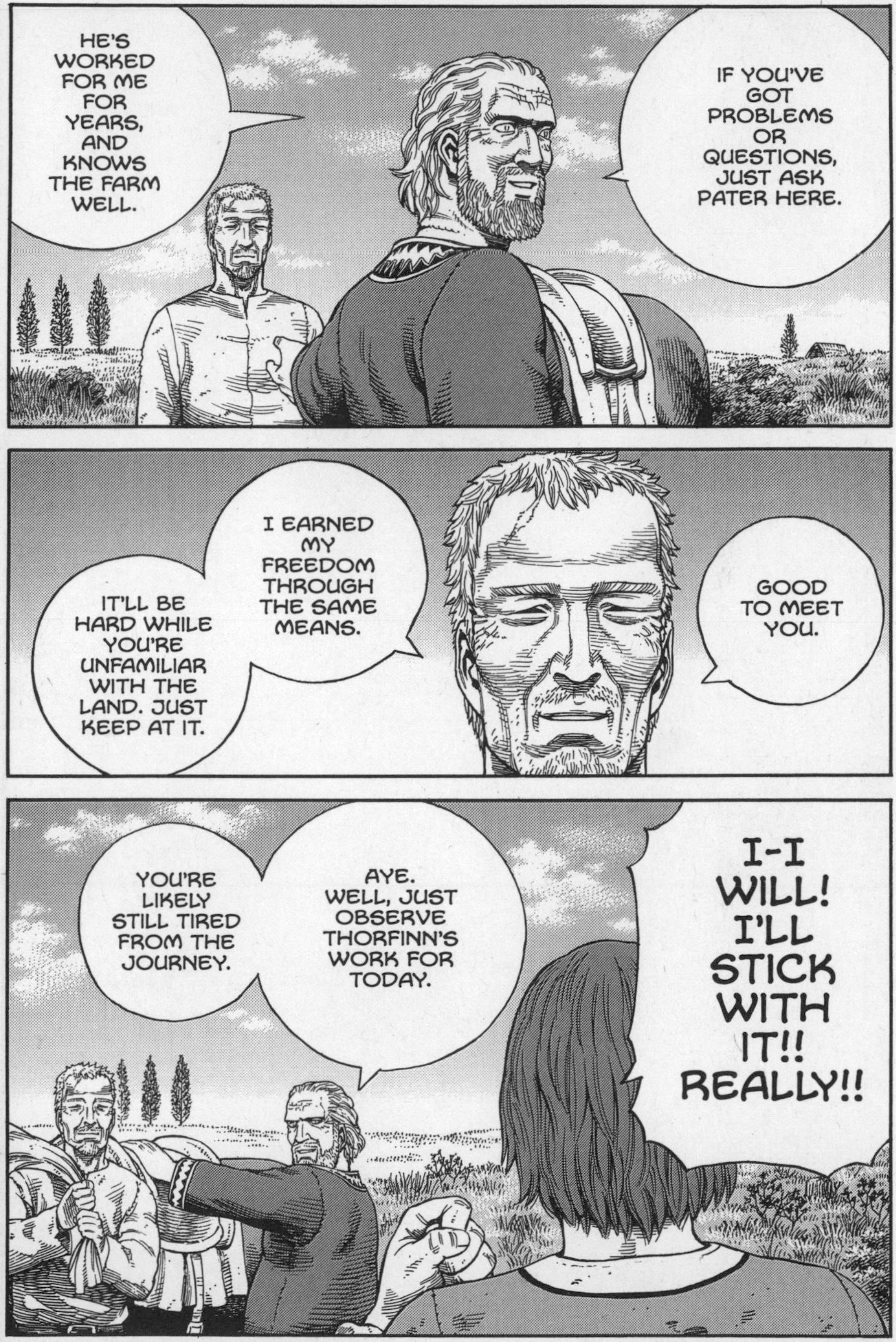
IF YOU'VE GOT PROBLEMS OR QUESTIONS, JUST ASK PATER HERE.
HE'S WORKED FOR ME FOR YEARS, AND KNOWS THE FARM WELL.
GOOD TO MEET YOU.
I EARNED MY FREEDOM THROUGH THE SAME MEANS.
IT'LL BE HARD WHILE YOU'RE UNFAMILIAR WITH THE LAND. JUST KEEP AT IT.
I-I WILL! I'LL STICK WITH IT!! REALLY!!
AYE. WELL, JUST OBSERVE THORFINN'S WORK FOR TODAY.
YOU'RE LIKELY STILL TIRED FROM THE JOURNEY.

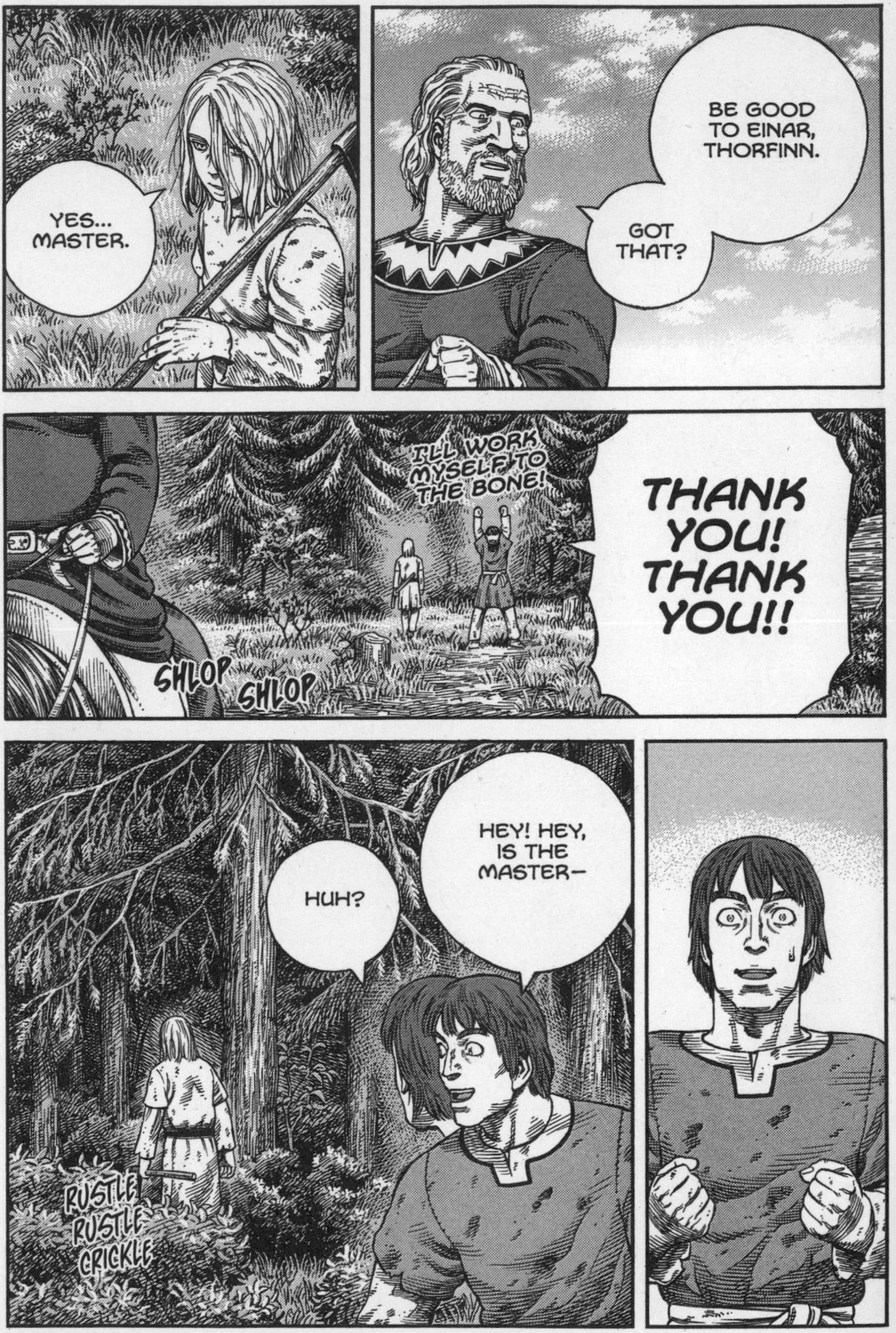
BE GOOD TO EINAR, THORFINN.
GOT THAT?
YES... MASTER.
THANK YOU! THANK YOU!!
I'LL WORK MYSELF TO THE BONE!
SHLOP
SHLOP
HEY! HEY, IS THE MASTER–
HUH?
RUSTLE RUSTLE CRICKLE

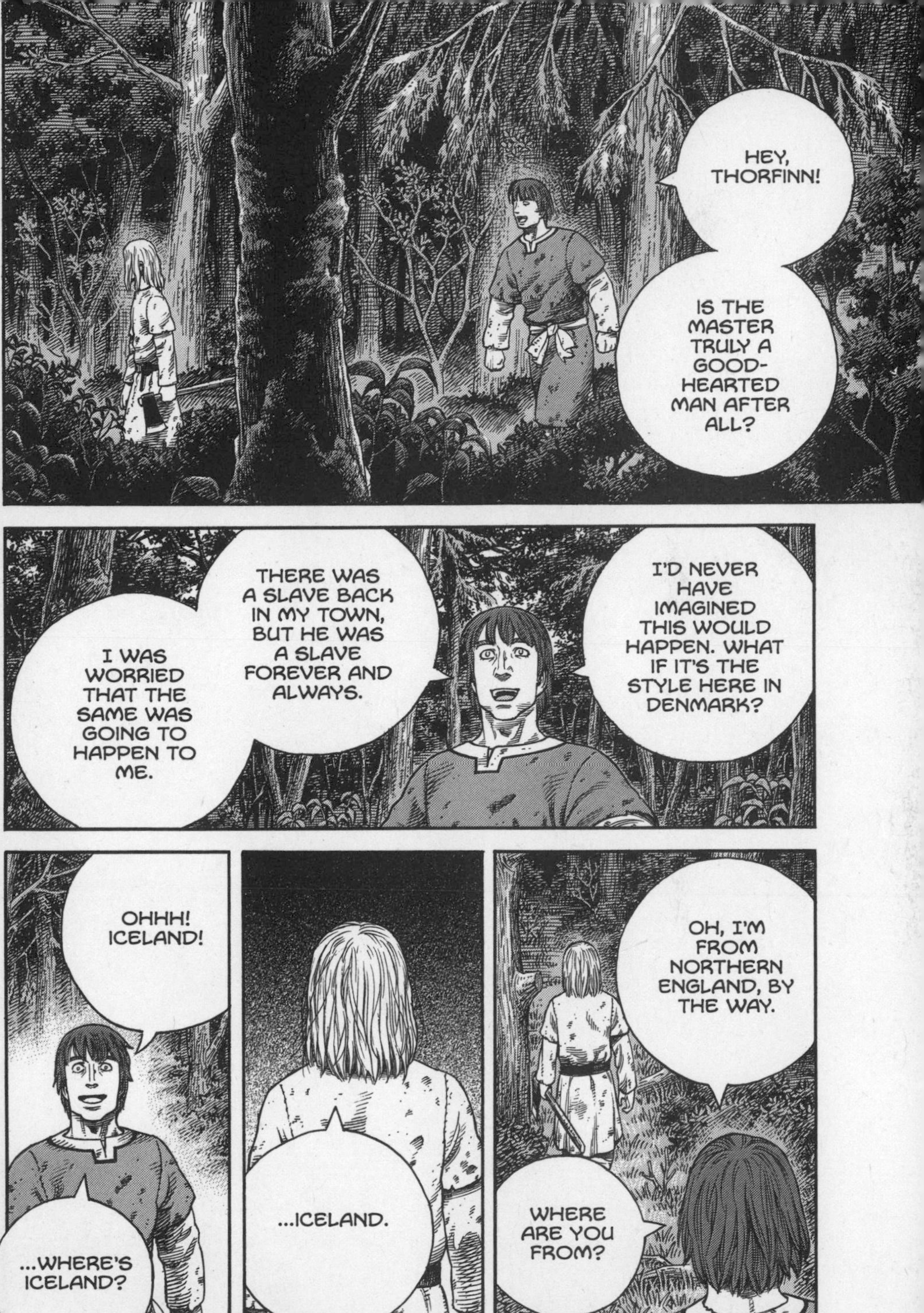
HEY, THORFINN!
IS THE MASTER TRULY A GOOD-HEARTED MAN AFTER ALL?
I'D NEVER HAVE IMAGINED THIS WOULD HAPPEN. WHAT IF IT'S THE STYLE HERE IN DENMARK?
THERE WAS A SLAVE BACK IN MY TOWN, BUT HE WAS A SLAVE FOREVER AND ALWAYS.
I WAS WORRIED THAT THE SAME WAS GOING TO HAPPEN TO ME.
OH, I'M FROM NORTHERN ENGLAND, BY THE WAY.
WHERE ARE YOU FROM?
...ICELAND.
OHHH! ICELAND!
...WHERE'S ICELAND?

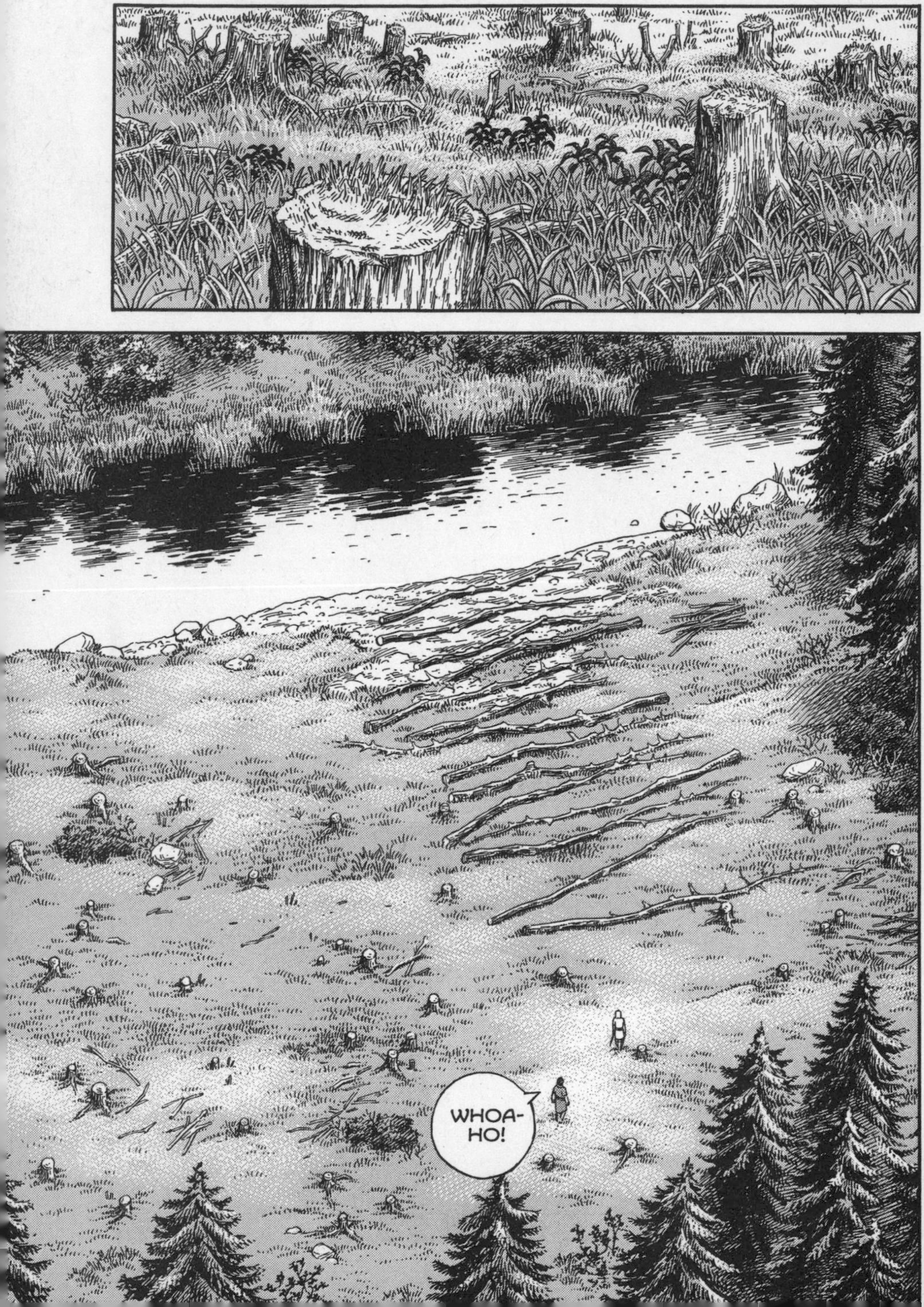
WHOA-HO!

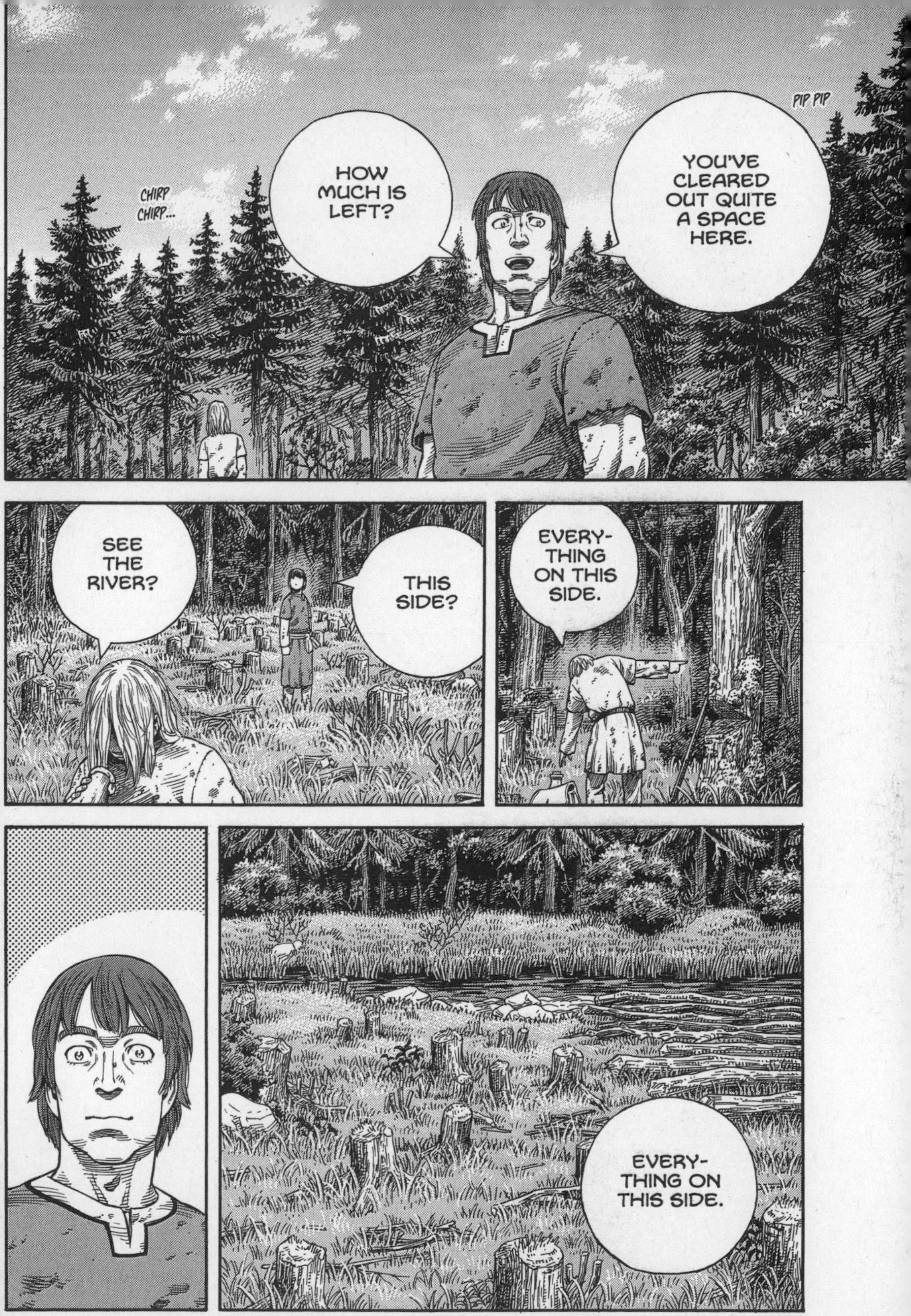
PIP PIP
YOU'VE CLEARED OUT QUITE A SPACE HERE.
HOW MUCH IS LEFT?
CHIRP CHIRP...
EVERY-THING ON THIS SIDE.
SEE THE RIVER?
THIS SIDE?
EVERY-THING ON THIS SIDE.

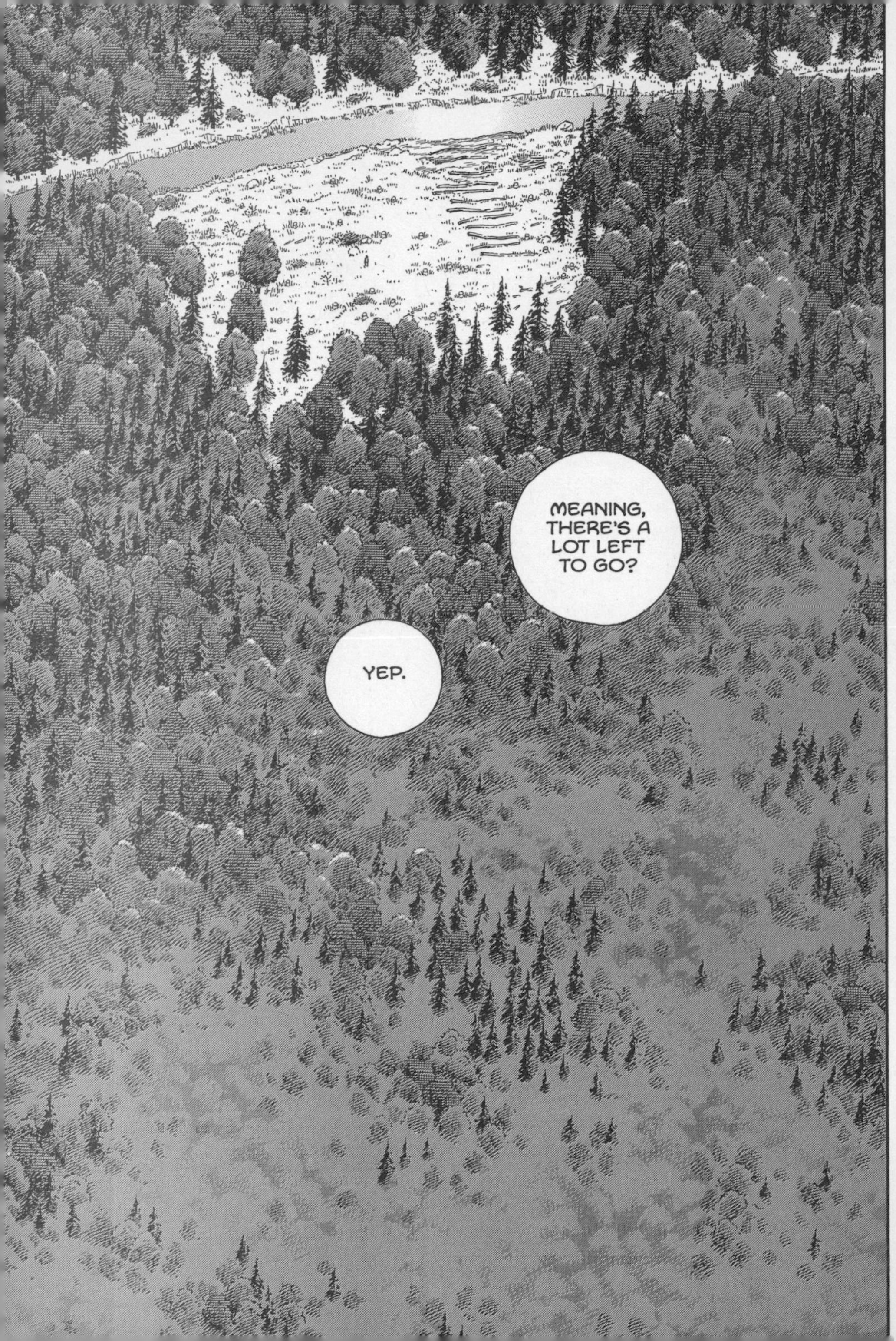
MEANING, THERE'S A LOT LEFT TO GO?
YEP.

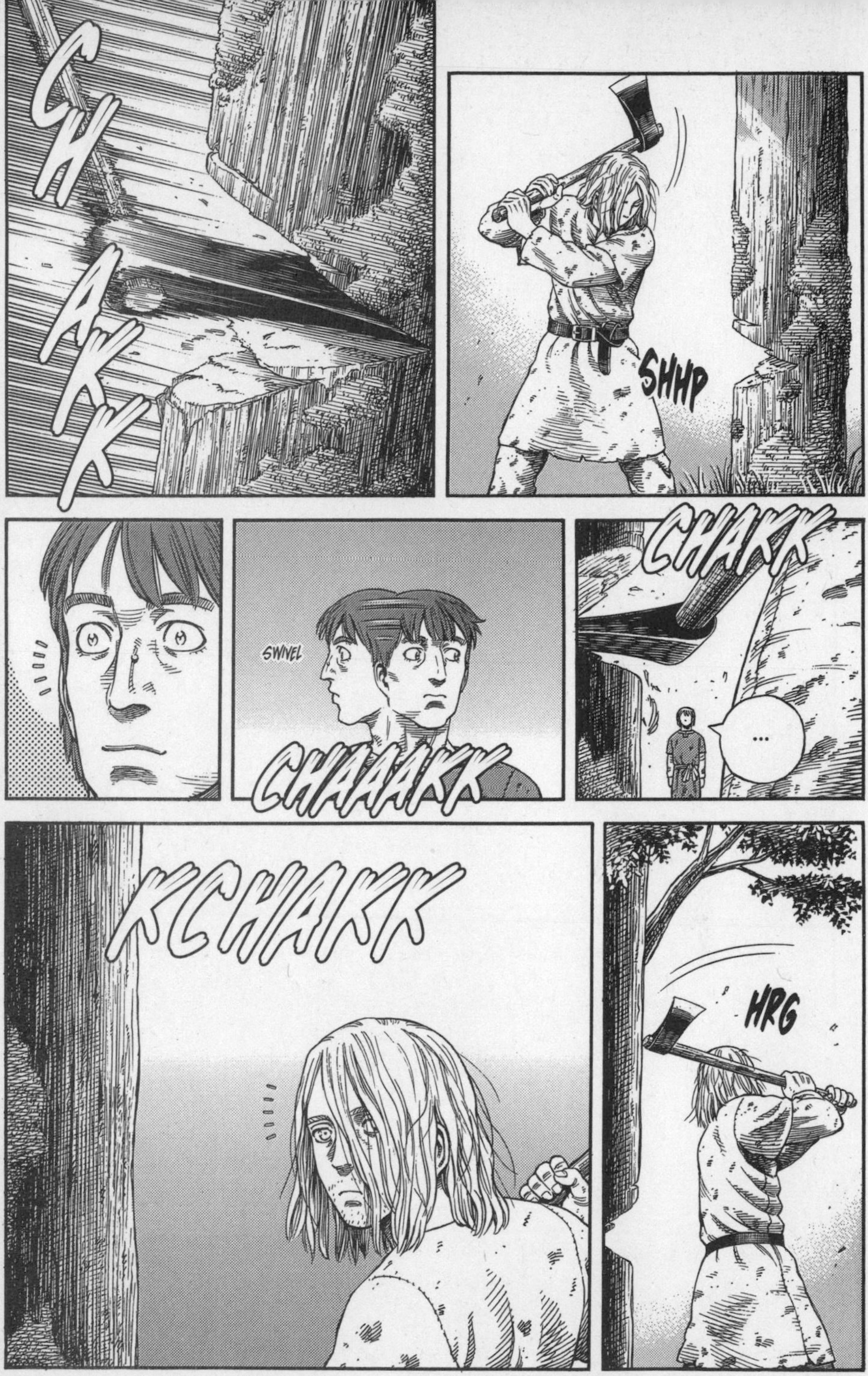
SHHP
CHAKK
CHAKK
...
SWIVEL
CHAAAKK
HRG
KCHAKK

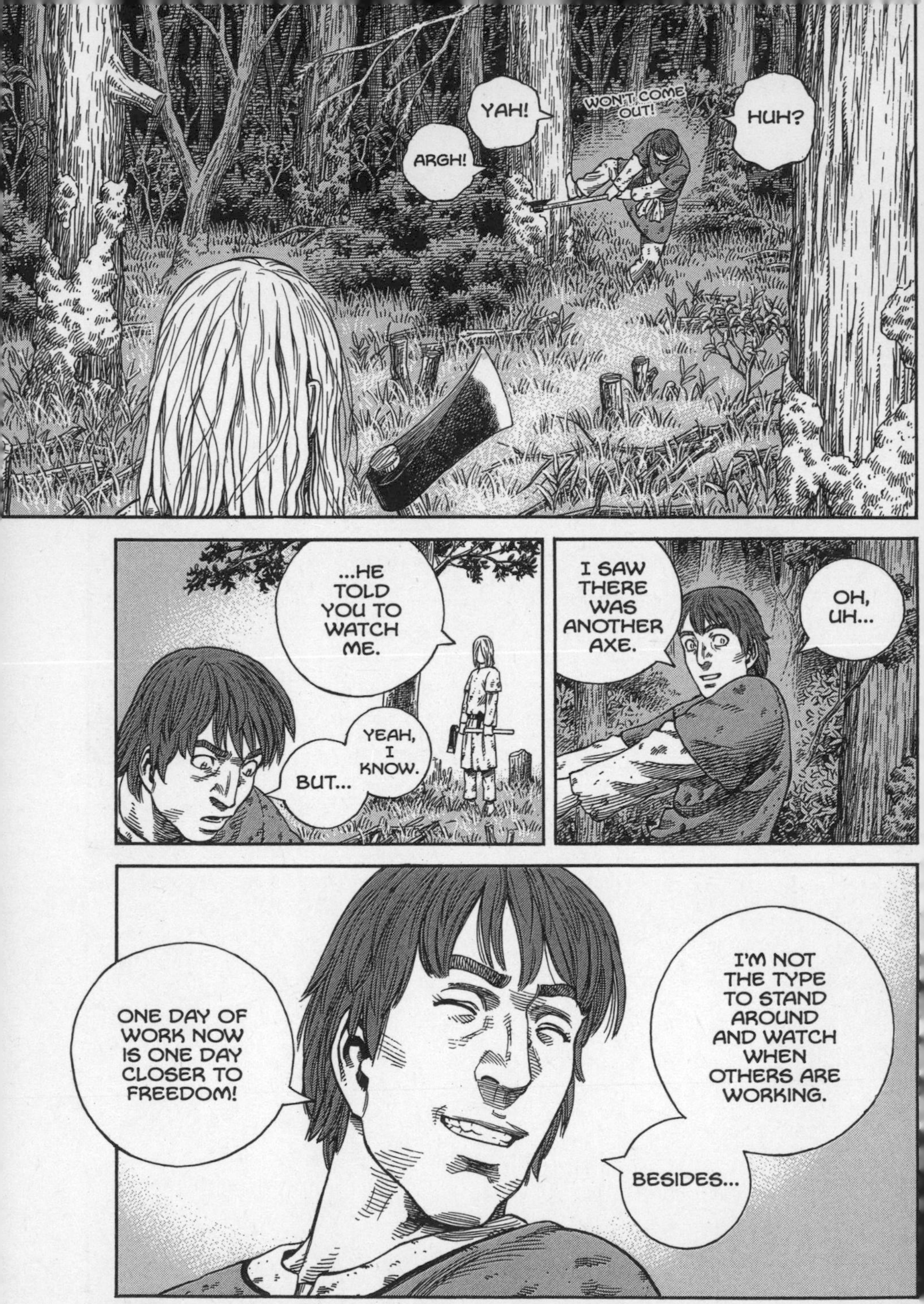
HUH?
WON'T COME OUT!
YAH!
ARGH!
OH, UH...
I SAW THERE WAS ANOTHER AXE.
...HE TOLD YOU TO WATCH ME.
YEAH, I KNOW.
BUT...
I'M NOT THE TYPE TO STAND AROUND AND WATCH WHEN OTHERS ARE WORKING.
BESIDES...
ONE DAY OF WORK NOW IS ONE DAY CLOSER TO FREEDOM!

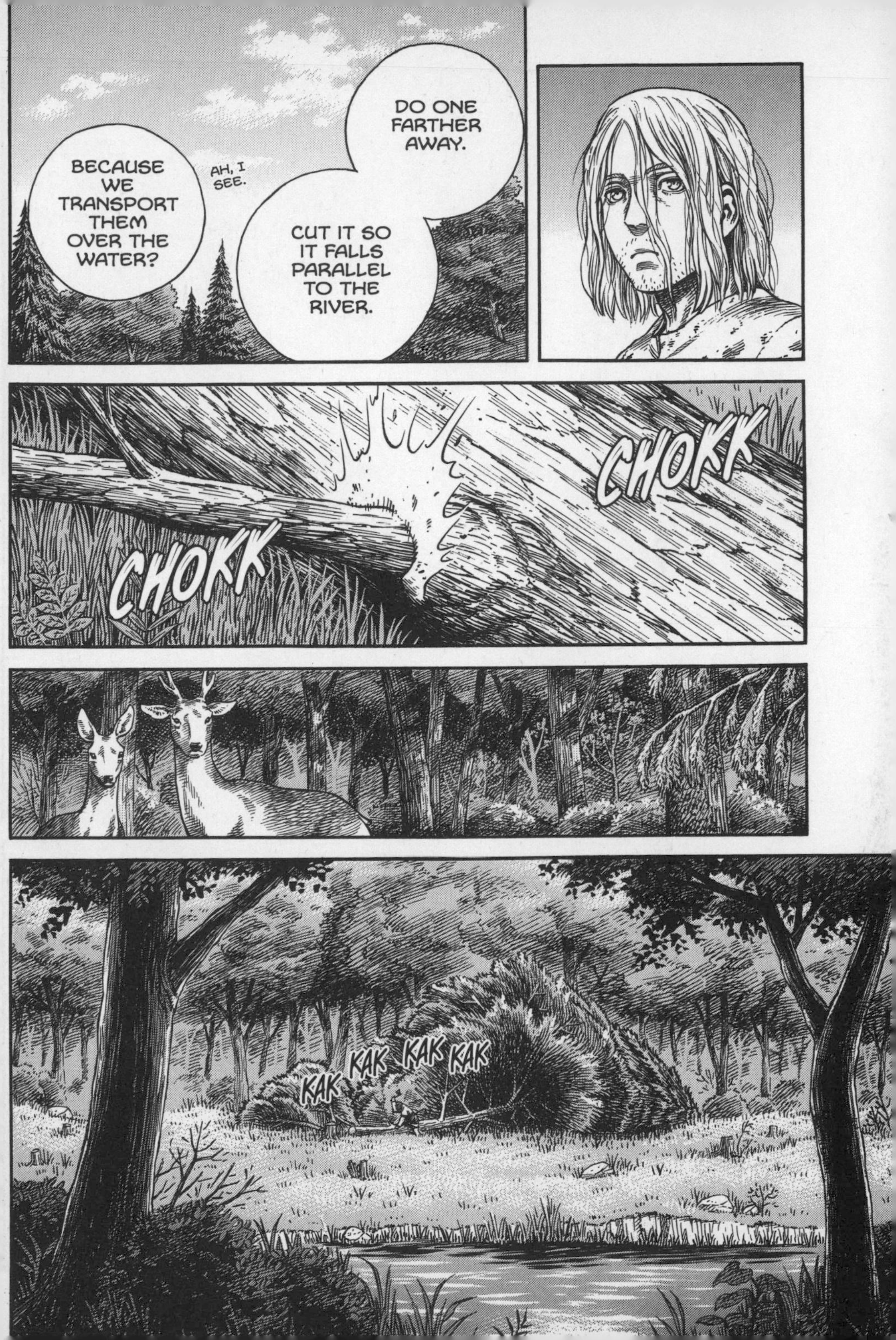

DO ONE FARTHER AWAY.
CUT IT SO IT FALLS PARALLEL TO THE RIVER.
AH, I SEE.
BECAUSE WE TRANSPORT THEM OVER THE WATER?
CHOKK
CHOKK
KAK KAK KAK KAK

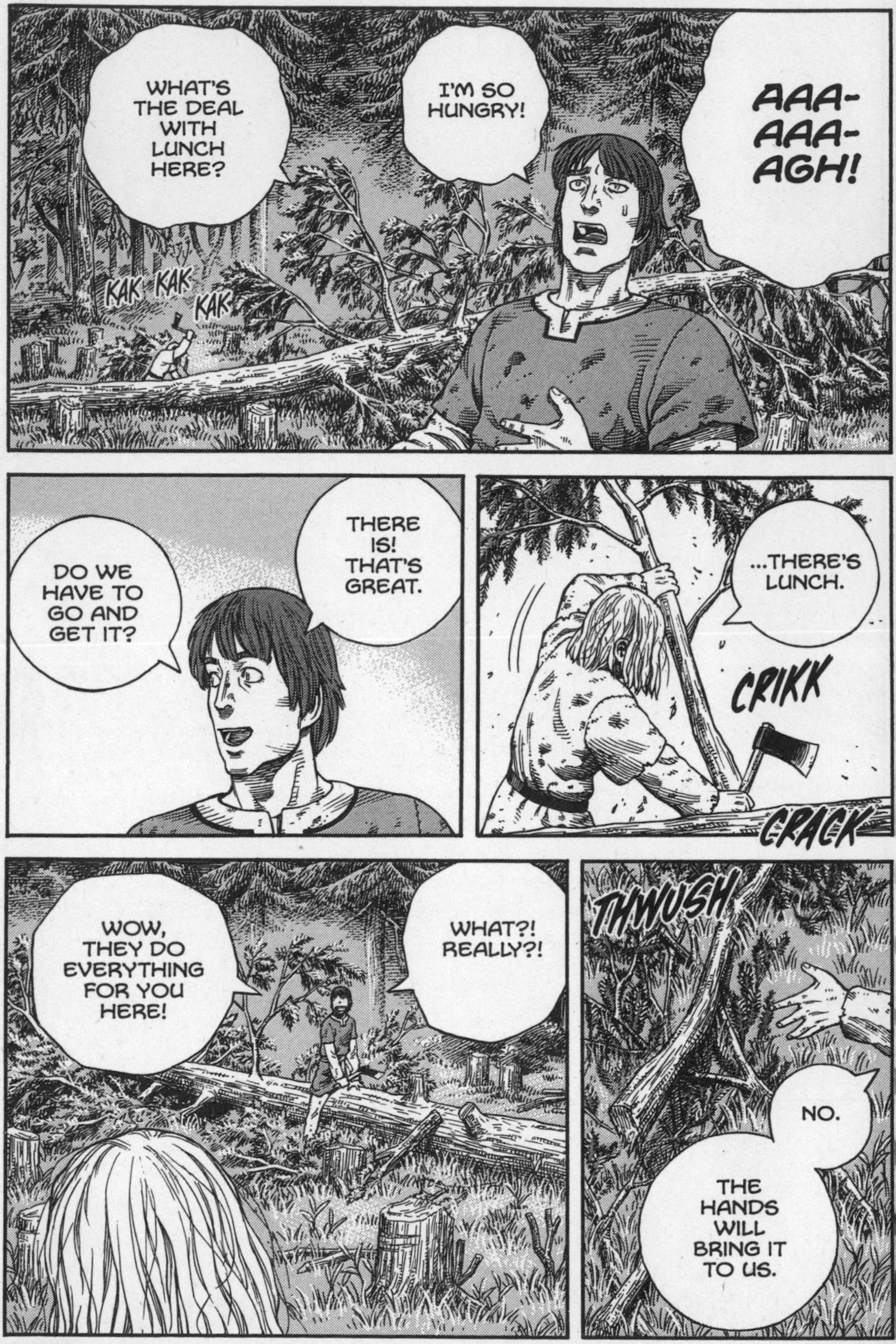
AAA-AAA-AGH!
I'M SO HUNGRY!
WHAT'S THE DEAL WITH LUNCH HERE?
KAK KAK KAK
...THERE'S LUNCH.
CRIKK
CRACK
THERE IS! THAT'S GREAT.
DO WE HAVE TO GO AND GET IT?
THWUSH
NO.
THE HANDS WILL BRING IT TO US.
WHAT?! REALLY?!
WOW, THEY DO EVERYTHING FOR YOU HERE!

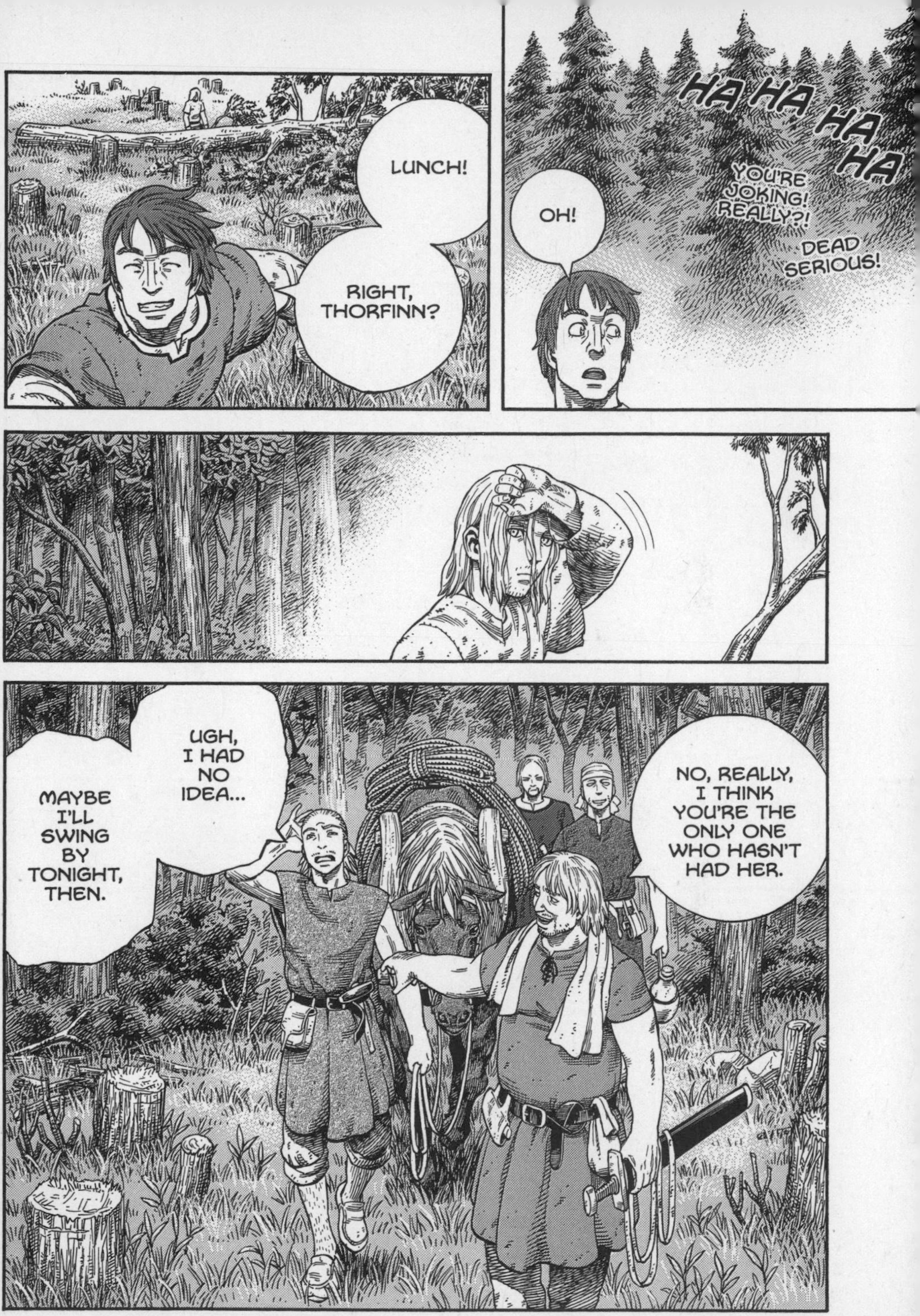
HA HA HA HA
YOU'RE JOKING! REALLY?!
DEAD SERIOUS!
OH!
LUNCH!
RIGHT, THORFINN?
NO, REALLY, I THINK YOU'RE THE ONLY ONE WHO HASN'T HAD HER.
UGH, I HAD NO IDEA...
MAYBE I'LL SWING BY TONIGHT, THEN.

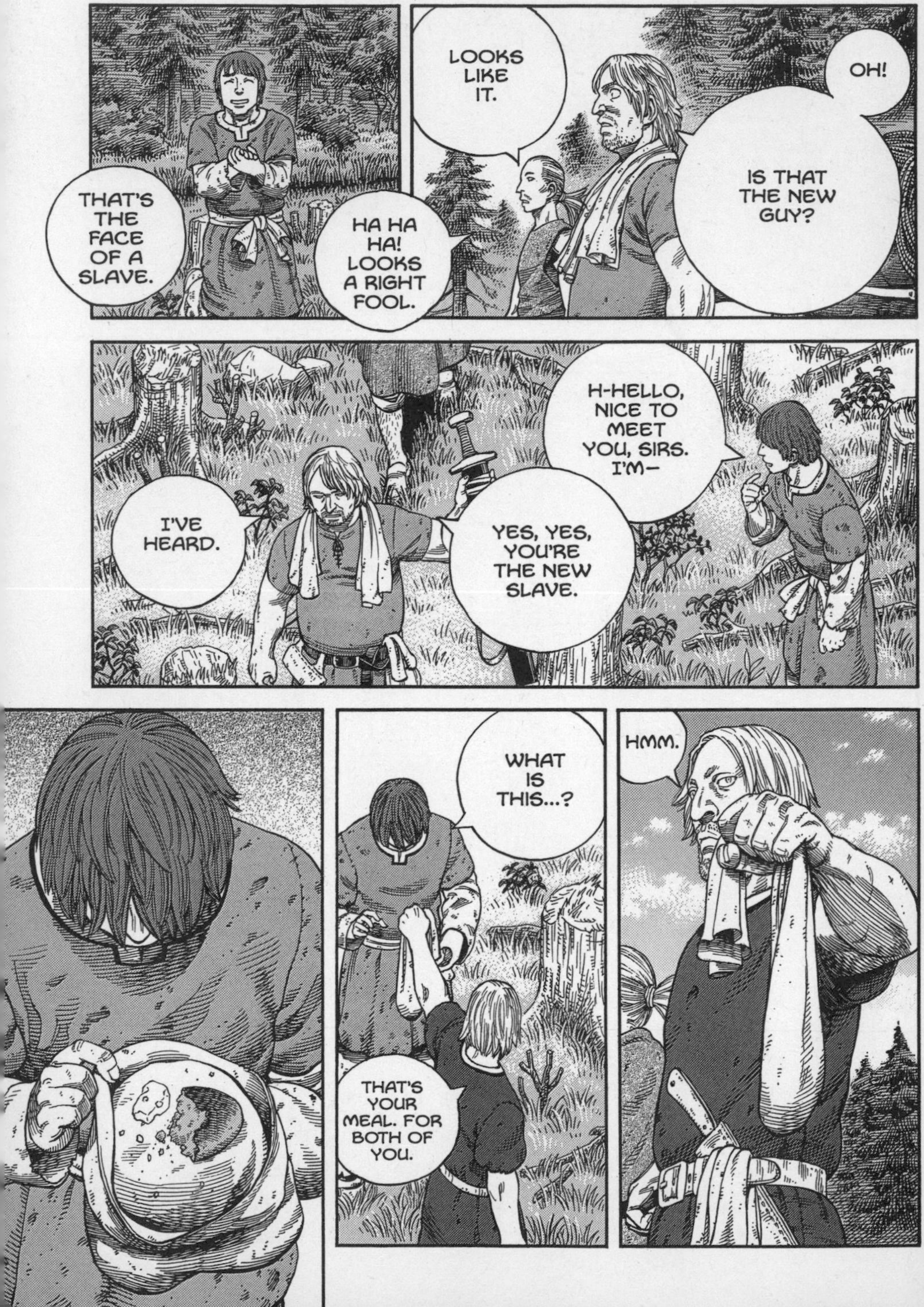
OH!
IS THAT THE NEW GUY?
LOOKS LIKE IT.
HA HA HA! LOOKS A RIGHT FOOL.
THAT'S THE FACE OF A SLAVE.
H-HELLO, NICE TO MEET YOU, SIRS. I'M—
YES, YES, YOU'RE THE NEW SLAVE.
I'VE HEARD.
HMM.
WHAT IS THIS...?
THAT'S YOUR MEAL. FOR BOTH OF YOU.

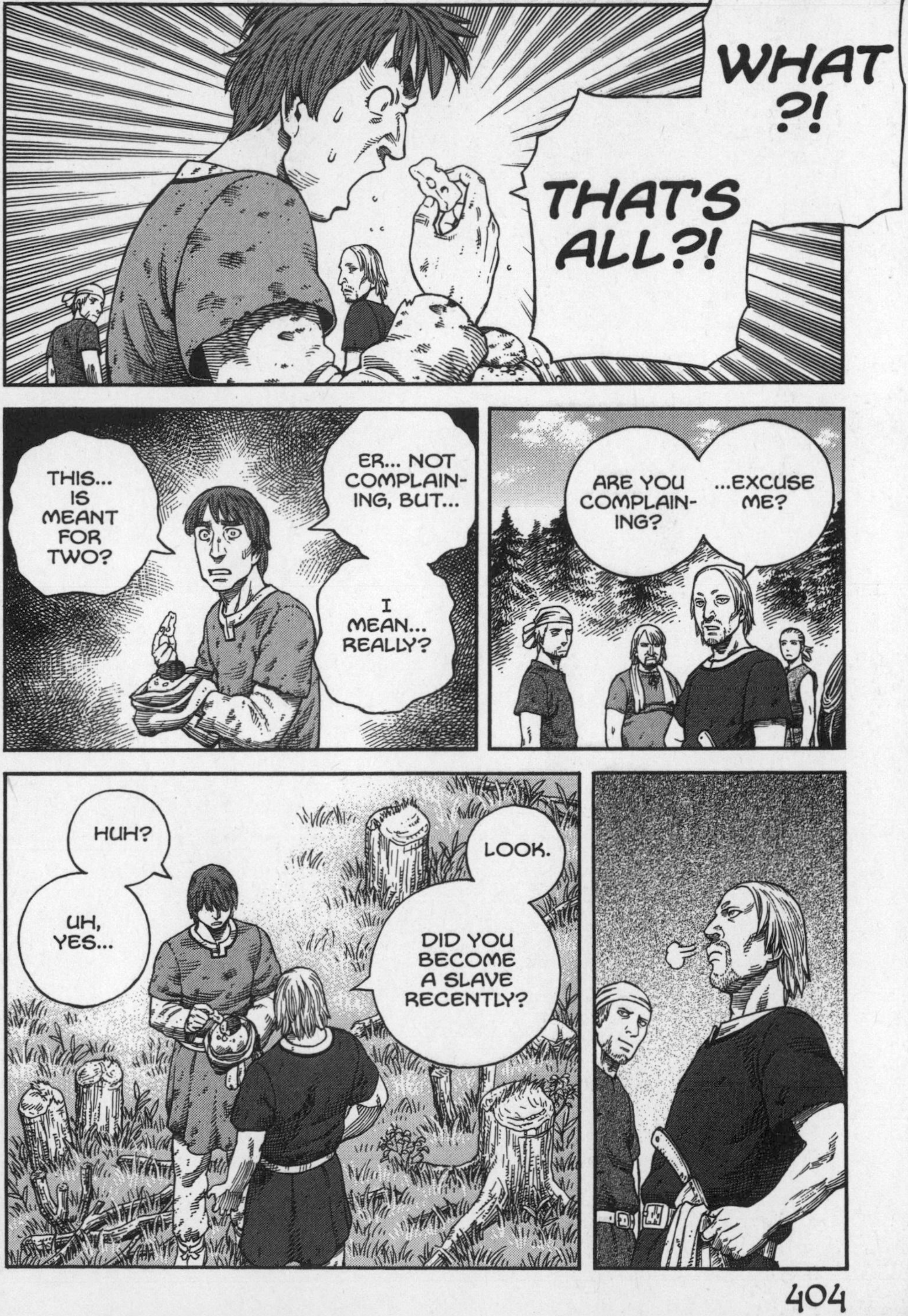
WHAT ?!
THAT'S ALL?!
...EXCUSE ME?
ARE YOU COMPLAINING?
ER... NOT COMPLAINING, BUT...
I MEAN... REALLY?
THIS... IS MEANT FOR TWO?
LOOK.
DID YOU BECOME A SLAVE RECENTLY?
HUH?
UH, YES...

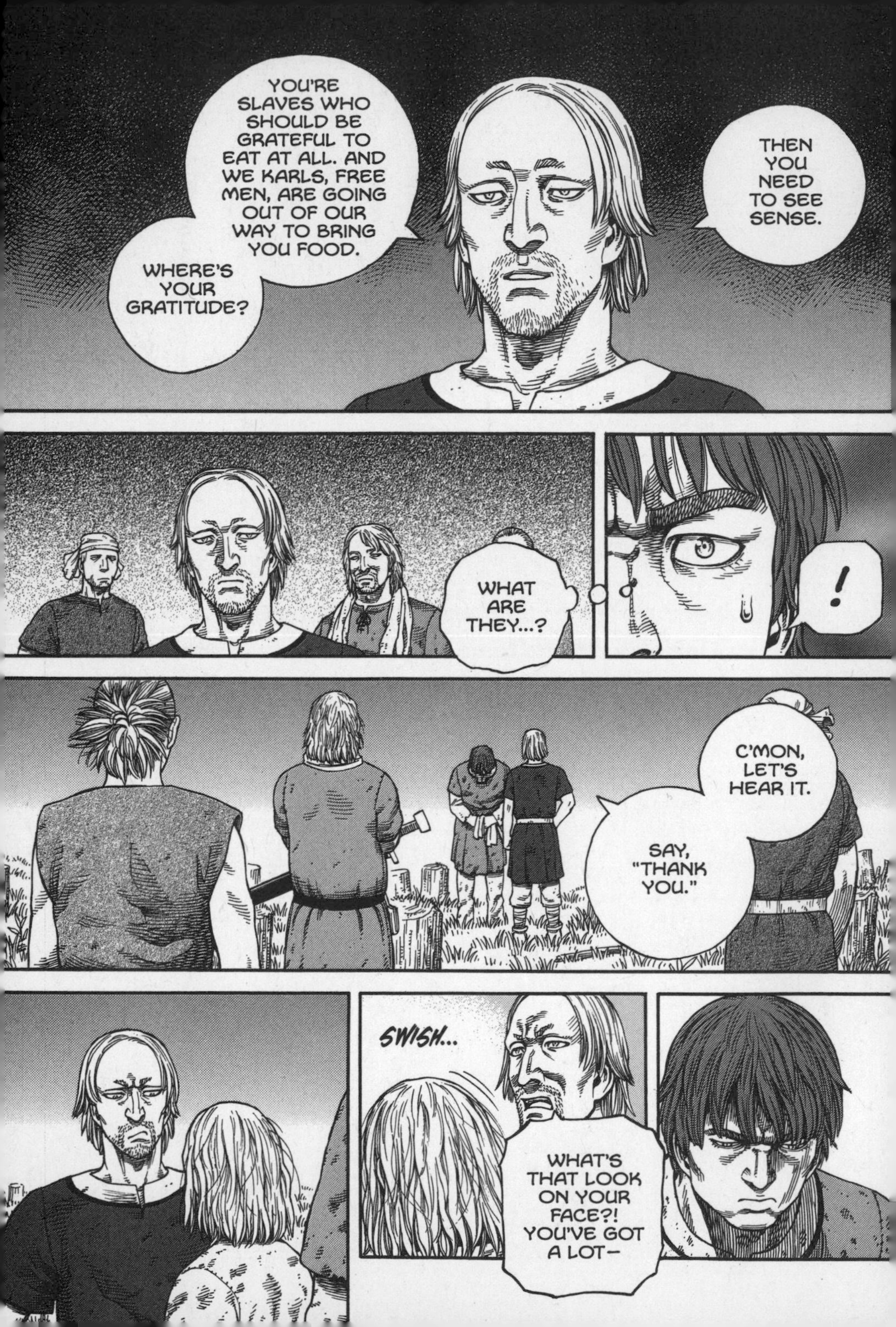
YOU'RE SLAVES WHO SHOULD BE GRATEFUL TO EAT AT ALL. AND WE KARLS, FREE MEN, ARE GOING OUT OF OUR WAY TO BRING YOU FOOD.
WHERE'S YOUR GRATITUDE?
THEN YOU NEED TO SEE SENSE.
!
WHAT ARE THEY...?
C'MON, LET'S HEAR IT.
SAY, "THANK YOU."
WHAT'S THAT LOOK ON YOUR FACE?! YOU'VE GOT A LOT—
SWISH...

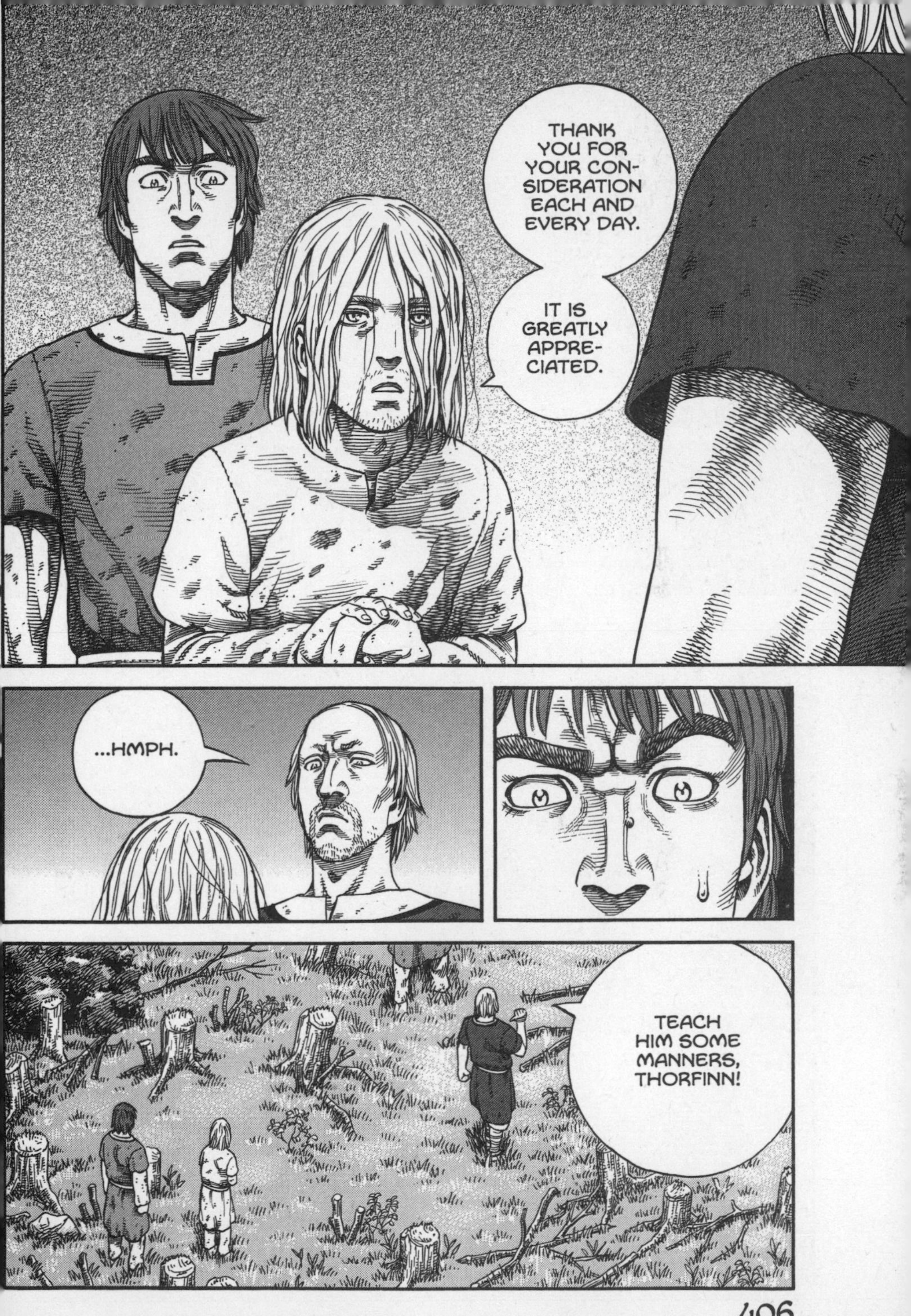
THANK YOU FOR YOUR CON-SIDERATION EACH AND EVERY DAY.
IT IS GREATLY APPRE-CIATED.
...HMPH.
TEACH HIM SOME MANNERS, THORFINN!

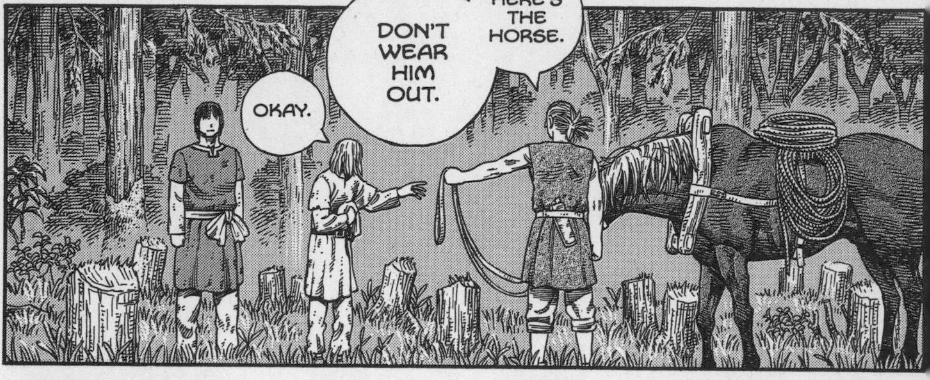
HERE'S THE HORSE.
DON'T WEAR HIM OUT.
OKAY.

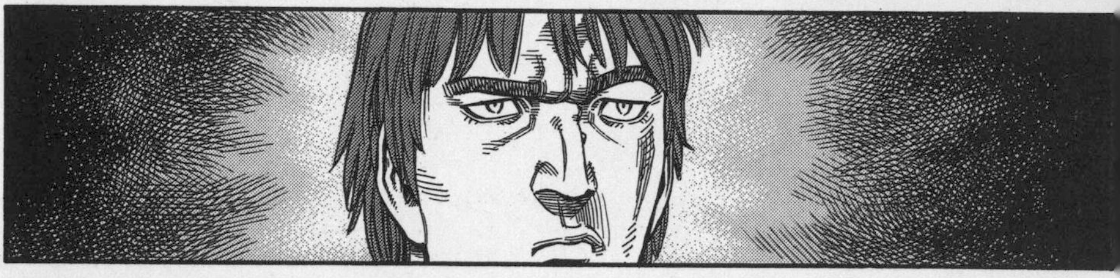

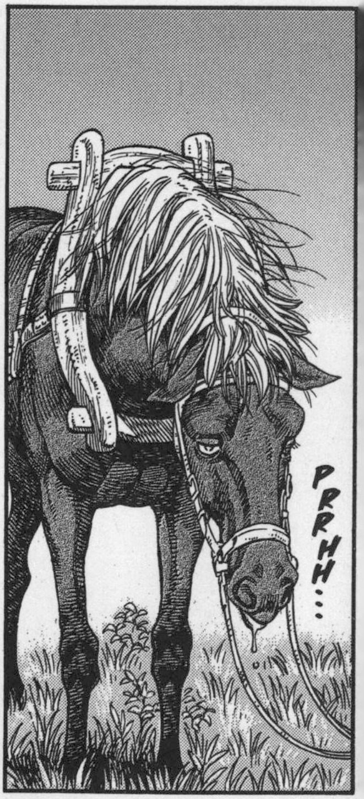
PRRHH...

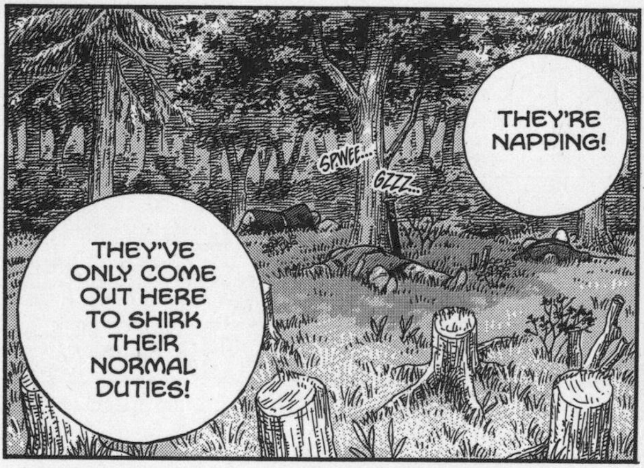
THEY'RE NAPPING!
SPWEE...
GZZZ...
THEY'VE ONLY COME OUT HERE TO SHIRK THEIR NORMAL DUTIES!

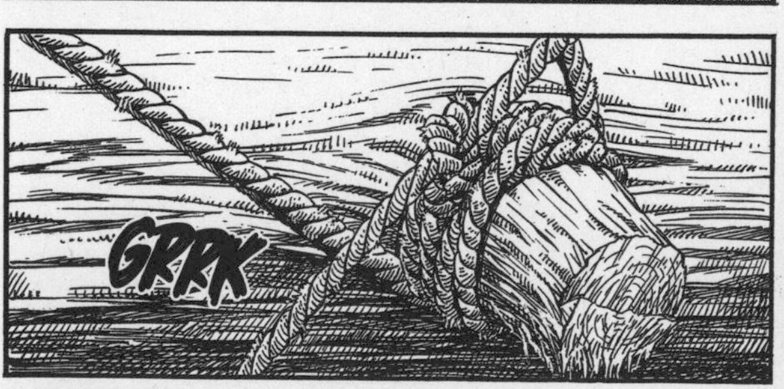
GRRK

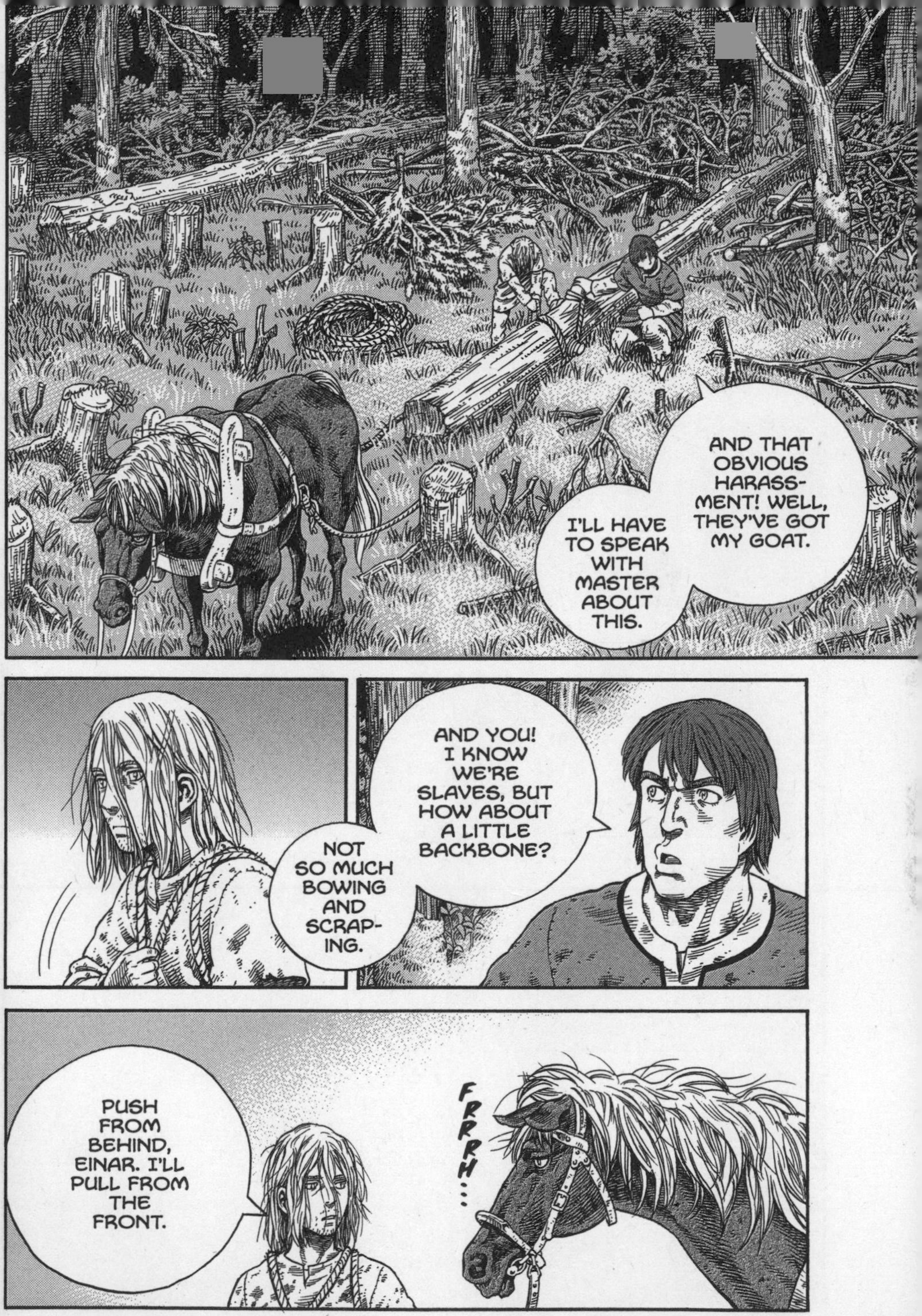
AND THAT OBVIOUS HARASSMENT! WELL, THEY'VE GOT MY GOAT.
I'LL HAVE TO SPEAK WITH MASTER ABOUT THIS.
AND YOU! I KNOW WE'RE SLAVES, BUT HOW ABOUT A LITTLE BACKBONE?
NOT SO MUCH BOWING AND SCRAPING.
FRRRH...
PUSH FROM BEHIND, EINAR. I'LL PULL FROM THE FRONT.

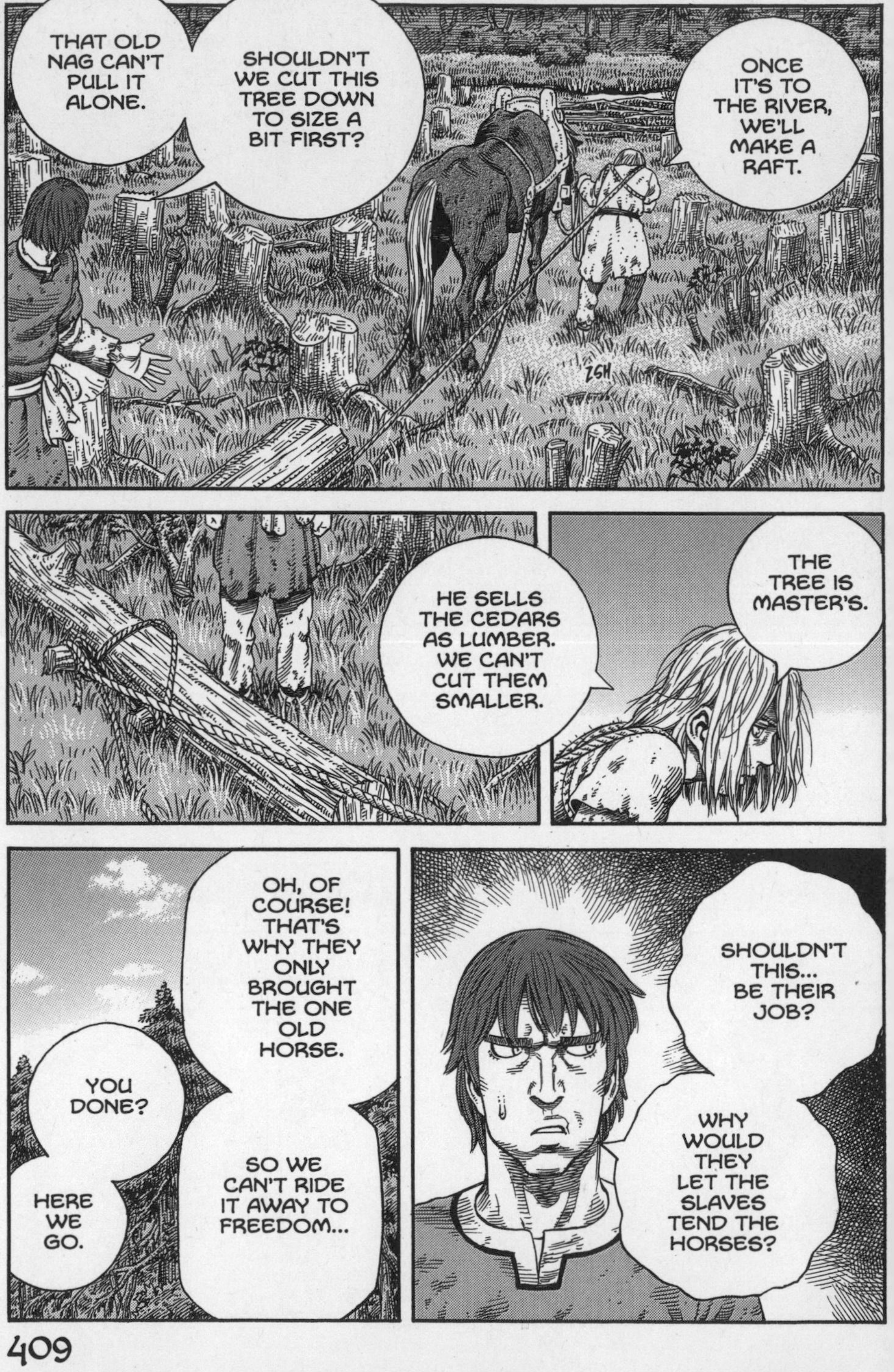

ONCE IT'S TO THE RIVER, WE'LL MAKE A RAFT.
SHOULDN'T WE CUT THIS TREE DOWN TO SIZE A BIT FIRST?
THAT OLD NAG CAN'T PULL IT ALONE.
ZSH
THE TREE IS MASTER'S.
HE SELLS THE CEDARS AS LUMBER. WE CAN'T CUT THEM SMALLER.
SHOULDN'T THIS... BE THEIR JOB?
WHY WOULD THEY LET THE SLAVES TEND THE HORSES?
OH, OF COURSE! THAT'S WHY THEY ONLY BROUGHT THE ONE OLD HORSE.
SO WE CAN'T RIDE IT AWAY TO FREEDOM...
YOU DONE?
HERE WE GO.

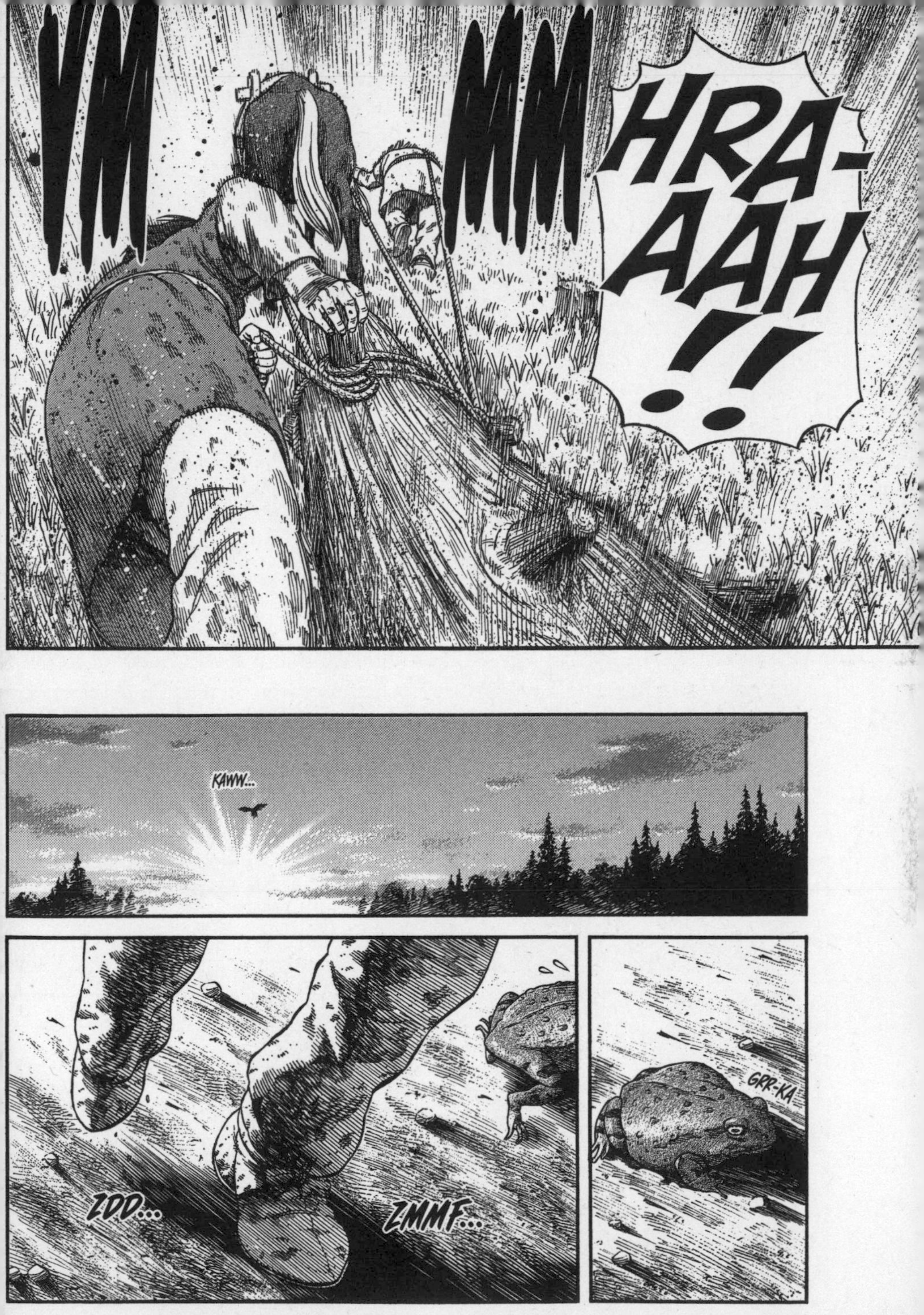
HRA-AAH!!
YM MMM
KAWW...
GRR-KA
ZMMF...
ZDD...

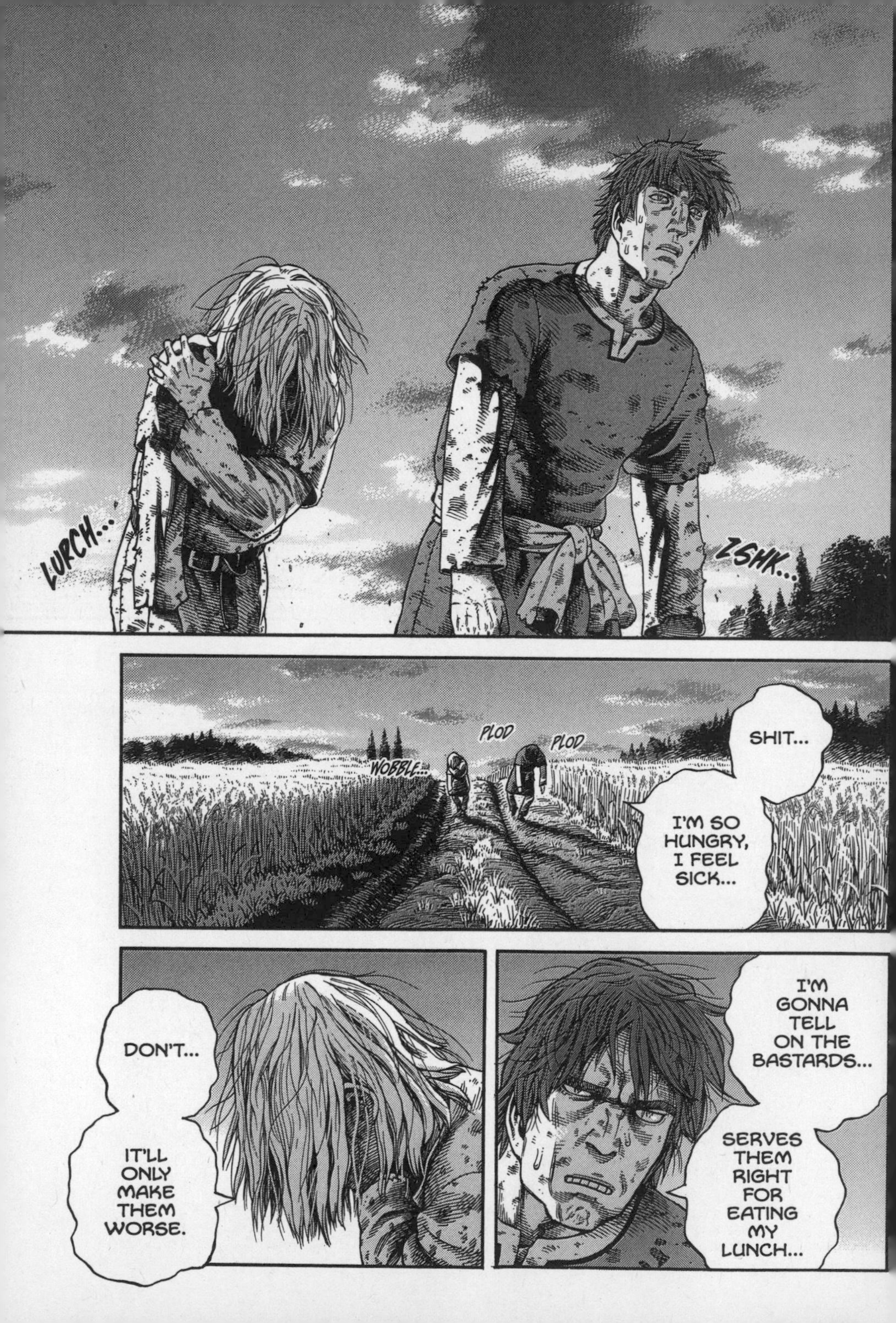
ZSHK...
LURCH...
SHIT...
PLOD
PLOD
WOBBLE...
I'M SO HUNGRY, I FEEL SICK...
I'M GONNA TELL ON THE BASTARDS...
SERVES THEM RIGHT FOR EATING MY LUNCH...
DON'T...
IT'LL ONLY MAKE THEM WORSE.

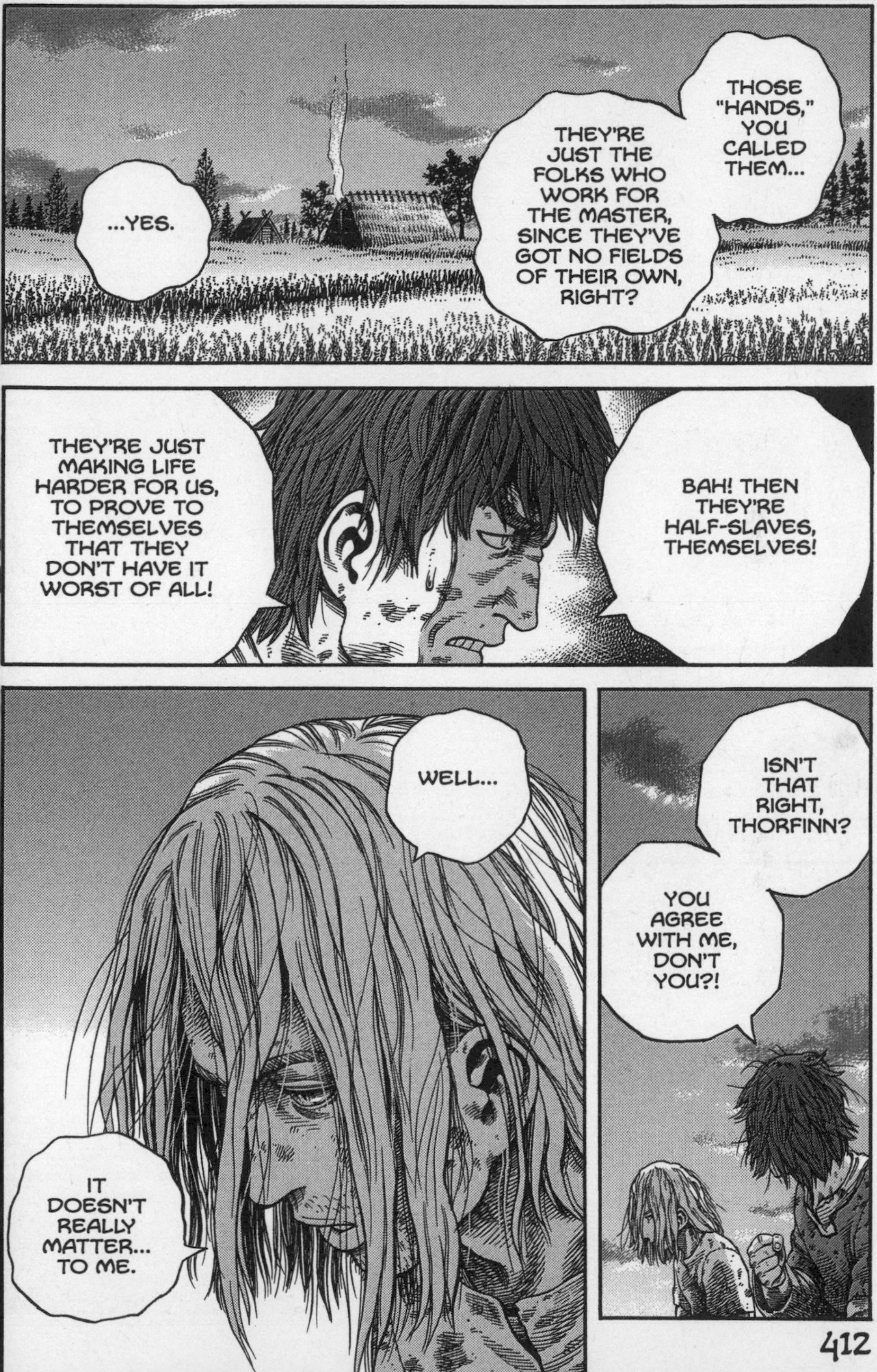
THOSE "HANDS," YOU CALLED THEM...
THEY'RE JUST THE FOLKS WHO WORK FOR THE MASTER, SINCE THEY'VE GOT NO FIELDS OF THEIR OWN, RIGHT?
...YES.
BAH! THEN THEY'RE HALF-SLAVES, THEMSELVES!
THEY'RE JUST MAKING LIFE HARDER FOR US, TO PROVE TO THEMSELVES THAT THEY DON'T HAVE IT WORST OF ALL!
ISN'T THAT RIGHT, THORFINN?
YOU AGREE WITH ME, DON'T YOU?!
WELL...
IT DOESN'T REALLY MATTER... TO ME.

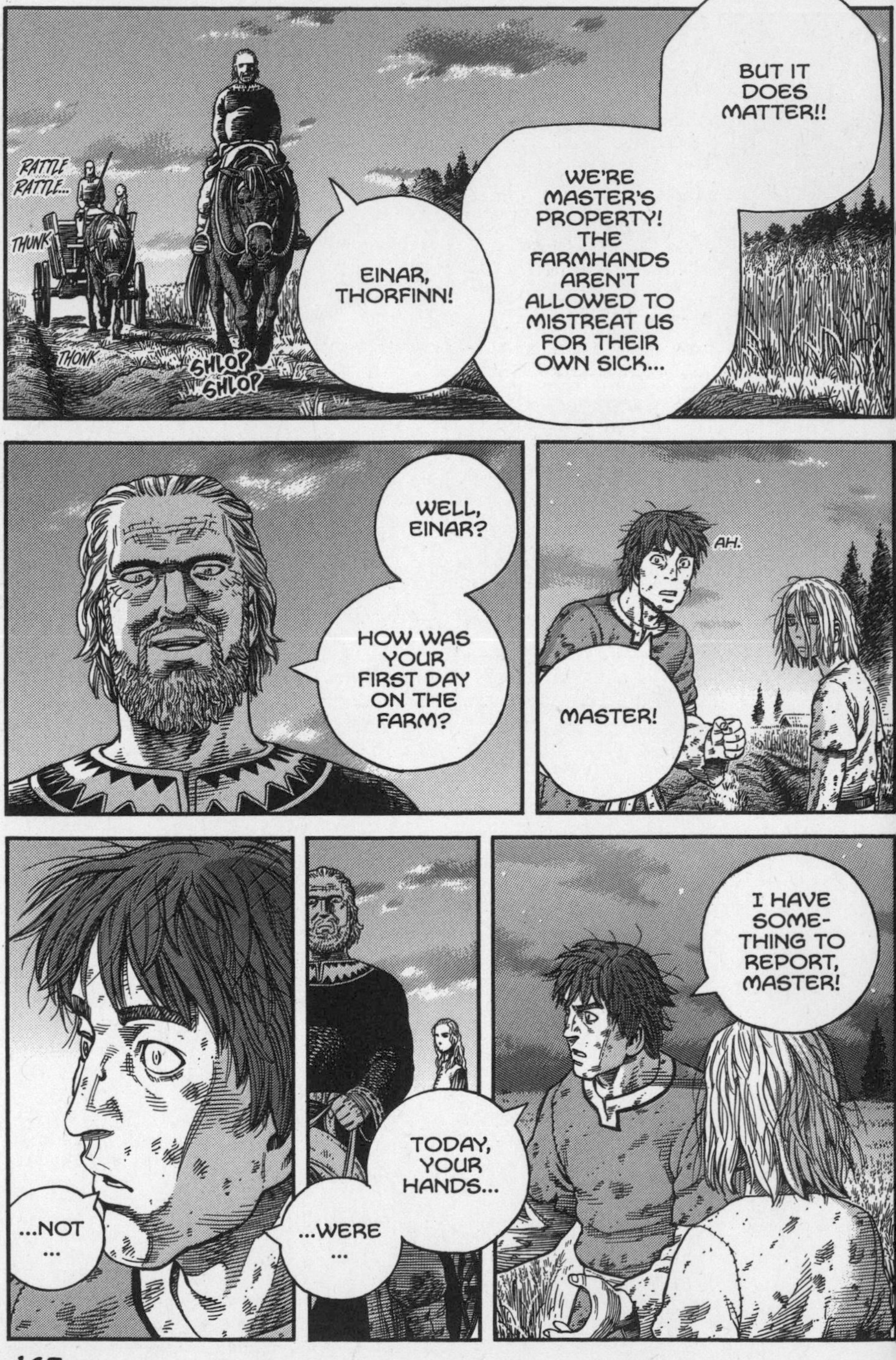
BUT IT DOES MATTER!!
WE'RE MASTER'S PROPERTY! THE FARMHANDS AREN'T ALLOWED TO MISTREAT US FOR THEIR OWN SICK...
EINAR, THORFINN!
RATTLE RATTLE...
THUNK
THONK
SHLOP SHLOP
AH.
MASTER!
WELL, EINAR?
HOW WAS YOUR FIRST DAY ON THE FARM?
I HAVE SOME-THING TO REPORT, MASTER!
TODAY, YOUR HANDS...
...WERE ...
...NOT ...

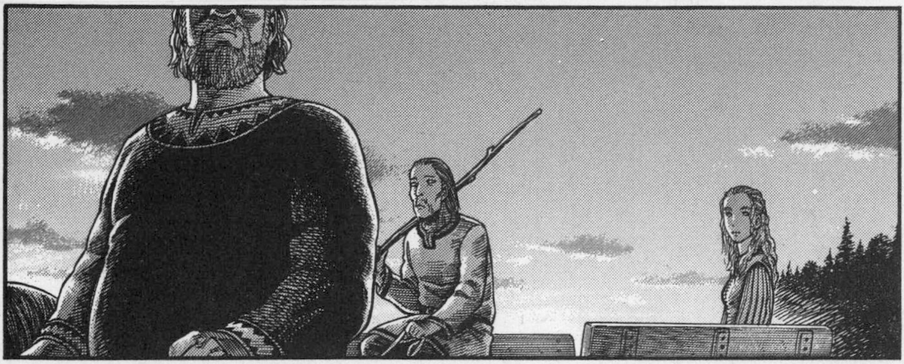
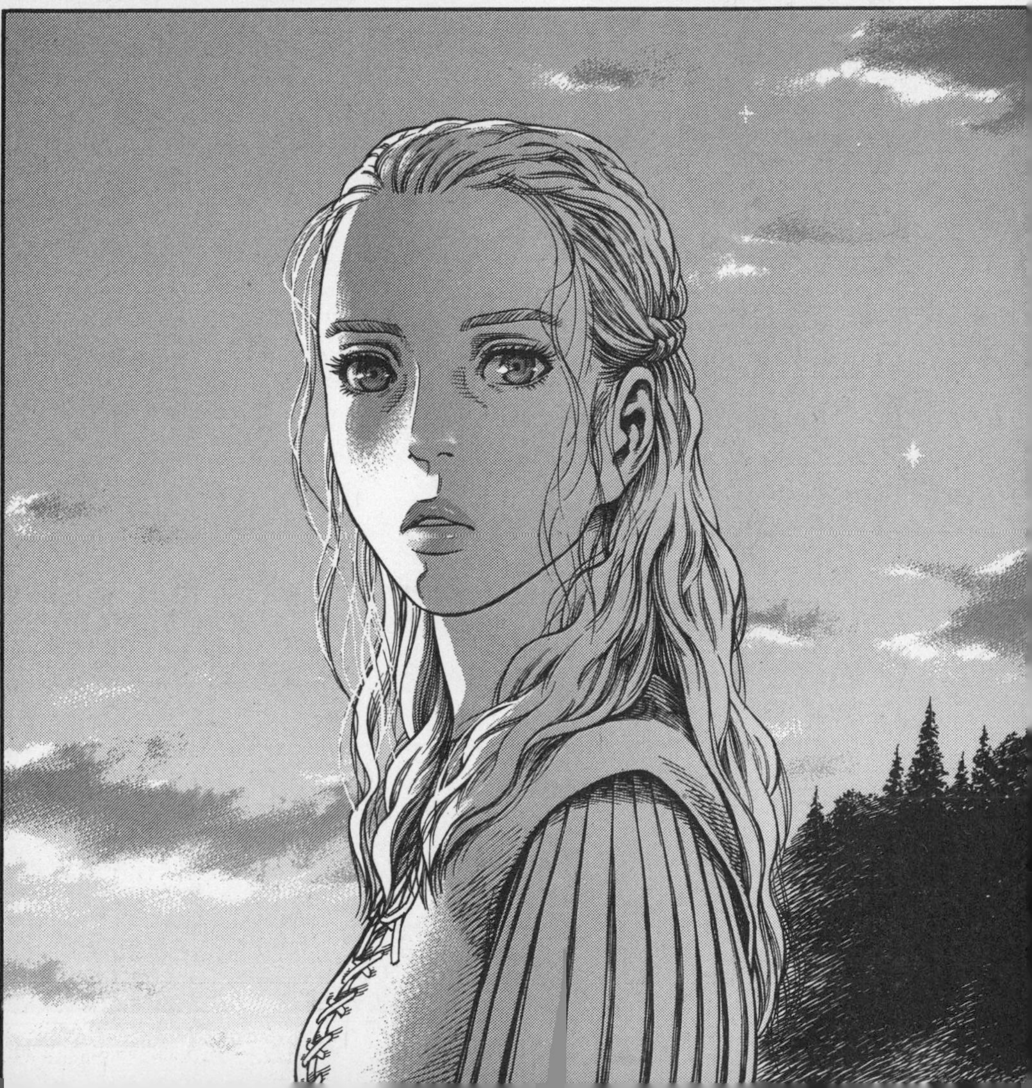

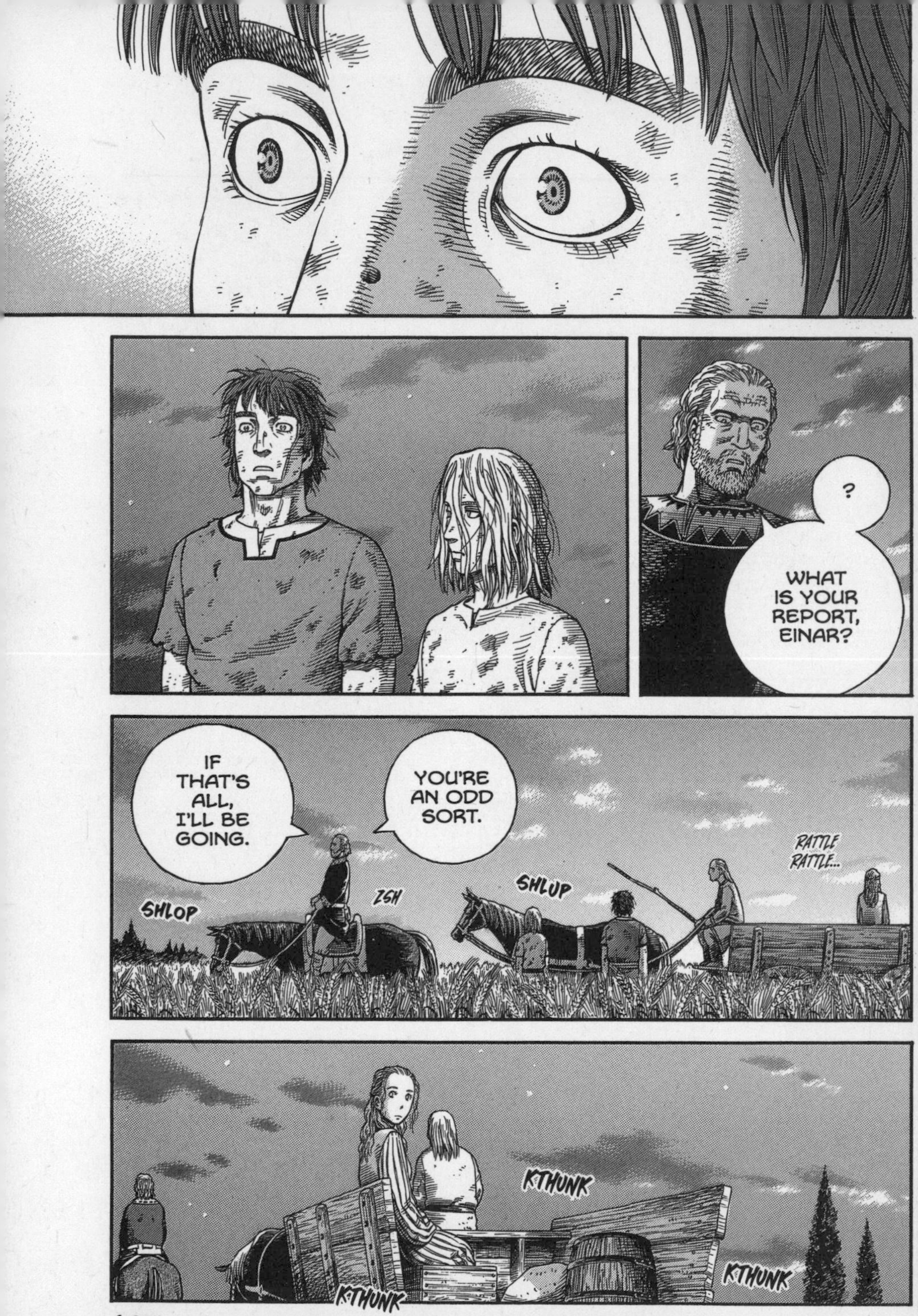
?
WHAT IS YOUR REPORT, EINAR?
RATTLE RATTLE...
SHLUP
YOU'RE AN ODD SORT.
ZSH
IF THAT'S ALL, I'LL BE GOING.
SHLOP
KTHUNK
KTHUNK
KTHUNK

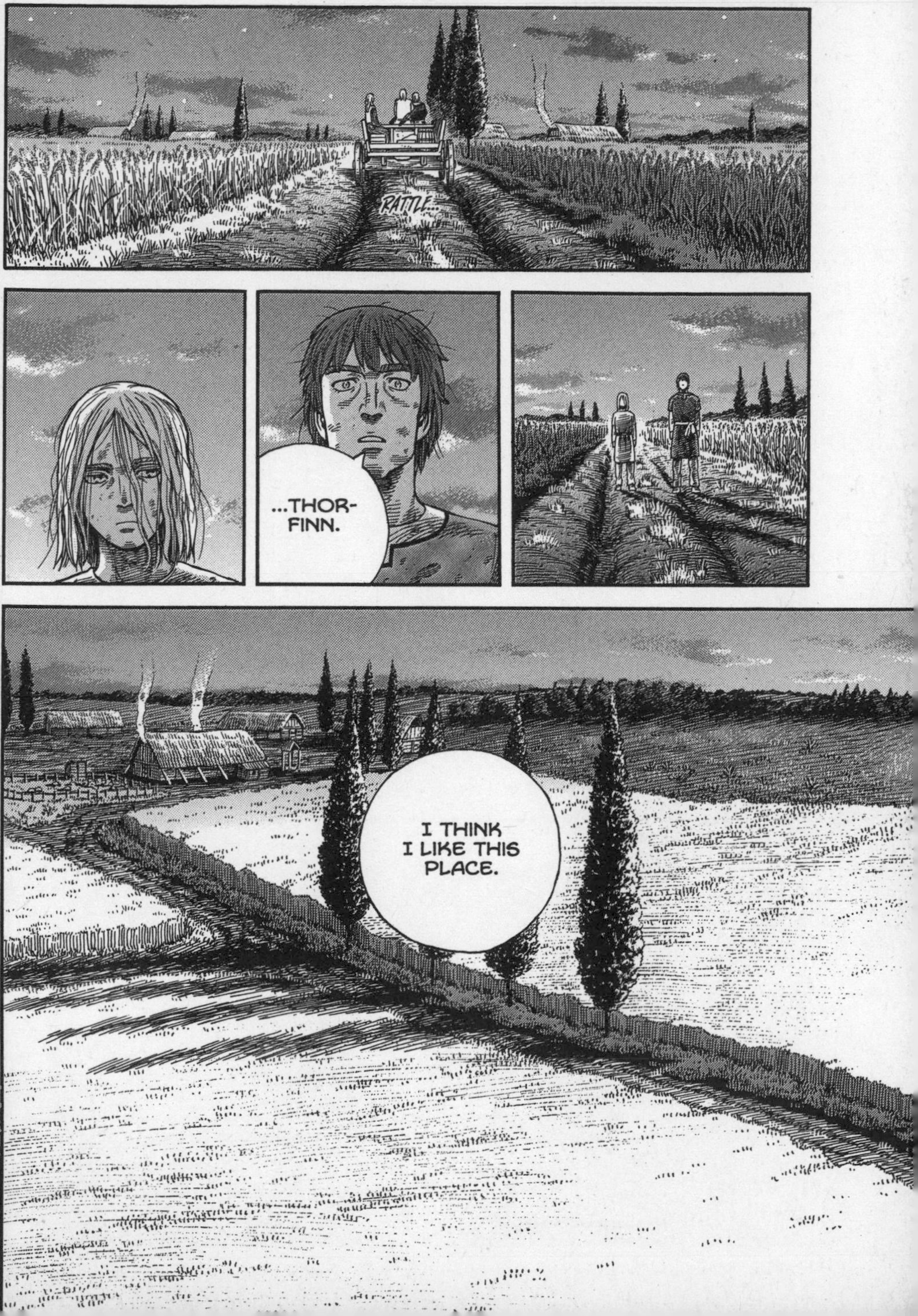
RATTLE...
...THOR-FINN.
I THINK I LIKE THIS PLACE.

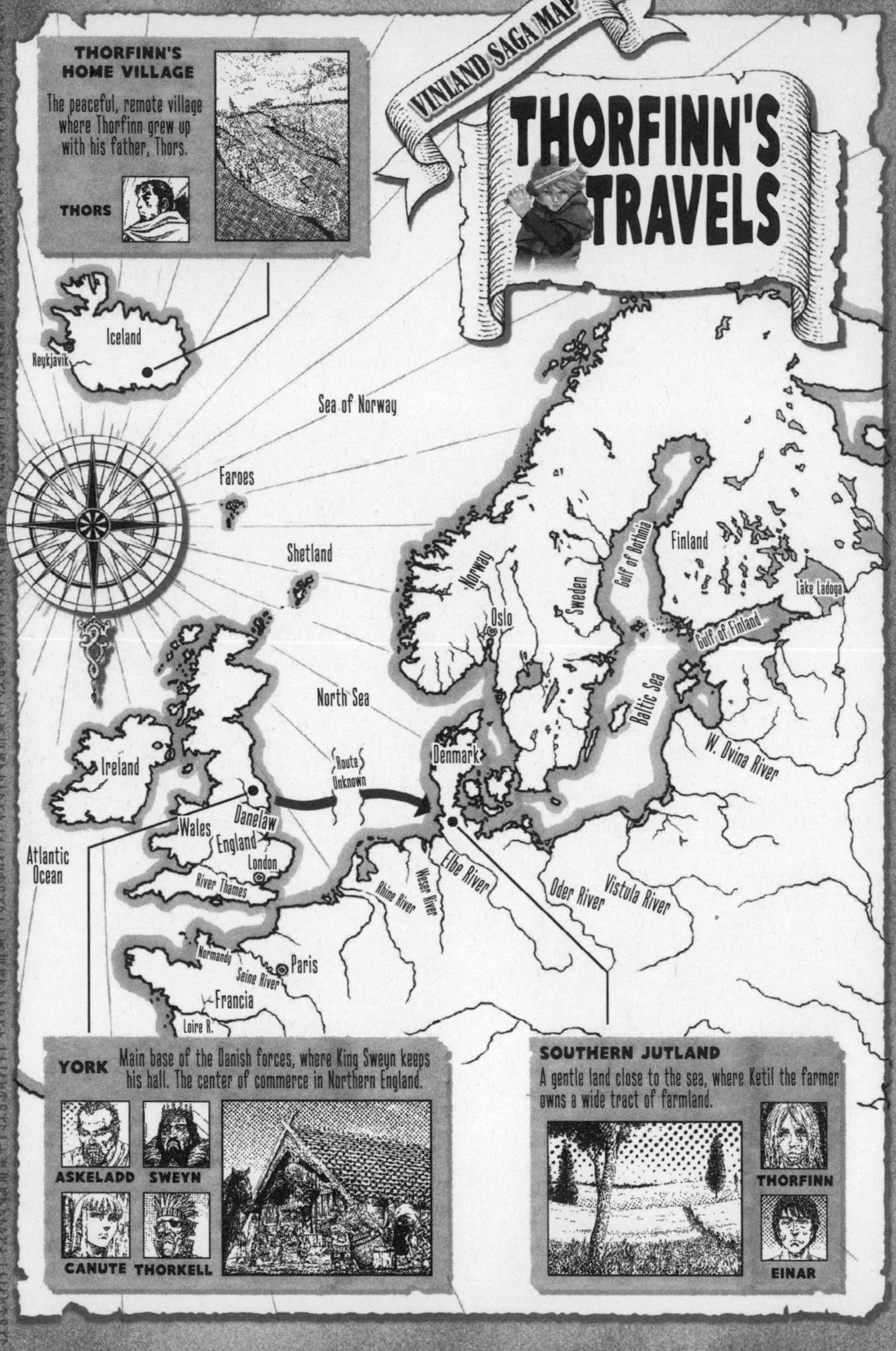

VINLAND SAGA MAP
THORFINN'S TRAVELS
THORFINN'S HOME VILLAGE
The peaceful, remote village where Thorfinn grew up with his father, Thors.
THORS
Iceland
Reykjavík
Sea of Norway
Faroes
Shetland
North Sea
Norway
Oslo
Sweden
Gulf of Bothnia
Finland
Lake Ladoga
Gulf of Finland
Baltic Sea
W. Dvina River
Denmark
Route Unknown
Ireland
Danelaw
Wales
England
London
Atlantic Ocean
River Thames
Rhine River
Weser River
Elbe River
Oder River
Vistula River
Normandy
Paris
Seine River
Francia
Loire R.
YORK
Main base of the Danish forces, where King Sweyn keeps his hall. The center of commerce in Northern England.
ASKELADD
SWEYN
CANUTE
THORKELL
SOUTHERN JUTLAND
A gentle land close to the sea, where Ketil the farmer owns a wide tract of farmland.
THORFINN
EINAR

SUPPLEMENTAL DESIGNS

KING SWEYN'S HALL

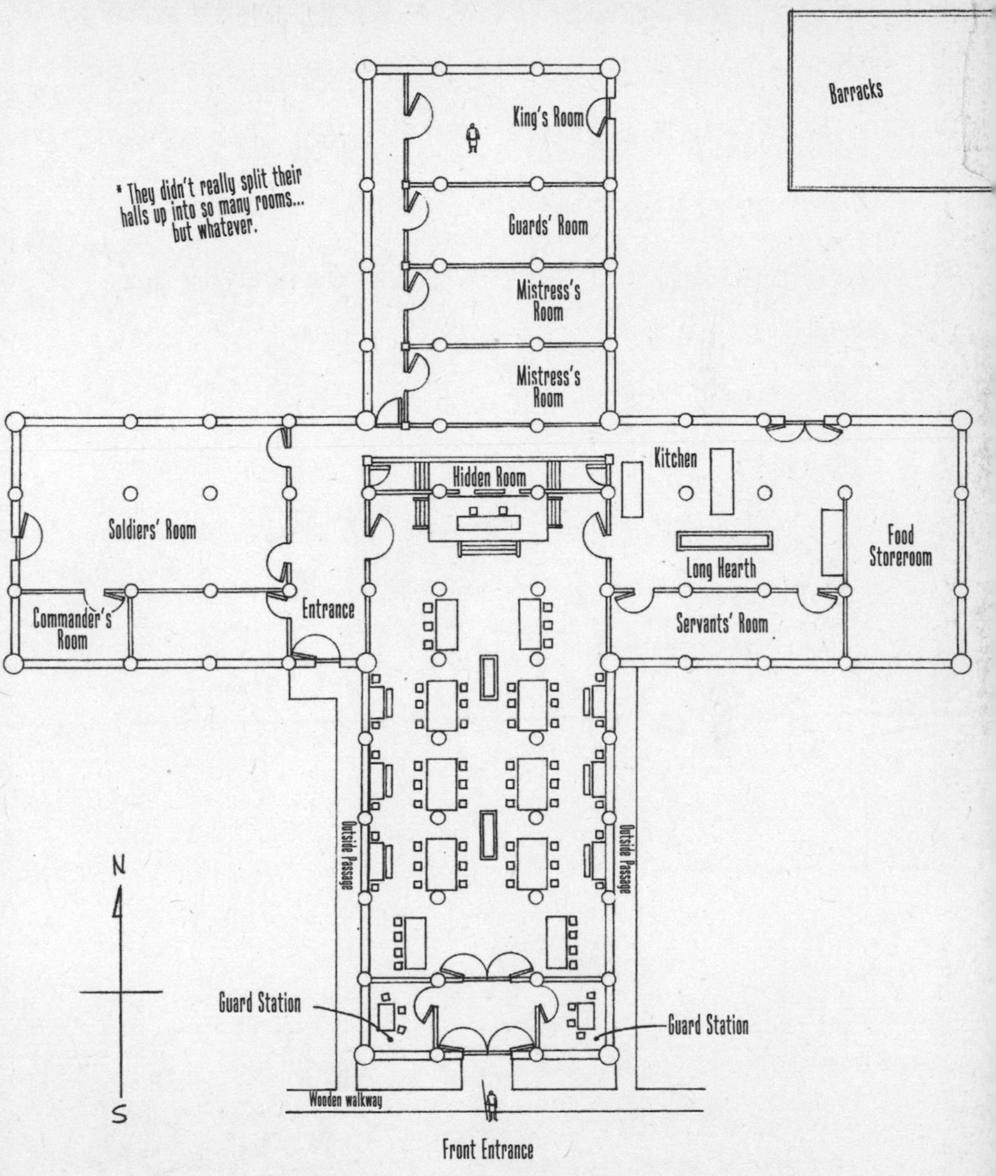
Barracks
King's Room
* They didn't really split their halls up into so many rooms... but whatever.
Guards' Room
Mistress's Room
Mistress's Room
Kitchen
Hidden Room
Soldiers' Room
Food Storeroom
Long Hearth
Commander's Room
Entrance
Servants' Room
Outside Passage
Outside Passage
N
S
Guard Station
Guard Station
Wooden walkway
Front Entrance

I keep trying to quit smoking, but it's not going well. I've been smoking for well over a decade now, so it's a fully ingrained habit. It has nothing to do with taste anymore. But given that we continue to transition to a non-smoking society, there might come a day when I can't smoke a cigarette, even if I want to. What if the world is totally smoke-free in the future, and they see old footage of me and think, "Gross! Did people in the past actually suck that smoke into their lungs? That's so stupid! Why would they do that?" Every era seems to have things that are destined to die out within that time. And the people of that era are always unable to objectively assess their own times. And yet here I am today, lighting up another historical relic. PUFF!

MAKOTO YUKIMURA

VINLAND SAGA

Translation Notes

Aegir, page 64

The Norse god of the sea. He was considered something of a party animal, and loved to throw lavish feasts for the rest of the gods. Thus, he could also be considered the god of drinking.

Askeladd, page 128

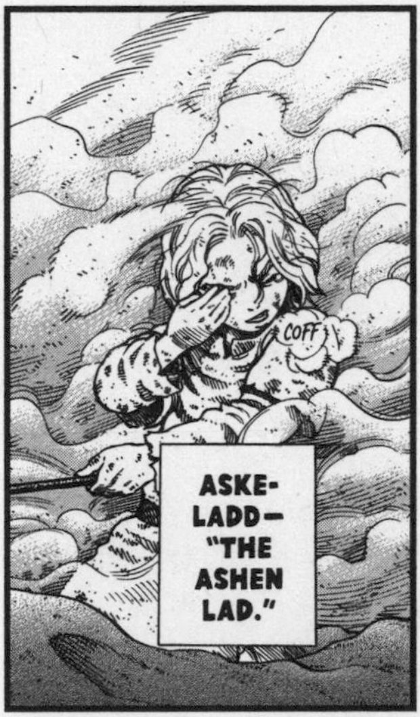
COFF
ASKE-LADD—"THE ASHEN LAD."

In Norwegian folk tales, Askeladden, or "Ashen Lad," is a clever and resourceful hero who shares many traits with the trickster god Loki. In the tales, he often outwits or tricks his opponents into doing his bidding. Askeladden is an example of a folk hero who succeeds not through strength or bravery, but creativity and quick thinking. Many of the tales hold that Askeladden is the youngest of three brothers, and must use his quick wits to get ahead in life, which is often conflated with the Norwegian historical position, overlooked by more powerful and wealthy Scandinavian cultures.

Jorvik, page 157

The Norse name for the town of York, particularly during their rule over the Northumbria region in the 9th and 10th centuries. Some places within York of certain historical value still bear the name, such as the popular Jorvik Viking Centre museum.

Karlsefni, page 190

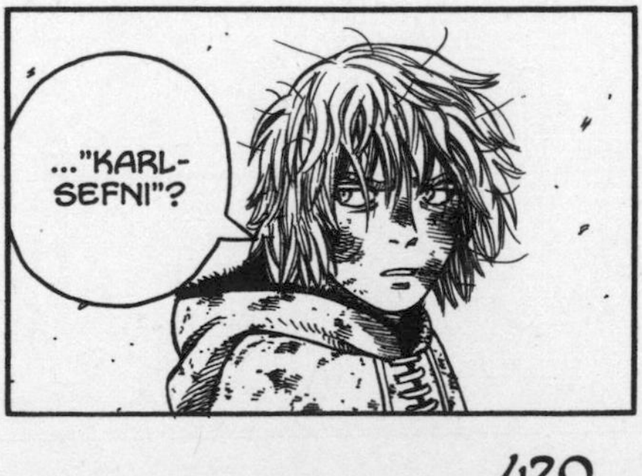
..."KARL-SEFNI"?

The character of Thorfinn is loosely based upon a real-life explorer named Thorfinn Karlsefni, whose attempts to reach the New World using Leif Ericson's routes were recounted in a number of Scandinavian sagas. The

name "Karlsefni" was not a surname, but an Icelandic epithet that others gave to Thorfinn. Translations of the name vary, from "the makings of a man" to "auspicious boy" to "a real man." In any case, they seem to suggest that he was viewed as likely to achieve great things.

Lucius Artorius Castus, page 282

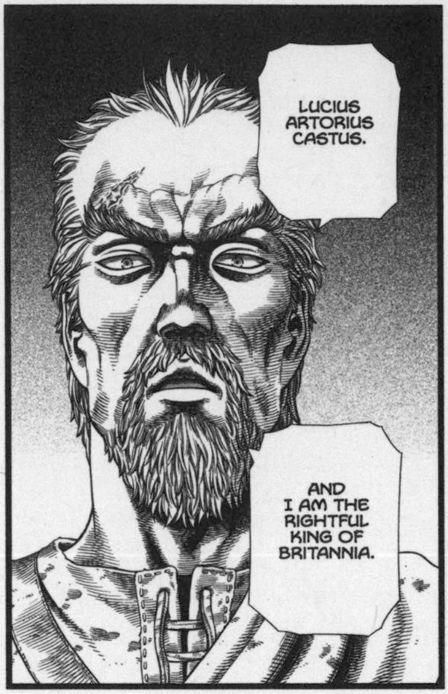
LUCIUS ARTORIUS CASTUS.
AND I AM THE RIGHTFUL KING OF BRITANNIA.

The name of a Roman general who was active in Britannia (the Roman colony on the British isles) in the 2nd or 3rd century AD. Though only a few historical records remain of him, some modern scholars have posited that he is the basis for the later legend of King Arthur.

Hávamál, page 353

A poem found within the Poetic Edda, a collection of Old Norse poems. The title translates to "sayings of the high one," and the contents of the poem are attributed to Odin. The Japanese translation, when not simply titled "Hávamál," is known as "the song of Odin" or "the proverbs of Odin." Hávamál is a gnomic poem, meaning that its verses are meant to serve as lessons or advice on customary topics, such as the laws of hospitality for both guest and host.

Karl, page 405

The Viking social class of free men, greater than thralls (slaves) but lower than noble jarls: in short, the common man. The Old English form of the word was "churl," which eventually evolved into its modern pejorative meaning: one who is so common as to be low class or boorish.

For Our Farewell Is Near Part 4
By Makoto Yukimura

Introduction

At the end of the Edo Period, the arrival of the "black ships" from abroad spelled the end of 260 years of isolation enforced by the shogunate. In response to the shogunate's desire to open the country's borders, disgruntled regional forces loyal to the emperor, such as the Choshu Domain, planned a rebellion. The imperial loyalists massed in Kyoto, where the emperor lived, growing increasingly bold until the city became, in effect, a lawless area. In an effort to restore order, the shogunate recruited ronin (masterless samurai) in Edo (Tokyo) and sent them to Kyoto.

Among these men were Kondo Isami and Okita Soji, students at the Shieikan dojo in Tama. Upon reaching Kyoto, they formed the "Shinsengumi" under the orders of the daimyo of Aizu Domain, who had been charged with keeping the peace in the city. But, unable to reverse the tide of history, the shogunate lost power, and the Shinsengumi were defeated at the Battle of Toba-Fushimi. In 1868, Kondo and Okita had fled to Edo. Okita's body was already wracked with tuberculosis at this time.

Note:
This story first appeared in 2004 in Kodansha's Evening magazine. This is the first time it has been published in English.

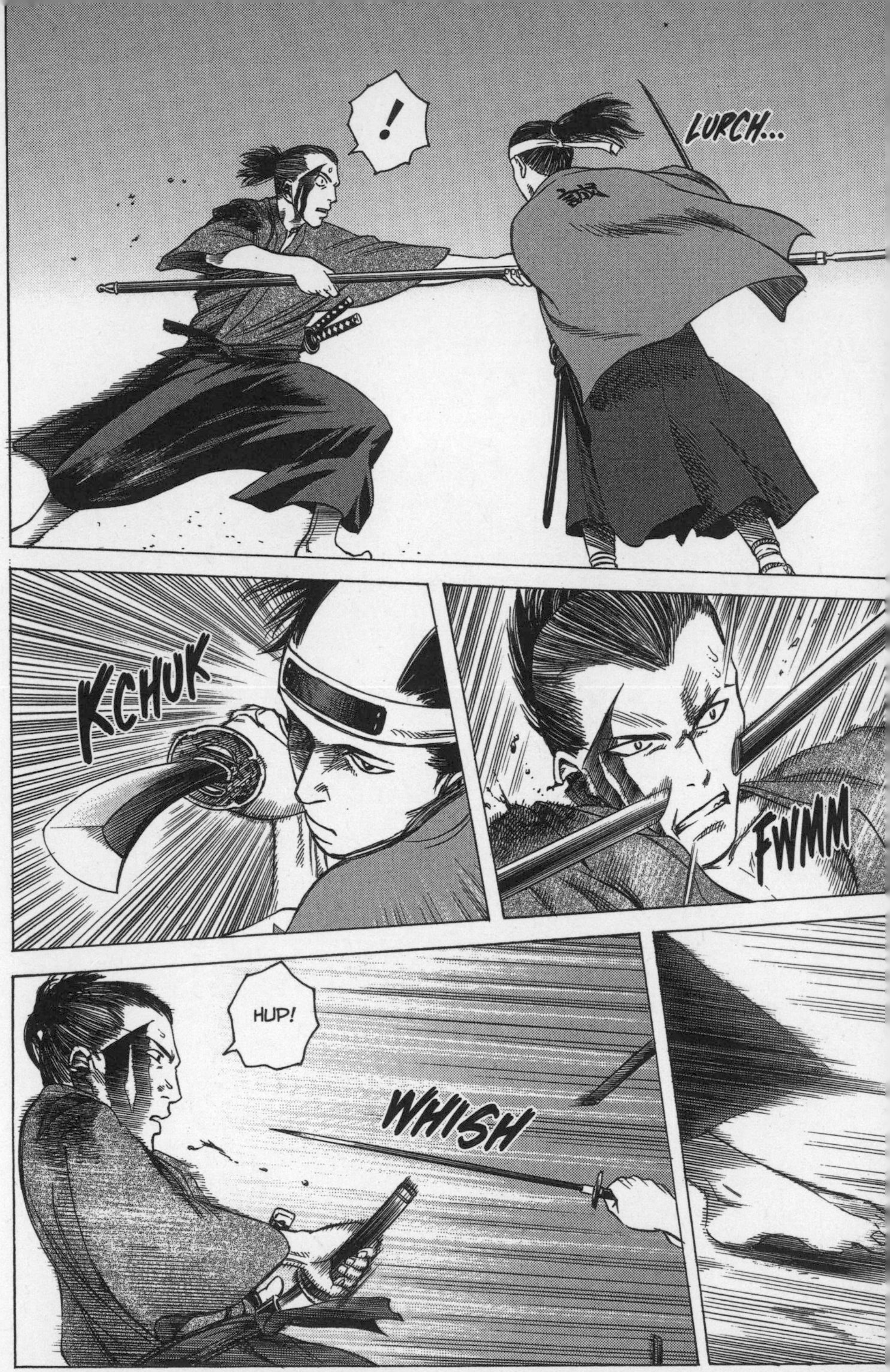
LURCH...
!
FWMM
KCHUK
HUP!
WHISH

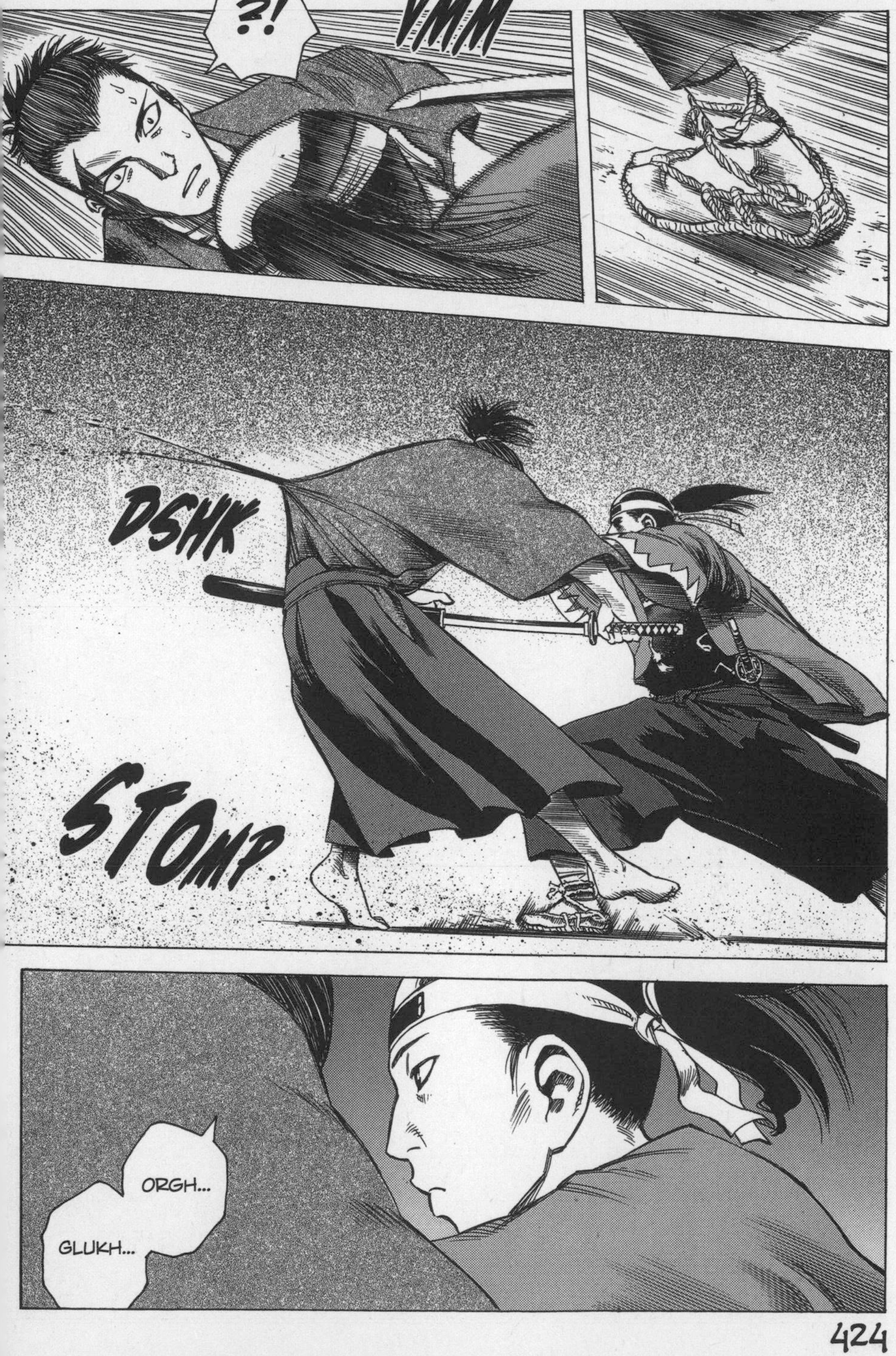
VMM
?!
DSHK
STOMP
ORGH...
GLUKH...

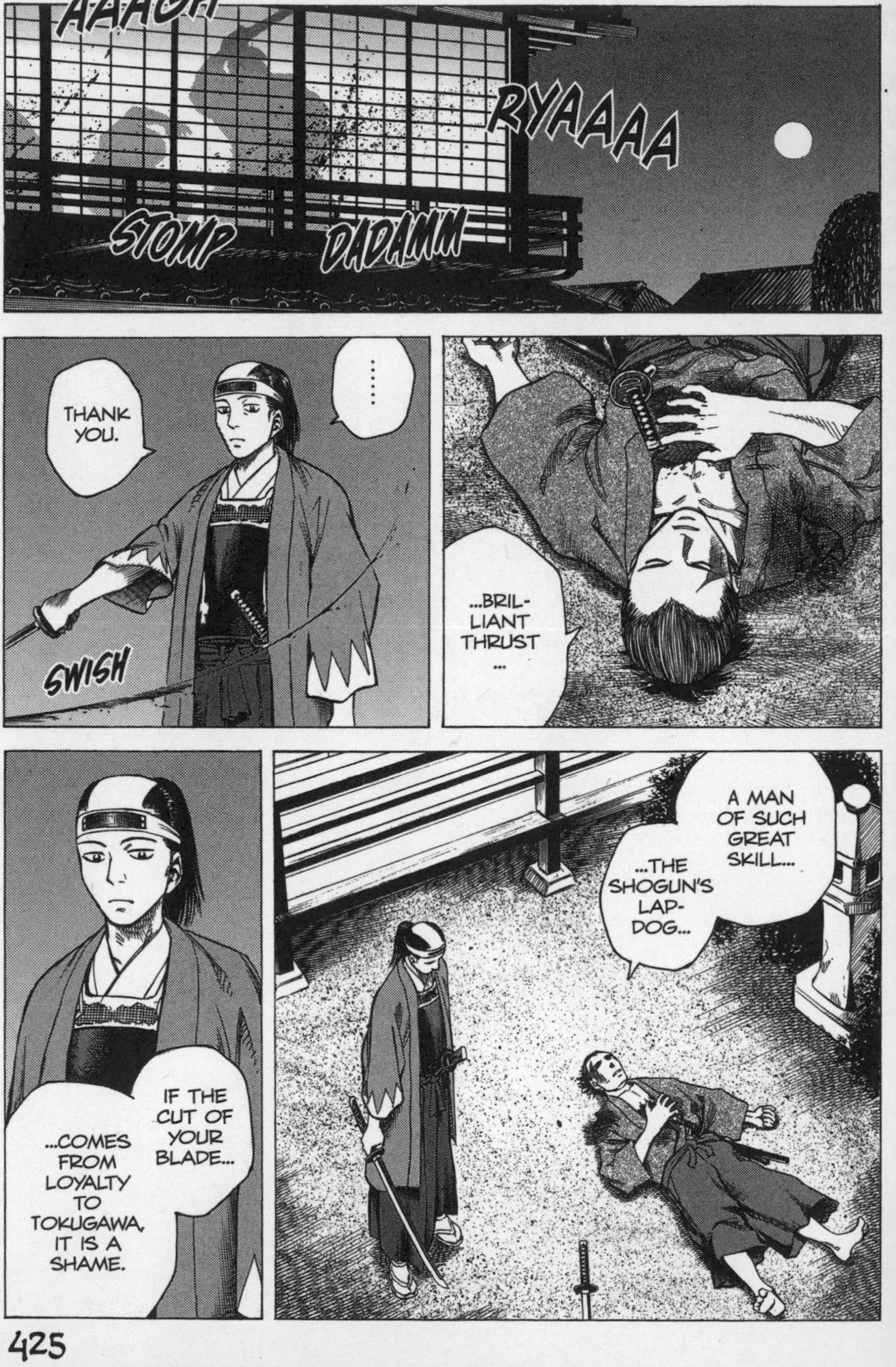
AAAGH
RYAAAA
STOMP
DADAMM
...BRIL-LIANT THRUST ...
......
THANK YOU.
SWISH
A MAN OF SUCH GREAT SKILL...
...THE SHOGUN'S LAP-DOG...
IF THE CUT OF YOUR BLADE...
...COMES FROM LOYALTY TO TOKUGAWA, IT IS A SHAME.

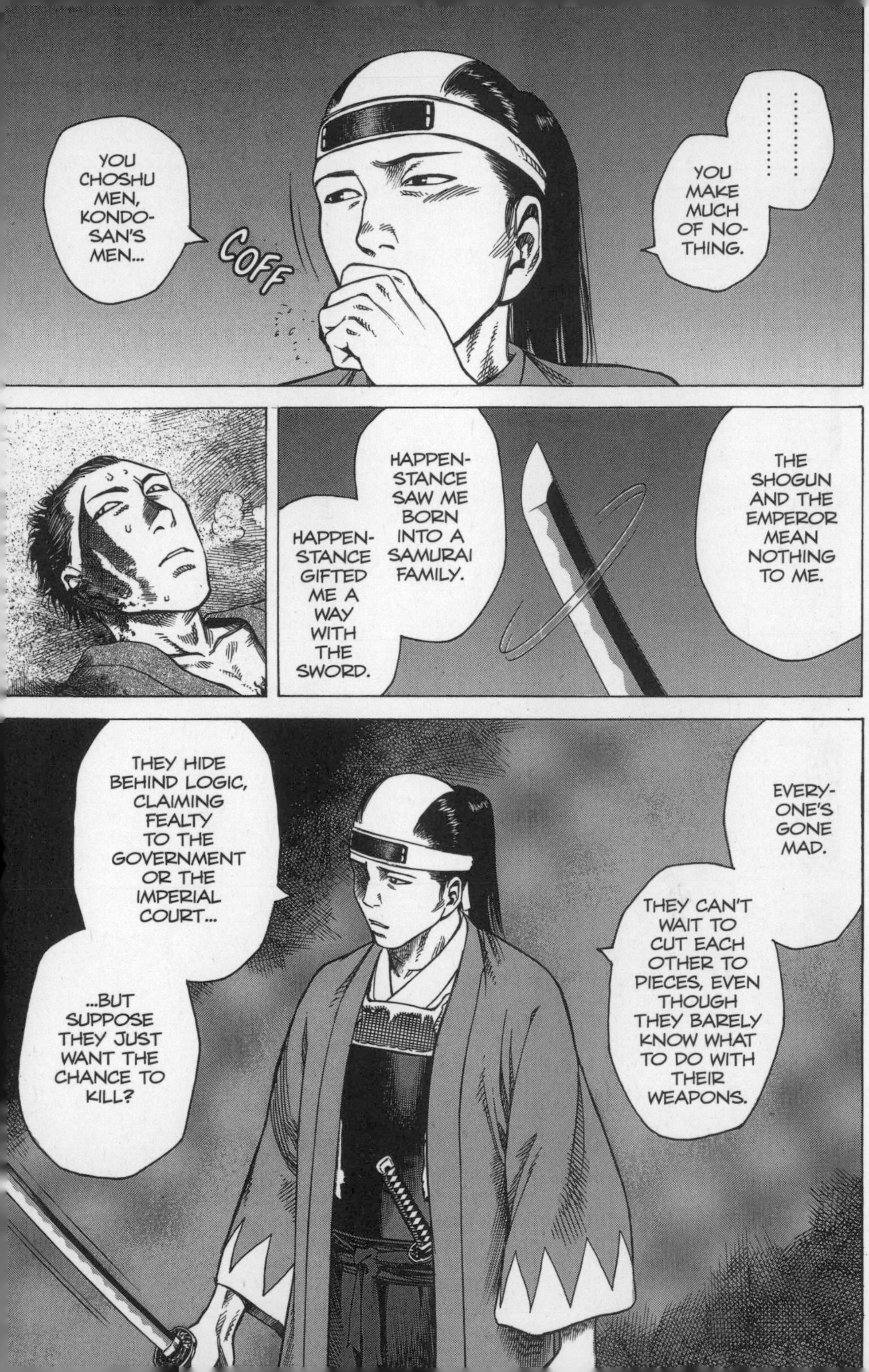
......
YOU MAKE MUCH OF NO-THING.
COFF
YOU CHOSHU MEN, KONDO-SAN'S MEN...
THE SHOGUN AND THE EMPEROR MEAN NOTHING TO ME.
HAPPEN-STANCE SAW ME BORN INTO A SAMURAI FAMILY.
HAPPEN-STANCE GIFTED ME A WAY WITH THE SWORD.
EVERY-ONE'S GONE MAD.
THEY CAN'T WAIT TO CUT EACH OTHER TO PIECES, EVEN THOUGH THEY BARELY KNOW WHAT TO DO WITH THEIR WEAPONS.
THEY HIDE BEHIND LOGIC, CLAIMING FEALTY TO THE GOVERNMENT OR THE IMPERIAL COURT...
...BUT SUPPOSE THEY JUST WANT THE CHANCE TO KILL?

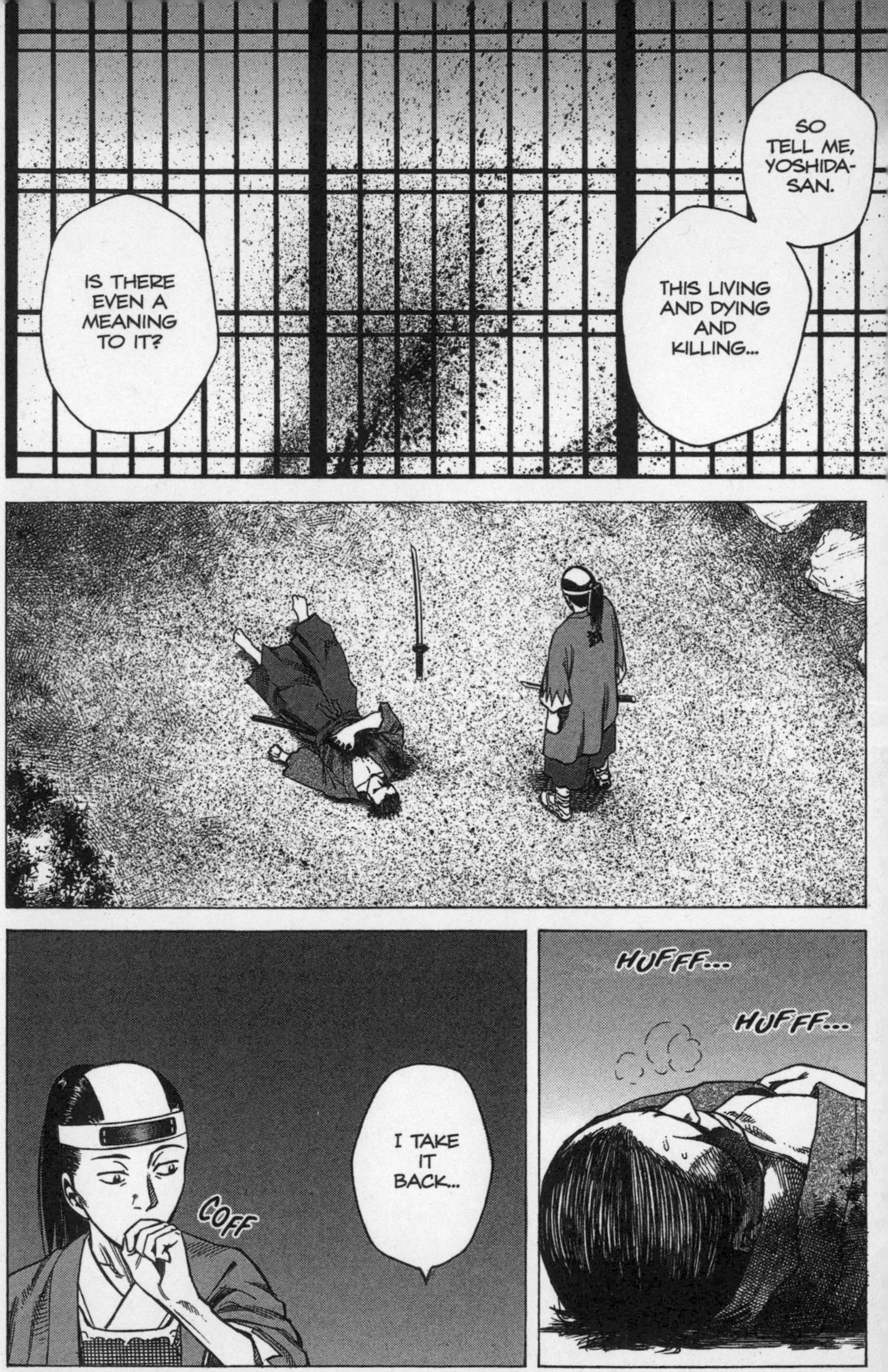
SO TELL ME, YOSHIDA-SAN.
THIS LIVING AND DYING AND KILLING...
IS THERE EVEN A MEANING TO IT?
HUFFF...
HUFFF...
I TAKE IT BACK..
COFF

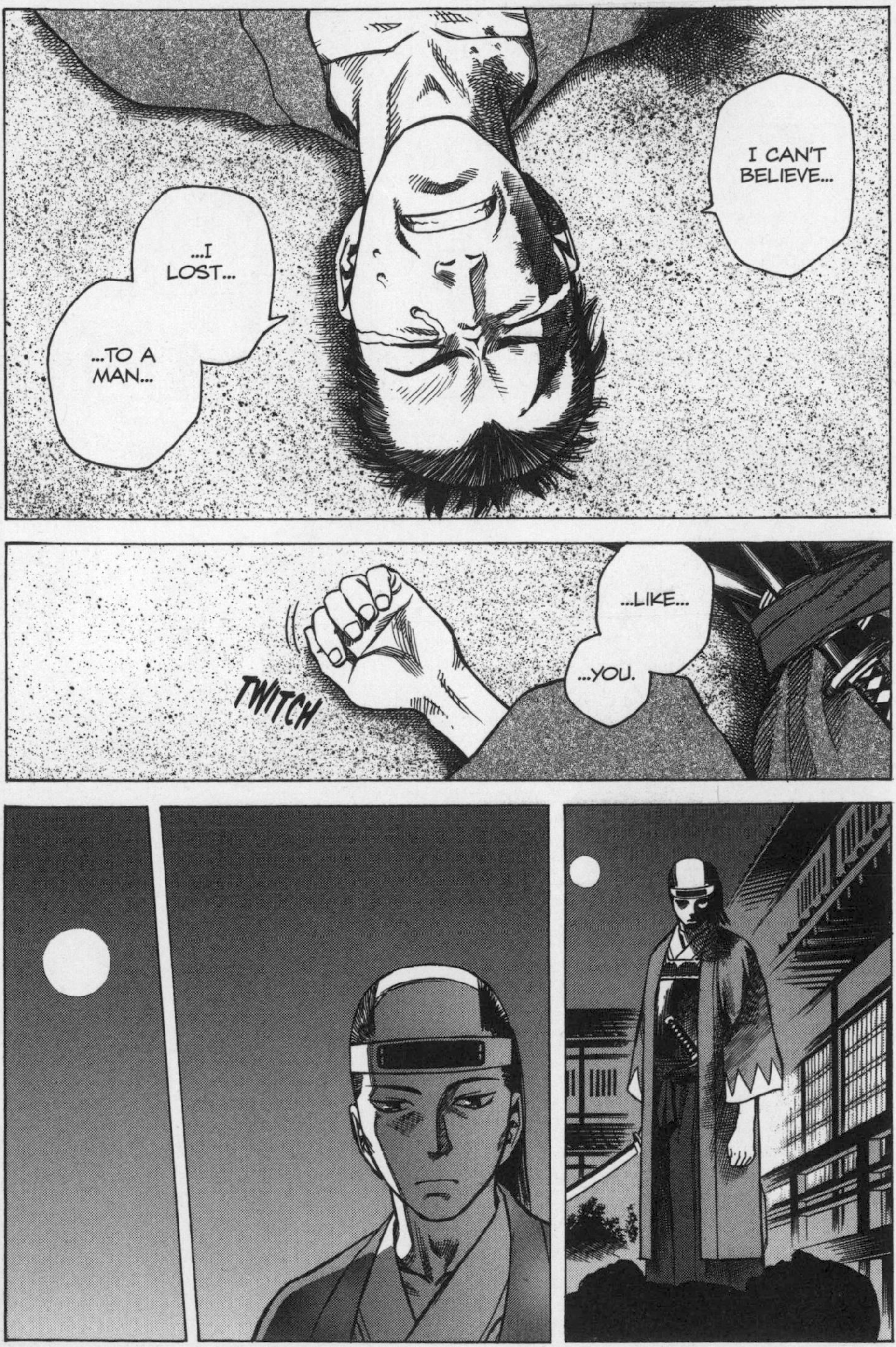
I CAN'T BELIEVE...
...I LOST...
...TO A MAN...
...LIKE...
...YOU.
TWITCH

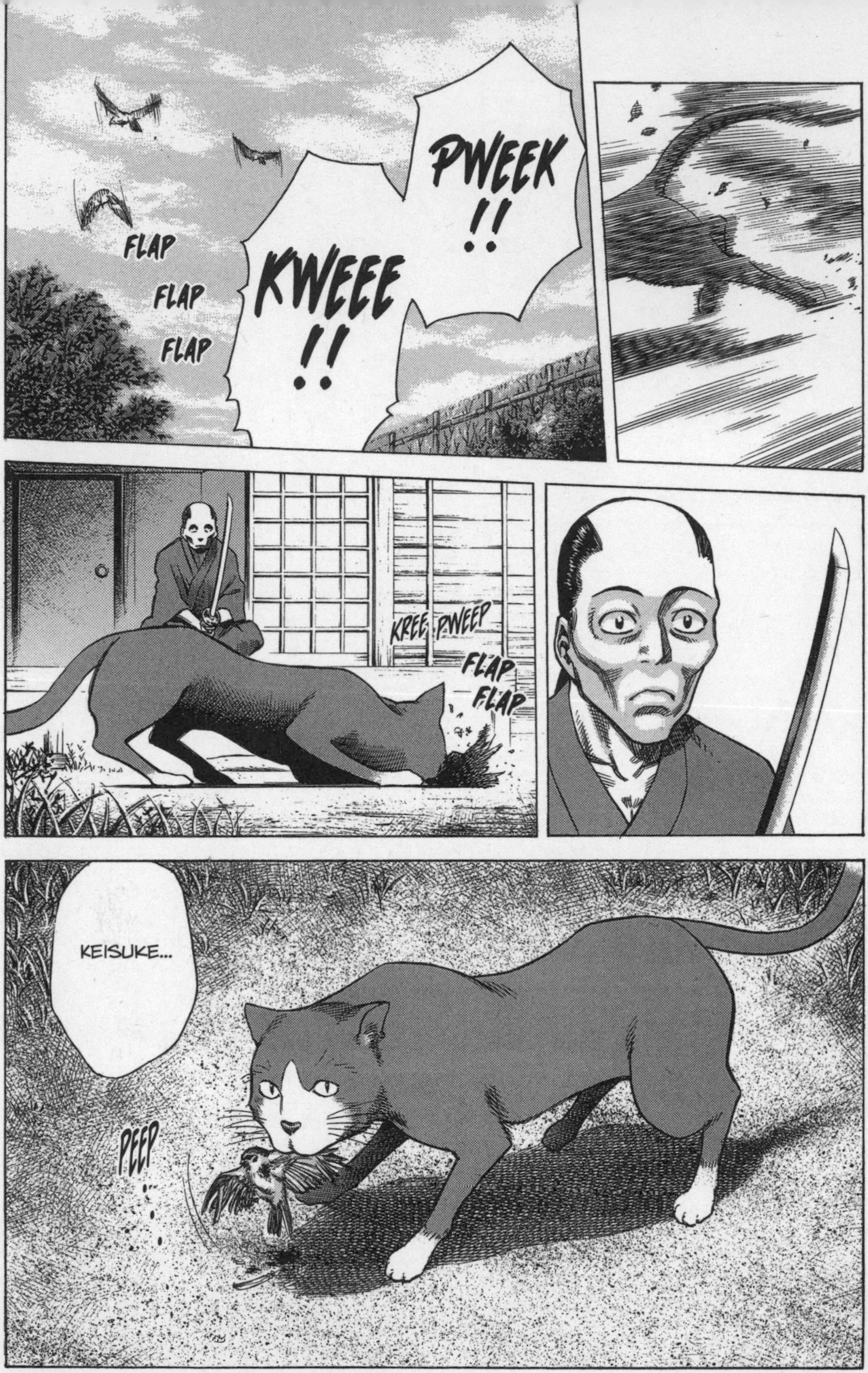
PWEEK !!
KWEEE !!
FLAP
FLAP
FLAP
KREE PWEEP
FLAP
FLAP
KEISUKE...
PEEP

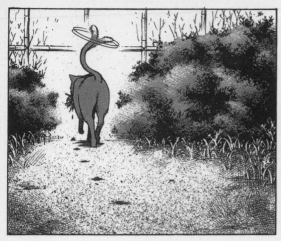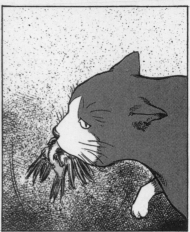
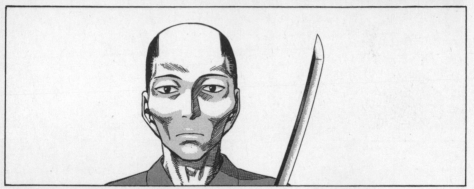
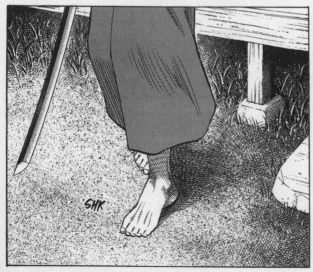

SHK

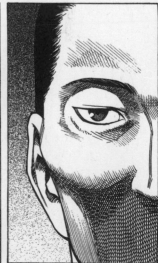

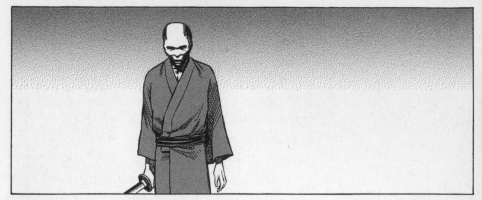

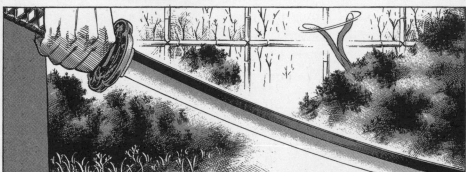

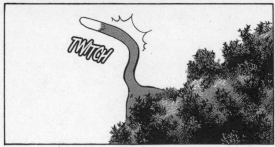

TWITCH

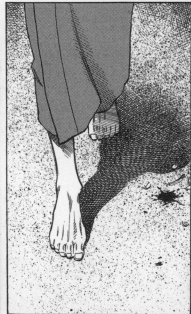

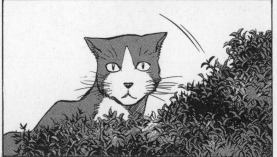

431

Concluded in Vinland Saga Book Five

ASK YUKIMURA

This exclusive Q&A with series creator Makoto Yukimura appears only in the U.S. edition of "Vinland Saga." Future volumes will include them, too, so if you have a question you'd like to ask Mr. Yukimura, please send it to kodanshacomics@randomhouse.com, or to:

Kodansha Comics
451 Park Ave. South, 7th floor
New York, NY 10016

Kodansha Comics: *Your action scenes often involve a lot of characters and background details. How difficult is it to keep track of where everyone is standing from page to page? Also, are there any artists or filmmakers whose action sequences you admire?*

Makoto Yukimura: These things happen inside my own head, so it's not that difficult. What I feel is difficult is getting the relative positions and emotional states of the characters that I have in my head across to the reader without causing misunderstandings or stress. I take care to make these things as clear as I possibly can.

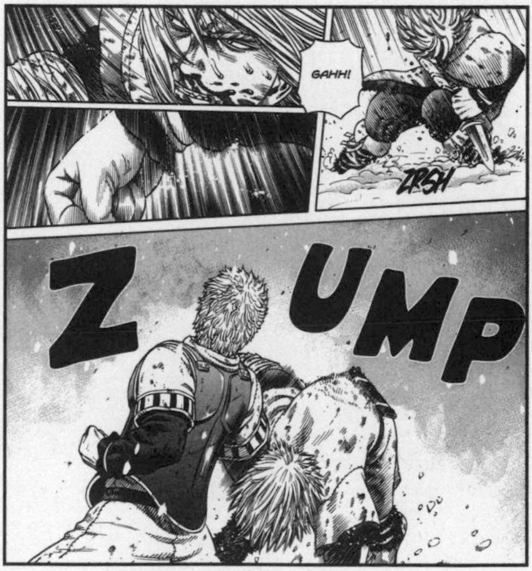
GAHH!
ZRSH
ZUMP

As for action scenes, there are countless wonderful action artists who are far beyond my level, but if I had to name one, it would be Yukito Kishiro, artist of the Japanese manga series *Gunnm.** When it comes to imagination, style, impact, composition, or anything else, he is one of the absolute masters of the Japanese manga world.

* Published in the United States as *Battle Angel Alita.*

KC: *What is a typical day of work like for you? When do you wake up and go to sleep? Do you have a set schedule for different tasks, or do you work on a more improvised schedule?*

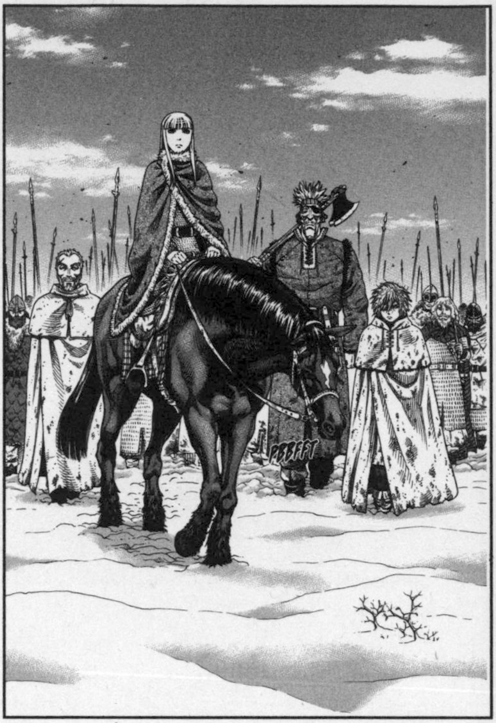
PBBFFT

Yukimura: Normally, my three staff members arrive at 10 in the morning and begin drawing. With breaks for lunch and dinner, I work with my staff until 10 at night. Most of the time, I go to sleep between 2 and 3 in the morning.

Before drawing comes the work of creating the story. This is something I tackle by myself, so the schedule is extremely flexible. Unlike drawing work, where as long as you move your hand you're making progress, you need to be patient until good ideas come. So I do other work, like non-Vinland Saga illustrations, while I wait.

I draw one chapter each month, which is 30 pages, give or take.

KC: *There is a lot of focus on father-son relationships in Vinland Saga, such as between Thors and Thorfinn, Sweyn and Canute, and even Thorfinn and his substitute father figure, Askeladd. What interests you about the father-son relationship in particular?*

In my personal experience, in my relationship with my own father, I don't think there were any dramatic events that might have had an influence on the manga. I probably drew fathers and sons in the manga so frequently because the motif was such an appropriate expression of the themes. It was a half-unconscious choice. Before I knew it, there were lots of fathers

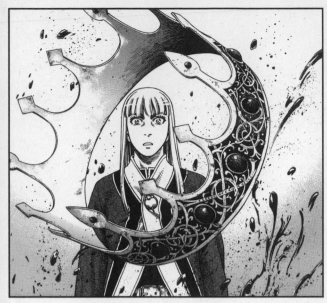

and sons appearing in the story. Even I was a little surprised.

If there was one thing I would mention about me and my own father, it would be about the time I left home to become a manga artist. This was 15 years ago, when I was 22 years old.

My father and mother both hoped that I would find a stable job after I left university, but I wanted to become a manga artist. It was a gamble, the kind of job where whether you can make a living depends on luck. I thought my father, a civil servant, would be against it.

But my father said, "If there's something you want to do, then do it," and sent me on my way. He even said, "You'll probably need this," put a not insignificant amount of money in an envelope, and made me take it. I was shocked.

My father didn't force me into anything. I'm sure he had lots of things he wanted to say to me, and lots of concerns about me, but he basically left me alone. It's not a dramatic story, but I am grateful that I had this relationship with my father where nothing in particular happened.

SEE YOU IN BOOK FIVE, COMING OCTOBER 2014!

W9-DGU-364